Security, Privacy, Trust, and Resource Management in Mobile and Wireless Communications

Danda B. Rawat
Georgia Southern University, USA

Bhed B. Bista
Iwate Prefectural University, Japan

Gongjun Yan
University of Southern Indiana, USA

A volume in the Advances in Information Security, Privacy, and Ethics (AISPE) Book Series

Information Science REFERENCE

An Imprint of IGI Global

Managing Director:	Lindsay Johnston
Editorial Director	Myla Merkel
Production Manager:	Jennifer Yoder
Publishing Systems Analyst:	Adrienne Freeland
Development Editor:	Christine Smith
Acquisitions Editor:	Kayla Wolfe
Typesetter:	John Crodian
Cover Design:	Jason Mull

Published in the United States of America by
Information Science Reference (an imprint of IGI Global)
701 E. Chocolate Avenue
Hershey PA 17033
Tel: 717-533-8845
Fax: 717-533-8661
E-mail: cust@igi-global.com
Web site: http://www.igi-global.com

Library of Congress Cataloging-in-Publication Data

Security, privacy, trust, and resource management in mobile and wireless communications / Danda B. Rawat, Bhed B. Bista, and Gongjun Yan, editors.
     pages cm
 Includes bibliographical references and index.
 Summary: "This book examines the current scope of theoretical and practical applications on the security of mobile and wireless communications, covering fundamental concepts of current issues, challenges, and solutions in wireless and mobile networks"-- Provided by publisher.
  ISBN 978-1-4666-4691-9 (hardcover) -- ISBN 978-1-4666-4692-6 (ebook) -- ISBN 978-1-4666-4693-3 (print & perpetual access) 1. Wireless communication systems--Security measures. 2. Mobile communication systems--Security measures. 3. Computer networks--Security measures. I. Rawat, Danda B., 1977- II. Bista, Bhed B., 1967- III. Yan, Gongjun, 1976-.
 TK5103.2.S444 2013
 005.8--dc23
                                                            2013025029

This book is published in the IGI Global book series Advances in Information Security, Privacy, and Ethics (AISPE) (ISSN: 1948-9730; eISSN: 1948-9749)

British Cataloguing in Publication Data
A Cataloguing in Publication record for this book is available from the British Library.

All work contributed to this book is new, previously-unpublished material. The views expressed in this book are those of the authors, but not necessarily of the publisher.

For electronic access to this publication, please contact: eresources@igi-global.com.

Advances in Information Security, Privacy, and Ethics (AISPE) Book Series

ISSN: 1948-9730
EISSN: 1948-9749

MISSION

In the digital age, when everything from municipal power grids to individual mobile telephone locations is all available in electronic form, the implications and protection of this data has never been more important and controversial. As digital technologies become more pervasive in everyday life and the Internet is utilized in ever increasing ways by both private and public entities, the need for more research on securing, regulating, and understanding these areas is growing.

The **Advances in Information Security, Privacy, & Ethics (AISPE) Book Series** is the source for this research, as the series provides only the most cutting-edge research on how information is utilized in the digital age.

COVERAGE

- Access Control
- Device Fingerprinting
- Global Privacy Concerns
- Information Security Standards
- Network Security Services
- Privacy-Enhancing Technologies
- Risk Management
- Security Information Management
- Technoethics
- Tracking Cookies

IGI Global is currently accepting manuscripts for publication within this series. To submit a proposal for a volume in this series, please contact our Acquisition Editors at Acquisitions@igi-global.com or visit: http://www.igi-global.com/publish/.

Titles in this Series

For a list of additional titles in this series, please visit: www.igi-global.com

Research Developments in Biometrics and Video Processing Techniques
Rajeev Srivastava (Indian Institute of Technology (BHU), India) S.K. Singh (Indian Institute of Technology (BHU), India) and K.K. Shukla (Indian Institute of Technology (BHU), India)
Information Science Reference • copyright 2014 • 237pp • H/C (ISBN: 9781466648685) • US $195.00 (our price)

Security, Privacy, Trust, and Resource Management in Mobile and Wireless Communications
Danda B. Rawat (Georgia Southern University, USA) Bhed B. Bista (Iwate Prefectural University, Japan) and Gongjun Yan (University of Southern Indiana, USA)
Information Science Reference • copyright 2014 • 413pp • H/C (ISBN: 9781466646919) • US $195.00 (our price)

Architectures and Protocols for Secure Information Technology Infrastructures
Antonio Ruiz-Martinez (University of Murcia, Spain) Rafael Marin-Lopez (University of Murcia, Spain) and Fernando Pereniguez-Garcia (University of Murcia, Spain)
Information Science Reference • copyright 2014 • 427pp • H/C (ISBN: 9781466645141) • US $195.00 (our price)

Theory and Practice of Cryptography Solutions for Secure Information Systems
Atilla Elçi (Aksaray University, Turkey) Josef Pieprzyk (Macquarie University, Australia) Alexander G. Chefranov (Eastern Mediterranean University, North Cyprus) Mehmet A. Orgun (Macquarie University, Australia) Huaxiong Wang (Nanyang Technological University, Singapore) and Rajan Shankaran (Macquarie University, Australia)
Information Science Reference • copyright 2013 • 351pp • H/C (ISBN: 9781466640306) • US $195.00 (our price)

IT Security Governance Innovations Theory and Research
Daniel Mellado (Spanish Tax Agency, Spain) Luis Enrique Sánchez (University of Castilla-La Mancha, Spain) Eduardo Fernández-Medina (University of Castilla – La Mancha, Spain) and Mario G. Piattini (University of Castilla - La Mancha, Spain)
Information Science Reference • copyright 2013 • 373pp • H/C (ISBN: 9781466620834) • US $195.00 (our price)

Threats, Countermeasures, and Advances in Applied Information Security
Manish Gupta (State University of New York at Buffalo, USA) John Walp (M&T Bank Corporation, USA) and Raj Sharman (State University of New York, USA)
Information Science Reference • copyright 2012 • 319pp • H/C (ISBN: 9781466609785) • US $195.00 (our price)

Investigating Cyber Law and Cyber Ethics Issues, Impacts and Practices
Alfreda Dudley (Towson University, USA) James Braman (Towson University, USA) and Giovanni Vincenti (Towson University, USA)
Information Science Reference • copyright 2012 • 343pp • H/C (ISBN: 9781613501320) • US $195.00 (our price)

www.igi-global.com

701 E. Chocolate Ave., Hershey, PA 17033
Order online at www.igi-global.com or call 717-533-8845 x100
To place a standing order for titles released in this series, contact: cust@igi-global.com
Mon-Fri 8:00 am - 5:00 pm (est) or fax 24 hours a day 717-533-8661

To Our Families

Editorial Advisory Board

Table of Contents

Section 1
Fundamentals of Mobile and Wireless Communication Networks

Section 2
Physical Layer Security

Section 3
Vehicular Communications and Networking

Section 4
Mobile Ad Hoc Networks

Section 7
Cloud and Mobile Communications

Section 8
Wireless Network Management and Analysis

Detailed Table of Contents

Section 1
Fundamentals of Mobile and Wireless Communication Networks

Chapter 1

Danda B Rawat, Georgia Southern University, USA
Bhed Bahadur Bista, Iwate Prefectural University, Japan
Gongjun Yan, University of Southern Indiana, USA

Wireless communication networks offer transmission of signals, such as voice, data, and multimedia, without using wires, which is the crucial part of mobile communications. After successful deployment of wireless cellular networks in licensed bands and Wi-Fi networks in unlicensed bands, such as Industry, Scientific, and Medical (ISM) and Unlicensed National Information Infrastructure (UNII), over the last decade, several wireless networks, application, and services are emerging. Furthermore, wireless networks offer several advantages including mobility while getting service, scalability for further extension, reduced cost-of-ownership, and so on. However, there are some disadvantages and concerns, such as security, data rate, reliability, range, etc. The demand of ubiquitous communications is driving the development of wireless and mobile networks. Wireless communication is the fastest growing segment of the communication industry. This chapter provides the fundamentals of wireless and mobile networks and their advantages and disadvantages.

Chapter 2

Lei Chen, Sam Houston State University, USA
Cihan Varol, Sam Houston State University, USA
Qingzhong Liu, Sam Houston State University, USA
Bing Zhou, Sam Houston State University, USA

Thanks to the much larger geographical coverage and pleasing bandwidth of data transmissions, Wireless Metropolitan Area Networks (WMANs) have become widely accepted in many countries for everyday communications. Two of the main wireless technologies used in WMANs, the Worldwide Interoperability for Microwave Access (WiMAX, also known as Wireless Local Loop or WLL) and Long Term Evolution (LTE), have generated billions of dollars in the ever-growing wireless communication market. While the IEEE 802.16 standards for WiMAX and the 3GPP standards LTE are updated and improved almost annually, it is inevitable that current standards still contain a number of security vulnerabilities, potentially leading to various security attacks. To address the security concerns in these two WMANs technologies, this chapter presents the technical details of security aspects of WiMAX and LTE. More specifically, the key generation, authentication, data, and key confidentiality and integrity of both technologies are deliberated. The chapter ends with a discussion of the security vulnerabilities, threats, and countermeasures of WiMAX and LTE.

Section 2
Physical Layer Security

Chapter 3

Rajesh K. Sharma, Ilmenau University of Technology, Germany

This chapter provides a survey of physical layer security and key generation methods. This includes mainly an overview of ongoing research in physical layer security in the present and next generation communication networks. Although higher layer security mechanisms and protocols address wireless security challenges in large extent, more security vulnerabilities arise due to the increasingly pervasive existence of wireless communication devices. In this context, the focus of this chapter is mainly on physical layer security. Some security attacks in general are briefly reviewed. Models of physical layer security, information theoretic works, and key generation methods including quantization and reconciliation are discussed. Some latest developments for enhanced security like Multiple-Input Multiple-Output (MIMO) systems, reconfigurable antennas, and multiple relay systems are also presented. Finally, some existing and emerging application scenarios of physical layer security are discussed.

Chapter 4

    Özge Cepheli, Istanbul Technical University, Turkey
    Güneş Karabulut Kurt, Istanbul Technical University, Turkey

Physical layer (PHY) security has become an emerging area of research recently. Wireless networks use unguided medium as communication channels, so gathering wireless data transmission is easier when compared to traditional cable systems. With the rise of new security challenges, many different solutions have been offered and are being developed. However, maintaining security in wireless networks still remains a challenge. Secure transmission techniques in these networks are discussed throughout this chapter. PHY security measures, the secrecy rate, the secrecy capacity, and the outage secrecy rate are introduced. Security needs of wireless networks are discussed and the related common attack types are described. Main countermeasures that are proposed to prevent these attacks are also presented with both practical and theoretical perspectives.

Section 3
Vehicular Communications and Networking

Chapter 5

Hamada Alshaer, Khalifa University, UAE
Sami Muhaidat, Khalifa University, UAE
Raed Shubair, Khalifa University, UAE
Moein Shayegannia, Simon Fraser University, Canada

Reliable Vehicular Ad-Hoc Networks (VANETs) require secured uninterrupted uplink and downlink connectivity to guarantee secure ubiquitous vehicular communications. VANET mobility, multi-fading wireless, and radio channels could result in unsecured and disrupted vehicular communications, isolating some vehicle nodes and making them vulnerable to security attacks. A VANET is considered to be connected and secured if there is a secured path connecting any pair of Communication-Enabled Vehicles (CEVs) in this network. Among many parameters, VANET connectivity depends on two main elements: communication transmission range and statistical distribution characterizing inter-vehicle spacing. To guarantee persistent VANET connectivity, a vehicle transmission radio range must be set properly based on the characteristic of the statistical distribution modeling the inter-vehicle spacing. This chapter analyzes three inter-vehicle spacing models based on exponential, Generalized Extreme Value (GEV), and Exponential with Robustness Factor (EwRF) statistical distributions. Based on vehicle nodes spatial density on a road segment, each vehicle node can adjust its transmission range to increase network connectivity and guarantee ubiquitous vehicular communications. Communications among vehicle nodes are secured through trusted Road-Side Units (RSUs) which distribute efficiently secret keys to vehicle nodes under their coverage to establish secure communication sessions.

Chapter 6

Gongjun Yan, University of Southern Indiana, USA
Danda B. Rawat, Georgia Southern University, USA
Bhed Bahadur Bista, Iwate Prefectural University, Japan
Lei Chen, Sam Houston State University, USA

In Vehicular Ad-Hoc Networks (VANETs), applications are based on one fundamental piece of information: location. Therefore, attackers will exploit location information to launch attacks. The authors present an in-depth survey of location security methods that have been recently proposed in literature. They present the algorithms or protocols of different methods and compare them with each other in this chapter. The methods are mainly in three aspects: position integrity, position confidentiality, and position availability. The position integrity methods focus on validating a vehicle's position to ensure the position information is correct. Position confidentiality ensures not only the confidentiality of position information but also the authentication of location that a location related message can only decrypt by the receiver which is "physically" present inside a decryption region that is specified by location, time, and speed. The position availability methods create and maintain a reliable routing path to delivery position information. The selection and maintenance of routing paths in literature can be based on multiple resources, for example wireless signal strength, computation resources, and probability models. The three aspects, position integrity, position confidentiality, and position availability, are the three basic requirements of information security based on the standard 200 of NIST.

Chapter 7

Vehicular Networks (VANETs) have received increased attention from researchers in recent years. VANETs facilitate various safety measures that help in controlling traffic and saving human lives. As VANETs consist of multiple entities, effective measures for VANET safety are to be addressed as per requirement. In this chapter, the authors review some existing schemes proposed for misbehavior detection. They categorize the schemes into two parts: data centric and non-data centric misbehaving detection. In data-centric misbehaving detection, the receiver believes the information rather than the source of the information. The authors compare schemes in each category with respect to their security strengths and weaknesses. The comparative results show that most of the schemes fail to address required security attributes that are essential for VANET safety

Vehicular Ad-Hoc Networks (VANETs) are a critical component of the Intelligent Transportation Systems (ITS), which involve the applications of advanced information processing, communications, sensing, and controlling technologies in an integrated manner to improve the functionality and the safety of transportation systems, providing drivers with timely information on road and traffic conditions, and achieving smooth traffic flow on the roads. Recently, the security of VANETs has attracted major attention for the possible presence of malicious elements, and the presence of altered messages due to channel errors in transmissions. In order to provide reliable and secure communications, Intrusion Detection Systems (IDSs) can serve as a second defense wall after prevention-based approaches, such as encryption. This chapter first presents the state-of-the-art literature on intrusion detection in VANETs. Next, the detection of illicit wireless transmissions from the physical layer perspective is investigated, assuming the presence of regular ongoing legitimate transmissions. Finally, a novel cooperative intrusion detection scheme from the MAC sub-layer perspective is discussed.

Section 4
Mobile Ad Hoc Networks

Chapter 9

A Mobile Ad hoc NETwork (MANET) is a self-organizing, infrastructure-less network of mobile nodes connecting by wireless links. In operation, the nodes of MANETs do not have a central control mechanism. It is known for its properties of routable network, where each node acts as a router to forward packets to other specific nodes in the network. The unique properties of MANET have made it useful for large number of applications and led to a number of security challenges. Security in the mobile ad hoc network is a very critical job and requires the consideration of different security issues on all the layers of communication. The countermeasures are the functions that reduce or eliminate security vulnerabilities and attacks. This chapter provides a comprehensive study of all prominent attacks in Mobile Ad Hoc Networks described in the literature. It also provides various proactive and reactive approaches proposed to secure the MANETs. Moreover, it also points to areas of research that need to be investigated in the future.

Chapter 10

In this chapter, first, the authors briefly introduce the two new systems "MASN-OLSR" (Mobile Ad Hoc Social Networks with OLSR) and "MASN-AODV" (Mobile Ad Hoc Social Networks with AODV). Then they choose wormhole and black hole attack methods, because they are not completely solved, especially in a setting where MASN is used as OLSR or AODV routing protocol. The authors give a definition of the wormhole and black hole attacks on an ad hoc network using OLSR or AODV as routing protocol and then examine the various existing proposals in the literature to overcome this attack. With an analysis of these methods, they then determine the advantages and disadvantages of each of these new systems.

Section 5
Trust and Privacy in Mobile and Wireless Communications

This chapter presents a novel trust model called Multi-Parameter Trust Framework for Mobile ad hoc networks (MTFM). A key feature of this proposed framework is its use of multiple rather than a single parameter to decide the resulting trust value, applying Grey theory. Results presented here demonstrate that the new framework can maintain consistent trust values in the presence of various types of mobility. Simulations conducted in an 802.11-based mobile ad hoc network also show that this framework offers good robustness in misbehaviour detection by employing multiple parameters. The detection capability of the new framework is examined for a range of misbehaviours and its performance is compared to existing single-parameter approaches, such as the Beta distribution method.

Trust management is an emerging technology to facilitate secure interactions between two communicating entities in distributed environments where the traditional security mechanisms are insufficient due to incomplete knowledge about the remote entities. With the development of ubiquitous computing and smart embedded systems, new challenges and threats come up in a heterogeneous environment. Trust management techniques that depend on a centralized server are not feasible in wireless peer-to-peer communication networks. Hence, the trust management and modeling strategies are becoming increasingly complex to cope with the system vulnerabilities in a distributed environment. The aim of this chapter is to have a thorough understanding of the trust formation process and the statistical techniques that are used at different stages of the trust computation process. The functional components of a trust management framework are identified and some of the existing statistical techniques used in different phases of the trust management framework are analyzed.

Chapter 13

Gongjun Yan, University of Southern Indiana, USA

Danda B. Rawat, Georgia Southern University, USA

Bhed Bahadur Bista, Iwate Prefectural University, Japan

Wu He, Old Dominion University, USA

Awny Alnusair, Indiana University – Kokomo, USA

The first main contribution of this chapter is to take a non-trivial step towards providing a robust and scalable solution to privacy protection in vehicular networks. To promote scalability and robustness the authors employ two strategies. First, they view vehicular networks as consisting of non-overlapping subnetworks, each local to a geographic area referred to as a cell. Each cell has a server that maintains a list of pseudonyms that are valid for use in the cell. Each pseudonym has two components: the cell's ID and a random number as host ID. Instead of issuing pseudonyms to vehicles proactively (as virtually all existing schemes do) the authors issue pseudonyms only to those vehicles that request them. This strategy is suggested by the fact that, in a typical scenario, only a fraction of the vehicles in an area will engage in communication with other vehicles and/or with the infrastructure and, therefore, do not need pseudonyms. The second main contribution is to model analytically the time-varying request for pseudonyms in a given cell. This is important for capacity planning purposes since it allows system managers to predict, by taking into account the time-varying attributes of the traffic, the probability that a given number of pseudonyms will be required at a certain time as well as the expected number of pseudonyms in use in a cell at a certain time. Empirical results obtained by detailed simulation confirm the accuracy of the authors' analytical predictions.

Section 6
Wireless Sensor Networks

Chapter 14

Meenakshi Tripathi, Malaviya National Institute of Technology, India

M.S. Gaur, Malaviya National Institute of Technology, India

V.Laxmi, Malaviya National Institute of Technology, India

Wireless Sensor Networks are a subset of ad hoc networks. Their unique characteristics are smaller node size, high node density, unattended operation in remote areas. Dynamic topology and wireless communication make them vulnerable to numerous types of attacks. In addition to that, memory, processing, and energy constraint make it difficult to incorporate compute-intensive security solutions in these networks. Existing solutions for developing cost and energy efficient algorithms do not fit the security parameters for these resource constrained networks. As a result, these networks remain vulnerable to several types of attacks. This chapter presents a survey of various attacks at the different layers of WSN protocol stack, their detection, and countermeasures. Although every layer of the stack has its own security challenges, the network layer is most vulnerable to many security attacks because it provides an excellent basis for traffic monitoring activities, which helps the attacker form a strategy to perform the attack. The most common attacks on this layer are the Sybil attack, selective forwarding attack, wormhole attack, sinkhole attack, etc. This survey provides a comprehensive view of present attacking strategies to disrupt the normal functioning of WSN.

Chapter 15

Nazar Elfadil, Fahad Bin Sultan University, Saudi Arabia

Yaqoob J. Al-Raisi, The Research Council of the Sultanate of Oman, Sultanate of Oman

The success of Wireless Sensor Network application monitoring relies on the accuracy and reliability of its nodes operation. Unfortunately, operation deviations of these nodes appear as regular occurrences not isolated events as in traditional networks. This is due to their special characteristics that reduce network manufacturing and deployment costs and maintain the nodes immunity against internal and external conditions. The goal of this chapter is to propose a real-time, distributed, passive, and low resources usage performance-monitoring algorithm that monitors Wireless Sensor Network functionality and isolates the detected deviated nodes from norm operation. Simulation and empirical experiments showed that the proposed algorithm has a slight processing and storage overhead. It is important to mention that these experiments showed that the proposed algorithm has a high reliability in tracking and isolating network nodes problems.

Section 7
Cloud and Mobile Communications

Chapter 16

Hassan Takabi, University of Pittsburgh, USA

Saman Taghavi Zargar, University of Pittsburgh, USA

James B. D. Joshi, University of Pittsburgh, USA

Mobile cloud computing has grown out of two hot technology trends, mobility and cloud. The emergence of cloud computing and its extension into the mobile domain creates the potential for a global, interconnected mobile cloud computing environment that will allow the entire mobile ecosystem to enrich their services across multiple networks. We can utilize significant optimization and increased operating power offered by cloud computing to enable seamless and transparent use of cloud resources to extend the capability of resource constrained mobile devices. However, in order to realize mobile cloud computing, we need to develop mechanisms to achieve interoperability among heterogeneous and distributed devices. We need solutions to discover best available resources in the cloud servers based on the user demands and approaches to deliver desired resources and services efficiently and in a timely fashion to the mobile terminals. Furthermore, while mobile cloud computing has tremendous potential to enable the mobile terminals to have access to powerful and reliable computing resources anywhere and anytime, we must consider several issues including privacy and security, and reliability in realizing mobile cloud computing. In this chapter, the authors first explore the architectural components required to realize a mobile cloud computing infrastructure. They then discuss mobile cloud computing features with their unique privacy and security implications. They present unique issues of mobile cloud computing that exacerbate privacy and security challenges. They also discuss various approaches to address these challenges and explore the future work needed to provide a trustworthy mobile cloud computing environment.

Chapter 17

This chapter provides an overview of Near Field Communication (NFC) technology. It first introduces the technology and gives a brief history. It examines what the technology is and how it works. It looks at the various operation modes and hardware architectures available for the technology. This is followed by some examples in use of the technology today, in particular NFC in use in mobile payment environment. The chapter then focuses on NFC technology from the perspective of security and privacy of personal information when using the technology. Finally, the chapter looks at the security and privacy challenges that are currently faced by the technology and suggests some possible solutions to these challenges.

Chapter 18

User-centric wireless networks are characterized by a community-scale objective aiming at the shared provision of user-generated services and contents. This may be contrasted by the reticence of individuals to share the limited resources of mobile devices. Hence, cooperation incentives play a key role to promote prosocial decisions and to isolate selfish nodes and cheating behaviors. In particular, trust-based incentives and remuneration are used to induce collaborative behaviors in Wi-Fi communities. Typically, these mechanisms are based on reputation infrastructures and virtual currency systems, the application of which should not hinder the normal operation of the network. In this chapter, the authors present an approach to the combined use of indirect rewards deriving from trust-based incentives and direct rewards deriving from remuneration. The effectiveness and efficiency of such an approach in the setting of user-centric wireless networks is verified by conducting a formal study of the benefits of the joint application of these rewards and of the related impact upon performance.

Section 8
Wireless Network Management and Analysis

Chapter 19

The next generation wireless networks will be heterogeneous wireless environments because of the coexistence of a large variety of wireless access technologies. The different networks have different architectures and protocols. So it is difficult for a user to roam from one radio system to another which can be solved by using the Internet protocol as a common interconnection protocol as it needs no assumptions about the characteristics of the underlying technologies. An all-IP wireless network is an IP-based wireless access system that makes wireless networks more robust, scalable, and cost effective. The nodes in such a network are mobile nodes as they change their location and point of attachment to the Internet frequently. The mobility management is an important research issue in an all-IP wireless network for providing seamless roaming facility to mobile nodes from one wireless system to another. The dynamic resource management is also required in this environment to ensure sufficient resource in the selected route for transmission or reception of the data packets during seamless roaming of the mobile nodes. This chapter is aimed at the researchers and the policy makers making them aware of the different means of mobility management and resource management for mobile nodes in all-IP wireless networks.

Refarming means re-arrangement of the traditionally allotted spectrum for a technology/application/service and carving out a part of the spectrum for technology/application/service with higher value. The refarming concept can be used for 3G network deployment in 2G bands or for 4G network deployment in 2G/3G bands. Relative to the UMTS core band (2100MHz), in the 900MHz band radio signal propagation loss is lower. Fewer base stations can be deployed in 900MHz band to achieve the same coverage. Especially in the rural areas, villages, etc., covering limited areas, the UMTS900 band coverage advantages are more obvious. The lower carrier frequency penetration capability becomes much stronger. It reduces the loss while penetrating the wall. This chapter aims to focus on the global UMTS900 refarming status, key advantages of UMTS900 refarming, major challenges of transitioning to UMTS900, technical feasibility of GSM/UMTS co-existence band, and UMTS900 frequency refarming case study in sandwich mode. ECC interference analysis and simulation results are provided for study on co-existence of GSM900 and UMTS900. In the later part of the chapter a detailed case study on 900MHz refarming on sandwich mode is provided with system simulation, frequency planning, capacity migration, and deployment strategy.

Preface

After successful deployment of Wi-Fi and cellular networks in the past decade, wireless and mobile communication systems became the fastest growing sector of the communication industry, and there are different networks based on the coverage area: Wireless Personal Area Network (WPAN), Wireless Local Area Network (WLAN), Wireless Metropolitan Area Network (WMAN), and Wireless Wide Area Network (WWAN). The vision of being connected anywhere and anytime is no longer just an idea; it is becoming a reality because of the combination of mobile devices with wireless communication technologies. Almost all businesses that rely on wireless and mobile networks expect the same or a similar level of security, privacy, and trust as the ones that exist in wired networks to ensure the integrity and confidentiality of communications among terminals, networks, applications, and services. Many physical, capacity, and economic limitations of wireless and mobile networks represent important challenges. Yet, it is very challenging to ensure security, privacy, trust, and resource management because of the mobility of network nodes.

Although higher layer security mechanisms and protocols address wireless security challenges to a large extent, more security vulnerabilities arise due to the increasingly pervasive existence of wireless communication devices. Secure transmission is a concern for wireless devices and networks due to the broadcast nature of signals. By exploiting variations in the transmission channel, wireless devices can generate a shared secret key to provide security in the physical layer. The physical layer security concept is linked to two main desired features. The first is system reliability, which means that a message intended for a specific user should be reliably received by that user. The second is message secrecy, which means that a transmitter wants to communicate a secret message to a legitimate receiver.

With the advent of ad hoc networking technologies, mobile users could form a Mobile Ad Hoc Network (MANET) where users have an opportunity to create their own wireless network on the fly. MANETs represent a milestone in the evolution of wireless networks; however, they inherit the traditional limitations of mobile and wireless communication systems, such as allocation of bandwidth, transmitting power, coverage, etc. In MANETs, each node can directly communicate with other nodes using a direct link (i.e., single hop) or multi-hop communications. In this case, each node works as a source, a router, or a destination node. Nodes rely on the message received from other nodes, and thus, it is important to measure the trustworthiness of the received messages. As a consequence, each node needs security, privacy, and trust management schemes to protect the MANET as a whole.

Vehicular Ad Hoc Networks (VANETs) are a special form of MANETs where vehicles exchange information with each other while they travel on the road. Because of the high speed of the vehicles, VANETs have highly dynamic topologies, which result in frequent communication link breakage. In addition, vehicles' identities are linked with the identities of owners/drivers. As a consequence, it is not secure to use Vehicle Identification Numbers (VINs) or other private information that is linked to the owner or driver. To provide security and privacy, anonymity of vehicles is commonly used to participate in communications. In this case, malicious drivers can easily mislead the communication by injecting false information when ad hoc networks do not have the capability of tracking malicious drivers. Therefore, security, privacy, and trust in VANETs are key components to realizing its full potential.

Recent advances in Micro-Electro-Mechanical Systems (MEMS) technology have made it easy to build small, inexpensive, and energy-efficient wireless nodes that make a Wireless Sensor Network (WSN) a reality. In WSN, each node is comprised of a sensing, processing, transmitting, and power unit. When sensor nodes are deployed in a remote location, they are supposed to coordinate with each other to perform a specific action. Each operation of the sensor node costs the battery life, and no one would be able to change the battery in the sensor or deploy new sensors, especially in war zones. WSN has wide range of applications including temperature sensing, pressure sensing, inventory tracking, seismic detection, mobility sensing, environment monitoring, homeland security, etc. Despite their diverse applications, WSN poses a number of unique technical challenges due to several factors, such as fault tolerance, scalability, operating environment, network topology, transmit media, power consumption, limited security implementation, etc.

In true mobile communications to provide seamless mobility, there is an intrinsic problem related to mobility in the data network that uses the IP address as the node's identifier and location within a sub network. When a mobile node moves from one network to another, the assigned IP can no longer serve as a locator for the node in the new network. Mobile IPv4 (MIPv4) and Mobile IPv6 (MIPv6) are emerging to provide macro-mobility support using IPv4 and IPv6 network protocol stacks. Mobility in this type of network is effective when the mobile nodes are one hop away from access routers. The emergence of cloud computing and its extension into the mobile domain creates the potential for a global, interconnected mobile cloud computing environment that will allow the entire mobile ecosystem to enrich their services across multiple networks.

This book is organized as follows:

- Section 1 introduces the fundamentals of mobile and wireless communications networks;
- Section 2 presents physical layer security;
- Section 3 discusses about vehicular communications and networking;
- Section 4 describes security in mobile ad hoc networks;
- Section 5 deals with trust and privacy in wireless networks;
- Section 6 discusses the wireless sensor network and its challenges;
- Section 7 describes the applications and issues of cloud and mobile communications;
- Section 8 deals with wireless network management and analysis.

In more detail:

- Section 1 includes chapters titled "Introduction to Mobile and Wireless Communications Networks" and "Security in Wireless Metropolitan Area Networks: WiMAX and LTE;"
- Section 2 includes "Physical Layer Security and Its Applications: A Survey" and "Physical Layer Security in Wireless Communication Networks;"

- Section 3 includes "Security and Connectivity Analysis in Vehicular Communication Networks," "Location Security in Vehicular Wireless Networks," "Misbehavior Detection in VANET: A Survey," and "Intrusion Detection in Vehicular Ad-Hoc Networks on Lower Layers;"
- Section 4 includes "Security Issues in Mobile Ad Hoc Networks: A Survey" and "Security and Privacy in Mobile Ad Hoc Social Networks;"
- Section 5 includes "A Multi-Parameter Trust Framework for Mobile Ad Hoc Networks," "Trust Management and Modeling Techniques in Wireless Communications," and "Privacy Protection in Vehicular Ad-Hoc Networks;"
- Section 6 includes "Security Challenges in Wireless Sensor Networks" and "Voting Median Base Algorithm for Measurement Approximation of Wireless Sensor Network Performance;"
- Section 7 includes "Mobile Cloud Computing and Its Security, Privacy, and Trust Management Challenges," "State of the Art for Near Field Communication: Security and Privacy within the Field," and "Modeling and Verification of Cooperation Incentive Mechanisms in User-Centric Wireless Communications;"
- Section 8 includes "Seamless Mobility Management: A Need for Next Generation All-IP Wireless Networks" and "900 MHz Spectrum Refarming Analysis for UMTS900 Deployment."

This book covers the fundamental concepts and current issues, challenges, and solutions in wireless and mobile networks. We hope it serves as a reference for graduate students, professors, and researchers in this emerging field.

Danda B. Rawat
Georgia Southern University, USA

Bhed B. Bista
Iwate Prefectural University, Japan

Gongjun Yan
University of Southern Indiana, USA

Acknowledgment

This book would not have been published without the contribution of several people. First and foremost, we would like to express our warm appreciation to the authors who work hard to contribute the chapters and have chosen this book as a platform to publish their research findings. Special thanks go to the contributors' universities and organizations who allowed them the valuable time and resources towards the effort of writing the chapters. We would also like to express our warm appreciation to the editorial advisory board members and reviewers who gave their valuable time to reviewing chapters and helping us select high quality chapters.

Finally, we want to thank our families who supported and encouraged us in spite of all the time this book took us away from them. Last and not least, we beg forgiveness of all we have failed to mention.

Danda B. Rawat
Georgia Southern University, USA

Bhed B. Bista
Iwate Prefectural University, Japan

Gongjun Yan
University of Southern Indiana, USA

Section 1
Fundamentals of Mobile and Wireless Communication Networks

Chapter 1
Introduction to Mobile and Wireless Communications Networks

Danda B Rawat
Georgia Southern University, USA

Bhed Bahadur Bista
Iwate Prefectural University, Japan

Gongjun Yan
University of Southern Indiana, USA

ABSTRACT

Wireless communication networks offer transmission of signals, such as voice, data, and multimedia, without using wires, which is the crucial part of mobile communications. After successful deployment of wireless cellular networks in licensed bands and Wi-Fi networks in unlicensed bands, such as Industry, Scientific, and Medical (ISM) and Unlicensed National Information Infrastructure (UNII), over the last decade, several wireless networks, application, and services are emerging. Furthermore, wireless networks offer several advantages including mobility while getting service, scalability for further extension, reduced cost-of-ownership, and so on. However, there are some disadvantages and concerns, such as security, data rate, reliability, range, etc. The demand of ubiquitous communications is driving the development of wireless and mobile networks. Wireless communication is the fastest growing segment of the communication industry. This chapter provides the fundamentals of wireless and mobile networks and their advantages and disadvantages.

DOI: 10.4018/978-1-4666-4691-9.ch001

INTRODUCTION

Wireless communications is the fastest growing segment of the communication industry. Wireless technologies and applications have been widely deployed in various areas. Generally, wireless networks are categorized into two different types based on the structure of the networks: Infrastructure-based wireless networks and infrastructure less wireless networks.

Wireless network where wireless devices communicate with each other through centralized infrastructure such as base station in cellular network and access point in Wi-Fi networks is known as infrastructure-based wireless network. In this type of network, generally, centralized infrastructure is fixed and wireless users are mobile. Mobile users connect to fixed equipment through wireless links and can move anywhere within a coverage area of a basestation or access point. Mobile users can also move from one basestation's coverage area to another by using handover features.

Wireless devices communicate with each other without using any centralized infrastructure forming a network called infrastructure-less network. This type of network is also known as wireless ad hoc network or peer-to-peer network and all users could move forming true mobile communications. The network topology of wireless ad hoc network is dynamic and changes constantly.

Both infrastructure and infrastructure-less wireless network can transmit voice, data or multimedia without using wires such as in cellular network, Wi-Fi with VoIP, etc. Wireless communication networks are popular because of several advantages such as mobility and convenience, cost efficiency, and ease of integration with other networks and network components, ease of expansion.

WIRELESS COMMUNICATION NETWORKS

Wireless networks are further classified as wireless personal area network, wireless local area network, wireless metropolitan network and wireless wide area network.

Wireless Personal Area Network (WPAN)

Wireless network for interconnecting wireless devices centered around an individual person's workspace using ISM bands is known as wireless personal area network. Examples of WPAN are Bluetooth, Z-Wave, ZigBee, UWB and Body Area Network. WPAN devices follow IEEE 802.15 standard.

Bluetooth

In Bluetooth networks, wireless users use a pairing or association process to establish encryption and authentication between two devices. The association process takes 1 to 4 seconds. Bluetooth was standardized as IEEE 802.15.1. Bluetooth provides theoretical data transfer speeds of up to 24 Mbit/s. Bluetooth devices form a master slave like structure while pairing and use 48-bit hardware address of a master, shared 128-bit random number, and a user-specified PIN of up to 128 bits. It is assumed that the Bluetooth network is secured; unfortunately it is possible to break the Bluetooth network [Shaked, Y., & Wool, A., 2005] by sniffing the packet or exploiting vendor specific flaws such as default setting of allowing any pairing. To protect Bluetooth devices, users need to change default setting and choose strong PINs.

ZigBee

ZigBee network operates in the ISM bands and its data transmission rates vary from 20 to 900 kb/s. Two devices take about 30 milliseconds to get associated. IEEE 802.15.4 standard defines the characteristics of ZigBee devices. To provide network security, ZigBee runs in two different security modes: Residential mode and Commercial mode. In residential mode, all users use pre-deployed key for the entire PAN and for all applications. Residential mode security protects the PAN from external eavesdroppers; however it does not provide the security from the user within the same PAN. In Commercial mode, the coordinator node in a trust center is used to pre-share the two master keys that provide extra security on top of residential mode. This method is costly since infrastructure is needed to have centralized coordinator node for the trust center to store sessions for each links.

Ultra Wide Band (UWB) Network

UWB network, IEEE 802.15.4a standard, uses low transmit-power and cover small coverage area. To attack this type of networks, the attacker should be close enough to the UWB network. The FCC in the US authorizes the unlicensed use of UWB in the range of 3.1 to 10.6 GHz. There are no standard security modes in UWB networks. According to WiMedia [ECMA International, 2013] there are three levels of link-layer security: Security Level 0 in which communication is fully unencrypted, Security Level 1 which has both encrypted communications with AES-128 for encrypted links and unencrypted communications for unencrypted links, and Security Level 2 in which all communications must be encrypted with AES-128.

Wireless Body Area Network

IEEE 802.15.6 - 2012 serves the wireless communications standard for wireless body area network. Body area network uses ultra-low power wearable computing devices operating in or around the human body to form a wireless body area network. In particular, the network consists of several miniaturized body sensor units together with a single body central unit.

Wireless Local Area Network

Wireless local area network (WLAN) is based on IEEE 802.11 standard for implementing wireless network in the 2.4, 3.6, 5 and 60 GHz frequency bands. IEEE standardized wireless LAN in 1997. Wireless communications has been tested in 1971 by researcher at the University of Hawaii. IEEE 802.11 Wireless LAN can be configured to operate in an infrastructure (AP) mode or in an ad-hoc mode.

In AP mode, wireless client stations (STAs) connect with each other through an Access Point (AP). In AP mode WLAN, all communications pass through an AP which means wireless clients cannot communicate with each other directly. When WLAN has only one AP, it is called Basic Service Set (BSS) as shown in Figure 1, in which

Figure 1. Wireless LAN in AP Mode (also known as BSS)

Figure 2. Extended service set

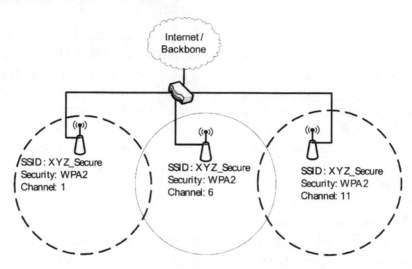

the network consists of an AP and several wireless devices. The area covered by a transmission range of an AP is called basic service area (BSA).

For roaming or mobility support, basic service sets can be combined to form an Extended Service Set (ESS) via single backbone system to provide roaming for wireless clients as shown in Figure 2.

In order to avoid interference, wireless APs should be configured in non-overlapping adjacent channels, otherwise, the performance of wireless LAN will be significantly degraded [Roshan, P., & Leary, J., 2004]. However the other configuration and network name should be the same for all APs in ESS setup.

In Ad hoc Mode WLAN, wireless devices communicate with each other directly without using centralized AP as shown in Figure 3, the wireless LAN configuration is called an Independent Basic Service Set (IBSS). One of the ad hoc wireless nodes (e.g. computer) should be configured to provide SSID for wireless ad hoc networking.

Figure 3. Wireless LAN in Ad Hoc Mode: IBSS

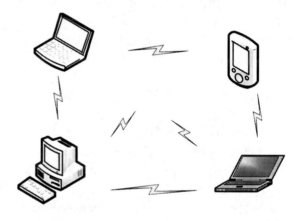

Wireless Metropolitan Area Network (WMAN)

A wireless metropolitan area network (WMAN) is intended to cover area of approximately the size of a city. Span of a WMAN spans a larger area than a WLAN but smaller than a wireless wide area network. Multiple base stations are used to coverage entire city area in WMAN.

Worldwide Interoperability for Microwave Access (WiMAX) [Pareek, D., 2006; Rawat, et al, 2013; WiMAX] is an example of WMAN that can offer data-transfer rates of up to 75 Mbps or an area of radius of about 50 km (30 miles). WiMAX bases on IEEE 802.16 standard. Radio frequency bands: 10 to 66 GHz (licensed bands), 2 to 11 GHz (licensed bands), 2 to 11 GHz (unlicensed bands) are used by the WiMAX IEEE 802.16 standard.

WiMAX still has some shortcomings in terms of security. Among different IEEE 802.16 standards, 802.16a/d standards make use of public-key encryption keys. However, it does not provide adequate protection against data forgery. IEEE 802.16e implements a 128-bit encryption key mode based on the Advanced Encryption Standard (AES) to remove the flaws that are present in 802.16a/d. The man-in-the-middle attacks launched using rouge basestation are mitigated by mutual authentication [Johnston, D., & Walker, J., 2004].

Wireless Wide Area Network (WWAN)

Wireless WAN consists of point-to-point or point-to-multi-point wireless connections between two or more wireless networks including different wireless technologies. WWANs have the capability of covering very large geographical area. The WWAN can provide wireless broadband communication for internet access through special adaptors. Data rate in WWAN is much lower than that in WLAN. Cellular wireless telephone network is an example of WWAN.

Cellular Wireless Telephone Network

Cellular telephone communications uses basestation to cover a certain area known as cell [Goldsmith, A., 2005]. Mobile users connect to their basestation to communicate with each other. Mobile users can move within a cell during communications and can move from one cell to another using handover technique without breaking communications. Wireless systems are prone to interference from other users who share same frequency for the communications. To avoid interference between cells, adjacent cell use different frequencies as shown in Figure 4.

Cellular networks have been commercially available since early 1980s. Japan implemented cellular telephone systems in 1979 and became the first country to deploy a cellular telephone network. European countries implemented Nordic Mobile Telephony (NMT) in 1982. In 1983, the US deployed Advanced Mobile Phone System (AMPS) as its first cellular telephone network [Lee, W. C., 2006].

There are different generations of cellular telephone systems [Goldsmith, A., 2005; Lee, W. C., 2006]. 1G network was able to transmit voice with maximum speed of about 9.6Kb/s. 1G telecommunication networks used analog modulation to transmit voice and are regarded as analog telecommunication networks.

1G cellular system has some limitations such as poor voice quality, no support of encryption, inefficient use of frequency spectrum, and poor interference handling techniques.

2G's primary focus was voice communications although it served as a remedy of several limitations of 1G. In the US, CDMA (Code Division Multiple Access), North American Time Division Multiple Access (NA-TDMA) and Digital AMPS (D-AMPS) have been deployed as 2G cellular network. In Europe, Time Division Multiplexing (TDM) based GSM (Global System for Mobile

Figure 4. Cells with different frequencies in cellular telephone networks (Rawat et al, 2013)

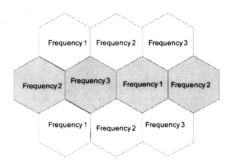

communication) has been deployed whereas in Japan Personal Digital Cellular (PDC) has been deployed. GSM based cellular system has become the most widely adopted 2G technology in the world.

Active research for data communications along with voice communication service resulted in data services over 2G developed and became 2.5G. The 1xEV-DO and 1xEV-DV have been deployed as 2.5G in the US.

The third generation (3G) cellular system was developed with the goal of providing fast internet connectivity, enhanced voice communication, video telephone, and so on. CDMA2000 in the US, Wideband-CDMA (WCDMA) in Europe, and Time Division-Synchronous Code Division Multiple Access (TD-SCDMA) in China were deployed as 3G cellular networks. 3G has been deployed in the most of the countries and is being used in major communication networks. Service providers have already started deploying the fourth generation (4G) cellular communication systems which offer data rate of up to 20Mbps and support mobile communication in moving vehicles with speed up to 250 km/hr.

Fourth generation (4G) aims of incorporating high quality of service and mobility in which a mobile user terminal will always select the best possible access available. 4G also aims of using mobile IP with IPv6 address scheme in which

each mobile device will have its own globally unique IP address.

In general, cellular network has two main parts [Yang, H., Ricciato, F., Lu, S., & Zhang, L.; 2006, Rawat *et al,* 2013],

- The Radio Access Network (RAN)
- The Core Network (CN)

Mobile users gain access wirelessly to the cellular network via radio access network (RAN) as shown in Figure 5. RAN is connected to core area network (CN). The core network is connected to internet via gateways through which mobile users can receive multimedia services. The core network is also connected to public switched network (PSTN).

The RAN consists of the existing GPRS, GSM or CDMA cellular telephone networks in which Radio Network Controller (RNC) or Basestation connector (BSC) is connected to packet switched core network (PS-CN) to provide the interaction between RAN and CN.

The core network consists of circuit switch networks, packet switched networks and IP multimedia networks. The high-end network servers facilitate the core network and provide several functions through Home Location Register (HLR) to maintain subscriber information, the visitor location register (VLR) to maintain temporary data

Figure 5. Cellular telephone network architecture (Rawat et al, 2013)

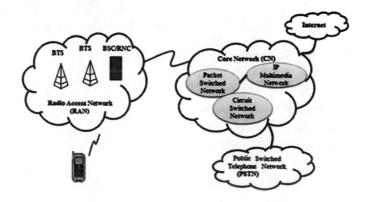

of subscribers, the mobile switching center (MSC) to interface the RAN and CN, and the gateway switching center (GMSC) to route the calls to the actual location of mobile users Xenakis, C., & Merakos, L., 2004].

Every subscriber is permanently assigned to a home network and is also affiliated with a visiting network through which subscribers can roam onto it. The home network is responsible to maintain subscriber profile and current location. The visiting network is the network where a mobile user is currently roaming. It is important to note that the visiting networks provide all the functionality to mobile users on behalf of the home network.

IP based servers such as DNS, DHCP and RADIUS servers interact with the gateways and provide control and management functions needed for mobile users while getting service from the Internet.

Other Wireless Ad Hoc Network

Mobile Ad-Hoc Network MANET

A mobile ad-hoc network (MANET) consists of mobile nodes equipped with wireless communication devices. There is no fixed infrastructure in pure MANET so when two wireless nodes are within the communication range of each other they can communicate with each other using single hop communication and when they out of their transmission ranges, other nodes located between them can forward their messages using multihop communications. In MANET, each node needs to be equipped with the capability of an autonomous system including computing, storing and routing. The mobile nodes can move arbitrarily in MANET and form a dynamic network topology. Some of the main characteristics of MANET are frequent communication link breakage due to mobile nodes, limited resources (bandwidth, computing power, battery lifetime, etc.) and instant deployment. There are several applications of MANET include military operation, emergency rescue, mesh networks, wireless sensor networks, multi-hop cellular networks, vehicular communications.

A Vehicular Ad-hoc Network (VANET) as shown in Figure 6 is a special case of MANET to enable exchange of information among nearby vehicles using vehicle-to-vehicle (V2V) communications and/or vehicle-to-roadside (V2R) communications. VANETs are expected to implement variety of wireless technologies like Wi-Fi or Dedicatee Short Range Communication (DSRC) as well as on long-range cellular systems to provide road safety and transport efficiency by providing timely information to drivers and concerned authorities, and provide Internet access on the move to ensure wireless ubiquitous connectivity. VANET is envisioned to be able to provide a wide range of applications, including safety applications (e.g., lane merge, collision

Figure 6. Vehicular ad hoc network (VANET) special case of mobile ad hoc network (MANET)

avoidance and safety warnings), traffic applications (e.g. real-time traffic congestion, speed and routing information), entertainment and information sharing applications (e.g. media and content sharing), and other applications. In VANET, there are several concerns to be addressed such as security and privacy of drivers or passengers since vehicle owners' information is directly related to the information of vehicle. Communication between highly mobile vehicles is very challenging as there will be limited time for connection setup and exchanging messages. Message transmission delay for time critical emergency messages in vehicular network is very important metric.

Wireless Sensor Networks

Wireless sensor network (WSN) consists of a number of sensor nodes and one or more sink nodes [Akyildiz, I. F. and Vuran, M. C., 2010]. A sensor node senses its environment and collects data which is sent to the sink node. The sink node processes data received from sensor nodes. The processed data may be automatically interpreted to action or it may be displayed to the user for making decision about the environment.

Sending data from a sensor node to the sink node may be triggered by an event or a sensor node may be configured to send data continuously or periodically. In some applications, a sensor node will send data upon receiving request from the sink node. In general, sensor nodes are assumed to be stationary whereas a sink node may be stationary or mobile. The communication between the stationary sink node and sensor nodes will be mutihop whereas the communication between the mobile sink node and sensor nodes will in general be single hop.

WSN is an application specific network and depending upon the application, sensor nodes are dropped from the air, for example for monitoring bush fire or monitoring enemy territory. Sensors may be put manually at a specific location for example monitoring wild life habitat, roads,

building structures and so on. Due to the nature of WSN, there are many challenges that need to be addressed and tackled for its successful deployment and operation.

Sensor nodes are battery operated and they self-organize to form a network to monitor an area or an object. One of the major challenges in WSN is how to increase the network's operation life. The major power consuming module in a wireless sensor node is the communication module which consumes a large portion of power for transceiving data and network management packets. Each sensor node sends its data to the sink node in mutihop manner. Nodes on the communication path to the sink node have to forward other nodes' data as well.

A large number of transceiving events occur in WSN for forming the network, maintaining it and transporting requests and data in between sensor nodes and the sink node. There are many research papers that address the energy efficient routing protocols and algorithms. Basically the aim of the researches is to reduce the number of transceiving events in WSN. To reduce the power consumption by other modules of a sensor node, sleep wakeup cycle of nodes are also considered. When a node is in sleep cycle its power consumption is minimal. There are still many challenges to tackle. Sensor nodes near to the sink node and on the communication path consume more energy as they have to transfer data for other nodes also. Scheduling sleep wake up cycle for sensor nodes is not trivial task.

Security and privacy in WSN is another major challenge. WSN is a wide open network. It is vulnerable for attack such as modifying the data, routing the data to an illegitimate node and so on. An illegitimate node may take the advantage of spectrum leakage of WSN and put itself within the WSN communication range and receive data without disrupting it. Due to the limitation of processing capacity of sensor nodes, the conventional security measure used in other wireless network cannot be easily implemented in WSN.

Any security related protocols and algorithms for WSN should not be computationally intensive. Privacy is also a major issue, especially where WSN is used for monitoring health, people's movement or anything that involves monitoring related to people.

Though individual sensor have been used extensively for monitoring health, objects, environment, fire, flood etc., the deployment of WSN is not wide spread yet even after many years of extensive research. This is because, among others, finding an appropriate communication protocol and algorithm, security and privacy management scheme for resources (computational, storage and power supply) limited sensor nodes is still a big challenge.

Cognitive Radio Network

Most of the current spectrum assignment rules in existing wireless communication networks around the world challenge the dynamic spectrum access aspects due to static RF spectrum assignment to the service providers for exclusive use on a long term basis. The exclusive spectrum licensing by government regulatory bodies, such the Federal Communications Commission (FCC) in the United States, and its counterparts around the world, is for interference mitigation among different service providers and their users. However, the static RF spectrum assignment to particular service provider leads to inefficient use of spectrum since most portion of the spectrum remains under-utilization [Akyildiz et al., 2006].

Cognitive radio (CR) system is an emerging concept to increase the spectrum efficiency which uses the spectrum opportunities dynamically without creating harmful interference to licensed primary users. The dynamic spectrum access for spectrum sharing in CR systems has two basic approaches [Akyildiz et al., 2006, Haykin, 2005]. One is *spectrum overlay* technique whereby un-

licensed CR users require to sense and identify the spectrum opportunities in licensed bands before using them for given time and geographic location, and exploit those opportunities dynamically. Whenever the primary users are active in given frequency band for given time and location, secondary CR users are not allowed to use that band. Once they find the spectrum opportunities they can use those opportunities dynamically until the primary systems want to use them and the CR users have to leave the band as quickly as possible [Haykin, 2005]. The other is *spectrum underlay* approach where secondary CR users coexist and transmit simultaneously with primary users sharing the licensed bands but CR users are not allowed to transmit with high power as they have to respect the active primary user transmissions. In this approach, secondary CR users do not have to sense the spectrum for opportunities however they are not allowed to transmit with higher than the preset power mask even if the primary system is completely idle. It is worth to note that the main goal in both approaches is to access the licensed spectrum dynamically and/or opportunistically without disturbing the primary user transmissions. In spectrum overlay approach, the major challenge to realize the full potential of CR systems is to identify the spectrum opportunities in the wide band regime reliably and optimally. And in spectrum underlay approach, the challenge is to transmit with low power so as not to exceed the tolerable interference level at primary users.

Main capabilities of CR users depend on sensed information from which they analyze and learned and then adapt their own operating parameters accordingly. All functionality of cognitive radio networks rely on sensed information. Therefore, robust spectrum sensing is a fundamental task in CR system.

CONCLUDING REMARKS

Over the past decade, there has been a rapid growth in wireless networks and several wireless networks, application and services are emerging as wireless personal area networks, wireless local area network, wireless wide area networks, and so on. The concluding remark is wireless networks have made successful mobile communications and made the entire world as a global e-village.

REFERENCES

Akyildiz, I. F., Lee, W. Y., Vuran, M. C., & Mohanty, S. (2006). NeXt generation/dynamic spectrum access/cognitive radio wireless networks: A survey. *Computer Networks, 50*(13), 2127–2159. doi:10.1016/j.comnet.2006.05.001.

Akyildiz, I. F., & Vuran, M. C. (2010). *Wireless sensor networks*. New York: John Wiley & Sons. doi:10.1002/9780470515181.

ECMA International. (2013). *ECMA international*. Retrieved May 5, 2013, from http://www.ecma-international.org

Goldsmith, A. (2005). *Wireless communications*. Cambridge, UK: Cambridge University Press. doi:10.1017/CBO9780511841224.

Haykin, S. (2005). Cognitive radio: Brain-empowered wireless communications. *IEEE Journal on Selected Areas in Communications, 23*(2), 201–220. doi:10.1109/JSAC.2004.839380.

Johnston, D., & Walker, J. (2004). Overview of IEEE 802.16 security. *IEEE Security & Privacy, 2*(3), 40–48. doi:10.1109/MSP.2004.20.

Lee, W. C. (2006). *Wireless and cellular telecommunications*. New York: McGraw-Hill.

Pareek, D. (2006). *WiMAX: Taking wireless to the max*. Boca Raton, FL: CRC Press. doi:10.1201/9781420013436.

Rawat, D. B. (April 15, 2013). *Computer and network security: An experimental approach*. CreateSpace Publishing Platform.

Rawat, D. B., Yan, G., Bista, B. B., & Chandra, V. (2013). *Wireless network security: An overview*. Boca Raton, FL: CRC Press.

Roshan, P., & Leary, J. (2004). *802. 11 wireless LAN fundamentals*. New York: Cisco Systems.

Shaked, Y., & Wool, A. (2005). Cracking the bluetooth pin. In *Proceedings of the 3rd International Conference on Mobile Systems, Applications, and Services* (pp. 39-50). ACM.

WiMAX. (2013). *Worldwide interoperability for microwave access*. Retrieved May 5, 2013, from http://www.wimax.com/

Xenakis, C., & Merakos, L. (2004). Security in third generation mobile networks. *Computer Communications, 27*(7), 638–650. doi:10.1016/j.comcom.2003.12.004.

Yang, H., Ricciato, F., Lu, S., & Zhang, L. (2006). Securing a wireless world. *Proceedings of the IEEE, 94*(2), 442–454. doi:10.1109/JPROC.2005.862321.

Chapter 2
Security in Wireless Metropolitan Area Networks:
WiMAX and LTE

Lei Chen
Sam Houston State University, USA

Cihan Varol
Sam Houston State University, USA

Qingzhong Liu
Sam Houston State University, USA

Bing Zhou
Sam Houston State University, USA

ABSTRACT

Thanks to the much larger geographical coverage and pleasing bandwidth of data transmissions, Wireless Metropolitan Area Networks (WMANs) have become widely accepted in many countries for everyday communications. Two of the main wireless technologies used in WMANs, the Worldwide Interoperability for Microwave Access (WiMAX, also known as Wireless Local Loop or WLL) and Long Term Evolution (LTE), have generated billions of dollars in the ever-growing wireless communication market. While the IEEE 802.16 standards for WiMAX and the 3GPP standards LTE are updated and improved almost annually, it is inevitable that current standards still contain a number of security vulnerabilities, potentially leading to various security attacks. To address the security concerns in these two WMANs technologies, this chapter presents the technical details of security aspects of WiMAX and LTE. More specifically, the key generation, authentication, data, and key confidentiality and integrity of both technologies are deliberated. The chapter ends with a discussion of the security vulnerabilities, threats, and countermeasures of WiMAX and LTE.

DOI: 10.4018/978-1-4666-4691-9.ch002

1. INTRODUCTION

A Metropolitan Area Network (MAN) can be described as a communication network that spreads over one or multiple adjacent neighboring cities and geographical areas (Ghosh, Wolter, Andrews, and Chen, 2005; MAN, 2009). The purpose of MANs is to enable an efficient transportation of data-oriented traffic in a much larger geographical area compared to Wireless Local Area Networks (WLANs) (WiMAX, n.d.; LTE, n.d.). Scalability is a main challenge in such a network that covers a relatively large range. Conventional wireless technologies would not survive in such situation when trying to meet the high capacity demands from nowadays users. As an example, researchers at Sprint's Applied Research & Advanced Technology Labs (AR&ATL) have proposed a next-generation, high-capacity metropolitan area network under their HORNET project that is designed to achieve cost-effective scaling using hybrid optoelectronic ring network (White, Rogge, Shrikhande, and Kazoysky, 2003).

A Local Area Network (or simply LAN), according to the IEEE 802-2002 standard (IEEE L/M SC, 2002), is generally owned and operated by a single organization whereas a MAN is usually designed to be used by more than one individuals and organizations, and sometimes also as public utilities. A variety of applications and services, such as file transfer, graphics, text and data processing, emails, database access and multimedia, are supported by both LANs and MANs. What makes a LAN and a MAN different mainly is the geographic regions covered: 0-2 miles for a typically LAN, and 2-30 miles for MANs. Both types of networks make used of a variety of network technologies, e.g. Asynchronous Transfer Mode (ATM), Fiber Distributed Data Interface (FDDI), Switched Multi-megabit Data Service (SMDS) and linked together using microwave, radio, infra-red or Ethernet-based connections. Some common examples of MANs can be found in large cities where the fire stations and emergency responder networks are interlinked across jurisdictions. Media companies such as newspapers, cable networks employ metro networks to coordinate their activities across different branch offices. In the next few sections, we will have a discussion of the basics and security aspects of two dominant WMAN technologies: WiMAX and LTE.

2. FUNDAMENTALS OF WIMAX AND LTE

WiMAX and LTE are the two most widely accepted and applied MAN technologies. WiMAX can provide up to 70 mbps of bandwidth over a radius of several miles (WiMAX, n.d.), and is a true 4G technology being used by consumers in over 150 countries and gaining acceptance in several industries. The WiMAX Forum is an industry-led, not-for-profit organization that certifies and promotes the compatibility and interoperability of broadband wireless products based on the IEEE 802.16 Standards. Its competitor LTE, based on the GSM/EDGE and UMTS/HSPA network technologies, as specified in the 3rd Generation Partnership Project (3GPP) Release 8 and 9 document series, was not originally considered as a true 4G technology, but was later decided by the International Telecommunication Union (ITU) and introduced, for marketing purpose, by major service providers such as Verizon Wireless as a 4G technology. LTE supports cell sizes from tens of meters to up to 62 miles with peak download rates up to 300 mbps and upload rates up to 70 mbps (LTE, n.d.).

In the rest of this section, we will examine the fundamentals of WiMAX, the IEEE 802.16 Standard, and LTE. The IEEE 802.16 working group was formed to address the projected increase in the demand for metropolitan and wide-area wireless internet access over the next few years. This working group has put forth a standard for Broadband Wireless Access (BWA) systems, namely the IEEE 802.16 Standards. In this section we will also discuss the applications, technical aspects of the standard, and the services that can be expected by the end users.

2.1 WiMAX and LTE Overview

In June of 2001, a number of technology corporations and service providers came together to establish the WiMAX Forum. The forum was created with the objective of accelerating wide-scale adoption of the Broadband Wireless Access technology. This forum had three primary goals in mind (WiMAX Forum prnewswire, 2011):

- To establish standards and build equipment profiles ensuring interoperability;
- To work with government agencies for releasing spectrum;
- To establish and grow an ecosystem for encouraging wide adoption of WiMAX technologies.

The success of the WiMAX forum can be seen from the fact that WiMAX has not only attracted the conventional communications services, but also industries ranging from aviation, education, energy, government and healthcare.

On the other hand, LTE was introduced by NTT DoCoMo in the year of 2004, and LTE services were first provided by TeliaSonera in Norway and Sweden in late 2009. This technology appeared in 2010 as Verizon Wireless launched large scale LTE as an upgrade from the traditional GSM and CDMA (LTE, n.d.). As GSM counted for 89% of the global cellular market, according to Gartner Inc., LTE, being the natural upgrade from GSM, is expected to be the dominant technology for the 4G era (Hamblen, 2008; LTE: 4gamericas, n.d.). The LTE Advance technology, submitted formally as a 4G candidate in 2009, was finalized in 2011 by 3GPP to support up to 3.3gbps peak download rate per sector of base station under ideal conditions (LTE Advanced, n.d.).

2.2 WiMAX and LTE Network Topologies

The current IEEE 802.16 Standards support four different network topologies: Point-to-Point (P2P), Point-to-Multiple-Point (PMP), Multi-Hop Relay (MHR), and Mobile (Scarfone, Tibbs, and Sexton, n.d.). The P2P topology involves a Base Station (BS), a Subscriber Station (SS), and a dedicated long-range, e.g. up to 30 miles using Line of Sight (LOS) or 5 miles using None-LOS (NLOS), and high-capacity wireless link between the two parties. The PMP adds more SSs to P2P topology which is commonly used to provide last-mile broadband access. Due to the cell configuration and the high density of obstacles and high interference to signals, the operating range reduces to less than 5 miles. The MHR topology was defined in IEEE 802.16j-2009 and it extends the network by allowing SSs to relay traffic by acting as Relay Stations (RSs). The operating range between two nodes is less than 5 miles. Similar to a cellular network, a Mobile topology WiMAX network has multiple BSs working together to provide seamless communications to SSs. The communication range is also within 5 miles.

While LTE is mainly deployed in cellular networks, the most notable advance in topology change is the X2 traffic, where intelligent base stations can transmit data directly to one another, unlike in most other technologies which only allow transmissions solely with core network. This change cuts down on data delivery latency as data can be routed close to the cell site rather than be transported to network core (LTE TEN, n.d.; LTE BTE, n.d.; Backhauling X2, n.d.). Future LTE topology advances may include integrating small cells of various types of networks, such as pico, femto, and micro cells, forming Heterogeneous Networks or HetNets (LTE TEN, n.d.).

2.3 The IEEE 802.16 Standards

The first IEEE 802.16 Standard, put forth by the IEEE Standards Board in late 2001, was based on LOS technology in the 10-66 GHz spectrum. Due to the lack of support for NLOS operations, this standard was not suitable for lower frequency applications. From 2002 to 2004, the IEEE 802.16a through 802.16d standards were published to accommodate this requirement. These standards were developed for consumers to use as a replacement for the 802.11 WLAN standards. In 2005, an amendment to 802.16a/d standard was made and the IEEE 802.16e was released. This standard has been commercialized under the name WiMAX by the WiMAX Forum Industry Alliance (WiMAX Forum, n.d.). This forum supports and certifies the compatibility and interoperability of commercial devices and equipment based on the IEEE 802.16 standards. Table 1 (Nguyen, 2009) summarizes the different standards in the IEEE 802.16 family.

Note that the standard 802.16a/d in Table 1 are "fixed", implying stationary and nomadic use with limitation that end devices cannot move between base stations but with the provision that they can enter the network at different locations (Nguyen, 2009). The IEEE 802.16e standard mitigates this limitation and addresses the mobility enabling Mobile Stations (MSs) to handover between base stations while communicating.

Besides the above IEEE 802.16 Standards, the IEEE 802.16-2009 Standard consolidated a number of previous 802.16 standards and amendments from 2004 through 2008. However the security aspects of IEEE 802.16-2009 is same as IEEE 802.16e and therefore is not considered separately as far as security is concerned.

The IEEE 802.16 Standards set different security requirements for various types of connections. Two types of connections are essential in WiMAX: management connections and data transport connections. Management connections have three subtypes: basic, primary, and secondary. A basic connection is created for each Mobile Station, or an SS with mobility, when it joins the network. This type of connection is used for short and urgent management messages. The primary connection is also created for each MS at the same time with the purpose for delay-tolerant management messages. The secondary management connection is used for IP encapsulated management messages such as DHCP and SNMP. Transport connections are set up as needed and they are used to carry user data.

Table 1. Summary of the IEEE 802.16 standards

Standards	802.16-2001	802.16a/802.16d	802.16e
Spectrum	10 to 63 GHz	< 11 GHz	< 6 GHz
Channel Conditions	Line-of-Sight only	Non-Line-of-Sight	Non-Line-of-Sight
Speed (bit rate)	32 to 134 Mbps	75 Mbps max, 20-MHz channelization	15 Mbps max, 5-MHz channelization
Modulation	QPSK 16QAM 64 QAM	OFDM 256 subcarrier QPSK 16QAM 64QAM	Same as 802.16a
Mobility	Fixed	Fixed	Pedestrian mobility, regional roaming
Channel Bandwidths	20, 25, and 28 MHz	Selectable between 1.25 and 20 MHz	Same as 802.16a with sub-channels
Typical Cell Radius	1 – 3 miles	3 – 5 miles (up to 30 miles, depending on tower height, antenna gain and transmit power)	1 – 3 miles

2.4 The 3GPP LTE Standards

3GPP is a collaborated project among organizational partners and telecommunication associations. The main purpose of 3GPP is to establish the third-generation (3G) mobile phone system specifications globally. Given the fact that LTE is an upgrade from the existing GSM services, it is no surprise that 3GPP holds the standards of LTE and its successors.

The first standard for LTE emerged in 2008 as Release 8, which specified that LTE supports technologies such as OFDMA and MIMO. Release 9 in 2009 extends its capability to support WiMAX and LTE interoperability. In an effort of pushing LTE to the true 4G realm, Release 10 in 2011 provided the specifications of LTE Advanced fulfilling IMT Advanced 4G requirements (3GPP, n.d.). Now LTE Advanced is considered as a true 4G technology and will still remain a major competitor of WiMax. The specifications of LTE are documented in the 3GPP's number 36 series. Details of these specifications can be found at www.3gpp.org (3GPP Specs, 2013).

3. SECURITY GOALS AND SOLUTIONS OF WIMAX AND LTE

The IEEE 802.16e Standard for WiMAX specifies a set of security mechanisms to protect confidentiality of data and secret keys, preserve integrity of data and control messages, and provide secure authentication as well as secure key generation and management (PKCS, n.d.; PKI, n.d.). These security goals are mainly addressed and achieved in the Security Sub-layer of the IEEE 802.16 Protocol Stack as shown in Figure 1 and are discussed in the rest of this section (PKCS, n.d.; Barbeau and Laurendeau, 2007). Acronyms used in the following discussions are listed and explained as follows.

- **RSA:** Currently the most widely used public key cipher in various secure authentication and communication protocols.

- **Security Association (SA):** A set of cryptographic methods and associated keying material containing the information about cryptographic ciphers and keys used. Each SS establishes at least one SA in the initialization process (WiMAX PKI, n.d.).

- **Extensible Authentication Protocol (EAP):** Defined in Request For Comments (RFC) 3748 and updated in RFC 5247, EAP is an authentication framework widely used in wireless networks and Point-to-Point connections (Xu, Matthews, and Huang, 2006). For WiMAX there are many methods defined by RFCs and a number of vendor specific methods each of which has

Figure 1. Security Sub-layer of IEEE 802.16 Protocol Stack

RSA-based Authentication	Authentication/SA Control	EAP Encapsulation/De-capsulation
PKM Control Management		
Traffic Data Encryption/Authentication Processing	Control Message Processing	
		Message Authentication Processing
Physical SAP		

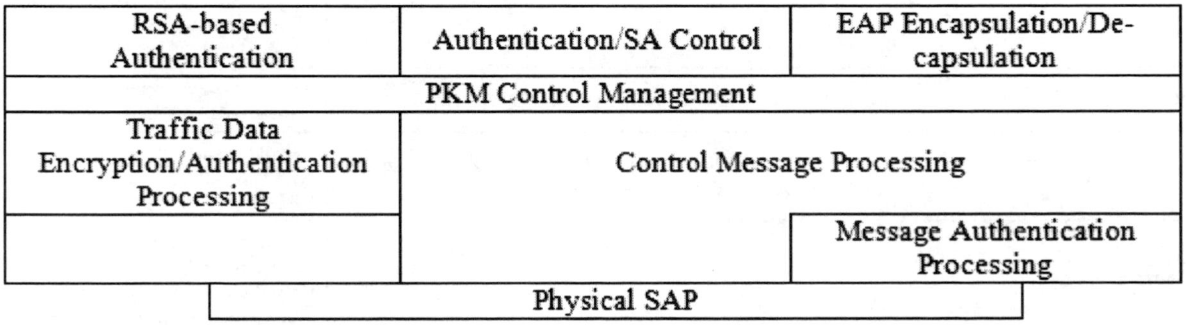

its own keying material and parameters (Xu et al, 2006).

- **Privacy Key Management Protocol (PKM):** PKM provides the secure distribution of keying data from the BS to the SS, and the synchronization of keying data. PKM is also used by the BS to enforce conditional access to network services. PKM Version 2 (PKMv2) was defined with enhanced security features in the 802.16e amendment (IEEE 802.16e, 2013).

The Security Sub-layer has been redefined in the IEEE 802.16e amendment to address a number of security vulnerabilities in the 802.16-2004 Standards. The 802.16e amendment defined PKMv2 with enhanced features. Table 2 summarizes the main differences between the two versions of PKM (IEEE 802.16e, 2013).

As a major competitor, LTE is designed and expected to have at least the same level of security in the current 3G networks (Zugenmaier and Aono, 2009). There are four main security requirements (Zugenmaier and Aono, 2009):

- While retaining user convenience, provide at least same security level as 3G networks
- LTE should defend the network and mobile devices from most current Internet attacks
- Smooth transition from 3G to LTE should not be affected by security functions introduced
- LTE should also continue supporting the use of Universal Subscriber Identity Module (USIM)

The 3GPP Authentication and Key Agreement (AKA) helps satisfy the security requirements 3 and 4. The TS33.210 standard specifications (3GPP TS33.210 V8.3.0, n.d.) protect the LTE core network by making use of Network Domain Security (NDS) just like in 3G networks. (Zugenmaier and Aono, 2009). On the other hand, due to the fact that some of the Radio Network Controller (RNC) functions are integrated in the network edge, or evolved Node B (eNB), the 3G security architecture cannon be reused in LTE. As eNB stores encryption key and provides integrity check, when the mobile terminal is not connected, the security relevant information will not be stored in eNB.

Table 2. The main differences between PKMv1 and PKMv2

Security Features	PKMv1	PKMv2
Authentication	RSA-based one-way authentication: the BS authenticates the SS	Mutual authentication. Supports two authentication methods: EAP or RSA
Security Association	One SA family: Unicast. Composed of three types of SAs: primary, dynamic and static.	Three SA families: Unicast SA, Group SA and MBS SA. Composed of the same three types of SAs as PKMv1
Key encryption	Use of three encryption algorithms: 3-DES, RSA and AES	New encryption method implemented: AES with Key Wrap
Data encryption	Two different algorithms are defined in the standard: DES in CBC mode, AES in CCM mode	Use of the same algorithms plus AES in CTR mode and AES in CBC mode implementation
Other additions		Management of security for: broadcast traffic, MBS traffic. Definition of a preauthentication procedure in the case of handover

3.1 WiMAX PKI and Digital Certificates

PKI is a set of hardware, software, people, policies, and procedures to create, manage, distribute, use, store, and revoke digital certificates (PKI, n.d.; DES, n.d.). The main purpose of PKI is to have trustworthy binding public keys with respective user identities by means of Certificate Authorities (CAs). In other words, if a certificate in the PKI is proven to be valid and genuine, the public key found in the certificate is then recognized as being genuine and the binding between this public key and the identity of the owner of the certificate is also validated (they are both from the same owner). According to the WiMAX PKI, each MS is preconfigured with an X.509 digital certificate (Barbeau and Laurendeau, 2007). The purpose of having X.509 certificates and their associated keys is to identify and authenticate the identity of devices or SSs and servers (WiMAX PKI, n.d.). The WiMAX CAs provide hosting of the WiMAX PKI hierarchy and supplies device and server certificates for used in WiMAX networks.

WiMAX PKI makes use of public key cryptography, e.g. RSA, to digitally sign certificates in a hierarchy of certificates. As shown in Figure 2, each certificate is digitally signed by a certificate at a higher level, back to a root certificate which signs itself to form a certificate chain. The format, content, and use of these X.509 certificates are described in RFC 3280. The cryptography related specifications, such as RSA cipher, can be found in the Public-Key Cryptography Standards (PKCS) #1 through #13 at RSA Laboratories website (WiMAX PKI, n.d.; PKCS, n.d.). Also illustrated in the figure, WiMAX has two hierarchies of PKI, one for the device identification and the other for the identification of the Authentication, Authorization and Accounting (AAA) servers.

Figure 3 shows a segment of a certificate chain. In each of the certificates, regardless of signing or being signed, the identity information, such as issuer identity and subject identity, the public key, and the validity dates are required (WiMAX PKI, n.d.). The signature of certificate issuer is attached to the certificate. Among the above information, signature of issuer, issuer identity, and subject identity are used to distinguish between a signing

Figure 2. Device and Server Hierarchies of WiMAX Public Key Infrastructure (PKI). Arrows refer to the process of signing

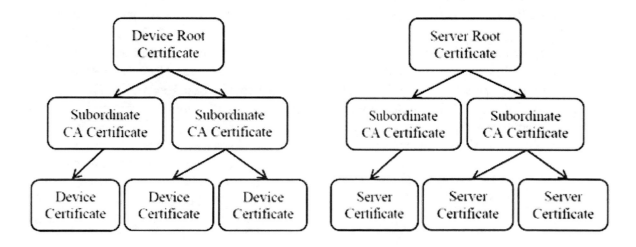

Figure 3. A segment of a certificate chain

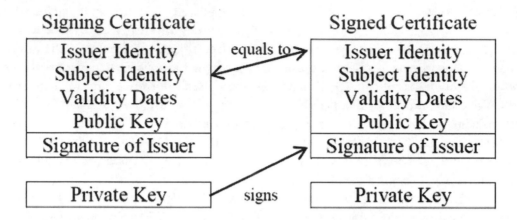

certificate and a signed certificate, e.g. the signature of issuer for a signed certificate is obtained from the signing using the issuer's private key, and the subject's identity of a signing certificate appears as the issuer identity of all signed certificates.

The exchange of certificates and other authentication information is needed when a WiMAX SS tries to connect to a BS using Transport Layer Security (TLS) (WiMAX PKI, n.d.). The SS sends the server its certificate chain which typically includes three to four certificates: its own certificate, the signing certificate, and all the higher signing certificates up to the root certificate, all of which are from the device hierarchy. On the other hand the AAA server sends its certificate chain, obtained from the server certificate hierarchy, to the SS. By accepting the digital certificates received, both the device and server accept the genuineness of the public keys included in the certificates, e.g. the public key found in a SS's certificate truly belongs to that SS. This process is essential in preparing for the key generation and management process as well as the authentication process.

3.2 Wimax Security Association, Key Generation and Management

Except for public keys, all other keys used in WiMAX are established during authorization, and they are subject to an aging process, therefore they must be refreshed periodically during reauthorization (Barbeau and Laurendeau, 2007). In WiMAX IEEE 802.16-2004, the following keys (not considering private keys as they are held only by the key owners) are defined in PKMv1 (Barbeau and Laurendeau, 2007; Nuaymi, 2007):

- **Public Key (PK):** The PK is included in an X.509 digital certificate that belongs to the same owner. The genuineness and binding to identity is proven when the certificate is validated. An SS mainly uses its PK for authentication with the BS and encrypting the Authorization Key using R5A cipher.

- **Authorization Key (AK):** The BS determines the 160-bit AK and encrypts it with the MS's PK. After the MS receives the encrypted AK, it uses its private key to decrypt and obtain AK. The lifetime for an AK is between one and 70 days with default value being seven days. To provide smooth transitions, two AKs may be active at the same time and they are distinguished using sequence numbers (from zero to 15).

- **Key Encryption Key (KEK):** A 128-bit KEK is determined by SS using AK. KEK is used as input to 3-DES cipher for encrypting the Traffic Encryption Key.
- **Traffic Encryption Key (TEK):** A 128-bit data encryption key with lifetime of 30 minutes to 7 days.
- **Hashed Message Authentication Code Key (HMAC Key):** The purpose of HMAC keys is to assure message integrity. There are three types of HMAC keys: 160-bit HMAC key for downlink (HMAC_KEY_D), 160-bit HMAC for uplink (HMAC_KEY_U), and HMAC key used in Mesh mode (HMAC_KEY_S). MS uses AK to determine HMAC keys. The sequence number of AK implicitly affects the value of HMAC keys.

In additional to the keys discussed above, PKMv2 protocol in 802.16e amendment enhanced the security of Authorization Key generation and introduced a number of new keys mainly for multicast services as shown in Table 3 (Xu et al, 2006)

WiMAX uses Security Association to specify the security parameters, such as keys and selected encryption algorithms, of a connection (Barbeau and Laurendeau, 2007). Among the four types of connections discussed previously, the basic and primary management connections do not have any associated SA, and SAs are optional for secondary management connections but required for all transport connections. A transport connection can either have one SA for both uplink and downlink or two separate SAs for the two directions (Barbeau and Laurendeau, 2007).

Each SA has a unique 16-bit identifier (SAID), a cryptographic suite identifier for selected algorithms, TEKs, and Initialization Vectors (IVs). SAs are managed by the Base Stations. There are three types of SAs: primary SA, static SA and dynamic SA (Barbeau and Laurendeau, 2007). For each MS a primary SA is established for its second-

Table 3. New keys introduced in PKMv2 and the 802.16e amendment

Keys	Functions/Derivation
Pairwise Master Key (PMK)	obtained from EAP authentication
Primary Authorization Key (PAK)	obtained from RSA-based authentication
Authorization Key (AK)	derived from PMK or PAK
Group Key Encryption Key (GKEK)	used for encrypting GTEK
Group Traffic Encryption Key (GTEK)	used for encrypting multicast data packets
Multicast Broadcast Service (MBS) Authorization Key (MAK)	authentication for MBS
MBS Group Traffic Encryption Key (GMTEK)	used for generating MTK with MAK
MBS Traffic Key (MTK)	used for protecting MBS Traffic; derived from MAK and MGTEK
H/CMAC/KEY_D	used for preserving message integrity for downlink
H/CMAC/KEY_U	used for preserving message integrity for uplink

ary management connection with the BS and it is established when the MS is initialized. This primary SA is unique and is only shared between a specific MS and BS. During the initialization of an MS, the BS creates one or multiple static SAs depending on the services that MS has subscribed, e.g. there may be a static SA for the basic unicast service and additional static SAs for each of other subscribed services. Dynamic SAs are only created when there are new traffic flows and they are closed when traffic flows are completed. In scenarios such as multicast, static SAs and dynamic SAs can be shared among multiple SSs.

3.3 LTE Key Hierarchy

Similar to 3G networks, LTE encrypts data by performing Exclusive OR (XOR) over the data stream with a generated key stream (Zugenmaier and Aono, 2009). The key hierarchy and relationship is described as follows (LTE: 4G, n.d.):

- **Key K:** 128-bit in length, is the master base key for GSM, UMTS, and Evolved Packet System (EPS); K is stored permanently in USIM and Authentication Center (AuC)
- **Cipher Key CK and Integrity Key IK:** Both 128-bit in length, are generated using K and established between AuC and USIM during AKA
- **KASME:** 256-bit in length, is an intermediate key derived in Home Subscriber Server (HSS) and User Equipment (UE) from CK and IK
- **KeNB:** 256-bit in length, is an intermediate key derived in Mobile Management Entity (MME) and UE from KASME; this key will be used to generate the next three keys used in UE and eNB
- **KUPenc, KRRCint, and KRRCenc:** All 256-bit in length, are relevant encryption keys and integrity key for protection of user plane data and Radio Resource Control (RRC) data derived in eNB and UE
- **KNASint and KNASenc:** Both 256-bit in length, are the integrity and encryption keys for protection of NAS data derived in MME and UE

3.4 WiMAX and LTE Authentication

This section discusses the authentication of WiMAX and LTE. Authentication in WiMAX includes three different types: BS authenticating SS as required in PKMv1, Mutual Authentication and Message Authentication required in PKMv2, which are elaborated in the next two subsections.

3.4.1 BS Authenticating SS in PKMv1 of WiMAX

In PKMv1, to start the authentication process, the SS sends the BS a PKM Authentication Information message which contains SS manufacturer X.509 certificate (Nuaymi, 2007). Then the SS

sends a PKM Authorization Request message containing the same certificate, the SS primary SAID, and a description of its security capabilities, e.g. supported ciphers. Upon receiving the request message, the BS uses the validated Public Key found within the received X.509 certificate to encrypt the Authorization Key and sends it, along with other information such as AK lifetime, sequence number, and SA descriptor(s), to the SS using a PKM Authorization Response Message. Replay attacks can be prevented with the help from the above-mentioned sequence number. After this point, the SS is required to periodically repeat authentication and key exchange to keep its key material up-to-date. The above process only implements one-way (BS to SS) authentication and the opposite direction authentication is missing. This security vulnerability is addressed and fixed in PKMv2.

3.4.2 Mutual Authentication in PKMv2 of WiMAX

Although both versions of PKM share the same security basis (Nuaymi, 2007), PKMv2 provides mutual authentication in which the SS also authenticates the BS. The mutual authentication process goes as follows.

- BS authenticates an SS.
- SS authenticates the BS.
- BS provides the authenticated SS with an AK.
- BS provides the authenticated SS with the identities and properties of primary and static SAs.

PKMv2 supports two different authentication protocols: X.509 digital certificates or Extensible Authentication Protocol (EAP). When X.509 certificate based authentication is used, the process is same in both directions as described in the previous subsection. If otherwise EAP is chosen, one of the defined and supported EAP authentication methods needs to be chosen, and corresponding security elements, such as subscriber identity module, password, X.509 certificate or others, will also be used in such method. Currently among the various available methods, Transport Layer Security (TLS) and Tunneled Transport Layer Security (TTLS) are recommended by the WiMAX Forum (IEEE 802.16e, 2013). EAP-TLS is an Internet Engineering Task Force (IETF) open standard and is defined in RFC 5216 (Simon, Aboba, and Hurst, 2008). It uses PKI to secure communication to a Remote Authentication Dial in User Service (RADIUS) or another type of authentication server (EAP, n.d.). EAP-TTLS extends EAP-TLS by providing a secure connection or "tunnel" for the BS to authenticate the SS (EAP, n.d.).

3.4.3 Message Authentication of WiMax

In versions before 802.16e, the authentication of messages is done by using the Hashed Message Authentication Code (HMAC) which makes use of the HMAC keys discussed earlier. Since only the communication parties involved in the same SAs will share the same HMAC keys, only the authenticated parties are able to provide the correct HMAC. The original HMAC authentication did not provide a counter to protect against replay attacks and subsequently it has been fixed in newer versions. Another message authentication method, One-key Message Authentication Code (OMAC), is supported by 208.16e (Barbeau and Laurendeau, 2007). The OMAC is Advanced Encryption Standard (AES)-based and it includes replay attack protection. As far as message authentication is concerned, both HMAC with anti-replay counter and OMAC are considered to have strong security.

3.4.4 LTE Authentication

The purpose of the Authentication and Key Agreement (AKA) procedure is to provide mutual authentication between the user and the network, as well as to agree on the KASME mentioned earlier in the key hierarchy. Defined in 3GPP LTE standard TS33.401 (3GPP TS33.401, n.d.), ASME is a security entity that receives the top level keys from the HSS (LTE: 4G, n.d.).

MME requests the authentication data from the HSS. This request includes the UE's permanent identity (IMSI), the serving network identity (mobile country code and network code), the network type, and the number of requested Authentication Vectors (AVs). Upon receiving the authentication data request, the HSS will request the AuC to generate the AVs if this has not been done before. By following the key hierarchy, a series of keys are generated and agreed (LTE: 4G, n.d.). These keys and credentials will be used for authentication of the UE through the NAS procedures.

3.5 WiMAX Confidentiality and Integrity

In this section, we discuss how WiMAX protects the confidentiality of both keys and data, as well as the integrity of data.

3.5.1 WiMAX Key Confidentiality

The BS generates Authorization Key and encrypts it using RSA cipher with SS's PK. No other party, except the SS who possesses the paired private key, is able to decrypt and obtain AK. Both KEK and HMAC Keys are derived on both sides using AK (IEEE 802.16e, 2013; Wongthavarawat, 2005). During their lifetime, these keys must be stored in a secure manner at both SS and BS. The TEK for encrypting data is encrypted using one of the following ciphers: 3DES with 112-bit KEK, AES with 128-bit KEK, or RSA with SS's PK (Wongthavarawat, 2005). In PKM2, the additional secret keys used for multicast and broadcast are also secured in a similar way.

3.5.2 WiMAX Data Confidentiality

The PKMv1 only uses Data Encryption Standard (DES) algorithm in the Cipher Block Chaining (CBC), or DES-CBC, to protect data confidentiality and PKMv2 adds AES-CCM with the active TEK (Scarfone, Tibbs, and Sexton, n.d.; Counter CTR, n.d.; Dekleva, Shim, Varshney, and Knoerzer, 2007).

The Data Encryption Standard (DES) is a symmetric-key block cipher using 56-bit key and was selected by the National Bureau of Standards (NBS) as an official Federal Information Processing Standard (FIPS) for the U.S. in 1976 (DES, n.d.). Mainly due to its small key size DES was found vulnerable about a decade ago. However, the algorithm is believed to be practically secure in the form of 3DES. In the Cipher-Block Chaining (CBC) mode, each plaintext block is XORed with the previous ciphertext block before being encrypted, as shown in Figure 4.

The Advanced Encryption Standard (AES) is a symmetric key block cipher announced by NIST as U.S. FIPS in 2001 superseding DES (AES, n.d.). The Counter with CBC-MAC (CCM) mode of a cipher combines the Counter mode with CBC-MAC in order to provide both authentication and confidentiality. Counter mode generates the next keystream block by encrypting successive values of a "counter", e.g. keystream block #1 is generated by encrypting counter "00000000" with a nonce, and the next keystream block is generated by encryption counter "00000001" with the same nonce. Although increment counter is most frequently used, counter function can be any function that produces a sequence that will not repeat for a long time (Counter CTR, n.d.). CBC-MAC stands for Cipher-Block Chaining Message Authentication Code, which constructs a MAC from a block cipher (CBC-MAC, n.d.). AES in CCM Mode in PKMv1 is considered a stronger cipher with longer key compared to DES-CBC and therefore is preferred in protecting data confidentiality.

In additional to the above ciphers, the 802.16e Amendment added a number of cryptographic algorithms, including AES in Counter for MBS, AES in CBC mode, and AES KeyWrap with 128-bit key (Dekleva et al, 2007). The KeyWrap combines both encryption/decryption with integrity check values and can therefore provide both confidentiality and integrity.

Figure 4. Operations of DES-CBC

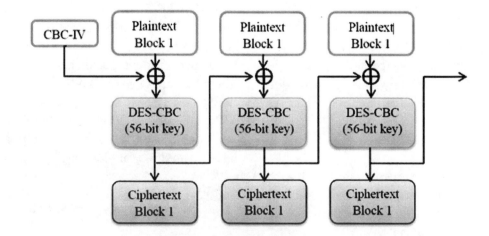

3.5.3 WiMAX Data Integrity

WiMAX preserves data integrity by using HMAC and Cipher-based Message Authentication Code (CMAC) (Dekleva et al, 2007)(Wongthavarawat, 2005), e.g. PKMv1 supports the use of HMAC for both downlink and uplink traffic and PKMv2 adds CMAC for the same purpose. The generation of HMAC or CMAC is illustrated in Figure 5 where the Secret Key refers to the integrity related keys introduced earlier: HMAC_KEY_D, HMAC_KEY_U, and MAC_KEY_S in PKMv1, and H/CMAC/KEY_D and H/CMAC/KEY_U in PKMv2. As addressed in the previous section, the AES KeyWrap in PKMv2 also provides integrity check of the traffic. When EAP exchange happens, the EAP messages are protected by an EAP Integrity Key (EIK) (Nasreldin, Asian, El-Hennawy, and El-Hennawy, 2008; Dekleva et al, 2007).

3.6 LTE Confidentiality and Integrity

Ciphering mechanisms are used in LTE to provide signaling and user data confidentiality, and integrity and replay mechanisms provide the integrity of signaling and user data 3, n.d.). The EPS Encryption Algorithms (EEA), specified in 3GPP standard TS 33.401 (3GPP TS33.401, n.d.), gives a list of available encryption ciphers using 128-bit keys:

128-EEA0: Null ciphering algorithm
128-EEA1: SNOW 3G
128-EEA2: AES

The EPS Integrity Algorithms (EIA), also specified in TS 33.401, lists two available ciphers for integrity check purpose (3GPP TS33.401, n.d.):

128-EIA1: SNOW 3G
128-EIA2: AES

4. SECURITY VULNERABILITIES, THREATS, AND COUNTERMEASURES OF WIMAX AND LTE

This section discusses the security vulnerabilities, threats, and countermeasures of WiMAX and LTE.

4.1 IEEE 802.16-2004 WiMAX Systems

In WiMAX systems that use versions prior to IEEE 802.16e, the major security vulnerabilities include (Nasreldin et al, 2008; Barbeau, 2005):

- **No Two-Way Authentication:** Not until 802.16e did WiMAX provide authentication of BS by SS. Therefore in earlier versions, SSs were susceptible to forgery attacks by a rogue BS. Threats making

Figure 5. Generation of HMAC or CMAC

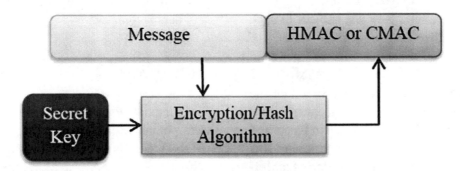

use of this vulnerability include degraded performance, information theft, Denial of Service (DoS) attacks, and Man-in-the-Middle (MiM) attacks. External authentication of devices and users should be used to identify the BS and enforce two-way authentication.

- **Weak Cryptographic Algorithm:** Only DES-CBC was available for protecting data confidentiality. This potentially leads to unauthorized disclosure of information, eavesdropping, DoS attacks, and MiM attacks. Stronger cipher algorithms, e.g. FIPS-validated algorithms such as AES, should be employed.

- **Reused TEK:** Due to the short identifier (only two-bit) of TEK, it repeats every four rekey cycles. Threats include reusing expired TEKs in replay attacks to disclose confidential information and further compromise the TEK. It is recommended to use FIPS-validated encryption algorithms as well as cryptographic modules.

4.2 All WiMAX Systems and LTE

The following vulnerabilities appear in all WiMAX and LTE systems regardless of the versions of the standards or amendments adopted (Nasreldin et al, 2008; Dekleva et al, 2007; Barbeau, 2005; Parkey, 2012):

- **Subject to RF Jamming Attacks:** This is not unique to WiMAX and LTE as all wireless technologies are subject to such attacks. Classified as a DoS attack, RF jamming adversary transmits powerful RF signals to overwhelm the WiMAX and LTE spectrum causing all SSs within the interference range not being able to communicate. While it is possible to locate and remove the source of the RF jamming, this is often not an easy task considering the rel-

atively large area covered by 4G networks, e.g. radius of 5 miles. Therefore out-of-band communications are recommended.

- **Subject to Scrambling Attacks:** While considered as a subcategory of RF jamming attacks, scrambling requires more precise injections of RF interference during the transmission of specific management messages in relatively short time periods and therefore is more difficulty to detect. Countermeasures to such attacks are similar to jamming attacks but require more sensitive and accurate detection and faster responses.

- **Unencrypted Management Messages and No Integrity Check for Multicast and Broadcast Traffic:** None of the WiMAX or LTE standards or amendments so far has addressed or required the encryption of management messages, and consequently puts confidential information involved in the processes of network entry, node registration, and bandwidth allocation in danger. Possible related attacks include eavesdropping, replay attacks, and scrambling. Integrity checks are only provided to unicast traffic which means multicast and broadcast traffics are subject to DoS attacks. There is no countermeasure to this threat given that no encryption is applied to management messages. AES-CCM however helps in fighting against MiM attacks. As far as DoS attacks are concerned, it is recommended to plan for out-of-band communications and the inclusion of incident responses.

5. SUMMARY

This chapter discussed the fundamentals of Metropolitan Area Networks (MANs), Wireless MANs (WMANs), as well as two competitive 4G technologies: WiMAX and LTE regarding their security elements, security goals and solutions, as well as vulnerabilities, threats, and counter-measures. Both WiMAX and LTE provide basic security needs such as Mutual Authentication and Message Authentication, Data and Key Confidentiality, and Data Integrity. While these two major 4G technologies are still subject to threats and attacks, their security will continue to be improved through the series of new standards and efforts from on-going 4G group projects.

REFERENCES

Advanced, L. T. E. (n.d.). *Wikipedia*. Retrieved April 20, 2013, from http://en.wikipedia.org/wiki/LTE_Advanced

Backhauling X2. (n.d.). Retrieved April 20, 2013, from http://cbnl.com/sites/all/files/userfiles/files/Backhauling-X2_0.pdf

Barbeau, M. (2005). WiMAX/802.16 threat analysis. In *Proceedings of the 1st ACM International Workshop on Quality of Service & Security in Wireless and Mobile Networks* (pp. 8-15). New York: ACM.

Barbeau, M., & Laurendeau, C. (2007). Analysis of threats to WiMAX/802.16 decurity. In C. Xhang, & H. H. Chen (Eds.), *Mobile WiMAX: Toward broadband wireless metropolitan area networks*. Boca Raton, FL: Taylor and Francis CRC Press.

CBC-MAC. (n.d.). *Wikipedia*. Retrieved April 20, 2013, from http://en.wikipedia.org/wiki/CBC-MAC

Counter, C. T. R. (n.d.). *Wikipedia*. Retrieved April 20, 2013, from http://en.wikipedia.org/wiki/Block_cipher_modes_of_operation#Counter_.28CTR.29

Data Encryption Standard. (n.d.). *Wikipedia*. Retrieved April 20, 2013, from http://en.wikipedia.org/wiki/Data_Encryption_Standard

Dekleva, S., Shim, J. P., Varshney, U., & Knoerzer, G. (2007). Evolution and emerging issues in mobile wireless networks. *Communications of the ACM–Smart Business Networks, 50*(6), 38–43.

Extensible Authentication Protocol (EAP). (2013). *Wikipedia*. Retrieved April 20, 2013, from http://en.wikipedia.org/wiki/Extensible_Authentication_Protocol

Ghosh, A., Wolter, D. R., Andrews, J. G., & Chen, R. (2005). Broadband wireless access with WiMax/802.16: Current performance benchmarks and future potential. *IEEE Communications Magazine, 43*(2), 129–136. doi:10.1109/MCOM.2005.1391513.

3GPP. Specs. (2013). *3GPP: Specifications series*. Retrieved April 20, 2013, from http://www.3gpp.org/ftp/Specs/html-info/36-series.htm

3GPP. (n.d.). *Wikipedia*. Retrieved April 20, 2013, from http://en.wikipedia.org/wiki/3GPP

3GPP: TS33.210 V8.3.0. (n.d.). Retrieved April 20, 2013, from http://www.3gpp.org/ftp/Specs/html-info/33210.htm

3GPP: TS33.401. (n.d.). Retrieved April 20, 2013, from http://www.3gpp.org/ftp/Specs/html-info/33401.htm

Guidelines for LTE Backhaul Traffic Estimation (LTE BTE). (n.d.). Retrieved April 20, 2013, from http://www.ngmn.org/uploads/media/NGMN_Whitepaper_Guideline_for_LTE_Backhaul_Traffic_Estimation.pdf

Hamblen, M. (2008, May 14). *WiMax vs. long term evolution: Let the battle begin*. Retrieved April 20, 2013, from http://www.computerworld.com/s/article/9085202/WiMax_vs._Long_Term_Evolution_Let_the_battle_begin

IEEE 802.16e. (2013). Retrieved from http://grouper.ieee.org/groups/802/16/tge/ on April 20, 2013

IEEE LAN/MAN Standards Committee (IEEE L/M SC). (2002). *IEEE standard for local and metropolitan area networks: Overview and architecture*. Retrieved April 20, 2013, from http://standards.ieee.org/getieee802/download/802-2001.pdf

LTE. (n.d.). *Wikipedia*. Retrieved April 20, 2013, from http://en.wikipedia.org/wiki/LTE_(telecommunication)

LTE: 4gamericas. (n.d.). Retrieved April 20, 2013, from http://www.4gamericas.org/index.cfm?fuseaction=page&sectionid = 249

LTE and the Evolution to 4G Wireless (LTE: 4G). (n.d.). Retrieved April 20, 2013, from http://www.home.agilent.com/upload/cmc_upload/All/Security_in_the_LTE-AE_Network.PDF?&cc=US&lc=eng

LTE Topology Evolving Networks (LTE TEN). (n.d.). Retrieved April 20, 2013, from http://www.rcrwireless.com/mobile-backhaul/lte-topology.html

MAN. (2009). *Wikipedia*. Retrieved April 20, 2013, from http://en.wikipedia.org/wiki/Metropolitan_area_network

Nasreldin, M., Asian, H., El-Hennawy, M., & El-Hennawy, A. (2008). WiMAX security. In *Proceedings of the Advanced Information Networking and Applications - Workshops, AINAW* (pp. 1335-1340). AINAW.

Nguyen, T. (2009, April 20). *A survey of wimax security threats*. Retrieved April 20, 2013, from http://www.cse.wustl.edu/~jain/cse571-09/ftp/wimax2.pdf

Nuaymi, L. (2007). *WiMAX: Technology for broadband wireless access*. Hoboken, NJ: Wiley. doi:10.1002/9780470319055.

Parkey, T. (2012, November 14). *LTE networks are easy prey for jamming attacks*. Retrieved April 20, 2013, from http://www.fiercebroadbandwireless.com/story/lte-networks-are-easy-prey-jamming-attacks/2012-11-14

Public-Key Cryptography Standards (PKCS). (n.d.). Retrieved April 20, 2013, from http://www.rsa.com/rsalabs/node.asp?id=2124

Public Key Infrastructure (PKI). (n.d.). *Wikipedia*. Retrieved April 20, 2013, from http://en.wikipedia.org/wiki/Public_key_infrastructure

Scarfone, K., Tibbs, C., & Sexton, M. (n.d.). *Guide to securing WiMAX wireless communications*. Retrieved April 20, 2013, from http://csrc.nist.gov/publications/nistpubs/800-127/sp800-127.pdf

Simon, D., Aboba, B., & Hurst, R. (2008). *The EAP-TLS authentication protocol*. Retrieved April 20, 2013, from http://tools.ietf.org/html/rfc5216

White, I. M., Rogge, M. S., Shrikhande, K., & Kazovsky, L. G. (2003). A summary of the HORNET project: A next-generation metropolitan area network. *IEEE Journal on Selected Areas in Communications, 21*(9), 1478–1494. doi:10.1109/JSAC.2003.818838.

Wikipedia. (n.d.). *Advanced encryption standard*. Retrieved April 20, 2013, from http://en.wikipedia.org/wiki/Advanced_Encryption_Standard

WiMAX. (n.d.). *Wikipedia*. Retrieved April 20, 2013, from http://en.wikipedia.org/wiki/WiMAX

WiMAX Forum. (n.d.). Retrieved April 20, 2013, from http://www.wimaxforum.org/

WiMAX Forum PRNewswire. (2011). Retrieved April 20, 2013, from http://www.prnewswire.com/news-releases/wimax-forum-celebrates-10-years-of-driving-broadband-innovation-123463264.html

WiMAX Public Key Infrastructure Users Overview (WiMAX PKI). (n.d.). Retrieved April 20, 2013, from http://www.wimaxforum.org/sites/wimax-forum.org/files/page/2009/12/wimax_pki_users_overview_4_28_10

Wongthavarawat, K. (2005, March 28). *IEEE 802.16 WiMAX securit.* Retrieved April 20, 2013, from http://www.nectec.or.th/nac2005/documents/20050328_SecurityTechnology-05_Presentation.pdf

Xu, S., Matthews, M., & Huang, T. C. (2006). Security issues in privacy and key management protocols of IEEE 802.16. In *Proceedings of the 44th Annual Southeast Regional Conference* (pp. 113-118). New York: SRC.

Zugenmaier, A., & Aono, H. (2009). Security technology for SAE/LTE. *NTT DOCOMO Technical Journal, 11*(3), 27–30.

Section 2
Physical Layer Security

Chapter 3
Physical Layer Security and Its Applications:
A Survey

Rajesh K. Sharma
Ilmenau University of Technology, Germany

ABSTRACT

This chapter provides a survey of physical layer security and key generation methods. This includes mainly an overview of ongoing research in physical layer security in the present and next generation communication networks. Although higher layer security mechanisms and protocols address wireless security challenges in large extent, more security vulnerabilities arise due to the increasingly pervasive existence of wireless communication devices. In this context, the focus of this chapter is mainly on physical layer security. Some security attacks in general are briefly reviewed. Models of physical layer security, information theoretic works, and key generation methods including quantization and reconciliation are discussed. Some latest developments for enhanced security like Multiple-Input Multiple-Output (MIMO) systems, reconfigurable antennas, and multiple relay systems are also presented. Finally, some existing and emerging application scenarios of physical layer security are discussed.

INTRODUCTION

Secure transmission is a concern for wireless devices and networks due to the broadcast nature of signals. As wireless devices become increasingly pervasive, they are more and more likely to serve both as targets for attack and as means for such attacks to be carried out successfully (Trappe et al., 2011). While there are a number of traditional methods for establishing secure keys using conventional secure channel or later developed public key cryptosystems and distribution systems (Diffie & Hellman, 1976), there have been numerous attempts to make various wireless

DOI: 10.4018/978-1-4666-4691-9.ch003

platforms secure by migrating traditional network security strategies to the wireless domain. In spite of these efforts, the security failures have also been continuously reported.

While conventional cryptographic security mechanisms are essential to the overall problem of securing wireless networks, they do not directly leverage the unique properties of the wireless domain to address security threats (Mathur et al., 2010). The wireless medium itself can be a powerful source of secure key that can complement and enhance traditional security mechanisms. New security paradigms which exploit physical layer properties of the wireless medium, such as the rapid spatial, spectral, and temporal decorrelation properties of the radio channel, can enhance confidentiality and authentication services (Mathur et al., 2010).

Figure 1 shows information flow in a traditional cryptographic system, where the key (K) is trans- mitted by the source to the receiver using a secure channel or an insecure public channel. In a wireless communication, the strongest notion of security is in an information theoretic sense, where the Transmitter (commonly known as Alice) and Receiver (commonly known as Bob) can share information up to the secrecy capacity, without providing any information to the Cryptanalyst (commonly known as Eve) (Massey, 1988). Although

Figure 1. Flow of information in a cryptographic system where the key (K) may be transmitted only to the legitimate receiver via a secure channel (conventional cryptography), or transmitted publicly (public cryptography) (Diffie & Hellman, 1976).

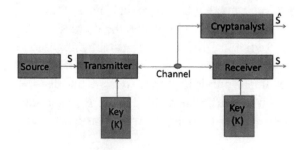

traditional systems employ private or public-key cryptography without considering the physical transmission, there is growing interest in physical layer security methods that exploit the properties of the propagation channel to strengthen existing cryptosystems (see (Bloch, Barros, Rodrigues, & McLaughlin, 2008) and references therein).

Several information-theoretic studies have been performed for secrecy in wireless communication. For example, in (Ahlswede & Csiszar, 1993), information-theoretic models of secret sharing are considered for "wiretap channel" where the concept of key-capacity has been provided and formulas and bounds to key-capacity for different models have been derived. In (Maurer, 1993) it has been proven that matching secret keys can be generated by Alice and Bob by exploiting knowledge of the physical channel and public discussion over an error-free channel. In the case of fading channels, it has been shown in (Barros & Rodrigues, 2006) that positive secrecy capacity exists without the need for a feedback channel or public discussion, and in (Bloch et al., 2008) a practical method for generating secret keys without public discussion has been developed. However, one drawback of such approaches is that both Alice and Bob require at least partial channel state information (CSI) of their own channel as well as the eavesdropper channel. The former may require a feedback channel, potentially sharing useful information with Eve, and the latter may not be obtainable in practice.

In recent years, there has been keen interest in physical layer security. There are several papers published whose contributions range from are largely theoretical to application related issues including channel properties, MIMO and Relay techniques, use of reconfiguration antennas, and new application areas like optical layer security, security in satellite communications and smart grids, etc. Some experimental works of physical layer security are also available. While many information-theoretic aspects and implementation issues of physical-layer security are still to be explored, it has gained significant maturity and the trend is that the future research will focus more on practical communication-theoretic and signal processing aspects of physical layer security (Bloch, Debbah, Liang, Oohama, & Thangaraj, 2012).

As an existing work, the tutorial article (Shiu, Chang, Wu, Huang, & Chen, 2011), has also provided a survey of several prevalent methods to enhance security at the physical layer in wireless networks. The authors have classified these methods based on their characteristic features into five categories, each of which has been discussed in terms of two metrics: secret channel capacities, and computational complexities in exhaustive key search. Using these metrics, the authors have also illustrated security requirements of the methods via some examples. In (Mathur et al., 2010), some basic constructions for confidentiality and authentication services have been outlined, and then a case study has been provided for how physical layer can be integrated into a broader security framework for a wireless network.

MODELS IN PHYSICAL LAYER SECURITY

Wiretap Model

In (Wyner, 1975), wiretap channel model was introduced in a security context which is shown in Figure 2. It is a channel with one input and two output terminals, one for legitimate receiver and the other for eavesdropper or "wiretapper." The message from the source is to be reliably sent to the legitimate receiver as fast as possible, while keeping the wiretapper as ignorant as possible about the message. Wyner showed that it was possible to keep the wiretapper fully unaware about the entire message by transmitting at a rate less than capacity on the main link. There are many works in the physical layer security based on this model. For example, low density parity check (LDPC) codes for the Gaussian wiretap channel

has been discussed in (Klinc, Ha, McLaughlin, Barros, & Kwak, 2011). Information-theoretic models of secret sharing for wiretap channel have been considered in (Ahlswede & Csiszar, 1993), where the concept of key-capacity along with the derivation of formulas and bounds to key-capacity for different models are given. Similarly, strongly secure communications over the two-way wiretap channel has been discussed in (Pierrot & Bloch, 2011). Strong secrecy on the binary erasure wiretap channel using large-Girth LDPC Codes has been discussed in (Subramanian, Thangaraj, Bloch, & McLaughlin, 2011). Secrecy degrees of freedom of the multi-antenna block fading wiretap channels have been discussed in (Kobayashi, Piantanida, Yang, & Shamai, 2011). Ergodic secrecy rate for multi-Antenna wiretap channels in a Rician fading environment is available in (Li & Petropulu, 2011).

In (Liang, Poor, & Shamai (Shitz), 2009), information theoretic security and the related principal results have been reviewed for basic and more specific wiretap channel models including Gaussian, MIMO, compound, and feedback wiretap channels, as well as the wiretap channel with side information. The wiretap formalism has been then extended to the basic channels of multi-user networks, including broadcast channels, multiple-

Figure 2. General case of a wiretap channel (Wyner, 1975).

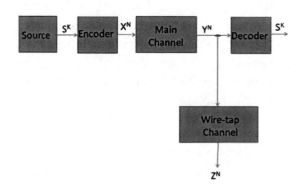

access channels (MACs), interference channels, relay channels, and two- way channels.

In (Goel, Aggarwal, Yener, & Calderbank, 2011), the effect of eavesdroppers on network connectivity has been investigated using a wiretap model and percolation theory, where connectivity exists if an infinite connected component exists in the corresponding secrecy graph. The authors have maintained that this approach attempts to bridge the gap between physical layer security under uncertain channel state information and network level connectivity under secrecy constraints. Bounds on the percolation threshold have been obtained for some secrecy graphs. The capacity of secret-key agreement over a wiretap channel with state parameters has been studied in (Khisti, Diggavi, & Wornell, 2011), where the transmitter, the legitimate receiver, and the eavesdropper are connected by a discrete memoryless wiretap channel with a memoryless state sequence. Based on some assumptions, the authors have derived lower and upper bounds on the secret-key capacity.

Source-Type Model

In (Ahlswede & Csiszar, 1993), source-type and channel-type models for information theoretic security were provided. This model gives a discrete memoryless multiple source (DMMS) with two component sources and generic variables (X, Y). Terminal X "can see" the source outputs $X^n = (X_1, \cdots, X_n)$ and terminal Y "can see" the source outputs $Y^n = (Y_1, \cdots, Y_n)$. Further, a noiseless public channel of unlimited capacity is available for communication between the two terminals.

This simple models can be generalized to the case when the third party (wiretapper) has access to more information than what is transmitted over the public channel. This is also known as source-type model with wiretapper. In this model a DMMS with three component sources and generic variables (X, Y, Z) are given. Terminal X "sees" the source outputs X^n, terminal Y "sees"

the source outputs Y^n, and the wiretapper "sees" the source outputs Z^n.

In source-type model with wiretapper a noiseless public channel of unlimited capacity is also available for communication between terminals X and Y, communication over this channel is completely known to the wiretapper.

In (Salimi, Salmasizadeh, & Aref, 2011), a source model has been considered where two users at one side communicate with another user at the other side via a public channel where all can observe i.i.d. outputs of correlated sources. Each of first two users intends to share a secret key with third user where first user acts as a wiretapper for second user and vice versa. In this model, two situations are considered: communication from first two users to third user (the forward key strategy) and from third user to other two users (the backward key strategy). In both situations, the goal is sharing a secret key between first and third user while leaking no effective information about that key to second user, and simultaneously, sharing another secret key between second and third user while leaking no effective information about the latter key to first user. This model has been motivated by considering third user as base station with two network users. For both the forward and backward key strategies, inner and outer bounds of secret key capacity regions have been derived.

Channel-Type Model

Here we discuss channel-type models for information theoretic security as provided in (Ahlswede & Csiszar, 1993). We are given a discrete memoryless channel (DMC) $W : X \to Y$. Terminal X can govern the input of this DMC, while Terminal Y observes the output. In addition to transmissions of length n over this DMC, which is considered a secure channel, also a noiseless public channel of unlimited capacity may be used for communication between the two terminals.

As in the case of source-type model, channel type model is also generalized as Model CW (channel- type model with wiretapper). In this case we are given a DMC $W: X \rightarrow Y \times Z$. Terminal X governs the input, Terminal Y "sees" the Y-outputs, whereas the wiretapper "sees" the Z-outputs. In this model, as in the case of source-type model with wiretapper, a noiseless public channel of unlimited capacity is also available for communication between terminals X and Y; communication over this channel is completely known to the wiretapper.

In (Lai, Liang, & Poor, 2012), a joint source-channel approach for key agreement over wireless fading channels has been developed. It is shown that, in general, to fully exploit the resources provided by time-varying channel gains, one needs to combine both the channel model, in which Alice sends a key to Bob over a wireless channel, and the source model, in which Alice and Bob generate a key by exploiting the correlated observations obtained from the wireless fading channel. Asymptotic analyses have been presented suggesting that the channel model is asymptotically optimal in the long coherence time regime and the source model is asymptotically optimal in the high power regime. Another study on the secret-key capacity in a joint source-channel coding setup is found in (Khisti, Diggavi, & Wornell, 2012), where the terminals are connected over a discrete memoryless channel and have access to side information, modeled as a pair of discrete memoryless source sequences. The bounds on the secret- key capacity have been established. In addition, when the eavesdropper also observes a correlated side information sequence, the authors have established the secret-key capacity when both the source and channel of the eavesdropper are a degraded version of the legitimate receiver. Finally, the case when a public discussion channel is available has also been treated.

TYPES OF SECURITY ATTACKS

A security attack may be defined as disruption or corruption in communication by an adversary. In general, the attacks can be divided into two categories: active and passive. In active attack, the attacker maintains active interactions with the legitimate system by sending some fake information and trying to get responses, in order to gain a physical control on the network and provide adverse effect on it. In passive attack, the attacker tries to listen and obtain secure information from legitimate users without performing interaction or communication with them. A survey of some active and passive attacks can be found in (Benjamin, 1990). In this section we discuss briefly some of the security attacks in wired as well as wireless networks.

Active Attacks

There are several types of active attacks. Here, some of them are discussed.

1. **Phishing:** Phishing is a security attack trying to obtain secret information from Internet users, typically by sending an e-mail that looks as if it is from a legitimate organization, but contains a link to a fake web-site that replicates the real one. The harm caused by phishing ranges from denial of access to e-mail to severe financial loss. Wireless smart-phones are at the same risk of phishing as desktop platforms. In fact, many users trust their mobile device more than their computers and thus are more vulnerable to phishing (Leavitt, 2011).

2. **Spoofing and Masquerading:** Spoofing, also known as masquerading, involves the attacker posing as a legitimate network host or application tricking the victim into revealing confidential information. The attacker uses a fake identity, such as a network identity, to gain unauthorized access to the

user network. In the absence of a fully secure authorization process, a network can become highly vulnerable to a masquerade attack. Such attacks can be initiated by using stolen passwords and logons, by locating gaps in programs, or by finding a way around the authentication process.

Spoofing is one of the common identity-based attacks in wireless networks which open doors for many other forms of attacks on the networks (Y. Chen, Yang, Trappe, & Martin, 2010). Among various types of attacks, identity-based spoofing attacks are especially easy to launch and can cause significant damage to network performance (Yang, Chen, Trappe, & Cheng, 2013). In (Yang et al., 2013), the spatial correlation of received signal strength (RSS) inherited from wireless nodes have been used to detect the spoofing attacks. The authors have also formulated a multi-class detection problem for determining the number of attackers. Similarly in (Y. Chen et al., 2010), the authors from same group have proposed a method for detecting both spoofing and Sybil attacks (to be discussed shortly) by using the same set of techniques.

3. **Sybil Attacks:** Like Spoofing attack, Sybil attack is also a common identity-based attack in wireless networks. In Sybil attack (Douceur, 2002), (Newsome, Shi, Song, & Perrig, 2004), a malicious node illegitimately claims a large number of identities and thus depletes system resources. Due to the broadcast nature of the wireless medium, wireless networks are especially vulnerable to Sybil attacks (Xiao, Greenstein, Mandayam, & Trappe, 2009). In (Newsome et al., 2004), the Sybil attack to wireless sensor networks has been analyzed demonstrating that the attack can be highly detrimental to many important functions of the sensor network such as routing, resource allocation, and misbehavior detection. A classification of different types of the Sybil attack has been established, enabling for better understanding of the threats posed by each type, and better design of countermeasures against each type. In (Xiao et al., 2009), an enhanced physical-layer authentication scheme exploiting the spatial variations of rich scattering radio channels has been proposed for detecting Sybil attacks.

4. **Man-in-the-Middle (MITM) Attack:** In this attack, an attacker may actively intercept, modify and inject messages between two parties without their knowledge (Shim, 2003). This attacker is sometimes called Mallory or Mallet (Scoville, 1999) instead of Eve used in passive attacks. The difficulty of securing a system against Mallory/Mallet is much greater than against Eve.

5. **Availability Attacks, or Denial-of-Service (DoS):** Availability attacks, or denial-of-service (DoS), pose significant problems to enterprise networks as they attack the network connectivity, which is the core of the information economy paradigm. These attacks prevent legitimate network users from accessing services or resources to which they are entitled. In addition, these attacks may target a remote host or network that would otherwise be used to serve legitimate users. Such attacks can be launched in a number of ways, from malicious use of common applications such as e-mail, to subverting Internet protocols (Haggerty, Shi, & Merabti, 2005). Irrespective of the attacking methods, DoS attacks are common as the tools needed for such attacks are easily available on the Internet, simple to launch, effective, and difficult to prevent. The quantitative estimation of DoS attacks in internet has been presented in (Moore, Shannon, Brown, Voelker, & Savage, 2006). A survey of denial-of-service threats and countermeasures in wireless sensor networks is available in (Raymond & Midkiff, 2008).

In (Haggerty et al., 2005), a distributed and scalable mechanism for early detection and prevention of DoS attacks at the router level within a network has been proposed.

Passive Attacks

A passive attack is the unauthorized interception of a communication system (Benjamin, 1990). Passive attack is also called eavesdropping which is a passive listening to the communication in general. Passive attacks try to disclose information or data files to the adversary without the consent or knowledge of the user. The attacker is sometimes known as Eve. It is very hard to validate eavesdropping attacks. If the key generation is not secure from information theoretic sense, the Eavesdropper can obtain the secret information by the brute force attack.

In general, passive adversaries perform traffic analysis to monitor the unprotected communications, then decrypt the weakly encrypted traffic, and capture the authentication information. Passive interception of network operations enables adversaries to see upcoming actions. A survey of some potential passive threats to secure communications and the defenses against them, primarily cryptographic can be found in (Benjamin, 1990).

1. **Brute Force Attack:** A brute force or exhaustive search attack attempts to break a key by trying all the possibilities. Although this is theoretically possible, it becomes practical only when the key size is inadequate. It requires no insight as the technique is to run test encryptions until the attacker finds the key or gives up. In the worst case, this would involve traversing the entire search space before finding the key. The cost is easily approximated since it depends only on the key-size and the cost of test encryptions. This is, therefore, sometimes used as a benchmark in evaluating any other attack.

2. **Algebraic Attack:** An algebraic attack is a method of cryptanalysis against a ci-

pher where the key is found by solving an overdefined system of algebraic equations (Courtois & Meier, 2003). Since a classical construction of stream ciphers is to combine several liner feedback shift registers (LFSRs) and a highly non-linear Boolean function, algebraic attack can be seen as solving a system of multivariate linear equations. It involves expressing the cipher operations as a system of equations, then substituting in known data for some of the variables, and solving for the key with some probability of success. In the context of algebraic attacks, the algebraic immunity of a Boolean function is an important notion. In (Rizomiliotis, 2010), a framework has been provided to assess the resistance of Boolean functions against the new algebraic attacks, including fast algebraic attacks. The analysis is based on the univariate polynomial representation of Boolean functions and necessary and sufficient conditions are presented for a Boolean function to have optimal behavior against all the new algebraic attacks.

3. **Code-Book Attack:** A code-book attack is an example of a known plain-text attack scenario in which the attacker is given access to a set of plain-texts and their corresponding encryptions for a fixed key. These pairs constitute a code-book which someone could use to listen to further communication and which could help him or her to partially decrypt the future messages even without the knowledge of the secret key. The attacker also uses this knowledge in a replay attack by replacing blocks in the communication or by constructing meaningful messages from the blocks of the code-book (SpringerReference, 2013). For this attack, the attacker needs very large amounts of resource in terms of intercepts and storage of the data, all encrypted with the same fixed key. If the user changes the keys at short intervals, this attack turns to be highly unsuccessful.

In (Lai, Liang, & Poor, 2012), assuming that the goal of the active attacker is to minimize the key rate that can be generated using the proposed protocol and the attacker will employ such an attack strategy, the attacker's optimal attack strategy has been identified and the key rate under this attack model has been characterized.

INFORMATION THEORETIC LIMITS OF PHYSICAL LAYER KEY GENERATION

Several information theoretic works focused on physical layer cryptography are available in literature. In (Maurer & Wolf, 2003a), which deals on secret-key agreement against active adversaries, a number of general impossibility results have been proved following the consideration of the important special case where the legitimate partners as well as the adversary have access to the outcomes of many independent repetitions of a fixed tripartite random experiment. The results shown indicate that either a secret key can be generated at the same rate as in the passive-adversary case, or such secret-key agreement is completely impossible. In (Maurer & Wolf, 2003c), the so-called simulatability condition has been analyzed in the context of unconditionally secure identification and authentication between parties sharing correlated information. A new formalism based on a mechanical model has been introduced for a simple and efficient characterization of the possibility of secret-key agreement. Finally, in (Maurer & Wolf, 2003b), the special case is considered where the mutual information shared by Alice and Bob is partially known to Eve. The problem of generating a secret key in this case has been well studied in the passive-adversary model- for instance, in the context of quantum key agreement - under the name of privacy amplification. The same problem has been also considered with respect to an active adversary and two protocols have been proposed. The authors claim that their protocols are secure even against adversaries knowing a substantial amount of the 'secret' key.

Shannon-theoretic secret key generation by several parties has been considered in (Csiszar & Narayan, 2008) for models in which a secure noisy channel with one input terminal and multiple output terminals and a public noiseless channel of unlimited capacity are available. In (Bloch et al., 2008), based on an information-theoretic formulation of the problem, and considering quasi-static fading channels, the important role of fading has been characterized in terms of average secure communication rates and outage probability. Based on the insights from this analysis, a practical secure communication protocol has been developed, which uses a four-step procedure to ensure wireless information-theoretic security: (i) common randomness via opportunistic transmission, (ii) message reconciliation, (iii) common key generation via privacy amplification, and (iv) message protection with a secret key. Finally, a set of metrics for assessing average secure key generation rates is established, and it is shown that the protocol is effective in secure key renewal-even in the presence of imperfect channel state information.

An upper bound for the secrecy capacity and a sufficient condition for its tightness are given for models in which the eavesdropper also possesses side information that is not available to any of the terminals cooperating in secrecy generation. A new upper bound for Eve's information in secret key generation from a common random number without communication has been derived in (Hayashi, 2011). This bound has been applied to a wire-tap channel to derive an exponential upper bound for Eve's information. The result has been applied to secret key agreement by public discussion.

More theoretical contributions in physical layer security for the next generation of communication systems are found in recent works. For example, an analysis on signal sets for secret key agreement with public discussion based on Gaussian and fading channels is available in (Isaka & Kawata, 2011). Secret key agreement from vector Gaussian sources by rate-limited public communication has been discussed in (Watanabe & Oohama, 2011). In (Agrawal, Rezki, Khisti, & Alouini, 2011), the authors have discussed on non-coherent capacity of secret-key agreement with public discussion. Coding for cryptographic security enhancement using stopping sets has been discussed in (Harrison, Almeida, McLaughlin, & Barros, 2011). Position-based jamming for enhanced wireless secrecy has been proposed in (Vilela, Pinto, & Barros, 2011). Secure wireless communication and optimal power control under statistical queuing constraints has been discussed in (Qiao, Gursoy, & Velipasalar, 2011). Stability and utility maximization with secure communications over wireless broadcast networks has been addressed in (Liang, Poor, & Ying, 2011). Similarly, the work in (X. Wang, Tao, Mo, & Xu, 2011) has dealt on power and subcarrier allocation for physical-layer security in OFDMA-based broadband wireless networks. As a new trend, a concept of optical layer security in fiber-optic networks has been introduced in (Fok, Wang, Deng, & Prucnal, 2011).

There are also some interesting works on network-focused physical layer security methods in recent literature. For example, the work in (Abdallah, Latif, Youssef, Sultan, & El Gamal, 2011) has discussed keys through automatic repeat request (ARQ) protocol in Wi-Fi networks. Information-theoretic traffic privacy in packet streams has been discussed in (Mathur & Trappe, 2011). A secure type-based multiple access method has been proposed in (Jeon, Hwang, Choi, Lee, & Ha, 2011). A generalized multiple access channel (MAC) model for secret key sharing between three terminals has been considered in (Salimi, Salmasizadeh, Aref, & Golic, 2011). An information secrecy game in cognitive radio networks has been discussed in (Wu & Liu, 2011).

Reciprocal Channel Key Generation

With reciprocity, instead of transmitting information through the fading channel and distilling common random information unobservable by Eve, Alice and Bob simply observe the reciprocal channel directly to form keys, suggested as early as (Hershey, Hassan, & Yarlagadda, 1995), (Hassan, Stark, Hershey, & Chennakeshu, 1996). Reciprocal channel key generation (RCKG) has several advantages compared to other existing physical-layer methods: (i) When the Alice-Bob channel is independent of Eve's channel, perfect secrecy is achievable without the knowledge on the quality of Eve's channel. (ii) Alice and Bob never transmit CSI, allowing them to exploit full randomness for key generation. (iii) Since CSI is passively observed, it can be used in a buffered, off-line fashion (unlike methods where transmission depends on channel state), and minor modification to existing protocols is required.

Practical examples of wireless systems where reciprocity can be achieved are those employing time-division duplex (TDD), such as 802.11, 802.16 (WiMAX), and LTE, where uplink and downlink use the same electromagnetic channel which is known to be reciprocal. In practical consideration, Non-reciprocity due to system effects can be removed through proper calibration procedures.

Recently, reciprocal channel key generation (RCKG) has been discussed for MIMO channel. For example, an important theoretical result on information theoretic security has been provided in (J. Wallace, 2009). The limits of RCKG for MIMO Gaussian channels have been derived and used to compute key generation rates for the measured channels in (J. W. Wallace & Sharma, 2010). Other RCKG methods include (Aono, Higuchi, Ohira, Komiyama, & Sasaoka, 2005), where reciprocal amplitude fluctuations arising from random switching of parasitic loads is exploited. More recently, (Sayeed & Perrig, 2008) presents a method based on phase quantization for scalar channels.

A quantum key distribution (QKD) protocol based on continuous-spectrum quantum carriers has been proposed in (Van Assche, Cardinal, & Cerf, 2004) allowing Alice and Bob to distill a binary secret key out of a list of correlated variables that they share after running the protocol. The authors present a construction that allows the legitimate parties to get equal bit strings out of correlated variables by using a classical channel, with as little leaked information as possible opening the way to securely correcting non-binary key elements. In particular, the construction is refined to the case of Gaussian variables to make it directly applicable to continuous-variable protocols for QKD. In (Ye, Reznik, & Shah, 2006), a method for secrecy extraction from jointly Gaussian random sources has been presented. In (Ye, Reznik, Sternberg, & Shah, 2007), a technique to generate a shared perfectly secret key by two terminals observing a multipath fading channel has been presented and the secrecy that can be generated from ITU cellular channels for the 2 GHz frequency range has been quantified.

In (Wilson, Tse, & Scholtz, 2007), a key distribution method exploiting ultra-wideband (UWB) channel pulse response is proposed. The maximum size of a secure key is characterized by the mutual information between the observations of two nodes, and an approximation and upper bound on mutual information is found for a general multipath channel. Various information-sharing strategies to achieve these bounds are considered and their performance is simulated. A qualitative assessment of the vulnerability of such a secret sharing system to attack from a radio in a nearby location is also given.

More recently, in (Mathur, Trappe, Mandayam, Ye, & Reznik, 2008), authors have presented a protocol that allows two users to establish a common cryptographic key by exploiting the underlying channel response between any two parties which is unique and decorrelates rapidly in space. Their algorithm uses level-crossings and quantization to extract bits from correlated stochastic processes. The algorithm have been validated through experimental studies using an 802.11 development platform with customized logic that extracts raw channel impulse response data from the preamble of a format-compliant 802.11a packet as well as using off-the-shelf 802.11 hardware. Similarly in (Ye et al., 2010), which is extended form of (Mathur et al., 2008), the authors have studied the key generation scheme for the Rayleigh and Rician fading models associated with a richly scattering environment and also proposed a more realistic and powerful approach suited for more general channel state distributions. It has been shown that reliable secret key establishment can be accomplished at rates on the order of 10 bits/second for the typical Wi-Fi channel.

A brief review of the system model of RCKG from (J. W. Wallace & Sharma, 2010) is provided here. This analysis uses the system model as shown in Figure 3. Nodes 1 (Alice) and 2 (Bob) are legitimate users requiring secure communications, while Node 3 (Eve) is a potential eavesdropper. Reciprocal vector channels $\mathbf{h}_a = \mathbf{h}_{a'}$ are referred to as the *forward* and *reverse* channels for legitimate communications, which are estimated by Bob and Alice, respectively. Channels $\mathbf{h}_b$ and $\mathbf{h}_c$ convey information to (and are estimated by) Eve.

Due to noise or synchronization error, the nodes have imperfect estimates of the channels, or

$$\begin{aligned} \hat{\mathbf{h}}_a &= \mathbf{h}_a + \epsilon_2, \hat{\mathbf{h}}_{a'} = \mathbf{h}_{a'} + \epsilon_1, \\ \hat{\mathbf{h}}_b &= \mathbf{h}_b + \epsilon_3, \hat{\mathbf{h}}_c = \mathbf{h}_c + \epsilon', \end{aligned} \qquad (1)$$

where ϵ_i (or ϵ') is zero-mean complex Gaussian estimation error at node i having variance σ^2. Based on this channel model, information theoretic rates

Figure 3.Wireless communications scenario with multiple antennas, where Alice and Bob are legitimate users and Eve is an Eavesdropper

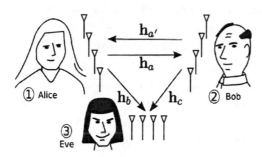

of key generation have been derived and applied to the measured MIMO channels.

QUANTIZATION METHODS

To obtain the key bits from the channel variation, the channel values must be sampled and quantized. The quantization must be done such that there is minimum mismatch in the obtained key bits by Alice and Bob. The small amount of error can be later resolved by error correction during the reconciliation process (to be discussed later). In this section, a brief review of state-of-the-art key generation (quantization) methods is presented. Two commonly used key generation methods

developed are channel quantization with guardband (CQG) and channel quantization alternating (CQA) (J. W. Wallace & Sharma, 2010).

Channel Quantization with Guardband (CQG)

CQG is a generalization of the simple CQ method in (Sayeed & Perrig, 2008) and (Mathur et al., 2008). To exploit both amplitude and phase fluctuations the space of observable complex channels is divided into M equally probable quantization sectors (QSs), where each sector is assigned a unique symbol and corresponding bit pattern. As Alice and Bob observe the channel at specified sample times, the symbols or bits in the corresponding QS are added to the key.

The work in (J. W. Wallace & Sharma, 2010) has assumed rectangular and symmetric QSs (similar to QAM decision regions), where the problem of defining the QSs is reduced to finding $M' = \sqrt{M}/2$ one-sided (positive axis), one-dimensional quantization intervals (QIs), which are then applied separately to real and imaginary parts. The one-sided QIs are defined as depicted in Figure 4, where guardband g helps avoid mismatch for channel observations near quantization boundaries. An iterative method for finding equal-probability QIs with specified guardband 'g' has been given in (J. Wallace, 2009).

Figure 4. Parameters for defining one-sided quantization intervals with guardband. Only one positive dimension is required, where x_m is the start of the mth out of M' total quantization intervals separated by guardband of size g (J. W. Wallace & Sharma, 2010)

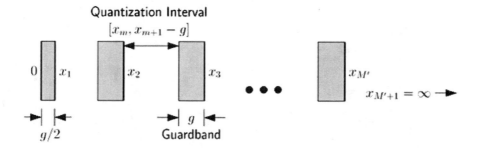

The idea of using guardband is for reducing the probability of key symbol mismatch by discarding channels observed in the guardband region. In a one-way handshake, Alice transmits a guardband indicator bit (GIB) to Bob over a public channel, where GIB=0 and GIB=1 indicate observation of the channel outside or inside the guardband, respectively. When GIB=1, both Alice and Bob discard that channel observation. In a two-way handshake, Alice and Bob exchange GIBs and discard the channel if either user declares GIB=1. Increasing guardband gradually reduces the efficiency of key generation, but dramatically reduces the symbol mismatch rate. The exact efficiency and error probability of CQG have been computed in this work.

Channel Quantization Alternating (CQA)

Instead of using guardband, the error probability can be reduced by simply adapting the quantization map to the channel observation, which is referred to as channel quantization alternating (CQA) (J. W. Wallace & Sharma, 2010), as illustrated in Figure 5. Here, a two-sided set of $4M'$ QIs with equal probability is generated, where each pair of QIs forms a single sector with a given QS index. A quantization map (QM) bit is generated by Alice that indicates which side of the sector the

channel is observed on and transmitted publicly to Bob. Given the QM bit, Bob quantizes his observation of the channel using one of the two alternate maps. Since the QM bit only indicates which side the channel was on, no information about QS is given to Eve. However, the QM bit helps Bob reduce the probability of a symbol error dramatically. Intuitively, for each observed channel the unused half intervals become guardband for the used interval. Key generation performance of CQA in terms of error probability and efficiency has been derived similar to CQG.

As a more realistic analysis of bit error rate (BER) of the practical key generation, performance of two practical key generation methods CQG and CQA considering Gray coded mapping has been computed in (Sharma & Wallace, 2010). An improved efficiency metric has been also presented giving a more realistic indication of key generation performance.

In (Sharma & Wallace, 2011), two methods have been developed that can be applied to generate secret keys automatically from reciprocal fading channels having arbitrary (i.e. non Gaussian) statistics. An improved channel quantization method compared to (J. W. Wallace & Sharma, 2010) has been developed, where the empirical cumulative distribution function (cdf) of the channel has been used directly to ensure equal probability of the key symbols. The idea of positional coding

Figure 5. Example illustrating CQA method for $M' = 2$

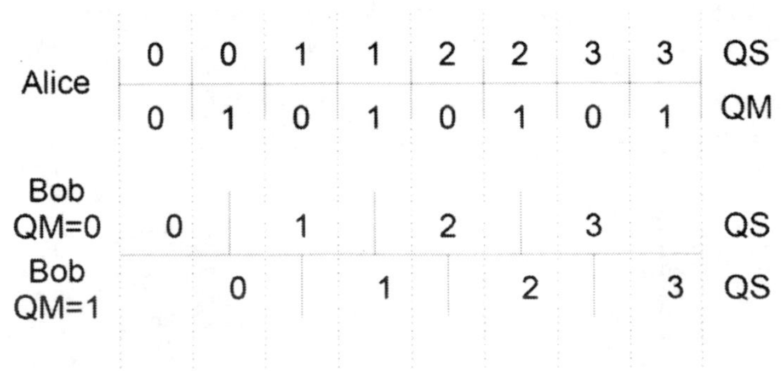

has been also developed, where a secret key can be transmitted by dividing empirical channel observations into multiple code-words and conveying a secret message from Alice to Bob in the sequence of channels fed forward from Alice to Bob. It has been shown that key mismatch rate can be made arbitrarily low by properly selecting the code-word length.

In (El Hajj Shehadeh, Alfandi, & Hogrefe, 2012), intelligent quantization mechanisms for key generation, achieving high secret bits generation rate have been proposed. Moreover, some practical issues affecting the performance of the key generation mechanism have been investigated including the enhanced key generation mechanisms under the effects of delay and mobility. The authors have indicated that this paper serves as a framework towards robust key generation from multipath wireless channels.

The key generation efficiency of the CQG protocol has been further analyzed in (Sun, Xu, Jiang, & Zhao, 2011) to obtain closed-form expressions of BER and key generation efficiency. In order to further improve the key generation efficiency, the authors have proposed to concatenate the CQG protocol with reconciliation (to be discussed in next section). The authors have also presented an upper bound of key generation efficiency, which can be maximized by carefully selecting the guardband region and LDPC codes. The key generation efficiency has also been analyzed by considering the attacks in the case of an unauthenticated wireless channel.

The work in (Patwari, Croft, Jana, & Kasera, 2010) addresses the extraction of secret key bits from noisy radio channel measurements at two nodes such that the two secret keys reliably agree. This work has introduced high-rate uncorrelated bit extraction (HRUBE), a framework for interpolating, transforming for decorrelation, and encoding channel measurements using a multibit adaptive quantization scheme which allows multiple bits per component. The authors have presented an analysis of the probability of bit disagreement in

generated secret keys, and have used experimental data to demonstrate the HRUBE scheme and to quantify its experimental performance.

In (Ren, Su, & Wang, 2011), the framework of the physical layer key generation schemes have been introduced and categorized into two classes: received-signal-strength-based and channel- phase- based protocols. A performance comparison of them has been presented in terms of key disagreement probability, key generation rate, key bit randomness, scalability, and implementation issues. A so called intelligent quantization mechanisms for key generation, achieving high secret bits generation rate has also been proposed in (El Hajj Shehadeh et al., 2012).

RECONCILIATION METHODS

One fundamental problem in secret key formation is the role of the discussion channel for secretly resolving the error in the shared bits. This is a classical problem that arises in physical-layer security, because of the estimation errors, even when channels are fully reciprocal. Practically, sharing information is performed via noisy channels meaning there is always an error in the key bits which are useless unless the error correction is performed. The receiver has to apply some error correcting procedures by the help of some additional bits transmitted in the public channel. In the context of secret key generation, this process of error correction is called reconciliation (Van Assche et al., 2004)(Brassard & Salvail, 1994).

It is observed from the several state of the art works that, LDPC codes have gained significant attention in physical-layer security, especially as the basis of resolving errors or discrepancies that might exist between two parties during the key establishment process (Klinc et al., 2011). A reconciliation procedure based on multilevel coding and optimized LDPC codes has been introduced in (Bloch et al., 2008), which allows to achieve communication rates close to the fundamental security limits in several relevant instances.

In (Wong, Wong, & Shea, 2011), an error-free public channel has been used for the source and destination to exchange messages in order to help the secret-sharing process. The wiretapper can perfectly observe all messages in the public channel. It is shown that a secret-sharing scheme that employs a random ensemble of regular LDPC codes can achieve the key capacity of the BPSK-constrained Gaussian wiretap channel asymptotically with increasing block length. To accommodate practical constraints of finite block length and limited decoding complexity, fixed irregular LDPC codes have also been designed.

The work in (Bloch, Thangaraj, McLaughlin, & Merolla, 2006) has investigated a practical secret key agreement protocol over the Gaussian wire-tap channel based on an LDPC code based efficient information reconciliation method. The reconciliation procedure outputs a binary string over a error-free channel and allows them to find and correct these discrepancies. The authors claim that using privacy amplification techniques (Bennett, Brassard, Crepeau, & Maurer, 1995), the performance approaches the secrecy capacity. Privacy amplification is a process that allows two parties to distill a secret key from a common random variable about which an eavesdropper has partial information.

In (Sun, Wu, Zhao, Jiang, & Xu, 2010), a method to compute the Slepian-Wolf lower bound for the reconciliation of physical layer secret keys has been shown. Two coding approaches, including the syndrome method and the parity method, have been proven to require the same number of bits exchanged between two terminals for the reconciliation in the noiseless environment. The authors have also presented a practical coding approach based on LDPC codes. A reconciliation procedure for physical key generation based on specially designed LDPC codes using Slepian-Wolf-type coding has been presented in (Etesami & Henkel, 2012). The authors have studied an LDPC-based

reconciliation method assuming the extra bit communication in a noisy channel. In (Subramanian et al., 2011) a sequence of LDPC code ensembles have been constructed using Ramanujan graphs to provide strong secrecy over the binary erasure wiretap channel.

It is to be noted that the necessity to eliminate the publicly disclosed bits for security reasons lowers the final key rate. To improve this key rate, the amount of disclosed bits should be minimized. In addition, decreasing the time spent on error reconciliation also improves the key rate. These issues have been addressed in (Cui et al., 2013) by introducing a practical method for expeditious error reconciliation implemented in a field programmable gate array (FPGA) for a discrete variable quantum key distribution system. Experimental results have been presented to demonstrate the rapidity of the proposed protocol.

In (Limmanee & Henkel, 2010), a method to protect vulnerable key symbols by means of physical-layer key encoding has been proposed. The authors have proposed some necessary and sufficient conditions on the code in order to achieve perfect secrecy, even when the eavesdropper knows the code, and derive the asymptotic code rate accordingly. The authors have also discussed how to design the code when the number of vulnerable key symbols is not known.

ENHANCED SECURITY WITH MIMO SYSTEM

There are some information-theoretic works available in literature on security over MIMO channels. The secrecy capacity region of the Gaussian MIMO multi-receiver wiretap channel has been derived in (Ekrem & Ulukus, 2011). A new proof technique in MIMO secrecy context has been provided which makes use of the relationships between the Fisher information and the differential entropy. The authors have shown that the capacity achieving coding scheme is a variant of dirty-paper coding with Gaussian signals.

In (Liu, Liu, Poor, & Shamai, 2010), the problem of secret communication over a two-receiver MIMO Gaussian broadcast channel has been considered, where transmitter has two independent messages, each of which is intended for one of the receivers but needs to be kept asymptotically perfectly secret from the other. It has been shown that under a matrix power constraint, both messages can be simultaneously transmitted at their respective maximal secrecy rates. In (Ly, Liu, & Liang, 2010), the problem of the MIMO Gaussian broadcast channel with two receivers (receivers 1 and 2) and two messages has been considered: a common message intended for both receivers and a confidential message intended only for receiver 1 but needing to be kept asymptotically perfectly secure from receiver 2. The secrecy capacity region of the system has been characterized.

The capacity of the Gaussian wiretap channel model with nodes (Alice, Bob and Eve) with multiple antennas has been analyzed in (Khisti & Wornell, 2010), assuming that the associated channel matrices are fixed and known to all the nodes. A computable characterization of the secrecy capacity has been established as the saddle point solution to a minimax problem. The converse is based on a Sato- type argument used in other broadcast settings, and the coding theorem is based on Gaussian wiretap codebooks. At high signal-to-noise ratio (SNR), it has been shown that the secrecy capacity is attained by simultaneously diagonalizing the channel matrices via the generalized singular value decomposition, and independently coding across the resulting parallel channels.

In (Ekrem & Ulukus, 2012), the Gaussian MIMO wiretap channel has been studied where the transmitter sends a common message to both the legitimate user and the eavesdropper and a private message only to legitimate user, which is desired to be kept hidden as much as possible from the eavesdropper. The authors have obtained the entire capacity-equivocation region for this channel. In particular, the sufficiency of jointly Gaussian auxiliary random variables and channel input to evaluate the existing single-letter description of the capacity-equivocation region due to Csiszar-Korner has been shown.

Secrecy rate analysis of MIMO wiretap channels driven by finite-alphabet input is found in (Bashar, Ding, & Xiao, 2012), where the effect of finite-alphabet input constraint on the secrecy rate of a multi- antenna wiretap channel has been investigated. The proposed precoding scheme converts the underlying multi-antenna system into a bank of parallel channels. Based on this precoding strategy, a decentralized power allocation algorithm based on dual decomposition has been developed to maximize the achievable secrecy rate. Substantial difference in secrecy rate between systems finite-alphabet inputs and systems with Gaussian inputs has been reported.

In (Shafiee, Liu, & Ulukus, 2009), secrecy capacity of Gaussian MIMO wiretap channel has been developed, which consists of a transmitter and a receiver with two antennas each, and an eavesdropper with a single antenna. The authors have determined the secrecy capacity of this channel by proposing an achievable scheme and then developing a tight upper bound that meets the proposed achievable secrecy rate. It has been shown that Gaussian signaling in the form of beam-forming is optimal for this channel, and no pre-processing of information is necessary.

Ergodic secrecy rate for multiple-antenna wiretap channels with Rician fading has been presented in (Li & Petropulu, 2011). The authors have studied the problem of finding the optimal input covariance that maximizes the ergodic secrecy rate subject to a power constraint, assuming that full information on the legitimate channel is available to the transmitter, but only statistical information on the eavesdropper channel is known. More specifically, the authors have investigated the case of MIMO Rician fading for the eavesdropper channel. They show that the optimal input covariance has rank one, allowing to reduce the original optimization problem to a smooth one variable optimization problem. A Newton-type method for a local maximizer, and Piyavskii's algorithm for the global maximizer have been proposed.

In (Alves, Souza, Debbah, & Bennis, 2012), the physical layer security of a multiple antenna transmitter and single antenna receiver system in the presence of a multiple antenna eavesdropper has been studied using transmit antenna selection (TAS). The authors have developed closed-form expressions for the secrecy outage probability showing that the PHY security can be considerably enhanced by using multiple antennas by the legitimate transmitter.

The analysis on achievable secrecy rate in MIMO interference channel with confidential messages along with the secure system design is available in (Fakoorian & Swindlehurst, 2011). MIMO authentication via deliberate fingerprinting at the physical layer can be found (Yu & Sadler, 2011). In (Baracca, Laurenti, & Tomasin, 2012), an authentication scheme has been proposed in the framework of hypothesis testing that suits a multiple wiretap channels environment with correlated fading, as is the case of MIMO systems and/or orthogonal frequency division multiplexing (OFDM) modulation. The performance of the proposed methods is evaluated in a MIMO/OFDM scenario and numerical results show the merits of the proposed approaches that can be adopted as a layer one authentication mechanism.

In (Madiseh, Neville, & McGuire, 2012), MIMO-based antenna systems and the use of random beamforming has been proposed for generating secret keys at the presence of temporal correlation (wideband systems)(Madiseh et al., 2012). The security of the resulting approach is assessed with respect to the worst case scenario whereby the eavesdropper, Eve, is assumed to possess perfect knowledge of Alice and Bob's MIMO channel and is able to estimate, with some degree of error, the coefficients of Alice and Bob's independent random beamformers.

Establishment of secret keys at the presence of spatial and temporal correlations of the channel coefficients have been considered in (C. Chen & Jensen, 2011). The authors have explored decorrelation of the channel coefficients in a MIMO channel demonstrating that this process cannot be separated into spatial and temporal decorrelation processes. The authors have maintained that that the insights gained from these studies assist in the development of a practical key generation protocol based on a published channel coefficient quantization method.

In (Prabhu & Rodrigues, 2011), the probability of secrecy-outage and the asymptotic high-SNR-outage secrecy-capacity for a single-input-single-output-multi-eavesdropper (SISOME) wireless system has been computed with eavesdroppers performing maximum ratio combining (MRC) or selection diversity combining (SDC) reception. The authors have also considered the SISO2E case with eavesdropper antenna-correlation and finally, analyzed the scenario where the eavesdropper has Rician fading links with the transmitter.

MIMO Measurement Campaigns and Testbed Implementations

Some measurement campaigns are reported on the key generation using MIMO channels. In (J. W. Wallace & Sharma, 2010) information theoretic limits for random key generation in MIMO wireless systems exhibiting a reciprocal channel response have been investigated experimentally with a three-node MIMO measurement campaign.

Building on the initial theoretical work in (J. Wallace, Chen, & Jensen, 2009),(J. Wallace, 2009), the paper (J. W. Wallace & Sharma, 2010) has studied limits of RCKG from an experimental perspective, where information theoretic expressions and RCKG protocols have been applied to three-node (for Alice, Bob, and Eve) MIMO measurements taken in an indoor environment using a multi-tone signal consisting of 8 discrete frequencies with 10 MHz separation and centered at 2.55 GHz.

Two methods for generating secret keys have been analyzed in the context of MIMO channels and their mismatch rate and efficiency have been derived. A new wideband indoor MIMO measurement campaign in the 2.51- to 2.59-GHz band has been presented, obtaining the number of available key bits in both line-of-sight (LOS) and non-line-of-sight (NLOS) environments. The key generation rates that can be obtained in practice for four-element arrays have been presented considering environment effects (LOS and NLOS), as well as the dependency on antenna numbers. Single-frequency key generation at a rate higher than 30 bits/m) with movement have been reported, even for LOS scenarios.

The performance of key extraction has been studied in (Premnath et al., 2012) in a MIMO-like sensor network testbed created using TelosB sensors. The authors have mentioned that their MIMO-like sensor environment produces high bit mismatch, which however, could be corrected by iterative distillation stage in key extraction process obtaining improved key rate with multiple sensors.

KEY GENERATION USING RECONFIGURABLE ANTENNAS

Recently, a new method of key generation using reconfigurable antennas has been proposed. In (Mehmood & Wallace, 2011), secret keys from parasitic reconfigurable aperture (RECAP) antennas has been investigated, showing that RCKG methods can employed even in the case of static and LOS channels. Since the artificial channel fluctuations created by RECAP structures are not necessarily Gaussian, a numerical procedure for computing available and secure key bits in arbitrary fading channel has been developed. A lower bound on the required RECAP complexity to avoid a possibility of reduced- complexity

brute-force attack has been also developed. This method has been investigated experimentally in (Mehmood & Wallace, 2012), where measurements with a 5×5 parasitic RECAP antenna at 2.54 GHz in an indoor laboratory environment have been reported. Analysis of the data have been presented to show that number secure key bits is lower when an eavesdropper is in the LOS path between legitimate nodes as opposed to a direction perpendicular to that path. Encouragingly, it has been reported that that around 80% of generated key bits are secure even in the worst case conditions.

In (Mookiah & Dandekar, 2010), the performance gains that can be achieved by using multiple uncorrelated channel realizations for user authentication at the physical layer has been investigated by employing a reconfigurable antenna. Ray tracing simulations using a reconfigurable circular patch antenna has been carried out and the intruder detection rate and false alarm rates have been studied as a function of the number of available antenna modes and the SNR at the receiver.

A new secret key generation and agreement scheme has been proposed in (Aono et al., 2005), that uses the fluctuation of channel characteristics with an electronically steerable parasitic array radiator (ESPAR) antenna. The authors have mentioned that the fluctuation of the channel characteristics can be increased using the beamforming technique of the ESPAR antenna. From experimental results, authors have concluded that the proposed scheme has the ability to generate secret keys from the received signal strength indicator (RSSI) profile with sufficient independence.

ENHANCED SECURITY WITH MULTIPLE RELAY SYSTEM

Recently, physical layer security enhancement using multiple relay systems have been studied with due interest. For example, in (Bassily & Ulukus, 2012), the role of cooperative relays to provide and improve secure communication rates through decode-and-forward (DF) strategies in a full-duplex multiple relay network with an eavesdropper has been studied. The authors have considered the DF scheme as a basis for cooperation and proposed several strategies that implement different versions of this scheme suited for cooperation with multiple relays. Numerical results have been presented to illustrate the performance the proposed strategies in terms of achievable rates in different practical scenarios.

In (Kim, Ikhlef, & Schober, 2012), a combined relay selection and cooperative beamforming schemes for physical layer security has been proposed, where only two of the available relays are selected for beamforming and data transmission. The proposed schemes have introduced a selection gain which partially compensates for the decrease in coding gain due to limiting the number of participating relays to two. Both the cases where full and only partial channel state information available for relay selection and cooperative beamforming have been considered.

The security of a two-way relay network in the presence of an eavesdropper has been addressed in (H.-M. Wang, Yin, & Xia, 2012), where each node is only equipped with single antenna. The authors have proposed two-phase distributed analog network coding, or distributed beamforming and power allocation to enhance the secrecy sum rate of the data exchange. In the first phase, the two terminals broadcast their information data simultaneously to all the relay nodes. In the second phase, three different security schemes have been proposed: optimal beamforming, null-space beamforming, and artificial noise beamforming. Numerical results are provided and analyzed to show the properties and efficiency of the proposed designs. Physical layer secret key agreement in two-way wireless relaying systems has also been discussed in (Shimizu, Iwai, & Sasaoka, 2011).

In (Lai, Liang, & Du, 2012), a relay-assisted key generation strategy has been proposed where the channels between legitimate nodes change slowly. Four practical scenarios are studied, for which relay-assisted key generation protocols are proposed and are shown to be optimal or order-optimal in terms of the key rate. It has also been shown that the multiplexing gain in the key rate scales linearly with the number of relays, indicating that relay-assisted schemes substantially increase the key rate. This is in sharp contrast to scenarios with relays helping information transmission, in which the multiplexing gain does not scale with the number of relays. Furthermore, a cooperative scheme has also been proposed in which relays help key generation but the generated keys are kept secure from these relays.

A physical layer security using cooperative wireless network in the presence of one or more eavesdroppers has been considered in (Li, Petropulu, & Weber, 2011). Two different cooperation schemes are considered. In the first scheme, cooperating nodes retransmit a weighted version of the source signal in a DF fashion. In the second scheme, referred to as cooperative jamming (CJ), while the source is transmitting, cooperating nodes transmit weighted noise to confound the eavesdropper. Two objectives have been investigated: i) maximization of the achievable secrecy rate subject to a total power constraint and ii) minimization of the total power transmit power under a secrecy rate constraint. Numerical results have been presented to illustrate the proposed results and compare them to existing work.

To overcome the limitations of physical layer key generation protocols, e.g., low key generation rate, lower entropy of key bits, and a high reliance on node mobility, the work in (Q. Wang, Xu, & Ren, 2012) has developed a cooperative key generation protocol in narrowband fading channels with the aid of relay node(s). The performance of the cooperative key generation scheme has been evaluated theoretically establishing theoretical and practical upper bounds based on Cramer-Rao bound (CRB).

A scheme called cooperative jamming (CJ) to increase the physical layer security of a wiretap fading channel via distributed relays has been studied in (Zheng, Choo, & Wong, 2011). The feasible conditions on the positiveness of the secrecy rate have been provided showing that the optimization problem can be solved using a combination of convex optimization and a one-dimensional search. Distributed implementations to realize the CJ solution and extension to deal with per group relays' power constraints have also been discussed.

In (Mo, Tao, & Liu, 2012), the problem of secure connection in cooperative wireless communication with two relay strategies, DF and randomize-and-forward (RF) has been studied. The four-node scenario (source, destination, relay, and eavesdropper), and cellular scenario have been considered. For the typical four-node scenario, the authors have derived the optimal power allocation for the DF strategy and found that the RF strategy is always better than the DF to enhance secure connection. In cellular networks, it has been shown that without relay, it is difficult to establish secure connections from the base station to the cell edge users.

In contrast to the other relay scenarios, an interesting security scenario has been considered in (Yuksel,

Liu, & Erkip, 2011), formulating a secure communication game with a relay helping the eavesdropper.

APPLICATION SCENARIOS

Security in Smart Grid

The smart grid is characterized by the two-way flow of electric power and information. For the information flow implementation and support, several wireless communication technologies and standards are being considered. Although there is no doubt that using wireless communications offers significant benefits over wired connections, the wireless technology introduces additional vul-

nerability in terms of network security. The work in (Lee, Gerla, & Oh, 2012) addresses physical layer security, a topic that has been hardly investigated in the smart grid domain. To understand new types of threats, fundamentals of wireless communication have been reviewed and physical attack models have been examined in depth. As a promising solution to physical security, a random spread-spectrum based wireless communication scheme that can achieve both fast and robust data transmission has been described.

For a power distribution grid, wireless communications provide many benefits such as low cost high speed links, easy setup of connections among different devices/appliances, and so on. Connecting power equipment, devices, and appliances through wireless networks is indispensable for a smart distribution grid (SDG) (X. Wang & Yi, 2011). Developing appropriate wireless communication architecture and its security measures is extremely important for an SDG. Some physical layer security like anti-jamming techniques (passive and active) and eavesdropping disable have been proposed in (X. Wang & Yi, 2011). In the proposed active anti-jamming schemes, physical layer techniques that are tolerable to jamming schemes are adopted for wireless communications. For example, spread spectrum (either frequency hopping or direct sequence) techniques can be applied to reduce the impact by intentional jamming signals. The proposed passive schemes are based on monitoring electromagnetic emissions in the frequency band of wireless mesh networks (WMNs) for an SDG. If abnormal jamming signals are detected, the next key step is to locate the jamming source. In this way, a security attacker can be captured. Physical layer security can be also used to disable eavesdropping by totally blocking eavesdropper in SDG. In (Zeng, Li, & Peng, 2012), a frequency hopping (FH) technology supporting multi-level quality-of-service (QoS) requirement has been considered as a promising candidate technology in the physical layer of smart gird communication infrastructure providing security as well as QoS.

Applying physical layer security to SDG wireless communications is a long term research effort instead of a short-term solution, for two reasons (X. Wang & Yi, 2011). Firstly, to date, physical layer security is still immature in terms of the practical implementation in realistic system. Secondly, a cross- layer design between MAC/routing protocols and physical layer security algorithms for SDG wireless communications still needs further research. However, physical layer security is a promising approach that can provide nearly perfect security in the physical layer for wireless communications. Power grids also can take advantage from this distinct feature of physical layer security.

Security in Satellite Communication

Security threats introduced due to the vulnerability of the transmission medium may hinder the proliferation of Ka band multibeam satellite systems for civil and military data applications (Zheng, Arapoglou, & Ottersten, 2012). The work in (Zheng et al., 2012) has studied physical layer security techniques for fixed legitimate receivers dispersed throughout multiple beams, each possibly surrounded by multiple (passive) eavesdroppers. The design objective is to minimize via transmit beamforming the costly total transmit power on board the satellite, while satisfying individual intended users' secrecy rate constraints. Assuming state-of-the-art satellite channel models when perfect CSI about the eavesdroppers is available at the satellite, a partial zero-forcing approach is proposed for obtaining a low-complexity suboptimal solution. Furthermore, the use of artificial noise as an additional degree-of-freedom for protection against eavesdroppers has been explored. When only partial CSI about the eavesdroppers is available, the authors have studied the problem of minimizing the eavesdroppers' received signal to interference-plus-noise ratios.

In (Lei, Han, Vaazquez-Castro, & Hjorungnes, 2011), a secure multibeam satellite communication using Physical-layer security has been addressed proposing system design that minimizes the satellite transmit power subject to the individual secrecy rate requested per user constraints. The performance is evaluated taking into account the impact of the channel condition with given individual secrecy rate requirement. Same group of authors have also studied in (Lei, Han, Vazquez-Castro, & Hjorungnes, 2011) joint power control and beamforming for improved performance. By first assuming that the CSI is available and the beamforming weights are fixed, a security has been investigated to minimize the transmit power with individual secrecy rate constraints. Moreover, suboptimal beamforming weights have been obtained by completely eliminating the co-channel interference and nulling the eavesdroppers' signal simultaneously. In order to obtain jointly optimized power allocation and a beamforming strategy in some practical cases, the authors have further evaluated the impact of the eavesdropper's CSI on the secure multibeam satellite system design. The results have been presented showing that the joint beamforming scheme is more favorable than the fixed beamforming scheme, especially in the cases of a larger number of satellite antenna elements and higher secrecy rate requirement.

Security in Optical Communication Networks

Optical physical layer security has also been considered in recent literature. Perhaps the most notable difference between optical layer security is the fact that the optical physical layer is being used as a "computation" engine for actually performing encryption at the physical layer (Trappe et al., 2011). Whereas physical layer security for wireless systems involves new forms of coding and communication strategies to extract as much confidentiality as possible from the wireless system, optical systems provide benefit on implementing conventional cipher algorithms with very high speed. For example, it has been shown in (Fok et al., 2011) that it is possible to create an XOR with feedback building block using the physical (nonlinear) properties of light.

In (Fok et al., 2011), the security threats in an optical network have been discussed and several existing optical techniques to improve the security have been presented. Various types of security threats that could appear in the optical layer of an optical network, include jamming, physical infrastructure attacks, eavesdropping, and interception. Real-time processing of the optical signal is essential in order to integrate security functionality at the physical layer while not undermining the true value of optical communications, which is its speed. Optical layer security benefits from the unique properties of optical processing-instantaneous response, broadband operation, electromagnetic immunity, compactness, and low latency. Various defenses against the security threats have been proposed including optical encryption, optical code-division multiple access (CDMA) confidentiality, self-healing survivable optical rings, anti- jamming, and optical steganography (Fok et al., 2011).

Security in RFID systems

Radio frequency identification (RFID) is a technology used for automated identification of objects and people. An RFID tag is a small electronic device with an antenna and has a unique serial number which can be used in many applications including libraries, payment transponders, passports, ID cards, etc. Although Physical layer attacks and security in RFID systems have not been studied extensively till now, the security enhancement using multiple communication layers has been discussed in some works (Juels, 2006). Physical layer attack on RFID systems that prevents the reception of communication has been discussed in (Vahedi, Shah-Mansouri, Wong, Blake, & Ward, 2011), where authors have studied the use of blocker tags for malicious attacks that can prevent nearby legitimate readers from correctly receiving the reply messages from the tags. The authors have proposed a lower-layer solution for the blocker attack which is a MAC-layer denial of service (DoS) threat.

In (Saad, Han, & Poor, 2012), the secrecy rate of ultra-high frequency (UHF) RFID backscatter systems has been characterized. A novel approach has been proposed for maximizing this secrecy rate by exploiting the nature and features of the RFID backscatter channel. To explore these features, the proposed approach allows the RFID readers to append artificial noise signals to their continuous wave (CW) signals which then propagate via the backscatter channel hence inducing interference at the eavesdroppers.

Since the existing research in the physical layer security in RFID is still immature, it can be a good field of investigation for the researchers in the physical layer security area.

Security in Cognitive Radio Networks

Security in cognitive radio networks (CRN) will likely play a significant role in the long-term commercial viability of the technology. Security in CRN is a challenging issue, since there is a lack of trusted network infrastructure, and more chances are given to attackers by cognitive radio (CR) technology compared to general wireless networks (Burbank, 2008). Thus, methods that can guarantee secure communication without the need for existing infrastructure are of high interest.

Among the different types of attacks common in wireless networks, primary user emulation attack (PUEA) is one that may have serious impact on CR (Chin, Tseng, Tsai, Kao, & Kao, 2012). In (Chin et al., 2012), a method has been proposed to identify the PUEA by using the characteristics of wireless channels themselves showing that the proposed physical layer based scheme is more efficient than conventional security schemes based on higher layer protocols in terms of the detection time.

Recently physical layer security in CRN has been given attention due to its features of providing secure key from the communication channel itself. In (Pei, Liang, Zhang, Teh, & Li, 2010), the physical layer security issue of a secondary user (SU) in a CRN has been addressed from an information- theoretic perspective. Specially, the authors have considered a secure multiple-input single-output (MISO) CR channel, where a multi-antenna SU transmitter sends confidential information to a legitimate SU receiver in the presence of an eavesdropper and on the licensed band of a primary user (PU). The secrecy capacity of the channel has been characterized, which is a quasiconvex optimization problem of finding the capacity-achieving transmit covariance matrix under the joint transmit power and interference power constraints. Three suboptimal but computationally efficient schemes have been presented.

The achievable rates of the MIMO secrecy channel with multiple single-/multi-antenna eavesdroppers has been studied in (Zhang, Zhang, Liang, Xin, & Cui, 2010), exploring a relationship between the secrecy channel and the CR channel. By constructing an auxiliary multi-antenna CR channel that has the same channel responses as the secrecy channel, the authors have shown that finding the optimal complex transmit covariance matrix for the secrecy channel becomes equivalent to searching over a set of real interference power constraints in the auxiliary CR channel. Based on this relationship, efficient algorithms have been proposed to solve the non-convex secrecy rate maximization problem by transforming it into a sequence of convex CR spectrum sharing capacity computation problems, under various setups of the secrecy channel.

The issue of optimal transmitter design to achieve physical layer security for a MISO CRN has been addressed in (Pei, Liang, Teh, & Li, 2011) with an assumption that all the CSI of the secondary, primary, and eavesdropper channels is not perfectly known at the SU transmitter. The optimal and sub- optimal transmitter designs reducing the computational complexity have been proposed and evaluated by simulation results.

In (Sakran, Shokair, Nasr, El-Rabaie, & El-Azm, 2012), a relay selection scheme has been proposed for the security constrained CRNs with single eavesdropper, multiple eavesdroppers, and PUs. The proposed scheme selects a trusted decode and forward relay to assist the SU transmitter and maximize the achievable secrecy rate that is subjected to the interference power constraints at the PUs for the different number of eavesdroppers and PUs under available channel knowledge. Secrecy rate and secrecy outage probability have been considered as two performance metrics of the proposed scheme.

Physical layer security in collaborative sensing of CR under malicious attacks has been also investigated in (H. Wang, Lightfoot, & Li, 2010). Similarly power allocation using Vickrey auction and sequential first-price auction games for physical layer security in cognitive relay networks has been discussed in (T. Wang, Song, Han, Cheng, & Jiao, 2012).

CONCLUSION

This chapter has provided a survey of physical layer security and key generation methods. Security models have been discussed and some security attacks have been reviewed. Some discussion on information theoretic works, and key generation methods including quantization and reconciliation have been presented. New trends on physical layer security including the MIMO, relays and reconfigurable antennas have also been discussed. Finally, some existing and emerging application scenarios of physical layer security have been discussed. Although much has been accomplished in the last few years towards understanding the potential of the physical layer to enhance the security in wireless communication systems, the future research should focus on the practical implementation of this concept. The trends show that this concept is very likely to be paid higher attention by researchers in incoming days.

REFERENCES

Abdallah, Y., Latif, M. A., Youssef, M., Sultan, A., & El Gamal, H. (2011). Keys through ARQ: Theory and practice. *IEEE Transactions on Information Forensics and Security, 6*(3), 737–751. doi:10.1109/TIFS.2011.2123093.

Agrawal, A., Rezki, Z., Khisti, A., & Alouini, M. (2011). Noncoherent capacity of secret-key agreement with public discussion. *IEEE Transactions on Information Forensics and Security, 6*(3), 565–574. doi:10.1109/TIFS.2011.2158999.

Ahlswede, R., & Csiszar, I. (1993). Common randomness in information theory and cryptography—Part I: Secret sharing. *IEEE Transactions on Information Theory, 39*(4), 1121–1132. doi:10.1109/18.243431.

Alves, H., Souza, R., Debbah, M., & Bennis, M. (2012). Performance of transmit antenna selection physical layer security schemes. *IEEE Signal Processing Letters, 19*(6), 372–375. doi:10.1109/LSP.2012.2195490.

Aono, T., Higuchi, K., Ohira, T., Komiyama, B., & Sasaoka, H. (2005). Wireless secret key generation exploiting reactance-domain scalar response of multipath fading channels. *IEEE Transactions on Antennas and Propagation, 53*, 3776–3784. doi:10.1109/TAP.2005.858853.

Baracca, P., Laurenti, N., & Tomasin, S. (2012). Physical layer authentication over MIMO fading wiretap channels. *IEEE Transactions on Wireless Communications, 11*(7), 2564–2573. doi:10.1109/TWC.2012.051512.111481.

Barros, J., & Rodrigues, M. R. D. (2006). Secrecy capacity of wireless channels. In *Proceedings of the 2006 IEEE International Symposium on Information Theory,* (pp. 356-360). Seattle, WA: IEEE.

Bashar, S., Ding, Z., & Xiao, C. (2012). On secrecy rate analysis of MIMO wiretap channels driven by finite-alphabet input. *IEEE Transactions on Communications, 60*(12), 3816–3825. doi:10.1109/TCOMM.2012.091212.110199.

Bassily, R., & Ulukus, S. (2012). Secure communication in multiple relay networks through decode-and-forward strategies. *Journal of Communications and Networks, 14*(4), 352–363.

Benjamin, R. (1990). Security considerations in communications systems and networks. *IEEE Proceedings I: Communications, Speech and Vision, 137*(2), 61-72.

Bennett, C., Brassard, G., Crepeau, C., & Maurer, U. (1995). Generalized privacy amplification. *IEEE Transactions on Information Theory, 41*(6), 1915–1923. doi:10.1109/18.476316.

Bloch, M., Barros, J., Rodrigues, M. R. D., & McLaughlin, S. W. (2008). Wireless information- Theoretic security. *IEEE Transactions on Information Theory, 54*, 2515–2534. doi:10.1109/TIT.2008.921908.

Bloch, M., Debbah, M., Liang, Y., Oohama, Y., & Thangaraj, A. (2012). Special issue on physical-layer security. *Journal of Communications and Networks, 14*(4), 349–351.

Bloch, M., Thangaraj, A., McLaughlin, S., & Merolla, J.-M. (2006). LDPC-based secret key agreement over the Gaussian wiretap channel. In *Proceedings of the 2006 IEEE International Symposium on Information Theory* (pp. 1179-1183). IEEE.

Brassard, G., & Salvail, L. (1994). Secret-key reconciliation by public discussion. In *Proceedings of the Workshop on the Theory and Application of Cryptographic Techniques on Advances in Cryptology* (pp. 410–423). Secaucus, NJ: Springer-Verlag. Retrieved from http://dl.acm.org/citation.cfm?id=188307.188368

Burbank, J. (2008). Security in cognitive radio networks: The required evolution in approaches to wireless network security. In *Proceedings of the 3rd International Conference on Cognitive Radio Oriented Wireless Networks and Communications* (CROWNCOM 2008) (pp. 1-7). CROWNCOM.

Chen, C., & Jensen, M. (2011). Secret key establishment using temporally and spatially correlated wireless channel coefficients. *IEEE Transactions on Mobile Computing*, 10(2), 205–215. doi:10.1109/TMC.2010.114.

Chen, Y., Yang, J., Trappe, W., & Martin, R. (2010). Detecting and localizing identity-based attacks in wireless and sensor networks. *IEEE Transactions on Vehicular Technology*, 59(5), 2418–2434. doi:10.1109/TVT.2010.2044904.

Chin, W.-L., Tseng, C.-L., Tsai, C.-S., Kao, W.-C., & Kao, C.-W. (2012). Channel-based detection of primary user emulation attacks in cognitive radios. In *Proceedings of the 2012 IEEE 75th Vehicular Technology Conference* (VTC Spring) (pp. 1-5). IEEE.

Courtois, N. T., & Meier, W. (2003). Algebraic attacks on stream ciphers with linear feedback. In *Proceedings of the 22nd International Conference on Theory and Applications of Cryptographic Techniques* (pp. 345–359). Berlin, Germany: Springer-Verlag. Retrieved from http://dl.acm.org/citation.cfm?id=1766171.1766200

Csiszar, I., & Narayan, P. (2008). Secrecy capacities for multiterminal channel models. *IEEE Transactions on Information Theory*, 54(6), 2437–2452. doi:10.1109/TIT.2008.921705.

Cui, K., Wang, J., Zhang, H.-F., Luo, C.-L., Jin, G., & Chen, T.-Y. (2013). A real-time design based on FPGA for expeditious error reconciliation in QKD system. *IEEE Transactions on Information Forensics and Security*, 8(1), 184–190. doi:10.1109/TIFS.2012.2228855.

Diffie, W., & Hellman, M. (1976). New directions in cryptography. *IEEE Transactions on Information Theory*, 22(6), 644–654. doi:10.1109/TIT.1976.1055638.

Douceur, J. R. (2002). The sybil attack. In *Revised papers from the first international workshop on peer-to-peer systems* (pp. 251-260). London, UK: Springer-Verlag. Retrieved from http://dl.acm.org/citation.cfm?id=646334.687813

Ekrem, E., & Ulukus, S. (2011). The secrecy capacity region of the Gaussian MIMO multi-receiver wiretap channel. *IEEE Transactions on Information Theory*, 57(4), 2083–2114. doi:10.1109/TIT.2011.2111750.

Ekrem, E., & Ulukus, S. (2012). Capacity-equivocation region of the Gaussian MIMO wiretap channel. *IEEE Transactions on Information Theory*, 58(9), 5699–5710. doi:10.1109/TIT.2012.2204534.

El Hajj Shehadeh, Y., Alfandi, O., & Hogrefe, D. (2012). Towards robust key extraction from multipath wireless channels. *Journal of Communications and Networks*, 14(4), 385–395.

Etesami, J., & Henkel, W. (2012). LDPC code construction for wireless physical-layer key reconciliation. In *Proceedings of the 2012 1st IEEE International Conference on Communications in China (ICCC)* (pp. 208-213). ICCC.

Fakoorian, S. A. A., & Swindlehurst, A. L. (2011). MIMO interference channel with confidential messages: Achievable secrecy rates and precoder design. *IEEE Transactions on Information Forensics and Security*, 6(3), 640–649. doi:10.1109/TIFS.2011.2156788.

Fok, M. P., Wang, Z., Deng, Y., & Prucnal, P. R. (2011). Optical layer security in fiber-optic networks. *IEEE Transactions on Information Forensics and Security, 6*(3), 725–736. doi:10.1109/TIFS.2011.2141990.

Goel, S., Aggarwal, V., Yener, A., & Calderbank, A. (2011). The effect of eavesdroppers on network connectivity: A secrecy graph approach. *IEEE Transactions on Information Forensics and Security, 6*(3), 712–724. doi:10.1109/TIFS.2011.2148714.

Haggerty, J., Shi, Q., & Merabti, M. (2005). Early detection and prevention of denial-of-service attacks: A novel mechanism with propagated traced-back attack blocking. *IEEE Journal on Selected Areas in Communications, 23*(10), 1994–2002. doi:10.1109/JSAC.2005.854123.

Harrison, W., Almeida, J., McLaughlin, S., & Barros, J. (2011, September). Coding for cryptographic security enhancement using stopping sets. *IEEE Transactions on Information Forensics and Security, 6*(3), 575–584. doi:10.1109/TIFS.2011.2145371.

Hassan, A. A., Stark, W. E., Hershey, J. E., & Chennakeshu, S. (1996). Cryptographic key agreement for mobile radio. *Digital Signal Processing, 6*(4), 207–212. doi:10.1006/dspr.1996.0023.

Hayashi, M. (2011). Exponential decreasing rate of leaked information in universal random privacy amplification. *IEEE Transactions on Information Theory, 57*(6), 3989–4001. doi:10.1109/TIT.2011.2110950.

Hershey, J. E., Hassan, A. A., & Yarlagadda, R. (1995). Unconventional cryptographic keying variable management. *IEEE Transactions on Communications, 43*, 3–6. doi:10.1109/26.385951.

Isaka, M., & Kawata, S. (2011). Signal sets for secret key agreement with public discussion based on Gaussian and fading channels. *IEEE Transactions on Information Forensics and Security, 6*(3), 523–531. doi:10.1109/TIFS.2011.2131132.

Jeon, H., Hwang, D., Choi, J., Lee, H., & Ha, J. (2011). Secure type-based multiple access. *IEEE Transactions on Information Forensics and Security, 6*(3), 763–774. doi:10.1109/TIFS.2011.2158312.

Juels, A. (2006). RFID security and privacy: A research survey. *IEEE Journal on Selected Areas in Communications, 24*(2), 381–394. doi:10.1109/JSAC.2005.861395.

Khisti, A., Diggavi, S. N., & Wornell, G. W. (2011). Secret-key agreement with channel state information at the transmitter. *IEEE Transactions on Information Forensics and Security, 6*(3), 672–681. doi:10.1109/TIFS.2011.2151188.

Khisti, A., Diggavi, S. N., & Wornell, G. W. (2012). Secret-key generation using correlated sources and channels. *IEEE Transactions on Information Theory, 58*(2), 652–670. doi:10.1109/TIT.2011.2173629.

Khisti, A., & Wornell, G. (2010). Secure transmission with multiple antennas— Part II: The MIMOME wiretap channel. *IEEE Transactions on Information Theory, 56*(11), 5515–5532. doi:10.1109/TIT.2010.2068852.

Kim, J., Ikhlef, A., & Schober, R. (2012). Combined relay selection and cooperative beamforming for physical layer security. *Journal of Communications and Networks, 14*(4), 364–373.

Klinc, D., Ha, J., McLaughlin, S., Barros, J., & Kwak, B.-J. (2011). LDPC codes for the Gaussian wiretap channel. *IEEE Transactions on Information Forensics and Security, 6*(3), 532–540. doi:10.1109/TIFS.2011.2134093.

Kobayashi, M., Piantanida, P., Yang, S., & Shamai, S. (2011). On the secrecy degrees of freedom of the multiantenna block fading wiretap channels. *IEEE Transactions on Information Forensics and Security, 6*(3), 703–711. doi:10.1109/TIFS.2011.2159376.

Lai, L., Liang, Y., & Du, W. (2012). Cooperative key generation in wireless networks. *IEEE Journal on Selected Areas in Communications, 30*(8), 1578–1588. doi:10.1109/JSAC.2012.120924.

Lai, L., Liang, Y., & Poor, H. V. (2012). A unified framework for key agreement over wireless fading channels. *IEEE Transactions on Information Forensics and Security, 7*(2), 480–490. doi:10.1109/TIFS.2011.2180527.

Leavitt, N. (2011, June). Mobile security: Finally a serious problem? *Computer, 44*(6), 11–14. doi:10.1109/MC.2011.184.

Lee, E.-K., Gerla, M., & Oh, S. Y. (2012). Physical layer security in wireless smart grid. *IEEE Communications Magazine, 50*(8), 46–52. doi:10.1109/MCOM.2012.6257526.

Lei, J., Han, Z., Vaazquez-Castro, M., & Hjorungnes, A. (2011). Multibeam satcom systems design with physical layer security. In *Proceedings of the 2011 IEEE International Conference on Ultra-Wideband (ICUWB)* (pp. 555-559). IEEE.

Lei, J., Han, Z., Vazquez-Castro, M., & Hjorungnes, A. (2011). Secure satellite communication systems design with individual secrecy rate constraints. *IEEE Transactions on Information Forensics and Security, 6*(3), 661–671. doi:10.1109/TIFS.2011.2148716.

Li, J., & Petropulu, A. P. (2011, September). Ergodic secrecy rate for multiple-antenna wiretap channels with Rician fading. *IEEE Transactions on Information Forensics and Security, 6*(3), 861–867. doi:10.1109/TIFS.2011.2158538.

Li, J., Petropulu, A. P., & Weber, S. (2011). On cooperative relaying schemes for wireless physical layer security. *IEEE Transactions on Signal Processing, 59*(10), 4985–4997. doi:10.1109/TSP.2011.2159598.

Liang, Y., Poor, H., & Ying, L. (2011, September). Secure communications over wireless broadcast networks: Stability and utility maximization. *IEEE Transactions on Information Forensics and Security, 6*(3), 682–692. doi:10.1109/TIFS.2011.2158311.

Liang, Y., Poor, H. V., & Shamai (Shitz), S. (2009). Information theoretic security. *Found. Trends Commun. Inf. Theory, 5*(4-5), 355-580. Retrieved from http://dx.doi.org/10.1561/0100000036

Limmanee, A., & Henkel, W. (2010). Secure physical-layer key generation protocol and key encoding in wireless communications. In *Proceedings of the 2010 IEEE GLOBECOM workshops (GC WKSHPS)* (pp. 94-98). IEEE.

Liu, R., Liu, T., Poor, H., & Shamai, S. (2010). Multiple-input multiple-output Gaussian broadcast channels with confidential messages. *IEEE Transactions on Information Theory, 56*(9), 4215–4227. doi:10.1109/TIT.2010.2054593.

Ly, H., Liu, T., & Liang, Y. (2010). Multiple-input multiple-output Gaussian broadcast channels with common and confidential messages. *IEEE Transactions on Information Theory, 56*(11), 5477–5487. doi:10.1109/TIT.2010.2069190.

Madiseh, M. G., Neville, S. W., & McGuire, M. L. (2012). Applying beamforming to address temporal correlation in wireless channel characterization-based secret key generation. *IEEE Transactions on Information Forensics and Security, 7*(4), 1278–1287. doi:10.1109/TIFS.2012.2195176.

Massey, J. (1988, May). An introduction to contemporary cryptology. *Proceedings of the IEEE, 76*, 533–549. doi:10.1109/5.4440.

Mathur, S., Reznik, A., Ye, C., Mukherjee, R., Rahman, A., Shah, Y., & Mandayam, N. (2010). Exploiting the physical layer for enhanced security [security and privacy in emerging wireless networks]. *IEEE Wireless Communications*, *17*(5), 63–70. doi:10.1109/MWC.2010.5601960.

Mathur, S., & Trappe, W. (2011). Bit-traps: Building information-theoretic traffic privacy into packet streams. *IEEE Transactions on Information Forensics and Security*, *6*(3), 752–762. doi:10.1109/TIFS.2011.2138696.

Mathur, S., Trappe, W., Mandayam, N., Ye, C., & Reznik, A. (2008). Radio-telepathy: Extracting a secret key from an unauthenticated wireless channel. In *Proceedings of the 14th ACM Intl. Conf. on Mobile Computing and Networking (MOBICOM '08)* (pp. 128–139). San Francisco, CA: ACM.

Maurer, U. (1993). Secret key agreement by public discussion from common information. *IEEE Transactions on Information Theory*, *39*, 733–742. doi:10.1109/18.256484.

Maurer, U., & Wolf, S. (2003a). Secret-key agreement over unauthenticated public channels—Part I: Definitions and a completeness result. *IEEE Transactions on Information Theory*, *49*(4), 822–831. doi:10.1109/TIT.2003.809563.

Maurer, U., & Wolf, S. (2003b). Secret-key agreement over unauthenticated public channels—Part III: Privacy amplification. *IEEE Transactions on Information Theory*, *49*(4), 839–851. doi:10.1109/TIT.2003.809559.

Maurer, U., & Wolf, S. (2003c). Secret-key agreement over unauthenticated public channels—Part II: The simulatability condition. *IEEE Transactions on Information Theory*, *49*(4), 832–838. doi:10.1109/TIT.2003.809560.

Mehmood, R., & Wallace, J. (2011, April). Wireless security enhancement using parasitic reconfigurable aperture antennas. In *Proceedings of the 5th European Conference on Antennas and Propagation (EUCAP)* (pp. 2761-2765). EUCAP.

Mehmood, R., & Wallace, J. (2012). Experimental assessment of secret key generation using parasitic reconfigurable aperture antennas. In *Proceedings of the 2012 6th European Conference on Antennas and Propagation (EUCAP)* (pp. 1151-1155). EUCAP.

Mo, J., Tao, M., & Liu, Y. (2012). Relay placement for physical layer security: A secure connection perspective. *IEEE Communications Letters*, *16*(6), 878–881. doi:10.1109/LCOMM.2012.042312.120582.

Mookiah, P., & Dandekar, K. (2010). Enhancing wireless security through reconfigurable antennas. In *Proceedings of the 2010 IEEE Radio and Wireless Symposium (RWS)* (pp. 593-596). IEEE.

Moore, D., Shannon, C., Brown, D. J., Voelker, G. M., & Savage, S. (2006). Inferring internet denial-of-service activity. *ACM Transactions on Computer Systems*, *24*(2), 115–139. Retrieved from http://doi.acm.org/10.1145/1132026.1132027 doi:10.1145/1132026.1132027.

Newsome, J., Shi, E., Song, D., & Perrig, A. (2004). The sybil attack in sensor networks: Analysis defenses. In *Proceedings of the Third International Symposium on Information Processing in Sensor Networks, 2004 (IPSN 2004)* (pp. 259-268). IPSN.

Patwari, N., Croft, J., Jana, S., & Kasera, S. K. (2010). High-rate uncorrelated bit extraction for shared secret key generation from channel measurements. *IEEE Transactions on Mobile Computing*, *9*(1), 17–30. doi:10.1109/TMC.2009.88.

Pei, Y., Liang, Y.-C., Teh, K. C., & Li, K. H. (2011). Secure communication in multiantenna cognitive radio networks with imperfect channel state information. *IEEE Transactions on Signal Processing*, *59*(4), 1683–1693. doi:10.1109/TSP.2011.2105479.

Pei, Y., Liang, Y.-C., Zhang, L., Teh, K. C., & Li, K. H. (2010). Secure communication over MISO cognitive radio channels. *IEEE Transactions on Wireless Communications*, *9*(4), 1494–1502. doi:10.1109/TWC.2010.04.090746.

Pierrot, A., & Bloch, M. (2011). Strongly secure communications over the two-way wiretap channel. *IEEE Transactions on Information Forensics and Security*, *6*(3), 595–605. doi:10.1109/TIFS.2011.2158422.

Prabhu, V. U., & Rodrigues, M. R. D. (2011). On wireless channels with M-antenna eavesdroppers: Characterization of the outage probability and ε-outage secrecy capacity. *IEEE Transactions on Information Forensics and Security*, *6*(3), 853–860. doi:10.1109/TIFS.2011.2159491.

Premnath, S., Jana, S., Croft, J., Lakshmane Gowda, P., Clark, M., Kasera, S., & Krishnamurthy, S. (2012). Secret key extraction from wireless signal strength in real environments. *IEEE Transactions on Mobile Computing*, *12*(5), 917–930. doi:10.1109/TMC.2012.63.

Qiao, D., Gursoy, M., & Velipasalar, S. (2011). Secure wireless communication and optimal power control under statistical queueing constraints. *IEEE Transactions on Information Forensics and Security*, *6*(3), 628–639. doi:10.1109/TIFS.2011.2155650.

Raymond, D., & Midkiff, S. (2008). Denial-of-service in wireless sensor networks: Attacks and defenses. *IEEE Pervasive Computing / IEEE Computer Society [and] IEEE Communications Society*, *7*(1), 74–81. doi:10.1109/MPRV.2008.6.

Ren, K., Su, H., & Wang, Q. (2011). Secret key generation exploiting channel characteristics in wireless communications. *IEEE Wireless Communications*, *18*(4), 6–12. doi:10.1109/MWC.2011.5999759.

Rizomiliotis, P. (2010). On the resistance of boolean functions against algebraic attacks using univariate polynomial representation. *IEEE Transactions on Information Theory*, *56*(8), 4014–4024. doi:10.1109/TIT.2010.2050801.

Saad, W., Han, Z., & Poor, H. (2012). On the physical layer security of backscatter RFID systems. In *Proceedings of the 2012 International Symposium on Wireless Communication Systems (ISWCS)* (pp. 1092-1096). ISWCS.

Sakran, H., Shokair, M., Nasr, O., El-Rabaie, S., & El-Azm, A. A. (2012). Proposed relay selection scheme for physical layer security in cognitive radio networks. *IET Communications*, *6*(16), 2676–2687. doi:10.1049/iet-com.2011.0638.

Salimi, S., Salmasizadeh, M., & Aref, M. (2011). Rate regions of secret key sharing in a new source model. *IET Communications*, *5*(4), 443–455. doi:10.1049/iet-com.2009.0777.

Salimi, S., Salmasizadeh, M., Aref, M. R., & Golic, J. D. (2011). Key agreement over multiple access channel. *IEEE Transactions on Information Forensics and Security*, *6*(3), 775–790. doi:10.1109/TIFS.2011.2158310.

Sayeed, A., & Perrig, A. (2008). Secure wireless communications: Secret keys through multipath. In *Proceedings of the 2008 IEEE International Conference on Acoustics, Speech, and Signal Processing* (pp. 3013-3016). Las Vegas, NV: IEEE.

Scoville, A.W. (1999) Clear signatures, obscure signs. Retrieved from http://www.bc.edu.bcorg/avp/law/st.org/iptf/articles/content/1999070101.html

Shafiee, S., Liu, N., & Ulukus, S. (2009). Towards the secrecy capacity of the Gaussian MIMO wiretap channel: The 2-2-1 channel. *IEEE Transactions on Information Theory, 55*(9), 4033–4039. doi:10.1109/TIT.2009.2025549.

Sharma, R., & Wallace, J. (2010). Bit error rate and efficiency analysis of wireless reciprocal channel key generation. In *Proceedings of the 2010 IEEE International Conference on Wireless Information Technology and Systems (ICWITS)* (pp. 1-4). IEEE.

Sharma, R., & Wallace, J. (2011). Physical layer key generation methods for arbitrary fading channels. In *Proceedings of the 2011 IEEE International Symposium on Antennas and Propagation (APSURSI)* (pp. 1368-1371). IEEE.

Shim, K. (2003). Some attacks on chikazawa-yamagishi id-based key sharing scheme. *IEEE Communications Letters, 7*(3), 145–147. doi:10.1109/LCOMM.2003.809992.

Shimizu, T., Iwai, H., & Sasaoka, H. (2011). Physical-layer secret key agreement in two-way wireless relaying systems. *IEEE Transactions on Information Forensics and Security, 6*(3), 650–660. doi:10.1109/TIFS.2011.2147314.

Shiu, Y.-S., Chang, S. Y., Wu, H.-C., Huang, S.-H., & Chen, H.-H. (2011). Physical layer security in wireless networks: A tutorial. *IEEE Wireless Communications, 18*(2), 66–74. doi:10.1109/MWC.2011.5751298.

Springer Reference. (2013). Retrieved from http://www.springerreference.com/docs/html/chapterdbid/317535.html

Subramanian, A., Thangaraj, A., Bloch, M., & McLaughlin, S. (2011). Strong secrecy on the binary erasure wiretap channel using large-girth LDPC codes. *IEEE Transactions on Information Forensics and Security, 6*(3), 585–594. doi:10.1109/TIFS.2011.2148715.

Sun, X., Wu, X., Zhao, C., Jiang, M., & Xu, W. (2010). Slepian-wolf coding for reconciliation of physical layer secret keys. In *Proceedings of the 2010 IEEE Wireless Communications and Networking Conference (WCNC)* (pp. 1-6). IEEE.

Sun, X., Xu, W., Jiang, M., & Zhao, C. (2011). Improved generation efficiency for key extracting from wireless channels. In *Proceedings of the 2011 IEEE International Conference on Communications (ICC)* (pp. 1-6). IEEE.

Trappe, W., Poor, V., Iwai, H., Yener, A., Prucnal, P., & Barros, J. (2011). Guest editorial special issue on using the physical layer for securing the next generation of communication systems. *IEEE Transactions on Information Forensics and Security, 6*(3), 521–522. doi:10.1109/TIFS.2011.2160572.

Vahedi, E., Shah-Mansouri, V., Wong, V. W. S., Blake, I. F., & Ward, R. K. (2011). Probabilistic analysis of blocking attack in RFID systems. *IEEE Transactions on Information Forensics and Security, 6*(3), 803–817. doi:10.1109/TIFS.2011.2132129.

Van Assche, G., Cardinal, J., & Cerf, N. (2004). Reconciliation of a quantum-distributed Gaussian key. *IEEE Transactions on Information Theory, 50*(2), 394–400. doi:10.1109/TIT.2003.822618.

Vilela, J., Pinto, P., & Barros, J. (2011). Position-based jamming for enhanced wireless secrecy. *IEEE Transactions on Information Forensics and Security, 6*(3), 616–627. doi:10.1109/TIFS.2011.2142305.

Wallace, J. (2009). Secure physical layer key generation schemes: Performance and information theoretic limits. In *Proceedings of the 2009 IEEE International Conference on Communications (ICC)* (pp. 1-5). Dresden, Germany: IEEE.

Wallace, J., Chen, C., & Jensen, M. (2009). Key generation exploiting MIMO channel evolution: Algorithms and theoretical limits. In *Proceedings of the 3rd European Conference on Antennas and Propagation (EUCAP '09)* (pp. 1499-1503). Berlin, Germany: EUCAP.

Wallace, J. W., & Sharma, R. K. (2010). Automatic secret keys from reciprocal MIMO wireless channels: Measurement and analysis. *IEEE Transactions on Information Forensics and Security, 5*(3), 381–392. doi:10.1109/TIFS.2010.2052253.

Wang, H., Lightfoot, L., & Li, T. (2010). On phy-layer security of cognitive radio: Collaborative sensing under malicious attacks. In *Proceedings of the 2010 44th Annual Conference on Information Sciences and Systems (CISS)* (pp. 1-6). CISS.

Wang, H.-M., Yin, Q., & Xia, X.-G. (2012). Distributed beamforming for physical-layer security of two-way relay networks. *IEEE Transactions on Signal Processing, 60*(7), 3532–3545. doi:10.1109/TSP.2012.2191543.

Wang, Q., Xu, K., & Ren, K. (2012). Cooperative secret key generation from phase estimation in narrowband fading channels. *IEEE Journal on Selected Areas in Communications, 30*(9), 1666–1674. doi:10.1109/JSAC.2012.121010.

Wang, T., Song, L., Han, Z., Cheng, X., & Jiao, B. (2012). Power allocation using vickrey auction and sequential first-price auction games for physical layer security in cognitive relay networks. In *Proceedings of the 2012 IEEE International Conference on Communications (ICC)* (pp. 1683-1687). IEEE.

Wang, X., Tao, M., Mo, J., & Xu, Y. (2011). Power and subcarrier allocation for physical-layer security in ofdma-based broadband wireless networks. *IEEE Transactions on Information Forensics and Security, 6*(3), 693–702. doi:10.1109/TIFS.2011.2159206.

Wang, X., & Yi, P. (2011). Security framework for wireless communications in smart distribution grid. *IEEE Transactions on Smart Grid, 2*(4), 809–818. doi:10.1109/TSG.2011.2167354.

Watanabe, S., & Oohama, Y. (2011). Secret key agreement from vector Gaussian sources by rate limited public communication. *IEEE Transactions on Information Forensics and Security, 6*(3), 541–550. doi:10.1109/TIFS.2011.2132130.

Wilson, R., Tse, D., & Scholtz, R. (2007). Channel identification: Secret sharing using reciprocity in ultrawideband channels. *IEEE Transactions on Information Forensics and Security, 2*(3), 364–375. doi:10.1109/TIFS.2007.902666.

Wong, C. W., Wong, T., & Shea, J. (2011). Secret-sharing LDPC codes for the BPSK-constrained Gaussian wiretap channel. *IEEE Transactions on Information Forensics and Security, 6*(3), 551–564. doi:10.1109/TIFS.2011.2139208.

Wu, Y., & Liu, K. J. R. (2011). An information secrecy game in cognitive radio networks. *IEEE Transactions on Information Forensics and Security, 6*(3), 831–842. doi:10.1109/TIFS.2011.2144585.

Wyner, A. (1975). The wiretap channel. *The Bell System Technical Journal, 54*, 1355–1387. doi:10.1002/j.1538-7305.1975.tb02040.x.

Xiao, L., Greenstein, L., Mandayam, N., & Trappe, W. (2009). Channel-based detection of sybil attacks in wireless networks. *IEEE Transactions on Information Forensics and Security, 4*(3), 492–503. doi:10.1109/TIFS.2009.2026454.

Yang, J., Chen, Y., Trappe, W., & Cheng, J. (2013). Detection and localization of multiple spoofing attackers in wireless networks. *IEEE Transactions on Parallel and Distributed Systems, 24*(1), 44–58. doi:10.1109/TPDS.2012.104.

Ye, C., Mathur, S., Reznik, A., Shah, Y., Trappe, W., & Mandayam, N. B. (2010). Information-theoretically secret key generation for fading wireless channels. *IEEE Transactions on Information Forensics and Security, 5*(2), 240–254. doi:10.1109/TIFS.2010.2043187.

Ye, C., Reznik, A., & Shah, Y. (2006). Extracting secrecy from jointly Gaussian random variables. In *Proceedings of the 2006 IEEE International Symposium on Information Theory* (pp. 2593-2597). IEEE.

Ye, C., Reznik, A., Sternberg, G., & Shah, Y. (2007). On the secrecy capabilities of ITU channels. In *Proceedings of the 2007 IEEE 66th Vehicular Technology Conference* (pp. 2030-2034). IEEE.

Yu, P., & Sadler, B. (2011). MIMO authentication via deliberate fingerprinting at the physical layer. *IEEE Transactions on Information Forensics and Security, 6*(3), 606–615. doi:10.1109/TIFS.2011.2134850.

Yuksel, M., Liu, X., & Erkip, E. (2011). A secure communication game with a relay helping the eavesdropper. *IEEE Transactions on Information Forensics and Security, 6*(3), 818–830. doi:10.1109/TIFS.2011.2125956.

Zeng, Q., Li, H., & Peng, D. (2012). Frequency-hopping based communication network with multi-level qoss in smart grid: Code design and performance analysis. *IEEE Transactions on Smart Grid, 3*(4), 1841–1852. doi:10.1109/TSG.2012.2214067.

Zhang, L., Zhang, R., Liang, Y.-C., Xin, Y., & Cui, S. (2010). On the relationship between the multi-antenna secrecy communications and cognitive radio communications. *IEEE Transactions on Communications, 58*(6), 1877–1886. doi:10.1109/TCOMM.2010.06.090063.

Zheng, G., Arapoglou, P.-D., & Ottersten, B. (2012). Physical layer security in multibeam satellite systems. *IEEE Transactions on Wireless Communications, 11*(2), 852–863. doi:10.1109/TWC.2011.120911.111460.

Zheng, G., Choo, L.-C., & Wong, K.-K. (2011). Optimal cooperative jamming to enhance physical layer security using relays. *IEEE Transactions on Signal Processing, 59*(3), 1317–1322. doi:10.1109/TSP.2010.2092774.

ADDITIONAL READING

Bloch, M., & Barros, J. (2011). *Physical-layer security: From information theory to security engineering*. Cambridge, UK: Cambridge University Press. doi:10.1017/CBO9780511977985.

Liu, R., & Trappe, W. (2010). *Securing wireless communications at the physical layer*. New York: Springer. doi:10.1007/978-1-4419-1385-2.

Shannon, C. E. (1949). Communication theory of secrecy systems. *The Bell System Technical Journal, 28*(4), 656–715. doi:10.1002/j.1538-7305.1949.tb00928.x.

Wen, H. (2013). *Physical layer approaches for securing wireless communication systems*. New York: Springer. doi:10.1007/978-1-4614-6510-2.

Zhou, X., Song, L., & Zhang, Y. (2013). *Physical layer security in wireless communications*. Boca Raton, FL: CRC Press.

KEY TERMS AND DEFINITIONS

Channel Quantization: The process of generation of key bits from the received channels values

Cognitive Radio: A brain-empowered radio which can sense the environment and acts by adjusting its parameters according to the radio environment conditions. It has been proposed as a new technology, in which opportunistic communication by unlicensed (secondary) users is possible where licensed (primary) users are already present.

Multiple-Input-Multiple-Output (MIMO): The wireless communication technology employing multiple antennas at both transmitter and receiver sides to increase the performance.

Physical Layer: The first layer in the Open Systems Interconnection (OSI) communications model, supporting the electrical or mechanical interface to the physical medium.

Reciprocal Channel: The channel which exhibits identical response for both uplink and downlink transmission modes.

Reconfigurable Antenna: The antenna which can change its radiation pattern related parameters dynamically by using a switching network.

Relay: An intermediate node between source (Transmitter) and destination (Receiver) for making communication possible or improving the performance of the system.

Wiretap: Intercept of information in legitimate channel by an unauthorized user (Wiretapper or Eavesdropper).

Chapter 4
Physical Layer Security in Wireless Communication Networks

Özge Cepheli
Istanbul Technical University, Turkey

Güneş Karabulut Kurt
Istanbul Technical University, Turkey

ABSTRACT

Physical layer (PHY) security has become an emerging area of research recently. Wireless networks use unguided medium as communication channels, so gathering wireless data transmission is easier when compared to traditional cable systems. With the rise of new security challenges, many different solutions have been offered and are being developed. However, maintaining security in wireless networks still remains a challenge. Secure transmission techniques in these networks are discussed throughout this chapter. PHY security measures, the secrecy rate, the secrecy capacity, and the outage secrecy rate are introduced. Security needs of wireless networks are discussed and the related common attack types are described. Main countermeasures that are proposed to prevent these attacks are also presented with both practical and theoretical perspectives.

INTRODUCTION

In order to highlight the effect of mobility in current security systems, the network model of the Open Systems Interconnect (OSI) reference model can be considered (ISO/IEC 7498-1, 1994). This model, proposing a composition of seven layers; physical, data link, network, transport, presentation, session and application layers, distributes network's functionalities to distinct layers that are assumed to act independently from other layers. Using the OSI reference model can provide a formal definition and practical terms that affects information security on a layer-by-layer basis.

DOI: 10.4018/978-1-4666-4691-9.ch004

Security can be seen as an aggregation of protection mechanisms of different layers.

A conceptual visualization of layered security solutions is shown in Figure 1. One should pass through the security layers in order to acquire private data. In such cases, physical layer (PHY) security becomes inevitably important, as it forms the first step of the security system.

PHY security has become popular with the arising of wireless technologies. Wireless medium is potentially unsafe as the communications signals are broadcasted into air and anyone in the antenna range can access the transmitted signals. In traditional wired technologies, the possibility of the transmit signals are gathered by an untrusted third party may not be a main trouble, as physical security is deployed by hiding cables in walls and cable endpoints locked up in server rooms or cabinets. If one use a special device to "line in" to the link, a physical attempt needs to be done. Hence, even though it is not impossible, there is a certain difficulty for gathering the signals from a cable unless you have the endpoint. As a result, traditional systems usually accept that cable is secure, meaning that it is assumed that no one can access the data unless they access the endpoints. However, this assumption cannot be made for

wireless networks, as wireless channels, unlike cables, are available to every node in a range equipped with a proper receiving antenna.

In this chapter, information theoretical approaches, which are also included in the initial PHY security studies, will be introduced. This will be followed by a discussion of physical vulnerabilities of wireless systems. Common PHY attacks, namely eavesdropping, traffic analysis, jamming, massage modification, information disclosure, masquerade, ID theft, man-in-the-middle and denial of service will be introduced to the reader afterwards. The book chapter will introduce PHY security methods under two titles; code based methods and signalling based methods, along with the corresponding attack types that they aim to prevent.

In this chapter, signalling based methods will be the main focus of the countermeasures. Beamforming and artificial noise techniques are proven to be effective countermeasures for privacy attacks and are therefore very important. *Beamforming* is a multi-antenna technique that enables the transmitter to focus signals spatially. *Artificial noise* (AN) is a recent concept that is utilized in PHY security methods, consisting of transmitting noise signals generated by the transmitter to non-legitimate users to degrade their signal reception quality. The AN studies in the literature usually follow isotropic AN and smart AN approaches (Liao, 2011). Isotropic AN approach is based on broadcasting the generated noise without spatial selectivity (except for the legitimate user's direction), whereas the smart AN approach is based on sending AN only to only the locations and/or frequency bands where eavesdropper exists. Here, we will give also a comparison of AN techniques. This chapter will be concluded with the open issues about implementations of PHY security countermeasures.

Figure 1. Layers of data

State of the Art

Security is an important issue in wireless networks due to the open nature of wireless medium. Several studies have been conducted to improve security systems for wireless networks. As a consequence, there exist many solutions offered in different layers. In this section, a background on PHY security will be provided along with the related work.

Most of the attacks in PHY can be categorised as eavesdropping-based attacks. Eavesdropping attacks are unauthorized compromise of the data traffic between the between legitimate nodes. Traffic analysis attacks are an example of eavesdropping-based attack type, where the content of the data is not compromised but the transmitter and receiver nodes are detected. These types of attacks are typically approached via cryptographic algorithms that are implemented at higher network layers. However, the new approach is to prevent the attack in PHY, by using physical characteristics of the wireless channel for secure communication.

In the pioneering work of Wyner (Wyner, 1975), the wiretap channel is introduced as seen in Fig 2(a) and it is showed that when an eavesdropper's channel is a degraded version of the main communication channel, perfect secrecy, as defined by Shannon (Shannon, 1949) can be achieved.

In the study (Csiszar, 1978), authors considered a general independent channel condition as seen in Fig. 2(b), by eliminating the degraded eavesdropper channel assumption and studied the transmission. The results of this study generalized the results of (Wyner, 1975), however it was stated that the channel of eavesdroppers should be still noisier than that of legitimate receiver's. These early studies showed that positive secrecy capacity can be achieved for a wireless communication network in the presence of eavesdroppers with noisier channels. The impact of these works remains limited until the arrival of enabling technologies such as smart antennas, increased computational capabilities of electronic devices and multi-input multi-output (MIMO) systems. The main reason was the requirement of the legitimate transmitter and receiver to have some advantage over the attacker in terms of channel quality, which cannot be guaranteed in a practical system. Moreover, almost at the same time, Diffie and Hellman published the basic principles of public-key cryptography (Diffie, 1976), which was adopted by nearly all security systems.

Later, in 2000s multi-antenna systems have enabled a very useful technique, referred to as beamforming. The first beamforming study for security discussed preventing jamming attacks by deploying beamforming (Noubir, 2004). In this study, the use of directional antennas is shown to

Figure 2. Channel model of a system with eavesdroppers, (a) Wiretap channel model of Wyner, (b) independent channel model.

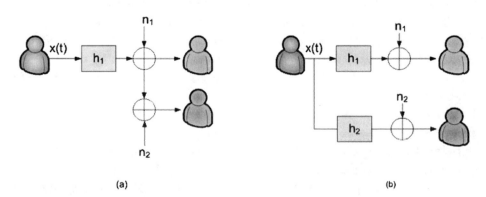

(a)   (b)

give higher performance than omni-directional antennas. A single input multi output (SIMO) system model is considered in (Li, 2007). In this study, beamforming transmission can provide maximization of secrecy rate in Gaussian channels, in multi-antenna systems. The secrecy capacity analysis in MIMO systems is conducted in (Khisti, 2007) and (Oggier, 2008). These studies assume that full channel state information (CSI) is provided, which may not be very practical to assume for real-world scenarios. However, it is shown that full CSI at transmitter case is an upper bound for secrecy rate (Bloch, 2008), meaning the secrecy rate will decrease in partial CSI systems. Following the lead of these studies, many theoretical and practical studies have been conducted to analyze the secrecy rates of different systems. The majority of these studies used information theoretic approaches and the *secret channel capacity, secrecy capacity* and *outage secrecy* bounds have become very common as performance metrics of PHY security systems. These metrics will be described in the next section.

The ergodic secrecy capacity in fading channels has been examined with and without CSI of eavesdropper. In (Liang, 2008), a fading broadcast channel is deployed and a scheme to find the optimal power allocation that minimizes the outage secrecy probability is proposed. Furthermore, various physical-layer techniques were introduced to achieve secure communication, even if the receiver's channel is worse than the eavesdropper's channel. One of these techniques is the use of interference or artificial noise to confuse the eavesdropper. With two base stations connected by a high-capacity backbone, one base station can simultaneously transmit an interfering signal to secure the uplink communication for the other base station (Jorgensen, 2007). In the scenario where the transmitter has a helping interferer or a relay node, the secrecy level can also be increased by having the interferer to send random noise signals independently at an appropriate rate. This scheme is referred to as cooperative jamming. When

multiple cooperative nodes are available to help the transmitter, the optimal weights of the signal transmitted from cooperative nodes, which maximize an achievable secrecy rate, were derived for decode-and-forward protocols in (Dong, 2008) and amplify-and-forward protocols in (Dong, 2009). The use of interference for secrecy is also extended to multiple access and broadcast channels with user cooperation (Ekrem, 2009).

With the use of multi-antenna systems, it is possible to simultaneously transmit both the information bearing signal and the artificial noise to achieve secrecy in a fading environment as shown in (Negi, 2005) and (Goel, 2008). In these studies, the artificial noise is transmitted in an isotropic sense and CSI of the eavesdropper is not required. However, it should be noted that the legitimate communication also gets affected by the transmitted noise. As a result, the transmit power allocation on data signals and AN are crucial in these systems. A suboptimal power allocation strategy was considered in (Swindlehurst, 2009), which aims to meet a target signal-to-interference-and-noise ratio at the intended receiver to satisfy a quality of service requirement. In the study (Prabhu, 2011), a scenario with multiple antenna eavesdroppers is deployed. The authors have shown that when selection combining (SC) is used one multiple antenna eavesdropper causes the same effect as of multiple single antenna eavesdroppers. Moreover, it was shown that as the number of the eavesdropper's antennas increases, the secrecy outage probability also rises. Many of the recent studies make use of convex optimization techniques to find the optimal AN and beamforming weights that satisfy signal to interference and noise ratio (SINR) with minimum power. In (Liao, 2010) space selective artificial noise is proposed and two minimization problems are constructed. The first minimization problem is to minimize total power while satisfying SINR constraints on eavesdropper on legitimate receiver and eavesdropper, while second problem is to maximize SINR of legitimate receiver for a given maximum SINR for eavesdropper and limiting the total power. The proposed space selective artificial noise scenario shown to be more power-effective compared to isotropic AN and no-AN scenarios, however the space selectivity requires the CSI of eavesdropper to be known by the transmitter. In (Li, 2012), this idea is further developed by changing the position of the AN source from the transmitter to the receiver. Authors state that self-interference cancellation techniques are used at receiver in order to eliminate the effects of the simultaneous artificial noise transmission on the receiver antennas. The results are shown to be effective compared to AN at transmitter systems under perfect self-interference cancellation, which is very hard to achieve.

The second direction of using PHY attributes in encryption systems, which is referred to as PHY based key generation in (Lai, 2012). This idea is based on channel reciprocity, which is the term for equality of transmitter to receiver and receiver to transmitter channel responses, in other words, uplink and downlink channels are the same. This specialty allows two communicating nodes to share a unique random data, as channel state information between two nodes cannot be gathered by any other nodes if it is not broadcasted. This random data can provide a common randomness source to system nodes. Eavesdroppers may only be able to detect the channel between transmitter and themselves, but they cannot estimate the channel between two legitimate nodes easily. As a result, the generated keys provides security with information theoretic guarantee. Hence, PHY-based encryption key generation has become a very promising area of research. Especially in mobile systems, common random source is very dynamic due the fast changing nature of the wireless channel as shown in (Quist, 2012). However, the slow changing environments may have limited source for key generation. Inevitably, generated key rate depends on the frequency of the changes in the channel.

REQUIREMENTS, ISSUES, AND SOLUTION APPROACHES

Physical Layer System Model and Performance Metrics

In this section we will first introduce the general signal and channel model of a wireless system in order to define performance metrics. The most basic wireless networks with eavesdropping can be simplified to have one transmitter node A, one legitimate receiver node B and an eavesdropper node E. Assume that all the nodes are equipped with single transmitting or receiving antenna for simplicity. Data bits are coded and modulated before transmission regarding to the selected modulation and coding scheme. Let $s(k)$ be the data signal that A wants to send to B at time k and let $x(k)$ represent the signal to be transmitted. For now, we assume A transmits only the data signal, without weighting or noise addition, so $x(k) = s(k)$ is transmitted signal from A, as seen in Figure 2(b). The received signals of A and E are given as $r_B(k)$ and $r_E(k)$ and they are defined as,

$$r_B(k) = h_{AB}(k)\, x(k) + n_B(k), \qquad (1)$$

$$r_E(k) = h_{AE}(k)\, x(k) + n_E(k), \qquad (2)$$

where $n_B(k)$ and $n_E(k)$ are the additive zero-mean Gaussian noise (AWGN) components and $h_{AB}(k)$ and $h_{AE}(k)$ are the channel coefficients of the channels between nodes A and B and nodes A and E, respectively. Estimates of these channel coefficients are referred to as channel state information, and modelled as a standard real AWGN channel. There are different channel models that are frequently being used in the literature such as Rayleigh, Rician or Nakagami-m fading channel models, as well as off-the-shelf solutions such as Stanford University Interim (SUI) radio propagation model (Erceg,1999), WINNER channel Model (WIN)-Phase II (WIM2) (Kyösti, 2008), or IMT-A channel models (ITU-R M.2135, 2008),

(ITU-R M.2135-1, 2009). Channel effects as path loss, shadowing, multipath and Doppler shift are included in these models. Channel noise powers of legitimate user's channel and eavesdropper's channel are σ_B^2 and σ_E^2, respectively.

A very useful measure of the channel quality is the signal to interference and noise ratio (SINR). This ratio gives how strong the received data signal power compared to non-data signal power caused by channel noise and interference

$$SINR_B(k) = P_{signal} |h_{AB}(k)|^2 / \sigma_B^2, \qquad (3)$$

$$SINR_E(k) = P_{signal} |h_{AE}(k)|^2 / \sigma_E^2, \qquad (4)$$

where the average transmit signal power is defined as P_{signal}. Note that SINR is equal to signal to noise ratio (SNR) when the interference power is zero, however SINR definition is important for the security system models with interference, as given in the following sections.

In the assumption of $\sigma_E^2 > \sigma_B^2$, the *secrecy capacity*, highest transmission rate at which the eavesdropper is unable to decode any information, is defined by (Barros, 2006) in Box 1.

Notice that in order for secrecy capacity to be non-zero, $SINR_B(k)$ should be higher than $SINR_E(k)$, meaning $\sigma_E^2 > \sigma_B^2$ should be satisfied. As in (Li, 2012), a complex AWGN channel is equal to two parallel real-valued AWGN channels, as a result the secrecy capacity of a complex AWGN channel can be defined in Box 2.

The upper bound of perfectly secret transmission rate from the source node to legitimate destination node is defined as the *secrecy rate*. Secrecy capacity is also the achievable maximum secrecy rate. The probability of outage in secrecy capacity is another important definition of information theoretic analysis of PHY security. *Outage secrecy capacity* (OSC) probability is defined in (Barros, 2006) as the probability that the instantaneous secrecy capacity being less than a target secrecy rate as:

Box 1.

$$C_{secrecy}(k) = C_B(k) - C_E(k) = \frac{1}{2} \log_2 \left(1 + SINR_B(k)\right) - \frac{1}{2} \log_2 \left(1 + SINR_E(k)\right). \qquad (5)$$

Box 2.

$$C_{sec\,recy}(k) = \begin{cases} \log_2(1 + SINR_B(k)) - \log_2(1 + SINR_E(k)), & \sigma_E^2 > \sigma_B^2 \\ 0, & otherwise \end{cases} \qquad (6)$$

$$P_{OSC}\left(R_S\right) = P\left(C_{secrecy} < R_S\right)$$
$$= P(C_{secrecy} < R_S | SINR_B > SINR_E) P(SINR_B > SINR_E).$$
$$(7)$$

After the transmitted signals arrive at the receiving antenna, the received signals are demodulated and decoded to bits, where it is possible to calculate the bit error rate (BER) of the system, which is one of the primary performance measures for digital communication systems. Usually a minimum BER requirement is defined for a successful communication, depending on the desired application. If BER of a system is below a minimum required level, a communication link cannot be properly established. As a result, it can be seen that satisfying a non-sufficient BER on unauthorized nodes can actually provide security. Hence, BER can also be used to define the quality of service (QoS) and the PHY security level of a network. It is obvious that SINR value of the channel is directly related to system BER, however, this relation varies according to the preferred modulation and coding schemes. For every system, higher SINRs point to lower BER values. In order to avoid the effect of modulation and coding techniques, SINR can be used for the definition of QoS and PHY security levels. For more information about channel models and wireless communication network basics, readers are referred to additional reading section.

Major Security Needs in Wireless Communication Systems

The main requirements of a wireless security network are the authentication, secrecy and data integrity along with robustness to physical attacks like jamming or natural effects like channel noise or interference. We give the detailed discussions of these requirements below.

Secrecy

Secrecy (data secrecy), in a communications system refers to the state that the information is obtainable solely by the legitimate receiver. This is a challenge that should be properly addressed especially for wireless communication systems. In wired communication networks, data secrecy is accepted to be guaranteed between two nodes, which means a cable is assumed to be secure and security is considered to be maintained on the network nodes on the way from sender to receiver. In another words, it is often accepted that if sender and receiver is directly connected by cable, then the data cannot be obtained by anyone else so secrecy is maintained on PHY. However, as mentioned, wireless medium has an open nature that makes it very hard to maintain secrecy. Any receiver in the coverage of sender antenna can capture the communication signals without being noticed. In wireless networks, non-legitimate receivers can execute such an attack, eliminating secrecy of data. In such case, maintaining physical security becomes very important.

Major attack types against data secrecy are eavesdropping and traffic analysis. *Eavesdropping* is the act of secretly listening to the private conversation of others without their consent, which projects to gathering of wireless communication data by non-legitimate users. Eavesdropping attacks are typically very easy to perform and very challenging to detect due to their passive nature. Such attacks can be performed with a proper receiving antenna and a system for decryption of the encrypted data, if encryption is made. *Traffic analysis* is a similar version of eavesdropping, in which the non-legitimate user cannot intercept the communication data but gathers the traffic information, like sender and receiver identities, data rates, data type, data protocols. Usually traffic analysis attack is performed where the encryption key cannot be gathered. Major countermeasures to eavesdropping and traffic analysis attacks are encryption, beamforming and artificial noise.

These security techniques will be detailed review will be given in the following section.

Authentication

User authentication is a means of identifying the user and verifying that the user is allowed to access some restricted service. Proper authentication mechanisms can be considered as the base of the security expedients, because of their importance. If a non-legitimate user is able to get authenticated by the system, every restricted service and information can be easily accessed. Moreover, the risk of the information and/or the system to be altered is highly considerable, for example a wireless remote system can be severely damaged causing destructive incidents, depending on the application.

Authentication is usually executed by using an authentication key mechanism. Authentication keys can be obtained from ID-based systems, hardware tokens, channel coefficients, pre-shared passwords and location information (Boyd, 2003).

ID-based cryptography, which is introduced in (Shamir, 1984), is rapidly emerging in the recent years. Now, identity based encryption (IBE) algorithm in (Franklin, 2001) and combined public key (CPK) algorithm in (Chen, 2006) are the two popular identity based cryptography systems. In IBE, user identity is its public key, and it cancelled the chain of certification authority (CA), but it still requires online databases. CPK-based authentication systems do not need online database or trusted third party which result in improved processing and efficiency ability. Nan Xiang-hao first proposed CPK in 1999 that overcomes disadvantages of IBE and awarded a national patent in 2006 (Nan, 2006). CPK can judge user identity by its key. The theoretical foundation of CPK is based on the elliptic curve discrete logarithm problem (ECDLP). In identification applications, CPK-based authentication system is expected to get increased attention in the near future.

Major authentication attack types can be outlined as brute-force attacks, eavesdropping attacks, man in the middle attacks, authentication cloning and ID theft attacks. *Man in the middle (MIM)* attacks are a form of active eavesdropping in which the attacker makes independent connections with the target nodes and messages between them, making them believe that they are talking directly to each other over a secure connection. In fact, during a MIM attack, the entire conversation is controlled by the attacker. Beyond the secrecy violation, it is clear that MIM attacks can be very dangerous to systems as the attacker gets authenticated and it is able to enter the system or change the communication data in a harmful manner. In an *authentication cloning attack*, an unauthorized user pretends to be a legitimate user by deceiving the authentication system. An authentication cloning attack can be implemented in many ways, including capturing the authentication sequences that are based on PHY attributes. For example, an intruder can imitate its location or channel information as the legitimate user and get authenticated to access resources. *Identity theft* occurs when an attacker captures network traffic and identifies the MAC address of a device with network privileges. Most wireless networks allow some kind of ID filtering to allow only authorized device with specific IDs to gain access and utilize the network. However, devices exist that have network "sniffing" capabilities, which means they are able to capture the transmitted data in a network. If these devices can imitate the authorized devices' ID as their own, they can easily get authenticated. Identity information can also be gathered by executing *brute force attack*, which means trying all the possible ID key options (Kurita, 2012).

Data Integrity Awareness

In its broadest meaning, data integrity refers to the trustworthiness of information over its entire life cycle. It is the representational faithfulness of information to the true state of the object that the information represents. Representational faithfulness has four essential attributes: completeness, currency/timeliness, accuracy/correctness and validity/authorization. Integrity is a critical requirement in wireless networks, because of the potential vulnerabilities originated from PHY. Major data integrity attacks are message modification and jamming attacks. Attacker can send forged control, management or data frames over wireless to mislead the recipient or facilitate another type of attack. Message modification is the general class of attack types that based on additions or deletions to actual data by malicious users. Jamming attacks are based on transmitting signals to depress or degrading the communication service performance. Jamming attacks usually aim to block legitimate communication, but can result in partial corruptions in data as well. Authentication based attacks can also lead to data integrity issues, as altering data is a possible action once the attacker gets authenticated. In order to detect data integrity issues, integrity checks like checksum checks are performed. If data is intentionally altered with a message modification attack, it is not likely to be detected. However, integrity checks are still an efficient way to deal with PHY errors during transmission. After integrity issue is detected, correction algorithms can be used as error correction coding (ECC) systems to correct some erroneous parts of data, a request for retransmission can be made.

Robustness

High degree of robustness against jamming and/or natural performance degrading effects such as noise or interference resulting from other wireless transmitters is one of the major design goals of wireless networks. The major attack type that a system should be robust against is denial of service (DoS) attack type. A DoS attack aims exhausting the available resources to system's legitimate users. DoS attacks may focus on any resource of a system in order to degrade or cancel

a service functionality. Jamming is widely used to execute DoS attacks at the physical layer. DoS attacks are sometimes executed by a number of distributed nodes to increase effectiveness and to reduce the risk of being detected, hence being prevented. These types of DoS attacks are named as distributed denial of service (DDoS) attacks and are accepted to be one of the most challenging security issues in communication systems. Countermeasures of DoS or DDoS attacks are not clear as these attacks can be executed in various ways. Anomaly detection systems are used to determine if an attack is being held for a resource (Karabatis, 2012). If the system decides that there is a DoS attack, it usually prevents the attacker by blocking its resource usage (Barna, 2012). This countermeasure is harder in DDoS attack scenarios as the attacker divides the attack into number of different nodes, therefore it is very hard to tell if any node is an attacker or not. Another way to enhance the robustness of a system is to use resource diversification techniques, which means having back up resources to use if one resource is under attack. For example, if a jammer is detected, the system switches to a different center frequency to avoid the quality degrading effects. Usually systems are designed to have back up communication lines in different networks to avoid connection losses. Robustness can also be achieved in the device side, wireless networks can be designed to have back up devices that can be switched to, if the master device is under a physical attack.

PHYSICAL LAYER SECURITY SOLUTIONS

In this section, we will present solutions to deal with aforementioned system secrecy vulnerabilities and attack types. We categorize the solutions to achieve maximum secrecy as code based methods, signaling based methods and PHY-based encryption methods.

Secrecy is the focus of PHY security in wireless networks, as it is the major vulnerability in wireless transmission. Code based and signaling based approaches exist for achieving maximum secrecy level and enhance robustness, which will be discussed in this section.

Code Based Methods

The main objective of code based approaches is to improve resilience against jamming and eavesdropping. These approaches include the use of error correction coding and spread spectrum coding.

Error Correction Coding

In a conventional cryptographic method, a single error in the received ciphertext will cause a large number of errors in the decrypted plain text after channel decoding. In order to address this problem, a combination of turbo coding and advanced encryption standard (AES) cryptosystem was proposed in (Chang, 2010). This scheme uses the encrypted turbo codes to set up a secure communication session based on the pseudo-random number generation algorithms. Depending on channel conditions, this method can be adopted to choose the number of redundant bits required to protect the information in order to achieve higher efficiency. The main advantages of secure turbo codes include higher-speed encryption and decryption with higher security, smaller encoder/decoder size, and greater efficiency.

Spread Spectrum Coding

Spread spectrum is a signalling technique in which a signal is spread by a pseudo-noise (PN) sequence over a wide frequency band with frequency bandwidth much wider than that contained in the frequency bandwidth of the original information. Spread spectrum is an effective solution to achieve physical layer security. Direct sequence spread-spectrum (DSSS) has been widely used to spread the transmitted data over multiple frequencies (Ozharar, 2011). Frequency-hopping spread-spectrum (FHSS) continuously changes the central frequency of a conventional carrier several times per bit duration (i.e., in a fast hopping system) in accordance with a randomly selected channel so that it is extremely difficult to illegally monitor the spread spectrum signals. The main difference between conventional cryptographic systems and spread-spectrum systems lies in their key sizes. Readers are referred to (Abdulkawi, 2012) for more information about this method.

Signalling Based Methods

Data protection can also be facilitated using signalling design approaches. The usual schemes in these approaches involve beamforming and the injection of artificial noise. Beamforming and AN methods can be used as countermeasures against secrecy or authentication targeted attacks by improving secrecy. These methods are detailed below.

Beamforming

Beamforming is a multi-antenna technique that enables the transmitter to focus signals spatially. Recently, beamforming techniques have received great interests and it can achieve performance and capacity enhancement without the need for additional power or spectrum. Beamforming is a type of radio frequency (RF) management in which an access point uses multiple antennas to send out the same signal. By sending out multiple signals and analyzing feedback from receivers, the wireless LAN infrastructure can adjust signals it sends out and can determine the best path the signal should take in order to reach a receiver node. In a sense, beamforming shapes the RF beam as it traverses the physical space. Early implementation of beamforming is switched beam technique, which refers to system that selects the optimum of pre-determined antenna patterns. A more dynamic way to spatially form the patterns is to use adaptive beamforming systems. These two systems are shown in Fig. 3(a) and Fig. 3(b). In switched beam scenario, the nearest pattern is chosen to the location of legitimate receiver. However, it should be noticed that the beam pattern is not perfectly focused on the intended target. Another drawback of switched beam is that side lobes cannot be controlled for eavesdropper locations, which is shown in Fig. 3(b). These drawbacks are resolved in adaptive beamforming systems, in which the weights of antenna arrays can be changed dynamically. As seen in Fig. 3(a), beam pattern can be designed as perfectly focused on the legitimate user and eavesdropper can be avoided.

In security studies, adaptive beamforming scenarios are more frequently deployed. However it should be noted that switched beam systems also provide a secrecy improvement, compared to traditional isotropic antenna systems.

In a beamforming scenario, transmitter device has multi-antenna transmitter and applies beamforming to the information signals transmitted to authorized receiver. An unauthorized receiver cannot gather information signal as the signal is focused spatially on the authorized receiver. Therefore, beamforming is a major concept in PHY security, due to the secrecy it provides.

Solely beamforming type of optimization scenario is a basic beamforming weight adjustment case, in which signal beam is targeted to legitimate user and not sent to anywhere else. When this problem is formed to minimize total transmit power, it can be expressed as a convex optimization problem and can be solved easily with convex optimization methods.

A system model of a beamforming system is very similar to the basic model that we have introduced earlier. Consider the system model with one legitimate transmitter (node A), one legitimate receiver (node B) and one eavesdropper (node E). This time the nodes are equipped with multi-antenna transmitter or receivers, with the quantity of N_A, N_B and N_E antennas, respectively.

Hence the signal $s(k)$ now will be multiplied with N_A sized weight coefficient matrix, $\mathbf{w}(k)$ and form the transmission signal vector $\mathbf{x}(k) = \mathbf{w}(k)\,s(k)$. The received signal vectors of legitimate receiver and eavesdropper will be,

$$\mathbf{r}_B(k) = \mathbf{H}^H_{AB}(k)\,\mathbf{w}(k)\,s(k) + \mathbf{n}_B(k), \qquad (8)$$

$$\mathbf{r}_E(k) = \mathbf{H}^H_{AE}(k)\,\mathbf{w}(k)\,s(k) + \mathbf{n}_E(k), \qquad (9)$$

where $\mathbf{H}_{AB}(k)$ is the channel matrix of MIMO channel between A and B having dimensions of $N_A \times N_B$ and $\mathbf{H}_{AE}(k)$ is the channel matrix of MIMO channel between A and E having dimensions of $N_A \times N_E$. The channels are assumed to be quasi-static in the time range of all k's, which means the change in channel CSI through time is infinitely slow through k, so $\mathbf{H}_{AB}(k) = \mathbf{H}_{AB}$ and $\mathbf{H}_{AE}(k) = \mathbf{H}_{AE}$. With this assumption we can also calculate $\mathbf{w}(k)$ for every different channel conditions i.e when the location of receiver changes, so we have $\mathbf{w}(k) = \mathbf{w}$ for a pre-defined time range. The terms $\mathbf{n}_B(k)$ and $\mathbf{n}_E(k)$ are AWGN component vectors, having length of N_B and N_E respectively. $\mathbf{r}_B(k)$ and $\mathbf{r}_E(k)$ have also length of N_B and N_E, defining one signal value for each receiver antenna. The received signals can be combined by many combining techniques. Assume maximal ratio combining (MRC) is deployed, which is the optimal combiner for AWGN channels as it maximizes the SINR by combining the received signals according to their channel noise level. SINR of an MRC receiver output is equivalent to the sum of all receive antenna SINRs.

Now we can define the SINRs as,

$$SINR_B = \sum_{i=1}^{N_B} P_{signal} \frac{\mathbf{w}^H \mathbf{R}_{H_{AB,i}} \mathbf{w}}{\sigma_B^2},$$
$$SINR_E = \sum_{j=1}^{N_E} P_{signal} \frac{\mathbf{w}^H \mathbf{R}_{H_{AE,j}} \mathbf{w}}{\sigma_E^2}, \qquad (10)$$

where $\mathbf{R}_{H_{AB,i}} = \mathbf{H}_{AB,i}\,\mathbf{H}^H_{AB,i}$ and $\mathbf{R}_{H_{AE,j}} = \mathbf{H}_{AE,j}\,\mathbf{H}^H_{AE,j}$ are defined as the instanta-

Figure 3. Beamforming, (a) adaptive beamforming, (b) switched beam system

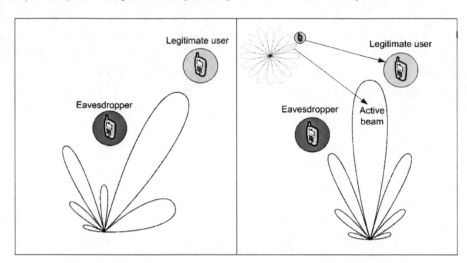

neous CSIs of B and E available to A. The notation of $\mathbf{H}_{AB,i}$ refers to the N_A-length channel vector of A to i^{th} antenna of B. The SINRs are defined for each antenna of the receiver antenna array.

After this, a simple minimization problem can be solved by,

$$\min_{w} \quad \|\mathbf{w}\|^2 \qquad (11.a)$$

$$\text{s.t.} \quad SINR_B \geq \gamma_B \qquad (11.b)$$

$$SINR_E \leq \gamma_E, \qquad (11.c)$$

where γ_B and γ_E are minimum and maximum SINR constraints that we require on B and E, respectively. By solving this optimization problem we can obtain the weight vector $\mathbf{w}$, which satisfies the required SINR on legitimate receiver, a required secrecy level for eavesdropper with minimum power.

As the beam width is inversely proportional to gain in a directional antenna, directional transmission can improve spatial reuse and enlarge the geographical coverage. Under jamming attacks, use of directional antennas and beamforming methods may also become advantageous. Ander a jamming attack the node would still be able to

receive data from the directions not covered by the jamming signals. Therefore, the employment of directional antennas can improve robustness also, by avoiding physical jamming attempts, and enhancing data availability.

Artificial Noise

Artificial noise (AN) is a novel concept that is utilized in PHY security methods, consists on sending generated noise by transmitter to non-legitimate users to degrade their signal reception quality. This method showed that perfect secrecy can be achieved when the intruder's channel is noisier than the receiver's channel. In this method, artificial noise is generated using multiple antennas or the coordination of helping nodes, and is injected into the null-subspace of the intended receiver's channel. AN is utilized to impair the intruder's channel, but it does not affect the intended receiver's channel since the noise is generated in the null-subspace of the legitimate receiver's channel. It was also shown in (Yang, 2012) that relying on AN, secret communications can be achieved even if the intruder enjoys a much better channel condition than the intended receiver.

Combined Beamforming and Artificial Noise

Beamforming and AN are proven to be effective PHY security methods. AN and beamforming can be used to maintain a defined secrecy level for eavesdroppers along with a defined service quality level for legitimate users. These methods can be divided into 2 categories as isotropic AN designs and smart AN designs.

In AN aided transmit beamforming scenarios, the transmit vector can be defined as

$$\mathbf{x}(k) = \mathbf{w}\, s(k) + \mathbf{z}(k), \tag{12}$$

where $s(k)$ is the complex data that legitimate transmitter wants to send to legitimate receiver, $\mathbf{w}$ is the transmit beamforming weight vector of $s(k)$ and $\mathbf{z}(k)$ is the generated artificial noise vector with the length of N_A. It is assumed that $\mathbf{z}(k) \sim CN(0,\Sigma)$, which means $\mathbf{z}(k)$ is a random vector following a complex Gaussian distribution with mean 0 and covariance $\Sigma > 0$.

Isotropic AN Designs: In isotropic AN design, the transmitter generates a determined amount of artificial noise to interfere eavesdroppers. In isotropic AN case, the locations and channel conditions of eavesdroppers are not known and generated noise is transmitted everywhere but the legitimate user (null space of the legitimate receiver's channel), in a isotropic manner to improve secrecy. In this method AN covariance can be chosen as $\Sigma = \beta \mathbf{P}_h^\perp$ where $P_h^\perp = \mathbf{I}_{N_t} - \mathbf{R}_{H_{AB}} / \| \mathbf{H}_{AB} \|^2$ is the orthogonal complement projector of $\mathbf{H}_{AB}$, and $\beta > 0$ is a scale factor determining the power invested on AN. It is shown in (Liao, 2011) that if we choose ρ and β as

$$\rho = \frac{\sigma_B^2 \gamma_B}{\left\| \mathbf{H}_{AB} \right\|^4} \tag{13}$$

$$\beta = \max\left\{ 0, \frac{\rho \mathbf{H}_{AB}^H \mathbf{R}_{H_{AE}} \mathbf{H}_{AB} - \sigma_E^2}{\mathrm{Tr}\left(P_h^\perp \mathbf{R}_{H_{AE}} \right)} \right\}, \tag{14}$$

then the optimum signal transmit weight vector and AN covariance can be obtained for a $N_B = N_E = 1$ single input multi output (SIMO) system, by

$$\mathbf{w} = \sqrt{\rho} \mathbf{H}_{AD}, \Sigma = \beta P_h^\perp. \tag{15}$$

Smart AN designs: Smart AN is a term that we use to categorize selective AN types. The generated noise can be formed selective in frequency, space and time, depending on the scenario. For example, it has been shown that pilot jammers are more effective then plain jammers on OFDM systems (Mingyan, 2010). It is a reliable countermeasure for eavesdropping like attacks, by performing jamming attack to malicious users. Please note that this scenario uses more optimized transmit by eliminating the eavesdropper-free areas in the selectivity domain. However, it is not very practical to assume that location of eavesdroppers' are known in any domain, as eavesdropping is a passive attack type. However, the idea is that AN can be designed as focused on important parts of the transmission so that same secrecy can be provided with less power consumption. Optimization problems with smart AN cases can be designed in theory and as a result, these designs give better results than previous AN designs. The power optimization problem of space-selective AN in (Liao, 2011) can be briefly given as,

$$\min_{\mathbf{W}.\Sigma} \quad \mathbf{w}^2 + Tr\left(\Sigma \right) \tag{16.a}$$

$$SINR_B\left(\mathbf{w},\Sigma \right) \geq \gamma_B \tag{16.b}$$

$$SINR_E\left(\mathbf{w},\Sigma \right) \leq \gamma_E \tag{16.c}$$

$$\Sigma > 0. \tag{16.d}$$

Figure 4. Comparison of AN techniques

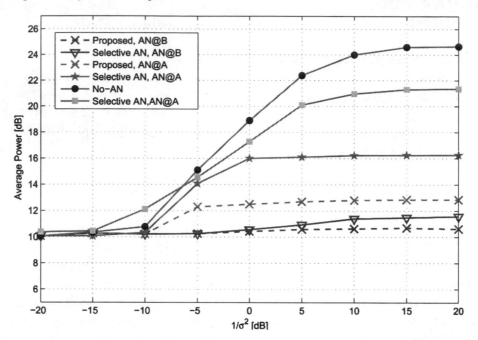

We also proposed a spatiotemporal selective smart AN for OFDM in (Cepheli, 2013), where AN is chosen as selective in both time and space to interfere with pilot signals. The problem in (16) is still valid, within the pilot signal transmission. The comparison of our proposed technique with other AN techniques can be seen in Figure 4.

The last thing that should be discussed is the solution of the optimization problems mentioned above. The problems (11) and (16) are unfortunately non-convex due to the $\mathbf{w}^H \mathbf{R}_H \mathbf{w}$ terms in the constraints on SINR of B. A common approach to deal with non-convex problems is to obtain a convex problem that approximates the original solution by relaxing the non-convex constraints with semi-definite relaxation (SDR) techniques. A crucial first step in deriving an SDR of these problems is to observe that

$$\mathbf{w}^H \mathbf{R}_H \mathbf{w} = \mathrm{Tr}(\mathbf{w}^H \mathbf{R}_H \mathbf{w}) = \mathrm{Tr}(\mathbf{R}_H \mathbf{w} \mathbf{w}^H) \qquad (17)$$

Notice that defining new variable $\mathbf{W} = \mathbf{w}\mathbf{w}^H$ is equivalent to $\mathbf{W}$ being a rank one symmetric positive semi-definite (PSD) matrix which adds

the constraints $\mathbf{W} \geq 0, \mathrm{rank}(\mathbf{W}) = 1$. However, the problem is still considered as very hard to solve due to the non-convex $\mathrm{rank}(\mathbf{W}) = 1$ constraint. Applying SDR approach to make the problem convex, we relax it by neglecting this constraint and we achieve the convex SDR problem as,

$$\min_{\mathbf{W}, \Sigma} \quad \mathrm{Tr}\left(\mathbf{W}\right) + \mathrm{Tr}\left(\Sigma\right) \qquad (18.\mathrm{a})$$

$$\mathrm{s.t.} \quad \frac{1}{\gamma_b} \mathrm{Tr}\left(\mathbf{W} \mathbf{R}_{H_{AB}}\right) - \mathrm{Tr}\left(\mathbf{R}_{H_{AB}} \Sigma\right) \geq \sigma_B^2$$

$$(18.\mathrm{b})$$

$$\frac{1}{\gamma_e} \mathrm{Tr}\left(\mathbf{W} \mathbf{R}_{H_{AE}}\right) - \mathrm{Tr}\left(\mathbf{R}_{R_{H_{AE}}} \Sigma\right) \leq \sigma_E^2$$

$$(18.\mathrm{c})$$

$$\Sigma \geq 0, \mathbf{W} \geq 0. \qquad (18.\mathrm{d})$$

As we omitted the non-convex rank-1 constraint, the problem in (18) is not actually equal to the original problem in (16). However, it can be verified that the solution of the SDR problem yields to the exact solution of the problem by using the rank reduction result of Lemma 3.1 in (Huang, 2010). Thus, we can compute the FDB secrecy optimization problem with a formulation that can be solved, in an efficient and numerically reliable fashion.

PHY Aided Encryption Key Extraction

Key exchange problem is one of the main challenges of encryption systems. The same encryption keys must be obtained in transmitter receiver pair for correctly decrypting the encrypted messages transmitted. However, if the key is transmitted through the insecure communication channel, the key can be gathered by non-legitimate users and encryption process becomes worthless as everyone can decrypt the transmitted signals especially in the shared wireless communication channels. Diffie and Hellman proposed a key exchange and key sharing method to solve the problem of key exchange in (Diffie, 1976). The purpose of this method is to allow only the authorized receiver transmitter obtain the encryption key, even if other nodes are able to hear the transmitted signals. Variations of this method have been proposed since then.

In almost all key exchange algorithms, length of public keys are chosen long, leading to increase in computational complexity and shortening of battery life on wireless devices (Zhuo, 2005). In recent years the idea of merging the physical layer attributes has emerged and a new class of key sharing technique is discovered (Ren, 2011). Many studies have been done on different physical layer key exchange methods which seem to have various advantages over the classical algorithms (Karas, 2011), (Soosahabi, 2012). These security methods can be classified both in data link layer and physical layer, merging advantages of encryption and physical layer privacy and enhancing existing encryption methods with PHY components.

CONCLUSION AND FUTURE RESEARCH DIRECTIONS

PHY security is a rather novel concept, implying that there are a lot of opportunities for researchers. Future research directions include new and more effective smart beamforming and AN techniques. Seeking of PHY countermeasures against specific attack types of wireless network is also a solid need of research. Practical implementation is also an open area of research for transferring PHY security techniques from theory into real world systems.

In this chapter, the basic definitions and state of the art on the area of PHY security were introduced. Most common PHY attacks, such as eavesdropping, jamming, man in the middle, ID theft, were explained along with the security needs of wireless systems. The countermeasure techniques offered in PHY were categorized and detailed. As a result, the importance of PHY security systems are obvious, while more practical techniques should be pioneered for the implementation in todays' wireless communication networks.

REFERENCES

Abdulkawi, A., Saleh, T. S., Khattab, S., & Farag, I. (2012). Anti-jamming defense in wireless networks using channel hopping and error correcting code. In *Proceedings of the 8th International Conference on Informatics and Systems (INFOS)* (pp. 12-17). INFOS.

Barna, C., Shtern, M., Smit, M., Tzerpos, V., & Litoiu, M. (2012). Model-based adaptive dos attack mitigation. In *Proceedings of the ICSE Workshop on Software Engineering for Adaptive and Self-Managing Systems (SEAMS)* (pp. 119-128). ICSE.

Barros, J., & Rodrigues, M. R. D. (2006). Secrecy capacity of wireless channels. *In Proceedings of the IEEE International Symposium on Information Theory*, (pp. 356–360). Seattle, WA: IEEE.

Bloch, M., Barros, J., Rodrigues, M. R. D., & McLaughlin, S. W. (2008). Wireless information-theoretic security. *IEEE Transactions on Information Theory*, *54*(6), 2515–2534. doi:10.1109/TIT.2008.921908.

Boyd, C., & Mathuria, A. (2003). *Protocols for authentication and key establishment*. New York: Springer. doi:10.1007/978-3-662-09527-0.

Cepheli, Ö., & Karabulut, K. G. (2013). *Efficient PHY layer security in MIMO-OFDM: Spatiotemporal selective artificial noise*. Paper presented at the Fourth International Workshop on Data Security and Privacy in wireless networks. Madrid, Spain.

Chang, Q., Zhang, Y. P., & Qin, L. L. (2010). A node authentication protocol based on ECC in WSN. In *Proceedings of the International Conference on Computer Design and Applications (ICCDA)* (pp. 606-609). ICCDA.

Chen, Z., & Nan, X. H. (2006). *CPK identity authentication*. Beijing, China: National Defence Industry Press.

Csiszár, I., & Korner, J. (1978). Broadcast channels with confidential messages. *IEEE Transactions on Information Theory*, *24*, 339–348. doi:10.1109/TIT.1978.1055892.

Diffie, W., & Hellman, M. (1976). New directions in cryptography. *IEEE Transactions on Information Theory*, *22*(6), 644–654. doi:10.1109/TIT.1976.1055638.

Dong, L., Han, Z., Petropulu, A. P., & Poor, H. V. (2008). Secure wireless communications via cooperation. In *Proceedings of the 46th Annual Allerton Conference on Communications, Control, Computing* (pp. 1132–1138). Monticello, IL: Allerton.

Dong, L., Han, Z., Petropulu, A. P., & Poor, H. V. (2009). Amplify-and-forward based cooperation for secure wireless communications. In *Proceedings of IEEE International Conference on Acoustics, Speech, and Signal Processing* (pp. 2613–2616). Taipei, Taiwan: IEEE.

Ekrem, E., & Ulukus, S. (2009). Cooperative secrecy in wireless communications. In R. Liu, & W. Trappe (Eds.), *Securing wireless communications at the physical layer*. New York: Springer-Verlag.

Erceg, V., Greenstein, L. J., Tjandra, S. Y., & Parkoff, S. R. (1999). An empirically based path loss model for wireless channels in suburban environments. *IEEE Journal on Selected Areas in Communications*, *17*(7), 1205–1211. doi:10.1109/49.778178.

Franklin, M., & Boneh, D. (2001). Identity based encryption from weil pairing. [Berlin: Springer Verlag.]. *Proceedings of CRYPTO, 2001*, 213–239.

Goel, S., & Negi, R. (2008, June). Guaranteeing secrecy using artificial noise. *IEEE Transactions on Wireless Communications*, *7*(6), 2180–2189. doi:10.1109/TWC.2008.060848.

Huang, Y., & Palomar, D. P. (2010). Rank-constrained separable semidefinite programming with applications to optimal beamforming. *IEEE Transactions on Signal Processing*, *58*(2), 664–678. doi:10.1109/TSP.2009.2031732.

ISO/IEC 7498-1. (1994). *Information processing systems, open systems interconnection (OSI) reference model, the basic model.* ITU-T Recommendation X.200.

ITU-R M.2135. (2008). *Guidelines for evaluation of radio interface technologies for IMT-advanced.* Geneva, Switzerland: ITU Rep. ITU-R M.2135.

ITU-R M.2135-1. (2009). *Guidelines for evaluation of radio interface technologies for IMT-advanced.* Geneva, Switzerland: ITU Rep. ITU-R M.2135-1.

Jorgensen, M. L., Yanakiev, B. R., Kirkelund, F. E., Popovski, P., Yomo, H., & Larsen, T. (2007). Shout to secure: Physical-layer wireless security with known interference. In *Proceedings of IEEE GLOBECOM* (pp. 33–38). Washington, DC: IEEE.

Karabatis, G., & Aleroud, A. (2012). Discovering unknown cyber attacks using contextual misuse and anomaly detection. *Science Journal, 1*(3), 106–120.

Karas, D. S., Karagiannidis, G. K., & Schober, R. (2011). Neural network based PHY-layer key exchange for wireless communications. In *Proceedings of the IEEE 22nd International Symposium on Personal Indoor and Mobile Radio Communications (PIMRC)* (pp. 1233-1238). IEEE.

Khisti, A., & Wornell, G. W. (2007). Secure transmission with multiple antennas: The MIMOME channel. *IEEE Transactions of Information Theory.* Retrieved from http://arxiv.org/abs/0708.4219

Kurita, S., Komoriya, K., & Uda, R. (2012). Privacy protection on transfer system of automated teller machine from brute force attack. In *Proceedings of the 26th International Conference on Advanced Information Networking and Applications Workshops (WAINA)* (pp. 72-77). WAINA.

Kyösti, P, Meinilä, J, Hentilä, L., Zhao, X., Jämsä, T., Schneider, C.,... Rautiainen, T. (2008). *WINNER II channel models.* IST-4-027756, WINNER II D1.1.2, v1.2.

Lai, L., Liang, Y., & Du, W. (2012). Cooperative key generation in wireless networks. *IEEE Journal on Selected Areas in Communications, 30*(8), 1578–1588. doi:10.1109/JSAC.2012.120924.

Li, W., Ghogho, M., Chen, B., & Xiong, C. (2012). Secure communication via sending artificial noise by the receiver: Outage secrecy capacity/region analysis. *IEEE Communications Letters, 16*(10), 1628–1631. doi:10.1109/LCOMM.2012.081612.121344.

Li, Z., Trappe, W., & Yates, R. (2007). Secret communication via multiantenna transmission. In *Proceedings of 41st CISS* (pp. 905–910). Baltimore, MD: CISS.

Liang, Y., Poor, H. V., & Shamai, S. (2008). Secure communication over fading channels. *IEEE Transactions on Information Theory, 54*(6), 2470–2492. doi:10.1109/TIT.2008.921678.

Liao, W. C., Chang, T. H., Ma, W. K., & Chi, C. Y. (2010). Joint transmit beamforming and artificial noise design for QoS discrimination in wireless downlink. In *Proceedings of the 2010 IEEE International Conference on Acoustics Speech and Signal Processing,* (pp. 2562-2565). IEEE.

Mingyan, L., Koutsopoulos, I., & Poovendran, R. (2010). Optimal jamming attack strategies and network defense policies in wireless sensor networks. *IEEE Transactions on Mobile Computing, 9*(8), 1119–1133. doi:10.1109/TMC.2010.75.

Nan, X. H., & Chen, Z. (2006). *Identifier-based private key generating method and device.* WO Patent WO/2006/074,611.

Negi, R., & Goel, S. (2005). Secret communications using artificial noise. In *Proceedings of IEEE Vehicular Technology Conference* (pp. 1906-1910). Dallas, TX: IEEE.

Noubir, G. (2004). On connectivity in ad hoc network under jamming using directional antennas and mobility. In *Proceedings of the 2nd International Conference on Wired and Wireless Internet Communications* (pp. 54–62). IEEE.

Oggier, F., & Hassibi, B. (2008). The secrecy capacity of the MIMO wiretap channel. In *Proceedings of the IEEE International Symposium on Information Theory*, (pp. 524–528). Toronto, Canada: IEEE.

Ozharar, S., Reilly, D. R., Wang, S. X., Kanter, G. X., & Kumar, P. (2011). Two dimensional optical code-division modulation with quantum-noise aided encryption for applications in key distribution. *Journal of Lightwave Technology*, 29(14), 2081–2088. doi:10.1109/JLT.2011.2156760.

Prabhu, V., & Rodrigues, M. (2011). On wireless channels with m-antenna eavesdroppers: Characterization of the outage probability and outage secrecy capacity. *IEEE Transactions on Information Forensics Security, 99*.

Quist, B. T., & Jensen, M. A. (2012). The impact of multiple antennas in physical layer encryption key establishment. In *Proceedings of the IEEE International Workshop on Antenna Technology (iWAT)* (pp. 24-27). IEEE.

Ren, K., Su, H., & Wang, Q. (2011). Secret key generation exploiting channel characteristics in wireless communications. *IEEE Wireless Communications, 18*(4), 6–12. doi:10.1109/MWC.2011.5999759.

Shamir, A. (1984). Identity-based cryptosystems and signature schemes. [Berlin: Springer Verlag.]. *Proceedings of CRYPTO, 84*, 47–53.

Shannon, C. E. (1949). Communication theory of secrecy systems. *The Bell System Technical Journal, 28*(4), 656–715. doi:10.1002/j.1538-7305.1949.tb00928.x.

Soosahabi, R., & Naraghi-Pour, M. (2012). Scalable PHY-layer security for distributed detection in wireless sensor networks. *IEEE Transactions on Information Forensics and Security, 7*(4), 1118–1126. doi:10.1109/TIFS.2012.2194704.

Swindlehurst, A. L. (2009). Fixed SINR solutions for the MIMO wiretap channel. In *Proceedings of the IEEE International Conference on Acoustics, Speech, and Signal Processing* (pp. 2437–2440). Taipei, Taiwan: IEEE.

Wyner, A. D. (1975). The wire-tap channel. *The Bell System Technical Journal, 54*, 1355–1387. doi:10.1002/j.1538-7305.1975.tb02040.x.

Yang, Y., Wang, W., Zhao, H., & Zhao, L. (2012). Transmitter beamforming and artificial noise with delayed feedback: Secrecy rate and power allocation. *Journal of Communications and Networks, 14*(4), 374–384.

Zhuo, C., Fan, H., & Liang, H. (2005). A new authentication and key exchange protocol in WLAN. In *Proceedings of the International Conference on Information Technology: Coding and Computing, ITCC*, (pp. 552-556). ITCC.

ADDITIONAL READING

Cepheli, Ö., & Karabulut, K. G. (2012). Effects of channel estimation error in AN-aided beamforming. In *Proceedings of the European Conference. on the Use of Modern Information and Communication Technologies (ECUMICT 2012)*. Gent, Belgium: ECUMICT.

Ekrem, E., & Ulukus, S. (2011). Secrecy in cooperative relay broadcast channels. *IEEE Transactions on Information Theory*, *57*(1), 137–155. doi:10.1109/TIT.2010.2090215.

Gopala, P. K., Lai, L., & El-Gamal, H. (2007). On the secrecy capacity of fading channels. In *Proceedings of IEEE International Symposium on Information Theory*. Nice, France: IEEE.

Gopala, P. K., Lai, L., & Gamal, H. E. (2008). On the secrecy capacity of fading channels. *IEEE Transactions on Information Theory*, *54*(10), 4687–4698. doi:10.1109/TIT.2008.928990.

Grant, M., & Boyd, S. (2009). *CVX: MATLAB software for disciplined convex programming*. Retrieved from http://stanford.edu/ boyd/cvx

Khisti, A., & Wornell, G. W. (2010). Secure transmission with multiple antennas: The MISOME channel. *IEEE Transactions on Information Theory*, *56*(7), 3088–3104. doi:10.1109/TIT.2010.2048445.

Lai, L., & Gamal, H. E. (2008). The relay-eavesdropper channel: Cooperation for secrecy. *IEEE Transactions on Information Theory*, *54*(9), 4005–4019. doi:10.1109/TIT.2008.928272.

Liao, W. C., Chang, T. H., Ma, W. K., & Chi, C. Y. (2011). QoS-based transmit beamforming in the presence of eavesdroppers: An optimized artificial-noise-aided approach. *IEEE Transactions on Signal Processing*, *59*(3), 1202–1216. doi:10.1109/TSP.2010.2094610.

Luo, Z. Q., Ma, W. K., So, A. M. C., Ye, Y., & Zhang, S. (2010). Nonconvex quadratic optimization, semidefinite relaxation, and applications. *IEEE Signal Processing Magazine*. doi:10.1109/MSP.2010.936019.

Parada, P., & Blahut, R. (2005). Secrecy capacity of SIMO and slow fading channels. In *Proceedings of IEEE International Symposium on Information Theory* (pp. 2152–2155). Adelaide, Australia: IEEE.

Proakis, J. G., & Manolakis, D. G. (2007). *Digital signal processing*. Upper Saddle River, NJ: Pearson Prentice Hall.

Rappaport, T. S. (2002). *Wireless communications: Principles and practice*. Upper Saddle River, NJ: Prentice Hall.

Shiu, Y. S., Chang, S. Y., Wu, H. C., Huang, S. C. H., & Chen, H. H. (2011). Physical layer security in wireless networks: A tutorial. *IEEE Wireless Communications*, *18*(2), 66–74. doi:10.1109/MWC.2011.5751298.

Simeone, O., & Popovski, P. (2008). Secure communications via cooperating base stations. *IEEE Communications Letters*, *12*(3), 188–190. doi:10.1109/LCOMM.2008.071836.

Tang, X., Liu, R., Spasojevic, P., & Poor, H. V. (2008). Interference-assisted secret communication. In *Proceedings of IEEE Information Theory Workshop* (pp. 164–168). Porto, Portugal: IEEE.

Tekin, E., & Yener, A. (2008). The general Gaussian multiple-access and two way channels: Achievable rates and cooperative jamming. *IEEE Transactions on Information Theory*, *54*(6), 2735–2751. doi:10.1109/TIT.2008.921680.

KEY TERMS AND DEFINITIONS

Artificial Noise (AN): A generated interference signal sent by a legitimate node in order to degrade reception quality of unauthorized receiver nodes.

Beamforming: A multi-antenna technique to design the transmit pattern of an antenna, by allocating proper weights to each antenna array element.

Eavesdropper: A type of attacker that listens to communication between two nodes in an unauthorized manner.

Jammer: A type of attacker who sends generated interference signals to block or degrade the communication between two nodes.

Outage Secrecy Capacity (OSC) Probability: The probability that the instantaneous secrecy capacity is less than a target secrecy rate.

Secrecy Capacity: The maximum of all achievable secrecy rates, defined as the difference between channel capacity of legitimate receiver and that of eavesdropper's.

Secrecy Rate: A transmission rate that satisfy an eavesdropper node cannot obtain the transmitted signals.

APPENDIX: REVIEW QUESTIONS

1. Which layers of the OSI reference model are directly related with the security functionalities?
2. Why maintaining security in wireless communication channels is more difficult than their wired counterparts?
3. Explain the conditions to achieve perfect information theoretic secrecy and their physical implications.
4. Describe the artificial noise concept. What are the required statistical properties of this concept to enhance security?
5. How can the wireless communication channel be used to generate the encryption keys for encryption based security?
6. In what kind of wireless networks can we use beamforming? How many antennas are needed to employ beamforming at the transmitter?
7. Is the channel reciprocity assumption valid for all wireless communication networks? What are the conditions that can invalidate this assumption?
8. Can beamforming and artificial noise solutions be used for wireless broadcast services?
9. How accurate should the channel state information be at the wireless transmitting node to employ PHY security precautions? What would be the effect of any channel state information error at the transmitter side?
10. How can artificial noise and beamforming concepts be used to avoid distributed denial of service attacks?
11. Is physical layer security sufficient to attain perfectly secure wireless communication networks?

Section 3
Vehicular Communications and Networking

Chapter 5
Security and Connectivity Analysis in Vehicular Communication Networks

Hamada Alshaer
Khalifa University, UAE

Sami Muhaidat
Khalifa University, UAE

Raed Shubair
Khalifa University, UAE

Moein Shayegannia
Simon Fraser University, Canada

ABSTRACT

Reliable Vehicular Ad-Hoc Networks (VANETs) require secured uninterrupted uplink and downlink connectivity to guarantee secure ubiquitous vehicular communications. VANET mobility, multi-fading wireless, and radio channels could result in unsecured and disrupted vehicular communications, isolating some vehicle nodes and making them vulnerable to security attacks. A VANET is considered to be connected and secured if there is a secured path connecting any pair of Communication-Enabled Vehicles (CEVs) in this network. Among many parameters, VANET connectivity depends on two main elements: communication transmission range and statistical distribution characterizing inter-vehicle spacing. To guarantee persistent VANET connectivity, a vehicle transmission radio range must be set properly based on the characteristic of the statistical distribution modeling the inter-vehicle spacing. This chapter analyzes three inter-vehicle spacing models based on exponential, Generalized Extreme Value (GEV), and Exponential with Robustness Factor (EwRF) statistical distributions. Based on vehicle nodes spatial density on a road segment, each vehicle node can adjust its transmission range to increase network connectivity and guarantee ubiquitous vehicular communications. Communications among vehicle nodes are secured through trusted Road-Side Units (RSUs) which distribute efficiently secret keys to vehicle nodes under their coverage to establish secure communication sessions.

DOI: 10.4018/978-1-4666-4691-9.ch005

INTRODUCTION

Next generation intelligent transport systems (NGITSs) enable vehicles to communicate with its neighbors through vehicular ad-hoc networks (VANETs) connectivity and exchange information with road-side units (RSUs) as well as road communication gateways (RCGs), installed along the roads, through vehicle-to-road (V2R) or vehicle-to-infrastructure (V2I) connectivity (Alshaer & Elmirghani, 2009; Alshae & Horlait, 2004; Alshaer & Horlait, 2005). Communication-enabled vehicles (CEVs) are equipped with small-sized wireless devices with increasing computing capabilities which can enable them to network together through peer-to-peer (P2P) communications without the need for fixed communication infrastructure (Blum & Eskandarian & Hoffman, 2004; Hartenstein & Laberteaux, 2008). Reliable VANETs require establishing security and privacy techniques to secure vehicular information messages delivery. VANET security should (i) ensure the information received by vehicle nodes is correct and (ii) verify message integrity and source authentication (Sun & Zhang & Zhang & Fang, 2010). Because of the high and fluctuating mobility of vehicle nodes and transmission power constraints, a VANET might suffer continuous and persistent disruptions. This makes it challenging to maintain security and connectivity of VANET at a determined level.

VANET connectivity ensures the relay of information messages from a vehicle to reach all the other vehicles in the network. To guarantee this connectivity, a road must be sufficiently dense. If the vehicles are too sparsely distributed, the distance between two consecutive vehicles may exceed their radio transmission range, which makes them unable to communicate, causing disconnections in the network connecting them. The number of vehicle nodes involved in VANETs may vary, depending on the change in the transmission ranges assigned to vehicle nodes. A vehicle node that transmits at a large transmission range will increase the probability of finding a receiver in the desired direction and significantly contribute in the successful data transmission range. But, this may result in a higher probability of collisions with other data transmissions and increase energy (power) consumption. The converse is correct for short transmission range.

Despite vehicles in VANETs are highly mobile, both velocity and flow of vehicles are dependent on vehicle density (Nagatani, 2002). The increase in vehicle density causes traffic to shift from free-flow stage, where vehicles movement is unrestricted, to traffic jams caused by dense traffic. While many research studies have been conducted on the connectivity of VANETs (Panichpapiboon & Atikom, 2008; Santi & Blough, 2003; Penrose,1999; Desai & Manjunath, 2002; Panichpapiboon & Pattara-atikom, 2008), most of them rely on the crucial assumption that the inter-vehicle spacing between consecutive vehicles is exponentially distributed. Although an exponential distribution is a good approximation for the inter-vehicle spacing in extremely light traffic conditions, a new empirical analysis (Cheng & Panichpapiboon, 2012) suggests that in a moderate condition the inter-vehicle spacing better be described by other statistical distributions. If the inter-vehicle spacing distribution is not exponential, how does it affect the connectivity analysis? To what extent would the density and the transmission range required for network connectivity change if the inter-vehicle spacing distribution was not exponential? This chapter answers these questions and associates connectivity analysis with security.

Some vehicular traffic information systems still rely on a centralized communication model, where the collected traffic data are sent to a central processing unit before being distributed back to drivers on the roads. This is inefficient in terms of delay and other quality-of-service (QoS) requirements; and the communication infrastructure required for the centralized communication model could be costly (Alshaer & Ernst & Fortelle, 2012). The whole communication system becomes more effective and less expensive if the traffic information could be directly exchanged in a secure manner among vehicle nodes through vehicular ad-hoc networks. Information messages exchanged in a vehicular ad-hoc network have different levels of importance, thus different security measures could be implemented to secure communication sessions among vehicle nodes. Securing communication sessions through symmetric encryption with implicit key safety messages requires the deployment of a scheme privileging authentication over confidentiality (Raya & Hubaux, 2007), since the information contained in the exchanged messages is not particularly sensitive and may be of interest to multiple vehicle nodes, while the legitimacy of the source is important.

Numerous applications and services could be provisioned in VANETs, which range from driver assistance systems to traffic information systems (Alshaer & Elmirghani, 2009). To successfully commercialize these applications, security and privacy issues, such as message authentication, integrity, non-repudiation should be considered in vehicular communications. By securing VANETs connectivity, intelligent transport service providers (ITSPs) can reliably provision next generation vehicular services to road users and enable vehicle nodes to safely run telematics applications. For example, vehicle nodes can run high-bandwidth applications that require both peer-to-peer communications and computations for optimal routing paths planning using GPS signal or remote diagnostics using data from sensors built on vehicles (Briesemeister & Hommel, 2000). Thus, reliable distribution of information in a VANET requires secure and robust network connectivity.

A vehicular public key infrastructure (VPKI) mechanism shares common keys between vehicles that are near each other, where public key infrastructure (PKI) mechanism (Weimerskirch & Hu & Laberteaux, 2009) makes use of public key cryptography (PKC) for information messages authentication. VPKI mechanism enables each vehicle node to have a public/private key.

When a vehicle node sends a safety message, this VPKI mechanism assigns it with its own private key and adds a certificate authority (CA). Vehicle nodes receiving this message obtain the public key of ''V'' using the certificate and then verify V's signature using its certified public key. The receiver, however, should have the public key of the certificate authority (CA). Note that a VPKI mechanism applies certificate revocation technique which is used to revoke the expired certificates to make other vehicles aware of the certificates invalidity. Vehicle nodes receive a list of all the revoked certificates, which enable them to detect the certificates of attackers.

This chapter analyses the major assumptions underlining the statistical distributions characterizing the inter-vehicle spacing. It analyses in-depth the exponential, generalized extreme value (GEV) and exponential with robustness factor inter-vehicle spacing distribution. Analytical formulas and equations are introduced to define the relationship between vehicle nodes density, transmission range and security of VANET connectivity. A vehicular public key infrastructure (VPKI) scheme is discussed to enable vehicles to establish secure pairwise connections with arbitrarily high probability of success and low communication complexity. The proposed mechanism exploits spatially bounded communication patterns that are present in VANETs by advertising the common keys between vehicles that are near each other. The obtained results highlight the efficiency of the proposed mechanism, as well as the trade-offs between the density of trusted nodes and the speed of information dissemination.

This Chapter is organized as follows. Section 2 describes vehicular ad-hoc network topology and communication connectivity models and characteristics. Section 3 defines the relationship between the vehicle nods density and their transmission range in three VANET connectivity models. Section 4 discusses inter-vehicle information security. Section 5 introduces security scheme based on public key infrastructure (PKI)

Figure 1. VANET nodes randomly distributed along a road segment of length L meter

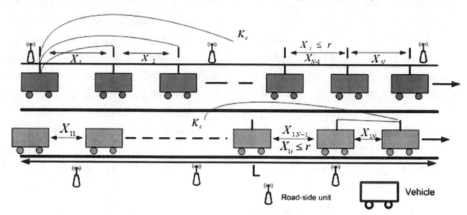

for securing VANET communications. Sections **6** and **7** draw a conclusion to this paper and provide some prospective for future.

1. VEHICULAR AD-HOC NETWORK MODEL

Figure 1 describes the considered VANET model in this chapter. A VANET is composed of vehicle nodes, where road-side units (RSUs) can support these nodes to communicate through fixed communication infrastructure.

Vehicle nodes travel on one-way two-lane road. A VANET topology can be represented as a communication graph G(V,E), where | V | represents the number of vehicle nodes and | E | represents the number of communication edges (links) forming this network. Note that VANET's mobility differs from other networks' mobility, as vehicle nodes' mobility is restricted to predetermined paths. This allows designers of VANET systems to consider one-dimensional VANET network (Wu & Fujimot & Riley, 2011). As the movement of vehicles is limited by a road structure, one can assume that a transmission range of vehicle node should cover the road's width. And, the inter-vehicle distances in the direction vertical to the road is ignored, where the communication connections mainly depend on the horizontal inter-

vehicle distances to the road (Vural & Ekici, 2007). A transmission range assignment for a d-dimensional network graph, $G_d = (V, E)$, is a function that assigns every vehicle node in V a value in $(0, r_{max}]$ (Se & Huson, 1996). A vehicle can transmit and receive within its wireless or radio transmission range, r. Obviously, vehicle nodes can be equipped with different wireless and radio communication technologies and therefore their transmission ranges could be also different (Baccelli & Jacquet & Rodolakis, 2008).

A communication channel (link), , between vehicle nodes and is active if and only if the Euclidean distance between these vehicle nodes is less than or equal to their shortest transmission range, i.e.,

$$E\left\{(v_i, v_j) \in V^2 \left\| x_i - x_j \right\| \leq \min(r_i, r_j)\right\} \qquad (1)$$

where x_i and r_i are the position and transmission range of the node v_i, respectively. Equation (1) results in a uni-directed graph. The forward link of node "i" starts at node "i" and terminates at node "j", where the forward or backward degree of a node is counted as the number of forward or backward-links of this node and represents the number of its forward or backward reachable neighbors. A path is established to connect network nodes, which can be a single link or formed of a set of consecutive links. A graph is said to be connected if at least one path exists between any two nodes in the graph. A graph is $k-$edge connected if and only if the removal of $k-1$ edges cannot disconnect the graph(Chartrand & Zhang, 2005). This chapter does not consider the influence of the operations underlining the deployed routing protocols on communication connections among vehicle nodes (Ni & Chandler, 1994).

A vehicular public key infrastructure (VPKI) mechanism is assumed to be operational along the road to enable vehicle nodes to possess at least one pair of public-private keys and the corresponding certificates issued by certificate authorities (CAs) (Zhou & Mutka & Ni, 2005). Each CA is responsible for a geographic region covering one or more highways, or an urban area, and acts as the root of trust for VANETs formed along the road. RSUs are infrastructure-based devices located next to the road, and therefore provide coverage within a given radio range. Ideally, the deployment coverage should be such that any vehicle can contact a RSU when entering a specific region controlled by a CA. This protocol can function even in environments with sparsely deployed RSUs, assuming that there is already a permanent connection between RSUs and some CAs. Key dissemination is enabled by RSUs, albeit a more general case can be considered where key dissemination is enabled by any other trusted node (static or mobile).

2. STATISTICAL DISTRIBUTIONS OF INTER-VEHICLE SPACING

Among many parameters, VANET connectivity depends on two main elements: inter-vehicle spacing and communication transmission range. To achieve network connectivity, the transmission range of each vehicle must be set properly based on the characteristics of the inter-vehicle spacing. Since the distance between each pair of consecutive vehicles on a road is a random variable, it is not possible to guarantee a surely connected network. Statistical modeling is often used to evaluate the probability that a network will be connected based on a given radio transmission range and the assumed statistical distribution of the inter-vehicle spacing. In most reported connectivity models, an exponential distribution is often assumed for the inter-vehicle spacing. However, it needs to be investigated if the inter-vehicle spacing indeed follows this specific distribution. If the exponential distribution cannot accurately represent the underlying inter-vehicle spacing distribution, the connectivity predicated may be invalid (Joerer & Sommer & Dressler, 2012).

Figure 2 depicts the main statistical distributions which have been proposed in the state-of-the-art to characterize the inter-vehicle spacing (Panichpapiboon & Pattara-atikom, 2008; Ukkusuri & Du, 2008; Cheng & Panichpapiboon, 2012). Basically, the designers of vehicular communications and intelligent transport systems are

Figure 2. Common inter-vehicle spacing distributions

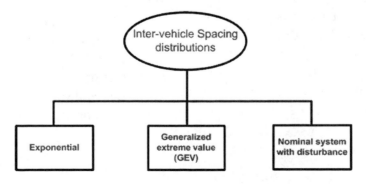

interested in determining the number of vehicles (i.e., the minimum penetration) necessary to form a connected network as well as the critical transmission range required to provide such connectivity. The following subsections summarize the different statistical distributions that could be used to characterize the inter-vehicle spacing and conceive vehicular connectivity models.

2.1 Exponential (EXP) Distribution

A number of research studies have been carried out on modeling the connectivity of VANETs. In (Desai & Manjunath, 2002; Panichpapiboon & Pattara-atikom, 2008), authors introduce analytical models to compute the connectivity probability of one-dimensional vehicular ad-hoc network. Their research studies are based on the assumption that the vehicle nodes are distributed on a linear line (e.g., a road segment) according to a Poisson point process, as shown in Figure 1. The probability that there are $|V|$ vehicles on a road segment of length "L" can be found from the following Poisson distribution (Chartrand & Zhang, 2005; Haenggi, 2005; Papoulis & Pillai, 2002)

$$f(V|,L) = \frac{(\rho L)^{|V|} e^{-\rho L}}{|V|!} \qquad (2)$$

where ρ denotes the number of vehicles per meter and $|V|$ represents the number of vehicles following Poisson process. Note that a Poisson assumption also implies that the inter-vehicle spacing is exponentially distributed. Thus, while the connectivity of VANET depends largely on how the vehicles are spatially distributed on a road, the distance between any two consecutive communication-enabled vehicles (CEVs) is exponentially distributed. Figure1 shows that a random variable X_i, $\forall$ $i = 1, 2, ..., |V| - 1$, represents a distance between V_i and V_{i+1}, which

is exponentially distributed with the following cumulative distribution function

$$F_{X_i}(x) = \begin{cases} 1 - e^{\rho x}, & \text{if } x \geq 0 \\ 0, & \text{if } x < 0 \end{cases} \qquad (3)$$

where $\rho = \dfrac{|V|}{L}$ and denotes the spatial density of communication-enabled vehicles.

Denote the probability that a vehicular ad-hoc network is connected by P_c. This VANET is considered to be connected if there is a path connecting any pair of CEVs. Assume that the vehicle nodes have the same transmission radio range, r, where $P_r\{X_i \leq r\}$, $\forall$ $i = 1, 2, ..., |V| - 1$. Then, P_c can be mathematically formulated as follows:

$$P_c = P_r\{X_1 \leq r, X_2 \leq r, ..., X_{|V|-1} \leq r\}. \qquad (4)$$

Since X_is are identical independent distributed (i.i.d) random variables, from Eqs.(3,4) it follows that the probability of network is connected, P_c, can be expressed as follows

$$P_c = \Pi_{i=1}^{N-1} Pr\{X_i \leq r\} = (1 - e^{-\rho r})^{|V|-1} \qquad (5)$$

where r could be taken any value based on the deployed communication technology connecting CEVs. For example, the assigned value of the transmission range, r, can be 100, 250 and 1000 m, which represent the typical transmission ranges of the 802.11b, 802.11n and WiMax (802.16) communication technologies, respectively (Santi & Blough, 2003). Figure 3 depicts the impact of communication-enabled vehicles density and transmission range of the deployed communication technologies on VANET connectivity.

Figure 3. VANET connectivity versus vehicle nodes 'transmission range

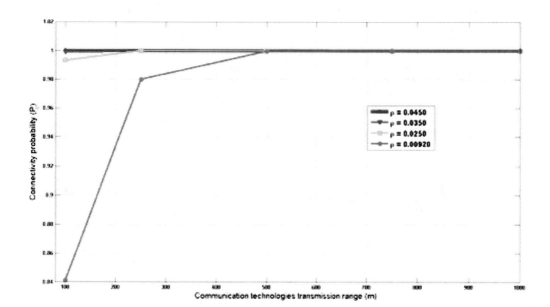

A VANET connectivity increases in terms of the transmission range and vehicle node density. Figure 4 shows that as the number of vehicle nodes decreases on a road segment, these nodes tend to transmit data at a larger transmission range to guarantee vehicle-ad hoc network connectivity.

This can help in determining the desired connectivity level by accurately determining the required number of CEVs on the road segment of length " L ". In other words, this determines the critical (minimum) transmission range, r_c, required for network connectivity based on the desired connectivity level and the CEV nodes spatial density. Assuming it is given CEV nodes spatial density and connectivity probability; from Equation (6), the critical transmission range can be derived algebraically and formulated as follows:

$$ r_c = -\frac{1}{\rho} \ln(1 - P_c^{\frac{1}{(|V|-1)}}). \tag{6} $$

Therefore, either the transmission range or the CEV nodes spatial density must increase to satisfy higher probability of VANET connectivity. If the connectivity probability is low, then it is possible that the network is divided into multiple isolated VANETs (clusters).

Figure 5 depicts VANET connectivity for different transmission ranges and vehicle densities. The transmission range has more impact on vehicular connectivity than the vehicular density on VANET connectivity. For example, vehicles get more connected when the transmission range of vehicle nodes increases from m to m for the same vehicle density in VANETs. Given the road segment and (number of vehicle nodes in VANETs), we can set the transmission range to a minimum value or disperse the minimum number of of vehicle nodes to ensure guaranteed network connectivity. However, in vehicular communication networks, vehicle nodes have high mobility which makes the analysis quiet complex. Instead of having a single cluster in the network, there might be some broken links with length greater than the transmission range. This splits in turn the network into multiple clusters. Note that the probability of having multiple clusters in a VANET is a

Figure 4. Critical transmission range versus number of vehicles

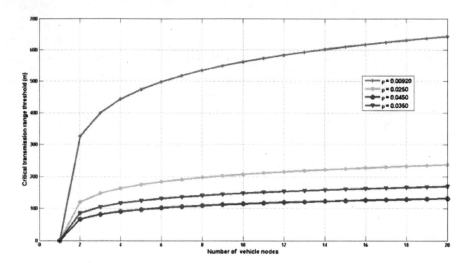

Figure 5. VANET connectivity versus vehicle nodes 'density

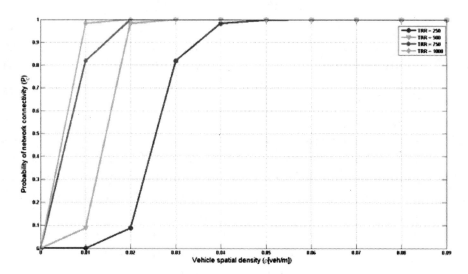

complement of the VANET connectivity probability. If the connectivity probability is low, then the probability of having multiple clusters is high and vice-versa. In the store-and forward routing strategy, the forwarding routing is used when there is a broken link (Kesting& Treiber & Helbing, 2010; Wisitpongphan& Bai & Mudalige& Sadekar & Tonguz, 2007). The network is regarded as connected, if all the broken links can be fixable. A broken link is fixable if a node at the upstream end of the link can find another node on the opposite to carry the packet. Denoting the probability that a broken link is not fixable by P_{nf}, then this can be mathematically expressed as follows:

$$P_{nf} = e^{-\rho r} \tag{7}$$

where $(P_{nf} = P(X_i > r)$. Applying Equation(3) the probability of fixable link is $1 - P_{nf}$.

The distances among vehicle nodes change according to their mobility and hence failures may occur on multiple links. Denote the number of broken links by $|J|$, then network connectivity can be calculated as follows

$$P_C = (1 - P_{nf})^J. \tag{8}$$

A link between two consecutive CEVs could be broken for different reasons, but a main reason might be referred to that the distance between any two consecutive CEVs is larger than their longest transmission range $"r"$. In this case, the probability of one-dimensional VANET connectivity, P_c, can be calculated using the binomial distribution function as follows:

$$P_c(J \mid (N-1)) = (P_{nf})^J (1 - P_{nf})^{N-1-J}. \tag{9}$$

2.2 Exponential Distribution with Disturbance (EDD)

Figure 6 represents a vehicular ad-hoc network as a nominal system operating under frequent disturbances. Under free flow conditions, the time headway follows an exponential distribution (Santi & Blough, 2003). As the velocity of ve-

Figure 6. VANET system with disturbance

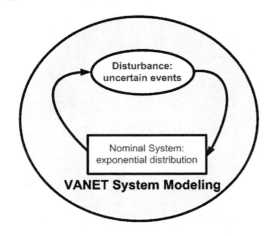

hicles in traffic flow follows uniform distribution, the space headway follows the same distribution with time headway. The unexpected behaviors of drivers not only interrupt the communication connections among vehicles, but also transform the exponential distribution into other variants of exponential distribution.

The state of traffic flow is impacted by disturbances, such as unexpected acceleration, deceleration and lane changing. In (Ukkusuri & Du, 2008), authors discuss the problem of integrating the initial space headway distribution and dynamic traffic flow features into modeling the nominal system with disturbances. A robustness factor is introduced to measure the impact of disturbances (uncertain events) on the connectivity of VANETs. In (Ukkusuri & Du, 2008), authors conceive a geometric VANET connectivity model based on a derived relationship between the transmission range of vehicle nodes and the number of their reachable neighbors $"K_c"$ under nominal system model. The probability that each vehicle has exactly (or can reach) K_c can be described as follows:

$$F(r, \lambda) = \frac{e^{-\lambda r} \cdot (\lambda r)^{K_c}}{K_c !} \tag{10}$$

where λ denotes the arrival rate of vehicles and r represents the transmission range of vehicle nodes. To find an optimal transmission range r' which not only maximizes F, but also keeps connecting each vehicle node to almost K_c reachable neighbors, we get the first derivative of $"F"$ described in Equation(10) in function of $"r"$, as follows:

$$\frac{dF}{dr} = K_c . \lambda . (\lambda r)^{(K_c - 1)} e^{(-\lambda r)} - \lambda . (\lambda r)^{K_c} e^{(-\lambda r)} = 0. \tag{11}$$

By solving Equation(11) for r', we get $r' = \dfrac{K_c}{\lambda}$. By substituting r by r' in Equation(10), the maximum value of "F" can be formulated as follows:

$$F_{max}(K_c) = \frac{e^{(-K_c)} K_c^{K_c}}{K_c!} \tag{12}$$

The probability that at least K_c reachable neighbors can be represented as

$$Q_{max}(K_c) = P(\sum_{i=1}^{K_c} X_i < r) = 1 - \sum_{i=0}^{K_c-1} \frac{e^{-K_c} K_c^i}{i!} \tag{13}$$

where X_i, $i = 1, ..., n$, is a random variable denoting the space headway and follows independent identical exponential distribution (i.i.d).

Figure 7. shows that $Q_{max}(r)$, which represents the maximum probabilities to maintain exactly K_c neighbours to each arrived CEV is low for all $K_c's$. As $K_c = 15$, the probability that a vehicle node will cover 15 neighbours when optimal transmission range is only 0.1. When K_c increases, $Q_{max}(r)$ decreases as vehicle nodes can reach easier their neighbour nodes. Figure 8 shows that the probability a communication-enabled vehicle node can reach at least K_c or $K_c + 1$ neighbors in its coverage range is nearly 0.6, which is relatively high. However, the probability that it has more than $2K_c$ reachable neighbours is less than 0.54 when $K_c > 6$. Thus, given r', it is reasonable to ignore the situation when more than $2K_c$ neighbors are reachable by a CEV vehicle node.

Each vehicle node can adjust its transmission range, $r = K_c/\lambda$, to reach almost Kc vehicle nodes. With this transmission range configured by each vehicle node, a k-connected VANET is created with the following lower bound connectivity probability (Ukkusuri & Du, 2008) on a freeway segment

$$P_c = \Pi_{j=1}^n (1 - (\sum_{k=0}^{2K_c} \frac{e^{-K_c} P_D K_c^k}{k!})) \tag{14}$$

$$\geq (\Pi_{j=1}^n (1 - \sum_{k=0}^{2K_c} \frac{e^{-K_c} (dK_c)^k}{k!}))$$

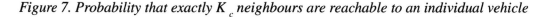

Figure 7. Probability that exactly K_c neighbours are reachable to an individual vehicle

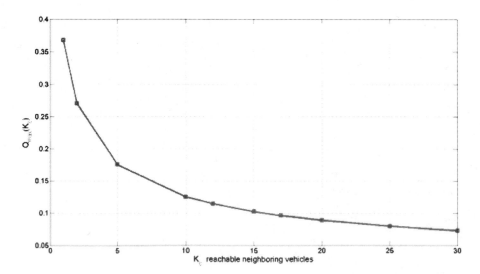

Figure 8. The probability that a CEV can reach at least K_c, $K_c + 1$ *and* $2K_c$

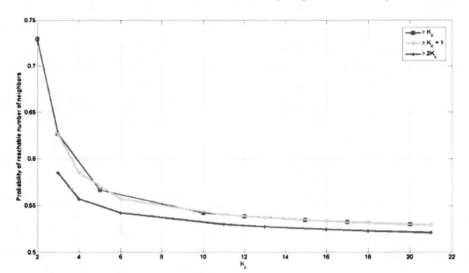

where $D_i, i = 1, 2, ..., k$ represent the event that a CEV node is separated with its ith forward or backward neighbour by the disturbance. P_D denotes the probability of the event $\bigcap_{i=1}^{k} D_i$. d is defined as a robustness factor to balance and adjust the negative influence from unexpected driver behaviors on VANET connectivity. Thus,

d indicates the extent of the disturbance impact on VANET connectivity on freeway segments. Note that the lower bound of the connectivity is only related to the number of reachable neighbors, K_c, and the parameter d ($0 \leq d \leq 1$).

For the lower bound of the connectivity a smaller d means that a smaller Kc can maintain the required VANET connectivity. Figure 9 depicts the VANET connectivity with CEV nodes

Figure 9. VANET connectivity probability when $r = r'$ *and* $d = 0.02$

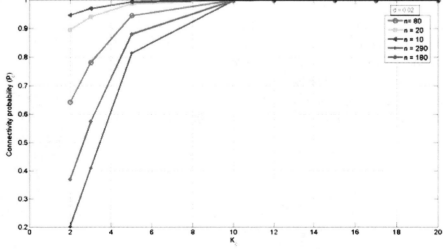

varying from 10 to 290 under different values of reachable neighbors Kc, which could be estimated from Equation(14).

Figure 9 along with Figure 7 confirm the fact that P_c increases with K_c. As the number of the reachable CEVs for each CEV node increases, VANET connectivity increases. Note that as the number of CEV nodes increases, each CEV node requires to reach more vehicles. This explains the fact that with low values of K_c, a VANET with $n = 290$ is less connected than a VANET with $n = 10$.

2.3 Generalized Extreme Value (GEV) Distribution

Extreme events that occur as a result of unpredictable driving behaviors have not been a matter of concern as the probability of extreme events occurrence in the dominant models of inter-vehicle spacing is considered to be negligible. The extreme value theory is a robust framework to analyze the tail behavior of inter-vehicle spacing distributions. This motivates the use of the Generalized Extreme Value (GEV) distribution in the context of modeling inter-vehicle spacing with view to overcoming the problems associated with existing inter-vehicle spacing models which do not accurately capture the real inter-vehicle spacing characteristics. Unlike the normal distribution that arises from the use of the central limit theorem on sample averages, the extreme value distribution arises from the limit theorem on extreme values or maxima in sample data (Qazi & Alshaer & Elmirghani, 2010; Papoulis, 1983) . In (Seeling & Reisslein& Kulapala, 2004), authors introduce a model which characterizes the inter-vehicle spacing distribution accurately by characterizing it through an empirical data analysis. These data are collected from the dual-loop detectors installed along a highway in New York. Each dual-loop is capable of sensing the presence of a vehicle passing over it as well as estimating the speed of the

passing vehicle (Qazi & Alshaer & Elmirghani, 2010; Cheng & Panichpapiboon, 2012). As a result, for each vehicle arriving at an observation point, a record of its arrival instant and speed is registered. The arrival instants are accurate within $1 / 60$ of a second. These two pieces of information are used to further compute a headway distance between two consecutive arrivals or an inter-arrival spacing.

Basically, an inter-vehicle spacing between two consecutive vehicles can be obtained from the product of their inter-arrival time and instantaneous speed. Naturally the statistics of the inter-vehicle spacing will be based on the hours of the day (Fraleigh, & Tobagi, & Diot, 2003; Joerer & Sommer & Dressler, 2012). For example, the inter-arrival spacing during rush hour, when vehicles arrive as a burst, is expected to be drastically different from that in an off peak period where the traffic is light (Papoulis, 1983). Therefore, this helps in identifying the exact statistical properties of the inter-vehicle spacing on an hourly basis. Two classes of distribution are used as hypothesized distributions: exponential distributions (EXP) and general extreme value (GEV) distributions. The vehicle density in each period can be obtained from the reciprocal of the average inter-arrival spacing. A GEV distribution is a flexible three parameter model that combines a family of common distributions, as described as follows:

$$F_{X_{\zeta,\mu,\sigma}}(x) = e^{[1+(\zeta(x-\mu)/\sigma)]^{-1/\zeta}}, \quad \forall\, 1 + (\zeta(x-\mu)\,/\,\sigma) > 0 \tag{15}$$

where ζ is the shape parameter that controls the size of the tail of this distribution, μ represents the location parameter and σ represents the scale parameter. This chapter discusses only the distributions associated with $\zeta > 0$, which are called Frechet. These include well known fat tailed distributions such as the Pareto, Cauchy, Student-t and mixture distributions (Papoulis, 1983; Puterman,1994).

Figure 10 along with Figure 5 confirm the fact that both of vehicle nodes density and their assigned transmission ranges can influence VANET connectivity, where the transmission range has more impact on connectivity probability than vehicle density. Figure 3 shows that for the same vehicle density around 0.02, VANET connectivity probability changes from zero to 1 as the transmission range (TRR) increases from 250m to 100m. This explains some cases where the VANET may be partitioned due to the limited radio transmission range become inevitable when traffic density is low- such as at night, or when few vehicles are communication-enabled.

Figure 11 compares the VANET connectivity probability under exponential and generalized extreme value (GEV) statistical distributions. It shows that the exponential distribution is more suitable for modeling the inter-vehicle spacing distribution than the GEV distribution, when the traffic densities are very light. But the GEV distribution can model the inter-vehicle spacing in light as well as in moderate traffic scenarios quite well. In some periods both distributions cannot

well characterize the inter-vehicle spacing. They are not good enough to fit the empirical distributions at the desired level of accuracy (95% critical level) (Seeling& Reisslein & Kulapala, 2004) .

Considering an accurate statistical distribution that captures the inter-vehicle spacing contributes in significantly improving the security of VANET connectivity and information messages exchanged among vehicle nodes. The following section explains schemes and mechanisms introduced for securing VANET connectivity independent of the statistical distribution characterizing inter-vehicle spacing.

3. INTER-VEHICLE INFORMATION SECURITY

Numerous applications such as lane changing assistance, collision warning, traffic light scheduling; and providing the location of gas stations and parking areas are functioning on reliable inter-vehicle connectivity based on the characteristics of VANETs (Sichitiu & Kihl, 2008). For example, the driving safety support system (DSS) assists drivers by preventing traffic accidents

Figure 10. The connectivity probability as a function of the vehicle density

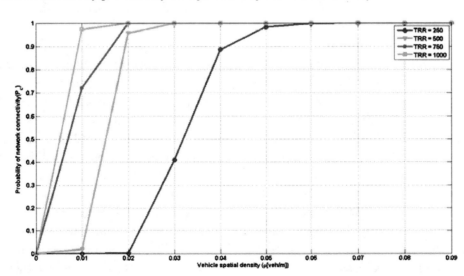

Figure 11. The connectivity probability obtained under the exponential distribution and the GEV distribution assumptions

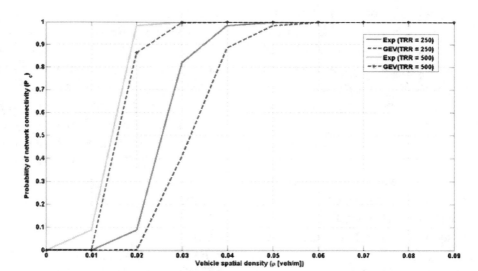

through securing exchanged inter-vehicle and road-to-vehicle (R2V) information messages. If the authentication of information messages is not guaranteed, it is difficult to ensure the authorization of information messages sent by their senders. Generally, public key infrastructure (PKI) is used to provide authentication and privacy protection in wireless networks. However, it is difficult to use conventional PKI-based approach in VANETs environment, as VANETs usually send messages at every $100 - 300$ ms following the Dedicated Short-Range Communication (DSRC) protocol (Xu &Mak& Ko&Sengupta, 2004). This means that VANETs users' signatures and certificates are constantly broadcasted, which can reveal users' real identity (Zhang &Wu & Solanas, 2010).

In (Verma& Huang,2009; Shin & Choi & Jeong, 2009), a research study is conducted to ensure the reliability of inter-vehicle transmitted information messages based on public key encryption and digital signature.

In (Yamamoto T., & Fukuta & Mohri & Hirotomo & Shiraishi, 2012), authors propose a network coded broadcast communication scheme for distributing certificate revocation list (CRL). Because of the mobility of vehicles, these cannot

always communicate with RSUs. A certificate cannot be verified reliably if CRL updating process is slow. If the distribution of CRL process is slow, a vehicle cannot correctly verify the validity of an issued certificate. In (Yamamoto T., & Fukuta & Mohri & Hirotomo & Shiraishi, 2012), authors use random network coding to propose a CRL distribution scheme for highly density road intersections. In (JaeHyu & Song, 2012), authors propose a pre-authentication method based on a scalable robust authentication protocol (SRAP). This modifies the key request stage of the SRAP and reduces the number of packets transmitted in the key request stage, which means that delays related to transmitting packets are reduced. The calculation time is also decreased by using symmetric key encryption function, resulting into a more efficient authentication process. In (Don& Pandit & Agrawal 2012), authors introduce a multi-variable symmetric polynomial based Group Key Management (GKM) GKM which eliminates the need for the re-distribution of keys up to a configurable number of membership changes, without compromising the forward or backward secrecy. The proposed scheme reduces the impact of mobility on the re-keying overhead by allowing vehicles to handoff between RSUs within the group without re-keying.

To provide confidentiality and ensure only the authorized users have access to information, group communication applications can use cryptographic tools and techniques. A common traffic encryption key (TEK) shared among all members of the group can be used to encrypt and decrypt data and this will ensure confidentially and legitimacy of access. In (Don& Pandit & Agrawal 2012), authors propose a Multi-variable Symmetric Polynomial based Group Key Management (MSPGKM) scheme which eliminates the need for the re-distribution of keys up to a configurable number of membership changes in a secure communication group without compromising either forward or backward secrecy. This is achieved by enabling vehicles to produce new group TEKs by themselves using information provided at the initiation. Under this scheme, vehicles do not have to update their keys if they must handoff between the RSUs already in the group. Furthermore, vehicles can continue to produce new TEKs as membership changes independent of RSUs as long as the membership changes do not increase or decrease the total number of members of the group beyond a given limit.

In (Hossain & Mahmud, 2006), authors propose a GKM for secure multicasting in remote software uploads to future vehicles. Their scheme functions as a decentralized GKM relying on road side infrastructure similar to mobile cellular infrastructure and works for situations where one-to-many sender oriented multicasting is used without the need for backward or forward secrecy as they use time driven periodic re-keying. However, their scheme cannot be used where secrecy is essential after every membership change. In (Park& Gwon &Seo& Jeong, 2011), authors propose a key tree based distributed GKM with backward and forward secrecy for VANETs and divide the key management responsibilities between RSUs and a Key Distribution Center (KDC) in order to reduce communication overhead. While KDC

takes care of revoking and updating the TEK in response to membership changes, RSUs handle key encryption keys and vehicle mobility between RSUs. This reduces the burden on KDC for keeping track of node mobility, which can be very high in VANETs. But, the communication overhead due to re-keying is still present at the RSU level.

In (Golle & Greene & Staddon.), authors propose the evaluation of message reliability by modeling the network. A scheme is presented which allows vehicles to detect and correct malicious messages in VANETs. Vehicles are assumed to maintain a"model" of the VANET, which contains all the knowledge that the vehicles possess about the VANET. A vehicle can then compare the messages received against the model of the VANET. A message that is consistent and agrees with the vehicle's model is likely to be accepted as valid. Inconsistent messages are addressed using a heuristic approach. A vehicle will search for explanations for the inconsistent messages and rank all possible explanations according to the heuristic approach. The message with the highest scoring explanation will be validated. However, requiring vehicles to possess a wide knowledge of the network may be infeasible and impractical.

In (Dotzer & Fischer & Magiera, 2005), authors propose a reputation system based on a mechanism called opinion piggybacking. In this approach, a vehicle generates a message and broadcasts it to neighboring vehicles. A receiving vehicle will append its own opinion about the reliability of the message, which may be based on the content of the message or the aggregated opinions already appended to the message. Upon receiving a message, a vehicle is required to compute and aggregate previous opinions appended to the message before it decides and generates its own opinion. This may create a computational burden on receiving vehicles.

In (Minhas & Zhang & Tran & Cohen, 2010), authors evaluate the message reliability using a hybrid approach to model the trustworthiness of the message generator. In this scheme, vehicle trustworthiness is modeled based on the combination of three trust models: (i) role-based trust, (ii) experience-based trust and (iii) majority based trust. Role-based trust exploits certain predefined roles that are enabled through the identification of vehicles. For example, vehicles may have more trust toward traffic patrol or law enforcement authorities compared with other vehicles. To avoid impersonation attacks, each vehicle is required to possess a certificate that includes its name, role, and public key, issued by a trusted authority for authentication purposes. Experience-based trust is established based on direct interactions: A vehicle determines who to trust based on how truthful they have been in their past interactions (Patwardhan &Joshi & Finin& Yesha, 2006). However, such a model requires vehicles to establish a long term relationship with each other, which may not be practical in a large VANET environment. Furthermore, it also requires vehicles to store information regarding vehicles that they have encountered in the past. This may lead to storage problems. In (Wang & Liu & Liu & Zhang, 2009), authors introduce a scheme for enhancing trust propagation in VANET. In VANETs, a source node must rely on other nodes to forward its packets on multi-hop routes to the destination. Trust propagation is the principle by which new trust relationships can be derived from pre-existing trust relationship.

A trust routing is achieved by introducing the concept of attribute similarity to find some potential friendly nodes among strangers. Based on similarity degree, a new forwarding behavior is considered. The following section evaluates the performance and efficiency of a scheme for securing VANET connectivity.

4. A SECURITY SCHEME FOR VANET

VANET connectivity should be secured by enabling any two vehicle nodes to establish secure communication connections. By deploying the vehicular public key infrastructure scheme (Almeida & Shintre & Boban& Barros, 2011) each vehicle entering a geographic region requests a set of keys from a road-side unit (RSU) configured within that region. Vehicle nodes can contact RSUs in one of two ways, either: i) through one-hop communication, where they directly communicate with RSUs or ii) through multi-hop routes connecting to the RSUs. . The former approach limits the number of messages flooded in VANETs. But, it requires higher RSU density for a timely bootstrap, i.e., to satisfy the key requests immediately (Du& Deng & Han & Chen & Varshney 2004) . The latter is more robust to sparse RSU densities, while being more prone to active attacks by intermediate nodes.

For example, let a vehicle node "V" sends a key request message to a RSU with its public key "K_V". The RSU draws a set of $K-$ring keys out of a pool of N keys, and sends the vehicle node the set of keys K_V encrypted with the node's public key, along with the respective identifiers. After the RSU gets the authentication request from the vehicle, it creates a challenge message by encrypting a random secret with the set of keys indicated in the request by using Cipher-Block Chaining (CBC) mode (Du& Deng & Han & Chen & Varshney 2004 ; Yu,2008). Upon receiving the challenge, the vehicle decrypts the challenge with the chosen keys and creates a response by encrypting the random secret with the session key. Finally, the RSU verifies the response and accepts the session key for the next communications with the vehicle (Du& Deng & Han & Chen & Varshney 2004 ; Yu, 2008).

To optimize the task of checking the key subset indicated in the request by the RSU, a tree-based version can be used where the central key pool of "N" keys is represented by a tree with "k " levels. Each vehicle node is associated to $s = k$ leaves, and each edge represents a secret key. In this way, the key-ring of each vehicle node is formed by several paths from the root to the leaves linked to it. During each authentication process the vehicle node chooses at random one of its paths, which may be shared by several vehicle nodes. In this way, to check the keys, the RSU has to determine which first-level key was used, then, it continues by determining which second-level key was used but by searching only through those second-level keys below the identified first-level key. This process continues until all " s " keys are identified, which at the end implies a positive and anonymous verification. Using this approach, the RSU reduces considerably the search space each time a vehicle is authenticated.

Also the RSU sends to the vehicle node "V" a list of identifiers of the common keys shared by V and the set $N(t)$ of vehicles that have contacted the RSU at most t seconds ago. The vehicle V then exploits this information about nearby vehicles to immediately establish a secure connection with the vehicles in $N(t)$ without further interaction, as long as they share some keys. The RSU informs its x − hop neighborhood, N_x, about the presence of vehicle node "V", broadcasting the identifiers of its keys. This enables the vehicles in N_x to have fresh information about incoming vehicles that are geographically close. Suppose that two vehicle nodes share s keys, $k_1, ..., k_s$, with $s > 0$. They secure a communication link by deriving a new shared secret

$K = f(k_1, ..., k_s)$, where $f(\bullet)$ is a cryptographic hash function (Du& Deng & Han & Chen & Varshney 2004 ; Yu,2008).

Figure 12 illustrates the key dissemination process in VANETs. Here, a vehicle node V_1 requests a set of keys to road-side unit RSU_1. Suppose this RSU_1 has been contacted by vehicle nodes $(V_2, ..., V_6)$ in the last t seconds, i.e. $N_1(t) = (V_2, ..., V_6)$. RSU_1, then, sends V_1 a list of all the key identifiers these nodes have in common with it. Now consider that RSU_1 will inform its first hop neighborhood, $N_1 = (V_2, ..., V_6)$, about the keys assigned to V_1. Assuming that V_1 shares keys with these nodes, then it can communicate securely with the set $(V_2, ..., V_6)$, while at the same time the set $(V_2, ..., V_4)$ can also communicate securely with V_1. Similarly V_5 and V_6 can communicate securely with V_4, while this V_4 can communicate securely with $(V_6, ..., V_{10})$ through RSU_2.

Information messages propagating in VANETs are asymmetric and change dynamically, thus nodes might not be aware of other vehicle nodes' keys. There are two cases that need to be taken into account with regard to the asymmetry of information sent in VANETs. If the transmitter is not aware of the receiver's keys, such as that information has not reached him yet, both vehicle nodes need to broadcast key identifiers to find the common keys and proceed as before to compute the shared secret. The other case is when they do not have shared keys. In this case, they can fall-

Figure 12. An example on requesting and distributing key process

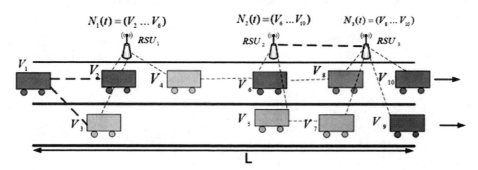

back to one of the standard key agreement approaches.

Note that a set of keys, instead of only one key, is proposed for authentication, because there is a high probability for an on-board unit (vehicle node) to have one key shared by a large number of vehicle nodes. This makes it difficult to identify a malicious vehicle node if just one key is used. However, there is a much lower probability that a set of keys be shared by a large number of vehicles, and so it is much easier to catch a malicious vehicle node. Thus exposing identifiers of the keys does not directly compromise secure communication, since an attacker has to possess all the keys used to secure the link (Du& Deng & Han& Chen& Varshney 2004 ;Yu,2008) . If an attacker compromises other vehicles security, the keys he obtains are still random keys and therefore knowing a priori the shared keys does not increase its probability of compromising a communication link.

4.1 Security Attack Model

Confidentiality and privacy in vehicular communications imply keeping the contents of information messages secret to all vehicle nodes, except the authorized ones. In this context it is assumed passive attackers and therefore this chapter mainly focuses on mitigating eavesdropping attacks. Although passive attacks impose fewer risks to the safety of the VANET, in general, they are also more difficult to detect than active attacks. It is also assumed that the messages exchanged over the wireless links are encrypted. Under the assumption that the eavesdropper is unable to break the underlying cipher, the goal of this security attack is to gain access to the key that is used to secure the communication link. Note that the presence of an eavesdropper is generally oblivious to legitimate vehicle nodes. Moreover, vehicle nodes that comply with the communication protocol and are part of the network may also eavesdrop on other vehicle nodes.

4.2 Analytical Security Analysis

The key used to encrypt a communication link in a VANET is a function of intersection of the key sets assigned to each vehicle node. This gives an opportunity to an attacker to successfully attack a link if they possess all the keys used to compute the shared secret. In this context, a group of eavesdroppers operating together can be seen as a single eavesdropper with access to a larger set of keys. Referring to Figure 12, let K_{V_1} and K_{V_2} denote the sets of keys possessed by vehicle nodes V_1 and V_2, respectively. In addition, let $|K_{V_1}| = |K_{V_2}| = k$, where the pool size is N. Let an eavesdropper contains a set of keys E, with $0 \leq |E| = k' \leq N$.

As the presence of this eavesdropper is not known in advance, we do not know which keys are compromised. Nevertheless, we can estimate the number of keys required to compromise the security of pairwise connections. Let $P(|K_{V_1} \cap K_{V_2}| = s)$ denote the probability that two legitimate nodes share exactly s keys, $0 \leq s \leq k$, then

$$P(|K_{V_1} \cap K_{V_2}| = s) = \frac{\binom{N}{s}\binom{N-s}{k-s}\binom{N-k}{k-s}}{\binom{N}{k}^2}. \quad (16)$$

Let the number of neighboring nodes at a given time be m. A link is secure with respect to its neighboring nodes if nodes share at least s keys, with $s > 0$, and these s keys are not compromised by m neighbors. The probability that a link is secure is given by

$$P_S = 1 - \sum_{s=0}^{k} P(|K_{V_1} \cap K_{V_2}| = s)(1 - (1 - \frac{k}{N})^m)^s. \quad (17)$$

The outage is defined as the event that an eavesdropper with access to a set of keys O_e is able to compromise the security of any communication link in VANET. The outage probability P_{outage} can then be determined as

$$P_{outage} = P(K_{V_1} \cap K_{V_2} \subseteq O_e) = \sum_{s=0}^{k} \frac{\binom{N}{s}\binom{N-s}{k-s}\binom{N-k}{k-s}\binom{N-s}{k'-s}}{\binom{N}{k}^2\binom{N}{k'}}.$$

(18)

Figure 13 shows the probability that a secure connection in VANET can be established in the presence of m neighbors reached by vehicle nodes having each k keys. Fig. 13 shows that as the number of neighbors increases, the probability of having a secure connection decreases rapidly.

However, the discussed vehicular public key infrastructure (VPKI) mechanism shows some strength for a reasonable number of neighbors: For a pool of N=30200 keys, distributing k−1550 keys are sufficient to getting a secure connection in the presence of 30 neighbors. This enables vehicle nodes to derive secret keys even in the presence of a possibly large amount of neighbors.

4.3 Reliability of Security Scheme

Analyzing the reliability of the discussed key distribution scheme in a dynamic scenario such as a vehicular network is a complex task. This chapter compares this scheme with a basic version of the Diffie-Hellman (DH) key agreement (Menezes & Oorschot & Vanstone, 2001; Zhou & Yung, 2010) assuming an end-to-end erasure model (Gharan O. S., & Fashandi S., & Khandani A. K. (2010)), where packets are lost with probability ϕ. Referring to Fig. 12, assume that vehicle node V_1 wishes to share a secret with vehicle node V_3. Following the DH protocol, each vehicle node transmits a message prior to computing a shared secret. In addition, the two nodes must acknowledge the reception of both packets, which gives four transmissions in total. In this discussed scheme, if V_1 and V_3 share keys assigned by the RSU_1 and are aware of the common keys, they already possess a shared secret. If they are unaware of the common keys, they will broadcast their key identifiers and acknowledge the reception of this information, i.e., they will use the same number

Figure 13. Probability of two vehicle nodes sharing a secret key not possessed by any of their m *neighbors*

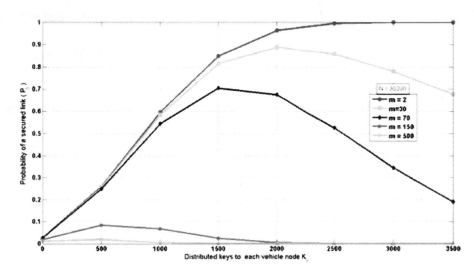

of transmissions as the DH scheme. If they do not share keys, they will fall-back to the DH scheme.

Denote the probability that two vehicle nodes are able to exchange keys without having to retransmit any packets by γ. For the basic DH scheme $\gamma_{dh} = (1 - \phi)$. Let the probability of two vehicle nodes sharing keys be denoted by P_S, the probability that a successful key exchange occurred by P_x and let $P_{V_3} = P(V_3 \in N_1(t))$. Also let the complement of the first two events be denoted by $P_{\bar{S}}$ and $P_{\bar{V}_3}$. Let $P_S = 1 - \alpha$, $P_{V_3} = 1 - \beta$ and $P_X = (1 - \phi)^4$. In this discussed security scheme, the probability that V_1 is able to share a secret with V_3 without the need for retransmissions is given by (Almeida& Shintre& Boban, &Barros, 2011)

$$\gamma = P_s[P_{V_3} + P_{\bar{V}_3}P_X] + P_{\bar{S}}P_X$$

$$= (1 - \alpha)[(1 - \beta) + \beta(1 - \phi)^4] + \alpha(1 - \phi)^4$$

$$= (1 - \phi)^4(\alpha + (1 - \alpha)\beta) + (1 - \alpha)(1 - \beta). \quad (19)$$

Figure 14 shows the values of the probability of key successful exchange between two vehicle nodes without packet retransmission (γ) for $\alpha = 10^{-2}$ and varying values of β.

Figure 14 shows that γ decays much slowly for small values of β, collapsing with the DH case when $\beta = 1$. The plot shows that the discussed security scheme is fairly robust to ϕ for small values of β, meaning that if the RSU is able to inform a large enough number of vehicle nodes, the consequences of channel errors can be then compensated. This is particularly useful in an unpredictable environment such as a VANET, where many packet losses occur sporadically because of network mobility and obstacles in signal propagation.

5. FURTHER RESEARCH DIRECTIONS

- Conduct vehicular traffic measurement to investigate the statistical distribution charactering inter-vehicle spacing.
- Develop a certificate revocation list (CRL) scheme for two-way roads and multiple roads intersections.

Figure 14. Probability that two vehicle nodes share a secret key without packets retransmission for

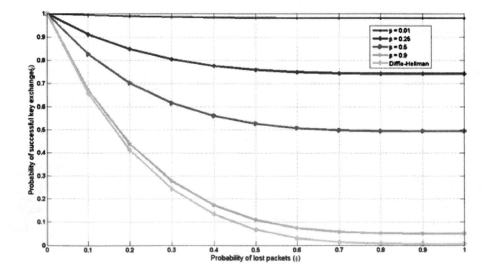

6. SUMMARY

This chapter has introduced the main connectivity models and a security scheme which can properly determine the key parameters in designing reliable and secure vehicular ad-hoc networks. The obtained results show that not only the transmission range of vehicle nodes and vehicle nodes density can have impact on VANET connectivity and vehicular communications, but also the considered statistical distribution characterizing the inter-vehicle spacing. This chapter has analyzed in-depth the critical transmission range assignment to vehicle nodes which can guarantee VANET connectivity. Although an exponential distribution is a very good assumption for describing an inter-vehicle spacing in a very light traffic condition, it has been found out that in a moderate traffic condition inter-vehicle spacing can be better described by other statistical distributions, such as generalized extreme value (GEV) statistical distribution. The developed VANET connectivity models can predict uplink and downlink connectivity probabilities in VANETs.

This chapter has also discussed a vehicular public key infrastructure (VPKI) mechanism which can guarantee the security of vehicular communications by the help of road-side units (RSUs). The obtained results and analysis have explained that robust vehicular ad-hoc networks are strongly dependent on their security and privacy features. The discussed security scheme enables vehicle nodes to share secret keys for establishing secure communication sessions. Unlike infrastructure-to-vehicle (I2V) communication, in vehicle-to-infrastructure (V2I) communications privacy is an essential ingredient. The discussed security scheme preserves vehicle nodes privacy due to the feature that each symmetric key is with a high probability shared by several vehicles. When a vehicle wants to communicate with the RSU, it sends an authentication request together with a set of s keys taken at random from its key-ring and a time stamp. All this information is then encrypted by the established session key.

The discussed VANET connectivity models and security scheme can be deployed by intelligent transport service providers (ITSPs) to (i) enable vehicles to securely run applications with different quality-of-service (QoS) requirements, (ii) engineer vehicular communication networks to guarantee secure services provisioning and performance, and (iii) effectively achieve road users (i.e., vehicle nodes or users on-board) satisfaction and guaranteed service coverage.

REFERENCES

Almeida, J., Shintre, S., Boban, M., & Barros, J. (2011). A dynamic key distribution protocol for PKI-based VANETs. In *Proceedings of the IEEE/IFIP Wireless Days (WD)* (pp. 1-3). Niagara Falls, Canada: IEEE.

Alshaer, H., & Elmirghani, J. J. M. (2009). Road safety based on efficient vehicular communications. In *Proceedings of the IEEE Intelligent Vehicle Symposium*. XI'an, China: IEEE.

Alshaer, H., Ernst, T., & Fortelle, A. D. L. (2012). An integrated architecture for multi-homed vehicle-to-infrastructure communications. In *Proceedings of 1the 3th IEEE/IFIP Network Operations and Management Symposium (NOMS)* (pp. 1042-1047). IEEE.

Alshaer, H., Ernst, T., & Fortelle, A. D. L. (2012). A QoS architecture for provisioning high quality in intelligent transportation services. In *Proceedings of the 13th IEEE/IFIP Network Operations and Management Symposium (NOMS)* (pp. 595-598). IEEE.

Alshaer, H., & Horlait, E. (2004). Emerging client-server and ad-hoc approach in inter-vehicle communication platform. In *Proceedings of the IEEE VTC-Fall*. Los Angeles, CA: IEEE.

Alshaer, H., & Horlait, E. (2005). An optimized adaptive broadcast scheme for inter-vehicle communication. In *Proceedings of the IEEE VTC-Spring*. Stockholm, Sweden: IEEE.

Baccelli, E., Jacquet, P., & Rodolakis, G. (2008). IEEE 802.11p: Towards an international standard for wireless access in vehicular environments. In *Proceedings of the Vehicular Technology Conference (VTC) Spring* (pp. 2036-2040). Singapore: IEEE.

Blum, J. J., Eskandarian, A., & Hoffman, L. J. (2004). Challenges of intervehicle ad hoc networks. *IEEE Transactions on Intelligent Transportation Systems*, 5(4), 347–351. doi:10.1109/TITS.2004.838218.

Briesemeister, L., & Hommel, G. (2000). Role-based multicast in highly mobile but sparsely connected and hoc networks. In *Proceedings of the IEEE/ACM Workshop on MobiHoc*, (pp. 45-50). IEEE/ACM.

Chartrand, G., & Zhang, P. (2005). *Introduction to graph theory*. Singapore: McGraw Higher Education.

Cheng, L., & Panichpapiboon, S. (2012). Effects of intervehicle spacing distributions on connectivity of VANET: A case study from measured highway traffic. *IEEE Communications Magazine*, 50(10), 90–97. doi:10.1109/MCOM.2012.6316781.

Desai, M., & Manjunath, D. (2002). On the connectivity in finite ad-hoc networks. *IEEE Communications Letters*, 6(10), 437–439. doi:10.1109/LCOMM.2002.804241.

Don, D. A., Pandit, V., & Agrawal, D. P. (2012). Multivariate symmetric polynomial based group key management for vehicular ad hoc networks. In *Proceedings of the IEEE International Conference on Communications (ICC)*. IEEE.

Dotzer, F., Fischer, L., & Magiera, P. (2005). VARS: A vehicle ad hoc network reputation system. In *Proceedings of the 6th IEEE International Symposium World Wireless Mobile Multimedia Networks* (Vol. 1, pp. 454-456). IEEE.

Du, W., Deng, J., Han, Y. S., Chen, S., & Varshney, P. K. (2004). A key management scheme for wireless sensor networks using deployment knowledge. In *Proceedings of IEEE Infocom* (pp. 1–8). Hong Kong: IEEE.

Fraleigh, C., Tobagi, F., & Diot, C. (2003). Provisioning IP backbone networks to support latency sensitive traffic. In *Proceedings of IEEE Infocom*. IEEE.

Gharan, O. S., Fashandi, S., & Khandani, A. K. (2010). Diversity-rate trade-off in erasure networks. In *Proceedings of the IEEE Infocom* (pp. 1-9). San Diego, CA: IEEE.

Golle, P., Greene, D. H., & Staddon, J. (2004). Detecting and correcting malicious data in VANETs. In *Proceedings of the 1st ACM International Workshop Vehicular Ad-Hoc Network* (pp. 29-37). ACM.

Haenggi, M. (2005). On distances in uniformly random networks. *IEEE Transactions on Information Theory*, 51(10), 3584–3684. doi:10.1109/TIT.2005.855610.

Hartenstein, H., & Laberteaux, K. P. (2008). A tutorial survey on vehicular ad hoc networks. *IEEE Communications Magazine*, 164–171. doi:10.1109/MCOM.2008.4539481.

Hossain, I., & Mahmud, S. (2006). *Group key management for secure multicasting in remote software upload to future vehicles*. Warrendale, PA: Society of Automotive Engineers. doi:10.4271/2006-01-1584.

JaeHyu. K., & Song, J. (2012). A pre-authentication method for secure communications in vehicular ad hoc network. In *Proceedings of the 8th International Conference on Wireless Communications, Networking and Mobile Computing (WiCOM)* (pp. 1- 6). WiCOM.

Joerer, S., Sommer, C., & Dressler, F. (2012). Toward reproducability and comparability of IVC simulation studies: A literature survey. *IEEE Communications Magazine, 50*(10), 82–88. doi:10.1109/MCOM.2012.6316780.

Kesting, K., Treiber, M., & Helbing, D. (2010). Connectivity statistics of store-and-forward intervehicle communication. *IEEE Transactions on Intelligent Transportation Systems, 11*(1), 172–181. doi:10.1109/TITS.2009.2037924.

Menezes, A., Oorschot, P. V., & Vanstone, S. (2001). *Handbook of applied cryptography (discrete mathematics and its applications)* (5th ed.). Boca Raton, FL: CRC Press.

Minhas, U., Zhang, J., Tran, T., & Cohen, R. (2010). Towards expanded trust management for agents in vehicular ad hoc networks. *International Journal of Computational Intelligence Theory and Practice, 5*(1), 3–15.

Nagatani, T. (2002). The physics of traffic jams. *Reports on Progress in Physics, 65*(9), 1331–1386. doi:10.1088/0034-4885/65/9/203.

Ni, J., & Chandler, S. A. G. (1994). Connectivity properties of a random radio network. *IEEE Proceedings-Communications, 141*(14), 289-296.

Panichpapiboon, S., & Atikom, W. P. (2008). Connectivity requirements for self-organizing traffic information systems. *IEEE Transactions on Vehicular Technology, 57*(6), 12–22. doi:10.1109/TVT.2008.929067.

Panichpapiboon, S., & Pattara-Atikom, W. (2008). Connectivity requirements for self-organizing traffic information systems. *IEEE Transactions on Vehicular Technology, 57*(6), 3333–3340. doi:10.1109/TVT.2008.929067.

Papoulis, A. (1983). *Probability, random variables and stochastic processes* (2nd ed.). New York: McGraw-Hill.

Papoulis, A., & Pillai, S. U. (2002). *Probability, random variables and stochastic processes* (4th ed.). New York: McGraw-Hill.

Park, M., Gwon, G., Seo, S., & Jeong, H. (2011). RSU-based distributed key management (RDKM) for secure vehicular multicast communications. *IEEE Journal on Selected Areas in Communications, 29*(3), 644–658. doi:10.1109/JSAC.2011.110313.

Patwardhan, A., Joshi, A., Finin, T., & Yesha, Y. (2006). A data intensive reputation management scheme for vehicular ad hoc networks. In *Proceedings of the 3rd Annual International Conference Mobile Ubiquitous System* (pp. 1-8). IEEE.

Penrose, M. D. (1999). On k-connectivity for a geometric random graph. *Random Structures and Algorithms, 15*(2), 145–164. doi:10.1002/(SICI)1098-2418(199909)15:2<145::AID-RSA2>3.0.CO;2-G.

Puterman, M. L. (1994). *Markov decision processes*. New York: Wiley Inter-Science. doi:10.1002/9780470316887.

Qazi, Q., Alshaer, H., & Elmirghani, J. M. H. (2010). Analysis and design of a MAC protocol and vehicular traffic simulator for multimedia communication on motorways. *IEEE Transactions on Vehicular Technology, 59*(2). doi:10.1109/TVT.2009.2033278.

Raya, M., & Hubaux, J. P. (2007). Securing vehicular ad hoc networks. *Journal of Computer Security, 15*(1), 39–68.

Santi, P., & Blough, D. (2003). The critical transmitting range for connectivity in sparse wireless ad hoc networks. *IEEE Transactions on Mobile Computing, 2*(1), 25–39. doi:10.1109/TMC.2003.1195149.

Santi, P., & Blough, D. (2003). The critical transmitting range for connectivity in sparse in wireless ad hoc networks. *IEEE Transactions on Mobile Computing, 2*(1), 25–39. doi:10.1109/TMC.2003.1195149.

Seeling, P., Reisslein, M., & Kulapala, B. (2004). Network performance evaluation using frame size and quality traces of single layer and two layer video: A tutorial. *IEEE Communications Magazine, 6*(3), 58–78.

Sen, A., & Huson, M. L. (1996). A new model for scheduling packet radio networks. In *Proceedings of the IEEE Infocom,* (pp. 1116-1124). IEEE.

Shin, K., Choi, H., & Jeong, J. (2009). A practical security framework for a VANET-based entertainment service. In *Proceedings of the 4th ACM Workshop on Performance Monitoring and Measurement of Heterogeneous Wireless and Wired Networks (PM2HW2N)* (pp. 175-182). Las Vegas, NV: ACM.

Sichitiu, M. L., & Kihl, M. (2008). Inter-vehicle communication systems: A survey. *IEEE Communications Surveys & Tutorials, 10*(2), 88–105. doi:10.1109/COMST.2008.4564481.

Sun, J., Zhang, C., Zhang, Y., & Fang, Y. (2010). An identity-based security system for user privacy in vehicular ad hoc networks. *IEEE Transactions on Parallel and Distributed Systems, 21*(9), 1227–1239. doi:10.1109/TPDS.2010.14.

Ukkusuri, S., & Du, L. (2008). Geometric connectivity of vehicular ad hoc networks: Analytical characterization. *Transportation Research Part C, Emerging Technologies, 16*(5), 615–634. doi:10.1016/j.trc.2007.12.002.

Verma, M., & Huang, D. (2009). SegCom: Secure group communication in VANETs. In *Proceedings of the 6th IEEE Consumer Communications and Networking Conference (CCNC)* (pp. 1-5). Las Vegas, NV: IEEE.

Vural, S., & Ekici, E. (2007). Probability distribution of multihop distance in one-dimensional sensor networks. *Computer Networks: The International Journal of Computer and Telecommunications Networking, 51*(13), 3727–3749.

Wang, J., Liu, Y., Liu, X., & Zhang, J. (2009). A trust propagation scheme in VANETs. In *Proceedings of the IEEE Intelligent Vehicles Symposium* (pp. 1067-1071). IEEE.

Weimerskirch, J. J., Hu, Y.-C., & Laberteaux, K. P. (2009). Data security in vehicular communication networks. In H. Hartenstein, & K. Laberteaux (Eds.), *VANET: Vehicular applications and internetworking technologies.* New York: John Wiley.

Wisitpongphan, N., Bai, F., Mudalige, P., Sadekar, V., & Tonguz, O. (2007). Routing in sparse vehicular ad hoc wireless networks. *IEEE Journal on Selected Areas in Communications, 25*(8), 1538–1556. doi:10.1109/JSAC.2007.071005.

Wu, H., Fujimoto, R., & Riley, G. (2011). Analytical models for information propagation in vehicle to vehicle networks. In *Proceedings of IEEE Vehicular Technology Conference* (pp. 26-29). Los Angeles, CA: IEEE.

Xu, Q., Mak, T., Ko, J., & Sengupta, R. (2004). Vehicle-to-vehicle safety messaging in DSRC. In *Proceedings of 1st ACM workshop on Vehicular Ad-hoc Networks* (pp. 19-28). ACM.

Yamamoto, T., Fukuta, Y., Mohri, M., Hirotomo, M., & Shiraishi, Y. (2012). A distribution scheme of certificate revocation list by inter-vehicle communication using a random network coding. In *Proceedings of the Information International Symposium on Theory and its Applications (ISITA).* Honolulu, HI: ISITA.

Yu, Z. (2008). A key management scheme using deployment knowledge for wireless sensor networks. *IEEE Transactions on Parallel and Distributed Systems*, *19*(10), 1411–1425. doi:10.1109/TPDS.2008.23.

Zhang, L., Wu, Q., & Solanas, A. (2010). A scalable robust authentication protocol for secure vehicular communications. *IEEE Transactions on Vehicular Technology*, *59*(4), 1606–1617. doi:10.1109/TVT.2009.2038222.

Zhou, H., Mutka, M. W., & Ni, L. M. (2005). Multiple-key cryptography-based distributed certificate authority in mobile ad-hoc networks. In *Proceedings of the IEEE Global Telecommunications Conference* (Vol. 5). St Louis, MO: IEEE.

Zhou, J., & Yung, M. (2010). Applied cryptography and network security (LNCS, vol. 6123). Berlin: Springer-Verlag.

Chapter 6
Location Security in Vehicular Wireless Networks

Gongjun Yan
University of Southern Indiana, USA

Danda B. Rawat
Georgia Southern University, USA

Bhed Bahadur Bista
Iwate Prefectural University, Japan

Lei Chen
Sam Houston State University, USA

ABSTRACT

In Vehicular Ad-Hoc Networks (VANETs), applications are based on one fundamental piece of information: location. Therefore, attackers will exploit location information to launch attacks. The authors present an in-depth survey of location security methods that have been recently proposed in literature. They present the algorithms or protocols of different methods and compare them with each other in this chapter. The methods are mainly in three aspects: position integrity, position confidentiality, and position availability. The position integrity methods focus on validating a vehicle's position to ensure the position information is correct. Position confidentiality ensures not only the confidentiality of position information but also the authentication of location that a location related message can only decrypt by the receiver which is "physically" present inside a decryption region that is specified by location, time, and speed. The position availability methods create and maintain a reliable routing path to delivery position information. The selection and maintenance of routing paths in literature can be based on multiple resources, for example wireless signal strength, computation resources, and probability models. The three aspects, position integrity, position confidentiality, and position availability, are the three basic requirements of information security based on the standard 200 of NIST.

DOI: 10.4018/978-1-4666-4691-9.ch006

INTRODUCTION

In the past few years, VANETs, specializing Mobile Ad-hoc Networks (MANET) to Vehicle-to-Vehicle and Vehicle-to-Roadside wireless communications, have received a huge amount of well-deserved attention in the literature. Indeed, because of their unmistakable societal impact that promises to revolutionize the way we drive, various car manufacturers, government agencies and standardization bodies have spawned national and international consortia devoted exclusively to VANET. Examples include the Car-2-Car Communication Consortium (Car 2 Car Communication Consortium (2009)), the Vehicle Safety Communications Consortium (US Department of Transportation, National Highway Traffic Safety Administration (2006)), and Honda's Advanced Safety Vehicle Program (Takahashi & Asanuma (2000); Yan et al. (2008)), among others. In addition, third party providers have already started to offer Internet access, distributed gaming, as well as other features of mobile entertainment.

The original impetus for the interest in VANET was provided by the need to inform fellow drivers of actual or imminent road conditions, delays, congestion, hazardous driving conditions and other similar concerns. In time, however, it was recognized that the veracity of the traffic advisories is as important as the advisories themselves. A fabricated or doctored traffic advisory distributed by a malicious driver or bystander is apt to create slow-downs and even congestion. This simple fact of life has, in turn, spawned a substantial body of research in information security in VANET. Almost all advisories and other traffic-safety related messages depend in a critical way on positional information. For example, traffic status reports, collision avoidance, emergency alerts, cooperative driving, or resource availability are directly related to positional information. Online payment services, online shopping, and the like, mainly focus on network access. However, most of the time, these applications involve local ser-

vices which need position information as well. Therefore accurate position information is of key importance. If position information is altered by malicious attackers, these applications will not work at all and will not be adopted by the public.

Therefore it is of importance to make sure location information is integrity. Location integrity means information is origin, correct, and not modified. There are two major methods which enhance or ensure the location integrity. One is encryption. The position information are encrypted. Only those who can decrypt the message can obtain the position information. The other way is validation. Validation can through checking the physical parameters, like the radio signal strength to locate the position. Validation can also be done by computational resources (vehicles failing to solve a puzzle are identified as fakes). Radar or camera can be enlisted to validate the position as well.

Moreover, we discuss the inter-cell position information availability as well because applications (for example, traffic notification, road view, etc.) often involve position information of remote vehicles or entities which are beyond a cell (ranging to miles). The location information of remote vehicles is often aggregated in one packet. Because of the high mobility of vehicles, the routing path which deliveries the aggregated location information packets is fragile. The position information that is not available when you need it, is almost as bad as none at all. It may be much worse for many applications like traffic view application because drivers may be used to these applications and rely on them. But these applications will not work when drivers need them most. The method to improve location availability, i.e., stable routing schemes are addressed.

On the other hand, it is vulnerable to use and store plaintext position information, especially aggregated position information because an attacker can easily modify the position information and harm the position integrity. Both encryption/decryption and access control mechanisms to provide location information confidentiality are needed. A direct method is to encrypt the location message by using current cryptographic algorithms, like PKI, DES, etc. Another method uses the geographic location-based encryption. The aggregated position message is encrypted by a key which is a geography location which specifies a decryption region. Vehicles have to be physically present in the specified decryption region to decrypt or access the aggregated position information.

The relationship of the above three aspects (location integrity, location confidentiality, and location availability) is shown in Figure 1. As we can ensure the position information confidentiality, integrity, and availability, we achieve the position information security based on the security requirement outlined in the NIST security standard 200 (Federal Information Processing Standards (FIPS) in National Institute of Standards and Technology (2009)).

Figure 1. Relationship of the proposed modules Yan et al. (2009)

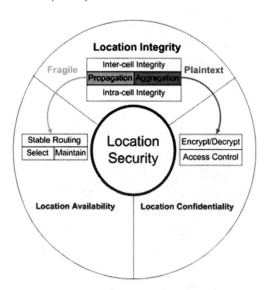

1.2 BACKGROUND AND TERMINOLOGIES

1.2.1 Security Requirements

Standard 200 (FIPS-National Institute of Standards and Technology) specifies the minimum requirement of security in computer systems (Federal Information Processing Standards (FIPS) in National Institute of Standards and Technology (2009)): confidentiality, integrity, and availability. Confidentiality refers to limiting information access and disclosure to authorized users and preventing access by or disclosure to unauthorized ones. We specify two properties of confidentiality. One is access control, i.e. that the operation to data is defined by the authorization control. The other is encryption/decryption of message, i.e. that the content of a message is kept secret from the nodes that are not authorized to access it. Integrity refers to the trustworthiness of position information. Position integrity means that position data have not been changed inappropriately, whether by accident or deliberately malicious activity. It also includes the "origin" of position information, i.e. the data actually came from the source vehicle or entity, rather than an imposter. Availability refers, unsurprisingly, to the availability of position information. The availability of position information means that the protocol and service should be operational even in the presence of malicious or benign faults. Papadimitratos et al. proposed security requirements in VANETs (Papadimitratos et al. (2006)). The requirements are based on although the minimum requirements of NIST (Federal Information Processing Standards (FIPS) in National Institute of Standards and Technology (2009)) are three: confidentiality, integrity, and availability, Papadimitratos extends the requirements in VANETs, for example, access control authorization, message confidentiality, integrity, non-repudiation, authentication, liability identification, availability, and privacy.

1.2.2 Position Information and its Applications

Position Information

Position information can be obtained from several devices, including GPS receiver, infrared scanner, etc. Since GPS imposes some constraints such as lack of coverage in some environments or its weak robustness for some critical applications, other positioning techniques have been proposed for the vehicular field, including cellular or WiFi localization, dead reckoning (by using last known last location information and velocity), and ultrasound range sensors (Bahl & Padmanabhan (2000)), and image/video localization (Spors et al. (2001)). Critical safety applications such as cooperative collision warning and incident management need highly accurate localization. Some comfort applications such as parking booking may benefit as well because an accurate positioning system can define the zone of relevance more precisely. Other services, however, do not require highly accurate localization, such as peer to peer applications, email clients, etc.

Position Applications

Location, such as GPS position or distance information, is important for almost all applications in vehicular wireless networks. Some typical applications are the following:

- Incident management is an application that manages operations and actions after an incident occurs. It includes incident detection, incident assistant, and traffic recovery from the incident. Incident detection finds out the exact incident location and is the basis of the rest of the incident management operations and actions.
- Collision warning is considered as the most important safety application. This application interactively warns vehicle drivers for collision by sensing and calculating safety distance from the obstacles, like other vehicles, buildings or anything that may cause collision.
- Vehicle tracking allows car manufacturers, logistic companies and other trusted parties, to remotely monitor vehicle's location and movement. The location information is collected, confirmed, and transmitted to the base station.
- Emergency vehicle avoidance is an application that alerts vehicle drivers to give way to those emergency vehicles like fire ambulance, medical ambulance, police vehicle, military vehicles, etc. To avoid these vehicles, drivers have to know the location of these vehicles and its own location.
- Resource awareness is an application that inform drivers resource nearby like gas station, parking lot, shopping center, etc.

Position-Based Security Applications

Examples of the proposed location-based security applications include the following:

- Military/police Applications specify only a certain region where the military/police can access or decrypt commands/files.
- Hospital Applications ensure that doctors and nurses inside a hospital building are authorized to access data only in a certain area.
- Copyright protection is an application that music or movies can only be accessed at a specified region.
- Secret Conferences/Rooms is an application that only authorized classrooms (e.g. business meetings, secret document rooms,

remote classroom) can access the multimedia content.

1.2.3 Cryptography

The terminologies specified here are only cryptography.

Ciphertext and Plaintext

In cryptography, plaintext is the information which the sender wishes to transmit to the receiver(s). It is text in the language of the communicating parties, such as email and word processor documents, or speech, music, pictures, videos data/files. The weakness of plaintext is that it is vulnerable in use and in storage, allowing an attacker to bypass the cryptography altogether.

Ciphertext is the output information after plaintext is transformed by encryption algorithm(s). The weakness of ciphertext is that there has extra cost (time and computing) in transforming from plaintext to ciphertext.

Symmetric and Asymmetric security algorithms

Symmetric security algorithms are a class of cryptography algorithms that use an identical key for both encryption and decryption. One example is Triple DES (TDES or simply DES). In cryptography, Triple DES is a block cipher formed from the Data Encryption Standard (DES) cipher by using it three times. Asymmetric security algorithms use two different keys for encryption and decryption. Public-key cryptography is the most widely used asymmetric security algorithm.

A decryption region is a geographic area which is specified by a security key. We expect vehicles will be in a certain a region where they can decrypt ciphertext and access data. We call this region as a decryption region. The geographic location information of a decryption region can serve as a security key to encrypt plaintext.

1.2.4 Vehicle Model

An important new concept in the automotive industry is neighborhood awareness. This allows a vehicle to know about the presence, location and even speed of neighboring vehicles. Today, new vehicles may have computer network devices, computing devices, and storage devices. Specifically, vehicles can be endowed with the following features (All sections in this chapter will use these features if no special specifying):

- A position black box, including a position receiver (PR) and a position key generator (PKG). The PR is GPS receiver in this work. The PKG is a key generating algorithm proposed in this work. We assume the whole position device is tamper-proofed. Figure 2 shows the device as a black box. Attackers cannot change the outputs of this black device. Except this device, attackers can announce faked GPS position or try different security keys to decrypt a message.

In the black box, one input is satellite signal. The other is the decryption region size. For example, we assume the decryption region is a square and suppose three types of squares: 10 meters, 100 meters and 1000 meters. Therefore, the inputs for region size are 1 for 10 meters, 2 for 100 meters and 3 for 1000 meters.

- A digital map, i.e. an electronic map of transportation. Attackers cannot change other vehicles' digital map.
- Radar (Sensor Technologies and Systems (2006); Toyota (2007)), such as microwave, infrared or ultrasonic radar. We assume that the omni-directional radar can detect neighboring cars with line of sight in a radius of 300 meters. Some cruise control systems already use this kind of radar. Although the driver can visually confirm

Figure 2. A position device includes a position receiver (PR) and a position key generator (PKG). It is tamper-proofed. The input is satellite signal. The outputs are two: GPS coordinates and the security key. The security key is based on the GPS position

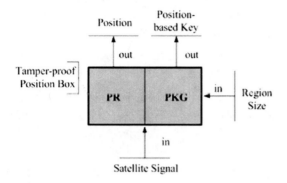

the objects detected by radar in some cases, the system does not require human interaction at all. Vehicular radar is only used active position integrity and general position integrity models.

- A wireless transceiver, using Dedicated Short Range Communications (DSRC) for fast communications which are short-range wireless communication channels specifically designed for automotive use and a corresponding set of protocols and standards IEEE 802.11p. The transmission range of DSRC is often 300 meters. We assume that position information can be modified by attackers before being transmitted by this device. DSRC for intelligent transportation system is working in the 5.9 GHz band (U.S.) or 5.8 GHz band (Japan, Europe).
- A computer center, which will provide data processing, computing and storage.
- A unique ID, such as an electronic license plate (Hubaux et al. (2004)), which is issued by a registration authority annually. It is an electronically tagged number plate which can identify all vehicles whether on

the move or stationary. It is also a standard-looking number plate with an embedded tamperproof, active, RFID tag (Electronic License Plate (2009)). The tag is self-powered and independent of the vehicle's power systems. This ID can be the vehicle registration mark or the vehicle identification number also known as the Vehicle Identification Number (VIN). Once the number plate is fitted to the vehicle, the unique id is installed. No further modifications are needed. We assume that the ID can be changed by attackers when construct a position message. Attackers can launch a Sybil attack, for example using an electronic license plate test unit to generate fake IDs.

- Existence of a trusted authority which will release the digital maps and issue vehicle IDs. In the confidentiality module, message can be encrypted by conventional cryptographic. In the conventional cryptographic, security keys will be distributed by authority but we do not use authority to distribute security key. The digital map is released by the authority and installed on vehicles. Once vehicles are one road, they do not communicate with authority any more. The digital map will update every year. Vehicles will update the digital map when they do annual inspection. In the model, the system is pure ad-hoc which means no centralized infrastructure.
- A virus checker. We will not discuss virus injection-based attacks.

A smart vehicle is proposed by Hubaux et al. (Hubaux et al. (2004)). Hubaux includes an event data recorder (EDR), a GPS receiver, and front-end radar in his smart vehicle model. Hubaux applies Public Key Infrastructure (PKI) to provide security of message. But the key management is not discussed in his work. In addition, delays will be caused by encryption/decryption, authentication and key exchanging (handshaking). Hubaux's system is working for messages which are not time-critical, for example, movies, emails, etc. But position information is time critical and 0.5 seconds will cause big difference in position if the vehicle's speed is high.

In reality, vehicles with some of these devices (GPS, radar, etc.) are already in production. For example, Toyota has developed a Pre-Crash Safety system (Toyota (2007)) which uses millimeter-wave radar to sense vehicles and obstacles on the road. Sensor Technologies and Systems developed forward looking vehicle radar (Sensor Technologies and Systems (2006)), which can detect obstacles with a 300-meters range. Furthermore, GPS and a computing center are popular vehicle accessories today. Since these components are already being installed in vehicles, there is no additional cost required to deploy the position security techniques except a wireless transceiver.

1.2.5 Network Model

Flooding Network

In VANET, the routing protocol is often based on flooding routing protocol because the topology is frequently changed. In flooding protocol, every incoming packet is sent out by wireless broadcasting. No routing table is existed. The major problem of flooding-based protocol is vast number of duplicated packets. Some means of controlling the expansion of packets is needed.

Static Network Cells

(Yan et al. (2008)) proposed static network cells which are virtual digital cells in digital maps. For example, every 300 meters there is a cell on the road, i.e., the cells' radius is 150 meters. All vehicles inside a cell can receive packets from each other directly. The diameter of cells matches the transmission range of radar, so that all the neighbors inside can be directly detected by radar when the line of sight is clear. The series of cell center coordinates are $(Xc_i, Yc_i),) < C_i < n$. Suppose the diameter is 300 meters, and the overlap is 30 meters because of the transmission range requirement of DSRC (Yan et al. (2008)). A vehicle is at coordinate (x_V, y_V) on the highway. The computer center in the vehicle will find the closest cell center coordinates (Xc_k, Yc_k) to the vehicle's coordinates. If the coordinates satisfy, $(x_v - Xc_k)^2 + (y_v - Yc_k)^2 \leq 150^2$ the vehicle is in cell k. There are two special nodes in the static network cells: cell leader and cell router. The main duty of the cell leader is to verify the GPS position of all the vehicles in its cell, aggregate these positions and broadcast this data to other vehicles in the cell. The main duty of cell router is to forward messages to conjuncted cells.

Dynamic Network Cells

Dynamic enclose cell routing is proposed by Yang et al. (Yang et al. (2004)). The cell is dynamically constructed in wireless sensor network. A node examines that two adjacent nodes can communicate with each other directly and construct a cell using the node and the two adjacent nodes, i.e. a triangle formed by the node and two adjacent nodes. If no triangle cell is found, the neighbor nodes begin to explore their adjacent nodes to construct a cell with the minimum number of nodes. If a new triangle is found, it keeps on exploring to construct a bigger cell. If no triangle can be found, no cell will be created. In this system, the cells are managed by nodes.

Comparison

Comparing flooding routing, cell routing saves bandwidth, reduces delay and increase security. The bandwidth is wasted by flooding message because all nodes are involved in communication/fowarding. The delay can be caused by the collision of flooding message and even the broadcasting storm may be caused in dense traffic. The last but not least, the more vehicles are involved in forwarding message, the more likely the message is modified. cell routing reduces the number of routing participators. In cell routing, position information is locally managed. Only a few nodes (a cell leader and a router) response the request from inter-cell nodes. The rest of nodes in the cell keep silence but monitor the behavior of the cell leader and cell router. Moreover, the cell-based structure improves the scalability of the system. In flood-based protocol, the number of duplicates will exponentially increase with the distance of message propagation. There is a scalability problem in flood-based protocol. In the cell-based structure, the system can scale in 30 km if we assume the number of message hops is less than 20. For each hop, there is only one or two routers are involved. It dramatically reduces the number duplicates of message.

Since vehicles move with high speed in vehicular ad hoc networks, the topology changes frequently. If we apply the dynamic cell construction, nodes have to frequently explore the triangle to maintain a cell. The frequent exploring will cause more delays and unstable of cells. In the model in this section, the cells are fixed and predefined. Therefore, vehicles do not even send any packets to know their cells. We take advantage a feature in VANET that vehicles are with digital maps. We can predefine cells on digital maps. Therefore, the preset cells, i.e. static network cells, avoid the need to undergo the complex process of forming a cell in dynamic network cell structure.

1.2.6 Trust Model

The following information usually can be trusted:

- Radar detection if radar exists. The famous adage: "*Seeing is believing*" is the basis of active position integrity. We trust the position which is "seen" by radar. There is precision for every radar device, for example

shifting. We consider the precision in our model by using angle tolerance $\Delta\Theta$ and radius tolerance $\Delta\gamma$.

- Oncoming traffic detection. We trust the oncoming traffic detection because it is hard to manage position attack. Even if there might have some attackers from the oncoming traffic, they pass away in a short time and the damage is trivial.

- Position security key and GPS coordinates from the position black box. Since we assume this device is tamper-proofed, the outputs of this device are trusted.

Threat Model

The attacker can announce faked GPS information, try position security key from key dictionary, and change ID. The message is not signed and can be changed by other vehicles. We achieve agreed positions under a certain precision range. For example, when the line of sight of radar is not blocked, position detections from different neighbors are same under a certain precision range because they have the same view. For the same reason, if the unsigned message is changed by one malicious vehicle, the malicious vehicle will be caught because the neighbors can hear the same unsigned the message, find the tampered message and monitor the behavior of others.

Attack Model

Since position information is fundamental and important in vehicular wireless networks, adversaries, such as pranksters and malicious attackers, tend to attack the location information to harm the system by perpetrating the following attacks (Harsch et al. (2007)):

- **Fabrication Attacks:** Create a bogus message or lie about congestion position or lie about identity, or the attacker claims to be at a different position than its actual one, e.g., by including it in a beacon, data packet, or a location reply. An attacker can fabricate its own position and announce the fake position to neighbors and cell leader. An attacker (as a router) can fabricate other vehicle's position as a forwarded position packet.

- **Alteration Attacks:** Modify the position in the message. An attacker can modify its own position information. As a cell leader or router, an attacker can modify other vehicles' position information as well.
- **Packet Dropping:** attackers selected as routers can simply drop packets. As a router, an attacker can drop packets directly to launch either black-hole attack (dropping all packets) or gray-hole attack (selectively dropping packets).
- **Replay:** The attacker re-injects previously received packets into the network. For example, the attacker can poison a node's location table by replaying beacons.

Attack Model to Geographic Key

The geographic key is computed by the proposed algorithm in the chapter. The attack model for geographic key is key dictionary attack. Attackers can select a set of possible keys and try these keys one by one to decrypt the message. As long as the attackers spend more time to find key than the time that the message keeps secret, we achieve the information confidentiality.

Attack Model to Combination of Position and ID

The Sybil attack (Douceur (2002)) is a well-known harmful attack in VANETs whereby a vehicle claims to be several vehicles either at the same time or in succession. The Sybil attack is harmful to network topologies, connections, network

bandwidth consumption, and there are some threats even related to human life under certain conditions. In some urgent situations, for example rescuing people at an accident site on the highway, the illusions will slow down the traffic, hampering the rescue vehicles from reaching the accident site. Geographic Sybil Attack (Harsch et al. (2007)) can be launched. The attacker advertises multiple IDs and/or positions, to mislead other nodes that high numbers of (non-existent) neighbors exist. Communication across non-existing nodes is in full control of the attacker; e.g., forwarded packets will be lost. This type of attack is also known as black-hole attack.

1.3 POSITION INTEGRITY

Based on the method used for position integrity, previous work on position security can be divided into three categories: cryptography-based, radio signal-based, and resource-based. Base on the way/attitude of achieving position integrity, there are active position integrity, passive integrity and mixture position integrity.

1.3.1 Cryptography-based Method

Cryptography-based methods ensure the reliability of the position and identities claimed by vehicles through encryption. Many of the published work on position security focuses on using Public Key Infrastructure (PKI)(Hubaux et al. (2004); Raya et al. (2006a); Capkun & Hubaux (2005)) and digital signatures (Armknecht et al. (2007); Choi et al. (2006); Parno & Perrig (2005); Plößl et al. (2006)). These methods work effectively and reliably when vehicles are in cities and with some infrasture, like base station, access point or roadside station, etc. While these solutions provide security, they add significant overhead to the system. The algorithms involved in encrypting and decrypting the messages along with the issue of distributing public keys and their certificates make the system complex. Moreover these method often use infrastrctures to distribute/revoke certificates, for example Certificate Authorities (CA). Therefore, key management is often a difficult task for pure adhoc networks. Therefore, validation methods are proposed. In validation methods, vehicles are allowed to send the information in plain-text. It is relied on receivers to verify the information.

1.3.2 Radio Signal-Based Method

Radio signal-based methods (Suen & Yasinsac (2005); Xiao et al. (2006)) determine false claimed positions based on the received signal power. The basic idea of this method is that the distance between two nodes can be computed from the received signal power. If there is a vehicle at a position which does not match the distance computed from the received radio power, the position of the vehicle is determined to be a fake. The advantage of this type of methods is that no extra hardware or devices needed. On the other hand, there are some risks. For example, a malicious node can use the same method to compute the transmission signal power to fool other nodes. Also, radio may bounce off vehicles and other obstacles. Detection based on these bounced radio signals may not be accurate. Therefore, this method needs the line-of-sight. Leinmüller et al. (Leinmüller et al. (2006)) proposed a method to secure position information by using hard thresholds (like, the geographic locationof bounds of vehicle positions, number of reports, etc.) to detect false locations. Vehicles monitor data to verify the reported position. If the geographic locations of reported position coordinates lie beyond a threshold, the location is determined to be false. If the number of nodes is larger than a threshold maximum number of nodes, the honest nodes know that there are some fake nodes. This method can work under a certain conditions but it is not flexible because of high mobility of vehicles in VANETs.

1.3.3 Resource-Based Method

Resource-based methods test vehicles' resources, such as radio resource (Newsome et al. (2004)), computational resources (vehicles failing to solve a puzzle are identified as fakes) (Douceur (2002)), and identification resources (vehicles whose MAC and IP addresses which are not recorded in a profile are identified as fakes) (Piro et al. (2006)). The basic idea of these methods is that vehicles are validated by examining the unique resorces. Therefore, the bogus position or fabriced location will be found and discarded. But Newsome et al. (Newsome et al. (2004)) claimed that the method for detecting Sybil attacks proposed by Douceur (Douceur (2002)) is not applicable to ad hoc networks and proposed other prevention methods including: radio resource testing, registration, and position verification. Radio resource testing is based on the assumption that no device can send and receive on more than one channel at a time. But, attackers in reality may have multiple channels. Registration does not apply to Sybil attacks, because the attackers can simply create multiple identities. Besides, registration creates a privacy concern. Position verification relies on roadside infrastructure, like base stations. Piro et al. (Piro et al. (2006)) records vehicles' MAC and IP addresses, as a passive ID, to create a profile about neighbors. However, attackers can have multiple devices to defeat this method. Moreover, privacy is an issue if MAC and IP addresses are recorded and tracked.

1.3.4 Active Position Integrity

Active position integrith mehod is proposed by (Yan et al. (2008)). In the model, all vehicles are enlisted with radar, GPS, and transceiver. The basic idea of active location integrity is to validate and enhance position integrity by enlisting the help of on-board radar to detect neighboring vehicles and to confirm their announce position coordinates. This method is inspired by a famous adage: seeing is believing. Radar is used as a vehicular virtual "eye" and transceiver as a vehicular virtual "ear". When vehicles receive the announced position information from the virtual ear, the receiver will actively detect the announced position by using the virtual eye. By comparing what is seen to what has been heard, a vehicle can corroborate the real position of neighbors and isolate malicious vehicles to achieve local security. The on-board radar device is expected to provide useful corroboration of reported location information, except for during short transient periods. For example, the line-of-sight that radar needs may be temporarily obstructed by a large truck. Due to the dynamic nature of traffic, even if there are transient obstructions, the line of sight will be restored eventually.

Since radar has limited radar range and transceiver has limited transmission range, network cells as security unit as well as communication unit are used. The authors use preset position-based cells as a basis for position integrith unit. Each vehicle in the cell can directly communicate with every other vehicle in the cell. To achieve intra-cell security, a vehicle may use its radar to verify its neighbors' positions or issue queries to verify the position of a specified vehicle in the cell. In this way, each vehicle in the cell knows the position of the other vehicles in the cell with high certainty.

In addition, The authors propose a method to provide inter-cell position information integrity for two reasons. The first reason is that applications often refer to position information of remote vehicles which are beyond a cell (ranging to miles). The second reason is that the on-board radar is not strong enough to verify vehicles in remote cells. When a vehicle receives an aggregated message which declares the position of remote vehicles, the vehicle can randomly challenge and confirm the position of a vehicle in a remote cell by using the on-board radar in oncoming traffic. The method that challenges and confirms the position of a remote vehicle with the help of radar is also

discussed. When radar is not available, position reports from the oncoming traffic or agreed position reports from neighbors can be employed. These reports will validate the announced position. If the announced position is validated, the announced position is accepted. Otherwise, it will be treated as faked position, and be disgarded. The vehicle which announced this faked position will be isolated.

1.3.5 Passive Position Integrity

For three major reasons, radar in the active position integrity is abandoned Yan et al. (2008). First, radar will not work when the line of sight is blocked, although the active position integrity model can prevent many position related attacks. In this scenario, we have to trust neighbors. But there definitely is a certain risk that the neighbors are position attackers. Another problem in the active position integrity model is that there is no relationship between identity and the location of a vehicle. Suppose two vehicles a and b are at position p_a and p_b. An attacker announces that vehicle a is at position p_b and b at p_a. By using radar, we cannot tell if the statement is true or not because radar can only detect the presence of vehicles. No identities are related to the presence of vehicles. The third, not all vehicles have radar installed in reality.

Therefore, *passive position integrity* model is proposed Yan et al. (2008). In this model, radar is removed but GPS and transceiver devices are remained. Vehicles collect location information from neighbors and the opposite traffic. After validating and filtering the false or inaccurate locations, vehicles store the validated locations into memory to create a history track of mobility of other vehicles, called "Map History". Based on the Map History, position prediction can be obtained and used to validate the announced positions. If the announced position is in the position prediction, it is fine, otherwise, it must be lying.

The lied vehilces will be isolated by using vehicle state tables. All vehicles in a cell maintain three tables in memory: trust table, question table and distrust table, shown in Figure 3 Each table consists of records indexed by vehicle ID. Vehicles record the history of other vehicles' mobility. The state of vehicles are placed in Map History. Each record consists of a set of Stacks. Each stack contains a map history in a certain time interval. All the records which are beyond the timeout limit (for example multiple times of Stack Interval) will be deleted. It is assumed that the trust table will be large and as a consequence, the task of determining a cell leader and routers will be always successful.

The passive position integrity model provides the intra-cell position information integrity. For the inter-cell position integrity, the intra-cell position integrity method is similar with the one discussed in section 1.3.4. The intra-cell position integrity method rely on vehicles of on-coming traffic and neighboring vehicles. Both vehicles of on-coming traffic and neighboring vehicles will use the same methods to figure out the loca-

Figure 3. State transitions. State transitions 1, 3, 5, 7: if confirmed by radar or opposite vehicles' radar, State Transitions 2, 4, 6, 8: if not confirmed by radar or opposite vehicles' radar Yan et al. (2008)

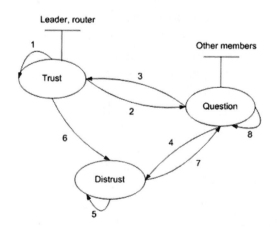

tion of vehicles. Suppose vehilce x announced position p_x and vehicle y receives this announcement. y wants to validate the p_x. y will send requests to both vehicles of on-coming vehicles and the neighboring vehicles. These vehicles which received the request will calculated position of x by radio signal strength computing or consulting the cell leaders. Once the location information is obtained, the position information will be send back the y as detected position p_y and y will validate the announced position p_x with p_y. If p_x with p_y agree each other, the announced position is accepted. Otherwise, p_x will be treated as faked position, and be disgarded. The vehicle x which announced this faked position will be isolated as well.

1.3.6 Mixture Position Integrity

In reality, some vehicles have GPS and transceiver, some have transceiver only, some old vehicles do not have any proposed devices. For example, 40% of vehicles have GPS and transceiver, 40% of vehicles have nothing, and 20% vehicle have radar, GPS and transceiver. Therefore, a validation system with a mixture of these vehicles is needed. A observer vehicle y which receive an positon p_x announced by vehicle x, will validate the announced position p_x under the misture of these vehicles. First, vehicle y will collect all position reports from the three types of vehicles. The position reports from each type of vehicles will be given a weight to indicate the significance of the position believability/credibility. For vehicles with radar, GPS and transceiver, a higher credibility weight, for example 0.7, is given. For oncoming vehicles with GPS and transceiver, a middle credibility weight, for example 0.35, is given. For vehicle with GPS and transceiver on the same directions, a low credibility weight, for example 0.15, is given. By apply data fusion or data processing method, like kalman filter, particle filter, etc., the position from malicious vehicles will be filtered out and a weighted average position with acceptable precision will be calculated.

1.4 Position Confidentiality

In VANETs, the messages of all sorts of applications (for example, aggregated position information) are transmitted over wireless media which is open to public. If the aggregated message is in plaintext format, it is vulnerable to be attacked by the attackers. The modification of the aggregated message will harm the messages integrity. One direct solution is to encrypt or to protect the plaintext message by using conventional cryptography (for example, symmetric and asymmetric cryptography), authentication (for example, user-password) and the access control schemes (for example, access matrix). A new geographyic location-based security is proposed by Denning & MacDoran (1996). The geographic location-based security is an extra layer over the conventional security methods (such as DES, PKI, user-password, access matrix, etc.)

1.4.1 Conventional Cryptographic Method

Generally, there are two categories encryption algorithms: symmetric (like Data Encryption Standard (DES), International Data Encryption Algorithm (IDEA), Advanced Encryption Standard (AES), etc.) and asymmetric algorithms (like RSA, Diffie-Hellman, ElGammal Signatures, etc.). Asymmetric algorithms are also known as Public Key Infrastructure (PKI). In symmetric algorithm, the communication peers share a secret key and use the secret key the encrypt and decrypt message. The secret key must be protected in a safe mode. In asymmetric algorithm, there are two keys for a server: a public key and a private key. The public key is well-know by all communicate nodes. The private is secretly kept by the server.

Both symmetric and asymmetric algorithm can encrypt and decrypt message. Usually, asymmetric algorithm is used to sign message to generate a signature of message.

PKI and digital signatures Armknecht et al. (2007); Choi et al. (2006); Parno & Perrig (2005); Plößl et al. (2006) are well-explored methods in VANET Hubaux et al. (2004); Raya et al. (2006b); Capkun & Hubaux (2005). A center of authentication will generate public key and private key for nodes. The public key is sent to unsecured channel and every nodes can obtain the public key. The private key will be kept as secret. When a node A sends encrypted message M to a node B, A will encrypt M by using the public key of B and send the ciphertext to B. Since B has private key, B can decrypt the ciphertext. If B wants to the message M to A with a signature, B will sign the message M with private key and send M and signature to A who will verify the signature by sign M by public key of B. If A obtains the same signature comparing the signature from B, A will accepted the M is sent by B because only B has the private key to generate the unique signature.

Scott & Denning (2003b) addressed a hybrid of symmetric and asymmetric method shown in Figure 4. This method combines both public key and private key with a symmetric key. The public key is, the private key is, and the symmetric key is *Key* in figure 1.4.1. The message is encrypted by symmetric key because symmetric encryption is faster than asymmetric encryption. The secret key is encrypted by the public key. Since only a right receiver has private key, the receiver can decrypt the ciphertext which includes the secret key and decrypt the ciphertext of message by using the secret key.

Laberteaux et al. (2008) discussed about the certification which follow the similar method to sign message. The purpose of signature is to validate and authenticate the sender. The purpose of encryption is to disclose the content of message only to the nodes with secret keys. The PKI or signatures are matured methods for security pur-

Figure 4. The hybrid of symmetric and asymmetric encryptionYan et al. (2008)

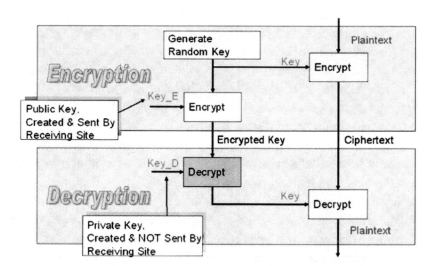

pose, especially for those roadside infrastructures, like roadside e-shops, internet access point, etc.

1.4.2 Geo-Encryption

Location-based encryption method is proposed by Denning *et al.* Denning & MacDoran (1996); Scott & Denning (2003b) that limits the area inside which the intended recipient can decrypt messages. This *geo-encryption* integrates geographic and mobility information (such as position, time, speed, etc) into the encryption and decryption processes. Denning proposes GeoLock that is computed with the receipient's position, velocity, and time, which is shown in Figure 5. Using the same notations in previous section, the GeoLock of *A* is moded with a secret key Key_S and then the result is encrypted by public key Key_E of *B* and sent to *B* which decrypts the ciphertext using private key Key_D of *B*. The secret key

Figure 5. Denning's geo-encryption Scott & Denning (2003b); Yan et al. (2008)

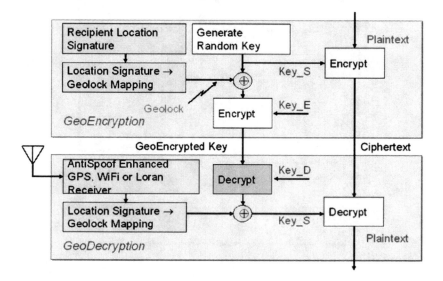

(symmetric key) Key_S is obtained and decrypted the message.

GeoLock is the key function of geo-encryption. Positions are signed and mapped to GeoLock which is like a value of a grid composed by xy-coordinates of positions. Figure 6 shows one example of the mapping function. Both location xy-coordinates and time are used to compose the GeoLock. But, the mapping function in practice is not specified in Denning's work. If the mapping function is preintsalled tables which is shown as example of the mapping function in Scott & Denning (2003b). It is extremely hard to ensure the synchronization of the key mapping grid in vehicular networks for two reasons. First, the population of nodes in the network is large, and it would be costly to replace the grid for all vehicles. Second, the mobility of nodes makes the nodes to immigrant from place to place. If the grid is not synchronized, the communication peers will not be able to communicate.

1.4.3 Decryption Region Prediction

Denning's geo-encryption model did not include details of an implementation of mobility support, so Al-Fuqaha *et al.* Al-Fuqaha & Al-Ibrahim (2007) proposed a model to provide for mobility when using GPS-based encryption. The decryption zone where the message is allowed to be decrypted contains a mobile node's estimated location. However, the decryption region predicted by Al-Fuqaha is designed for slow or constant mobility nodes. The location predicted by Al-Fuqaha does not include prediction errors. But in VANETs, the nodes have high mobility which will definitely cause a certain prediction errors. Vehicles can move about 33 meters per second (75 miles/hour) and can turn at street intersections, stop, accelerate, decelerate, etc. The dynamics of a vehicle's mobility will make the prediction from a sender difficult and inaccurate. For example, the delay caused by decryption will cause a certain distance of movement of vehicles. This movement will make the decryption prediction inaccurate.

Figure 6. Key mapping function/grid. Yan et al. (2008)

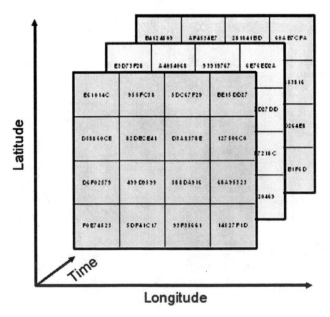

1.4.4 An Overlook of Encryption and Decryption

In this section, we discuss the geographic location-based security in a client-server scenario that the server is a fixed end and its public information such as GPS location and public key are known by all clients. We extend the scheme of encryption/decryption on the basis of geo-encryption algorithm in Scott & Denning (2003b). A major problem of the geo-encryption algorithm in Scott & Denning (2003b) is that vehicle's public key is not well-known by other nodes including the server if each vehicle maintains a pair of security keys: a public key and a private key. If symmetric encryption algorithm is used on client, a secret key is not known/shared by the server as well. Therefore, the public key or the secret key must be transmitted to the server. We assume that the symmetric encryption algorithm is used on client because transmitting a secret key to server is more challenging than transmitting a public key. Public key can be transmitted through wireless channel directly but a secret key must be encrypted before transmission. In addition, symmetric algorithm has a faster encryption/decryption rate than asymmetric algorithm.

There are two stages: security key hand-shaking stage and message exchanging stage, shown in Figure 7. The client and server negotiate security key in key hand-shaking stage. Clients generate two random numbers as two keys: Key_S and Key_C. Key_S is a secret key to encrypt messages. Key_C is a secret key to encrypt GeoLock value and the Key_S. Both Key_S and Key_C are shared by a client and a server. Key_C is appended to the first request message (including request, location, speed, acceleration) to form a combo message. The combo message is encrypted by a symmetric algorithm for example DES by using Key_S. The encrypted message is $E\{Req\}$ in figure 1.4.4. GeoLock maps the geographic location of the decryption region of the server into a lock value. The lock value is moded by Key_S to output a mixture of keys. The mixture of keys is encrypted by asymmetric algorithm using the server's public key Key_E to result a ciphertext: $E\{Key\}$. Both $E\{Req\}$ and $E\{Key\}$ are transmitted to the server through wireless channel. When the server receives the $E\{Key\}$, the $E\{Key\}$ is de-

Figure 7. The scheme of encryption and decryption. Yan et al. (2008); Yan & Olariu (2009)

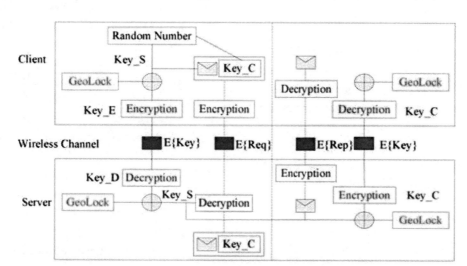

crypted by asymmetric algorithm using the server's public key Key_D to recover the mixture of keys. The mixture of keys is moded with the lock value generated from GeoLock on the GPS location of the server. The secret key Key_S will be recovered. The recovered Key_S can decrypt $E\{Req\}$ to obtain the request message and the secret key Key_C. The Key_C will encrypt the mixture in future communication. Both the Key_S and Key_C is transmitted securely to the server. This completes the security key hand-shaking stage.

In the message exchanging stage, both sever and client will use the symmetric algorithm and the shared Key_C to communicate. Suppose the server wants to reply a message to the client. A random number is generated as Key_S. Then the reply message is directly encrypted by the symmetric algorithm and Key_S to generate a ciphertext: $E\{Rep\}$. The decryption region of client is recited by the server and the location of the decryption region is mapped into a lock value by GeoLock. The lock value is moded with Key_S to generate a mixture of keys. The mixture of keys is encrypted by symmetric algorithm and Key_C to generate a ciphertext: $E\{Key'\}$. Notice that $E\{Key'\}$ is different to $E\{Key\}$ because of a new random number Key_S. Both $E\{Rep\}$ and $E\{Key'\}$ are transmitted to the server through wireless channel. The $E\{Key'\}$ is then decrypted by Key_C to recover the mixture of keys on the client. The GeoLock generates a lock value based on the current location of client. The lock value is moded with the mixture of keys to recover the secret key Key_S. The $E\{Rep\}$ is decrypted by Key_S and the reply message is recovered. The client repeat the algorithm in the message exchanging stage to communicate with the server.

1.4.5 Decryption Region in Vehicular Networks

In VANETs, the geo-encryption protocol allows nodes to securely communicate with nodes at a particular location and time period. We can use the special features of vehicular networks to enhance the geo-encryption methods. The movement of vehicles are constrained by roads, and the map of the roads can be accessed by all vehicles. Therefore, we can predict vehicles' position based on the map and vehicles' mobility. Based on the prediction of decryption region, the communication messages are checked by geographic location. Because of dynamics of vehicles, the predicted position will be updated by the real position of vehicles. The real position is piggybacked in communication messages.

1.4.6 Prediction of the Decryption Region

The position coordinates use Universal Transverse Mercator (UTM). Therefore, GPS coordinates received by GPS receiver will be converted into UTM coordinates. An example of UTM coordinates is a location called Hilltop 3705 which is located at grid 0577591395 or Zone 13 705775E 3391395N N.G. Terry (1996). One of the great features of UTM coordinates is the ability to provide a more precise location by simply adding a pair of digits to abbreviated coordinates N.G. Terry (1996), for example 8 digits UTM location, accurate to 10 meters, approximately the size of a house. Another example is 10 digits UTM location, accurate to 1 meter. The secret key is used for symmetric cryptography algorithm (for example Data Encryption Standard (DES)) which use trivially related, often identical, cryptographic keys for both decryption and encryption.

Suppose the target decryption region starts from position $P_0(x_0, y_0)$. The decryption region is assumed as a square region. Since a square region must have two components: starting point, length (length equals to width). Since the starting position can be predicted by the methods discussed earlier, the length of square needs to be determined. The length of square are listed as a series scales: *L*. For 10 digits Universal Transverse Mercator (UTM) position, $1 < L < 10^1$ because the precision is about 1 meter. For 8 digits UTM position, $10 < L < 10^7$ because 8 digits UTM position is accurate to 10 meters (N.G. Terry (1996)). For 6 digits UTM position, $L < 10^1$ because 6 digits UTM position is accurate to 100 meters. No smaller than 6 digits can be use in this chapter. Therefore, the length of square is selected from one of the three possible lengths.

The decryption region can be predicted in several ways in vehicular networks based on the map of roads and mobility of vehicles. The methods that predict the receiver's region are the following.

1. The location of communication peers can be calculated. This is the major method. The mobility parameters including current speed, current position, current acceleration, etc. A new position after a certain time interval can be computed. Suppose at time t_0, the target vehicle is at location (x_0, y_0) with speed v_{x0}, v_{y0} and acceleration a_{x0}, a_{y0}, where x_0, v_{x0}, a_{xo} are the x-axis value of initial location, relative speed on x-axis direction, and relative acceleration on x-axis direction; y_0, v_{y0}, a_{y0} are the y-axis value of initial location, relative speed on y-axis direction, and relative acceleration on y-axis direction;. After time interval t, We can roughly predict that the vehicle will at a place near location region: x_1, or

$$x_1 \in \left[x_0 + v_0 t + \cdot \frac{1}{2} a_0 t^2 - a * XDeviation \right]$$

$$x_0 + v_0 t + \frac{1}{2} a_0 t^2 - a * XDeviation \quad (1.1)$$

and y_1, or

$$y_1 \in \left[y_0 v_0 t + \cdot \frac{1}{2} a_0 t^2 - a * XDeviation \right] \quad (1.2)$$

$$x_0 + v_0 t + \cdot \frac{1}{2} a_0 t^2 - a * YDeviation \quad (2)$$

where $x_1, XDEviation$ are the location prediction on x-axis and the deviation of position value of x-axis; $y_1, XDeviation$ are the location prediction on y-axis and the deviation of position value of y-axis and α is the coefficient which implies the affection of the deviation, $0 \geq \alpha \geq 1$. Finally, the value of (x_1, y_1) are randomly selected from the possible region which is the overlapping area of the road on digital map and region specified by 1.1 and 1.2.

2. If the target receiver region is a fixed area, we can directly check the map of roads and calculate the GPS coordinates. This is the simplest scenario. Usually the e-business location is known on digital map. A location of a new business can be registered by the digital map generator.

3. If the target received region is dynamically moving, we can calculate the position of the target received region by querying the target receiver. This method is addressed in (Al-Fuqaha & Al-Ibrahim (2007); Scott & Denning (2003a); Yan & Olariu (2009)).

1.4.7 Updating The Decryption Region

Although the decryption region is predicted, there are prediction errors to the real positions because of dynamics of vehicles. Therefore, the decryption region needs to be updated to improve prediction precision for next communication. The predicted position will be updated by the real position which is piggybacked in communication messages. The speed, acceleration and direction of move will be piggybacked as well. Therefore, the updating step includes the following assignment:

$$x_1 = x_{real} \quad (3)$$

$$y_1 = y_{real} \quad (4)$$

$$XDeviation = (1 - \beta) * XDeviation + \left| x_{real} - x_0 \right| \quad (5)$$

$$YDeviation = (1 - \beta) * YDeviation + \left| y_{real} - y_0 \right| \quad (6)$$

where (x_{real}, y_{real}) is the real position piggybacked, β is the coefficient value which implies the effect of the prediction error $\left| x_{real} - x_0 \right|$.

The updating frequency is depended on the mobility of receiving vehicles, the precision requirement of decryption region and the bandwidth of control channel. For example, the frequency of updating on highways is much higher than the frequency of updating on urban area because the velocities on highway are much higher than the ones in urban area. Similarly, precision of decryption region and the bandwidth of control channel impact the updating frequency as well.

1.4.8 GeoLock Mapping Function

The GeoLock mapping function convert geographic location, time and mobility parameters into a unique value as a lock. This unique lock value validates that the recipients satisfy certain restriction, for example the decryption region at a certain time interval. The mapping function can be composed by several parameters: position coordinates, (x_0, y_0) time interval T, and speed interval V. The concept of GeoLock is proposed by Denning & MacDoran (1996); Scott & Denning (2003b). Our contribution of the mapping function is to provide a feasible and detailed method in VANETs. The mapping function can convert lock value on the fly. There is no preinstalled mapping tables.

From the Sender's View

The process of generating a key is shown in Figure 8a. First of all, all the input parameters are operated respectively. For example, the location (x_0, y_0) can be divided by the length of decryption region (square) L. For example, the length of target decryption region is 100 meters or $L=100$, each of coordinate number of $P_0(x_0, y_0)$ will be divided by 100. The integral part after division will be obtained. Therefore, bigger L will cause less digital numbers of the output from step one. Less digital numbers will result in weaker lock value. In extreme scenario, a weak lock value may be computed by brute force. Second, the output of the first step is multiplexed or reshuffled. Third, the output of the second step is hashed by a hash function. The hash function in practice can be designed as mod operation or as standard hash function, like Secure Hash Algorithm (SHA) functions which are are a set of cryptographic hash functions designed by the National Security

Figure 8. GeoLock mapping function. Yan & Olariu (2009).

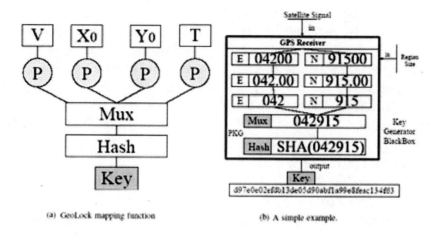

(a) GeoLock mapping function.   (b) A simple example.

Agency (NSA) and published by the NIST as a U.S. Federal Information Processing Standard.

A simple example of mapping GeoLock is shown in Figure 9. Assume P_0 is located at location (04200,91500) and $L=100$. In this example, only location coordinates are used. First step, two numbers are divided by the length of the region 100, i.e. (042.00, 915.00). The integer part after division, i.e. (042, 915) is kept. Second step, the two numbers: (042,915) are multiplexed as 042915. Third step, the multiplexed number is hashed by SHA to generate the lock value.

From the Recipient's View

After the receiver vehicle b receives the message and decrypts the message by the private key, the

Figure 9. A simple example. Only position of vehicles are used to compose a GeoLock. Yan & Olariu (2009).

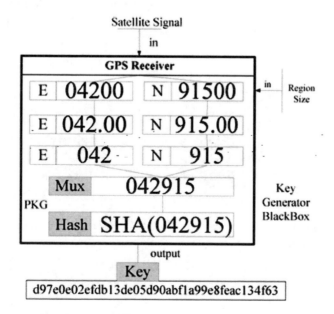

secret key will be recovered. The recipient's GPS coordinates is read from the enlisted GPS receiver. The other parameters can be obtained on the recipient vehicle *b*. Once all the parameters are obtained, the same mapping function discussed in section 1.4.8 is employed. If the vehicle *b* is restricted by the decryption region, the exact same lock value will be generated.

An example of the mapping function on the receiver's view is shown as Figure 10 The receiver vehicle *b* is located at location (04250,91520) (UTM 10 digital coordinates) shown in Figure 10 and the decryption region *L* is 100 meters. Figure 9 shows GeoLock on recipients. First step, the xy-axis value of location (04250,91520) are divided by the length of the region 100, i.e. (042.50, 915.20). The integer part after division, i.e. (042, 915) is obtained. Second step, the two numbers (042, 915) are multiplexed as 042915. At this point, the multiplexed number is exactly same as the one in key generator on sender side. Hash function (SHA) will generate exactly same key as well. We show That the lock value generated on the receiver side is exactly same as the one computed in GeoLock from the sender's view. It is obvious that the vehicles will pass the geographic validation.

1.5 POSITION AVAILABILITY

The position information/message will be propagated among vehicles in VANETs. This propagation is done by multihop routing path. Comparing with Ethernet, Mobile Adhoc Network, and Cellular networks, VANET's has special features: vehicles is location depended, the distance between two vehicles is dynamically changed (big holes may be created), vehicles are restricted on roads, the vehicle traffic is highly directional, etc. These features produce different routing protocols. It can be classified into: broadcasting based routing, geographic location-based routing, role-based routing, mobility-based routing, probabilistic model-based routing.

The simplest routing protocol is broadcasting-based routing protocol. The basic idea of broadcasting is to have each vehicle rebroadcast messages through wireless channel. broadcasting is reliable and has more chances to delivery packets to the destination because all the possible routes will be exploited to send the packet. In addition it is easy to implement. But broadcasting creates multiple duplicates on each node. The bandwidth is wasted exponentially to the number of nodes and it is often regarded as inefficient. When the number of node is sufficient big, broadcast storm witch extremely decrease the throughput of

Figure 10. Computing decryption key. Yan & Olariu (2009).

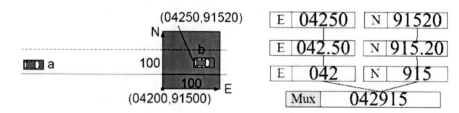

(a) A decryption region specified by a position and a length. (b) Computing decryption key.

system will be caused. Sun et al. (2000) collects the positions of neighbors and selects bordering neighbors which are on direction toward to the target node. Only those selected neighbors will rebroadcast the message. Others will discard the message without rebroadcast the message. Schwingenschlogl & Kosch (2002) enhances the AODV by adding position-based RREQ (Routing REQest control message). The position-based RREQ is forwarded to keep the messages from flooding the whole network.

1.5.1 Geographic Location-Based Routing

GVGrid (Sun et al. (2006b)) is a good example of routing which exploits geographic information. It divides a routing area into grid where messages are propagated among grids. The idea of this method includes two aspects: finding a network route and maintaining/rebuilding a new network route. Based on the position information of vehicles and the digital map, several metrics that specify the network routing path are defined. For example, the metrics include the number of red lights, vehicle's average speed, the distance between two consecutive vehicles, etc. These metrics have impact on stability. Therefore, the network route, i.e. the driving route, is selected on the basis of best stability. The maintenance of the network route is also built on the stability. Each intermediate node/vehicle remembers information of the route. When the current routing path is broken, a new network route can be built on the basis of the remembered information. Bernsen & Manivannan (2008) reviews several position-based greedy vehicle to vehicle protocols. The geographic source routing (GSR) algorithm (Lochert et al. (2003)) and the Spatially-Aware Packet Routing (SAR) (Tian et al. (2003)) use both digital maps and nodes' locations to compute the network route. The algorithm can prevent "holes" in routing path. Giudici & Pagani (October 05, 2005) extends the SAR by by only forwarding packets along streets

that are occupied by vehicles and avoiding the streets without vehicles. The Greedy Traffic Aware Routing (GyTAR) protocol (Jerbi et al. (2007)) improves the GSR and STAR by considering the direction of vehicles. In this algorithm, local routing optimum is achieved by selecting neighbors which are closest to intersection.

1.5.2 Probability Model-based Routing

Probability Model

The first paper was (Cheng & Robertazzi (1989)). The distance of a broadcast message can be propagated in a network which contains homogeneous Poisson distributed nodes. Several bounded areas (e.g. a straight line, a circle, etc.) are studied. Piret addressed the connectivity issues on a one-dimensional line segment where nodes are uniformly distributed (Piret (1991); Gupta & Kumar (1998); Bettstetter (2002); Santi & Blough (2003)). In VANETs, the vehicles move on roads which form maps. But roads can be circles, rectangles, straight lines, etc. It is not sufficient to limit the road as a certain bounded shape. Bettstetter et al. give a tight lower bound of connectivity of multihop radio networks for the minimum node density (Bettstetter & Hartmann (2005)). The basic assumptions are: 1) the wireless network is in a log-normal shadow fading environment; 2) nodes are with equal transmission capabilities; 3) the number of nodes at any time is randomly distributed according to a homogeneous Poisson process. Based on the three assumptions, the probability of the link and the node degree are derived. As noticed by the authors, Bettstetter's model can be used in sensor networks and ad hoc network. However, in vehicular networks, the mobility of vehicles can greatly change the topology of network. For example, a network with high speed nodes is less likely to have a stable link. But the velocity of nodes is not shown in the probability of a link. In our model, we analyze the probability model based on the mobility and a log-normal shadow fading environment. Nekovee et al. (Nekovee & Ko (2005)) assumed that the distribution of car velocity is normal. The path loss is also formalized as an exponential function of velocity. This formula is also the basis of (Nekovee (2006)). Nekovee (Nekovee (2006)) proposed a model to compute the probability of a link in wireless vehicular ad-hoc networks. The distance headway is expressed by a constant mean speed times the time. This paper only considers the slow fading/shading radio propagation model. Moreover, this work only considered the radio signal without considering the mobility of vehicles. Sun et al. (Sun et al. (2006a)) proposed an analytical model to compute the probability density function (pdf) of link lifetime. Their model is based on several assumptions, namely (1) intermediate nodes are equally spaced, and (2) vehicle speed is normally distributed. However, assumption (1) is not reasonable since, as known, the inter-vehicle distance is a random variable and certainly not constant.

Routing Based on the Probabilistic Model

Regarding selection and maintenance of network route, some work has been proposed in wireless ad hoc networks. Tarng et al. (Tarng et al. (April, 2007)) proposed a method based on the stability from the radio propagation: signal strength and path loss. The link stability is defined as the probability of the receiving signal strength exceeding a pre-defined threshold. Agarwal et al. (Agarwal et al. (2000)) stated a stable routing path by the Route Lifetime Assessment Based Routing (RABR). The authors calculate the average change in received signal strength to predict the duration time of a routing path. In sensor networks, location information is collected. The location information helps to create routing paths (Barria & Lent (2006); Yang & Sikdar (May 2003)). For example, the most stable path is selected on the location information. Zhu et al. (Zhu et al. (June 19-21, 2006)) proposed an

efficient scheme by sending green, yellow and red tickets to collect the delay, cost and stability information and construct a routing path based on the collected information at the sender. The stability is based on the physical feature of the links which compose the routing path.

1.6 SUMMARY

This chapter summarizes the current state-of-art location security algorithms in VANETs. It shows three aspects to support the location security. The three aspects are position integrity, position confidentiality, and position availability. Each aspects has several algorithms/protocols, which were explained. Two of the most important methods in each aspect were explained in more detail.

REFERENCES

Agarwal, S., Ahuja, A., Singh, J. P., & Shorey, R. (2000). Route-lifetime assessment based routing (RABR) protocol for mobile ad-hoc networks. In *Proceedings of the IEEE International Conference on Communications (ICC)* (pp. 1697-1701). IEEE.

Al-Fuqaha, A., & Al-Ibrahim, O. (2007). Geo-encryption protocol for mobile networks. *Computer Communications, 30*(11-12), 2510–2517. doi:10.1016/j.comcom.2007.04.016.

Armknecht, F., Festag, A., Westhoff, D., & Zeng, K. (2007). Cross-layer privacy enhancement and non-repudiation in vehicular communication. In *Proceedings of the Workshop on Mobile Ad-Hoc Networks (WMAN)*. Bern, Switzerland: WMAN.

Bahl, P., & Padmanabhan, V. N. (2000). Radar: An in-building rf-based user location and tracking system. In *Proceedings of the IEEE Infocom* (pp. 775-784). Tel Aviv, Israel: IEEE.

Barria, J., & Lent, R. (2006). Manet route discovery using residual lifetime estimation. In *Proceedings of International Symposium on Wireless Pervasive Computing ISWPC 2006* (pp. 1-4). Phuket, Thailand: ISWPC.

Bettstetter, C. (2002). On the minimum node degree and connectivity of a wireless multihop network. In *Proceedings of the 3rd ACM International Symposium on Mobile Ad Hoc Networking & Computing* (pp. 80-91). New York: ACM.

Bettstetter, C., & Hartmann, C. (2005). Connectivity of wireless multihop networks in a shadow fading environment. *Wireless Networks, 11*(5), 571–579. doi:10.1007/s11276-005-3513-x.

Capkun, S., & Hubaux, J.-P. (2005). Secure positioning of wireless devices with application to sensor networks. []. IEEE.]. *Proceedings - IEEE INFOCOM, 3*, 1917–1928.

Car 2 Car Communication Consortium. (2009). Retrieved from http://www.car-to-car.org/

Cheng, Y.-C., & Robertazzi, T. (1989). Critical connectivity phenomena in multihop radio models. *IEEE Transactions on Communications, 37*(7), 770–777. doi:10.1109/26.31170.

Choi, J. Y., Golle, P., & Jakobsson, M. (2006). Tamper-evident digital signatures: Protecting certification authorities against malware. In *Proceedings of the IEEE International Symposium on Dependable, Autonomic and Secure Computing (DASC)* (pp. 37-44). IEEE.

Denning, D., & MacDoran, P. (1996). Location-based authentication: Grounding cyberspace for better security. *Computer Fraud & Security, 2*, 12–16. doi:10.1016/S1361-3723(97)82613-9.

Douceur, J. (2002). The sybil attack. In *Revised Papers from the First International Workshop on Peer-to-Peer Systems* (LNCS), (vol. 2429, pp. 251-260). Berlin: Springer.

Electronic License Plate. (2009). *Electronic license plate.* Retrieved from http://www.identec-solutions.com/electroniclicenseplate.html

Federal Information Processing Standards (FIPS) in National Institute of Standards and Technology. (2009). *Minimum security requirements for federal information and information systems.* Reetrieved from http://csrc.nist.gov/publications/fips/fips200/FIPS-200-final-march.pdf

Giudici, F., & Pagani, E. (2005). *Spatial and traffic-aware routing (STAR) for vehicular systems.* Berlin, Germany: Springer. doi:10.1007/11557654_11.

Gupta, P., & Kumar, P. (1998). Critical power for asymptotic connectivity. In *Proceedings of the 37th IEEE Conference on Decision and Control,* (Vol. 1, pp. 1106-1110). IEEE.

Harsch, C., Festag, A., & Papadimitratos, P. (2007). Secure position-based routing for vanets. In *Proceedings of Vehicular Technology Conference,* (pp. 26-30). IEEE.

Hubaux, J.-P., Capkun, S., & Luo, J. (2004). The security and privacy of smart vehicles. *IEEE Security and Privacy Magazine, 2*(3), 49–55. doi:10.1109/MSP.2004.26.

Jerbi, M., Senouci, S.-M., Meraihi, R., & Ghamri-Doudane, Y. (2007). An improved vehicular ad hoc routing protocol for city environments. In *Proceedings of IEEE International Confernece on Communications* (pp. 3972-3979). IEEE.

Laberteaux, K. P., Haas, J. J., & Hu, Y.-C. (2008). Security certificate revocation list distribution for vanet. In *Proceedings of the Fifth ACM International Workshop on VehiculAr Inter-NETworking* (pp. 88-89). ACM.

Leinmüller, T., Schoch, E., Kargl, F., & Maihöfer, C. (2006). Improved security in geographic ad hoc routing through autonomous position verification. In *Proceedings of the ACM Workshop on Vehicular Ad Hoc Networks (VANET)* (pp. 57-66). Los Angeles, CA: ACM.

Lochert, C., Hartenstein, H., Tian, J., Fuessler, H., Hermann, D., & Mauve, M. (2003). A routing strategy for vehicular ad hoc networks in city environments. In *Proceedings of the IEEE Intelligent Vehicles Symposium* (pp. 156-161). IEEE.

Nekovee, M. (2006). Modeling the spread of worm epidemics in vehicular ad hoc networks. In *Proceedings of the 63rd IEEE Vehicular Technology Conference VTC Spring 2006* (pp. 841-845). Melbourne, Australia: IEEE.

Nekovee, M., & Ko, M. (2005). Throughput analysis of wi-fi based broadband access for mobile users on the highway. In *Proceedings of 13th IEEE International Conference on Networks 2005*, (p. 6). Boston, MA: IEEE.

Newsome, J., Shi, E., Song, D., & Perrig, A. (2004). The Sybil attack in sensor networks: Analysis & defenses. In *Proceedings of International Symposium on Information Processing in Sensor Networks (IPSN)* (pp. 259-268). Berkeley, CA: IPSN.

Papadimitratos, P., Gligor, V., & Hubaux, J. (2006). Securing vehicular communications—Assumptions, requirements, and principles. In *Proceedings of Fourth Workshop on Embedded Security in Cars (ESCAR)*. Berlin, Germany: ESCAR.

Parno, B., & Perrig, A. (2005). Challenges in securing vehicular networks. In *Proceedings of ACM HotNets*. ACM.

Piret, P. (1991). On the connectivity of radio networks. *IEEE Transactions on Information Theory*, *37*(5), 1490–1492. doi:10.1109/18.133276.

Piro, C., Shields, C., & Levine, B. N. (2006). Detecting the Sybil attack in mobile ad hoc network. In *Proceedings of the International Conference on Security and Privacy in Communication Networks* (pp. 1-11). IEEE.

Plößl, K., Nowey, T., & Mletzko, C. (2006). Towards a security architecture for vehicular ad hoc networks. In *Proceedings of the International Conference on Availability, Reliability and Security (ARES)* (pp. 374-381). Washington, DC: ARES.

Raya, M., Aziz, A., & Hubaux, J.-P. (2006a). Efficient secure aggregation in VANETs. In *Proceedings of the ACM Workshop on Vehicular Ad Hoc Networks (VANET)* (pp. 67-75). Los Angeles, CA: ACM.

Raya, M., Papadimitratos, P., & Hubaux, J.-P. (2006b). Securing vehicular communications. *IEEE Wireless Communications Magazine*, 8-15.

Santi, P., & Blough, D. M. (2003). The critical transmitting range for connectivity in sparse wireless ad hoc networks. *IEEE Transactions on Mobile Computing*, *2*(1), 25–39. doi:10.1109/TMC.2003.1195149.

Schwingenschlogl, C., & Kosch, T. (2002). Geocast enhancements of aodv for vehicular networks. *SIGMOBILE Mobile Computing and Communications Review*, *6*(3), 96–97. doi:10.1145/581291.581307.

Scott, L., & Denning, D. (2003a, April 1). Geoencryption: Using GPS to enhance data security. *GPS World*.

Scott, L., & Denning, D. E. (2003b). Location based encryption technique and some of its applications. In *Proceedings of Institute of Navigation National Technical Meeting 2003* (pp. 734-740). Anaheim, CA: IEEE.

Sensor Technologies and Systems. (2006). *Forward looking vehicle radar system (FLVRS)*. Retrieived from http://www.sensor-tech.com/sub\%20pages/products/AUTOMOTIVE/flvrs.html

Spors, S., Rabenstein, R., & Strobel, N. (2001). A multi-sensor object localization system. In *Proceedings of the Vision Modeling and Visualization Conference 2001* (pp. 19-26). Aka GmbH.

Suen, T., & Yasinsac, A. (2005). Ad hoc network security: Peer identification and authentication using signal properties. In *Proceedings of the Systems, Man and Cybernetics (SMC) Information Assurance Workshop* (pp. 432-433). IEEE.

Sun, M.-T., Feng, W.-C., Lai, T.-H., Yamada, K., Okada, H., & Fujimura, K. (2000). GPS-based message broadcasting for inter-vehicle communication. In *Proceedings of the 2000 International Conference on Parallel Processing* (pp. 279-286). Toronto, Canada: IEEE.

Sun, W., Yamaguchi, H., & Yukimasa, K. (2006). Gvgrid: A qos routing protocol for vehicular ad hoc networks. In *Proceedings of the Fourteenth IEEE International Workshop on Quality of Service (IWQoS 2006)* (pp. 130-139). New Haven, CT: IEEE.

Takahashi, A., & Asanuma, N. (2000). Introduction of Honda ASV-2 (advanced safety vehicle-phase 2). In *Proceedings of the IEEE Intelligent Vehicles Symposium* (pp. 694-701). Detroit, MI: IEEE.

Tarng, J., Chuang, B., & Wu, F. (2007). A novel stability-based routing protocol for mobile ad-hoc. *IEICE Transactions on Communications, E90-B*(4), 876–884. doi:10.1093/ietcom/e90-b.4.876.

Terry, N. G. (1996). How to read the universal transverse mercator (utm) grid. *GPS World, 32*.

Toyota. (2007). *Pre-crash safety*. Retrieved from http://www.toyota.co.jp/en/about_toyota/in_the_world/pdf2007/safety.pdf

US Department of Transportation, National Highway Traffic Safety Administration. (2006). *Vehicle safety communications consortium*. Retrieved from http://www-nrd.nhtsa.dot.gov/pdf/nrd-12/CAMP3/pages/VSCC.htm

Xiao, B., Yu, B., & Gao, C. (2006). Detection and localization of Sybil nodes in VANETs. In *Proceedings of the Workshop on Dependability Issues in Wireless Ad Hoc Networks and Sensor Networks* (pp. 1-8). Los Angeles, CA: IEEE.

Yan, G., & Olariu, S. (2009). An efficient geographic location-based security mechanism for vehicular ad hoc networks. In *Proceedings of the 2009 IEEE International Symposium on Trust, Security and Privacy for Pervasive Applications (TSP-09)*. Macau, China: IEEE.

Yan, G., Olariu, S., & Weigle, M. C. (2008). Providing VANET security through active position detection. *Computer Communications, 31*(12), 2883–2897. doi:10.1016/j.comcom.2008.01.009.

Yan, G., Olariu, S., & Weigle, M. C. (2009). Providing location security in vehicular ad-hoc networks. *IEEE Wireless Communications, 16*(6), 48–55. doi:10.1109/MWC.2009.5361178.

Yang, H., & Sikdar, B. (2003). A protocol for tracking mobile targets using sensor networks. In *Proceedings of IEEE Workshop on Sensor Network Protocols and Applications* (pp. 71-81). IEEE.

Yang, Y., Lee, D.-H., Park, M.-S., & In, H. P. (2004). Dynamic enclose cell routing in mobile sensor networks. In *Proceedings of the 11th Asia-Pacific Software Engineering Conference* (pp. 736-737). Washington, DC: IEEE Computer Society.

Zhu, W., Song, M., & Olariu, S. (June 19-21, 2006). Integrating stability estimation into quality of service routing in mobile ad-hoc networks. In *Proceedings of the Fourteenth IEEE International Workshop on Quality of Service (IWQoS 2006)*. New Haven, CT: Yale University.

Chapter 7
Misbehavior Detection in VANET:
A Survey

Shefali Jain
Dhirubhai Ambani Institute of Information and Communication Technology, India

Anish Mathuria
Dhirubhai Ambani Institute of Information and Communication Technology, India

Manik Lal Das
Dhirubhai Ambani Institute of Information and Communication Technology, India

ABSTRACT

Vehicular Networks (VANETs) have received increased attention from researchers in recent years. VANETs facilitate various safety measures that help in controlling traffic and saving human lives. As VANETs consist of multiple entities, effective measures for VANET safety are to be addressed as per requirement. In this chapter, the authors review some existing schemes proposed for misbehavior detection. They categorize the schemes into two parts: data centric and non-data centric misbehaving detection. In data-centric misbehaving detection, the receiver believes the information rather than the source of the information. The authors compare schemes in each category with respect to their security strengths and weaknesses. The comparative results show that most of the schemes fail to address required security attributes that are essential for VANET safety.

INTRODUCTION

Vehicular ad-hoc networks (VANETs) allow vehicles to exchange information for human safety and convenience. VANETs consist of multiple entities such as vehicles (e.g. cars, trucks, and buses), on-board units (OBUs), road side units (RSUs) and a Trusted Authority (TA). The TA acts as the root of the VANET safety architecture. On-board units (OBUs) installed on vehicles which allow vehicles to communicate with other entities (e.g., vehicles, RSUs). OBU also has capability of storing information and verifying incoming messages. Road side units (RSUs) are typically

DOI: 10.4018/978-1-4666-4691-9.ch007

fixed infrastructure, installed in some designated places of roads. OBUs regularly broadcast safety related messages useful in gaining information of current traffic situation, which enables receiving vehicle to take early action for any abnormal situation like road blocks or accidents. Typically, whenever a potential warning message for road condition is detected by the OBU, it generates an appropriate message and disseminates the same to its neighbours. For example, consider a scenario where the attacker (misbehaving vehicle) attempts to either prevent other vehicles from taking some road segment or indirectly suggest an alternative one. In such a situation, the attacker can create a false traffic-jam warning message for the identified route and disseminate the message in bulk. As a result, vehicles who have received that message from the attacker will be misguided and chose a longer path than the actual ones.

VANETs and MANETs (mobile ad-hoc networks) share many common characteristics, but they also have some differences. The main differences between VANETs and MANETs are:

- In VANETs, there is no limitation of power consumption, as vehicle is assumed to have sufficient amount of power and computing resources. In case of MANETs, due consideration needs to be given for power consumption.
- VANETs are highly dynamic networks compared to MANETs, as vehicles are always moving at high speed.
- In VANETs, all vehicles are registered with a trusted authority so that they have a unique identity. In MANETs, this is not enforced.

Vehicles in VANET can communicate directly with other vehicles using vehicle-to-vehicle (V2V) mode through their respective OBUs and/or using vehicle-to-infrastructure (V2I) mode through RSUs. The Figure 1 depicts the architecture of VANET (Wasef, Lu, Lin, & Shen, 2010).

There are various applications of VANETs, some of which are important for safety reasons and others for user convenience. Safety by providing prior information of road situation helps driver to change the route and avoids accidents.

Figure 1. Architecture of VANET (Wasef, Lu, Lin, & Shen, 2010)

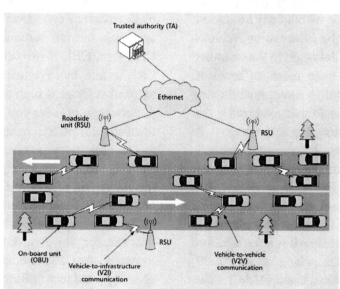

For example, scenarios like information about vehicle collision, identifying alternative routes in case of road blocks, shortest routes for medical emergency, and so on. This helps driver to choose the best and economical path that reduces fuel consumption and time (Raya, Papadimitratos, Aad, Jungels, & Hubaux, 2007). Furthermore, toll collection, access to Internet and location based services are some of the utility in VANETs. With the help of location based services, drivers can locate nearest food restaurant or fuel station.

In VANETs, OBUs communicate to each other by means of two types of messages: *beacon messages* and *alert messages*. A beacon message, sent periodically, includes location, speed, direction, steering angle and other information of vehicle. On the other hand, alert messages ensure safety of vehicle on road and are sent only when a vehicle detects any unintentional events on the road. By receiving these messages, drivers would be in a position to understand traffic situation and because of this advance information of emergency (by alert messages) like accident, road block or car crash, they can change the route suitably. However, all these advantages of VANETs come along with some challenges. For example, it is important to recognize that the sender vehicle is legitimate so that receiver's vehicle could relay the received messages to other destination without any hesitation; otherwise, due to the false information, vehicles may experience a long delay, go to the unknown route, pay penalty or even meet an accident. Therefore, it is important to detect misbehaving vehicle at an early stage so that road traffic can be controlled and monitored in better way.

VANETs security should guarantee authentication of communication entities, data integrity, and in some specific application scenarios, data confidentiality to protect the network against unauthorized message injection and alteration. Authentication and data integrity can be achieved by digital signature (Sha, Wang, & Shi, 2009) or message authentication code (MAC) (Sha, Wang, & Shi, 2009). Data confidentiality can

be achieved by using some standard cipher with required mode of operation (Sha, Wang, & Shi, 2009). In addition, VANETs may require some more security attributes such as location privacy, anonymity, non-repudiation, message freshness, and timelines. Although, one could achieve authentication, data integrity and confidentiality using symmetric key cryptography, services like anonymity and non-repudiation require public key cryptographic primitives. There have been many schemes (Huang, 2011), addressed to security concern for VANETs, which are based on public key infrastructure (PKI). Some schemes (Wasef, Jiang, & Shen, 2008), (Raya & Hubaux, 2007), (Lin, Sun, Ho, & Shen, 2007) have considered identity based infrastructure (IBC) (Shamir, 1985). for VANETs security.

One of the major concerns in PKI-based VANETs security is how effectively one can revoke misbehaving vehicles' keys/credentials. There are several reasons for timely key revocation because of malicious activity, equipment malfunction, change of ownership, and private key/public key compromise (Studer, Shi, Bai, & Perrig, 2009). Furthermore, identity of revoked vehicle needs to be sent to others active vehicles in VANETs to inform them that messages from the revoked vehicles should be ignored. Public key revocation by Certificate Revocation List (CRL) is a classic approach, but has some drawbacks such as the CRL size, CRL distribution, periodicity of the CRL update, etc. For instance, if the number of revoked vehicles is high as well as if for privacy preservation pseudonyms are used then for per revoked vehicle CRL contains about 43,800 identities for each anonymous certificate of that vehicle (Studer, Shi, Bai, & Perrig, 2009). According to the estimation of size of CRL based on the data of Annual Revocation Rate Triggers 2005, 1.37×10^{12} pseudonyms are required to be revoked every year (Studer, Shi, Bai, & Perrig, 2009). In order to reduce the CRL size, alternative methods are also suggested such as Bloom filter (Liu, Zhong, & Zhang, 2007), (Lu, Lin, Zhu, Ho, & Shen, 2008), group signature (Wasef, Jiang, & Shen, 2008), (Huang, 2011), (Abumansoor & Boukerche, 2011) and short term anonymous certificates (Lin, Sun, Ho, & Shen, 2007), (Nowatkowski, 2010). Another drawback in CRL approach is that, if we revoke a vehicle that has sent some false information only once for some selfish reason then we also end up ignoring useful information later sent by that vehicle. For example, vehicle might send false information for getting congestion free road (Ruj, Cavenaghi, Huang, Nayak, & Stojmenovic, 2011). Haas, Hu, & Laberteaux (2009) argued that it is necessary to distinguish between false or correct information rather than good or bad node efficiently, because a delay of even one second might cause traffic disturbance and accident. Ruj, Cavenaghi, Huang, Nayak, and Stojmenovic (2011) termed this problem as data-centric misbehavior detection. Ruj, Cavenaghi, Huang, Nayak, and Stojmenovic (2011) assumed that vehicle that misbehaves is not revoked but instead appropriate punishment must be imposed (by TA) in terms of some monetary fine, assuming the node will be discouraged and will not send any false information further. In (Ruj, Cavenaghi, Huang, Nayak, & Stojmenovic, 2011), each node independently detects false alert message (and misbehaving node) by observing behavior of node, after sending out the alert message. The decision is based on estimated vehicle position, freshness of messages, order of the vehicles (sender and receiver), and event on the road. Rawat, Bista, Yan, and Weigle (2011) proposed an algorithm to secure vehicular communication with the help of trust measured for the given period using a probabilistic approach. In their proposed algorithm they measure the trust of the received message by making observations for a given time interval to verify whether the received message is from a legitimate vehicle or not. Recently, Adigun, Amar Bensaber, and Biskri (2012) proposed a protocol that preserves authentication, non repudiation, and location privacy for vehicles' node while exchanging pseudonyms with other nodes. They

use both symmetric and asymmetric cryptographic primitives to exchange pseudonyms.

In this chapter, we discuss VANETs security attributes and misbehavior vehicle detection based data centric and non data centric approaches. We review some existing schemes, observe merits and limitations, and compare the schemes. The contribution of the chapter is summarized as follows.

- Discuss essential security requirements and potential threats of VANETs;
- Review data-centric misbehavior detection schemes;
- Review non data-centric misbehavior detection schemes; and
- Compare schemes in terms of their security strengths and weaknesses.

The chapter is organized as follows: Section 2 gives some preliminaries – security requirements for VANETs, attacks and threats scenarios, and possible defense mechanisms. Section 3 reviews misbehaviour detection schemes. We conclude the chapter in Section 4.

PRELIMINARIES

Security Requirement for VANETs

In order to make VANETs safe, following security properties assist in achieving VANETs security (Raya, Papadimitratos, Aad, Jungels, & Hubaux, 2007), (Wasef, Jiang, & Shen, 2008):

- **Data Origin Authentication:** Incoming messages are to be authenticated by the receiver in order to confirm that messages are actually sent by the sender vehicle. As messages are transmitted over-the-air, it is important to resist bogus message attack, impersonation attack, and Sybil attack.
- **Entity Authentication:** Apart from data origin authentication, authentication of

the communicating entity is an important factor, as the receiving entity requires to confirm authentication of the sender side before accepting or forwarding its request.

- **Data Integrity:** Data integrity means none of the bits are altered during message transmission. It provides assurance to the receiving entity that messages are exactly same as sent by the sender vehicle. It is also important to detect message alteration (if any) and discard it accordingly.

- **Non-Repudiation:** Non-repudiation prevents a vehicle denying sending of a message after committing it previously. This property is useful for identifying vehicle misbehaving or misguiding traffic situation.

- **Availability:** In VANETs, required information may not reach the intended recipients on time. A delay of even few seconds may cause abnormal situations like accident. To prevent this, VANETs need to be denial-of-service resistant so that availability of service and information as well is guaranteed.

- **Revocation:** When a vehicle misbehaves, it is necessary to revoke the vehicle for making VANETs safe and economically sound. It is also important to broadcast identities of all revoked vehicles in a VANET in a timely manner.

- **Anonymity:** A vehicle may not want to reveal its real identity. For such purpose, anonymous identities can be used. A unique identity needs to be assigned to vehicle for identification which can be used in case of any dispute.

Attacks/Threats in VANETs

VANETs may suffer from one or more attacks (Raya, Papadimitratos, Aad, Jungels, & Hubaux, 2007), (Wasef, Jiang, & Shen, 2008) as mentioned below:

- **Bogus Message Attack:** Adversary can send false (fake) messages to target vehicle to take advantage of the situation. For example, the adversary can send fake message to show congestion on some uncongested road so that adversary himself gets better traffic conditions.

- **Message Replay Attack:** Adversary can send a message that has already been sent previously, in order to disturb the traffic.

- **Message Modification Attack:** Adversary can modify a valid message during or after transmission, and then tries to fool the receiver of the message.

- **Impersonation Attack:** Adversary can behave as another legitimate vehicle or RSU to serve its own purpose.

- **Denial-of-Service (DoS) Attack:** Adversary could jam the communication channel by flooding large number of messages to target system. Adversary can also drop important messages before they reach to destination. As the communication channel in VANETs is wireless, DoS attack is a major concern in VANETs security.

- **Sybil Attack:** Sybil attack is a kind of impersonation attack in which a single vehicle impersonates multiple vehicles. By means of Sybil attack, adversary creates a scenario in which other vehicle observes that there are more number of vehicles around him but actually there is only one vehicle controlled by adversary.

- **Movement Tracking Attack:** Adversary may trace a vehicle's physical position and its moving patterns by observing the messages on wireless communication channel.

- **Identity Reveal Attack:** Adversary may find out the real identity of a legitimate vehicle by eavesdropping and analyzing the messages that were communicated on a wireless channel.

Defense Against Attacks in VANETs

The Trusted Authority (TA) requires managing an infrastructure for vehicles certificates issuance and revocation. The traditional public key infrastructure is a well-studied setup, which could provide required services (with certain customization) for VANETs security. Below is a brief review of mechanisms (Sun & Fang, 2009) that are in place for VANETs certificate/credential management.

Certificate-Based Revocation by TA

Certificate revocation by certificate revocation list (CRL) is not suitable for VANETs, as the size of the CRL is large and revocation of certificate may happen very often. The CRL needs to be distributed across the entire network timely, which is a bottleneck in VANETs. In order to mitigate the weakness of the traditional CRL-based revocation approach in the context of VANETs security, Raya, Papadimitratos, Aad, Jungels, and Hubaux (2007) proposed credential revocation protocols for VANETs as follows:

- **Revocation Protocol of the Tamper-Proof Device (RTPD):** RTPD is aimed at revoking the tamper-proof device (TPD) equipped with each vehicle. With this protocol, the TA sends a revocation message encrypted with the target vehicle's public key as and when revocation is required. Upon receiving the revocation request, the TPD decrypts the message and erases all the stored keys, which prevent the vehicle from signing any more messages. It is noted that the revocation messages have to be sent through RSUs, which is again a bottleneck of the system.
- **Distributed Revocation Protocol (DRP):** This protocol can be used in ad-hoc mode when fixed infrastructure is unavailable. Once an infrastructure point is reached, neighbouring nodes (vehicles/RSUs) will report accusations to the TA who, then, will distribute the updated CRL.

CRL-Based Revocation by RSU

CRL-based revocation is an indirect approach by which the infrastructure points (i.e., RSUs) require to revoke credential of the vehicle. If RSUs are physically unreachable or are blocked intentionally by misbehaving vehicles, receiving vehicles locally validate the signature on received message. The advantage of this approach is that vehicles never download the entire CRL. Instead, they will be informed by the RSUs about the revoked vehicle.

MISBEHAVIOR DETECTION SCHEMES

Detection of misbehaving node (OBUs/RSUs) is necessary for getting maximum benefits from all the applications of VANETs. Misbehavior detection schemes broadly divided into two categories - *data-centric* misbehavior detection and *non data-centric* misbehavior detection. The meaning of data-centric is to believe on information rather than source of information. Some of the misbehavior detection schemes run on every vehicle whose work is to detect misbehavior on the basis of collected information. This information is gathered by means of received messages (e.g., beacons and alert message). After misbehavior detection, vehicle reports to nearest TA. While in some schemes, misbehavior is detected by TA itself which may require additional overhead, as it may take long time for detection.

Evaluation Criteria

We consider following evaluation criteria in order to compare reviewed schemes of VANETs safety.

- **Sybil Attack**: In Sybil attack, a single vehicle impersonates multiple vehicles. This criterion should be satisfied by any misbehavior detection schemes for detecting correct misbehavior.

- **Location Privacy**: This criterion compares various misbehavior detection schemes according to the capability of location privacy of each vehicle by other vehicles of network.

- **Message Loss**: Various misbehavior detection schemes exist which are based on information gathered by neighboring vehicle and/or voting. Therefore, it is important to evaluate scheme for message loss.

- **False Message**: Vehicles may send *alert* and/or *beacon* messages with false information to satisfy their selfish motive. This criterion shows whether, misbehavior detection schemes consider false message or not.

Data-Centric Misbehavior Detection

Golle, Greene, and Staddon (2004) proposed a scheme for detecting incorrect information and identifying misbehaving node. Their scheme is based on two assumptions: 1) nodes can tell "at least some" other node apart from one another, and 2) a prudence argument that accurately reflects adversarial behavior in a VANET. In (Golle, Greene, & Staddon 2004), every node follows a model that has knowledge about all possible events and actions. Every node validates received message and if it agrees with all the conditions of the model then node accepts the message otherwise rejects that message and treats the corresponding node as malicious. The approach in (Golle, Greene, & Staddon 2004) defends against Sybil attack. The scheme did not discuss for location privacy as well as there is no mechanism for updating the model in future, which is necessary, because new

adversary might join network after construction of model (Haas, Hu, & Laberteaux, 2009).

Abumansoor and Boukerche (2011) proposed a trust model for the issue of None Line of Sight (NLOS), created by moving obstacles (e.g. trucks). In this approach, delivery of messages is affected among those vehicles that are in the range of each other. For example, in Figure 2 vehicle A, observes that an emergency vehicle is approaching. It responds to this event by sending an alert message to the vehicle behind it, so that they slow down their speeds. But, vehicle B is not able to get this alert message because of the position of bus C (moving obstacle). This type of NLOS situation gives impression that a neighbor is a malicious node (Abumansoor & Boukerche 2011), because it does not give response to the corresponding messages. To establish trust between vehicles and to overcome effects of moving obstacle, proposed trust model (Abumansoor & Boukerche 2011) consists of five modules. In the first module, vehicles determines its own and neighbor's location information by localization services and received beacons and alert messages, respectively. In the second module, each vehicle maintains a database of neighbor's current location and their mobility

Figure 2. Obstacles can prevent a vehicle from receiving safety messages (Abumansoor & Boukerche 2011)

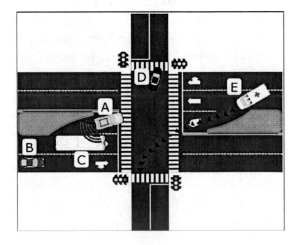

pattern. This module continuously monitors database to check inconsistency. If any inconsistency is determined then third module comes into existence which works for the verification of neighbor's location and updates awareness database. In the fourth model, trust score for each neighbor is calculated according to the location reachability. With the basic node information, vehicle records three more information - NLOS flag indicator, number of hops and a trust score. The last module is related to the trust evaluation according to the requirement of application and services.

In Vehicle Analysis and Evaluation Scheme (VEBUS) (Schmidt, Leinmueller, Schoch, Held, & Schaefer, 2008), each vehicle is classified as trustworthy, untrustworthy or neutral. The VEBUS contains various modules. The first module is related to behavior analysis, which contains several sub-modules. Previously received beacons messages are basis of the behavior analysis. Each sub-module gives positive or negative rating according to the analysis of specific properties such as movement analysis, maximum beaconing frequency and sensor-proofed position. The second module is output aging function, in which a weighted average of past history, for each sub-module is considered. Influence of each sub-module is decided by a gain function g_{mod} which is specified in compound module. In next module, positive votes of other vehicles known as recommendation are considered. Final evaluation (r_{agg}) is done by including this recommendation into local trust (r_{local}). In final module, trustworthiness is checked by applied threshold on (r_{agg}). This approach has advantage of prevention from message loss.

Molina-Gil, Caballero-Gil, and Caballero-Gil (2010) proposed a scheme based on cooperative groups for detecting false traffic warning messages. In (Molina-Gil, Caballero-Gil, & Caballero-Gil 2010), every node maintains two reputation lists. One is individual reputation list (IRL), based on direct observation and other one is global reputation list whose value is shared between other

nodes in the network and RSUs. When vehicle V detects an event, it behaves as leader and forms a cooperative group. When vehicle receives message that does not correspond to its real environment, it enters identity of sender to IRL. All vehicle of the group view and confirm the existence of this event by sending a signed message to the leader. The leader will aggregate all signatures and generate warning message. However, leader may create aggregate message with false data by using signature of other opponents. Haas, Hu, and Laberteaux (2009) proposed an idea to impose fine on such type of vehicle. This may discourage vehicle to further sending false information. To achieve location privacy, pseudonyms are used with some restriction on its lifetime so that working of the proposed algorithm is not affected.

Sha, Wang, and Shi (2009) proposed a role-differentiated cooperative deceptive data-detection and filtering mechanism called RD[4] for detecting false data. They classify data into two categories: redundant data that share similar information with the data reported previously and false data that generated by malfunction vehicle and vehicles into four categories: RSU, public vehicle, regular vehicle and vehicle itself. When vehicle V receives an alert message on accident, it firstly makes a judgment about the truth of this alert, based on its own signal strength observation and the signal strength reporting the same event from others.

We summarize the strengths and weaknesses of the reviewed schemes in Table 1.

Non Data-Centric Misbehavior Detection

Ghosh, Varghese, Gupta, Kherani, and Muthaiah (2010) proposed a scheme based on root-cause analysis. The scheme is specially designed for detecting misbehavior in case of post crash notification (PCN). The scheme considers two cases for sending false PCN alerts by misbehaving vehicle. One is the absence of crash (false alert message) and second one is the incorrect crash

Table 1. Comparisons of Data-Centric Misbehavior Detection Schemes

Scheme	Sybil Attack	Location Privacy	False Message	Message loss
Golle, Greene, and Staddon (2004)	No	Yes	No	Yes
Abumansoor and Boukerche (2011)	Yes	Yes	No	Yes
Ruj, Cavenaghi, Huang, Nayak, and Stojmenovic (2011)	No	No	No	Yes
Molina-Gil, Caballero-Gil, and Caballero-Gil (2010)	Yes	Yes	No	Yes
Sha, Wang, and Shi (2009)	No	Yes	No	No
Schmidt, Leinmueller, Schoch, Held, and Schaefer (2008)	Yes	No	No	No

Yes: the scheme suffers from the attack No: the scheme does not suffer from the attack

location information (true message with incorrect location information). The basis of the scheme is deviation between actual and expected trajectory of vehicle. The major drawback of this scheme is that it does not work with frequently changing pseudonyms. Moreover, authors make an assumption that malicious node always sends its correct location information, which looks unreasonable.

Kim, Studer, Dubey, Zhang, Perrig, Bai, Bellur, and Iyer (2010) proposed a multisource detection model to filter out invalid messages. They assume less number of malicious vehicles as compared to legitimate. Their model is based on two main components: a threshold curve that rate the event according to the relative distance between the vehicle and event and a Certainty of Event (CoE) curve that represents the confidence level of received messages.

Raya, Papadimitratos, Aad, Jungels, and Hubaux (2007) proposed a distributed scheme, Local Eviction of Attackers by Voting Evaluators (LEAVE), with the assumption of large set of honest vehicles. The vehicle, who detects a misbehaving neighbor, broadcasts warning messages to other vehicles. If a vehicle receives a warning message from another vehicle, it adds it to an accusation list. If the number of warning messages for a particular vehicle is greater than a predefine threshold (exclusion threshold) then it is added to a blacklist and a disregard message is sent to other vehicle to inform them (see Figure 3). Finally, the vehicle reports to its nearest TA. After receiving this report, TA uses RTC (Revocation of the Trusted Component) and RC²RL (Revocation using Compressed Certificate Revocation Lists) (Raya, Papadimitratos, Aad, Jungels, & Hubaux,

Figure 3. Example of LEAVE (Raya, Papadimitratos, Aad, Jungels, & Hubaux, 2007)

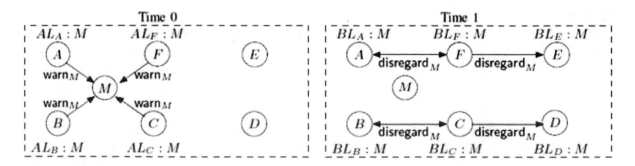

2007) for permanent revocation of misbehaving vehicle. In RC²RL, Bloom filter compression (probabilistic data structure) (Lu, Lin, Zhu, Ho, & Shen, 2008), (Raya, Papadimitratos, Aad, Jungels, & Hubaux, 2007) is used for reducing the size of CRL. In RTC, TA instructs the misbehaving vehicle to erase all cryptographic material it stores and halts its operation upon completion of the protocol.

Sun, Zhang, and Fang (2007) proposed a scheme based on identity based cryptosystem (IBC). In the initialization phase of the scheme, pseudonyms are assigned to vehicles by TA for a period of time. The pseudonyms are used to encrypt messages. Vehicles periodically transfer data to storage site at RSU. With the help of storage site and TA, traffic management and accident monitoring are being supervised.

Lin, Sun, Ho, and Shen (2007) proposed a scheme called as GSIS for security assurance and privacy preserving in VANETs. In GISS, group signature is used for V2V communication and identity based cryptography for V2I communication. In GISS, four types of entities are considered - MM (membership manager), TM (tracing manager), RSU and OBU. Before joining to the vehicular network, vehicles need to be registered to MM, and preloaded with system parameter and their own private key. The interesting feature of GISS is that if number of revoked vehicles is less than some predefined threshold then the verifier-local revocation scheme is invoked; otherwise, group public key and private key of all unrevoked vehicles are updated.

Moore, Raya, Clulow, Papadimitratos, Anderson, and Hubaux (2008) proposed a scheme, known as Stinger, for removing misbehaving vehicle. This scheme is based on suicide attack and removes both accused and accuser from the network. The motivation behind Stinger is that, removing a malicious vehicle is much simpler and faster when decision is taken by a single vehicle without waiting for voting result by all other neighbor vehicles. In Stinger, when a benign

Figure 4. Stinger (Moore, Raya, Clulow, Papadimitratos, Anderson, & Hubaux 2008)

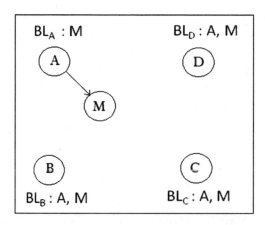

vehicle A detects some misbehaving vehicle M, it broadcasts a sting (A, M) after receiving this sting, all other vehicles blacklist both A and M (see Figure 4). The benign vehicle comes out from blacklist by means of voting, similar to LEAVE (Raya, Papadimitratos, Aad, Jungels, & Hubaux, 2007).

Vulimiri, Gupta, Roy, Muthaiah, and Kherani (2010) proposed a probabilistic framework for identifying misbehavior in case of PCN alert which uses SVA alerts as secondary information. They believe that, in response to alert message called as primary alert, correlated information or alerts, called as secondary alerts are generated. All events in (Vulimiri, Gupta, Roy, Muthaiah, & Kherani, 2010) are partitioned into event classes, which characterized by set of attributes. The probability of primary alert is being true, is calculated by combining, the probability of each event class and probability of secondary event corresponding to this primary alert. The main limitation of this framework is that it does not consider message loss and Sybil attack.

Tsang, Au, Kapadia, and Smith (2007) proposed a system in which service provider can blacklist misbehaving user (vehicle's owner) without revealing user's identity. In their scheme, user first obtains the credentials from Group Manager and then uses it for anonymously authenticating to Service Providers (SPs). All SPs maintain their own blacklist and they first check communicating user's status whether the user is in the blacklist or not. If the user is not in the blacklist then the ticket for requested service is granted.

Daeinabi and Rahbar (2011) proposed a misbehavior detection scheme, called DMV (Detection of Malicious Vehicle), for detecting vehicle that drops or duplicates received packets. In DMV, every vehicle is tagged by some distrust value (*Td*) and whole network is divided into cluster. Each cluster has one main cluster-head and one spare cluster-head (with lowest distrust value). Each vehicle *V* is monitored by its neighbors (say, verifier) which has lower or equal *Td*. If verifier nodes observe some abnormal behavior, they report the identification code of vehicle *V* to TA. The limitation with this approach is that, it has not considered messages with false information and anonymity of vehicles. It noted that consideration of Sybil attack is not required because it is based on packet drop and duplicate received packets and if an adversary impersonates as multiple vehicles and sends false information then it is not an issue.

Palomar, de Fuentes, Gonzlez-Tablas, and Al-caide (2012) proposed an approach in which sender has to perform some non-negligible amount of computation prior to sending the warning message. The scheme assumed that the computation cost (Proof of Work) will discourage vehicle to send false information. However, false data can still be created.

Cao, Kong, Lee, Gerla, and Chen (2008) proposed a Proof-of-Relevance (PoR) scheme for detecting false data injection attack. The scheme is designed to verify that the vehicle is authentically relevant to the event it has reported. PoR includes three phases as follows. In first phase of report generation, a report is generated and signed by vehicle *V*, when it detects some event on road. The validity of report requires at least *T* signature on it. For this purpose vehicle *V* should try to collect signed message for the same event broadcasted by the other witnesses which is done in second phase of signature collection. Report verification is third phase of this approach in which report is verified by means of validity of signature. The main drawback of this scheme is

Table 2. Comparisons of Non Data-Centric Misbehavior Detection Schemes

Scheme	Sybil Attack	Location Privacy	False Message	Message loss
Ghosh, Varghese, Gupta, Kherani, and Muthaiah (2010)	Yes	Yes	No	Yes
Kim, Studer, Dubey, Zhang, Perrig, Bai, Bellur, and Iyer (2010)	No	No	No	Yes
Raya, Papadimitratos, Aad, Jungels, and Hubaux (2007)	Yes	No	No	Yes
Moore, Raya, Clulow, Papadimitratos, Anderson, and Hubaux (2008)	Yes	Yes	No	Yes
Vulimiri, Gupta, Roy, Muthaiah, and Kherani (2010)	Yes	Yes	No	Yes
Daeinabi and Rahbar (2011)	Yes	Yes	Yes	No
Palomar, de Fuentes, Gonzlez-Tablas, and Al-caide (2012)	Yes	No	No	Yes
Cao, Kong, Lee, Gerla, and Chen (2008)	Yes	Yes	No	Yes
Sun, Zhang, and Fang (2007)	Yes	No	No	Yes
Lin, Sun, Ho, and Shen (2007)	Yes	No	No	No
Tsang, Au, Kapadia, and Smith (2007)	Yes	No	Yes	Yes

Yes: the scheme suffers from the attack No: the scheme does not suffer from the attack that it has significant amount of delay to detect false data because vehicle will spend time for collecting digital signature.

Table 2 shows comparison of non data-centric misbehavior detection schemes discussed above.

CONCLUSION

Safety in VANET is an important concern, as VANET involves human lives. Misbehavior detection on time could not only optimize traffic, money, but also prevent road accident. VANETs safety can be achieved with cryptographic primitives and non cryptographic primitives. However, schemes for VANETs safety should guarantee authentication of entities and data integrity, in order to protect the network against unauthorized message injection and alteration. Depending on VANETs application, suitable primitives need to be chosen and the scheme should be carefully design such that VANET can resist to Sybil attacks and message loss, achieves location privacy, and minimizes false positives. We reviewed some schemes, classifying them into *data centric* and *non data centric* misbehaving detection, aiming at identifying strengths and weaknesses of the schemes. We compare the schemes in each category with respect to schemes' security against Sybil attacks, location privacy, false message and message loss. The result in Table 1 and 2 shows that most of the schemes fail to address these important attributes, which are essential for VANETs safety.

We note that conventional CRL based misbehaving nodes revocation is insufficient to address the safety measures of VANET. As a result, structures like hashing, tree based identity revocation could, possibly, enable faster revocation mechanism in VANETs.

REFERENCES

Abumansoor, O., & Boukerche, A. (2011). A cooperative multi-hop location verification for non line of sight (NLOS) in VANET. In *Proceedings of the IEEE Wireless Communications and Networking Conference (WCNC)* (pp. 773-778). IEEE.

Adigun, A., Amar Bensaber, B., & Biskri, I. (2012). Proof of concept of a security based on lifetime of communication's pseudonyms for the VANETs. In *Proceedings of the Second ACM International Symposium on Design and Analysis of Intelligent Vehicular Networks and Applications* (pp. 111-114). ACM.

Akhlaq, M., Aslam, B., Alserhani, F., Awan, I. U., & Mellor, J. (2009). Empowered certification authority in VANETs. In *Proceedings of the International Conference on Advanced Information Networking and Applications Workshops* (pp. 181-186). IEEE.

Cao, Z., Kong, J., Lee, U., Gerla, M., & Chen, Z. (2008). Proof-of-relevance: Filtering false data via authentic consensus in vehicle ad-hoc networks. In *Proceedings of the IEEE Conference on Computer Communications Workshops* (pp. 1-6). IEEE.

Daeinabi, A., & Rahbar, A. G. (2011). Detection of malicious vehicles through monitoring in vehicular ad-hoc networks. *Multimedia Tools and Applications*, 1–14.

Ghosh, M., Varghese, A., Gupta, A., Kherani, A. A., & Muthaiah, S. N. (2010). Detecting misbehaviors in VANET with integrated root-cause analysis. *Ad Hoc Networks*, 8(7), 778–790. doi:10.1016/j.adhoc.2010.02.008.

Golle, P., Greene, D., & Staddon, J. (2004). Detecting and correcting malicious data in VANETs. In *Proceedings of the ACM International Workshop on Vehicular Ad Hoc Networks* (pp. 29-37). ACM.

Haas, J. J., Hu, Y. C., & Laberteaux, K. P. (2009). Design and analysis of a lightweight certificate revocation mechanism for VANET. In *Proceedings of the ACM International Workshop on Vehicular Internetworking* (pp. 89-98). ACM.

Huang, Z. (2011). *On reputation and data-centric misbehavior detection mechanisms for VANETs (Technical report)*. Ottawa, Canada: University of Ottawa.

Kim, T. H. J., Studer, A., Dubey, R., Zhang, X., Perrig, A., & Bai, F. … Iyer, A. (2010). VANET alert endorsement using multi-source filters. In *Proceedings of the ACM International Workshop on Vehicular Internetworking* (pp. 51-60). ACM.

Lin, X., Sun, X., Ho, P. H., & Shen, X. (2007). GSIS: A secure and privacy-preserving protocol for vehicular communications. *IEEE Transactions on Vehicular Technology, 56*(6), 3442–3456. doi:10.1109/TVT.2007.906878.

Liu, B., Zhong, Y., & Zhang, S. (2007). Probabilistic isolation of malicious vehicles in pseudonym changing VANETs. In *Proceedings of International Conference on Computer and Information Technology* (pp. 967-972). IEEE.

Lu, R., Lin, X., Zhu, H., Ho, P. H., & Shen, X. (2008). ECPP: Efficient conditional privacy preservation protocol for secure vehicular communications. In *Proceedings of the IEEE Conference on Computer Communications* (pp. 1229-1237). IEEE.

Menezes, A. J., van Oorschot, P. C., & Vanstone, S. A. (1996). *Handbook of applied cryptography*. Boca Raton, FL: CRC Press, Inc. doi:10.1201/9781439821916.

Molina-Gil, J., Caballero-Gil, P., & Caballero-Gil, C. (2010). Enhancing collaboration in vehicular networks. In *Proceedings of International Conference on Cooperative Design, Visualization, and Engineering* (pp. 77-80). IEEE.

Moore, T., Raya, M., Clulow, J., Papadimitratos, P., Anderson, R., & Hubaux, J. P. (2008). Fast exclusion of errant devices from vehicular networks. In *Proceedings of the IEEE Conference on Sensor, Mesh and Ad Hoc Communications and Networks (SECON)* (pp. 135-143). IEEE.

Nowatkowski, M. E. (2010). *Certificate revocation list distribution in vehicular ad hoc networks (Technical report)*. Atlanta, GA: Georgia Institute of Technology.

Palomar, E., de Fuentes, J. M., Gonzlez-Tablas, A. I., & Al-caide, A. (2012). Hindering false event dissemination in VANETs with proof-of-work mechanisms. *Transportation Research Part C, Emerging Technologies, 23*, 85–97. doi:10.1016/j.trc.2011.08.002.

Rawat, D. B., Bista, B. B., Yan, G., & Weigle, M. C. (2011). Securing vehicular ad-hoc networks against malicious drivers: A probabilistic approach. In *Proceedings of International Conference on Complex, Intelligent and Software Intensive Systems (CISIS)*, (pp. 146-151). CISIS.

Raya, M., & Hubaux, J. P. (2007). Securing vehicular ad hoc networks. *Journal of Computer Security, 15*(1), 39–68.

Raya, M., Papadimitratos, P., Aad, I., Jungels, D., & Hubaux, J. P. (2007). Eviction of misbehaving and faulty nodes in vehicular networks. *IEEE Journal on Selected Areas in Communications, 25*(8), 1557–1568. doi:10.1109/JSAC.2007.071006.

Ruj, S., Cavenaghi, M. A., Huang, Z., Nayak, A., & Stojmenovic, I. (2011). On data-centric misbehavior detection in VANETs. In *Proceedings of the IEEE Vehicular Technology Conference* (pp. 1-5). IEEE.

Schmidt, R. K., Leinmueller, T., Schoch, E., Held, A., & Schaefer, G. (2008). Vehicle behavior analysis to enhance security in VANETs. In *Proceedings of the IEEE Vehicle-to-Vehicle Communications Workshop*. IEEE.

Sha, K., Wang, S., & Shi, W. (2009). RD⁴: Role-differentiated cooperative deceptive data detection and filtering in VANETs. *IEEE Transactions on Vehicular Technology, 59*(3), 1183–1190.

Shamir, A. (1985). Identity-based cryptosystems and signature schemes. In *Proceedings of Advances in Cryptology (CRYPTO'84)* (pp. 47-53). Springer.

Studer, A., Shi, E., Bai, F., & Perrig, A. (2009). Tacking together efficient authentication, revocation, and privacy in VANETs. In *Proceedings of the IEEE Communications Society Conference on Sensor, Mesh and Ad Hoc Communications and Networks* (pp. 484-492). IEEE.

Sun, J., & Fang, Y. (2009). Defense against misbehavior in anonymous vehicular ad hoc networks. *Ad Hoc Networks, 7*, 1515–1525. doi:10.1016/j.adhoc.2009.04.013.

Sun, J., Zhang, C., & Fang, Y. (2007). An ID-based framework achieving privacy and non-repudiation in vehicular ad hoc networks. In *Proceedings of the IEEE Military Communications Conference* (pp. 1-7). IEEE.

Tsang, P., Au, M. H., Kapadia, A., & Smith, S. W. (2007). Blacklistable anonymous credentials: Blocking misbehaving users without TTPs. In *Proceedings of the ACM Conference on Computer and Communications Security* (pp. 72-81). ACM.

Vulimiri, A., Gupta, A., Roy, P., Muthaiah, S. N., & Kherani, A. A. (2010). Application of secondary information for misbehavior detection in VANETs. In *Proceedings of the IFIP International Conference on Networking* (pp. 385-396). IFIP.

Wasef, A., Jiang, Y., & Shen, X. (2008). ECMV: Efficient certificate management scheme for vehicular networks. In *Proceedings of the IEEE Globecom*. New Orleans, LA: IEEE.

Wasef, A., Lu, R., Lin, X., & Shen, X. (2010). Complementing public key infrastructure to secure vehicular ad hoc networks. *Wireless Communications, 17*(5), 22–28. doi:10.1109/MWC.2010.5601954.

Chapter 8
Intrusion Detection in Vehicular Ad-Hoc Networks on Lower Layers

Chong Han
University of Surrey, UK

Ibrahim Abualhaol
Khalifa University, UAE

Sami Muhaidat
Khalifa University, UAE

Mehrdad Dianati
University of Surrey, UK

Rahim Tafazolli
University of Surrey, UK

ABSTRACT

Vehicular Ad-Hoc Networks (VANETs) are a critical component of the Intelligent Transportation Systems (ITS), which involve the applications of advanced information processing, communications, sensing, and controlling technologies in an integrated manner to improve the functionality and the safety of transportation systems, providing drivers with timely information on road and traffic conditions, and achieving smooth traffic flow on the roads. Recently, the security of VANETs has attracted major attention for the possible presence of malicious elements, and the presence of altered messages due to channel errors in transmissions. In order to provide reliable and secure communications, Intrusion Detection Systems (IDSs) can serve as a second defense wall after prevention-based approaches, such as encryption. This chapter first presents the state-of-the-art literature on intrusion detection in VANETs. Next, the detection of illicit wireless transmissions from the physical layer perspective is investigated, assuming the presence of regular ongoing legitimate transmissions. Finally, a novel cooperative intrusion detection scheme from the MAC sub-layer perspective is discussed.

DOI: 10.4018/978-1-4666-4691-9.ch008

INTRODUCTION

Intelligent Transportation Systems (ITS) and related applications have been designed and deployed in recent years. ITS applications, which consist of safety-related and non-safety-related applications, provide timely life-critical information, help drivers and traffic controlling centre with efficient decision making, and provide commercial, leisure, and convenience services. As the key component of ITS, Vehicular Ad-Hoc Networks (VANETs) have attracted the attention in both industrial and academic communities because of the commercial potentials and the required research for their realization. The cooperative, self-organizing communication terminals in VANETs relay information with each other and also exchange data with fixed network infrastructure (Seyfi, Muhaidat, Jie, & Uysal, 2011). Communications are enabled among vehicles and infrastructure to enhance transportation safety, efficiency, and entertainment via Vehicle-to-Vehicle (V2V) communications and Vehicle-to-Infrastructure (V2I) communications. New research is required for developing many of the components and the architecture of such communications systems. Potential applications are diverse and pervasive. Safe and efficient transportation systems can be realized through fast dissemination of road and traffic information (i.e., updates regarding collisions, incidents, congestion, surface, and weather conditions) and coordination of vehicles at critical points such as highway entries and other intersections. In addition, many new applications will be facilitated, e.g., cooperative high-speed internet access from within the vehicular network, cooperative downloading, network gaming among passengers of adjacent vehicles, and virtual, video-enabled meetings among co-workers travelling in different vehicles, and previously unimagined products which tend to be spawned by new communications services. Currently, it is easy to imagine realistic-experience multimedia meetings for personal or business purposes, as well as for emergency services. In medical services, paramedics and other first responders could link with hospitals and other expert bases from incident sites and from ambulances and other emergency vehicles. For public transport, streaming multimedia offers new possibilities for security, fleet management, and advertising, in particular for buses and trains. New data services also enable new user-charging strategies for new or improved efficiency public services. Such services are only possible with enabling communication and networking technologies. Different service requirements must be addressed piecemeal-wise with different mobile technologies and different standards. The goal of VANETs is to offer economical, common, reliable, high rate, low latency systems for terrestrial communications-based services. They will use many industry standard components and cooperatively share the radio spectrum, a finite and shared resource.

Designs of protocols for different layers take into account the special characteristics of VANETs, such as the real-time constrains, high node mobility, frequent changing topology, large network scale, and the ad hoc communication structure. However, the vehicular networks turn to be vulnerable to various attacks naturally. Security in VANETs has attracted more attentions recently, since any malicious intruder with access to the open medium of VANET can threaten the information security and as a consequence affects the passengers' safety. Safety related applications have to be protected from malicious manipulation, such as altered messages, false alarm, and repudiation, in order to avoid potential harm to vehicle drivers due to failure to make correct decisions. Non-safety applications needs to avoid attacks from illicit users in terms of traffic jamming, overloading, and/or having a non-cooperative behavior (e.g., dropping packets). Moreover, manufactures and service providers need protection of their commercial profit. Hence, there is a need for a secure and reliable system to ensure that messages with life-critical information will not be modified, discarded or forged by any attacker. Since existing prevention based techniques are limited in their effectiveness and emerging intrusions, intrusion detection becomes an indispensable part to maintain the security in VANETs.

This chapter focuses on the problems of intrusions in vehicular networks. The chapter starts by presenting the security requirements of vehicular networks and their impacts on the security of these networks. A literature review is given on the existing efforts on the security for vehicular networks. Then, different types of intrusions in such networks are classified, and some relevant intrusion examples are introduced. To tackle the intrusion problem, we present novel intrusion detection schemes from PHY and MAC layers perspectives. Analytical and simulation results demonstrate how the proposed schemes on PHY and MAC layers help maintain a secure VANET.

BACKGROUND

Security Requirements in Vehicular Ad Hoc Networks

Security has become an important challenge in vehicular ad hoc networks, since it is essential to assure that life-critical information cannot be inserted, modified, or truncated by an attacker, where only authorized users should be able to generate/manipulate the transmitted information. Due to the special characteristics of VANETs, security protocols and techniques used in traditional wired networks cannot be applied directly. In VANETs, the following security requirements are worth consideration:

- **Authentication:** Entity authentication is required to ensure that the communicating entities are legitimate. In other words, authentication helps avoid illegitimate vehicles to generate and disseminate ITS data. In addition, data authentication is also needed to ensure that the contents of the received data is neither altered nor replayed.

- **Availability:** Network unavailability may be resulted in by Denial of service (DoS) intrusion attacks due to channel jamming, or traffic overloading. Legitimate users could temporarily lose access to the network to share life-critical information.

- **Non-Repudiation:** Non-repudiation is necessary to prevent users from denying the transmission or contents of their messages. Vehicles causing accidents or injecting malicious data must be reliably identified.

- **Privacy:** Preserving users' privacy is mainly related to preventing disclosure of their real identities. Besides identity privacy, location privacy needs to be protected from malicious users since it may expose the places of interest of legitimate users. Complete privacy preservation can achieve users' privacy, however, it helps intruders to cover malicious behaviors as well. Hence, conditional privacy preservation is of vital importance to secure vehicular communications.

- **Access Control:** It is necessary to define the operations that each entity in the network can perform to realize access control in the networks. In addition, any misbehaving entity should be revoked from the network to protect the safety of other legitimate entities in the network.

State-of-the-Art of Security in VANETs

Standardization and deployment efforts have been made in the domain of vehicular network security. The IEEE 1609.2 ("IEEE Trial-Use Standard for Wireless Access in Vehicular Environments - Security Services for Applications and Management Messages," 2006) has been proposed as the security service standard for Wireless Access in Vehicular Environments (WAVE) networking stack. The IEEE 1609.2 security infrastructure is based on industry standards for Public Key Infrastructure (PKI), including the support of Elliptic Curve Cryptography (ECC), WAVE certificate formats, and the hybrid encryption methods, in order to provide secure services for WAVE communications. The security requirements of data authentication and non-repudiation can be achieved by employing digital signatures, thus asymmetric cryptography (i.e., each entity has a public/private key pair) has been used to implement digital signatures. Any entity can use its unique private key to generate a unique digital signature for outgoing messages. When a message is received, the receiver node verifies the digital signature of the message by using the sender's public key. Successful digital signature verification implies that the content of the message has not been altered, and only the sender can generate this message. In this way, data authentication and non-repudiation are achieved. For entity authentication, the public key of each entity must be authentic to all the entities in the network. Therefore, Certificate Authorities (CAs) need to generate an authentic certificate for each entity in the network binding the entity's public key to its identity in this PKI. The IEEE 1609.2 standard considers the issues of authentication and non-repudiation, but it does not define protection mechanisms for other abovementioned concerns. In addition, the IEEE 1609.2 has left a lot of open issues including

1. **Privacy:** Although anonymous certificates in PKI can guarantee identity privacy, they do not support location privacy. Even though anonymous keys do not indicate the relationship between the identity and the key holders to non-CAs, privacy can still be hijacked by logging the messages containing the same given key (Raya & Hubaux, 2005b). Therefore, it is possible for attackers to track legitimate users in order to collect informa-

tion about places of interest of other users, or even discover a user's identity (e.g., by associating the user with the place of living).

2. **Revocation:** A Certificate Revocation List (CRL), which contains the certificate identities of misbehaving nodes, has to be issued by the CA and broadcast by the infrastructure, so as to revoke a vehicle in PKI. Since the network scale of VANETs is expected to be large, the dissemination of CRLs may suffer from long delays. In addition, efficient revocation scheme is required especially in vehicular networks with few numbers of RSUs. Meanwhile, it is also important to avoid revoking innocent vehicles, which may broadcast disputed message due to an unintentional misoperation.

3. **Authentication Efficiency:** Taking into account the frequent broadcast of messages, which include the current position of the vehicle, driving speed, and other telematic information, the efficiency of authentication is challenging. Each vehicle has to check the CRLs against a large number of certificates and verify senders' signatures on the received messages in a timely manner. Hence, there is a necessity for mechanisms that can accelerate the authentication in PKI to ensure reliable VANETs (Wasef, Rongxing, Xiaodong, & Xuemin, 2010).

Besides the IEEE 1609.2 standard, efforts are also put into the design of security mechanisms. Authors in (Abdalla, Abu-rgheff, & Senouci, 2007) suggest using the keys in another way by using short-term and long-term certificates. The long-term certificates are used for authentication, while short term certificates are employed for data transmission using public/private key cryptography. The multiple certificates help reduce the overhead of certificates notification and maintain good cryptography for data transmission.

Authors in (Ren, Ren, Lou, & Zhang, 2008), (Rongxing, Xiaodong, Haojin, Pin-Han, & Xuemin, 2008) and (Xiaodong et al., 2008) suggest employing the group signature to guarantee the requirements of authentication and privacy. However, a major drawback of this kind of proposals is that it causes a great overhead and verification delay. Every time a new vehicle enters a reference area, the group public key and the vehicle session key for each vehicle that belongs to the group must be changed and transmitted. Due to the node mobility in VANETs, the group is changing all the time, and the signatures and keys frequently changed and transmitted.

Privacy is also one of the most important security requirements of VANETs. Anonymous certificates are used for vehicles to authenticate other legitimate users while preserving their privacy, since anonymous certificates do not contain any information about the real identity of the certificate holder. Only the CA has the ability to identify the real identity of a vehicle from its anonymous certificate. However, vehicles can be tracked by malicious entities because of the same certificate they use all the time. To avoid being tracked, randomly changing identities (also called pseudonym) is suggested. However, the changing identities may lead to a situation where malicious users can easily change their identities to avoid punishment. To keep malicious users away from exploiting the use of pseudonyms in the networks, Liu et al. propose a probabilistic scheme in (Bisheng, Yiping, & Shiyong, 2007) which records both dishonest and trustable users using Bloom filters. The authors assume that each car has tamper-proof device (TPD) carrying out secure operations. In the scheme, feedbacks are periodically broadcast by each vehicle to its neighbours. Every feedback message is parsed and used to update its credit to indicate the honesty level.

Certificate Authority (CA) can certainly help secure the networks from illicit users, but the centralized controlling structure requires infrastructure support. The CA has been suggested by (Raya & Hubaux, 2005a) and (Xiaodong et al., 2008) to handle all the operations of certificates such as the generation, renewing and revoking. CAs must be responsible in initiating keys, storing, managing and broadcasting the CRLs. The dissemination of CRLs and the centralized certificate operations result in large latency to the networks.

Besides the use of PKI and CRL, additional security mechanisms providing location privacy, distributed and fair revocation, and efficient authentication can be designed to efficiently secure VANETs. Due to the special opportunities in VANETs, vehicles are equipped with on-board radar sensors, which makes it possible to check claimed positions in received messages with sensor data. Yan et al. (Yan, Olariu, & Weigle, 2008) present a system where an omni-directional radar sensor is equipped as the virtual 'eye' of a vehicle in order to verify the positions of nodes in the neighborhood. Due to the limited observation range of radar sensors, the authors propose a routing topology that allows the usage of radar information cooperatively in the neighborhood. In addition, although the radar transmission range is quite limited, vehicles receive reports of their neighbours' GPS coordinates. By comparing the information from radar sensors and reports with the received messages, vehicles can corroborate the real position of their neighbours and isolate malicious vehicles. In (Malaney, 2005), an approach based on techniques using Received Signal Strength (RSS) analysis is proposed to offer a robust position based verification system for secure network access. In (Abumansoor & Boukerche, 2012), the authors present a location verification protocol among cooperative neighbouring vehicles to overcome a non-line-of-sight (NLOS) condition and secure the integrity of localization services for VANETs. The simulation results show that the proposal improves neighborhood awareness in NLOS scenarios, and help maintain localization service integrity and reliability.

While most of the existing studies on VANET security focus on security mechanisms and solutions on VANET communications, there are not many works on intrusion detection on lower layers, (i.e., Physical Layer and Medium Access Control sub-layer). Design of efficient intrusion detection solutions on lower layers can improve the ability of protecting legitimate users from intruders, as well as collaborate with security mechanisms on higher layers. Intrusion detection on the lower layers helps add a second defense wall to enhance the security of VANETs. Therefore, a secured and reliable system to ensure that messages with life critical information will not be inserted or modified or delayed or even discarded by attackers.

INTRUSION IN VANETS

The special characteristics of VANETs make the networks susceptible to a wide range of intrusion attacks. In this section we discuss the most relevant intrusions threatening VANETs and inter-vehicular communications. A classification of these intrusions is provided and some concrete intrusion examples are discussed. As reviewed in the Section Background, there are no works on intrusion detection on lower layers (i.e., PHY and MAC) in VANETs. Hence, we propose two solutions on PHY and MAC layers to detect intrusions in VANETs, which are able to operate separately and cooperatively. These two schemes are elaborated in details in this section.

Intrusion Classification

It is very important to define the various intrusion attacks in the networks before considering corresponding protection mechanisms. This subsection presents the possible types of intrusions in VANETs.

- **Intentional or Unintentional Intrusion:** An intentional intrusion is mounted by an entity aiming voluntarily to intrude the networks, in order to undermine transmission between other nodes, obtain users privacy, or benefit itself by disseminating faulty information. Conversely an unintentional intrusion includes unintentional interruption of transmission, working on the same frequency band, or even just transmission errors.

- **Internal or External Intrusion:** An internal intrusion attack comes from a legitimate member of the networks. In other words, other nodes identify this member as an authenticated member, which means messages from this internal intrude member are likely to be accepted and believed as true information. This type of attack is probably the most critical one because it is not easy to identify the credibility of the message, if the protection mechanism works purely on the check of authentication. External intruders are non-authenticated entities, which are considered as intruders by legitimate members. However, the impact of the interruption of data transmission and occupation of the shared medium may cause difficulties for legitimate users to communicate with each other in the networks. In addition, if the external intruder is able to mock the identity of other legitimate users, the intrusion is also difficult to detect.

- **Independent or Coordinated Intrusion:** Independent intrusion usually occurs more frequently than a coordinated attack, since intruders need to know other intruders' identity and intention in order to collaborate to make a successful intrusion. Although coordinated intrusion appears rarely, it cannot be easily detected and may result in fatal danger or inconvenience to legitimate users in VANETs.

Intrusion Examples

This section shows several example scenarios with intrusions.

- **Denial of Service (DoS):** In this type of intrusion attack, the intruder tries to prevent legitimate vehicles from accessing the network services and disrupt the functioning of the system. This can be done by jamming the shared wireless channel, overloading the network, or having a non-cooperative behavior (e.g., dropping packets). With a DoS attack, critical information for safety-related ITS applications couldn't be delivered through the networks.

- **Information Inconsistency:** In this case, the intruder injects and disseminates false information in the network to affect the behavior of other vehicles. The motive might be to introduce flawed information to convince other legitimate users to take an alternative route, giving themselves a clear path. Relay nodes can easily mount such attacks. In general, an intruder can modify messages including location, vehicle status, identifier, and critical information (e.g. emergency break, and car crash). To punish the malicious users, the non-repudiation is very important.

- **Masquerading:** In masquerading attack, the intruder uses a false identity pretending to be another legitimate user, hence to be granted another vehicle privileges.

- **Identity Disclosure:** An illicit user could try to track other vehicles in order to gather information about a particular user. The adversary may only deploy a single DSRC receiver to collect information about a single compromising location, or couple information gained by the DSRC receiver with other information such as digital camera pictures. In addition, RF fingerprinting can be used to identify and recognize a vehicle.

- **Selfish Behavior:** It is natural that some drivers (even legitimate users) may try to obtain specific advantages from the network. Selfish drivers send false information to divert traffic and gain a clear path on their own routes.

- **Eavesdropping:** The malicious user monitors the network traffic to extract any sensitive/private information.

INTRUSION DETECTION ON PHY LAYER

In this section, we address the problem of detecting malicious roadside attackers that transmit forged warning messages to the vehicles passing its transmission range. We consider the scenario as shown in Figure 1, where the Road Side Unit (RSU) is transmitting the real legitimate messages to the vehicles within its transmission range, while the intruder disseminates false alarms to other users. In our system, we assume the presence of one legitimate transmission and one intrusion in the reference area. Local detection based on energy detection is implemented individually by collecting samples, which correspond to the time

Figure 1. System model

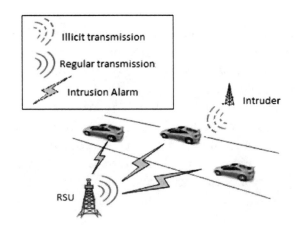

bandwidth product to produce its decision based on the collected energy. If the detected power is within a specific area, it transmits an intrusion alarm to the RSU, which warns the rest vehicles in the reference area about the intrusion.

The performance of intrusion detection depends on two factors: 1) the probability of false alarm P_{fa}, i.e., when it reports an intrusion while the received signal is just an interfering noise or a regular legitimate signal; 2) the probability of miss detection P_{md}, i.e., whenever the intruder is present while the node declares no intrusion. We aim to minimize P_e, i.e., the joint probability of P_{md} and P_{fa}, by using a new detection scheme with multiple detection thresholds.

Multi-Thresholds Intrusion Detection Algorithm for VANETs

When studying intrusion detection in VANETs, we need to consider the regular communications ongoing in the network, hence with assuming the presence of legitimate signal, the detection problem will become as the following:

$$H_0 : y_j \begin{cases} n_j & with\ 1-p \\ S_j + n_j & with\ p \end{cases}$$

$$(1)$$

$$H_1 : y_j \begin{cases} I_j + n_j & with\ 1-p \\ I_j + S_j + n_j & with\ p \end{cases} \quad (2)$$

Where p denotes the probability of legitimate transmission presence, which means that $(1-p)$ refers to the case of legitimate signal absence. Then the energy of the received signal at the energy detector is the test statistics, denoted as Y if M samples are collected in both cases:

$$H_0 : Y = \sum_{j=1}^{M} y_j^2 = \begin{cases} \sum_{j=1}^{M} n_j^2 & (1-p) \\ \sum_{j=1}^{M} [S_j + n_j]^2 & p \end{cases}$$

$$(3)$$

$$H_1 : Y = \sum_{j=1}^{M} y_j^2 = \begin{cases} \sum_{j=1}^{M} [I_j + n_j]^2 & (1-p) \\ \sum_{j=1}^{M} [I_j + S_j + n_j]^2 & p \end{cases}$$

$$(4)$$

It is difficult to detect malicious intruders in the presence of regular legitimate transmissions especially if they use the same transmission system, thus we propose a multi-threshold detection strategy that improves the detection performance and enables the detector to distinguish between the different received signals indirectly based on each signal's SNR.

In our system, we assume the legitimate signal is present in the network with probability p, while the intrusion signal appears in the network with probability α. To compute the probability of detection in the presence of legitimate signals, we need to evaluate the expectation and variance of the received signal in both hypotheses.

The test statistics Y with Gaussian approximation will have the following mean and variance assuming the legitimate signal absence:

$$Y \sim \begin{cases} N\left(M\sigma_n^2, 2M\sigma_n^4\right) & H_0 \\ N\left(M(\sigma_I^2 + \sigma_n^2), 2M\left(\sigma_I^2 + \sigma_n^2\right)^2\right) & H_1 \end{cases}$$

$$(5)$$

On the other hand, when we take into account the legitimate transmission presence, the decision statistics becomes:

$$Y \sim \begin{cases} N\left(M(\sigma_S^2 + \sigma_n^2), 2M(\sigma_S^2 + \sigma_n^2)^2\right) & H_0 \\ N\left(M(\sigma_I^2 + \sigma_S^2 + \sigma_n^2), 2M(\sigma_I^2 + \sigma_S^2 + \sigma_n^2)^2\right) & H_1 \end{cases}$$

$$(6)$$

Applying Gaussian approximation, the probability of false alarm can be found from (6) in H_0 considering the presence of a legitimate signal as:

$$P_{fa} = P\{Y > \lambda \mid H_0\} = Q\left(\frac{\lambda - M \sigma_n^2}{\sqrt{2M}\sigma_n^2}\right)(1-p) + Q\left(\frac{\lambda - M\left((\sigma_S^2 + \sigma_n^2)\right)}{\sqrt{2M}\left((\sigma_S^2 + \sigma_n^2)\right)}\right)p \quad (7)$$

While the probability of detection based on the expectation and variance of Y in H_1 can be evaluated as:

$$P_d = P\{Y > \lambda \mid H_1\} = Q\left(\frac{\lambda - M\left(\sigma_I^2 + \sigma_n^2\right)}{\sqrt{2M}\left(\sigma_I^2 + \sigma_n^2\right)}\right)(1-p) + Q\left(\frac{\lambda - M\left((\sigma_I^2 + \sigma_S^2 + \sigma_n^2)\right)}{\sqrt{2M}\left((\sigma_I^2 + \sigma_S^2 + \sigma_n^2)\right)}\right)p \quad (8)$$

Each detection threshold λ relates to a pair of (P_d, P_{fa}) which represents the Receiver Operation Characteristics (ROC) of the energy detector. When a legitimate signal exists in the network, we have to be aware of its transmission power to differentiate it from malicious attacks, thus deriving a one fixed threshold value based on the probability of false alarm in (7) will not reduce the false alarms caused by the legitimate presence, since a fixed value will not reflect the cases for different hypotheses tests: no transmission, just legitimate or just intrusion, and the existence of both signals in the network at the same time. Hence, a new multi-threshold algorithm is proposed and explained in the following.

In energy detection, the detector cannot distinguish between two signals given that it performs blind detection based on the signal's energy level without any information about its structure, modulation type, or any signal features. This will cause a high false alarm rate by detecting the legitimate signal instead of the intruder. We know that the key enabling for raising the detection probability and reducing the false alarm rate is to set an optimal detection threshold taking the tradeoff between the probability of miss detection and the probability of false alarm into account. Motivated by this requirement, the need for a multi-thresholds algorithm is essential.

Based on the transmission power of each signal, there are 3 possible cases: 1) the legitimate power is higher than the intruder's power (i.e., $\sigma_S^2 > \sigma_I^2$), which represents the worst case with high false alarm rate based on the traditional detection threshold algorithm. When, the high legitimate power affects the detector ability to detect the intruders transmitted with lower power, and any signal with energy higher than the threshold of intrusion triggers alarms. Hence, we propose a new three-threshold algorithm to overcome the false alarm issue and improve the system performance. We first define three thresholds for the case as shown in Figure 2.

As shown in Figure 2, the three thresholds λ_1, λ_2 and λ_3 are defined by:

$$\lambda_1 = \sigma_n^2\left(\sqrt{2M}Q^{-1}(P_{fa}) + M\right) \quad (9)$$

$$\lambda_2 = \left(\sigma_S^2 + \sigma_n^2\right)\left(\sqrt{2M}Q^{-1}\left(P_{fa}\right) + M\right) \quad (10)$$

Figure 2. The proposed three-thresholds when $\sigma_S^2 > \sigma_I^2$

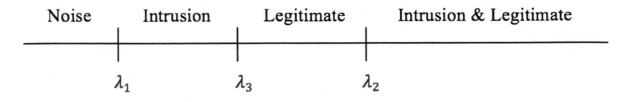

$$\lambda_3 = \left(\sigma_I^2 + \sigma_n^2\right)\left(\sqrt{2M}Q^{-1}\left(P_{fa}\right) + M\right) \qquad (11)$$

The flow chart of the proposed three-threshold algorithm for the case when $\sigma_S^2 > \sigma_I^2$ is given in Figure 3. In this algorithm, the detector compares the received energy with λ_1, if it is less, then there is no intruder since there is no transmission ongoing in the network. If the received energy is above λ_1 then there is a transmission either legitimate or intrusion or both. Then received energy is compared with λ_3 that depends on the intruder's power (shown in (11)), if it is less, it declares the presence of intruder by transmitting an intrusion alarm to the RSU which will broadcast a warning message regarding the detected intruder. On the other hand, if received energy above λ_3, the algorithm compares the energy with λ_2 to determine if the received signal is just a legitimate signal (e.g., when the energy is lower than λ_2), or both legitimate and intrusion signals exist (e.g., when it is higher than λ_2).

In the second case, the legitimate signal power is less than the intruder power ($\sigma_S^2 < \sigma_I^2$). In this case, two-threshold algorithm is enough for efficient detection as given in Figure 4, since it is easy to detect the higher power intrusion signal by comparing the received energy with λ_1 to check if there is a need to continue the detection process or stop it based on the presence of any transmissions. When there is a transmission the algorithm compares the energy with λ_2 to announce the detection of an intrusion if it is above λ_2. If the energy is less than λ_2, this means it is just a legitimate transmission and no attacks predicted as given in Figure 5.

Finally, in the third case the legitimate power equals the intruders' ($\sigma_S^2 = \sigma_I^2$), which basically means a higher false alarm rate because of the detector's inability to differentiate the intruder from legitimate signals (Figure 6). Similar to the previous case, the algorithm starts comparing the received signal energy with λ_1 to ensure the existence of a transmission. However, as shown in Figure 7, since the intrusion and legitimate

Figure 3. Flow chart of the proposed three-thresholds algorithm when $\sigma_S^2 > \sigma_I^2$

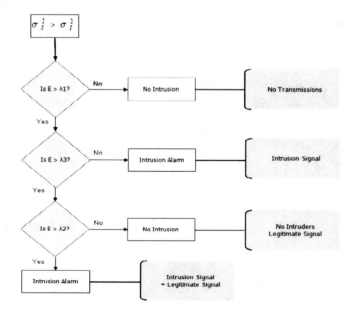

Figure 4. The proposed two-thresholds scheme when $\sigma_S^{\ 2} < \sigma_I^{\ 2}$

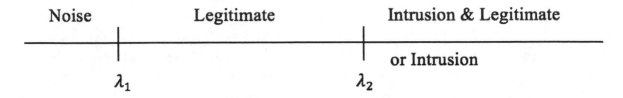

Figure 5. Flow chart of the proposed two-thresholds algorithm when $\sigma_S^{\ 2} < \sigma_I^{\ 2}$

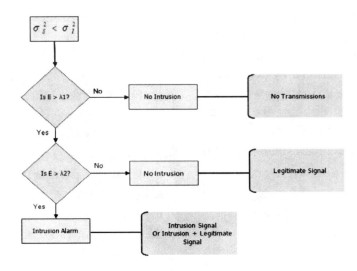

transmissions transmit at exactly the same power, the detector would detect the legitimate as intruder falsely, which lead to higher probability of false alarm.

The detection and false alarm probabilities P_d and P_{fa} with multiple thresholds can be given as:

$$P_d = Q\left(\frac{\lambda_1 - M\left(\sigma_I^2 + \sigma_n^2\right)}{\sqrt{2M}\left(\sigma_I^2 + \sigma_n^2\right)}\right)(1-p) + Q\left(\frac{\lambda_2 - M\left(\sigma_S^2 + \sigma_I^2 + \sigma_n^2\right)}{\sqrt{2M}\left(\sigma_S^2 + \sigma_I^2 + \sigma_n^2\right)}\right)p \quad (12)$$

$$P_{fa} = Q\left(\frac{\lambda_1 - M\sigma_n^2}{\sqrt{2M}\sigma_n^2}\right)(1-p) + Q\left(\frac{\lambda_2 - M\left(\left(\sigma_S^2 + \sigma_n^2\right)\right)}{\sqrt{2M}\left(\left(\sigma_S^2 + \sigma_n^2\right)\right)}\right)p \quad (13)$$

The effects of the new multi-threshold algorithm on the system performance will be shown

in the simulation results. The evaluation of the proposed algorithm performance in terms of the probability of false alarm P_{fa}, and the probability of miss detection P_{md} that formulates the probability of error P_e as

$$Pe = P\left(fa, H_0\right) + P\left(md, H_1\right) = P_{fa|H_0}P\left(H_0\right) + P_{md|H_1}P\left(H_1\right) \quad (14)$$

where

$$P_{md} = 1 - P_d, \ P\left(H_0\right) = 1 - \alpha, \ P\left(H_1\right) = \alpha.$$

Performance Analysis

To evaluate the performance of the proposed multi-threshold intrusion detection algorithm, simulations results from MATLAB are given in

Figure 6. The proposed two-thresholds scheme when $\sigma_S^2 = \sigma_I^2$

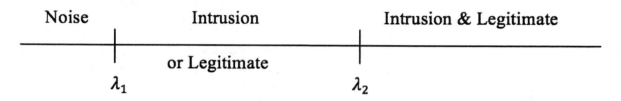

Figure 7. Flow chart of the proposed two-thresholds algorithm when $\sigma_S^2 = \sigma_I^2$

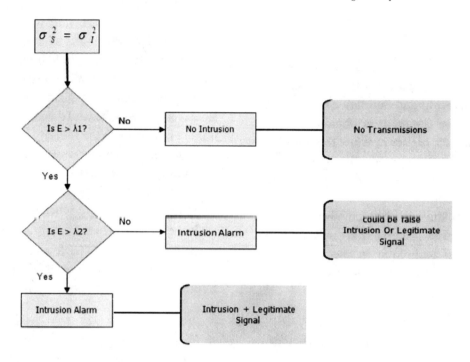

this sub-section. Major simulation parameters are given in Table 1.

To illustrate the behavior of the conventional energy detector, we plot the probability of detection versus the probability of false alarm with different intrusion's SNR without considering the presence of legitimate transmissions in Figure 8. It is obvious that increasing the probability of false alarm leads to higher probability of detection that includes both the right and the false detections. Figure 8 implicitly highlights the fact that reducing the detection threshold will improve the detection probability for given false alarm probability.

To check at which SNR the detector performance reaches the maximum in terms of probability of detection and minimum false alarms, we plot P_d versus SNR by varying P_{fa} in Figure. 9. The optimum performance exists when SNR is greater than -10 dB when P_{fa} is 0.01 as stated in Table 1.

To evaluate the proposed scheme, both analytical and simulation probability of error for

Table. 1 Simulation parameters

Number of samples M	5000
Probability of false alarm P_{fa}	0.01
Probability of legitimate presence p	0.4
Probability of intrusion presence α	0.5
Noise variance σ_n^2	1
Transmission modulation	BPSK

different values of α (the intruder's presence probability) is given in Figure 10. It can be seen that the analytical results and simulation results match very well in the figure. It is obvious from the Figure 10 that for higher α, when the intruder is present more in the network, the probability of error increases due to the increase in the miss detection probability.

To evaluate the performance of the proposed intrusion detection system based on the proposed multi-threshold technique in the presence of regular legitimate transmissions, we compare its

functionality based on three metrics (i.e., P_{md}, P_{fa}, and P_e) respectively in the three scenarios.

In scenario 1 ($\sigma_S^2 > \sigma_I^2$), Figure 11 shows the comparison of P_{md} among traditional one threshold, two thresholds, and three-threshold schemes. From Figure 11, we can see that the three-threshold algorithm achieves higher P_{md}, while the other two algorithms produce more reliable detection.

From Figure 12, the three-threshold algorithm reaches lower false alarm rate, which also reduces the overall error probability as shown in Figure 13. The proposed three-threshold intrusion detection algorithm outperforms the other two algorithms on the performance of false alarm and errors. However, since successful detection of intrusions is more important to the security, a reliable detection system instead of the decreased false alarm probability is more important to VANETs. Hence, the optimum detection performance is obtained by using just two-threshold scheme in this scenario.

In the scenario when $\sigma_S^2 < \sigma_I^2$, the performance of the three metrics differ from that in the previous case, as shown in Figure 14-Figure 16. The figures illustrate that the two-threshold and the

Figure 8. Conventional detector performance vs. probability of false alarm

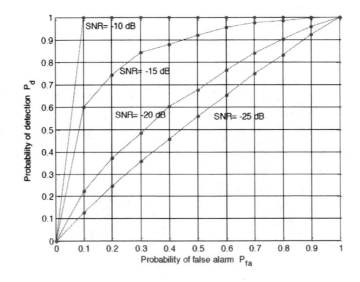

Figure 9. Conventional energy detector P_d vs. SNR

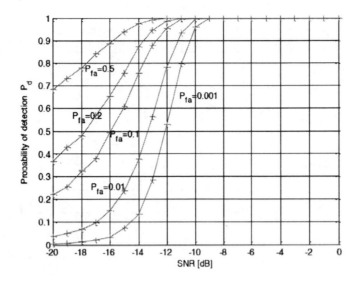

Figure 10. The proposed scheme P_e vs. intrusion SNR for different values of α

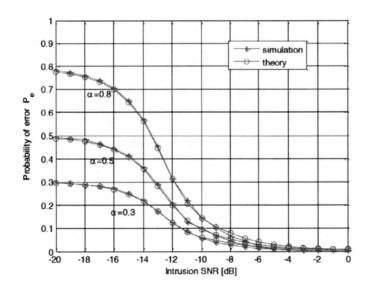

three-threshold algorithms have similar performance in terms of miss detection, and false alarm which yield the same error probability. Their performance outperforms the one-threshold algorithm. In this case, two-threshold algorithm is enough since it achieves the similar improvement on the performance in terms of the three metrics.

In the last scenario, when $\sigma_S^2 = \sigma_I^2$, the three algorithms all have the same performance in terms of false alarm rate and probability of miss detection, as shown in Figure 17 and Figure 18. In Figure 19, the minimum value of probability of error is 0.2 instead of 0, because of the existence of false alarm due to the detector's incapability to distinguish between the legitimate signal and

Figure 11. P_{md} vs. intruder's SNR for different thresholds when $\sigma_S^2 > \sigma_I^2$

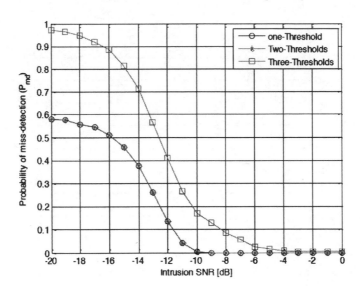

Figure 12. P_{fa} vs. intruder's SNR for different thresholds when $\sigma_S^2 > \sigma_I^2$

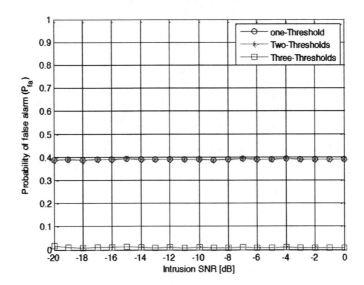

the intrusion signal based on their equal average power.

In this subsection, a novel multi-threshold intrusion detection scheme for vehicular networks is proposed, which operates on the PHY layer. The proposed multi-threshold scheme enhances the reliability of the intrusion detection in VANET, and improves the performance in terms of the probability of miss detection, the probabilities of

false alarm and error. The performance of the proposed multi-threshold scheme can be affected by the transmission powers of both legitimate and intrusion signals and the estimated noise variance. The trade-off between detection efficiency and the probability of false alarms should be considered for specific requirements of the network.

Figure 13. P_e vs. intruder's SNR for different thresholds when $\sigma_S^2 > \sigma_I^2$

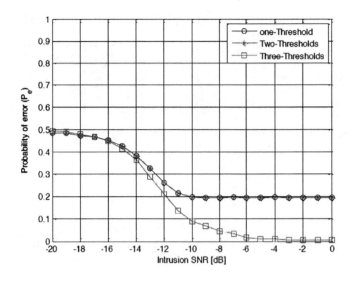

Figure 14. P_{md} vs. intruder's SNR for different thresholds when $\sigma_S^2 < \sigma_I^2$

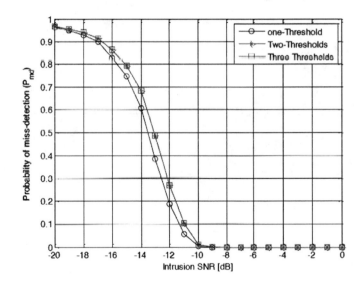

Intrusion Detection on MAC Sub-layer

Most of the existing security schemes for VANETs operate on higher layers, such as the link layer, the network layer, and the application layer. However, either from the perspective of the efficiency of transmission or from the concern of energy efficiency, security algorithms which work on lower layers are desired in vehicular networks. In this chapter, we have introduced a novel multi-threshold intrusion detection algorithm from a physical layer perspective. The proposed intrusion detection scheme is based on energy detection. From the simulation results, it can be seen that in the worst case (i.e., the transmission power of

Figure 15. P_{fa} vs. intruder's SNR for different thresholds when $\sigma_S^2 < \sigma_I^2$

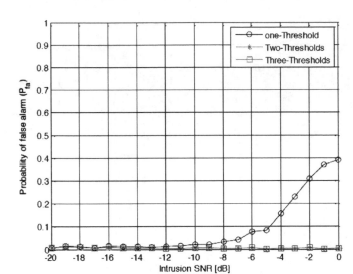

Figure 16. P_e vs. intruder's SNR for different thresholds when $\sigma_S^2 < \sigma_I^2$

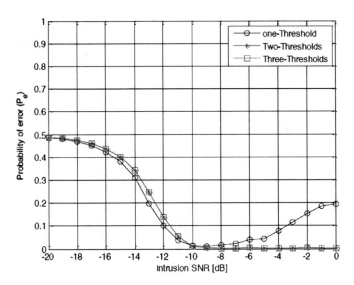

the legitimate user and malicious user are equal), the multi-threshold scheme cannot distinguish the intruder from legitimate user. Moreover, the results shown in Figure 18 and Figure 19 demonstrate higher false alarm probability and higher probability of errors, comparing to results in the other two scenarios as shown in Figure 12 and Figure 13, and Figure 15 and Figure 16. The intrusion

detection in such scenarios needs to be improved to obtain acceptable probabilities of false alarm and errors. In addition, if multiple intruders appear in the networks or multiple users attempt the channel at the same time, algorithms purely based on energy detection will fail to detect intrusions.

Hence, we propose an intrusion detection scheme which is implemented on the MAC sub-

Figure 17. P_{md} vs. intruder's SNR for different thresholds when $\sigma_S^2 = \sigma_I^2$

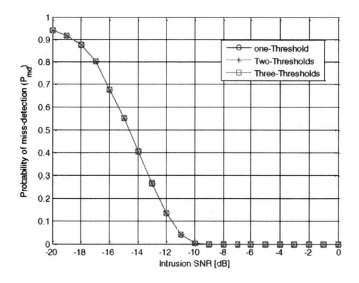

Figure 18. P_{fa} vs. intruder's SNR for different thresholds when $\sigma_S^2 = \sigma_I^2$

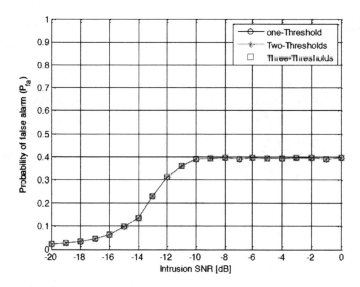

layer to help detect intruders. The main objective of the design is to detect intrusions (e.g., jamming and overloading attacks from external intruders) on the MAC sub-layer. The objectives of this study also include the investigation of the impacts on the system performance from the load of intrusion traffic and the numbers of intruders in the networks. This scheme works on each legitimate user, and can work in the scenarios without RSUs providing the user already knows the public key and transformation mechanism. Figure 20 shows a typical intrusion scenario with multiple intruders, a RSU, and legitimate users. It should be noted that intrusions could come from fixed devices and mobile users.

Figure 19. P_e vs. intruder's SNR for different thresholds when $\sigma_S^2 = \sigma_I^2$

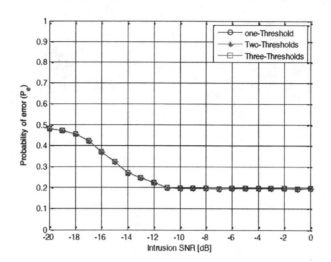

As discussed in the review of existing intrusions, external intruders may cause severe interruption of data transmission and occupation of the shared medium for legitimate users. The intrusions from external intruders differ from each other in particular scenarios. Some external intruders are not intentional to intrude the network. For instance, interruption can be caused by unintentional channel jamming when an external entity transmits on the same frequency. Some external intrusions aim to overload the network in order to block or limit the occupation of the channel by legitimate users. External intruders can be recognized as illicit users if the corresponding security mechanism is taken in the system. However, if the external intruder is able to mock the identity of other legitimate users, the intrusion becomes difficult to be detected, especially when the intruders are mobile.

In this proposed security scheme on MAC sublayer, we focus on the detection of external intrusions. The masquerading problem is also tackled in the proposal. We assume that: legitimated users communicate with RSUs via authentic certificates; RSUs and legitimated share a public key and a special mechanism of the transformation; and external intruders cannot figure out the public key and the transformation mechanism. Hence, legitimate users and the RSUs embed a special value in the header of each packet they transmit. This value is calculated using the public key and the transformation mechanism. To avoid being decoded, the transformation mechanism utilizes the time. For example, if the time is 13:02:63.897347, one transformation could be to use the last three digits' square plus the public key (i.e., 347^2 + public key). The encrypted information will be checked once a packet is received on the MAC sub-layer by legitimate users. Considering the transmission delay and processing delay, a small range of values will be accepted as correct encrypted value. In this example, if the value of three last digits derived by receivers is between 343 and 351, the sender will be authenticated by other legitimate receivers. On the contrary, external intruders do not know the existence of the encryption or the concrete algorithm of the encryption; hence they cannot receive any response from legitimate users since the packets they send are dropped on the MAC layer directly.

Although the standard IEEE 1609.2 provides security in terms of authentication and non-repudiation, the corresponding mechanisms work on higher layers in the protocol stack. It means

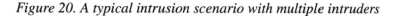

Figure 20. A typical intrusion scenario with multiple intruders

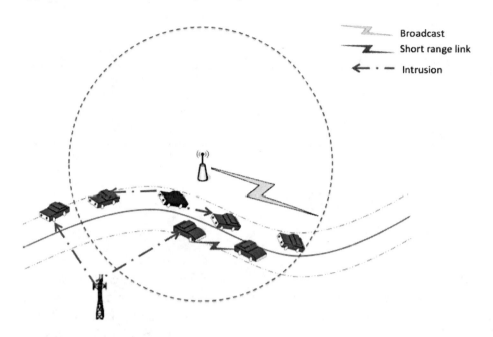

the packets need to be passed through link layer to network layer or application layer before the intrusion can be detected. In addition, on the MAC sub-layer, time is wasted on the transmissions of packets to and from the intruders as illustrated in the example given in Figure 21. In the conventional RTS/CTS mode of the IEEE 802.11p, a CTS packet is to be generated by the receiver and send to the source node, followed by the transmissions of the data and acknowledgement. Then, the packet is forwarded to upper layers for routing and taking actions on the application layer. Comparing with the conventional 802.11p, the proposed algorithm allows the receiver to drop the received RTS packet directly if an intrusion is detected. Hence, no more transmission (CTS, DATA, and ACK packets) between the legitimate user and the intruder will be started on the shared channel.

We evaluate the proposed intrusion detection MAC scheme using NS-2 (NS-2), from Lawrence Berkeley National Laboratory. The simulation scenario considers a reference area, where legitimate nodes, external intruders, and RSUs send messages to each other. The scenario comprises a 500 m by 500 m square area with Manhattan Grid pattern traffic, where nodes travel along the grids (i.e., representing lanes). We use Bonnmotion (Bonnmotion), which is a scenario generation and analysis tool, to define the mobility patterns in our Manhattan Grid and export it to ns-2 environment. The mobility model allows nodes to travel along the grids, change speed, stop for a while, and turn at the intersection, which is similar to mobility models in SUMO (SUMO). The maximum speed of vehicles is set to be 15 m/s. The communication range of the radios is set to 1000 m. The total number of intruders and legitimate users is 20 in the network. One RSU locates in the middle of the reference area. The data rate for the shared channel is set to 6 Mbps. The rest of the major simulation parameters are chosen from the IEEE 802.11p standard as listed in Table 2.

The objective of the first set of simulations is to investigate the impact of the traffic load of intrusions on the system performance. We consider scenarios with emergency messages generated in low frequency (i.e., 1 packet/second). The fre-

Figure 21. Channel access in IEEE 802.11p and the proposed scheme

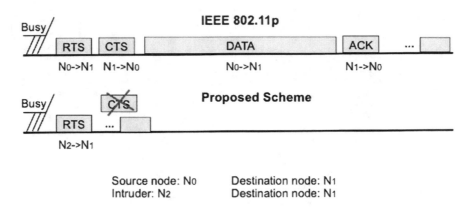

quency of AC0 flow is configured at a low level since emergency messages do not frequently occur in the network, while the frequency of traffic flows with higher priorities (i.e., AC1, AC2 and AC3) varies to offer the changing load of traffic flows. For legitimate users, the frequency of AC1, AC2 and AC3 is fixed to 10 Hz, which means they generate 10 packets for each access category per second. Intrusions vary from 10 Hz to 1000 Hz for each access category. In this scenario, we choose a user among the 20 nodes to behave as an intruder. To alleviate the impact from the geographical aspect (i.e., different positions of nodes, and different distance between two nodes), each node is selected as intruder once. The average value of the metric is calculated through multiple simulations. Minimum and maximum value are also recorded. Figure 22 shows the percentage of time when

the channel is occupied for transmissions due to intrusions verse the traffic load of the intruder.

It can be seen that as the load of intrusions increases, the time cost on intrusions increases in both schemes. When there is only one intruder in the network, the wasted time finally reaches the maximum value due to the fact that the intruder get saturated traffic flows. The proposed scheme can restrain the time wasted on intrusions within 10%, while the channel is occupied by intrusions in the IEEE 802.11p during half of the simulation time. In this kind of intrusion (e.g., overloading the network), the proposed scheme helps reduce the time on transmissions for intruders, and offers more opportunities to legitimate users.

Then, we use another set of simulations to observe the impact of number of intruders on the system performance. Changing the number

Table 2. Simulation parameters

Slot Time	13	Propagation delay	2
SIFS	32	DIFS	58
DataRate	6 Mbps		
AIFS[0]	2	AC0: CW(min, max)	(3, 7) time slots
AIFS[1]	3	AC1: CW(min, max)	(3, 15) time slots
AIFS[2]	6	AC2: CW(min, max)	(7, 1023) time slots
AIFS[3]	9	AC3: CW(min, max)	(15, 1023) time slots

Figure 22. Impact of the load of intrusions on the time spent due to intrusions

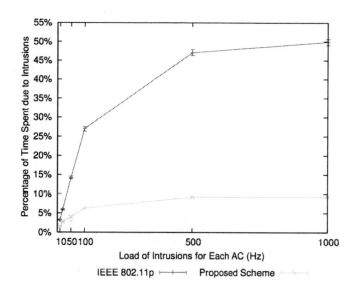

of intruders in the range of [0, 5], we vary the density of illicit users in the reference area. In this set of simulations, the frequencies of traffic flows of legitimate users are the same as previous simulations, while the frequency of traffic flows of AC1, AC2 and AC3 of intruders are fixed at 100 Hz. Figure 23 shows the percentage of time when the channel is occupied for transmissions due to intrusions verse the number of intruders. This figure also shows the improvement on channel occupancy of the proposed scheme comparing to the IEEE 802.11p. When 1/4 of the users are intruders, about 60% of the time is spent on the intrusions in the original 802.11p; while the proposed scheme saves 20-30% time for transmissions of legitimate users.

The proposed intrusion detection mechanism operates separately on MAC sub-layer for VANETs. The simulation results demonstrate significant improvement on the system performance in terms of the channel utilization comparing the benchmark 802.11p standard. Further enhancement can be designed on top of the scheme, such as cooperative intrusion detection algorithm. Information, e.g., the list of intruder IDs, can be shared among legitimate users and the RSUs.

However, selfish legitimate users may report peers as intruders in order to occupy the channel for themselves. Corresponding algorithms need to be designed taking into the potential threats in VANETs. Finally, the proposed scheme can also work with other security mechanisms on other layers.

FUTURE RESEARCH DIRECTIONS

Future vehicular network security mechanisms should comply with the special characteristics of the vehicular networks, i.e., high mobility, limited bandwidth, dynamic topologies, large scale, high node density, heterogeneous administration, and real-time constraints. Besides the types of intrusions mentioned in this chapter, emerging intrusions such as the group intruders and experienced hackers may bring potential danger to the security of VANETs. In the literature, some security schemes make decisions according to the reports collected from users. If a group of legitimate users (e.g., friends travelling together) turn into intruders, their reports can be identical to each other in order to fool the RSU or other users.

Figure 23. Impact of the number of intruders on the time spent due to intrusions

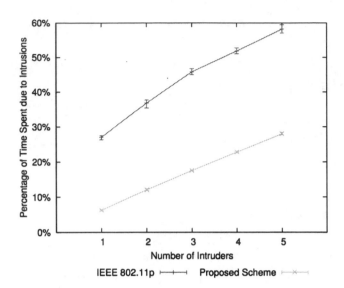

On the other hand, intruders or selfish users move from time to time and are able to change identities; hence it is difficult for legitimate users and RSUs to punish malicious users. Efficient non-repudiation intrusion detection mechanism is desired in the future ITS. It also has to be noted that sometimes the flaw messages transmitted by legitimate users may come from channel errors. Thus, the security mechanism has to take unintentional intrusions into account.

Finally, most of existing intrusion detection mechanisms operate on different layers on their own without utilizing the useful information collected on other layers. Hence, cross-layer cooperation for intrusion detection can be investigated in the future research. For instance, the proposed intrusion detection schemes in this chapter could be the first step of detection. Alarms may be alerted on the PHY/MAC layer; hence, other layers will start corresponding detection strategy to determine the attribute of the node behaviour. Meanwhile, other layers could make use of metrics (e.g., RSSI, transmission power, SNR) or alert from lower layers to assist the decision making in the intrusion detection system.

CONCLUSION

Security of vehicular ad hoc network is a major challenge, having a great impact on the future deployment and applications of ITS. A number of challenging intrusions exist in the vehicular environment. In this chapter we first give an overview of challenges for VANET security, and described potential security protocols for a variety of security objectives (e.g., authentication, encryption, privacy preservation, secure positioning, and identification of misbehaving nodes). Consequently, appropriate security mechanisms need to be in place to prevent messages of safety-related applications being modified by malicious entities, to protect legitimate users from eavesdropping and tracking, and to revoke illicit entities efficiently from the networks.

It is noticed that the existing security contributions are mainly working on higher layers such as network layer and application layer, which waste the occupation of the channel on transmissions to/from intruders. For instance, PHY and MAC layers pass all the packets to upper layers before giving any alert or dropping malicious packets. Channel is occupied for the transmissions due to intrusions instead of useful information dissemination for legitimate users. Hence, two intrusion detection mechanisms on the perspective of lower layers are proposed in this chapter. Actions are taken on lower layers to prevent the waste of time, which is usually cost on transmissions of flaw messages. The numerical and simulation-based results demonstrate significant improvement on system performance comparing to the IEEE 802.11p standard.

REFERENCES

Abdalla, G. M. T., Abu-rgheff, M. A., & Senouci, S. M. (2007). *Current trends in vehicular ad hoc networks*. Paper presented at the UBIROADS Workshop. New York, NY.

Abumansoor, O., & Boukerche, A. (2012). A secure cooperative approach for nonline-of-sight location verification in VANET. *IEEE Transactions on Vehicular Technology, 61*(1), 275 285. doi:10.1109/TVT.2011.2174465.

Bisheng, L., Yiping, Z., & Shiyong, Z. (2007). *Probabilistic isolation of malicious vehicles in pseudonym changing VANETs*. Paper presented at the Computer and Information Technology, 2007. New York, NY.

Bonnmotion. (n.d.). Retrieved from http://net.cs.uni-bonn.de/wg/cs/applications/-bonnmotion/

IEEE Trial-Use Standard for Wireless Access in Vehicular Environments—Security Services for Applications and Management Messages. (2006). *IEEE Std 1609.2-2006*, 0. doi: 10.1109/IEEESTD.2006.243731

Malaney, R. A. (2005). *Securing internal wi-fi networks with position verification*. Paper presented at the Global Telecommunications Conference. New York, NY. *NS-2*. (n.d.). Retrieved from http://www.isi.edu/nsnam/ns/

Raya, M., & Hubaux, J.-P. (2005a). The security of VANETs. In *Proceedings of the 2nd ACM International Workshop on Vehicular Ad Hoc Networks*. Cologne, Germany: ACM.

Raya, M., & Hubaux, J.-P. (2005b). The security of vehicular ad hoc networks. In *Proceedings of the 3rd ACM Workshop on Security of Ad Hoc and Sensor Networks*. Alexandria, VA: ACM.

Ren, W., Ren, K., Lou, W., & Zhang, Y. (2008). Efficient user revocation for privacy-aware PKI. In *Proceedings of the 5th International ICST Conference on Heterogeneous Networking for Quality, Reliability, Security and Robustness*. Hong Kong: ICST.

Rongxing, L., Xiaodong, L., Haojin, Z., Pin-Han, H., & Xuemin, S. (2008). *ECPP: Efficient conditional privacy preservation protocol for secure vehicular communications*. Paper presented at INFOCOM 2008. New York, NY.

Seyfi, M., Muhaidat, S., Jie, L., & Uysal, M. (2011). Relay selection in dual-hop vehicular networks. *IEEE Signal Processing Letters, 18*(2), 134–137. doi:10.1109/LSP.2010.2102017.

SUMO. (n.d.). Retrieved from http://sumo.sourceforge.net/

Wasef, A., Rongxing, L., Xiaodong, L., & Xuemin, S. (2010). Complementing public key infrastructure to secure vehicular ad hoc networks. *IEEE Wireless Communications, 17*(5), 22–28. doi:10.1109/MWC.2010.5601954.

Xiaodong, L., Rongxing, L., Chenxi, Z., Haojin, Z., Pin-Han, H., & Xuemin, S. (2008). Security in vehicular ad hoc networks. *IEEE Communications Magazine, 46*(4), 88–95. doi:10.1109/MCOM.2008.4481346.

Yan, G., Olariu, S., & Weigle, M. C. (2008). Providing VANET security through active position detection. *Computer Communications, 31*(12), 2883–2897. doi:10.1016/j.comcom.2008.01.009.

ADDITIONAL READING

Aslam, B., & Zou, C. C. (2011). *One-way-linkable blind signature security architecture for VANET.* Paper presented at the Consumer Communications and Networking Conference (CCNC), 2011. New York, NY.

Chaurasia, B. K., Verma, S., & Tomar, G. S. (2011). *Attacks on anonymity in VANET.* Paper presented at the 2011 International Conference on Computational Intelligence and Communication Networks (CICN). New York, NY.

Dharmaraja, S., Vinayak, R., Xiaomin, M., & Trivedi, K. S. (2012). *Reliability and survivability of vehicular ad hoc networks.* Paper presented at the 2012 International Symposium on Performance Evaluation of Computer and Telecommunication Systems (SPECTS). New York, NY.

Gowtham, G., & Samlinson, E. (2012). *A secured trust creation in VANET environment using random password generator.* Paper presented at the 2012 International Conference on Computing, Electronics and Electrical Technologies (ICCEET). New York, NY.

Haas, J. J., Yih-Chun, H., & Laberteaux, K. P. (2011). Efficient certificate revocation list organization and distribution. *IEEE Journal on Selected Areas in Communications, 29*(3), 595–604. doi:10.1109/JSAC.2011.110309.

Hsin-Te, W., Wei-Shuo, L., Tung-Shih, S., & Wen-Shyong, H. (2010). *A novel RSU-based message authentication scheme for VANET.* Paper presented at the 2010 Fifth International Conference on Systems and Networks Communications (ICSNC). New York, NY.

Isaac, J. T., Zeadally, S., & Cámara, J. S. (2010). Security attacks and solutions for vehicular ad hoc networks. *IET Communications, 4*(7), 894. doi:10.1049/iet-com.2009.0191.

Jinyuan, S., Chi, Z., Yanchao, Z., & Yuguang, F. (2010). An identity-based security system for user privacy in vehicular ad hoc networks. *IEEE Transactions on Parallel and Distributed Systems, 21*(9), 1227–1239. doi:10.1109/TPDS.2010.14.

Jiun-Long, H., Lo-Yao, Y., & Hung-Yu, C. (2011). ABAKA: An anonymous batch authenticated and key agreement scheme for value-added services in vehicular ad hoc networks. *IEEE Transactions on Vehicular Technology, 60*(1), 248–262. doi:10.1109/TVT.2010.2089544.

Jung, C. D., Sur, C., Park, Y., & Rhee, K.-H. (2009). A robust and efficient anonymous authentication protocol in VANETs. *Journal of Communications and Networks, 11*(6), 607–614. doi: doi:10.1109/JCN.2009.6388414.

Lei, Z., Qianhong, W., Solanas, A., & Domingo-Ferrer, J. (2010). A scalable robust authentication protocol for secure vehicular communications. *IEEE Transactions on Vehicular Technology, 59*(4), 1606–1617. doi:10.1109/TVT.2009.2038222.

Leinmuller, T., Schoch, E., & Kargl, F. (2006). Position verification approaches for vehicular ad hoc networks. *IEEE Wireless Communications, 13*(5), 16–21. doi:10.1109/WC-M.2006.250353.

Peksen, Y., & Acarman, T. (2012). *Multihop safety message broadcasting in VANET: A distributed medium access mechanism with a relaying metric.* Paper presented at the 2012 International Symposium on Wireless Communication Systems (ISWCS). New York, NY.

Rawat, D. B., Bista, B. B., Yan, G., & Weigle, M. C. (2011). Securing vehicular ad-hoc networks against malicious drivers: A probabilistic approach. In *Proceedings of the 2011 International Conference on Complex, Intelligent and Software Intensive Systems (CISIS)* (pp. 146-151). doi: 10.1109/cisis.2011.30

Rongxing, L., Xiaodong, L., Luan, T. H., Xiaohui, L., & Xuemin, S. (2012). Pseudonym changing at social spots: An effective strategy for location privacy in VANETs. *IEEE Transactions on Vehicular Technology, 61*(1), 86–96. doi:10.1109/TVT.2011.2162864.

Rongxing, L., Xiaodong, L., Xiaohui, L., & Xuemin, S. (2012). A dynamic privacy-preserving key management scheme for location-based services in VANETs. *IEEE Transactions on Intelligent Transportation Systems, 13*(1), 127–139. doi:10.1109/TITS.2011.2164068.

Sabahi, F. (2011). The security of vehicular adhoc networks. In *Proceedings of the International Conference on Computational Intelligence, Communication Systems and Networks* (pp. 338-342). doi: 10.1109/CICSyN.2011.77

Samara, G., Al-Salihy, W. A. H., & Sures, R. (2010). Security analysis of vehicular ad hoc networks (VANET). In *Proceedings of the 2010 Second International Conference on Network Applications, Protocols and Services* (pp. 55-60). doi: 10.1109/netapps.2010.17

Sampigethaya, K., Mingyan, L., Leping, H., & Poovendran, R. (2007). AMOEBA: Robust location privacy scheme for VANET. *IEEE Journal on Selected Areas in Communications, 25*(8), 1569–1589. doi:10.1109/JSAC.2007.071007.

Serna, J., Luna, J., & Medina, M. (2008). *Geolocation-based trust for VANET's privacy.* Paper presented at the Information Assurance and Security, 2008. New York, NY.

Shuhaimi, N. I., & Juhana, T. (2012). *Security in vehicular ad-hoc network with identity-based cryptography approach: A survey.* Paper presented at the 2012 7th International Conference on Telecommunication Systems, Services, and Applications (TSSA). New York, NY.

Studer, A., Bai, F., Bellur, B., & Perrig, A. (2009). Flexible, extensible, and efficient VANET authentication. *Journal of Communications and Networks, 11*(6), 574–588. doi: doi:10.1109/JCN.2009.6388411.

Sumra, I. A., Ahmad, I., Hasbullah, H., & bin Ab Manan, J. L. (2011). *Classes of attacks in VANET.* Paper presented at the 2011 Saudi International Electronics, Communications and Photonics Conference (SIECPC). New York, NY.

Yong, H., Yu, C., Chi, Z., & Wei, S. (2011). A distributed key management framework with cooperative message authentication in VANETs. *IEEE Journal on Selected Areas in Communications, 29*(3), 616–629. doi:10.1109/JSAC.2011.110311.

KEY TERMS AND DEFINITIONS

Illicit Users: Users who are not authorized to access a certain service. Illicit users could be legitimate users for other service.

Intruders: Intruders could be either legitimate users or illicit users, whenever the entity behaves to generate intrusion to the system.

Intrusion Detection System: The system which includes entities that adopt specific detection strategy to detect intrusions to themselves or the system.

Legitimate Users: Users who are authenticated as legal users to use a specific service in the system.

Lower Layers: Physical layer and MAC sublayer are usually referred as the lower layers in the Open Systems Interconnection (OSI) model.

VANETs: Vehicular Ad-hoc Networks, which enables the communication among vehicles and between vehicle and infrastructure to improve the safety, traffic efficiency, and quality of experience for both drivers and passengers.

Security: Security in VANETs focuses on issues such as authentication, availability, non-repudiation, privacy, and access control, which usually refer to information access/dissemination.

APPENDIX: REVIEW QUESTIONS

1. Why is intrusion detection important to VANETs?
2. What is the benefit of designing intrusion detection strategy on lower layers?
3. What is the difference between intentional and unintentional intrusions?
4. Which one might result in more harm, the internal or external intruders?
5. How many types of intrusion examples are described in the chapter? Can you give other intrusion scenarios in VANETs?
6. What are the possible threats of identity disclosure to the drivers?
7. What are the basic requirements on security in VANETs?
8. How does IEEE 1609.2 function to secure VANETs?
9. Why should authentication efficiency be taken into account during designing protocols for the security of VANETs?
10. Is there any good solution to the coordinated intrusion?

Section 4
Mobile Ad Hoc Networks

Chapter 9
Security Issues in Mobile Ad Hoc Networks:
A Survey

Sunil Kumar
National Institute of Technology, Hamirpur, India

Kamlesh Dutta
National Institute of Technology, Hamirpur, India

ABSTRACT

A Mobile Ad hoc NETwork (MANET) is a self-organizing, infrastructure-less network of mobile nodes connecting by wireless links. In operation, the nodes of MANETs do not have a central control mechanism. It is known for its properties of routable network, where each node acts as a router to forward packets to other specific nodes in the network. The unique properties of MANET have made it useful for large number of applications and led to a number of security challenges. Security in the mobile ad hoc network is a very critical job and requires the consideration of different security issues on all the layers of communication. The countermeasures are the functions that reduce or eliminate security vulnerabilities and attacks. This chapter provides a comprehensive study of all prominent attacks in Mobile Ad Hoc Networks described in the literature. It also provides various proactive and reactive approaches proposed to secure the MANETs. Moreover, it also points to areas of research that need to be investigated in the future.

DOI: 10.4018/978-1-4666-4691-9.ch009

INTRODUCTION

Wireless cellular system has been in operation since the 1980s. Wireless system operates through a centralized support structure such as an access point. Recent advancement of wireless technologies such as Bluetooth (Karygiannis, & Owens, 2002), IEEE 802.11 (Borisov, Goldberg, & Wagner, 2001) introduced a new type of wireless system known as Mobile ad hoc networks (MANETs), which operate in the absence of a central access point (Toh, 2001; Chlamtac, Conti, & Liu, 2003). It provides high mobility and portability of the device, which allows a node to communicate with the network and communication with each other in the network.

In Latin "Ad hoc" means "For a particular purpose only". The ad hoc Network is a spontaneous network and it is especially useful where installation of fixed network is not so easy (Chlamtac et al., 2003). A mobile ad hoc network is infrastructure–less network comprising of autonomous collection of mobile nodes connected by wireless medium and is capable of organizing itself into arbitrary changeable topologies (Perkins, 2001; Stallings, 2009). It is a system of mobile nodes with routing capabilities where each node oper-

ates both as host as well as router to forward the packets to each other as shown in Figure 1. The mobile ad hoc network has the following typical characteristics (Murthy, & Manoj, 2004; Ilyas, 2010):

- Autonomous in Behaviour
- Multi-Hop Routing Paths
- Dynamic Topology
- No Infrastructure
- Distributed Operation
- Very Limited Transmission Range
- Device Size Limitation

A MANET environment has to overcome certain issues of limitation and inefficiency:

- Limited Range of Wireless transmissions
- Unreliability of wireless links between nodes
- Packet loss due to errors in the transmission
- Route Changes due to Mobility
- Frequent network Partition
- Limited Battery Life
- Bandwidth and Slower Data Transfer Rate
- Resource Constraints

Figure 1. Mobile ad hoc network

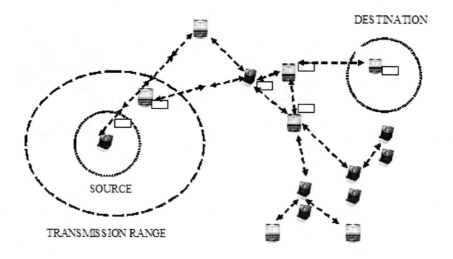

- Weaker In Security (Lack of Centralized Management Facility)
- Limited Physical Security

Apart from these limitation MANET has many extensive application like: Military communication and operations, Automated battlefields, Search and rescue operations, Disaster recovery, Policing and fire fighting, supporting doctors and nurses in hospitals, Conferences, meeting rooms, Virtual classrooms, Wireless P2P networking etc. The unique properties of MANETs present a new set of non trivial challenges to the security design. Unlike traditional networks, ad hoc networks use dedicated nodes to support their basic functions like packet forwarding, routing, and network management (Komninos, Vergados, & Douligeris, 2006; Mohamad, Hassan, Patel, & Razali, 2009).

Wu, Chen, Wu, & Cardei (2007) presented the detailed survey of security attacks and their countermeasures in mobile ad hoc networks. Islam, & Shaikh (2013) also discussed some security issues in mobile ad hoc networks. In mobile ad hoc network there can be node that will try to disrupt the proper network functioning by modifying packets, injecting packets or creating routing loops. These nodes can be malicious or selfish (Buchegger, & Buddec., 2001). The existing security solutions for wired networks cannot be directly applied to the MANETs due to its unique properties. Attacks from both external and internal nodes can easily affect the functioning of the ad hoc networks. The degree of the influence depends largely on the active level of the malicious nodes. There is no clearly defined place means any central management facility where traffic monitoring or access control mechanisms can be deployed such as the firewall etc. As a result, the border that separates the internal network from the outside world becomes blurred.

SECURITY CHALLENGES IN MANETS

Among the various research issues of the MANETs, Security is considered the most critical job. While designing a mobile ad hoc network, we need to consider the following security issues (Mohapatra, & Krishnamurthy, 2010). Table 1 summarizes these security challenges in MANETs in contrast to traditional wired system.

From the description held in this table, we can conclude that the mobile ad hoc network is insecure by its nature as there is no such a clear line of defense. In short, following are the goals of OSI security architecture that are to defend against all the kinds of attacks.

Table 1. Security Challenges in MANETs

Challenge	Description
Wireless Medium	Wireless medium is free to access by everyone and its prone to bit errors or interfacing problem.
Lack of Centralized Management	There is no central authority to monitor the traffic in a highly dynamic and large scale ad-hoc network and that makes the detection of attacks difficult.
Resource Availability	An attacker can easily become an important routing agent and disrupt the network operation by disobeying the protocol specifications as a Mobile ad hoc network is based on cooperative environments.
Infrastructure less	There are no specific infrastructure for addressing, key distribution, certificates etc.
Scalability	The protocols and services that are applied to the ad hoc network should be compatible to the continuously changing scale of the ad hoc network.
Dynamic topology	Dynamic topology may violate the trust relationship among the nodes.
Restricted power supply	Node in mobile ad-hoc network can behave in a selfish manner when there is consumption of battery to support some functions in the network.
Bandwidth constraint	Cooperation based security solutions must consider the bandwidth limitation associated with links.
Multihop Routing	As the nodes are dependent on each other for routing, adversaries can generate fabricated routes to create routing loops, false routes etc.

- **Availability:** The network must be available at all times to send and receive messages despite if it is under attack.
- **Confidentiality:** Provides secrecy to sensitive data being sent over the network and unauthorized nodes cannot read the data.
- **Integrity:** It ensures that messages being sent over the network are not modified.
- **Privacy:** It prevents adversaries from obtaining information that may have private content i.e. frequency, source node, routes, etc.
- **Authentication:** It is the process of verifying a claimed identity of a node as the originator of a message (message authentication) or the identity of a node as the end point of a channel (entity authentication).
- **Non-Repudiation:** Non-repudiation prevents the source from denying that it sent a packet.
- **Authorization:** Authorization is a process to assign different access rights to different level of users.
- **Access Control:** It is to prevent unauthorized use of network services and system resources.
- **Anonymity:** Neither the mobile node nor its system software should default expose any information that allows any conclusions on the owner or current user of the node.
- **Freshness:** It ensures that a malicious node does not resend previously captured packets.
- **Resilience to attacks:** It required sustaining the network functionalities when a portion of nodes is compromised or destroyed.

CLASSIFICATION OF THE SECURITY ATTACKS

Classification of the Attacks on the Basis of Nature: Active vs. Passive Attacks

The security attacks in MANETs can be broadly classified into two major categories on the basis of nature (Yang, Luo, Ye, Lu, & Zhang, 2004):

- **Passive Attacks:** Passive attacks are mainly against data confidentiality. In passive attacks the attacker does not violate the functioning of the network, instead try to extract the valuable information like node hierarchy and network topology by listening to the channel or monitoring the transmission over the channel. Selfish Nodes perform passive attacks with the aim of saving battery life. Selfish nodes can severely degrade the performance of the network and results into the partition of the network.
- **Active Attacks:** Active attacks are mostly against data confidentially and data integrity. Active attacks involve some changes in the data packets or creation of false routing through which the malicious nodes should bear some costs of energy in order to perform some harmful work. Malicious nodes are nodes that perform active attacks attempting to damage resources for the other nodes in the network.

Classification of the Attacks on the Basis of Domain: Internal vs. External Attacks

The security attacks in MANETs can also be classified into two categories on the basis of the Domain (Menezes, Van Oorschot, & Vanstone, 2010):

- **External Attacks:** Carried out by external nodes that do not belong to the network in order to cause overload, spread false routing information or disrupt the node from the providing of the network services.
- **Internal Attacks:** From the compromised nodes that belong to the network as authorized parties. Since malicious insider nodes are thus protected by the security mechanisms of the network and perform internal attacks.

ATTACKS ON DIFFERENT LAYERS OF THE INTERNET MODEL FOR MANETS

The attacks can be further classified according to the five layers of the Internet model. Some other attacks can be launched at multiple layers.

Physical Layer Attacks

The security of Physical layer is very important as it is lowest layer of TCP/IP model. The nodes in MANETs share a wireless medium and use the RF spectrum. It is vulnerable to various types of security attacks as it is easy to jam or intercept (Karygiannis, & Owens, 2002). Attacks at this layer are:

- **Eavesdropping:** Eavesdropping also known as disclosure attacks, are passive attacks by external or internal nodes. The term eavesdrops implies listening to wireless medium without expending any extra effort. In this intercepting and reading and conversation of message by unintended receiver take place by tuning to the proper frequency (Nichols, & Lekkas, 2002).
- **DoS in the Physical Layer:** A denial-of-service (DoS) attack mainly targets the availability of network services. A DoS is defined as any event that diminishes a network's capacity to perform its expected function correctly or in a timely manner (Wu, Chen et al., 2007).
- **Jammer Attack:** Jammer attack responsibility is to stop the nodes send and receive packets over the network. Jammer function at the physical layer is to create a package for steady speed over the wireless medium to preserve the busy environment; therefore a host cannot access the wireless environment because of the noise created by jammer in a wireless environment.
- **Interference Problem:** Unconstrained transmission in broadcast media may lead to the time overlap of two or more packet receptions, called *collision* or *interference*. Radio Frequency (RF) occupies the unwanted interference RF signals that interrupt the normal operations as 802.11 protocol defined by IEEE get interfering RF single of sufficient amplitude and frequency which can appear as bogus 802.11 nodes transmitting a packet. This cause genuine 802.11 station to wait for indefinite periods of time until interfering signal goes away. Many other types of devices besides those that support wireless networking also use 2.4GHz frequency range, or cause interference at the same frequencies. These include cordless phones, microwave ovens etc.
- **Device Tampering Attack:** The adversary can get useful data from the stolen devices and communication on behalf of the owner.
- **De-Packaging Attack:** De- packaging is the process of removal of chip which is mostly attached in nodes for transmitting signal. The first step towards decode the chip is to dissolve the chip in resin silicon fuming acid and then use the micro probing or electrobeam microscopy to read the useful information easily from ALU in processor, ROM cell etc. One the process of de-packaging chip is done it can provide useful information for launching attack to the network.

Defense Against Physical Layer Attacks

Two Spread Spectrums – Frequency Hopping Spread Spectrum (FHSS) and Direct Sequence Spread Spectrum (DSSS) technology can be used to make it difficult to interfere or jam the signals. Spread spectrum technology changes the frequency of the signal or spreads the energy of the signal to a wider spectrum. Spread spectrum technology also minimizes the possibility of interference from other radio and electromagnetic devices. It becomes very difficult to detect the signal without multiplication by the pseudo-random sequence (Zafer, Agrawal, & Srivatsa, 2009).

- **DSSS:** It is one of the most widely known spread spectrum system. The signal is spread across a frequency band using a spreading code. The carrier phase of the transmitted signal is changed as per code sequence. The code sequence is generated by a pseudo-random generator. The code repeats itself in the transmitted signal, after a given number of bits. The speed of the code sequence is called chipping rate and its unit is in chips per second (cps). At the receiver end, the information is recovered using replica of the code sequence.
- **FHSS:** The signal is modulated by a seemingly random series of radio frequencies, which hops from frequency to frequency at fixed intervals. The order of frequencies selected by the transmitter is given by the code sequence, which is synchronized with the transmitter, to recombine the spread signals in their original form. The receiver tracks these frequency changes and produces a constant signal. With the transmitter and the receiver synchronized correctly, the data is transmitted over a key channel. However, the signal seems to be unintelligible impulse noise duration for eavesdroppers.

Meanwhile, interference is minimized as the signal is spread over several frequencies.

- **Defense Against Device Tampering and De-Packaging Attack:** Anti-Tamper and defence acquisition process are required using some security modules like smart cards requires PIN codes or biometrics for access.

Link (MAC) Layer Attacks

IEEE 802.11 is considered as key enabler for MANETs and vulnerabilities associated with these standards can be exploited for different types of security attacks (Borisov et al., 2001).

- **Traffic Analysis & Monitoring:** Traffic analysis is a passive attack used to gain some useful information e.g. important information about the networking topology can be derived by analyzing traffic patterns. One of the following techniques may be used for traffic analysis (Cayirci, & Rong, 2008):
  - **Traffic analysis at the physical layer:** In this attack only the carrier is sensed and the traffic rates are analyzed for the nodes at a location.
  - **Traffic analysis in MAC and higher layers:** MAC frames, and data packets can be demultiplexed and headers can be analyzed. This can reveal information about the routing topology and friendship trees.
  - **Traffic analysis by event correlation:** Events like transmission by an end user can be correlated with the traffic and more detailed information e.g. routes can be obtained.
  - **Active traffic analysis:** Traffic analysis can also be performed as an active attack. For example, a certain number of nodes can be destroyed, which stimulates the self-organizing

networks, and valuable information about the topology can be collected.

- **Threats in IEEE 802.11 WEP:** The first security scheme provided by IEEE 802.11 standards is Wired Equivalent Privacy (WEP) to provide security for WLAN systems a modest level of privacy by encrypting the radio signals. To prepare a protected frame, first integrity check value (ICV) of the frame payload is computed using a cyclic redundancy check (CRC) function. The clear text payload concatenated with ICV is then encrypted using a bit-wise exclusive-or operation with a key stream as long as the payload concatenated with ICV. The key stream is a pseudorandom bit stream generated by the RC4 algorithm from a 40-bit secret key prepended with a 24-bit Initialization Value (IV). The resulting protected frame includes the clear text frame header, the clear text IV, the result of the encryption and a clear text frame check sequence field. WEP suffers from many design flaws and some weaknesses in the way the RC4 cipher is used in WEP (Wu, Chen et al., 2007):

  - **Key management and key size:** Key management is not specified in the WEP protocol. Lack of key management is a potential exposure for most of the attacks.
  - **Small initialization vector:** The initialization vector (IV) used in WEP is a 24-bit field which is sent in clear and is a part of the RC4 leads to probabilistic cipher key recovery attack or most commonly known as analytical attack.
  - **Poor ICV algorithm:** The combined use of a non-cryptographic integrity algorithm, CRC 32 with the stream chipper is a security risk and may cause message privacy and message integrity attacks.

- **DoS Attacks in Link layer:** To launch the DoS attack the attacker may exploit the binary exponential backoff scheme in IEEE 802.11(Wood, & Stankovic, 2002; Denko, 2005). Network allocation vector (NAV) in the RTS /CTS frame provides a different vulnerability to DoS attacks in the link layer (Kyasanur, & Vaidya, 2003; Yang et al., 2004). The algorithms in the link layer, especially MAC schemes present many exploitation opportunities for DoS attacks (Cayirci, & Rong, 2008).

  - **Reactive RTS jamming attack:** Whenever an RTS signal is received, a signal that collides with the CTS signal is transmitted. It disrupts these messages by immediately initiating a transmission. Since the nodes cannot start transmitting data before receiving the CTS, they continue sending RTS signals.
  - **Active periodic jamming attack:** If the MAC scheme is based on sleeping and active periods, jamming only the active periods can continuously block the channel.
  - **Corrupt RTS/CTS signal:** False RTS or CTS signals with long data transmission parameters are continuously sent out, which makes the other nodes that do virtual carrier sensing wait forever.
  - **Acknowledgement spoofing:** Where an adversary sends false link layer acknowledgements for overheard packets addressed to neighboring nodes can also be an effective link layer DoS attack.
  - **Selfish attack:** The selfish nodes will reduce the resource of wireless channel for other nodes of the network, thereby affect the network performance, and even interrupt the network service.

○ **Capture effect**: To capture the channel, loaded the network by sending data continuously, thereby resulting lightly loaded neighbors to back-off endlessly (Yang et al., 2004). Malicious nodes may cause a chain reaction in the upper level protocols using backoff scheme by taking the advantage of this effect (Wu, Chen et al., 2007).

- **Virtual jamming attack 802.11:** In this attack malicious node sent continuously RTS packets on the network for unlimited period of time and effectively jams the transmission with small expenditure of power.

Defense Against Link (MAC) Layer Attacks

To counter these attacks, a possible approach is to limit the data rate of nodes on the network. An alternative approach is to use Time Division multiplexing, where a fixed time slot is allocated for every node to transmit the data. One of the vulnerabilities in this layer is its binary exponential back off scheme and the security solution to this problem based on monitoring mechanism is proposed in (Kyasanur, & Vaidya, 2002). Traffic analysis is prevented by using strong encryption techniques and traffic padding at data link layer (IEEE Std. 802.11i/D30, 2002). Biswas, & Ali (2007) have proposed the mechanism RSN/ AESCCMP as countermeasures to improve the security in WEP. WEP encryption scheme is also defined that uses link encryption to hide information of the traffic. Gunasekaran, & Uthariaraj (2009) have proposed a DoSP-MAC protocol to improve the fairness of the network at link layer. The consumption of network resources using NAV field is still an open problem for research though some schemes have been proposed such as ERA-802.11 (Kyasanur, & Vaidya, 2003). Intrusion detection system using the concept of cross layer or running at link layer

also resolve some security attacks by monitoring for misbehaviours nodes.

Network Layer Attacks

Nodes in MANETs are required to route their packets through unknown nodes as mechanism of MANETs is cooperative in nature (Deng, Li, & Agrawal, 2002). The intermediate nodes can add, delete, or modify the routing and data packets or delay the forwarding packets unnecessarily and the entire network can be paralysed. So, it is necessary to protect the routing layer from malicious attacks for the smooth functioning of the network (Ghaffari, 2006; Kannhavong, Nakayama, Nemoto, Kato, & Jamalipour, 2007). Attacks at different stages of the network layer are:

Attacks on Autoconfiguration

All existing autoconfiguration algorithms for MANETs assume secure environments. They cannot function properly in the case of attacks from malicious nodes.

- **IP spoofing attack**: An attacker can perform an IP spoofing attack by sending a packet containing its own MAC address and a victim's IP address.
- **Sybil attack**: If a malicious node impersonates some non-existent nodes, it will appear that several malicious nodes conspire together, which is called a Sybil attack where a malicious node introduces itself as multiple nodes (Douceur, 2002). This attack aims at network services when cooperation is necessary and affects the autoconfiguration as well.
- **Neighbor attack:** The attacker, however, simply forwards the packet without recording their Id in the packet to make the two nodes that are not the communication range to each other believe that they are neighbors (e.g. one hop from each other)

resulting in violation of the routing function (Nguyen, & Nguyen, 2008).

- **State pollution attack:** If a malicious node does not give correct parameters in the reply, it is called the "state pollution" attack. This attack is difficult to be differentiated from the case when the global allocation states are not properly synchronized among all the mobile nodes because of the unreliable broadcast transmission (Zhou, 2008).

Fabrication Attack

Fabrication is an attack in which an unauthorized party not only gains the access but also inserts counterfeit objects into the system (Razak, Furnell, & Brooke, 2004). Here the attacker forges network packets. The fabrication attack is further classified in following categories:

- **Sleep deprivation attacks**: In a routing protocol, sleep deprivation attacks might be launched by flooding the targeted node with unnecessary routing packets. Attackers could flood any node in the networks by sending a huge number of route request (RREQ) towards targeted node in AODV (Perkins, & Royer, 1999), route replies (RREP) or route error (RERR) packets to the targeted node by which that particular node is unable to participate in the routing mechanisms and finally rendered unreachable by the other nodes in the networks.
- **Route salvaging attacks:** In a mobile ad hoc network, there is no guarantee that each transmitted packet will successfully reach the desired destination node. Route salvaging attacks are launched by the greedy internal nodes in the networks. Therefore, to salvage their packets from such failures, misbehaving internal nodes might duplicate and retransmit their pack-

ets although no sending error messages received to drain off more resources in intermediate and destination nodes and this attack might also cause the consumption of unnecessary bandwidth (Tseng, Ni, Chen, & Sheu, 2002).

- **Routing table poisoning attack:** Misbehaving or selfish nodes create fabricated routing updates and modifies the original routing route and re-broadcasting the modified original packet to other nodes on the network.
- **Route cache poisoning attack:** Route cache poisoning are mostly used in on demand routing protocols, as each node had a cache route that has the information regarding the route it has been routed to know nodes in the network and this attack is very much similar to eavesdropping attack.

Interruption Attack

Interruption attacks are launched to deny routing messages from reaching the destination nodes this by either attacking the routing messages or attacking the mobile nodes in the networks. Attacks that could be classified as under:

- **Packet dropping attacks**: In packet dropping attack, a malicious node collaborates as usual in the routing process of the MANETs and launches the constant packet dropping attacks if it is included as one of the intermediate nodes. In addition to above, instead of constantly dropping all the packets, malicious node might drop the randomly or selective packets (Medidi et al., 2003).
- **Lack of cooperation attacks**: Lack of cooperation from the internal nodes to participate in the network operations can also be seen as an attempt to launch a refusal of service attack. A selfish node wants to preserve own resources. Misbehaviour in-

ternal nodes might refuse to forward the other node's packets. This can be dangerous for the correct operation of the network just not involved in the forwarding packets of the other nodes by violating the routing function of MANETs (Razak et al., 2004).

Modification Attack

Modification is a type of attack when an unauthorized party not only gains access to the network but also modifies the packets or modifies the forwarding route (Sanzgiri, Dahill, Levine, Shields, & Belding-Royer, 2002). Examples of modification attacks that can be classified are as under:

- **Packet misrouting attacks**: In a packet misrouting attack, malicious nodes reroute the traffic from their correct path to wrong destinations and resulted into dropping the packets from the network (Medidi et al., 2003). As a result, the source node has to re-transmit the lost packets and this it will consume more bandwidth and increased the overhead in the network.
- **Impersonation attacks**: In this attack, a compromised node can access the network management as a super-user who has special privileges and change the configuration of the system as a super-user who has privileges (Burg, 2003; Tamilselvan, & Sankaranarayanan, 2007b).
  - **Man-in-the-middle attack:** It is a type of impersonation attack. In this attack, the attacker exists as intermediate node to any one node in the routing path and change contents of the packet that is being transmitted and injects the modified packet into the network (Caballero, 2006).
- **Byzantine attack:** This attack is launched by a set of compromised intermediate nodes or a compromised intermediate node. This type creates routing loops or

longer paths or packet dropping misroute attack which results in disruption of the routing services (Awerbuch, Holmer, Nita-Rotaru, & Rubens, 2002).

- **Blackmail attack**: It causes false identification of a good node as malicious node. An attacker can blackmail a good node and inform the other nodes in the network to add the node to their blacklists, and thus avoiding the victim node in future routes.

DoS Attacks Against Routing Schemes

These attacks generally fall into one of two categories routing disruption attacks to make the routing scheme dysfunction, making it unable to provide the required networking services or resource consumption attacks to consume network resources such as bandwidth, memory, computational power and energy.

- **Hello flood attacks:** The attacker broadcasts many Hello packets to detect one-hop neighbour nodes with large enough transmission power that each node receiving Hello packets assumes the adversary node to be its neighbour (Karlof, & Wagner, 2003).
- **Flooding attack (Route disruption attack):** The main aim of this attack is to consume network resources, such as bandwidth or node's resources, such as computational and battery power. In flooding attack, attackers disrupt the routing operation by sending a large number of route request packets to a destination node that does not exist in the network to cause severe degradation in network performance this could lead to denial-of-service due continue consumption of battery power as well as network bandwidth for the node (Guo, & Perreau, 2010).

- **Black hole attack:** In a black hole attack, a malicious node shows its interest in forwarding a packet towards a destination during route discovery phase. The attacker rushes during route discovery to ensure that a route is established through it, later on in the forwarding phase, it drops the packets intended for the destination (Al-Shurman, Yoo, & Park, 2004; Anita, & Vasudevan, 2010; Ghonge, Jawandhiya, & Ali, 2011). The black hole attack has two properties. First, the node uses a routing protocol such as in AODV to advertise itself as having a valid route to the destination node although the route is false in order to intercept the packets. Second, the node uses the captured packets to drop the packets to perform a denial-of-service attack (Kurosawa, Nakayama, Kato, Jamalipour, & Nemoto, 2007). Distribution routing messages referring to non-existent nodes not only increases the load on the network, but also add non-existing routes to the routing tables of other nodes. According to the original protocol AODV, when a source node S wants to communicate with the destination node D, the source node S broadcasts a route request (RREQ) packet, as shown in the example in Figure 2. So all the in-

termediate nodes update their routing table entry for the source node S and check if it is the destination node or has a fresh enough route to the destination. If not, then the intermediate node updates RREQ (increasing the number of hops) and flooding the network with RREQ to the destination node D until it reaches node D, or any other intermediate node that has a fresh route to D. The destination node D or an intermediate node with a fresh route to D initiates a route reply (RREP) in the reverse direction, as shown in Figure 3. Node S starts to send data packets to the neighbor, who replied first and discards replies of other nodes. The malicious nodes can send fake RREP (including fake serial number of destinations that are fabricated to be equal to or greater than that contained in the RREQ) to the source node, showing that it has fresh enough route to the destination. This leads to the source node to choose the route that passes through the attacker. Therefore, all traffic will be routed through this path as replied by attacker and thereafter attacker can misuse or discard the traffic.

Figure 3 shows an example of a black hole attack where an attacker B2 sends a fake RREP to the source node S, claiming that it

Figure 2. Network flooding of RREQ

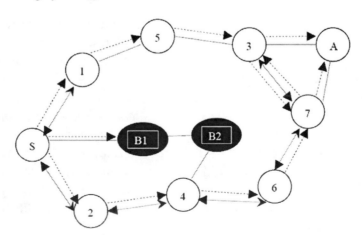

has fresh route to the destination D. Since the sequence number of the advertised by the attacker is higher than sequence number of the advertised by other nodes and source node S will choose the route that passes through the attacker node B1.

- **Cooperative black hole attack**: When multiple black hole nodes are acting in coordination with each other as a group then this type of attack is called cooperative black hole attack and the security of the network is compromised (Agrawal, Ghosh, & Das, 2008).

- **Gray hole attack**: Where the malicious node is not initially malicious, but as soon as it receives the packets from the neighboring node, it drop the packets. This is a type of active attack and launch Denial of Service (DoS) attack. In Gray Hole attack, attacker node behaves maliciously for the time until the packets are dropped and then go to their normal behavior (Xiaopeng, & Wei, 2007).

- **Link spoofing attack:** In a control message, signalization of an incorrect set of links is called link spoofing. In the links spoofing attack, malicious node advertises fake links with the neighbors and disrupts routing operations e.g. in OLSR protocol (Adjih et al., 2003), the attacker can advertise fake links with the neighbors with a target's two-hop neighbors . This causes the target node to select the malicious site to be its MPR. As MPR (Multi Relay Point) node, the malicious node can modify the data and routing traffic (Ngadi, Khokhar, & Mandala, 2008). Figure 4 shows an example of the link spoofing attack in an OLSR. In this figure, during the link spoofing attack, node A advertises a fake link with node 1's two-hop neighbor, that is, node 3. According to the OLSR protocol, node 1 will select the malicious node A as its only MPR since node A is the minimum set that reaches node 1's two-hop neighbors.

Figure 3. Propagation of RREP messages

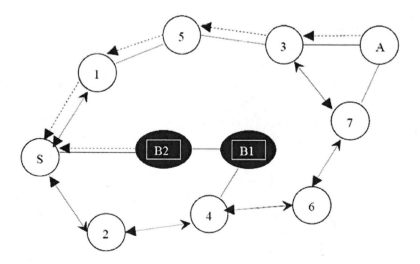

Figure 4. An example of a Link spoofing attack

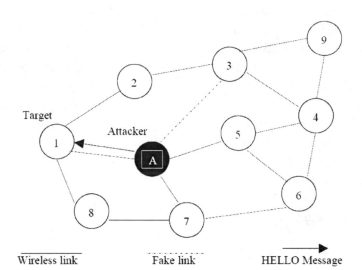

- ○ **Wormhole attack:** A wormhole attack is against authenticity and confidentiality. A wormhole attack is one of the most severe attacks in MANETs. It is also known as tunneling attack. Wormhole attacks use two cooperating network nodes to re-route data traffic. In this attack, first two nodes who are not one hop neighbors establish an additional channel outside normal network serving as a tunnel (Hu, Perrig, & Johnson, 2003a). Then node at one end records the packets and tunnels them to another end node by using wired network or using an off link wireless channel at different radio frequency as shown in figure 5 (Sen, J., 2013). As sending the packets through these paths which are not a part of the proper network results in to wormhole attack. Wormholes are not necessarily only negative for a network as such a shortcut can also have positive benefits such as relief for network traffic or

shorter transfer times for the packets on routes containing the tunnel.

Wormhole attacks can be classified into further five categories as proposed (Khalil, Bagchi, & Shroff, 2005):

- ▪ **Wormhole using encapsulation:** In this type M1 will encapsulate the packets coming from its neighbors and send them to M2 using the nodes in the network. M2 will broadcast the packets to its neighbors after demarshalling them. Note that, the original encapsulated packets are not viewed by the nodes on the route and thus the hop counts on these packets are not increased thus the nodes at M2 side will think that the nodes at M1 side are one-hop away.
- ▪ **Wormhole using out of band channel:** This stage the attack used a wireless band which is in different frequency as compare to the frequency of the target network.

Figure 5. An example of a wormhole attack (Sen, 2013)

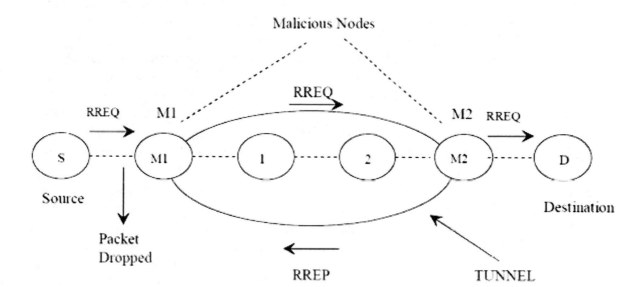

- **Open wormhole attack:** In this type of wormhole, the attackers include themselves in the packet header following the route discovery procedure.
- **Closed wormhole attack:** Attacker simply tunnels the packet from one side of wormhole to another side without modifying the content of the packet in a route discovery process and it rebroadcasts the packet.
- **Half-open wormhole attack:** Attacker at one side of wormhole does not modify the packet but attacker at another side modifies the packet in route discovery procedure.
  - **Wormhole with high power transmission:** In this mode, when a single malicious node gets a route request, it broadcasts the request with a very high power level. Any node that hears the high-power level packets at the

network rebroadcasts it towards the destination and a route between the source and the destination is established without the participation of a colluding node.
  - **Wormhole using packet relays:** In this case, malicious node at one end will simply amplify and further send the packets. This will increase the one-hop neighbor list of the sender.
- **Colluding misrelay attack:** In colluding misrelay attack, Multiple internal malicious nodes collude together to perform a misrelay attack, such as dropping or altering control messages to disrupt routing operation in a MANETs. This attack is difficult to detect by using the monitoring techniques such as watchdog and pathrater (Marti et al., 2000).
- **Jellyfish attack:** In this type of attack, the attacker node first get access to the network, once it get into the network and became a part of the network. The attacker then enter the network delays, delaying all the packets it receives, once delays are propagated then

packets are released in the network (Aad, Hubaux, & Knightly, 2008).

- **Rushing attack:** An attacker as intermediate node floods the route request packets quickly throughout the network before other nodes which also receive the same route request packet can react. Nodes that receive route request packets and consider these packets are duplicate packets of the packet have already been received through the attacker and therefore, reject those packets.

- **Packet replication:** In the case of packet replication, an attacker replicates stale packets. This requires more bandwidth and battery resources available at the nodes as well as causing unnecessary confusion in the routing process.

- **Attacks that Exploit Node-Penalizing Schemes:** If a malicious node can report error messages for a node which is actually performing well. Therefore, the routing scheme may avoid using a route that includes this node. Similarly, a link may be jammed for a short time but since error messages are generated about the link during that time interval, the routing scheme may continue to avoid the link even though it is not jammed any more.

- **Detour Attack:** It adds a number of virtual nodes in route, diverting the traffic through a longer/ malicious node. The attacking node itself can save energy by forwarding packets.

Defense Against Network Layer Attacks

Secure routing protocols provide the first line of defense against most of security threats at this layer (Biswas, & Ali, 2007). IPSec is mostly used on the network layer to provide packet confidentiality. It also protects against IP spoofing attacks. Source authentication and message integrity mechanism are required to protect against most of the attacks. Following are the some defense mechanisms against the network layer threats:

- **Defense Against Packet Dropping:** Marti et al. proposed a mechanism called watchdog that identifies misbehaving nodes based on monitoring mechanism and another module called pathrater that helps the routing protocols to bypass these misbehaving nodes detected by watchdog (Marti et al., 2000). According to Watchdog a node may measure a neighboring node's frequency of dropping or misrouting packets, or its frequency of invalid routing information advertisements. In the same way, Zeshan, Khan, Cheema, & Ahmed (2008) proposed a two folded approach: the first approach detects misbehavior nodes in network, other approach will isolate the malicious nodes from the network. Fahad, Djenouri, & Askwith (2007) proposed another approach for detecting the misbehaving nodes that drop data packets in MANETs with a low communication overhead. Medidi et al. (2003) provided an unobtrusive monitoring mechanism that monitors the system activity and logs offline to detect wireless link failure, misroute packets and packet dropping attacks.

- **Defense Against Flooding:** Balakrishnan, Varadharajan, & Tupakula (2006) have proposed a mechanism based on obligation-based model to defend against the packet drop and flooding attacks in MANETs by identifying the malicious, selfish nodes and then penalize them. Trust based security protocols can be used to further enhance the efficiency and improve the security in MANETs.

- **Defense against Modification & Impersonation Attacks:** A new key management scheme has been implemented in the NTP (Node transition probability) protocol for the efficiently utilization of bandwidth during heavy traffic with less communication overhead (Gracelin, Edna, & Radha, 2010). NTP determines stable routes using received power but the packet delivery cannot be guaranteed in this scheme because it is not protected by the protocol. This protocol detects modification and impersonation attacks.

A packet leash protocol can be added to the routing packet to restrict its transmission beyond some constraints (Hu et al., 2003a; Wu, & Yau, 2007). It is a mechanism to defend against the wormhole attack. Two types of leashes are distinguished-geographical leashes and temporal leashes. In temporal leashes, an extremely precise clock synchronized mechanism is assumed to be present. In the geographical, the scheme assumes geographical location information and loosely synchronized clocks. Similar to packet leash, SEAD protocol uses a one-way hash chain to prevent malicious nodes from increasing the sequence number or decreasing the hop count in routing advertisement packets (Hu, Johnson, & Perrig, 2003b). This protocol is used as defense mechanism against modification attacks. The routing protocol ARAN has been proposed to defend against impersonation and repudiation attacks (Sanzgiri et al., 2002; Ghonge et al., 2011). ARAN provides end to end authentication and non-repudiation services using predetermined cryptographic certificates. In ARAN, Route is discovered by broadcasting a route discovery message-RDP from the source node and reply message-REP is unicast only from the destination node to the source node. The routing messages are authenticated at each intermediate hop in both directions to provide protection against Blackmail attack in mobile ad hoc networks.

- **Defense Against Byzantine Attacks:** A secure on-demand MANET routing protocol named Robust Source Routing (RSR) is proposed as a countermeasure of Byzantine attacks (Crepeau, Davis, & Maheswaran, 2007). Yu, Zhou, & Su (2009) introduced an integrated protocol called secure routing against collusion (SRAC) as a countermeasure of Byzantine attacks in which routing decision is based on the trust values of a node provided by its neighboring nodes and route-discovery messages are protected by using public key cryptographic mechanisms with pairwise secret keys between a source and destination.

- **Defense Against Sybil Attack:** A robust Sybil attack detection framework is proposed for MANETs based on co-operative monitoring of network activities (Tangpong, Kesidis, Hsu, & Hurson, 2009). Each mobile node in the network in this framework observes packets passing through it and periodically exchanges its observations in order to determine the presence of an attack. Sybil attack cannot be detected in the absence of any centralized identification authority (Douceur, 2002). The protocols used for securing ad hoc networks against Sybil attacks can be classified as follows:

  - **PKI-Based protocols:** One way to prevent Sybil attack is to maintain a central identification mechanism to confirm identity of each node along with the identity of others nodes.

  - **Threshold-Based protocols:** When a group of trusted nodes distributes cryptographic material only if the new members meet certain threshold criteria.

  - **Reputation schemes:** Reputation schemes include protocols determining and maintaining information regarding the trustworthiness about the nodes in the group.

- **Defense Against Sleep Deprivation Attacks:** Shortest path algorithms or Public key cryptography should be preferred at the time of creating of the route for large networks to protect against the sleep deprivation attack.

- **Defense Against Black Hole Attacks:** Security-aware ad hoc routing protocol (SAR) based on on-demand routing protocols, such as AODV or DSR (Johnson, & Maltz, 1996) can be used to defend against black hole attacks (Yi, Naldurg, & Kravets, 2001). In SAR, securities metric are embedding into the RREQ packet itself and a different route discovery procedure is used w.r.t. RREQs. Intermediate nodes forward the packet only if it can provide the required authorization or trust level otherwise drop the RREQ packets. Hu et al. (2003b), Hu, Perrig, & Johnson (2005) and Sanzgiri et al.(2002) present their solutions to overcome the black hole attack. These solutions are to disable the ability of the intermediate nodes to reply the route against the route request, so that route reply message should be replied by the destination node only. A DPRAODV (Detection, Prevention and Reactive AODV) has been proposed to detect black hole attack based on sequence number of RREP and it also notifies other nodes in the network of the incident (Raj, & Swadas, 2009). Kurosawa et al.(2007) have proposed a mechanism to recognize a black hole attack by analyzing the sequence no of the packets. Wait and check the replies mechanism is also proposed to find a safe route for packets (Tamilselvan, & Sankaranarayanan, 2007a). Two authentication mechanisms based on the hash based Message Authentication Code (MAC) and pseudo-random function (PRF) are proposed to provide a quick verification of the messages to identify cooperative black hole attack and avoid the cooperative black

hole attack to discover safe route (Min, & Jiliu, 2009). TOGBAD-a centralized approach has been proposed using topology graphs to identify nodes that are creating a black hole in the network (Gerhards-Padilla, Aschenbruck, Martini, Jahnke, & Tolle, 2007).

- **Defense Against Wormhole Attacks:** Roy, Chaki & Chaki (2009) have presented a cluster based counter-measure for the wormhole attack that efficiently mitigates the effect of wormhole attack in MANET. A cluster based counter-measure Wormhole Attack Prevention (WAP) protocol is also proposed as countermeasure for the wormhole attack without using any specialized hardware as proposed in to prevent the wormhole attack (Choi, Kim, Lee, & Jung, 2008). A True Link mechanism which is timing based countermeasure to the wormhole attack has been proposed (Eriksson, Krishnamurthy, & Faloutsos, 2006). A packet leash protocol can be added to the routing packet to restrict its transmission beyond some constraints as a countermeasure to the wormhole attack (Hu et al., 2003a). A temporal packet leash specifies time a packet should take to reach to the destination by avoiding wormhole attacks. A sender includes the time and location in the message at the time of transmission. The receiver checks that the packet has traveled the distance between the sender and itself within the time frame. Temporal packet leashes require tightly synchronized knowledge of clocks and location. SECTOR mechanism has been proposed primarily based on distance bounding techniques (Capkun, Buttyán, & Hubaux, 2003b), one-way hash chain and the Merkle hash tree have been proposed to detect wormhole without the need of clock synchronization (Ghonge et al., 2011). SECTOR can also be used to secure

MANET routing protocols using the last counters and detect malicious nodes based on topology tracking. Directional antennas based approach has been proposed to prevent wormhole attacks (Hu, & Evans, 2004). This approach does not require any information about the location or timing, and is more energy efficient. Jain, & Jain (2010) have proposed a novel trust-based scheme for identifying and isolating nodes that create a wormhole in the network without using any cryptographic technique.

- **Defense Against Denial of service (DoS) Attack**: A DoS attack mitigation technique based on digital signatures has been proposed to verify legitimate packets and if the packets do not pass verification process, they are dropped to prevent DoS-attacks (Wu, & Yau, 2007). Kim, Sankhla, & Helmy (2004) proposed an efficient search technique to trace back DoS attackers. They used the Traffic Patterns Matching (TPM) that would be very beneficial to address the spoofing problems in DoS attacks and Traffic Volume Matching (TVM) to identify the attacker.

- **Defense Against Location Disclosure Attacks**: Chapkin, Bako, Kargl, & Schoch (2006) proposed a defense mechanism against location disclosure attack that uses geometric constraints and heuristics to find node positions efficiently. Blazevic, Le Boudec, & Giordano (2005) discussed some of the issues related to the protection mechanism from location disclosure attacks and then proposed Terminode routing mechanism for MANET that uses a combination of location-based routing (Terminode Remote Routing, TRR) and link state based routing (Terminode Local Routing TLR), where TRR is used when the destination is far away and TLR is used when the destination is very near. TRR uses anchored paths, a list of geographic points (not nodes) used as loose source routing information. Anchored paths discovered and managed sources, using one of two low overhead protocols: Friend Assisted Paths Discovery and Geographical Maps based on the path discovery to addresses the issues of the location of the disclosure attack.

- **Defense Against Gray Hole Attack**: Agrawal et al. (2008) have proposed a network model to trace the packet dropping nodes. Xiaopeng, & Wei (2007) proposed a signature based aggregate algorithm consisted of three related algorithms: the creating proof algorithm, the checkup algorithm and the diagnosis algorithm to trace packet dropping nodes. The first was for creating the proof and the second was for checking up source route nodes, and the last was for locating the malicious nodes.

- **Defense Against Impersonation Attack**: Hash Chaining and Digital signatures are generally used against Impersonation Attack. A Hash chain is used to secure mutable fields of the messages e.g. hop count information and Digital signature are used to authenticate the non-mutable fields of the messages.

- **Defense Against Man-in-the-middle attack**: On-Demand Public Key Management can be fully performed by nodes themselves without the need of any trusted third party in the network while providing dynamic public key management services against the various man-in-the-middle attacks. So, Strong Key management system is required as a defense mechanism against Man-in-the-middle attack, where an initiator (new joining node) sends its public key to central node. In the response of request, central node generates a session key encrypted with initiator's public key and sends it to the initiator (Boukerche, & Ren, 2008).

- **Defense Against Neighbor Attack:** Inter Switch Message Protocol (ISMP) was designed to facilitate the Inter switch communication within distributed connection-oriented switching networks. Switches use the Switch Neighbor Discovery and Maintenance protocol (SNDM) which is a part of ISMP to discover their neighboring switches and establish the topology of the switch fabric. SNDM is a new mechanism that prevents the neighbor attack.

- **Defense Against Jellyfish Attack:** There is a requirement of cross-layer approach that monitors the end-to-end "good" throughput at the transport layer to detect abnormities and reacts to those abnormities at the network layer.

Transport Layer Attacks

The security issues related to transport layer are authentication, securing end-to-end communications through data encryption, handling delays, packet loss and so on.

- **Session Hijacking:** All mobile nodes are authenticated only at the beginning of the session setup for the communication. The attacker may take the advantage of this and perform session hijacking attack. At first, in session hijacking the malicious node spoofs the IP address of the victim and concludes the right sequence number and after that malicious node performs a DoS

attack on the victim. As a result, the target system becomes unavailable for some time with giving opportunity to a malicious node to act as an authorized node and the attacker continues the session with the other system as a legitimate system (Biswas, & Ali, 2007).

- **TCP ACK Storm:** In this attack, the attacker launches the TCP session hijacking attack at the beginning. An attacker sends the injected session data and node 1 will acknowledge the receipt of the data by sending an ACK packet to node 2 as shown in Figure 6. This packet will not contain a sequence number that node 2 is expecting, so when node 2 receives this packet, it will try to resynchronize the TCP session with node 1 by sending it an ACK packet with the sequence number that it is expecting. The cycle goes on and on, and the ACK packets passing back and forth create an ACK storm (Wu, Chen et al., 2007).

- **Desynchronization Attack:** By targeting the transport layer, a "desynchronization" attacker can break an existing connection between two nodes by sending fabricated packets exceeding the sequence number to either node of the connection which request transmission of missed frames. But in some cases desynchronization attack alters the sequence numbers of the packets in order to disrupt the communication protocol and it can prevent the end points from exchanging any useful information. This

Figure 6. TCP ACK Storm Attack

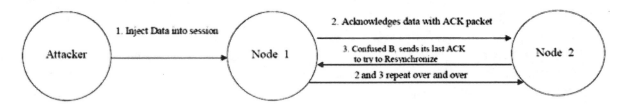

will cause a considerable drainage of energy of legitimate node (Clancy, 2005).

- **DoS in the Transport Layer:** Transport layer protocols are also susceptible to DoS security threats (Denko, 2005). Some DoS attack scenarios applicable at this layer are listed below (Cayirci, & Rong, 2008):

  ○ **Transport Layer Acknowledgement Spoofing:** False acknowledgement or acknowledgement with large receiver windows may make the source node generate more segments than the network can handle, causing congestion and degrading the network capacity.

  ○ **Replaying Acknowledgement:** A malicious node can replay an acknowledgement multiple times indicates negative acknowledgement and the source node believe that the message was not delivered successfully.

  ○ **Changing Sequence Number:** A malicious node may change the sequence number of a fragment and make the destination to believe that some fragments have been lost (Wu, Chen et al., 2007).

  ○ **Syn Flooding Attack:** The attacker uses the weakness of the TCP handshake. It sends an abundance of TCP SYN packets to the victim. The victim opens a lot of TCP connections and responds with ACK. But the attacker does not end the handshake, as a result, causes the half-open TCP connections to overflow the victim's incoming queue (Wang, Zhang, & Shin, 2002; Yi, Zhong, Zhang, & Dai, 2006).

  ○ **Jamming Acknowledgements:** A malicious node can jam the segments that convey the acknowledgements. This may lead to the termination of a connection.

  ○ **Connection Request Spoofing:** A malicious node can send many connection requests to a node, using up its resources such that it cannot accept any other connection request.

Defense Against Transport Layer Attacks

TCP feedback (TCP-F), TCP explicit failure notification (TCP-ELFN), ad-hoc Transmission Control Protocol (ATCP), ad hoc Transport Protocol (ATP) have been developed for securing end to end communication in MANETs but none one covers all the security issues involved at TCP layer in MANETs. Secure Socket Layer (SSL), Transport Layer Security (TLS) and Private Communications Transport (PCT protocols were designed based on public-key cryptography for securing end to end communication in MANETs (Hsieh, & Sivakumar, 2002; Biswas, & Ali, 2007).

Application Layer Attacks

This layer supports many protocols such as FTP, SMTP, HTTP and TELNET which have many vulnerabilities and access points for attackers. Some of main attacks in application layer are listed below:

- **DoS in the Application Layer:** Application layer protocols can also be exploited in DoS attacks. Protocols like node localization, time synchronization, data aggregation, association and data fusion can be cheated or hindered (Cayirci, & Rong, 2008).

- **Repudiation Attack:** Repudiation refers to a denial of participation in all or part of the communications. Different security solutions have been proposed at Network and Transport layer do not solve the authentication or non-repudiation problems for Application Layer.

- **Malicious Code Attack:** Malicious code such as worms, viruses, spywares and Trojan Horses can attack both operating systems as well as user applications. In MANETs, an attacker can produce similar attacks to the system of the mobile ad hoc network.

Defense Against Application Layer Attacks

Anti-spyware software can detect spyware and malicious software running on the system. However, using a firewall is not enough because in certain situations an attacker can penetrate even the firewall and make an attack. Another mechanism, Intrusion Detection System (IDS) is effective to prevent certain attacks such as the attempt to gain unauthorized access to the service, making it appear as a legitimate user (Zhang, & Lee, 2000; Anjum, & Mouchtaris, 2007). The application layer can detects a DoS attack more quickly than the lower layers.

Table 2 summarizes various types of security attack on MANETs at different layers and the countermeasures that can be used to protect against these attacks.

Other Attacks

Stealthy and Non-Stealthy Attacks: Stealthy attacks are more serious as compared to above discussed attacks as some security attacks use stealth, whereby the attackers try to hide their actions from either an individual who is monitoring the system or an intrusion detection system (IDS) and to detect this types of attack is very hard (Jakobsson, Wetzel, & Yener, 2003). Stealth attacks are classified into two classes (Stallings, 2005). The first class of attacks attempts to "hijack" or perform traffic analysis on filtered traffic to and from victim nodes. An attacker can divert traffic by using authentic routing messages to fool honest nodes into disrupting their routing tables. The second class partitions the network and reduces throughput by disconnecting victim nodes in several ways with the aim to consume the node's energy resources or create a perception of unavailability due the large quantities of messages being dropped by the victim. The most possible attacks were misrouting, power control, identity delegation and colluding collision (Khalil, & Bagchi, 2011).

- **Drop through Misrouting:** In the misrouting attack, a malicious node relays the packet to the wrong next hop, which results in a packet drop.
- **Drop through Power Control:** In this type of attack, a malicious node relays the packet by carefully reducing its transmission power thereby reducing the range and excluding the legitimate next-hop node. In the power control attack, the attacker narrows the guards that can detect the packet drop into the lightly shaded area while the majority of the guards are satisfied.
- **Drop through Colluding Collision:** The colluding node creates a collision in the vicinity of the expected next-hop node at an opportune time. In the colluding collision attack and identity delegation attack, the attacker completely evades detection by satisfying all the guards.
- **Drop through Identity Delegation:** In this form of the attack, the attacker uses two malicious nodes to drop the packet. One node is spatially close to the sender. The other node is the next hop from the sender. The first malicious node could be externally or an internally compromised node while the latter has to be an internally compromised node.

Following are the some defense mechanisms against the Stealthy attacks (Khalil, & Bagchi, 2011):

Table 2. Layer wise Security Issues and Solutions for MANETs

Layer	Security Issues	Attacks				Solutions
		Active Attacks	**Passive Attacks**			
Application Layer	Detecting and preventing Viruses, worms, malicious codes, and Applications	Repudiation attack and Malicious code attacks				Cooperation enforcement (Nuglets, Confidant, CORE) mechanisms, Detecting and preventing virus, worms, malicious codes by use of Distributed Firewalls, IDS, authentication Applications, trusted computing, etc.
Transport Layer	Authentication and Securing end-to-end communication	Session hijacking, Desynchronization, and SYN Flooding				Authentication and securing end-to-end communication by use of public cryptography (SSL, TLS, PCT, etc.)
Network Layer	Protecting the ad hoc routing and forwarding protocols	Byzantine Attack, IP Spoofing Attack, Sybil Attack, Fabrication Attack, Interruption Attack, Modification Attack, Routing Attacks, Hello flood attacks, Black hole attack,Link spoofing attack, Wormhole attack, Colluding misrelay attack, Packet Dropping etc.	DoS Attacks	Location Disclosure Attack	Eavesdropping, Traffic Analysis & Monitoring	Source authentication and message integrity mechanisms to prevent routing message modification, Securing routing protocols (e.g. IPSec, SAR, ARAN etc.) to overcome black hole, impersonation attacks, Packet leashes and SECTOR mechanism for wormhole attack, authentication and monitoring, verification, redundancy checking, probing, packet leashes by using geographical and temporal information etc.
Data Link Layer	Protecting the wireless MAC protocol and providing link layer security support	Threats in IEEE 802.11 MAC, Threats in IEEE 802.11 WEP				Providing link layer security support by using secure link layer protocols and Error –correction code, rate limitation, small frames, etc.
Physical Layer	Preventing Signal jamming	Interference and Jamming				Spread Spectrum Mechanism e.g. FHSS, DSSS, priority messages, mode change etc.

- **Mitigating Misrouting Packet Drop:** The local monitoring mechanism has to be incorporate with some additional functionality and information to detect this attack. The basic idea is to extend the knowledge at each guard to include the identity of the next hop for the packet being relayed. This additional knowledge can be collected during route establishment phase.

- **Mitigating Other Stealthy Drop Attacks:** The key observation behind the other types of the stealthy packet dropping attack is

that the attack defeats local monitoring-based detection by reducing the number of guards, so that overhear of packet reduce to zero or to a number that is less than the confidence index.

Cryptography vs. Non-Cryptography Related Attacks in MANETs

Cryptographic primitives are considered to be secure; however some problems related to cryptography were discovered such as pseudorandom number attacks (Kaufman, Perlman, & Speciner, 2002), digital signature attacks (Mehuron, 1994), and hash collision attacks (Wang, Feng, Lai, & Yu, 2004) as listed below (Wu, Chen et al., 2007):

- **Pseudorandom Number Attacks**: A timestamp or random number (nonce) is generated for a fresh session key and the shared secret key in public key infrastructure to prevent a replay attack (Khan, & Hasan, 2008). The shared secret key and session key are generated from a random number. The conventional random number generators are generally designed using statistical randomness to make very difficult to prediction by the cryptanalysts. Pseudorandom numbers are used when it is difficult to generate true random numbers in some cases. Therefore, the pseudorandom generators can be very easily a weak point in the system.
- **Digital Signature Attacks:** RSA public key algorithm can be used to create a digital signature, and the scheme is problem: it may suffer from a blind signature attack. As a protection, it was proposed ElGamal signature, which was updated in 1994 for the digital signature arithmetic. DSA was then chosen as the Digital Signature Standard (DSS) (Mehuron, 1994).
- **Hash Collision Cttacks:** The goal of a collision attack is to find two messages with the same hash. Hash collision attacks are used to modify existing certificate e.g. an attacker can construct a valid certificate corresponding to the hash collision (Wang et al., 2004).
- **Key Management Vulnerability:** The key management system must be secure, efficient and robust as it deal with the key generation, storage, distribution, updating, revocation, and certificate service for the cryptographic systems (Burnett, &

Paine, 2001; Menezes et al., 2010; Misra, & Goswami, 2010). Any secure communication is based upon it and that's why it is the weak point of system security as attackers can launch attacks to disclose the cryptographic key at the local host or during the key distribution procedure. Due to limited physical security at each node, in ad hoc networks this can create real problems related to key management (Wu, Wu, Fernandez, Ilyas, & Magliveras, 2007; Yi, & Kravets, 2004).

SECURITY MECHANISM

Preventive Mechanism

In a preventive mechanism, the conventional approaches such as authentication, access control, encryption, and digital signature are used as first line of defense in Mobile Ad Hoc Networks. Daza, Herranz, Morillo, & Ràfols (2007) proposed some cryptographic techniques to securely set up a mobile ad-hoc network. Cryptographic primitives such as hash value (message digest) is sufficient to ensure the integrity of data in transmission as well. Threshold cryptography can be used to hide data by dividing it by the number of shares. Digital signatures can also be used to achieve data integrity and authentication.

Secure Key Management: Preventing External Attacks

Key management is one of the main mechanisms for the security of applications and network services over a network (Mohapatra, & Krishnamurthy, 2010). Encryption, authentication, and key management are widely used to prevent external attacks. Key management scheme includes key distribution and key revocation. A trusted third party (TTP) is an entity trusted by the communicating parties to provide the key management services.

The TTPs are distinguishable into three categories in-line, online and off-line (Misra, & Goswami, 2010). There are several reasons which can call for key revocation before a key's expiry(Kocher, 1998; Wohlmacher, 2000). Centralized Certificate Authorities cannot be used for certificate management in mobile ad hoc network due to its dynamic environment. Thus many efforts have been made to adapt Certificate Authority's (CA) tasks to the dynamic environments of MANETs and distribute the tasks of CA among the nodes of MANETs. These distributed CAs are created dynamically and perform their operations distributed by cooperation of ad hoc network nodes. In a Distributed Certificate Authority (DCA) private key is distributed among the shareholder nodes. When operations such as issuing or revoking certificates are required, threshold of shareholders participate to perform the requested service (Chaddoud, Martin, & TW20, 2006). Various survey have been done for key management approaches in MANETs and classify them based on clustering, identity, routing, offline authority, mobility aware, contributed, distributed and chaining approaches (Aziz, Nourdine, & Mohamed, 2008; Eschenauer, & Gligor, 2002; Hegland et al., 2006; Manousakis, Sterne, Ivanic, Lawler, & McAuley, 2008; Masdari et al., 2011; Merwe, Dawoud, & McDonald, 2007). Investigations by the authors within the available publications have led to the classification of the current schemes into the following categories:

Symmetric Key Management Schemes in MANETs

- **Distributed Key Pre-distribution Scheme (DKPS):** Symmetric Key Management Schemes based on pre distribution of key information have been proposed for mobile ad hoc networks (Eschenauer, & Gligor, 2002). Chan (2004) has proposed a technique that removes the need of TTP (trusted third party) and basically consists

of three important phases Distributed Key Selection (DKS): In the first phase every node takes the key on random basis from the universal set by using exclusion property. Secure shared key Discovery (SSD): This is the second stage DKPS, in which each node have a common key with another node. Key Exclusion Property Testing (KEPT): This is last phase of DKPS symmetric key management scheme. To allow a node to test whether its set of keys satisfy the exclusion property, the information about the keys shared with other nodes is arranged in a data structure called incidence matrix through which they derive a simple testing algorithm KEPT.

- **Fully Distributed Certificate Authority:** Luo, Zerfos, Kong, Lu, & Zhang (2002) have presented the fully distributed certificate authority protocol that preserves the symmetric relationships between the communication entities in MANETs by distributing the burden of key management to all communication entities.

- **Peer Intermediaries for Key Establishment (PIKE):** PKIE is a symmetric key agreement scheme and uses a unique secret key in a set of nodes with the help of sensor nodes (Aziz et al., 2008).

- **Key Infection (INF):** This model is simple and each mobile node participates equally to make key creation process (Anderson, Chan, & Perrig, 2004).

Asymmetric Key Management Schemes in MANETs

- **Partially Distributed Threshold CA Scheme:** Zhou, & Haas (1999) have presented this scheme using the concept of CA distribution by employing threshold cryptography. Wu, Wu et al. (2007) have also proposed a key management schemes based on threshold cryptography and multicast server groups. Dong, Sui, Yiu, Li, & Hui (2007) have proposed a partially distributed clustered based approach when every cluster head node maintains detail about the certificate authority in the local clustering.

- **Mobile Certificate Authority (MOCA):** Yi, & Kravets (2003) have presented asymmetric key management scheme called mobile certificate authority (MOCA). In MOCA, the mobile nodes having great computational power and physically more secured are used as MOCA nodes on the basis of heterogeneity in the network.

- **Mobility-Based Key Management:** Capkun, Hubaux, & Buttyán (2006) have presented a mobility based key management scheme. This scheme exploits mobility and node encounters to establish security associations and ensures mutual authentication between the users.

- **Self Organized Key Scheme (SOKS):** A fully distributed scheme based on users has been proposed to issue the certificates to each other on the basis of personal acquaintance (Capkun, Buttyán, & Hubaux, 2003a). However, there is no trusted anchor trust structure. Certificate chain is used to verify the authenticity of public key in this scheme.

- **Partially Distributed CA Scheme:** The partially distributed certificate authority group of protocols distributes the trust in the certificate authority to a subset of the network communication entities for the efficient key management (Yi, & Kravets, 2003).

- **Identity-Based Key Asymmetric Management Scheme:** ID-based cryptography typically involves a global trusted authority (TA) that has a master secret key and is responsible for generating private keys for other nodes based on their IDs. Shamir (1985) has proposed first Identity

based key management scheme and a survey of the identity based approaches has been provided (Da Silva, Dos Santos, Albini, & Lima, 2008). Khalili, Katz, & Arbaugh (2003) have proposed identity-based key management approach that borrows concepts from the partially distributed certificate authority protocols, but uses as an identity-based cryptosystem to reduce the storage requirement compared to conventional public key cryptosystems. Kapil, & Rana (2009) have proposed four phase secure key management approach. During the initialization phase, each user gets their long term public and private key. Yu, Tang, Mason, & Wang (2010) have proposed a polynomial based key management approach in Hierarchical network, which is based on multiple variables polynomial with ID based threshold cryptography.

- **Ubiquitous and Robust Access Control (URSA):** Luo, Kong, Zerfos, Lu, & Zhang (2004) have proposed a localized key management scheme called URSA. In this scheme all nodes act as servers.

- **Composite Trust Model:** Yi, & Kravets (2004) have provided a composite trust model consisting of combination of the central trust and the fully distributed trust models.

- **Certificate Chaining-Based Key Management:** In the certificate chaining-based key management approach, communication entities can authenticate certificates by means of finding certificate chains between them. Certificate chaining based key management scheme has been proposed for the efficient authentication (Gordon, & Dawoud, 2009). In this approach, before the propagation route requests or reply the intermediate nodes perform certificate distribution step. Anita, & Vasudevan (2010) also presented a certificate chain based scheme to avoid black hole attack in ODMRP routing protocol. The chaining based key management approach also detailed by Hubaux, Buttyán, & Capkun, (2001) and Capkun et al., (2003a).

- **Secure and Efficient Key Management (SEKM):** This is one of decentralized asymmetric key management scheme based on a virtual CA trust model which provides safe procedure for interaction and coordination between the secret shareholders and efficient for those who have more responsibility (Wu, Wu et al., 2007).

- **Three Level Key Management Scheme:** Xiong, & Gong (2011) have proposed Secure and Highly Efficient Three Level Key Management scheme for MANETs to achieve three level securities in MANETs. This model uses ID-Based Cryptography with threshold secret sharing, Elliptic Curve Cryptography (ECC) (Menezes, 1993) and Bilinear Pairing Computation. ECC provides small keys to mobile nodes and high security level. Pairing technology provides confidentiality and authentication.

Group Key Management Schemes in MANETs

- **Simple and Efficient Group Key Management (SEGK):** Wu, Wu, & Dong (2009) proposed a SEGK model by using the concept of two multicast trees where one multicast tree as a blue tree and another multicast tree as a red tree. Computation and distribution of intermediates keying materials to all members is done by group coordinator through the use of underlying tree links. Konstantinou (2011) proposed a binary tree like clustering based key management protocol for energy constraint wireless ad hoc networks.

- **Hybrid or Composite Key Management Schemes in MANETs:** Ngai, Lyu, & Chin (2004) presented the cluster-based key management scheme that relies on a clustering algorithm to subdivide the network into smaller groups. Group members in the same proximity can monitor their neighbors and make recommendations to members from other groups on the authenticity of their neighbor's certificates. The CA private key is distributed to a set of clustered nodes for efficient key management in MANETs (Chaddoud et al., 2006).

- P. John, & Samuel (2011) proposed a predictive key management approach for minimizing the congestion and traffic overhead during the key management.

By using two or more of the above approaches in parallel, call the parallel key management so that the advantages of the one scheme is used to mitigate the disadvantages of the other. The parallel key management scheme introduced by Yi, & Kravets (2004) combines a partially distributed certificate authority proposed by Yi, & Kravets (2003) and the certificate chaining-based key management approach proposed by Capkun et al. (2003a).

We found that most of key management schemes do not comply with resource limitation and other constraints imposed by MANETs. The design of secure & efficient key management system is still open area for research.

Secure Routing Protocols: Preventing Attacks

The above mechanisms are useful to authenticate the MANETs nodes and prevent outsiders from masquerading as internal nodes. They however cannot prevent internal attacks such as misbehaving nodes attacking on ad-hoc routing. To prevent the internal attacks, several secure MANETs routing protocols have been proposed to enhance or replace existing ones. For example, SEAD (Secure Efficient Ad Hoc Distance Vector) has been proposed to replace DSDV (Perkins, & Bhagwat, 1994) as a secure distance-vector-based MANET routing protocol (Hu et al, 2003b). It does not rely on asymmetric encryption primitive but instead it relies on one-way hash chain for the security.

ARIADNE is secure extension of DSR (Johnson, & Maltz, 1996; Zhu, Lee, & Saadawi, 2003) relies on symmetric cryptography to provide security against willful active attackers and prevent its most severe attacks such as modifying the discovered routes (Hu et al., 2005). ARIADNE ensures end-to-end authentication of a routing message by using a shared key between the two parties and the MAC. Nevertheless, it relies on the TESLA to broadcast authentication message in a routing (Perrig, Canetti, Tygar, & Song, 2005). endairA is an inspiration of ARIADNE protocol that instead of verifying the request, verifies the route reply message and authors presents a solution that identifies routing anomalies using sequence number field of the routing packet (Acs, Buttyan, & Vajda, 2006). APALLS is also inspiration of ARIADNE that is designed for providing non-repudiable secure routing in MANET (Kulasekaran, & Ramkumar, 2011).

Two new protocols (ARAN and SAODV) have been proposed to secure the AODV (Perkins, & Royer, 1999) protocol with public key cryptography:

ARAN is an on-demand routing protocol that requires the presence of an online certification authority. Every node has a certificate issued by a Trusted Third party in ARAN (Sanzgiri et al., 2002).

SAODV is approach based on signing the non-mutable field of AODV routing sequences header. It is an on-demand routing approach that assumes the presence of an online key management scheme for association and verification of the public keys (Zapata, 2002).

SAR (Security-Aware Ad Hoc Routing protocol), which defines a level of trust as a metric for routing and as an attribute for security for routing. This is on-demand routing protocol assumes the existence of a key distribution or secret sharing mechanism. SAR using AODV uses encryption and decryption process using a common key (Yi et al., 2001).

Secure –MADOV is a secure multicast on-demand routing protocol in which each node (multicast group members as well as non-members) possesses a pair of public/private keys and a certificate signed by a CA (Roy, Addada, Setia, & Jajodia, 2005). The certificate binds the public key of a node to its IP address. Papadimitratos, & Haas (2002) have proposed a completely different routing protocol called SRP (Secure Routing Protocol) that assumes the existence of a security association between each source and destination node. SRP uses a Secure Message Transmission (SMT) protocol to disperse a message into pieces and transmits them through different paths, given a topology map of the network (Papadimitratos, & Haas, 2003b). SMP is an on-demand routing approach that assumes an initial trust between source and destination using public key cryptography. SRP is a symmetric key approach based on establishing a security association between source and destination using shared key. In these secure routing protocols, cryptographic mechanisms are widely used to protect the routing messages. The cost of using pair wise shared keys can be further reduced by adopting TESLA (Perrig, Szewczyk, Tygar, Wen, & Culler, 2002). It is a source authentication scheme for multicast communication which is based on loose time synchronization between the sender and the receivers followed by a delayed release of the authentication key by the sender. The sender attaches a MAC (message authentication code) to each packet using the key which initially is known to the sender only; the receiver buffers it without being able to authenticate the packet. A short while late, the sender disclosed the key and the receiver is then able to authenticate the packet.

A single MAC per packet is able to ensure source authentication if the receiver has a synchronized clock which is ahead in time as that of the sender, TESLA is light-weight, scalable and can be used in the network or in the application layer.

SLSP is a table-driven (proactive) protocol to secure OLSR protocol and assumes that the nodes have their public keys certified by a trusted third party (TTP) (Papadimitratos, & Haas, 2003a).

SOLAR is a table-driven (proactive) link state routing protocol and assumes loose clock synchronization for time-stamping the messages (Adjih et al., 2003). A key distribution center is also assumed to be present to manage the public keys or generation of the secret keys for message authentication, integrity and other security-related operations.

An on-demand (reactive) routing protocol ODSRB has been proposed that assumes bi-directional communication links and requires pair wise shared keys among the nodes which are established on-demand (Awerbuch et al., 2002; Awerbuch, Curtmola, Holmer, Rubens, & Nita-Rotaru, 2005). A multicast routing protocol BSMR has been proposed to protect against routing attacks by insider nodes that assumes a public key infrastructure to enable public key cryptographic operations (Curtmola, & Nita-Rotaru, 2007). For multicast communication, a multicast tree is constructed in BSMR.

Lou, Liu, Zhang, & Fang (2009) have proposed a mechanism in which the original routing message is first decomposed in to small shares using threshold secret sharing algorithm and send to destination using multiple routes to secure the routing message. By using the threshold secret sharing algorithm, it ensured that if some share gets corrupted by malicious node, the whole message can still be reconstructed. Rangara, Jaipuria, Yenugwar, & Jawandhiya (2010) proposed a scenario that employ multiple routing protocols are prone to different types of attacks. The idea is to switch the routing protocol upon a particular type of attack detected on the network. Trust models for secure routing using trust vector and trust value have been proposed respectively (Gong et al., 2010; Elizabeth, Radha, Priyadarshini, Jayasree, Swathi, 2012). Yang, Shu, Meng, & Lu (2006) provide a security solution for routing and data forwarding operation. It is based on collaborative monitoring performed by nodes. Awerbuch, Curtmola, Holmer, Nita-Rotaru, & Rubens (2008) proposed ODSBR an on-demand routing protocol that is based on adaptive probing technique. For a path of length n, if log n faults have been detected a misbehaving link is detected. Sen (2013) presents the detailed study of security and privacy issues in wireless mesh networks with the covering of most of the schemes for providing security in mobile ad hoc networks also. Most of the current routing protocols provide a security against specific types of attacks; in addition the current protocols do not take a global approach towards security as illustrated in Table 3 (Sen, 2013).

Intrusion Detection Techniques: Reactive Techniques

Although much attention in building a secure mobile ad-hoc network is still focused on prevention techniques as shown in the previous section, researchers have begun to investigate detection and response schemes as well. An intrusion detection system (IDS) provides a second line of defense for MANETs. Intrusion detection systems are used to detect misuse and anomalies (Mishra, Nadkarni, & Patcha, 2004). Zhang, & Lee (2000) were the first who discussed the need for a general intrusion detection framework in MANET. An IDS collects data from legitimate user behavior over a period of time and then analyzes it to determine whether there are any activities that violate the security rules, it then generates an alarm to alert the security administrator. Cooperation enforcement such as Nuglets, Confidant (Buchegger, & Le Boudec, 2002b), CORE and Token-based

Table 3. Secure Routing Mechanisms in MANETs

Protocol	Resident to Security Attacks	Vulnerable to Security Attacks
APALLS (Kulasekaran, & Ramkumar, 2011)	Reply, DOS, routing table poisoning and non repudiation attacks	Location disclosure, black hole and wormhole attacks
ARAN (Sanzgiri et al., 2002)	Reply and routing table poisoning attacks.	Location disclosure, black hole, wormhole and DoS attacks.
ARIADNE (Hu et al., 2005)	Reply, DOS and routing table poisoning attacks.	Location disclosure, black hole and wormhole attacks
BSMR (Curtmola, & Nita-Rotaru, 2007)	Replay, byzantine attacks, packet dropping, false packet injection, Packet modification, false route advertisement, intentional collision of frames at the MAC layer and jamming at the physical layer.	DoS attacks.
endairA (Acs et al., 2006)	Reply, DOS, routing table poisoning and black hole attacks.	Wormhole attack
ODSRB (Awerbuch et al., 2005; Awerbuch et al., 2002)	Byzantine attacks and selectively dropping packets	DoS and wormhole attacks.
Packet Leashes (Hu et al., 2003a; Wu, & Yau, 2007)	Wormhole attack	Invisible node attack
SAODV (Zapata, 2002)	Reply and routing table poisoning attacks.	Location disclosure, black hole, wormhole and DoS attacks.
SAR (Yi et al., 2001)	Reply and routing table poisoning attacks.	Location disclosure, black hole, wormhole and DoS attacks.
SEAD (Hu et al., 2003b)	Reply, DoS and routing table poisoning attacks.	Location disclosure, black hole, and wormhole attacks.
Secure MAODV (Roy et al., 2005)	Internal and External Attacks on route discovery process.	DoS attack.
SLSP (Papadimitratos, & Haas, 2003a)	Reply, DoS and routing table poisoning attacks.	Location disclosure, black hole and wormhole attacks.
SMT (Papadimitratos, & Haas, 2003b)	Reply and routing table poisoning attacks.	Location disclosure, black hole, wormhole and DoS attacks.
SOLAR (Adjih et al., 2003)	Reply attack, routing table poisoning attacks, incorrect HELLO flooding message, ID and Link spoofing, and malicious topology control (TC) message generation attacks.	Location disclosure, black hole, wormhole and DoS attacks.
SRP (Papadimitratos, & Haas, 2002)	Reply, DoS and routing table poisoning attacks.	Location disclosure, black hole and wormhole attacks.
TESLA (Perrig et al., 2005)	DoS attack on the sender if indirect time synchronization is used.	DoS attack on the sender if direct time synchronization is used.

reduce selfish node behavior (Anjum, & Mouchtaris, 2007) have been proposed for the detection of the nodes having selfish in nature. The early trend in the intrusion detection was designing of the efficient architecture. Depending upon the detection engine used in the architecture, the intrusion detection engines can be classified in three categories:

1. Anomaly / Behavior based IDS
2. Signature / Misuse based IDS
3. Specification based IDS.

A misuse detection system attempts to define improper behavior based on the patterns of well-known attacks. Anomaly detection attempts to define normal or expected behavior statistically.

Specification based detection defines a set of constraints that describe the correct operation of a protocol or program and oversees the program with the constraints defined. When considering the area, which is the source of data used for intrusion detection and another classification of intrusion detection systems can be used in terms of the type of the protected system. There is a family of IDS tools, which use information from one host (system)-host-based IDS (HIDS) and those IDS using information obtained from a local network segment (network based IDS i.e. NIDS).

The architectures for intrusion detection in mobile ad hoc network can be classified in to Stand-alone, Distributed and Co-operative and Hierarchical architectures.

Stand-Alone Architectures: For intrusion detection in mobile ad hoc network uses detection engine installed at each node utilizing only the node's local audit record. Nadkarni, & Mishra (2004) proposed a Threshold Based stand-alone IDS architecture that uses compound detection aiming at reducing the amount of false positive alerts, which typically appear in anomaly detection. It employs adjusting thresholds to determine malicious behaviors based on the initial normalized profile. Jacoby, & Davis (2007) proposed a standalone system that is based on monitoring the power consumption of nodes. Da Silva et al. (2008) proposed a mechanism in which every node maintains a miss-incident value that is calculated during the system initialization.

Distributed And Cooperative Architectures: Include intrusion detection engine installed in each node of the network, which monitors local audit data and sharing of audit data and / or detection results with neighboring nodes to resolve inconclusive. Bhargava, & Agrawal (2001) adopts similar approach where mal counts are maintained by node for other nodes, if a mal count for a node exceeds a threshold an alert is issued. Partridge et al. (2002) presented that basic signal processing techniques can be used to perform traffic analysis on packet streams, even if the data is encrypted. Buchegger, & Le Boudec (2002a) propose a routing protocol extension that detects and isolates nodes that do not cooperate in routing and forwarding due to selfishness. A follow-up work with focus on a preliminary investigation of anomaly detection approaches for MANETs with the use of local IDS has been proposed and it performs the anomaly detection using nodes profiles (Zhang, Lee, & Huang, 2003). Huang, Fan, Lee, & Yu (2003) used the data-mining techniques to automatically construct an anomaly detection model for MANETs. They used an analysis technique that targets multiple features and which acknowledges the characteristic patterns of correlation between them. The basic assumption here for anomaly detection is that normal and abnormal events have different feature vectors that can be differentiated. Bose, Bharathimurugan, & Kannan (2007) proposed a multilayer intrusion detection system that operates at all layer of protocol stack. Ramachandran, Misra, & Obaidat (2008) proposed agent based intrusion detection approach that is based on the performance of the nodes during intrusion detection phase. Razak, Furnell, Clarke, & Brooke (2008) have proposed a cooperative two-tier (i.e., one for local and one for global detection) friend-assisted intrusion detection architecture for MANETs, where each tier includes two detection engines, and first performs a signature based detection then an anomaly-based detection respectively.

Hierarchical Architectures: Multi-layer approach where dividing the entire network into clusters. Specific nodes are selected as cluster heads and a more comprehensive engine are running on these nodes and undertake various responsibilities and roles in intrusion detection functions, which are usually different from the ordinary members of the cluster, where only lightweight intrusion detection engine installed only to perform intrusion detection from local audit data. Manousakis et al. (2008) presented a mechanism in which the nodes are structured in the form of a dynamic tree, the upper nodes have the higher authority and they can pass directives to below nodes; the lower nodes pass the data to upper nodes that are aggregated and useful for the detection of the intrusion detection. Ma, & Fang (2009) proposed an IDS system in which cluster heads are selected based on an election algorithm. These nodes perform network intrusion detection.

Marti et al. (2000) proposed to use "watch-dog" to identify nodes with routing misbehavior and to avoid such nodes in the route used. It also uses "pathrater" to choose better path based on the reputation of intermediate nodes if multiple paths are available. CONFIDANT further extends these approaches to evaluate the level of trust of alert reports and to include a reputation system to rate each node (Buchegger, & Le Boudec, 2002b). Hsin, & Liu (2002) proposed a power-efficient distributed neighbor monitoring mechanism where alarms are transmitted back to a control center using a static sensor network. Urpi, Bonuccelli, & Giordano (2003) proposed a general framework for cooperation without any incentive mechanism. Their solution is based on the idea that each node monitors the behavior of other nodes in the neighborhood. Fahad et al. (2007) introduced a new approach for detecting misbehaving nodes that drop data packets in MA-NETs. It consists of two stages: first stage is the monitoring stage in which each node monitors its direct neighbours with respect to forwarding data packets and the second stage is decision stage in which direct neighbouring nodes decide whether the monitored node misbehave or not. Rachedi, & Benslimane (2009) proposed a novel IDS that is based on monitoring to assess the node behavior.

Cross layer are formed to be very efficient in the detection of intrusion. Joseph, Das, Seet, & Lee (2007) have demonstrated through simulation the need for cross layer design. CRADS is a cross layer IDS for routing attack identification (Joseph, Das, Seet, & Lee, 2008). Hortos (2009) proposed a multi level IDS system for wireless Ad Hoc network using un-supervised & supervised algorithms. XIDR is a dynamic cross layer intrusion

detection and responses system (Svecs, Sarkar, Basu, & Wong, 2010). The model comprises of multiple intrusions detection sources.

Game theory has been employed in intrusion detection system. A number of IDS solutions based on game theory have been proposed in literature. Luo et al. (2004) uses game theory to determine if it is essential runs an IDS always on nodes of the network. They modeled the interaction between attacker and IDS through two players non–cooperative and non zero sum model. Sen, & Clark (2011) presented genetic programming approach towards IDS in MANETs. In genetic programming, a set of candidate solutions are evolved towards the target solution. During each step, the current candidates solutions are cross over and mutated to generate new solutions. The new solutions are evaluated against a fitness function. Those solutions that passed the fitness criteria are selected as candidate solution and next iteration is iterated. The process is repeated until the termination criterion is satisfied. Sen, & Clark (2011) evaluated the programs for each type of attack with the consideration of the features related to mobility and packets as input variable to the genetic programming. Tournament selection algorithm is used for selecting individuals for cross over. The algorithm is evolved using training data. The fitness function is defined as the difference between detection rate and false positive rate. Ford, Carvalho, Allen, & Ham (2009) proposed a biological inspired tactical infrastructure for intrusion detection in mobile ad hoc networks. There are systems that consider only a specific type of attacks. The performance and accuracy of the intrusion detection also plays a critical role in MANETs security.

CONCLUSION AND FUTURE DIRECTIONS

This chapter has made a comprehensive presentation on the various attacks on different layers of the communication protocol. After identifying various security threats, the chapter has presented a comprehensive state of the art survey on various defense mechanisms for defending those attacks. Most of the proposals deliberated on an individual security problem. The security mechanisms presented in the literature has solved many security issues but a comprehensive security solution for MANETs is still not available that completely cover all the security issue related to MANETs. Moreover, there are many threats and attacks or combined of different attacks that have not been discovered yet and a lot of research is still on the way to identify new security threats and create secure mechanisms to counter those threats. Proper and efficient Key management is more required to enhance the security in MANETs. The effectiveness of key agreement and distribution in MANETs is an area of ongoing research. However, the attack prevention methods are not sufficient. So, to resist against attacks, Intrusion Detection Systems (IDS) and cooperation enforcement mechanisms are required to monitor the activities that violate the security policy in mobile ad hoc networks. The intrusion detection system should be designed in such a way that it can work independently without minimum human supervision and provide a necessary level of protection to the node and network. Finally some of the emerging trends in research and future research issues related to security in MANETs are also discussed in this chapter.

REFERENCES

Aad, I., Hubaux, J. P., & Knightly, E. W. (2008). Impact of denial of service attacks on ad hoc networks. *IEEE/ACM Transactions on Networking, 16*(4), 791–802. doi:10.1109/TNET.2007.904002.

Acs, G., Buttyan, L., & Vajda, I. (2006). Provably secure on-demand source routing in mobile ad hoc networks. *IEEE Transactions on Mobile Computing, 5*(11), 1533–1546. doi:10.1109/TMC.2006.170.

Adjih, C., Clausen, T., Jacquet, P., Laouiti, A., Muhlethaler, P., & Raffo, D. (2003). Securing the OLSR protocol. In *Proceedings of Med-Hoc-Net* (pp. 25–27). IEEE.

Agrawal, P., Ghosh, R. K., & Das, S. K. (2008). Cooperative black and gray hole attacks in mobile ad hoc networks. In *Proceedings of the 2nd International Conference on Ubiquitous Information Management and Communication* (pp. 310-314). ACM.

Al-Shurman, M., Yoo, S. M., & Park, S. (2004). Black hole attack in mobile ad hoc networks. In *Proceedings of the 42nd Annual Southeast Regional Conference* (pp. 96-97). ACM.

Anderson, R., Chan, H., & Perrig, A. (2004). Key infection: Smart trust for smart dust. In *Proceedings of the 12th IEEE International Conference on Network Protocols,* (pp. 206-215). IEEE.

Anita, E. M., & Vasudevan, V. (2010). Black hole attack prevention in multicast routing protocols for mobile ad hoc networks using certificate chaining. *International Journal of Computers and Applications, 1*(12), 21–22.

Anjum, F., & Mouchtaris, P. (2007). *Security for wireless ad hoc networks*. New York: Wiley-Interscience. doi:10.1002/0470118474.

Awerbuch, B., Curtmola, R., Holmer, D., Nita-Rotaru, C., & Rubens, H. (2008). ODSBR: An on-demand secure Byzantine resilient routing protocol for wireless ad hoc networks. *ACM Transactions on Information and System Security, 10*(4), 6. doi:10.1145/1284680.1341892.

Awerbuch, B., Curtmola, R., Holmer, D., Rubens, H., & Nita-Rotaru, C. (2005). On the survivability of routing protocols in ad hoc wireless networks. In *Proceedings of the First International Conference on Security and Privacy for Emerging Areas in Communications Networks,* (pp. 327-338). IEEE.

Awerbuch, B., Holmer, D., Nita-Rotaru, C., & Rubens, H. (2002). An on-demand secure routing protocol resilient to byzantine failures. In *Proceedings of the 1st ACM Workshop on Wireless Security* (pp. 21-30). ACM.

Aziz, B., Nourdine, E., & Mohamed, E. K. (2008). A recent survey on key management schemes in manet. In *Proceedings of the 3rd International Conference on Information and Communication Technologies: From Theory to Applications,* (pp. 1-6). IEEE.

Balakrishnan, V., Varadharajan, V., & Tupakula, U. K. (2006). Fellowship: Defense against flooding and packet drop attacks in MANET. In *Proceedings of the Network Operations and Management Symposium,* (pp. 1-4). IEEE.

Bhargava, S., & Agrawal, D. P. (2001). Security enhancements in AODV protocol for wireless ad hoc networks. In *Proceedings of the Vehicular Technology Conference,* (Vol. 4, pp. 2143-2147). IEEE.

Biswas, K., & Ali, M. L. (2007, March). Security threats in mobile ad hoc network. *Department of Interaction and System Design School of Engineering,* 9-26.

Blazevic, L., Le Boudec, J. Y., & Giordano, S. (2005). A location-based routing method for mobile ad hoc networks. *IEEE Transactions on Mobile Computing, 4*(2), 97–110. doi:10.1109/TMC.2005.16.

Borisov, N., Goldberg, I., & Wagner, D. (2001). Intercepting mobile communications: The insecurity of 802.11. In *Proceedings of the 7th Annual International Conference on Mobile Computing and Networking* (pp. 180-189). ACM.

Bose, S., Bharathimurugan, S., & Kannan, A. (2007). Multi-layer integrated anomaly intrusion detection system for mobile adhoc networks. In *Proceedings of the International Conference on Signal Processing, Communications and Networking,* (pp. 360-365). IEEE.

Boukerche, A., & Ren, Y. (2008). The design of a secure key management system for mobile ad hoc networks. In *Proceedings of the 33rd IEEE Conference on Local Computer Networks,* (pp. 320-327). IEEE.

Buchegger, S., & Buddec, J. L. (2001). *The selfish node: Increasing routing security in mobile ad hoc network (IBM Research Report: RR 3354).* IBM.

Buchegger, S., & Le Boudec, J. Y. (2002a). Nodes bearing grudges: Towards routing security, fairness, and robustness in mobile ad hoc networks. In *Proceedings of the 10th Euromicro Workshop on Parallel, Distributed and Network-Based Processing* (pp. 403-410). IEEE.

Buchegger, S., & Le Boudec, J. Y. (2002b). Performance analysis of the CONFIDANT protocol. In *Proceedings of the 3rd ACM International Symposium on Mobile Ad Hoc Networking & Computing* (pp. 226-236). ACM.

Burg, A. (2003). Ad hoc network specific attacks. In *Seminar on ad hoc networking: Concepts, applications, and security.* Technische Universität München.

Burnett, S., & Paine, S. (2001). *The RSA security's official guide to cryptography.* New York: McGraw-Hill, Inc..

Caballero, E. J. (2006). Vulnerabilities of intrusion detection systems in mobile ad-hoc networks—The routing problem. In *Proceedings of TKK T-110.5290 Seminar on Network Security* (pp. 1-2). TKK.

Capkun, S., Buttyán, L., & Hubaux, J. P. (2003a). Self-organized public-key management for mobile ad hoc networks. *IEEE Transactions on Mobile Computing, 2*(1), 52–64. doi:10.1109/TMC.2003.1195151.

Čapkun, S., Buttyán, L., & Hubaux, J. P. (2003b). SECTOR: Secure tracking of node encounters in multi-hop wireless networks. In *Proceedings of the 1st ACM Workshop on Security of Ad Hoc and Sensor Networks* (pp. 21-32). ACM.

Capkun, S., Hubaux, J. P., & Buttyan, L. (2006). Mobility helps peer-to-peer security. *IEEE Transactions on Mobile Computing, 5*(1), 43–51. doi:10.1109/TMC.2006.12.

Cayirci, E., & Rong, C. (2008). *Security in wireless ad hoc and sensor networks*. New York: Wiley.

Chaddoud, G., & Martin, K. (2006). Distributed certificate authority in cluster-based ad hoc networks. In *Proceedings of the Wireless Communications and Networking Conference* (Vol. 2, pp. 682-688). IEEE.

Chan, A. F. (2004). Distributed symmetric key management for mobile ad hoc networks. In *Proceedings of INFOCOM 2004 Twenty-Third Annual Joint Conference of the IEEE Computer and Communications Societies* (Vol. 4, pp. 2414-2424). IEEE.

Chapkin, S., Bako, B., Kargl, F., & Schoch, E. (2006). Location tracking attack in ad hoc networks based on topology information. In *Proceedings of the 2006 IEEE International Conference on Mobile Adhoc and Sensor Systems (MASS)* (pp. 870-875). IEEE.

Chlamtac, I., Conti, M., & Liu, J. J. N. (2003). Mobile ad hoc networking: imperatives and challenges. *Ad Hoc Networks, 1*(1), 13–64. doi:10.1016/S1570-8705(03)00013-1.

Choi, S., Kim, D. Y., Lee, D. H., & Jung, J. I. (2008). WAP: Wormhole attack prevention algorithm in mobile ad hoc networks. In *Proceedings of the IEEE International Conference on Sensor Networks, Ubiquitous and Trustworthy Computing,* (pp. 343-348). IEEE.

Clancy, T. C. (2005). *Security review of the light-weight access point protocol draft-ohara-capwap-lwapp-02.*

Crepeau, C., Davis, C. R., & Maheswaran, M. (2007). A secure MANET routing protocol with resilience against Byzantine behaviours of malicious or selfish nodes. In *Proceedings of the 21st International Conference on Advanced Information Networking and Applications Workshops,* (Vol. 2, pp. 19-26). IEEE.

Curtmola, R., & Nita-Rotaru, C. (2007). BSMR: Byzantine-resilient secure multicast routing in multi-hop wireless networks. In *Proceedings of the 4th Annual IEEE Communications Society Conference on Sensor, Mesh and Ad Hoc Communications and Networks,* (pp. 263-272). IEEE.

Da Silva, E., Dos Santos, A., Albini, L. C. P., & Lima, M. (2008). Identity-based key management in mobile ad hoc networks: Techniques and applications. *IEEE Wireless Communications, 15*(5), 46–52. doi:10.1109/MWC.2008.4653131.

Daza, V., Herranz, J., Morillo, P., & Ràfols, C. (2007). Cryptographic techniques for mobile ad-hoc networks. *Computer Networks, 51*(18), 4938–4950. doi:10.1016/j.comnet.2007.08.002.

Deng, H., Li, W., & Agrawal, D. P. (2002). Routing security in wireless ad hoc networks. *IEEE Communications Magazine, 40*(10), 70–75. doi:10.1109/MCOM.2002.1039859.

Denko, M. K. (2005). Detection and prevention of denial of service (DoS) attacks in mobile ad hoc networks using reputation-based incentive scheme. *Journal of Systemics. Cybernetics and Informatics, 3*(4), 1–9.

Dong, Y., Sui, A. F., Yiu, S. M., Li, V. O., & Hui, L. C. (2007). Providing distributed certificate authority service in cluster-based mobile ad hoc networks. *Computer Communications, 30*(11), 2442–2452. doi:10.1016/j.comcom.2007.04.011.

Douceur, J. R. (2002). The Sybil attack. In *Peer-to-peer systems* (pp. 251–260). Berlin, Germany: Springer. doi:10.1007/3-540-45748-8_24.

Elizabeth, N. E., Radha, S., Priyadarshini, S., Jayasree, S., & Swathi, K. N. (2012). SRT-secure routing using trust levels in MANETs. *European Journal of Scientific Research, 75*(3).

Eriksson, J., Krishnamurthy, S. V., & Faloutsos, M. (2006). Truelink: A practical countermeasure to the wormhole attack in wireless networks. In *Proceedings of the 2006 14th IEEE International Conference on Network Protocols,* (pp. 75-84). IEEE.

Eschenauer, L., & Gligor, V. D. (2002). A key-management scheme for distributed sensor networks. In *Proceedings of the 9th ACM Conference on Computer and Communications Security* (pp. 41-47). ACM.

Fahad, T., Djenouri, D., & Askwith, R. (2007). On detecting packets droppers in manet: A novel low cost approach. In *Proceedings of the Third International Symposium on Information Assurance and Security,* (pp. 56-64). IEEE.

Ford, R., Carvalho, M., Allen, W. H., & Ham, F. (2009). Adaptive security for MANETs via biology. In *Proceedings of the 2nd Cyberspace Research Workshop*. IEEE.

Gerhards-Padilla, E., Aschenbruck, N., Martini, P., Jahnke, M., & Tolle, J. (2007). Detecting black hole attacks in tactical MANETs using topology graphs. In *Proceedings of the 32nd IEEE Conference on Local Computer Networks,* (pp. 1043-1052). IEEE.

Ghaffari, A. (2006). Vulnerability and security of mobile ad hoc networks. In *Proceedings of the 6th WSEAS International Conference on Simulation, Modelling and Optimization* (pp. 124-129). World Scientific and Engineering Academy and Society (WSEAS).

Ghonge, M. M., Jawandhiya, P. M., & Ali, D. M. (2011). *Countermeasures of network layer attacks in MANETs*. IJCA.

Gong, W., You, Z., Chen, D., Zhao, X., Gu, M., & Lam, K. Y. (2010). Trust based routing for misbehavior detection in ad hoc networks. *Journal of Networks, 5*(5), 551–558. doi:10.4304/jnw.5.5.551-558.

Gordon, R. L., & Dawoud, D. S. (2009). Direct and indirect trust establishment in ad hoc networks by certificate distribution and verification. In *Proceedings of the 1st International Conference on Wireless Communication, Vehicular Technology, Information Theory and Aerospace & Electronic Systems Technology,* (pp. 624-629). IEEE.

Gracelin, S. R., Edna, E. N., & Radha, S. (2010). A novel method for detection and elimination of modification attack and TTL attack in NTP based routing algorithm. In *Proceedings of the 2010 International Conference on Recent Trends in Information, Telecommunication and Computing (ITC)* (pp. 60-64). IEEE.

Gunasekaran, R., & Uthariaraj, V. R. (2009). Prevention of denial of service attacks and performance enhancement in mobile adhoc networks. In *Proceedings of the First International Communication Systems and Networks and Workshops,* (pp. 1-6). IEEE.

Guo, Y., & Perreau, S. (2010). Detect DDoS flooding attacks in mobile ad hoc networks. *International Journal of Security and Networks, 5*(4), 259–269. doi:10.1504/IJSN.2010.037666.

Hegland, A. M., Winjum, E., Mjolsnes, S. F., Rong, C., Kure, O., & Spilling, P. (2006). A survey of key management in ad hoc networks. *IEEE Communications Surveys and Tutorials*, 8(3), 48–66. doi:10.1109/COMST.2006.253271.

Hortos, W. S. (2009). Unsupervised algorithms for intrusion detection and identification in wireless ad hoc sensor networks. In SPIE Defense, Security, and Sensing (pp. 73520J-73520J). International Society for Optics and Photonics.

Hsieh, H. Y., & Sivakumar, R. (2002). Transport over wireless networks. Handbook of Wireless Networks and Mobile Computing, 289.

Hsin, C. F., & Liu, M. (2002). A distributed monitoring mechanism for wireless sensor networks. In *Proceedings of the 1st ACM workshop on Wireless security* (pp. 57-66). ACM.

Hu, L., & Evans, D. (2004). Using directional antennas to prevent wormhole attacks. In *Network and Distributed System Security Symposium (NDSS)*. NDSS.

Hu, Y. C., Johnson, D. B., & Perrig, A. (2003b). SEAD: Secure efficient distance vector routing for mobile wireless ad hoc networks. *Ad Hoc Networks*, 1(1), 175–192. doi:10.1016/S1570-8705(03)00019-2.

Hu, Y. C., Perrig, A., & Johnson, D. B. (2003a). Packet leashes: A defense against wormhole attacks in wireless networks. [IEEE.]. *Proceedings of INFOCOM, 2003*, 1976–1986.

Hu, Y. C., Perrig, A., & Johnson, D. B. (2005). Ariadne: A secure on-demand routing protocol for ad hoc networks. *Wireless Networks*, 11(1-2), 21–38. doi:10.1007/s11276-004-4744-y.

Huang, Y. A., Fan, W., Lee, W., & Yu, P. S. (2003). Cross-feature analysis for detecting ad-hoc routing anomalies. In *Proceedings of the 23rd International Conference on Distributed Computing Systems, 2003* (pp. 478-487). IEEE.

Hubaux, J. P., Buttyán, L., & Capkun, S. (2001). The quest for security in mobile ad hoc networks. In *Proceedings of the 2nd ACM International Symposium on Mobile Ad Hoc Networking & Computing* (pp. 146-155). ACM.

Ilyas, M. (2010). *The handbook of ad hoc wireless networks*. Boca Raton, FL: CRC Press.

Islam, N., & Shaikh, Z. A. (2013). Security issues in mobile ad hoc network. In *Wireless Networks and Security* (pp. 49–80). Berlin, Germany: Springer Verlag. doi:10.1007/978-3-642-36169-2_2.

Jacoby, G. A., & Davis, N. J. (2007). Mobile host-based intrusion detection and attack identification. *IEEE Wireless Communications*, 14(4), 53–60. doi:10.1109/MWC.2007.4300984.

Jain, S., & Jain, S. (2010). Detection and prevention of wormhole attack in mobile ad-hoc networks. *International Journal of Computer Theory and Engineering*, 2(1).

Jakobsson, M., Wetzel, S., & Yener, B. (2003). Stealth attacks on ad-hoc wireless networks. In *Proceedings of the 58th Vehicular Technology Conference*, (Vol. 3, pp. 2103-2111). IEEE.

John, S. P., & Samuel, P. (2011). A predictive clustering technique for effective key management in mobile ad hoc networks. *Information Security Journal: A Global Perspective, 20*(4-5), 250-260.

Johnson, D. B., & Maltz, D. A. (1996). *Dynamic source routing in ad hoc wireless networks*. Dordrecht, The Netherlands: Kluwer. doi:10.1007/978-0-585-29603-6_5.

Joseph, J. F. C., Das, A., Seet, B. C., & Lee, B. S. (2007). Cross layer versus single layer approaches for intrusion detection in MANETs. In *Proceedings of the 15th IEEE International Conference on Networks*, (pp. 194-199). IEEE.

Joseph, J. F. C., Das, A., Seet, B. C., & Lee, B. S. (2008). CRADS: Integrated cross layer approach for detecting routing attacks in MANETs. In *Proceedings of the Wireless Communications and Networking Conference,* (pp. 1525-1530). IEEE.

Kannhavong, B., Nakayama, H., Nemoto, Y., Kato, N., & Jamalipour, A. (2007). A survey of routing attacks in mobile ad hoc networks. *IEEE Wireless Communications, 14*(5), 85–91. doi:10.1109/MWC.2007.4396947.

Kapil, A., & Rana, S. (2009). Identity-based key management in MANETs using public key cryptography. *International Journal of Security, 3*(1), 1.

Karlof, C., & Wagner, D. (2003). Secure routing in wireless sensor networks: Attacks and countermeasures. *Ad Hoc Networks, 1*(2), 293–315. doi:10.1016/S1570-8705(03)00008-8.

Karygiannis, T., & Owens, L. (2002). Wireless network security. *NIST Special Publication, 800,* 48.

Kaufman, C., Perlman, R., & Speciner, M. (2002). *Network security: Private communication in a public world.* Upper Saddle River, NJ: Prentice Hall Press.

Khalil, I., & Bagchi, S. (2011). Stealthy attacks in wireless ad hoc networks: Detection and countermeasure. *IEEE Transactions on Mobile Computing, 10*(8), 1096–1112. doi:10.1109/TMC.2010.249.

Khalil, I., Bagchi, S., & Shroff, N. B. (2007). Liteworp: Detection and isolation of the wormhole attack in static multihop wireless networks. *Computer networks, 51*(13), 3750-3772.

Khalili, A., Katz, J., & Arbaugh, W. A. (2003). Toward secure key distribution in truly ad-hoc networks. In *Proceedings of the 2003 Symposium on Applications and the Internet Workshops, 2003* (pp. 342-346). IEEE.

Khan, M. A., & Hasan, A. (2008). Pseudo random number based authentication to counter denial of service attacks on 802.11. In *Proceedings of the 5th IFIP International Conference on Wireless and Optical Communications Networks,* (pp. 1-5). IEEE.

Kim, Y., Sankhla, V., & Helmy, A. (2004). Efficient traceback of DoS attacks using small worlds in MANET. In *Proceedings of the Vehicular Technology Conference,* (Vol. 6, pp. 3979-3983). IEEE.

Kocher, P. C. (1998). On certificate revocation and validation. In *Financial Cryptography* (pp. 172–177). Berlin, Germany: Springer Verlag. doi:10.1007/BFb0055481.

Komninos, N., Vergados, D., & Douligeris, C. (2006). Layered security design for mobile ad hoc networks. *Computers & Security, 25*(2), 121–130. doi:10.1016/j.cose.2005.09.005.

Konstantinou, E. (2011). Efficient cluster-based group key agreement protocols for wireless ad hoc networks. *Journal of Network and Computer Applications, 34*(1), 384–393. doi:10.1016/j.jnca.2010.05.001.

Kulasekaran, S., & Ramkumar, M. (2011). APALLS: A secure MANET routing protocol. *Mobile Ad Hoc Networks: Applications.*

Kurosawa, S., Nakayama, H., Kato, N., Jamalipour, A., & Nemoto, Y. (2007). Detecting blackhole attack on AODV-based mobile ad hoc networks by dynamic learning method. *International Journal of Network Security, 5*(3), 338–346.

Kyasanur, P., & Vaidya, N. (2003). Detection and handling of MAC layer misbehavior in wireless networks. In *Proceedings of the International Conference on Dependable Systems and Networks* (pp. 22-25). IEEE.

Kyasanur, P., & Vaidya, N. H. (2002). Handling MAC layer misbehavior in wireless networks. In *Proceedings of MOBICOM'02*. Atlanta, GA: ACM.

Lou, W., Liu, W., Zhang, Y., & Fang, Y. (2009). SPREAD: Improving network security by multipath routing in mobile ad hoc networks. *Wireless Networks*, *15*(3), 279–294. doi:10.1007/s11276-007-0039-4.

Luo, H., Kong, J., Zerfos, P., Lu, S., & Zhang, L. (2004). URSA: Ubiquitous and robust access control for mobile ad hoc networks. *IEEE/ACM Transactions on Networking*, *12*(6), 1049–1063. doi:10.1109/TNET.2004.838598.

Luo, H., Zerfos, P., Kong, J., Lu, S., & Zhang, L. (2002). Self-securing ad hoc wireless networks. In *Proceedings of the Seventh IEEE Symposium on Computers and Communications (ISCC'02)* (Vol. 8). IEEE.

Ma, C. X., & Fang, Z. M. (2009). A novel intrusion detection architecture based on adaptive selection event triggering for mobile ad-hoc networks. In *Proceedings of the Second International Symposium on Intelligent Information Technology and Security Informatics*, (pp. 198-201). IEEE.

Manousakis, K., Sterne, D., Ivanic, N., Lawler, G., & McAuley, A. (2008). A stochastic approximation approach for improving intrusion detection data fusion structures. In *Proceedings of the Military Communications Conference*, (pp. 1-7). IEEE.

Marti, S., Giuli, T. J., Lai, K., & Baker, M. (2000). Mitigating routing misbehavior in mobile ad hoc networks. In *Proceedings of the 6th Annual International Conference on Mobile Computing and Networking* (Vol. 6, pp. 255-265). ACM.

Masdari, M., Jabbehdari, S., Ahmadi, M. R., Hashemi, S. M., Bagherzadeh, J., & Khadem-Zadeh, A. (2011). A survey and taxonomy of distributed certificate authorities in mobile ad hoc networks. *EURASIP Journal on Wireless Communications and Networking*, *1*, 1–12.

Medidi, S. R., Medidi, M., & Gavini, S. (2003). Detecting packet-dropping faults in mobile ad-hoc networks. In *Proceedings of the Conference Record of the Thirty-Seventh Asilomar Conference on Signals, Systems and Computers, 2003* (Vol. 2, pp. 1708-1712). IEEE.

Mehuron, W. (1994). *Digital signature standard (DSS)*. Washington, DC: NIST.

Menezes, A. J. (1993). *Elliptic curve public key cryptosystems*. Boston: Kluwer Academic Publishers. doi:10.1007/978-1-4615-3198-2.

Menezes, A. J., Van Oorschot, P. C., & Vanstone, S. A. (2010). *Handbook of applied cryptography*. Boca Raton, FL: CRC Press.

Merwe, J. V. D., Dawoud, D., & McDonald, S. (2007). A survey on peer-to-peer key management for mobile ad hoc networks. *ACM Computing Surveys*, *39*(1), 1. doi:10.1145/1216370.1216371.

Min, Z., & Jiliu, Z. (2009). Cooperative black hole attack prevention for mobile ad hoc networks. In *Proceedings of the International Symposium on Information Engineering and Electronic Commerce*, (pp. 26-30). IEEE.

Mishra, A., Nadkarni, K., & Patcha, A. (2004). Intrusion detection in wireless ad hoc networks. *IEEE Wireless Communications*, *11*(1), 48–60. doi:10.1109/MWC.2004.1269717.

Misra, S., & Goswami, S. (2010). Key management in mobile ad hoc networks. In A. K. Pathan (Ed.), *Security of self-organizing networks: MANET, WSN, WMN, VANET*. Boca Raton, FL: CRC Press. doi:10.1201/EBK1439819197-10.

Mohamad, O., Hassan, R., Patel, A., & Razali, R. (2009). A review of security parameters in mobile ad hoc networks. In *Proceeding of the International Conference on Information and Communications Systems (ICICS2009)* (Vol. 7). ICICS.

Mohapatra, P., & Krishnamurthy, S. (2010). *Ad hoc networks: Technologies and protocols*. New York: Springer Publishing Company, Incorporated.

Murthy, C. S. R., & Manoj, B. S. (2004). *Ad hoc wireless networks: Architectures and protocols*. Upper Saddle River, NJ: Prentice Hall.

Nadkarni, K., & Mishra, A. (2004). A novel intrusion detection approach for wireless ad hoc networks. In *Proceedings of the Wireless Communications and Networking Conference,* (Vol. 2, pp. 831-836). IEEE.

Ngadi, M., Khokhar, R. H., & Mandala, S. (2008). A review current routing attacks in mobile ad-hoc networks. *International Journal of Computer Science and Security*, 2(3), 18–29.

Ngai, E. C., Lyu, M. R., & Chin, R. T. (2004). An authentication service against dishonest users in mobile ad hoc networks. In *Proceedings of the Aerospace Conference,* (Vol. 2, pp. 1275-1285). IEEE.

Nguyen, H. L., & Nguyen, U. T. (2008). A study of different types of attacks on multicast in mobile ad hoc networks. *Ad Hoc Networks*, 6(1), 32–46. doi:10.1016/j.adhoc.2006.07.005.

Nichols, R. K., & Lekkas, P. C. (2002). *Wireless security*. New York: McGraw-Hill.

Papadimitratos, P., & Haas, Z. J. (2002). Secure routing for mobile ad hoc networks. In *Proceedings of the SCS Communication Networks and Distributed Systems Modeling and Simulation Conference (CNDS)* (pp. 193-204). SCS.

Papadimitratos, P., & Haas, Z. J. (2003a). Secure link state routing for mobile ad hoc networks. In *Proceedings of the 2003 Symposium on Applications and the Internet Workshops, 2003* (pp. 379-383). IEEE.

Papadimitratos, P., & Haas, Z. J. (2003b). Secure data transmission in mobile ad hoc networks. In *Proceedings of the 2nd ACM Workshop on Wireless Security* (pp. 41-50). ACM.

Partridge, C., Cousins, D., Jackson, A. W., Krishnan, R., Saxena, T., & Strayer, W. T. (2002). Using signal processing to analyze wireless data traffic. In *Proceedings of the 1st ACM Workshop on Wireless Security* (pp. 67-76). ACM.

Perkins, C. E. (2001). *Ad hoc networking*. Reading, MA: Addison-Wesley.

Perkins, C. E., & Bhagwat, P. (1994). Highly dynamic destination-sequenced distance-vector routing (DSDV) for mobile computers. *Computer Communication Review*, 24(4), 234–244. doi:10.1145/190809.190336.

Perkins, C. E., & Royer, E. M. (1999). Ad-hoc on-demand distance vector routing. In *Proceedings of the Second IEEE Workshop on Mobile Computing Systems and Applications,* (pp. 90-100). IEEE.

Perrig, A., Szewczyk, R., Tygar, J. D., Wen, V., & Culler, D. E. (2002). SPINS: Security protocols for sensor networks. *Wireless Networks*, 8(5), 521–534. doi:10.1023/A:1016598314198.

Rachedi, A., & Benslimane, A. (2009). Toward a cross-layer monitoring process for mobile ad hoc networks. *Security and Communication Networks*, 2(4), 351–368. doi:10.1002/sec.72.

Raj, P. N., & Swadas, P. B. (2009). Dpraodv: A dyanamic learning system against blackhole attack in aodv based manet. *arXiv preprint arXiv:0909.2371*.

Ramachandran, C., Misra, S., & Obaidat, M. S. (2008). FORK: A novel two-pronged strategy for an agent-based intrusion detection scheme in ad-hoc networks. *Computer Communications, 31*(16), 3855–3869. doi:10.1016/j.comcom.2008.04.012.

Rangara, R. R., Jaipuria, R. S., Yenugwar, G. N., & Jawandhiya, P. M. (2010). Intelligent secure routing model for MANET. In *Proceedings of the 3rd IEEE International Conference on Computer Science and Information Technology (ICCSIT), 2010* (Vol. 3, pp. 452-456). IEEE.

Razak, S. A., Furnell, S. M., & Brooke, P. J. (2004). Attacks against mobile ad hoc networks routing protocols. In *Proceedings of the 5th Annual Postgraduate Symposium on the Convergence of Telecommunications, Networking & Broadcasting (PGNET'04)*. PGNET.

Razak, S. A., Furnell, S. M., Clarke, N. L., & Brooke, P. J. (2008). Friend-assisted intrusion detection and response mechanisms for mobile ad hoc networks. *Ad Hoc Networks, 6*(7), 1151–1167. doi:10.1016/j.adhoc.2007.11.004.

Roy, D. B., Chaki, R., & Chaki, N. (2009). A new cluster based wormhole intrusion detection algorithm for MANET. *International Journal of Network Security & Its Applications, 1*(1).

Roy, S., Addada, V. G., Setia, S., & Jajodia, S. (2005). Securing MAODV: Attacks and counter-measures. In *Proceedings of the IEEE International Conference on Sensing, Communication, and Networking*. IEEE.

Sanzgiri, K., Dahill, B., Levine, B. N., Shields, C., & Belding-Royer, E. M. (2002). A secure routing protocol for ad hoc networks. In *Proceedings of the 10th IEEE International Conference on Network Protocols, 2002* (pp. 78-87). IEEE.

Sen, J. (2013). Security and privacy issues in wireless mesh networks: A survey. In *Wireless Networks and Security* (pp. 189–272). Berlin, Germany: Springer. doi:10.1007/978-3-642-36169-2_7.

Sen, S., & Clark, J. A. (2011). Evolutionary computation techniques for intrusion detection in mobile ad hoc networks. *Computer Networks, 55*(15), 3441–3457. doi:10.1016/j.comnet.2011.07.001.

Shamir, A. (1985). Identity-based cryptosystems and signature schemes. In *Advances in Cryptology* (pp. 47–53). Berlin, Germany: Springer. doi:10.1007/3-540-39568-7_5.

Stallings, W. (2005). *Cryptography and network security principles and practices* (4th ed.). Upper Saddle River, NJ: Prentice Hall.

Stallings, W. (2009). *Wireless communications & networks*. Delhi, India: Pearson Education India.

Std, I. E. E. E. 802.11i/D30. (2002). Wireless medium access control (MAC) and physical layer (PHY) specifications: Specification for enhanced security. IEEE.

Svecs, I., Sarkar, T., Basu, S., & Wong, J. S. (2010). XIDR: A dynamic framework utilizing cross-layer intrusion detection for effective response deployment. In *Proceedings of the 34th Annual Computer Software and Applications Conference Workshops (COMPSACW)*, (pp. 287-292). IEEE.

Tamilselvan, L., & Sankaranarayanan, D. V. (2007b). Prevention of impersonation attack in wireless mobile ad hoc networks. *International Journal of Computer Science and Network Security, 7*(3), 118–123.

Tamilselvan, L., & Sankaranarayanan, V. (2007a). Prevention of blackhole attack in MANET. In *Proceedings of the 2nd International Conference on Wireless Broadband and Ultra Wideband Communications*, (pp. 21-21). IEEE.

Tangpong, A., Kesidis, G., Hsu, H. Y., & Hurson, A. (2009). Robust Sybil detection for MANETs. In *Proceedings of the 18th Internatonal Conference on Computer Communications and Networks*, (pp. 1-6). IEEE.

Toh, C. K. (2001). *Ad hoc mobile wireless networks: Protocols and systems*. Upper Saddle River, NJ: Prentice Hall.

Tseng, Y. C., Ni, S. Y., Chen, Y. S., & Sheu, J. P. (2002). The broadcast storm problem in a mobile ad hoc network. *Wireless Networks*, 8(2/3), 153–167. doi:10.1023/A:1013763825347.

Urpi, A., Bonuccelli, M., & Giordano, S. (2003). Modelling cooperation in mobile ad hoc networks: A formal description of selfishness. In Proceedings of WiOpt'03: Modeling and Optimization in Mobile, Ad Hoc and Wireless Networks. WiOpt.

Wang, H., Zhang, D., & Shin, K. G. (2002). Detecting SYN flooding attacks. In *Proceedings of INFOCOM 2002*, (Vol. 3, pp. 1530-1539). IEEE.

Wang, X., Feng, D., Lai, X., & Yu, H. (2004). *Collisions for hash functions MD4, MD5, HAVAL-128 and RIPEMD*. Cryptology ePrint Archive, Report 2004/199.

Wohlmacher, P. (2000). Digital certificates: A survey of revocation methods. In *Proceedings of the 2000 ACM workshops on Multimedia* (pp. 111-114). ACM.

Wood, A. D., & Stankovic, J. A. (2002). Denial of service in sensor networks. *Computer*, 35(10), 54–62. doi:10.1109/MC.2002.1039518.

Wu, B., Chen, J., Wu, J., & Cardei, M. (2007). A survey of attacks and countermeasures in mobile ad hoc networks. In *Wireless Network Security* (pp. 103–135). New York: Springer. doi:10.1007/978-0-387-33112-6_5.

Wu, B., Wu, J., & Dong, Y. (2009). An efficient group key management scheme for mobile ad hoc networks. *International Journal of Security and Networks*, 4(1), 125–134. doi:10.1504/IJSN.2009.023431.

Wu, B., Wu, J., Fernandez, E. B., Ilyas, M., & Magliveras, S. (2007). Secure and efficient key management in mobile ad hoc networks. *Journal of Network and Computer Applications*, 30(3), 937–954. doi:10.1016/j.jnca.2005.07.008.

Wu, X., & Yau, D. K. (2007). Mitigating denial-of-service attacks in MANET by distributed packet filtering: a game-theoretic approach. In *Proceedings of the 2nd ACM Symposium on Information, Computer and Communications Security* (pp. 365-367). ACM.

Xiaopeng, G., & Wei, C. (2007). A novel gray hole attack detection scheme for mobile ad-hoc networks. In *Proceedings of the IFIP International Conference on Network and Parallel Computing Workshops*, (pp. 209-214). IEEE.

Xiong, W. A., & Gong, Y. H. (2011). Secure and highly efficient three level key management scheme for MANET. *WSEAS Transactions on Computers*, 10(1), 6–15.

Yang, H., Luo, H., Ye, F., Lu, S., & Zhang, L. (2004). Security in mobile ad hoc networks: Challenges and solutions. *IEEE Wireless Communications*, 11(1), 38–47. doi:10.1109/MWC.2004.1269716.

Yang, H., Shu, J., Meng, X., & Lu, S. (2006). SCAN: Self-organized network-layer security in mobile ad hoc networks. *IEEE Journal on Selected Areas in Communications*, 24(2), 261–273. doi:10.1109/JSAC.2005.861384.

Yi, P., Zhong, Y., Zhang, S., & Dai, Z. (2006). Flooding attack and defence in ad hoc networks. *Journal of Systems Engineering and Electronics*, 17(2), 410–416. doi:10.1016/S1004-4132(06)60070-4.

Yi, S., & Kravets, R. (2003). MOCA: Mobile certificate authority for wireless ad hoc networks. In *Proceedings of the 2nd Annual PKI Research Workshop Program (PKI 03)* (pp. 3-8). Gaithersburg, MD: PKI.

Yi, S., & Kravets, R. (2004). Composite key management for ad hoc networks. In *Proceedings of the First Annual International Conference on Mobile and Ubiquitous Systems: Networking and Services* (pp. 52-61). IEEE.

Yi, S., Naldurg, P., & Kravets, R. (2001). Security-aware ad hoc routing for wireless networks. In *Proceedings of the 2nd ACM International Symposium on Mobile Ad Hoc Networking & Computing* (pp. 299-302). ACM.

Yu, F. R., Tang, H., Mason, P. C., & Wang, F. (2010). A hierarchical identity based key management scheme in tactical mobile ad hoc networks. *IEEE Transactions on Network and Service Management, 7*(4), 258–267. doi:10.1109/TNSM.2010.1012.0362.

Yu, M., Zhou, M., & Su, W. (2009). A secure routing protocol against Byzantine attacks for MANETs in adversarial environments. *IEEE Transactions on Vehicular Technology, 58*(1), 449. doi:10.1109/TVT.2008.923683.

Zafer, M. A., Agrawal, D., & Srivatsa, M. (2009). Bootstrapping coalition manets: Physical-layer security under active adversary. In *Proceedings of the Annual Conference of ITA (ACITA) 2009*. ACITA.

Zapata, M. G. (2002). Secure ad hoc on-demand distance vector routing. *ACM SIGMOBILE Mobile Computing and Communications Review, 6*(3), 106–107. doi:10.1145/581291.581312.

Zeshan, M., Khan, S. A., Cheema, A. R., & Ahmed, A. (2008). Adding security against packet dropping attack in mobile ad hoc networks. In *Proceedings of the International Seminar on Future Information Technology and Management Engineering,* (pp. 568-572). IEEE.

Zhang, Y., & Lee, W. (2000). Intrusion detection in wireless ad-hoc networks. In *Proceedings of the 6th Annual International Conference on Mobile Computing and Networking* (pp. 275-283). ACM.

Zhang, Y., Lee, W., & Huang, Y. A. (2003). Intrusion detection techniques for mobile wireless networks. *Wireless Networks, 9*(5), 545–556. doi:10.1023/A:1024600519144.

Zhou, H. (2008). Secure prophet address allocation for mobile sd hoc networks. In *Proceedings of the International Conference on Network and Parallel Computing,* (pp. 60-67). IEEE.

Zhou, L., & Haas, Z. J. (1999). Securing ad hoc networks. *IEEE Network, 13*(6), 24–30. doi:10.1109/65.806983.

Zhu, C., Lee, M. J., & Saadawi, T. (2003). Rtt-based optimal waiting time for best route selection in ad hoc routing protocols. In *Proceedings of the Military Communications Conference,* (Vol. 2, pp. 1054-1059). IEEE.

ADDITIONAL READING

Adibi, S., & Agnew, G. B. (2008). Security measures for mobile ad-hoc networks (MANETs). In Y. Zhang, J. Zheng, & M. Ma (Eds.), *Handbook of research on wireless security* (pp. 500–514). Hershey, PA: IGI Global. doi:10.4018/978-1-59904-899-4.ch031.

Anantvalee, T., & Wu, J. (2007). A survey on intrusion detection in mobile ad hoc networks. In *Wireless Network Security* (pp. 159–180). New York: Springer. doi:10.1007/978-0-387-33112-6_7.

De Fuentes, J. M., González-Tablas, A. I., & Ribagorda, A. (2011). Overview of security issues in vehicular ad-hoc networks. In M. Cruz-Cunha, & F. Moreira (Eds.), *Handbook of research on mobility and computing: Evolving technologies and ubiquitous impacts* (pp. 894–911). Hershey, PA: IGI Global. doi:10.4018/978-1-60960-042-6.ch056.

Dhar, S. (2009). Mobile ad hoc network. In D. Taniar (Ed.), *Mobile computing: Concepts, methodologies, tools, and applications* (pp. 952–960). Hershey, PA: IGI Global.

Djenouri, D., Khelladi, L., & Badache, N. (2005). A survey of security issues in mobile ad hoc networks. *IEEE Communications Surveys, 7*(4).

Elboukhari, M., Azizi, M., & Azizi, A. (2011). Key management protocols in mobile ad hoc networks. In R. Aquino-Santos, V. Rangel-Licea, & A. Edwards-Block (Eds.), *Emerging technologies in wireless ad-hoc networks: Applications and future development* (pp. 181–201). Hershey, PA: IGI Global.

Huang, D., & Medhi, D. (2008). A secure group key management scheme for hierarchical mobile ad hoc networks. *Ad Hoc Networks, 6*(4), 560–577. doi:10.1016/j.adhoc.2007.04.006.

Joseph, J. F. C., Lee, B. S., Das, A., & Seet, B. C. (2011). Cross-layer detection of sinking behavior in wireless ad hoc networks using SVM and FDA. *IEEE Transactions on Dependable and Secure Computing, 8*(2), 233–245. doi:10.1109/TDSC.2009.48.

Lauf, A. P., Peters, R. A., & Robinson, W. H. (2010). A distributed intrusion detection system for resource-constrained devices in ad-hoc networks. *Ad Hoc Networks, 8*(3), 253–266. doi:10.1016/j.adhoc.2009.08.002.

Li, W., & Joshi, A. (2007). *Security issues in mobile ad hoc networks—A survey.* College Park, MD: University of Maryland.

Lu, B. (2008). Security in mobile ad hoc networks. In Y. Zhang, J. Zheng, & M. Ma (Eds.), *Handbook of research on wireless security* (pp. 412–430). Hershey, PA: IGI Global. doi:10.4018/978-1-59904-899-4.ch026.

Lu, B. (2008). Security in mobile ad hoc networks. In *Handbook of research on wireless security*. Hershey, PA: IGI Global. doi:10.4018/978-1-59904-899-4.ch026.

Marchang, N., & Datta, R. (2008). Collaborative techniques for intrusion detection in mobile ad-hoc networks. *Ad Hoc Networks, 6*(4), 508–523. doi:10.1016/j.adhoc.2007.04.003.

Mehul, E., & Limaye, V. (2009). Security in mobile ad hoc networks. In B. Unhelkar (Ed.), *Handbook of research in mobile business* (2nd ed., pp. 541–558). Hershey, PA: IGI Global.

Mishra, A., & Nadkarni, K. M. (2003). Security in wireless ad hoc networks. In *The handbook of ad hoc wireless networks* (pp. 499–549). Boca Raton, FL: CRC Press, Inc..

Mitrokotsa, A., & Dimitrakakis, C. (2012). Intrusion detection in MANET using classification algorithms: The effects of cost and model selection. *Ad Hoc Networks, 11*(1), 226–237. doi:10.1016/j.adhoc.2012.05.006.

Papadimitratos, P., & Haas, Z. J. (2003). Securing mobile ad hoc networks. In *The handbook of ad hoc wireless networks*. Boca Raton, FL: CRC Press, Inc..

Pathan, A. S. K. (2010). *Security of self-organizing networks: MANET, WSN, WMN, VANET*. Auerbach Pub. doi:10.1201/EBK1439819197.

Rawat, D. B., Yan, G., Bista, B. B., & Chandra, V. (2013). Wireless network security: An overview. In *Building next-generation converged networks: Theory and practice*. Boca Raton, FL: CRC Press. doi:10.1201/b14574-10.

Şen, S., & Clark, J. A. (2009). *Intrusion detection in mobile ad hoc networks* (pp. 427–454). London: Springer.

Sen, S., Clark, J. A., & Tapiador, J. E. (2010). Security threats in mobile ad hoc networks. In Security of self-organizing networks: MANET, WSN, WMN, VANET (pp. 127-147). Auerbach Publications.

Singh, A., Kumar, M., Rishi, R., & Madan, D. K. (2011). A relative study of MANET and VANET: Its applications, broadcasting approaches and challenging issues. In *Advances in networks and communications* (pp. 627–632). Berlin, Germany: Springer. doi:10.1007/978-3-642-17878-8_63.

Singh, S. (2012). Security threats and issues with MANET. In K. Lakhtaria (Ed.), *Technological advancements and applications in mobile ad-hoc networks: Research trends* (pp. 247–263). Hershey, PA: IGI Global. doi:10.4018/978-1-4666-0321-9.ch015.

Venkataraman, R., & Rao, T. R. (2012). Security issues and models in mobile ad hoc networks. In K. Lakhtaria (Ed.), *Technological advancements and applications in mobile ad-hoc networks: Research trends* (pp. 219–227). Hershey, PA: IGI Global. doi:10.4018/978-1-4666-0321-9.ch013.

Wu, B. (2006). *Key management in mobile ad hoc networks*. Miami, FL: Florida Atlantic University.

Wu, B., Wu, J., & Cardei, M. (2008). A survey of key management in mobile ad hoc networks. In Y. Zhang, J. Zheng, & M. Ma (Eds.), *Handbook of research on wireless security* (pp. 479–499). Hershey, PA: IGI Global. doi:10.4018/978-1-59904-899-4.ch030.

Xenakis, C., Panos, C., & Stavrakakis, I. (2011). A comparative evaluation of intrusion detection architectures for mobile ad hoc networks. *Computers & Security*, *30*(1), 63–80. doi:10.1016/j.cose.2010.10.008.

Zhang, Y., & Lee, W. (2005). Security in mobile ad-hoc networks. In *Ad Hoc Networks* (pp. 249–268). New York: Springer. doi:10.1007/0-387-22690-7_9.

KEY TERMS AND DEFINITIONS

Authentication: Authentication often involves of verifying the validity of source of information.

Certification Authority (CA): A certification authority, or CA, holds a trusted position because the certificate that it issues binds the identity of a system to the public and private keys (asymmetric cryptography).

Cryptography: Cryptography can be defined as the conversion of data into a scrambled code that can be deciphered and sent across a public or private network.

Denial of Service (DoS) Attacks: In a denial-of-service (DoS) attack, an attacker attempts to prevent legitimate users from accessing information or services.

Dropping Attacks: Packet dropping attacks are performed by selfish or malicious nodes in the network that do not forward the packets they just drop the packets routing through them.

Eavesdropping Attacks: When an attacker gains access to the data path in a network and has the ability to monitor and read the traffic. They don't interfere with the network's operation.

Group Key: A common secret key known by the group members.

Intrusion: Any set of actions that attempt to compromise the integrity, confidentiality, or availability of a resource.

Intrusion Detection System (IDS): A system to detect the intrusions against computers and the network, and respond to these detected intrusions.

Key: A set of values that a cryptographic algorithm operates on.

Key Distribution Center (KDC): The Key Distribution Center (KDC) is part of a symmetric cryptosystem intended to reduce the risks inherent in exchanging keys between two parties.

Key Management: The process of generating, distributing, using, exchanging, and updating keys in a cryptography system design.

Key Ring: A set of public or private keys used in PGP.

Mobile Ad Hoc Networks (MANETs): It is a self-configuring infrastructure network of mobile devices connected by wireless links and forming a temporary network without centralized administration.

Promiscuous Monitoring: The monitoring all packets in a node's transmission range regardless of their destinations in wireless networks.

Routing Attack: Attacks that seek to disrupt the routing operations of a network or denial-of-service (DoS) to deny the services to legitimate nodes.

APPENDIX: REVIEW QUESTIONS

1. What are the main differences between a wired network and a Mobile Ad Hoc Network (MANET)?
2. What are the major aspects of OSI security architecture?
3. What is the need for security in a Mobile Ad Hoc Network (MANET)?
4. What are the major challenges in implementing the security policy for MANET?
5. What are the unique characteristics of MANETs make new attacks possible?
6. What are the selfish & malicious nodes in a MANET and how do they lead to security vulnerabilities?
7. List the various possible attacks on different layers of the internet model for MANETs.
8. In how many ways is it possible to target a MANET on the network layer?
9. How can we prevent Sybil attacks?
10. Describe session hijacking in MANETs. Why and how?
11. What is the prospect of the protocols using key management schemes in enhancing the security level in MANETs?
12. Explain the two types of group key management techniques for Mobile Ad Hoc Network: group key agreement and group key distribution.
13. Why conventional intrusion detection and prevention schemes cannot be directly applicable in MANETs?
14. What are different benefits that can be provided by an intrusion detection system MANETs?
15. What techniques are used for detecting misbehaving nodes in MANETs?

Chapter 10
Security and Privacy in Mobile Ad hoc Social Networks

Mohamed Amine Ferrag
University of Badji Mokhtar – Annaba, Algeria

Mehdi Nafa
University of Badji Mokhtar – Annaba, Algeria

Salim Ghanemi
University of Badji Mokhtar – Annaba, Algeria

ABSTRACT

In this chapter, first, the authors briefly introduce the two new systems "MASN-OLSR" (Mobile Ad Hoc Social Networks with OLSR) and "MASN-AODV" (Mobile Ad Hoc Social Networks with AODV). Then they choose wormhole and black hole attack methods, because they are not completely solved, especially in a setting where MASN is used as OLSR or AODV routing protocol. The authors give a definition of the wormhole and black hole attacks on an ad hoc network using OLSR or AODV as routing protocol and then examine the various existing proposals in the literature to overcome this attack. With an analysis of these methods, they then determine the advantages and disadvantages of each of these new systems.

INTRODUCTION

Since their introduction, the wireless local area networks have attracted the interest of professionals, faced with the needs of mobility and network connectivity to their organization. 802.11 networks, standardized by the IEEE in 1997, has rapidly become until, in some cases, replace traditional wired networks like Ethernet. Since their arrival on the market, the steady evolution of their performance and lower their cost of acquisition helped accelerate their dissemination.

The IEEE 802.11 provides two modes: infrastructure mode and ad hoc mode. Infrastructure mode, also called cellular mode, uses a topology built around fixed access points. The latter is responsible for managing exchanges between mobile nodes located in their area transceiver. Multiple

DOI: 10.4018/978-1-4666-4691-9.ch010

access points can be interconnected by a backbone network, called the distribution system to provide connections to a larger number of nodes or increase the space of node mobility. Ad hoc mode, it establishes an exchange point to point between two mobile nodes. If two nodes do not share the same areas transceiver, a direct connection is impossible. In this case, the intermediate nodes are used to establish a path between the source and destination nodes. These networks, whose architecture evolves according to the movement and appearance of nodes are called MANET (Mobile Ad hoc NETwork) or spontaneous networks (M.A. Ferrag 2012).

In some contexts, users can benefit from the features of MANET to exchange information. A frequently cited example, in civil and military, is an ad hoc network formed by the interconnections between moving vehicles. In the industrial networks catch (Sensor Networks) can form a MANET to adapt to different environments. But many other situations of everyday life are adapted to the use of MANET. We consider, for example, a network created for the purposes and duration of a meeting of participants from different organizations, or created a network between students and their teacher in a classroom for the duration of a course.

There are primarily two types of routing protocol in ad hoc networks. The reactive routing protocols (AODV, DSR) that initiates the search for a route when trying to reach a destination that is not contained in the routing table. The proactive routing protocols (OLSR, FSR) that maintain regularly update the information in the routing table with route discovery requests. Note that the hybrid algorithms exist. They then make use of both protocols under different conditions.

Two types of algorithms used to maintain accurate routing tables. This is the distance vector algorithms and link state. In general, the route discovery is as follows. When a node wants to transmit a message to another node it broadcasts a route request different denominations according to

the protocols. The road was then built as and when his discovery to the recipient once attached can return a message back to sender. The road is then set and the actual data exchange can take place. In the absence of authentication, confidentiality, integrity, etc. Ensuring the smooth running of these protocols, network stability can be greatly compromised.

The issue of privacy is almost solved but major gaps remain in terms of routing protocols. For this reason, the subject of this chapter focuses on the security of routing protocols in MASN. We chose both OLSR and AODV routing protocol because they are most widely used in ad hoc community.

MASN (Mobile Ad Hoc Social Networks) is inherited from the MANET (Mobile Ad Hoc Networks). So the attacks which exist in MANET necessarily exist in MASN. The design consideration for MANET made a number of differences with the traditional centralized networks, namely:

1.   Dynamic Topology
2.   Resource Constraints
3.   Low Cost
4.   Limited Physical.

MANET is subject to a number of attacks. For example, an attacker in the MANET may not be willing to route packets to other nodes. On the other hand, more sophisticated attacks against MANET routing can disrupt the route discovery. In addition, they may interfere with maintaining ride disobedient routing protocols. Blackhole Attack, Byzantine Attack, Wormhole Attack , and Spoofing Attack are illustrations of various threats for MANET. For the purposes of group communication security, cryptography has been integrated in MANETs. Among the most popular techniques, symmetric and public key infrastructure (PKI).

First in this chapter, we briefly introduce the two routing protocols OLSR and AODV then the two new systems MASN- OLSR (Mobile Ad Hoc

Social Networks with OLSR) and MASN - AODV (Mobile Ad Hoc Social Networks with AODV).

Secondly, we choose the two attacks wormhole and black hole because are not completely solved, especially in a setting where MASN is used as OLSR or AODV routing protocol. We gave a definition of the wormhole attack and black hole on an ad hoc network using OLSR or AODV as routing protocol, and then examine the various existing proposals in the literature to overcome this attack was an analysis of these methods we will then determine the advantages and disadvantages of each of these proposals. In the next section, we present the type of social network completely mobile and its characteristics.

MOBILE AD HOC SOCIAL NETWORKS (MASN)

Definition of MASN

A mobile social network is a network created by a spontaneous meeting of mobiles can communicate through their interfaces "wireless", without any prior configuration or infrastructure. The nodes of such a network cooperate to manage the network. MASN is shown in Figure 1. Consists of two layers: (a) a physical layer of ad hoc network and (b) a layer of virtual social network. In the network layer (virtual) social are connected by virtual links when a routing protocol is used. Each virtual link is to a communication channel which may be composed of several hops. Once the friendly relations are established, friends can perform social such as resource sharing, sending messages, and navigation from each other. From this general definition, we present the main characteristics that differentiate an MASN to a network with a fixed architecture.

Characteristics of MASN

MASN is characterized by:

The properties of mobile nodes in MASN

- **The Mobility of All Mobile Nodes**: An intrinsic characteristic of MASNs. The movement of mobile nodes causes random changes and non predictable architecture of the network. Therefore, the routing techniques conventional networks, based on pre-determined routes with specialized equipment and dedicated, can no longer function properly.

- **The Equivalence of The Mobile Nodes:** Specific to MASNs. In a typical network, there is a clear distinction between the terminal nodes (stations, hosts) that support applications and internal network nodes (routers), responsible for routing data. This difference does not exist in the network MASN because all nodes may be required to provide routing functions.

- **The Number of Mobile Nodes**: Present in a MASN varies according to the needs or the position of each node. On a more general limitation is made on the size or number of nodes in an ad hoc network.

- **Energy Resources of Mobile Nodes**: Powered by sources of energy autonomous (batteries) are limited. These devices incorporate energy modes and it is important that the protocols implemented in the network MASN take into account this feature.

- **The Absence of a Centralized Server**: Complicates the control and management architecture that forms and grows with the appearance and movements of the mobile nodes. As a result, there is no hierarchy between mobile nodes and no network service can claim to be centralized.

Figure 1. Overview of Mobile Ad Hoc Social Network

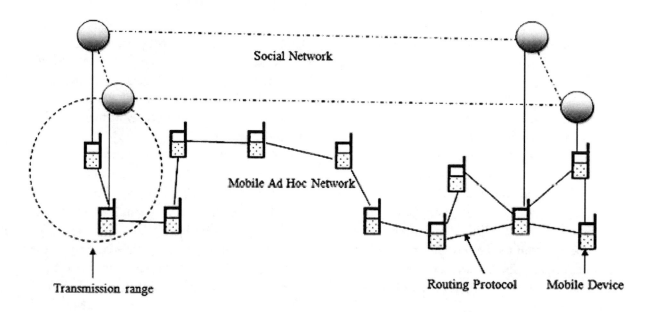

- **Physical Link:** Based on wireless communication technologies, essential to the establishment of an ad hoc network.

In the next section, we present the main principles and characteristics of routing protocols in MASN.

ROUTING PROTOCOLS IN MASN

A routing protocol determines the path between two mobile nodes based on a predefined strategy. In a network MASN, the routing protocol, distributed across all mobile nodes is more to minimize the time of establishment of the road, also called latency, and the use of resources for this operation. We limit our presentation to routing protocols point to point, also called unicast routing protocols.

When two mobile nodes in MASN directly exchange data packets without using intermediate mobile nodes, the connection is direct. If the path between source and destination nodes requires the presence of several intermediate nodes, the connection is called a multi hop.

In a network with fixed architecture, routes to the various networks are predefined and maintained by fixed interconnection equipment called routers. The dynamic architecture of a network MASN, resulting from the movement, the emergence of mobile nodes or the state of the physical connection, requires regular updating of routing tables located in each mobile node. To route a packet between two nodes mobile network MASN, the basic mechanism is flooding. It is to forward the packet to all nodes in the network. Flooding is performed by successive broadcasts to all neighbors of each node.

Complementary mechanisms of control can be used to avoid closures or duplication of packets. This flooding mechanism, very expensive in network resources can be applied to very small networks. Routing protocols aim, them, to limit the spread of packet flooding. Depending on the role played by the mobile nodes in the dissemination of messages, we can achieve a first differentiation of routing protocols:

- When all nodes have the same functionality, the protocol is referred to as uniform,
- If some nodes have special features in the dissemination of messages, the protocol is no uniform.

We can also distinguish the "standard protocols" by their mode of operation. Come in fixed architecture, both technical link-state and distance vector have a routing table at each node combines the address of the next node, the vector, and the number of intermediate nodes, the distance.

Routing protocols use link-state, them, a database that allows them to build the network topology and know well the path to all mobile nodes in the network MASN. Usually a metric based on several parameters relating to connections is used to select the best route.

To reduce the network load due to updated packages, some routing protocols trigger the search for a route only when it is requested. The time to obtain a route is longer. Protocols that use this operating mode are called reactive.

To reduce the number of control messages required to discover routes, routing protocols no uniform select some mobile nodes to create dynamic and hierarchical architectures. Thus, protocols for the selection of neighbors, each mobile node discharge the routing function to a subset of direct neighbors. While for partitioning protocols, the network is cutting areas in which routing is performed by a single master node. Some of these protocols, called hybrid, jointly use routing link state and distance vector routing. The main routing protocols are presented according to their mode of operation in Figure 2

Since July 2003, only protocols AODV (C. Perkins et al., 2003) and OLSR (T. Clausen et al., 2003) are subject to an RFC that is why we have based on these two routing protocols. Both protocols belong each to a family of protocols and each of them have a strategy. In the remainder of this section, we present the strategies of these two protocols in the two new systems "MASN with OLSR" and "MASN with AODV".

Mobile Ad Hoc Social Networks with OLSR (MASN- OLSR)

OLSR (Optimized Link State Routing Protocol (T. Clausen et al., 2003)) is a proactive protocol based on the regular exchange of information on the network topology. The algorithm is optimized by reducing the size and number of messages exchanged: only particular nodes, the MPR broadcast control messages to the entire network.

All nodes periodically send HELLO messages to their neighbors (HELLO_INTERVAL timer) on each node. OLSR uses a single message format, transported by UDP. The header specifies whether the message should be sent only in the immediate vicinity or to the entire network. Each node stores the description of its neighborhood: 2-hop neighbors interface, MPR and MS. This description is updated each receiving a HELLO message, and old information is erased.

OLSR routing is based on the routing of messages by the nodes that have a symmetric neighborhood. A link can participate in a way that it is symmetrical. Routing to remote stations over a hop (1 + N hops) is due to the MPR, which periodically broadcast messages TC (Topology Control). A sequence number can eliminate duplicates. These messages are used to maintain a table in each station topology.

The routing table is built and updated from the information contained in the interface table and the table adjacent to the topology uses a shortest path algorithm. The metric considered is the number of hops.

Figure 3 shows a flowchart of a process of communication in MASN using OLSR and AODV. First, a mobile node creates a personal profile and then connects to the network that includes at least one mobile node configured to use a routing protocol OLSR or AODV. The mobile node can store information about the topology of the mobile node discovered in neighboring groups. Alternatively, the mobile node can save the newly joined node mobile in its routing table. Secondly, if the routing protocol supports security with

Figure 2. Routing protocols in MASN

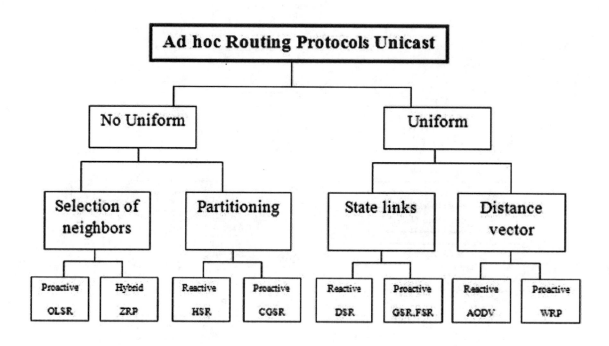

another mobile node, the node mobile communications allows messaging to be exchanged. For example, the mobile node can add online identities to a list of co-user, initiate a conversation or an instant messaging session, and / or launch a file exchange with the other mobile node. Finally, for using OLSR, the mobile node continues to periodically disseminate its messages HELLO containing information about its neighbors and their link status. These control messages are transmitted in broadcast mode. They are received by all neighbors to hop, but they are not relayed to additional nodes.

Mobile Ad Hoc Social Networks with AODV (MASN- AODV)

AODV (Ad hoc On Demand Distance Vector (C. Perkins et al., 2003)) is a reactive protocol, uniform and oriented destination. The route chosen is

bidirectional and is the shortest path (in number of nodes) between the source and destination. Each node maintains a routing table which stores the entries for a destination:

- The identifier of the destination,
- The identifier of the next node to the destination,
- The number of nodes to the destination.

In Figure 3, which represents a communication process MASN in the link using "AODV" as the routing protocol, the node broadcasts a RREQ. If a response "RREP" is received, then the operation of the route discovery is completed. Otherwise, after a timeout NET_TRANVERSAL_TIME, it rebroadcasts RREQ message and waits for a period longer than the first. A node receiving a RREQ packet will issue a RREP (route reply) if the destination or if it has a route to the destination. In

Figure 3. A flowchart of a process of communication in MASN using OLSR and AODV

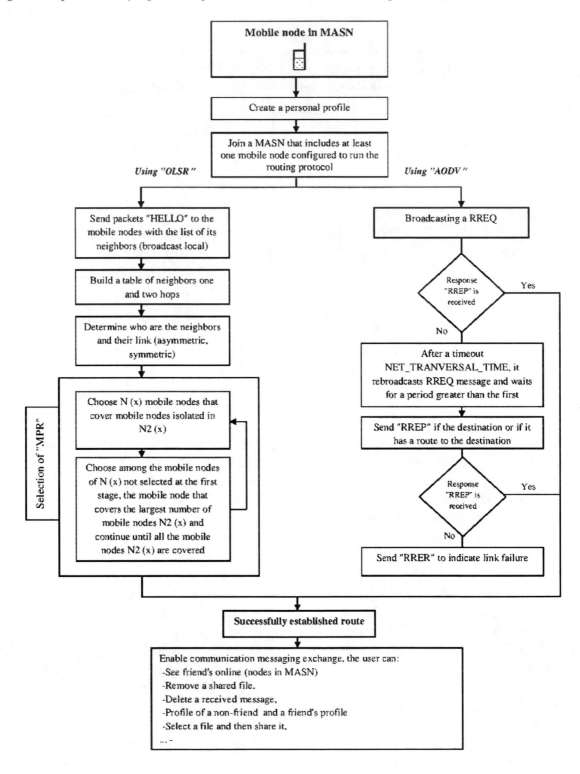

Figure 4. Taxonomy of attacks against MASN

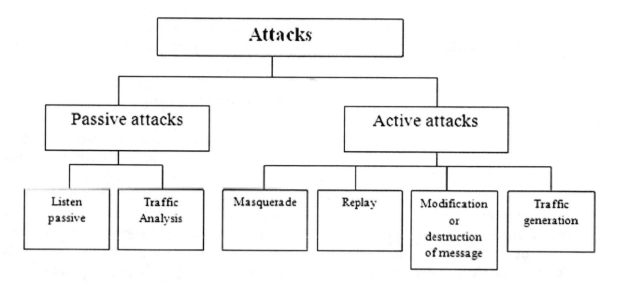

case of loss the link, the end node sends a packet RERR. Once the route is established, the node can send messages functional (Add online identities to a list of co-user, initiate a conversation ...).

In the next section, we examine the vulnerabilities and protection tools for MASN.

VULNERABILITIES AND PROTECTION TOOLS FOR MASN

In this section we present first a typology of attacks and their consequences for ad hoc networks. Then we present the main security mechanisms developed to mitigate these attacks.

MASNs are vulnerable to the same attacks as other types of networks and they are against easier to implement because in an ad hoc network, we cannot control access to the transmission medium, or define the limits of network.

The routing protocol, specific MASN and unavailable to its operation, is a prime target. MASN is inherited from the MANET (Mobile Ad Hoc Networks). So the attacks which exist in MANET necessarily exist in MASN. The taxonomy of attacks against WLANs proposed in

(T.Karygiannis et al., 2002) and shown in Figure 4 identifies two families of attacks: passive attacks and active attacks.

Passive attacks are based on access by an unauthorized node, the frames that pass over the network to collect information without altering the data exchanged. Passive listening is to read the content of messages exchanged between two nodes. Traffic analysis is to infer based on the different trading networks, information about the organization or network configuration.

Active attacks aim to allow a node authorized to edit a message, data or a data stream. The masquerade is an attack that is for an attacker to impersonate another user to benefit from his rights of access to different resources. To perform a replay attack, the attacker starts by recording a sequence of traffic compatible security policy and then regenerates the exchange instead of a party power to deceive the other. Partial modification of the contents of a message exchanged between two entities, or non-legitimate traffic generation techniques are also exploited by attackers to compromise the operation of a network MASN.

In an ad hoc network attacks can be directed against a service station or of the network. In the latter case, primarily targeting routing protocol to disrupt communications between nodes (Y.Huang et al., 2000). The main consequences of the attacks presented in (P. Papadimitratos et al., 2002), are summarized below:

- The introduction of a routing loop.
- The creation of a black hole is to redirect traffic to a node that does not transmit information.
- Dividing the network into several subnets to block exchanges between nodes belonging to different subnets.
- No retransmission node some messages.
- The node stops due to his lack of energy.
- Denial of service of a node is unable to send or receive packets.

To mitigate these threats, different security mechanisms can be put in place. Shown in Figure 5, they are based on cryptographic algorithms and applied to different levels of the OSI model to provide security services.

With the arrival of the standard "802.11i", responsible for providing optimum safety to Wi-Fi networks, manufacturers have proposed an improvement of WEP called WPA (Wi-Fi Protected Access). WPA compatible with existing equipment offers:

- Different authentication mode based on the protocol 802.1x/EAP [3] (Extensible Authentication Protocol) ;
- The use of a checksum integrity MIC (Message Integrity Control);
- The new encryption keys by using TKIP (Temporal Key Integrity Protocol).

Traditional security technologies applied at higher levels, such as VPN (Virtual Private Network) for level 3 or protocols SSL and SSH applications, can also be used to enhance the security level. These require local processing and transfer additional network and not solve the problem of key distribution in MASN.

In the remainder of this section, we present the vulnerability of the routing protocol OLSR and AODV.

Vulnerability of the Protocol OLSR

Routing protocols operate in two distinct phases: a phase of discovered network topology in which control information about network topology knowledge are exchanged, then a phase retransmission of data messages in which the data are sent from a source to a destination. Unlike wired networks, where routing operations are usually performed by physical equipment interconnection and managed by a dedicated administration legitimate, in MASN, these operations are entirely the responsibility of the nodes that compose them. This operating characteristic raises many security concerns. Look at the OLSR routing protocol, it is expected that each correctly generates control messages HELLO and TC and maintain a view of the network topology derived from the messages it receives.

The identification of attacks against OLSR studied in (B.Celine, 2009) is presented in Figure 6 and solutions discussed in (D. Raffo et al., 2004) are presented in Table 1.

Figure 7 shows an example of a MASN containing mobile nodes attackers. Attacks against OLSR are created in this network as follows:

- Incorrect Generation HELLO:
  - Identity spoofing:
    - "D" sends messages with "G" as the destination,
    - "B" and "E" will announce their neighborhood with "C"
    - "D" chooses "B" and / or "E" as its MPRs with the identity of "G", the MPR will say that they can provide connectivity to "G"

Figure 5. The main security mechanisms

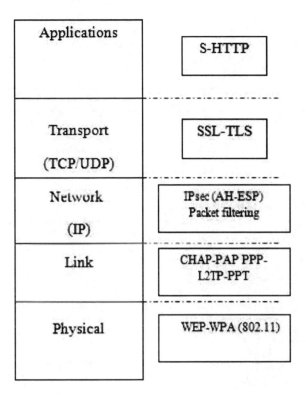

- Conflicts routes to "G", loss of connectivity.
  - Link spoofing:
    - "E" says a sym link with "H",
    - "F" chooses as its MPR set probably {E, I}, messages of "E" will not join "H",
    - Possible loss of connectivity, neighbors ignored.
- Incorrect generation of TCs:
  - Identity spoofing:
    - "D" sends a message with the identity of "G" stating "B" as a neighbor,
    - Wrong topology.
  - Link spoofing:
    - "D" sends a message saying "C" neighbor,
    - Wrong topology, not sending TC, so the topology unscattered.

- MPR attack:
  - "F" = MPR of "I", "E" = MPR of "F" and "H" = no MPR,
  - "I" sends a message to "H" and "F",
  - "H" relays the message to "E",
  - "F" relays the message to "E",
  - "E" does not relaying the message because he has already received "H",
  - Loss of messages.
- Attack ANSN:
  - "D" sends a TC with original "Y" falsified and ANSN high any TC message of "Y" with a lower ANSN is ignored.
- Replay attack:
  - Requires changing "MSN" (HELLO or TC) and / or ANSN (TC),
  - Results in a loss of messages according to its MSN / ANSN.

Figure 6. Attacks against OLSR routing protocol

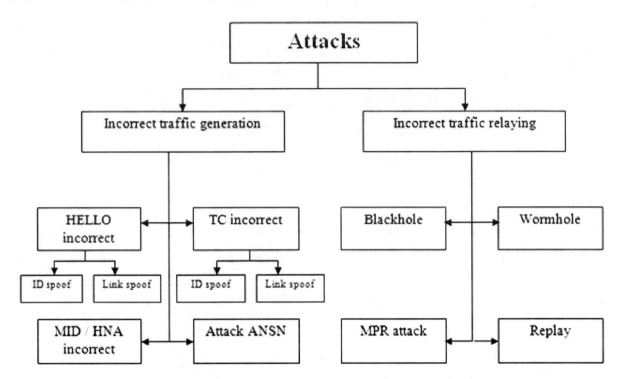

Table 1. Existing solutions to secure the OLSR routing protocol (M.A. Ferrag & M. NAFA, 2011)

Attacks			Semantic properties of OLSR (F. Cuppens et al., 2007)	AdvSig (L. Chen et al., 2006)	Environment or trusted third party
Generation traffic incorrect	HELLO	Usurpation Identity	Yes	No	Yes
		Usurpation Link	Yes	Yes	Yes
	TC	Usurpation Identity	Yes	No	Yes
		Usurpation Link	Yes	Yes	Yes
	Attaque ANSN		No	No	Yes
Relaying traffic incorrect	Changing Message		No	Yes	Yes
	Black hole		No	No	Possible
	Replay		No	Yes	Yes
	Wormhole		No	No	Possible
	MPR		No	No	Yes

Figure 7. An example of a MASN containing mobile nodes attackers using OLSR

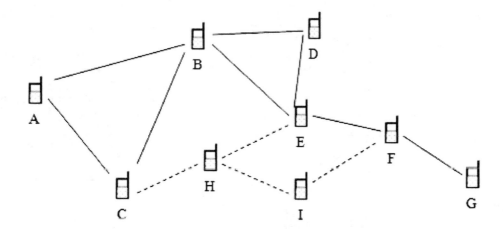

For Blackhole and Wormhole attacks, we present after the presentation of the vulnerability of the AODV routing protocol.

Vulnerability of the Protocol AODV

In (P. Ning et al., 2003), (Y. Huang et al., 2004) the authors propose two approaches to analyze attacks against the AODV routing protocol, called respectively *anomalous basic events* and *atomic misuse*.

The first approach classifies attacks against AODV into two categories:

1. Atomic, resulting from manipulation of a single message routing,
2. Composed, defined as a collection of atomic actions.

The second approach classifies attacks into a series of elementary events. Each set can contain one or more operations performed in order as follows:

1. Receiving a packet,
2. Changing packet fields,

3. The retransmission of the packet is a set of three operations.

Below, summarized in Table 2 provides a list of attacks against the AODV routing protocol.

- **Detour attack**
  - "A" = Source, "D" = Destination,
  - "A" sends the packet "RREQ" to request the road,
  - "B" makes the roads no longer pass through it.
- **Routing table poisoning**
  - "A" = Source, "D" = Destination,
  - "F" and "E" send packets back to "A" for say that the optimal path is "A, F, E, D",
  - The injection of false routing messages causes no-optimal network congestion, or a division of the network.
- **Sybil attack**
  - "A" = Source, "E" = Destination,
  - "B" takes the identity of "C",
  - The attacker has many identities and behaves as if it were a set of nodes.
- **Man-in-the-middle attack**

Table 2. Attacks against the AODV routing protocol and their influence on the security property (M.A. Ferrag et al., 2013)

Attacks	Influence on the security property				Target	Result
	Confidentiality	Authentication	Integrity	Availability		
Detour attack (L. Guang et al., 2006)			X		Nodes in the direct vicinity of the opponent	Not participate in routing
Black hole attack (H. Deng et al., 2002)			X		Nodes specific	Creating a tunnel and disrupt routing
Wormhole attack (Y.C. Hu et al., 2006)			X		Subset of nodes close to the hole	Creating a tunnel and disrupt routing
Routing table poisoning (T. Condie et al., 2006)			X		Subset of node	Division of routing
Sybil attack (J. Douceur, 2002)	X	x	X		Nodes specific	Create of multiple identities
Man-in-the-middle attack (C.Y. Tseng et al., 2003)	X	x	X		Nodes specific	Use impersonation
Rushing attack (Y.C. Hu et al., 2003)			X		Nodes in the direct vicinity of the opponent	Attract traffic
Resource consumption (I. Stamouli et al, 2005)	X	x		x	All nodes	Weakening battery
Routing table overflow (S. Gupte et al., 2003)				x	Nodes in the direct vicinity of the opponent	Overflow of routing table
Location disclosure (G. Vigna et al., 2004)	X	x			Nodes forming the path to a destination	Discover the location of mobile nodes

- ◦ "A" = Source, "E" = Destination,
- ◦ "B" takes the identity of the "E",
- ◦ "B" takes the identity of "A",
- ◦ The attacker impersonates the destination towards the source and the source towards the destination without any of them realizes that he is being attacked.
- **Rushing attack**
  - ◦ "A" = Source, "E" = Destination,
  - ◦ "F" forwards messages faster,
  - ◦ The attacker relays messages faster for the road that passes by it is taken.
- **Resource consumption**

- ◦ "A" = Source, "E" = Destination,
- ◦ "B" modifies packets for messages pass through it.
- **Routing table overflow**
  - ◦ "A" = Source, "E" = Destination,
  - ◦ "F" beyond the routing table of the target.
- **Location disclosure**
  - ◦ "A" = Source, "E" = Destination,
  - ◦ "B" tent to obtain the identity of the nodes forming the path to "E".

In the next section, we choose the two attacks wormhole and black hole because are not com-

Figure 8. An example of a MASN containing mobile nodes attackers using AODV

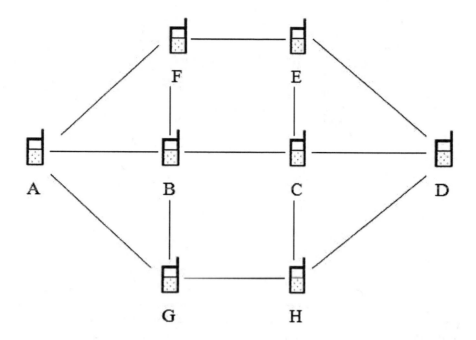

pletely solved, especially in a setting where MASN is used as OLSR or AODV routing protocol. We gave a definition of the wormhole attack and black hole on an ad hoc network using OLSR or AODV as routing protocol, and then we examine the various existing proposals in the literature to overcome this attack was an analysis of these methods we will then determine the advantages and disadvantages.

WORM/BLACK HOLE ATTACK

Both attacks "Wormhole and Blackhole" have the same characteristic except in the location of the node attacker; the wormhole attack is external while blackhole is internal. For this, we use the abbreviation "Worm / hole" for both attacks. However, this attack based on replay messages. It requires the cooperation of two or more nodes and the establishment of a private communication tunnel between them which heard the packets is forwarded from one side to the other side. The

tunnel can be created direct physical link or a virtual link, as is the case in (K. Sanzgiri et al, 2002) where the attackers use encapsulation of messages.

The Worm/Block hole attack is illustrated in Figure 9. It involves placing a tunnel between two attackers "X, Y" and one attacker "C" in MASN. We present their creations in both routing protocols OLSR and AODV.

Worm/Black Hole Attack in OLSR

When the mobile node "A" broadcasts its HELLO message, the node "X" (an attacker) copies the HELLO message and sends it to node "Y" through the vortex. "Y" gets the message HELLO and he plays in his speech. When the node "B" receives the message replayed node "B" judge the node "A" as a neighbor. After some time, a symmetrical link can be established between "A" and "B" according to the mechanism of OLSR. Once this link is symmetric is established, "A" and "B" are very likely to choose each other as multipoint

Figure 9. Worm/Black hole Attack led by two attackers "X, Y" and one attacker "C" in MASN

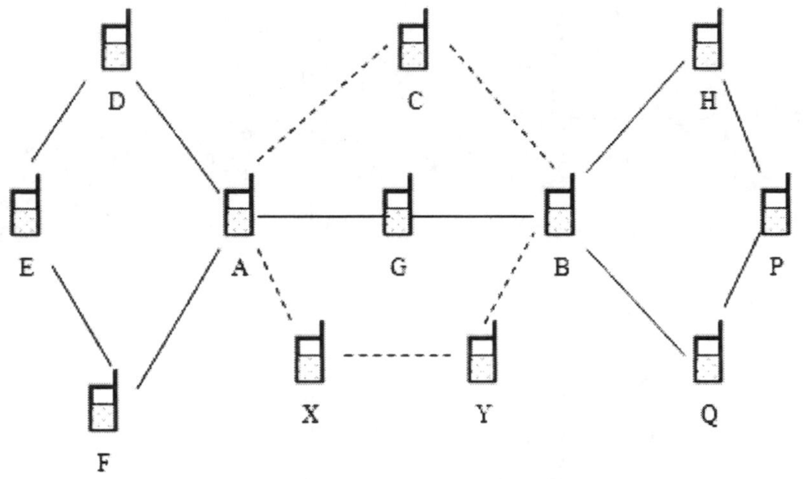

relays (MPR), which then leads to an exchange of certain message TC and data packets through the tunnel. In our example Figure 9. "B" can wait 1 hop neighbors of "A", which are parts of the neighbors "B" to 2 hops that part "A". Therefore, "B" must choose "A" as MPR and wait for the neighbors hop of A, so transmission of erroneous information, this leads to disruption of routing and loss of connectivity.

Worm/Black Hole Attack in AODV

For AODV routing protocol is different from the OLSR routing protocol on the operation of the attack. When the mobile node "A" needs a way to "B" and no route is available, it broadcasts a packet broadcast route request RREQ. This package contains an identifier (RREQ_ID) associated with the node address "B" used to uniquely identify an application route. The attacker "C" receives the route request and adds or updates its routing table, and then generates a false RREP packet response. The route reply reaches the source "A". A false bidirectional path is established between the source "A" and the destination "B". The mobile node "A" sends messages through the link established by the attacker "C".

Mechanisms Against Measure for Worm/Black Hole Attack

Many solutions have been proposed to secure ad hoc routing protocols. We classify these solutions into two categories (Figure 10):

1. Proactive security systems, in the sense that mechanisms are established in advance to ensure the safety enhancing system resilience to attacks with solutions based on cryptography and cons-measurement at the physical layer.
2. Reactive security systems that react according to the behavior of the neighborhood and is divided into reputation management solutions and trust and directional antennas.

Figure 10. The mechanism for secure ad hoc routing protocols

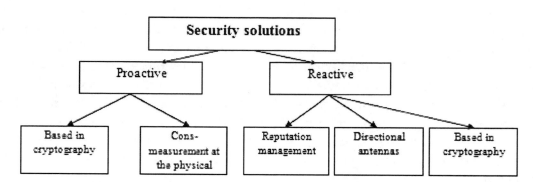

Counter Measurement at the Physical Layer

The first work dealing with the wormhole attack based on a hardware and signal processing techniques. It is suggested that a secret method of modulating radio signal bits. The signal can be demodulated only by authorized nodes. Vulnerability of this method is that the method is not kept in a safe space, which can lead to unauthorized adversaries to compromise legitimate nodes in the network to obtain the necessary access or opponents authorized to disclose their knowledge of the method. (It may be considered complementary mechanisms security code modulation / demodulation such as obfuscation, or the starch environment resistant to weathering). In terms of safety, this method only allows a defense against wormhole attack led by nodes outside attackers (unauthorized) to the network, that is to say, nodes that do not have key cryptography. There is also the question of establishing / negotiating the secret method between nodes in the network legitimate.

Solutions Based on Cryptography

Solutions based on cryptography are often used against external attackers. Some approaches are based on cryptographic hashes strings for authentication. This is the case of "SEAD" (Y.C. Hu et al., 2003), a proactive routing protocol based on DSDV which protects against attacks by changing the sequence number and the number of hops in the update messages. The same authors also propose an extension to DSR called "ARIADNE" (Y.C. Hu et al., 2005). This solution provides an authentication point-to-point routing messages using hash functions secret key (HMAC Hash-based Message Authentication Code). However, to ensure secure authentication, ARIADNE is based on TESLA (A. Perrig et al., 2002), a protocol to ensure secure authentication during broadcasts.

In (C. Adjih et al., 2003) propose M-SOLSR (Message based Secure OLSR) which uses the signature to ensure that the message comes from a trusted node and thus ensure the authentication of the source. With ARAN (K. Sanzgiri et al, 2002), the authors not only authentication only nodes from end to end, they offer a non-repudiation service using certificates pre-established distributed by a trusted server.

These security mechanisms based on cryptographic methods are used to secure the transfer of data so that only the relevant nodes can recover original data. A message is transformed to make incomprehensible to unauthorized persons and to prevent any changes. The recipient can retrieve the data clearly and to ensure that they have not been altered. The changes in question are based on mathematical functions known cryptographic algorithms. We distinguish two types of cryptographic algorithms reversible ones using the same key (symmetric) and those using two different keys (asymmetric).

Symmetric Cryptography: A mechanism of symmetric encryption secret key allows entities (generally two) perform encryption / decryption using a single key. In this sense, anyone can encrypt messages and so who knows the secret key can also decipher. This encryption mode behaves like a closed box with a lock where entities wishing to communicate must have each a key allowing them to open and close the box. In Figure 11, the node A wants to send a message to B. So it encrypts the message with the key k. Upon receiving the message, B decrypts the message using the same key k. It is important to note that there is an initial phase or two nodes agree on the secret key that will be used. Among the symmetric encryption algorithms is the best known "DES" (M.G. Zapata et al., 2002) (Data Encryption Standard).

Asymmetric Cryptography: A mechanism of asymmetric encryption is a function of two encryption keys: a public key that is provided to all those wishing to send a confidential message to one entity and a private key used to decrypt messages intended for it. These two keys are related in such a way that only the private key can decrypt

a message encrypted by the corresponding public key. In Figure 12, the node A wants to send the message to B. It then retrieves the public key of the destination Kpub (B) and encrypts the message. The encrypted message is sent over the communication channel. Destination B decrypts the received message using his secret key Kpriv (B) to obtain the plaintext message sent by A. A public key algorithm is the most popular "RSA" (A. Kahare, 2003) named after its developers, Rivest, Shamir and Adleman.

Cryptographic Hash Functions: To ensure the integrity of messages, a cryptographic hash function can be used. This is a non-reversible producing condensed with the following properties:

- Unique and fixed size;
- It is impossible to recover the original message from the digest;
- Knowing a given message and imprint using a hash function, it is very difficult to generate another message that gives the same impression;
- It is impossible to find two messages producing the same hash.

Message Authentication Code: The algorithm MAC (Message Authentication Code) is a special

Figure 11. Symmetric encryption

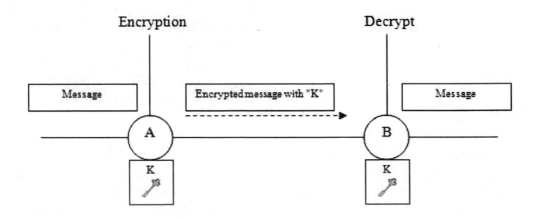

Figure 12. Asymmetric encryption

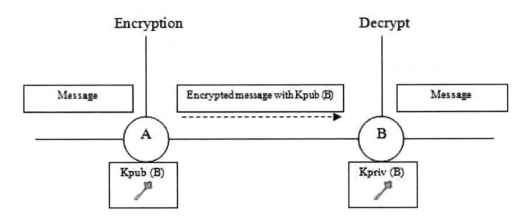

case of hash function. As a hash function, the MAC algorithm produces a digest of fixed size (called message authentication code - MAC). But unlike the latter, it uses a secret key in addition. MAC can be used to simultaneously verify the data integrity like any other hash function and the authenticity of the source data. In practice, a calculation method based MAC hash function more sophisticated and safer is used: it is the HMAC (keyed-Hash Message Authentication Code (R.L. Rivest et al., 1978)) has been the subject of the RFC 2104.

Systems Reputation Management

The proposed solutions are based on reputation systems. In [30], the authors define the reputation as the perception that another node has about its intentions, given a set of old shares and can be combined with other items view. Thus, for a node's behavior cannot decide on its reputation but can influence its own reputation. A numerical value is associated with the reputation of a node whose calculation is different from a solution to another, but that is mainly based on neighborhood watch and the first-hand information and / or second hand obtained.

One of the first works (L. Mui et al., 2002) proposes to use a watchdog and a miss path to mitigate the consequences of dishonest behavior.

While the former is used to monitor the neighborhood and detect non-transmission of a packet from a neighbor, the second allows the reputation management and routing evaluating each path used which avoids those with nodes attackers. TAODV (S. Marti et al., 2000) (Trusted AODV) AODV extended by adding a model of reputation management, a specific routing protocol for reputation information management system and key.

Confidant (X. Li et al., 2004) (Cooperation of Nodes Fairness in Dynamic Ad hoc Networks) proposes to combine the use of positive and negative assessments. Thus, each node monitors the behavior of its neighbors while keeping track of estimates (positive or negative) reputation as well as the views of neighbors. These estimates are then combined to give a level of confidence in a way as nodes through which the packet will be routed.

Directional Antennas

Nodes equipped with directional antennas using sectors (8 in numbers, namely N, S, E, W, NE, NW, SE, SW) to communicate between them. A node that receives a message from one of its neighbors gets a rough (N, S, E, W) on its position. It knows the relative orientation with respect to its neighbor itself. These are additional bits of information (angle of arrival of the signal) are exploited in some way to facilitate the detection / discovery of wormhole.

In (L. Hu et al., 2004), the authors propose a method for checking the neighborhood using directional antennas. Neighboring nodes examine the direction of the received signal for each of the other nodes and shared a witness. The neighbor relation is only confirmed when the directions of all the pairs match.

CONCLUSION

In this chapter, we are interested in security level routing protocol in mobile ad hoc social networks. We presented two new systems "MASN with OLSR" and "MASN with AODV". Then, we studied the vulnerability of the two routing protocols AODV and OLSR. We focused on two attacks "black hole and wormhole". At the end, we examined the various existing proposals in the literature to overcome this attack and an analysis of these methods. Then, we determined the advantages and disadvantages of each of these proposals.

REFERENCES

Buchegger, S., & Le Boudee, J. Y. (2005). Self-policing mobile ad hoc networks by reputation systems. *IEEE Communications Magazine*, *43*(7), 101–107. doi:10.1109/MCOM.2005.1470831.

Celine, B. (2009). *Contribution to securing the routing in ad hoc networks*. (PhD thesis). Limoges University, Limoges, France.

Clausen, T., & Jacquet, P. (n.d.). *Optimized link state routing protocol*. Retrieved from http://tools.ietf.org/id/draft-ietf-manet-olsr-11.txt

Condie, T., Kacholia, V., Sankararaman, S., Hellerstein, J., & Maniatis, P. (2006). Induced churn as shelter from routing-table poisoning. In *Proceedings of the 13th Annual Network and Distributed System Security Symposium (NDSS'06)*. NDSS.

Cuppens, F., Cuppens-Boulahia, N., Nuon, S., & Ramard, T. (2007). Property based intrusion detection to secure OLSR. In *Proceeding of the Third International Conference on Wireless and Mobile Communications*. Washington, DC: IEEE Computer Society.

Deng, H., Li, W., & Agrawal, D. P. (2002). Routing security in wireless ad hoc networks. *IEEE Communications Magazine*, *40*(10), 70–75. doi:10.1109/MCOM.2002.1039859.

Douceur, J. (2002). The Sybil attack. *Peer-to-Peer Systems*, *1*, 251–260. doi:10.1007/3-540-45748-8_24.

Ferrag, M. A. (2012, November 3). *Study of attacks in ad hoc networks*. Saarbrücken, Germany: LAP LAMBERT Academic Publishing.

Ferrag M. A., & Nafa M. (2011). Securing the OLSR routing protocol for ad hoc networks detecting and avoiding wormhole attack. *Journal of Selected Areas in Telecommunications*, 51-58.

Ferrag, M. A., Nafa, M., & Ghanmi, S. (2013). A new security mechanism for ad-hoc on-demand distance vector in mobile ad hoc social networks. In *Proceedings of the 7th Workshop on Wireless and Mobile Ad-Hoc Networks (WMAN 2013) in Conjunction with the Conference on Networked Systems NetSys/KIVS*. Stuttgart, Germany: WMAN.

Guang, L., Assi, C., & Benslimane, A. (2006). Interlayer attacks in mobile ad hoc networks. In *Proceedings of the Second International Conference on Mobile Ad-Hoc and Sensor Networks (MSN 2006)*, (pp. 436-448). New York: Springer.

Gupte, S., & Singhal, M. (2003). Secure routing in mobile wireless ad hoc networks. *Ad Hoc Networks*, *1*(1), 151–174. doi:10.1016/S1570-8705(03)00017-9.

Hu, L., & Evans, D. (2004). Using directional antennas to prevent wormhole attacks. In *Proceedings of the Network and Distribution Systems Security Symposium*. San Diego, CA: IEEE.

Hu, Y. C., Johnson, D. B., & Perrig, A. (2003). SEAD: Secure efficient distance vector routing for mobile wireless ad hoc networks. *Ad Hoc Networks*, *1*(1), 175–192. doi:10.1016/S1570-8705(03)00019-2.

Hu, Y. C., Perrig, A., & Johnson, D. B. (2003). Rushing attacks and defense in wireless ad hoc network routing protocols. In *Proceedings of the 2nd ACM Workshop on Wireless Security*. ACM.

Hu, Y. C., Perrig, A., & Johnson, D. B. (2005). Ariadne: A secure on-demand routing protocol for ad hoc networks. *Wireless Networks*, *11*, 21–38. doi:10.1007/s11276-004-4744-y.

Hu, Y. C., Perrig, A., & Johnson, D. B. (2006). Wormhole attacks in wireless networks. *IEEE Journal on Selected Areas in Communications*, *24*(2), 370–380. doi:10.1109/JSAC.2005.861394.

Huang, Y., & Lee, W. (2000). A cooperative intrusion detection system for ad hoc networks. In *Proceedings of the 1st ACM Workshop on security of Ad Hoc and Sensor Networks*. Fairfax, VA: ACM.

Huang, Y., & Lee, W. (2004). Attack analysis and detection for ad hoc routing protocols. In *Proceedings of the 7th International Symposium on Recent Advances in Intrusion Detection (RAID)* (Vol. 3224, pp. 125-145). New York: Springer.

Kahate, A. (2003). *Cryptography and network security* (2nd ed.). New York: Tata McGraw-Hill.

Karygiannis, T., & Owens, L. (2002). *Wireless network security*. Washington, DC: NIST.

Krawczyk, H., Bellare, M., & Canetti, R. (1997). *HMAC: Keyed-hashing for message authentication*. Retrieved from http://www.ietf.org/rfc/rfc2104.txt

Li, X., Lyu, M. R., & Liu, J. (2004). A trust model based routing protocol for secure ad-hoc networks. In *Proceedings of the Aerospace Conference*, (Vol. 2, pp. 1286-1295). IEEE.

Marti, S., Giuli, T. J., Lai, K., & Baker, M. (2000). Mitigating routing misbehavior in mobile ad hoc networks. In *Proceedings of the 6th Annual International Conference on Mobile Computing and Networking (MobiCom'00)*, (pp. 255-265). ACM.

Mui, L., Mohtashemi, M., & Halberstadt, A. (2002). A computational model of trust and reputation. In *Proceedings of the 35th Annual Hawaii International Conference on System Sciences (HICSS)*, (pp. 2431-2439). IEEE. Chen, L., Xue, X., & Leneutre, J. (2006). A lightweight mechanism to secure OLSR. [IMECS.]. *Proceedings of IMECS, 2006*, 887–895.

Papadimitratos, P., & Haas, Z. J. (2002). Secure routing for mobile ad hoc networks. In *Proceedings of the Communication Networks and Distributed Systems Modeleing and Simulation*. CNDS. Ning, P., & Sun, K. (2003). How to misuse AODV: A case study of insider attacks against mobile ad-hoc routing protocols. In *Proceedings of the IEEE Systems, Man and Cybernetics Society, Information Assurance Workshop (IAW'03)*, (pp. 60-67). IEEE.

Perkins, C., Belding-Royer, E., & Das, S. (2003). *Ad hoc on-demand distance vector (AODV) routing*. Retrieved from http: //tools.ietf.org/html/rfc3561

Perrig, A., Canetti, R., Tygar, J. D., & Song, D. (2002). The TESLA broadcast authentication protocol. *RSA CryptoBytes*, *5*(2), 2–13.

Raffo, D., Adjih, C., Clausen, T., & Muhlethaler, P. (2004). An advanced signature system for OLSR. In *Proceedings of the 2nd ACM Workshop on Security of Ad Hoc and Sensor Networks,* (pp. 10-16). New York: ACM.

Rivest, R. L., Shamir, A., & Adleman, L. (1978). A method for obtaining digital signatures and public-key cryptosystems. *Communications of the ACM, 21*(2), 126. doi:10.1145/359340.359342.

Sanzgiri, K., Dahill, B., Levine, B. N., Shields, C., & Belding-Royer, E. M. (2002). A secure routing protocol for ad hoc networks. In *Proceedings of the 10th IEEE International Conference on Network Protocols (ICNP'02),* (pp. 78-89). IEEE.

Stamouli, I., Argyroudis, P. G., & Tewari, H. (2005). Real-time intrusion detection for ad hoc networks. In *Proceedings of the Sixth IEEE International Symposium on a World of Wireless Mobile and Multimedia Networks (WoWMoM'05),* (pp. 374-380). IEEE Computer Society.

Tseng, C. Y., Balasubramanyam, P., Ko, C., Limprasittiporn, R., Rowe, J., & Levitt, K. (2003). A specification-based intrusion detection system for AODV. In *Proceedings of the 1st ACM Workshop on Security of Ad Hoc and Sensor Networks (SASN'03),* (pp. 125-134). ACM. Adjih, C., Clausen, T., Jacquet, P., Laouiti, A., Muhlethaler, P., & Raffo, D. (2003). Securing the OLSR protocol. In *Proceedings of Med-Hoc-Net,* (pp. 25-27). ACM.

Vigna, G., Gwalani, S., Srinivasan, K., Belding-Royer, E. M., & Kemmerer, R. A. (2004). An intrusion detection tool for AODV-based ad hoc wireless networks. In *Proceedings of the 20th Annual Computer Security Applications Conference (ACSAC'04),* (pp. 16-27). IEEE Computer Society.

Zapata, M. G., & Asokan, N. (2002). Securing ad hoc routing protocols. In *Proceedings of the 1st ACM Workshop on Wireless Security (WiSE'02),* (pp. 1-10). ACM.

KEY TERMS AND DEFINITIONS

Mobile Ad Hoc Network (MANET): A wireless network that does not require any fixed infrastructure.

Mobile Ad Hoc Social Network (MASN): A wireless network using a social network.

Node: An entity in the network, e.g., Laptop, PC, PDA.

Network State: State of connectivity of a node to other neighbor nodes is referred to as network state.

Routing: The process of deciding which is the best node sequence to send a message through the network.

Routing Attack: Attacks targeted at the routing protocol and with intent to disrupt the routing mechanism of the network.

Security: The process of denying access to unauthorized users and preventing unauthorized access to data.

Secure Routing: A system that deploys security mechanism to authenticate and verify the integrity of communication.

Security System: A system designed based on an in-depth understanding of the security vulnerabilities for preventing or detecting malicious behavior.

APPENDIX: REVIEW QUESTIONS

1. What is Mobile Ad hoc Social Networks (MASN)? What are the characteristics of a MASN?
2. Explain how the topology control is done in a MASN? Why MASN are highly vulnerable to security attacks?
3. What is a routing protocol of a MASN ? How does a routing protocol of a MASN differ from that of a traditional wire line or fixed network routing protocol ?
4. What is the difference between the routing protocol AODV and OLSR in MASN? Explain the process of communication in MASN using OLSR and AODV
5. What is the difference between the passive attacks and active attacks? Why are only two types of attacks?
6. What are the approaches of analysis attacks against AODV and OLSR? Give some examples of how the attacker attack routing.
7. What are the consequences of attackers in MASN? Why is the security in MASN important?

Section 5

Trust and Privacy in Mobile and Wireless Communications

Chapter 11
A Multi-Parameter Trust Framework for Mobile Ad Hoc Networks

Ji Guo
Queen's University Belfast, UK

Alan Marshall
Queen's University Belfast, UK

Bosheng Zhou
Queen's University Belfast, UK

ABSTRACT

This chapter presents a novel trust model called Multi-Parameter Trust Framework for Mobile ad hoc networks (MTFM). A key feature of this proposed framework is its use of multiple rather than a single parameter to decide the resulting trust value, applying Grey theory. Results presented here demonstrate that the new framework can maintain consistent trust values in the presence of various types of mobility. Simulations conducted in an 802.11-based mobile ad hoc network also show that this framework offers good robustness in misbehaviour detection by employing multiple parameters. The detection capability of the new framework is examined for a range of misbehaviours and its performance is compared to existing single-parameter approaches, such as the Beta distribution method.

DOI: 10.4018/978-1-4666-4691-9.ch011

INTRODUCTION

Wireless communication technologies have brought great changes in modern daily life, by letting people be able to access the Internet, whenever and wherever. A mobile ad hoc network (MANET) defined by (Corson & Macker, 1999) is a term of wireless network that does not have fixed network infrastructure, without centralized administration, where wireless nodes are free to move, communicate with each other over limited bandwidth links, fulfil routing discovery, and maintain routing in self-organized and cooperative ways.

Such MANETs were imaged to "have dynamic, sometimes rapidly-changing, random, multihop topologies which are likely composed of relatively bandwidth-constrained wireless links" (Corson & Macker, 1999). MANETs can be employed into situations without fixed infrastructures or some special environments that ignores costs, such as emergency aid, disaster recovery, military field communications, or some crisis services. Today MANETs are also applied in our daily life. For example, some academic conferences where a meeting or collaborative discussion assignment is required to be conducted outside the office building, or in some public buses and ships where people want to play online games with other passengers who take mobile phones within WiFi or Bluetooth modules.

The ad hoc topology of MANET may vary uncertainly and rapidly, as the mobile nodes are independent and have high mobility. Due to the network decentralization, any node in a MANET may act as a router to discover a routing path or to forward the data packets. Unlike wired networks and infrastructured wireless networks, the functional design of MANET should consider many factors such as power limitation, wireless link quality, and multiple user interference.

The main characteristics of MANETs have been summarized by (Corson & Macker, 1999) as follows:

1. **Dynamic Topologies:** That means nodes moving free and arbitrarily. Thus, the network topology, typically with multihop paths, may change randomly and rapidly along with time, which is unpredictable. The topology is dynamic, consisting of both bidirectional and unidirectional links.

2. **Bandwidth-Constrained:** variable capacity links. Usually, wireless connections have much lower capacity than their hardwired counterparts. Additionally, the realized throughput of a wireless connecting link is much less than a channel radio's maximum data transmitting rate, due to the effects of many physical factors, like signal fading, noise, multiple access, interference conditions, and so on.

3. **Energy-Constrained Operation:** The node battery or other power consumption methods can introduce many limits to the nodes in a MANET. In the system design, one essential criteria for optimization should be taken account of, that is energy conservation.

4. **Limited Physical Security**: The successful operation of MANETs depends upon the activities of all of the participants in the networks. However, in distributed mobile environments, nodes lack sufficient information about each other, which increases the risk of being compromised. Additionally, nodes in this kind of network may belong to different self-interested individuals and have limited power and bandwidth; therefore, some of them may tend to be selfish or malicious, during the interactions with their neighbours.

Wireless networks have been threatened by various attacks and intrusions, high-tech crimes and Internet fraud, which are growing in recent years. Thus, security has become as a highlighted research topic, for those designers who intend to utilize wireless technologies and obtain Internet services. (Koc, 1996) summarized the security attributes as follows:

- **Confidentiality:** Only the authorized parties can access to stored or transmitted information.
- **Authenticity:** The identification for the origin of the message can be executed correctly.
- **Integrity:** Authorized parties can be allowed to alter stored or transmitted information.
- **Availability:** Authorized parties can get available network resources.
- **Access Control:** Information resources are controlled.
- **Non-Repudiation:** Sender or receiver can not disallow the transmission.

For MANETs, self-organization, decentralization and openness are main advantages, but these characteristics also introduce vulnerability. In MANETs, nodes may not have enough information about other partners, which increases the risk of being harmed by attackers either outside or inside the MANETs. Malicious nodes can also join the network freely and perform various kinds of attacks to the network, to eavesdrop data packets, disrupt normal communications, or even perform the denial-of-service attack into the network.

Generally, based on their origin and nature, these attacks can be classified into categories, *passive attacks* and *active attacks*, while an origin-based classification divides the attacks into *external* and *internal* types. Various attacks take vulnerability for MANETs, such as Eavesdropping, Masquerading, Modification, Man-In-Middle, Flooding and Tunnelling. Many more complex attacks are combinations of these, and new types of attacks are still emerging. Therefore, security mechanisms must be designed to protect the individual node and the entire network from these types of attacks.

The nature of a MANET is to have wireless nodes cooperate with each other, to improve the connectivity and throughput of the whole network, and carry out some specific functions in the network. However nodes in a MANET may belong to different authorities or individual entities. Thus they have their respective interests. Because of the limitation of their individual resources (power, bandwidth, and so on), they are inherently reluctant to forward packets for other nodes. Such behaviour is called *selfishness*. For the selfishness problem, a few particular misbehaviours et al., 2008) and (J. Li, et al., 2008) need to be identified, such as selective misbehaviour, on-off, conflicting and bad mouthing.

Substantial research efforts have been contributed to tackle the attacks and misbehaviours described above. A widespread range of algorithms and techniques have been developed; anti-virus software, firewalls, intrusion detection and prevention systems, and encryption algorithms are examples. For designing a secure application in a MANET, there exists an essential challenge, which is to determine how one network entity can trust another one. Researchers have begun to design trust models that classify trust relationships, for the purposed of dynamically monitoring, and adjusting trust relationships. A number of models and algorithms have been proposed to implement trust schemes in distributed environments, such as policy language, public-key cryptography, the resurrecting duckling model (Stajano & Anderson, 2000), and various approaches such as Probabilistic estimation (J. Li et al., 2008), Information theory (Sun, et al., 2006), Dempster-Shafer theory (Aparicio-Navarro, et al., 2011), Game theory (Tuan, 2006) and Fuzzy theory et al., 2008) that have been used to design trust models. Trust models have also been included in security applications for e-commerce, peer-to-peer networks, and some other distributed systems.

The MTFM shown in this chapter utilizes multiple parameters to measure trust values, and these are not limited to the probability of successful interactions or the packet loss rate. In MTFM, the use of Grey theory allows the comparison of different types of parameters so that we can incorporate both quantitative as well as qualitative (i.e. probability-based parameter) in the evaluation algorithms. Grey theory can help to make a quantitative analysis, of a system's dynamic developing processes. The main idea is to investigate the relationships among different factors, depending on the degree of similarity between data. This chapter shows that the MTFM can compare the parameters with different types, and process the various types of observed data, and then can give an integrated value for final decision, especially for misbehaviour detection.

This chapter is about organized as follows: The introduction is given in this section and background for related work in next section; Section 3 presents the motivations of the research work shown in this chapter; Section 4 describes the new trust framework and Section 5 shows simulation results for different mobility scenarios; Section 6 shows multiple parameters are useful in misbehavior detection, and presents the performance of the framework in detecting a range of misbehaviors, and the results compared to currently single-parameter scheme such as Beta distribution method and shown to produce much improved detection capability. Conclusions and further work are then presented in Section 7 and 8.

BACKGROUND

Trust is a complicated subject. There is no unanimous definition of it. The *Merriam-Webster's Dictionary* describes trust as "assured reliance on the character, ability, strength, or truth of someone or something." Dictionary.com defines trust as the "firm reliance on the integrity, ability, or character of a person or thing." For the trust metrics used in communication systems, especially wireless networks, trust is defined as the belief degree that an entity is capable of behaving reliably and securely to a specific action.

Trust relationship has a list of characteristics and different forms from different points of view. This section describes several basic properties and forms of trust relationship as follows:

1. **Trust Relationship:** A trust relationship can be a one-to-one relation between two entities. From (Grandison & Sloman, 2000), relationships may also be one-to-multiple and multiple-to-one relations. There can also be multiple-to-multiple relationships, for example, in a class of 50 students and 5 teachers.

2. **Asymmetry:** Generally, trust relationships are not symmetric, (Poortinga & Pidgeon, 2004). A trust relationship is usually a one-way or unidirectional relation. For example, one entity can trust another one, but the converse may not be true. In other words, the trustworthiness in the reverse direction may not come into existence at the same time. If for the two ways between a pair of entities, the trust relations both exist, they can be represented as two separate trust relationships.

3. **Transitivity:** Some trust relationship scenarios perform transitivity, (Alfarez & Stephen, 1997). The delegation of trust relationship is a classical example for the application of trust transitivity. For example, when Alice delegates her trust decisions to Bob, it means she authorizes Bob to make trust decisions on her behalf. Thus, if Bob trusts an unknown entity such as Chuck, Alice will trust Chuck to some extent.

4. **Relativity:** Trust relationship is not absolute. One trust relationship can be founded, changed or removed for specific environment. In other words, two entities just keep a trust relationship only in certain contexts. Faced with various and numerous information about trust, people usually decide to

trust some specific information to a certain degree. Because of the relativity, many trust models use trust categories to represent which aspect of trust they are referring to and how much they trust.

5. **Measurability**: Trust can be measured. Through this concept, a level is often attached to a trust relationship. The trust level or trusted degree is used to assess an entity's belief in the honesty, competence and dependability, (Grandison & Sloman, 2002). An entity's trust may be evaluated by many neighbours before performing certain actions relevant to that entity. The valuation method varies, and the values of trust can be either discrete or continuous. If using discrete values, qualitative key words like high, medium and low are often chosen.

6. **Uncertainty:** In many situations, trust is uncertain. There exists a grey zone between trust and distrust, that is, one may be ignorant or uncertain about an entity's trustworthiness, if there is lack of context, experience or complete information, (Cheshire & Cook, 2004). Some certainty mechanisms specify trust values only according to known facts and desired behaviours, but ignore the existence of uncertainty.

In distributed environments, highly autonomous entities want network services available in open networks that dynamically adopt the topology based on the modes of mobility, which makes the entire network become vulnerable to various attacks. With the growth in the requirement for open services, the uncertainty of nodes' behaviours is increasing. Trust can help deal with uncertainty. Trust models can be integrated into secure network applications and have become a very important design aspect of modern communication systems (H. Li & Singhal, 2007).

A key point in the design is to determine how one network entity is able to trust another one. In recent years, researchers have designed many trust

metrics; these are usually obtained by collecting the necessary information, and then dynamically monitoring, establishing and modifying the trust relationships. The main purpose of employing trust metrics is to provide more detailed and better-informed authorisation decisions, for wireless networks with a higher level of automation.

A lot of trust models and algorithms have been designed for distributed environments, such as policy language, the resurrecting duckling model, public-key cryptography, and so on. Moreover, a number of distributed trust models have also been well-developed for distributed systems and MANETs.

Credential-Based Model and Policy language

The roots of credential-based trust models are within authentication and authorisation. The certificates are viewed as the main proof for judging nodes' reputations. One credential-based trust model with negotiation strategies is discussed in (Winsborough, Seamons, & Jones, 1999). Policy languages, (Blaze, et al., 1998; Chu, et al., 1997), helps to automatically determine whether certain credentials are enough to authorise the trustee, for a specific action. For some credential-based models, like PolicyMaker in (Blaze et al., 1998), and REFEREE by (Chu et al., 1997), the basic idea is to use languages for specifying trust policies or trusted actions and trust relationships.

The Sultan trust management framework, which is presented by (Grandison & Sloman, 2002), introduced a language to describe the trust relationships of a system. (Damianou, Dulay, Lupu, & Sloman, 2001) proposed the Ponder policy language linked with trust relationships, in which certain constraints were attached to these relationships.

At the authentication level, the degree of trust changes little over time and usually means a certain identity or membership. The above models do not consider updating trust levels based on evidence of actual behaviours, rather, the focus of those models is on credentials matching policy. Therefore, when establishing a trust management system in decentralized infrastructure networks, one essential element of the design is having adequate flexibility to adapt to changing relationships.

Resurrecting Duckling Model

(Stajano & Anderson, 2000)'s *resurrecting duckling* model has a hierarchical structure. The network entities are usually within a master-slave relationship. The master entity is named as the mother duck, while setting the slave entity as the duckling. The process by which a slave entity recognizes the first entity as the master and sends it a secret key via an out-of-band secret channel, is called *imprinting* (Stajano & Anderson, 2000). The master passes the instructions and lists of access control to its slaves. And the salves always obey their master. However, the relationship between a master and a slave can be broken by a time-out, or a specific event. Then other entities may imprint, or resurrect the slave. During the imprinting process, a slave entity can also become as a master for other entities. Thus, the trust relationship among those entities is tree-like. A node controls its neighbour nodes in its sub-tree. If there is a break in the relation between two nodes, the relationships in the entire subtree will be destroyed. The *resurrecting duckling model* is suitable for environments that cannot perform public-key cryptography. But the model is required to deliver the secret key via an out-of-band secret channel, which may be unable to be applied in some wireless networks.

Recommendation-Based Trust Model

(Alfarez & Stephen, 1997) presented a distributed recommendation-based trust model. The model proposed *conditional transitivity of trust*, which presented that trust could be transitive under certain conditions. The initial idea of this model comes from networking in human society. In the society, people know each other through direct interaction and via broadcasting and exchanging relationships. Similarly in distributed systems, any entity cannot get all the first-hand/direct information about all the other entities, and optionally, entities may obtain recommendations from other neighbours, or collect second-hand information. This distributed trust model from (Alfarez & Stephen, 1997) assumes asymmetrical trust. It classifies trust relationships into two types: *direct trust* and *recommender trust*, and categorizes a trust relationship between two nodes in terms of different interactions.

A number of research works have been developed on the calculation of nodes' trust values in distributed systems like MANETs. Most consider reputation or trust values that can express the risk level of communicating with neighbour nodes. Existing studies focus on the evaluation of the degrees of trust for nodes. A number of approaches like Probabilistic Estimation, Information Theory, Fuzzy theory and Game theory have been utilized in the design of distributed trust models. The main methods of these theories can be summarized as follows.

Evidence Theory

(Eschenauer, et al., 2004) presented a framework for trust management in mobile ad hoc networks, based on the distribution of trust evidence. They also considered trust as a set of relationships established by the support of evidence. In their framework, evidence could be a policy for establishing a trust relationship, such as public key, identity, and address. Evidence can be obtained either online or offline, such as via physical connection. An entity can generate evidence for itself and for other entities. One way of generating evidence is by using public-key cryptography. Any entity can create a piece of evidence, set the valid time, sign with its private key, and broadcast this evidence to other entities. Other entities, who receive this piece of evidence, need the original entity's public key and certificate, so as to verify the evidence. (Eschenauer et al., 2004) also proposed that, if there is no Certification Authority (CA) in an ad hoc network, Pretty Good Privacy (PGP) could be another option. In their model, an entity could withdraw other entities' evidence by generating and broadcasting conflicting evidence. At any time, an entity can invalidate its evidence by creating a certificate for annulment.

However, allowing such actions is open to attack. A malicious node can distribute fake evidence to invalidate other nodes' legitimate evidence, which may introduce chaos into the network. A malicious node may also generate bogus evidence for its own purposes; for example, an attacker intending to impersonate other normal nodes. To avoid these attacks, (Eschenauer et al., 2004) proposed using redundant and independent evidence from various sources. However, they did not investigate the evaluation of evidence. In fact, evaluating evidence is very important in trust management. Because each node's trustworthiness is not dynamically adjusted, the framework is mainly useful for initial authentication.

Probabilistic Estimation

(Buchegger & Boudec, 2005) presented an approach using the probability of normal observations to calculate trust values, which could be viewed as the probabilistic estimation method. (Ganeriwal, Balzano, & Srivastava, 2008) improved the method based on Beta distribution probability. The main idea is to build the trust relationships, according to a basic probabilistic principle, called the posterior probability distribution of the node behaviours, which is subject to Beta distribution. The paper assumed that the data samples should be consistent with the probability distribution.

Information theory

(Sun et al., 2006) proposed an information theoretic framework with modelling and evaluating trust. They viewed trust as a measure of uncertainty. The concept described the certainty of whether a neighbour entity performed a cooperating action or not, from the view of the subject entity. Therefore, different subject entities could define different probability values for an entity's one behaviour, due to different points of view.

(Cover & Thomas, 2006) states that "entropy is a natural measure for uncertainty", from information theory. Hereupon, (Sun et al., 2006) defined the entropy based trust value. The authors defined the axioms, which can be viewed as the basic rules of trust. These axioms are used to build trust by a third party (*concatenation propagation*), and by recommendations from multiple sources (*multi-path propagation*). The trust values are derived from observation. This paper designed two trust models, for handling with the concatenation and multi-path trust propagation problems in mobile ad hoc networks. In particular, the paper investigated building trust relationships and making recommendations, associated with packet forwarding. It also presented a distributed scheme for generating, maintaining, and updating trust values for MANETs. The trust value records can be applied to take route selections, and to detect malicious nodes.

Dempster-Shafer Theory

Dempster-Shafer (D-S) is a theory of evidence, which can be viewed as an extended approach of Bayesian theory about subjective probability. The basic idea of D-S is to obtain the degree of belief for a question, according to the relative subjective probability about another related question (Singh, Vatsa, & Noore, 2006). That is, D-S is an approach to describe unknown uncertainty.

A number of researchers have used it to design Intrusion Detection System (IDS) and trust evaluation in wireless networks. One research (Aparicio-Navarro et al., 2011) presents an on-line IDS for wireless networks with using data fusion technique based on D-S. The system is effective in detecting attacks and limiting false alarms from different layers of networks. Another article (Konorski & Orlikowski, 2009) gives a data-centric trust evaluation for selfishness detection in MANETs and WSNs (Wireless Sensor Networks), with maintaining the balance between robustness to false alarms and convergence of selfish misbehaviour detection.

However, most systems that employ data fusion techniques, have to collect large amounts of data samples, and process them, which means requiring a training period before intrusion detection beginning. In other words, these systems need to compare with historical data. Therefore it is hard for these systems to automatically adapt to changes of nodes' behaviours in real-time, without enough previous data.

For the issue above, (Aparicio-Navarro, Kyriakopoulos, & Parish, 2012) proposes a novel Basic Probability Assignment (BPA) methodology, which can adjust its detection capability to the changes of real-time characteristics of wireless networks, without intervention from an IDS administrator.

Game Theory

Game theory has been successfully applied for modelling and analyzing with uncertainty, particularly, in the fields related to trust. In a distributed network, uncertainty and belief among nodes are distinct characteristics. Nodes in MANETs or peers in P2P systems are not sure about their partners' actions, intentions, and trust valuations. As a result, nodes are unable to choose an appropriate strategy to interact. Though nodes may have some prior belief about others' behaviours, their belief will be changed because of updating information.

Game-theoretic analysis mainly focuses on pure strategic games, in which a player is fully sure of the action that he or she should do. However, mixed strategies are generally not well considered. (Tuan, 2006) gives a view of game-theoretic analysis, in which a mixed strategy could fit well within the context.

By modelling a game with mixed strategy, the trust model (Tuan, 2006) can deal with uncertainty, when making nodes' decisions. The means of solving uncertainty can use the probability analysis. Rather than having a fully certain strategy, nodes can assign a probability of a concrete strategy. In other words, the model can gain a distribution about all the possible strategies.

Another point of view models the change of belief by using game theory. In many situations, nodes or peers may be not perfectly informed about others' behaviours; or a node may know about others' actions well, but may not know how well other nodes are informed about its own characteristics. A game-theoretic approach applying the Bayesian method (Tuan, 2006) can fit well within the context, to mitigate uncertainty.

Fuzzy Theory

Fuzzy mathematics can be applied to conceptualize the subjectivity and uncertainty of the trust, (Qin et al., 2008). Many researchers have studied fuzzy theory in the application of trust evaluation. (Ni & Luo, 2008) proposed a method of clustering analysis to evaluate grid nodes' trust. (Chen, Luo, & Ni, 2008) designed a two-level trust evaluation model for grid environment, with fuzzy math theory, based on access control. (Tao, Huang, & Hong, 2010) adopted fuzzy mathematics to put forward a method of expressing subjective trust, based on multiple-element connection number. (Zhang, Zou, & Wang, 2009) suggested a dynamic trust class definition scheme, and gave the trust calculation by a fuzzy comprehensive evaluation algorithm.

However, most existing trust models evaluate nodes' degrees of trust using pre-defined and static classifications. One disadvantage is that determining the proper number of trust classes is not easy. Too detailed (fine-grained) definitions may affect system efficiency, while rough (coarse-grained) definitions will bring risks to system security. Another disadvantage is that one entity may obtain different or even conflicting judgments from otter entities.

Grey Theory

Deng Julong proposed the method named *grey relational analysis* in (Deng, 1989). Grey theory can help to make a quantitative analysis of a system's dynamically developing process. Grey theory has been widely used in various fields like agriculture, aerographs and environmental science. The main idea of grey theory is to investigate the relationships among different factors, depending on the degree of similarity between data. One advantage of this approach is that it does not require a lot of sample data. Moreover, the data samples do not have to be consistent with any special distribution rules.

(Fu et al., 2009), used an improved analysis method based on grey theory, to design risk assessment. This method can process multiple-attribute data effectively, and create the Grey Relational Grades (GRG) about different sorts of original data. In addition, it can mitigate the uncertainty through the distinguishing coefficient of GRG. The author presented a feasible method for risk assessment in distributed environments. Currently some researchers have applied Grey theory into improving network performance or designing trust models, such as (Fu et al., 2009), (Guo, Marshall, & Zhou, 2011).

(Fu, Huang et al., 2009) developed a risk assessment method for mobile ad hoc networks based on a combination of grey theory and vector projection, based on (Fu et al., 2009). (Ye et al., 2010) proposed a model on basis of Projection Pursuit theory to realize both risk assessment and attributes analysis. The proposed design of this paper is based on principle component analysis

with projection pursuit theory (Friedman et al., 1973), which is a flexible assessment method to analyze multi-attribute data and determine inherent laws of ad hoc working nodes behaviours. Principle component analysis (Dunteman, 1989) and component matrix can help to make evaluation of ad-hoc node, and also determines importance of each different attribute. Though trust evaluation is related with risk assessment, trust is not always proportional to trust. The considerations of selecting multiple types of parameters for trust and risk are different. Moreover, the papers intend to give flexible importance values for different attributes; however, when the model once calculates the importance values, these values will be fixed.

With developing of the research on trust design, various distributed algorithms are invented; however, they are largely based on the classical method- probabilistic estimation, and focus on processing probability-based parameters. For the purpose of employing and processing multiple types of parameters (it is hard to use probability-based algorithms to do those), some researchers have applied grey theory to process many parameters in the field of secure wireless communication systems. However, research such as (Fu et al., 2009) uses grey theory in other aspects such as risk assessment of networks, which cannot be directly used for trust evaluation in distributed environment. In addition, (Fu et al., 2009) used the Grey Relational Grade, but with fixed weight vectors for the input parameters. If fixed weight vectors are used for calculating trust values, a problem is that if attackers know which factor is the most important one in the trust model, the attackers or malicious nodes can get high trust values by only behaving well in that specified factor; however, in fact they do not cooperate well with other normal nodes. (Cho et al., 2011) summarized a few trust models with the purpose for misbehaviour detection. Due to the limit of the probability-based methods, it is hard for these previous models to detect those misbehaviours, which malicious nodes do not behave in probability parameter.

MAIN FOCUS OF THE CHAPTER

Motivations of this Chapter

For a MANET, one particular feature, caused by the nodes' limited resources, can offer incentives for some nodes to act selfishly. Trust management can help to mitigate the selfishness and make the efficient utilization of network resources. However, currently in trust design, most existing algorithms are based on the methods for processing qualitative parameters (probability-based), such as probability estimation. For example, some trust metrics such as Objective Trust Management Framework (OTMF) presented by (J. Li et al., 2008), a subjective trust model with two-dimensional measurement (Chang, Liu, & Wang, 2009) and a trust establishment framework using Dempster-Shafer theory (Karami & Fathian, 2009), usually employ the probability of successful interactions as their main input parameter, in the calculation of trust value. Selfish or malicious nodes can take advantage of this to either gain unfair trust values for themselves, or to degrade the trust values of other nodes.

In fact, the trusted degree of one node for another node can be expressed not only by the successful (or unsuccessful) outcomes like packet loss rate, but also through the physical factors such as data rate, and signal strength. These are not considered in existing trust models. For example, a selfish node or a malicious one may make use of the knowledge that the packet loss rate is the main parameter employed in the calculation of trust values. Accordingly, the trust value of the attacker can be given a very high value. In fact, the selfish node only cooperates with close neighbour nodes, while abandoning or dropping data packets with the nodes further away. In comparison, normal behaving nodes have the interactions with all neighbours, either near or far. Thus, one possible situation may arise, when a normal node communicating with a far-away neighbour, experience a packet loss rate much higher than

that of the selfish one which just interacts with near neighbours. If the trust value calculation only chooses the packet loss rate as the deciding factor, it will result in a normal node's trust value being lower than the selfish node's, which selectively chooses its partners. It is therefore essential for a trust model to detect such cheating behaviour, and thus, it should consider multiple parameters, particularly those factors involved in the communications processes. Moreover, the trust scheme should also consider different types of parameters.

Conventionally a classical approach such as probabilistic estimation is used to process probability-based parameters. These parameters, such as the packet loss rate (PLR) generally have the form of *s/(s+f)*, where *s=number of successful interactions, f=number of failed interactions*. However, many of the parameters in MANETs such as signal strength, delay, and throughput, are quantitative in their nature. Therefore, it is difficult to apply the probabilistic estimation methods to process these types of quantitative values.

The MTFM shown in this chapter utilizes multiple parameters to measure trust values, and these are not limited to the probability of successful interactions or the packet loss rate. Using more than one parameter is based on the assertion that one node's behaviour, whether that interaction is successful or not, is influenced by various factors. For example, the signal strength, delay of forwarding packets, throughout, and data rate, may all affect the cooperation between two nodes. Whether one node could be trusted or not, is not only determined by the probability of successful interactions, but also by various parameters from the physical and MAC layers. However if the trust model only adopts the classical algorithm – probability estimation, it is hard to calculate trust values based on various input parameters. In MTFM, the use of Grey theory allows the comparison of different types of parameters so that we can incorporate both quantitative as well as qualitative (i.e. probability-based parameter) in the evaluation algorithms.

In (Deng, 1989), Deng Julong presented the relational analysis method of grey theory to determine the relationships of different factors, based on the degree of similarity among data samples. Nor does it need a high quantity of samples. Moreover, the data samples are not required to be consistent with any kind of distribution. Meanwhile, a very convincible result can be still obtained, which is consistent with qualitative analysis. With applying Grey theory, it can help with designing algorithms to process multiple parameters.

Some researchers have applied grey theory in the field of secure wireless communication systems; however, research such as (Fu et al., 2009) uses grey theory in other aspects such as risk assessment of networks, and not for trust evaluation in distributed environment. (Fu et al., 2009) used the Grey Relational Grade, but with fixed weight vectors for the input parameters. If fixed weight vectors are used for calculating trust values, a problem is that if attackers know which factor is the most important one in the trust model, the attackers or malicious nodes can get high trust values by only behaving well in that specified factor; however, in fact they do not cooperate well with other normal nodes.

The proposed trust framework not only considers multiple and different types of input parameters, but also sets several groups of weight vectors to calculate trust values. Based on groups of weight vectors, MTFM can obtain different trust values for a node; this can identify which aspect of a node's behaviour is abnormal. With this new design, this framework can deduce selfish nodes' behaviour strategies.

Multi-Parameter Trust Framework for Mobile Ad Hoc Networks

A novel trust framework, called a multi-parameter trust framework for mobile ad hoc networks (MTFM), is proposed in this section. Three new concepts of the trust relationships are introduced, which play a key role throughout the proposed

framework. The work presented here views the wireless network neighbourhood from three levels in (Guo, Marshall, & Zhou, 2011). For the neighbourhood of one node, according to the node' interaction situations, trust relationships are classified into *direct, indirect,* and *recommendation trust,* on behalf of the trust opinions of anyone node's different neighbours'.

- **Direct trust** is a type of trust relationship, when the related interactions between the observing and observed node exist. For example, *node A* (observing node) wants to know *node B's* (observed node) information, for which observations obtained directly from *B* are called *direct trust.*

- **Indirect trust** means the trust information transited from third parties, which the observing node do not have interactions with the third parties. For example, *Node E and F* are the indirect trust nodes, which have interactions with *B*, but *A* does not communicate with *E and F*. The trust values of *B* that *A* gets from *E* and *F* are called *indirect trust.*

- **Recommendation trust** is a special type of trust relationship. We assume the observing node communicates with another node that also has interactions with the observed node. This new node is denoted as the recommendation node for the observing node. For example (Guo, Marshall, & Zhou, 2011), *node A* can calculate the trust values of *B* and *C* from *A's* view. If *A* wants to know the trust records of *B* from *C*, *C* will provide the trust value of *B* based on the observations of interactions between *B and C*.

In a wireless mobile ad hoc network, MTFM views a node as an agent for generating the trust values. The functional blocks of the framework are shown in Figure 1. The observing node processes multiple input parameters using algorithms based

Figure 1. Functional blocks of the framework

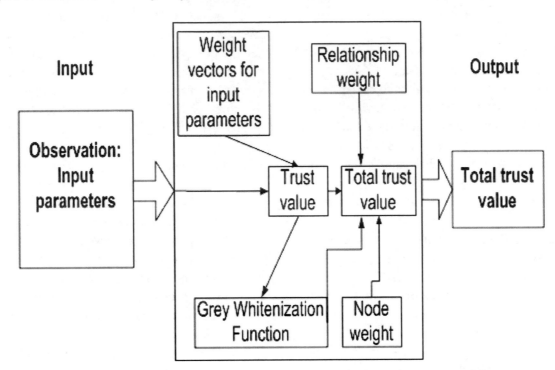

on grey theory to obtain direct, recommendation, and indirect trust values (these values can be called individual trust values). Then, the total trust values are calculated using nodes' weights, relationship weights, and grey whitenization weights as described in the following parts.

Trust models compute the trust values based upon input information that one node can gather about other nodes. The particular question is what are the appropriate parameters or events of input information in MANETs. Many current trust models for distributed environments just select the probability of successful interactions, (or the packet loss rate), as the main parameter in the calculation of trust values. However, in fact, the probability of one node well-cooperating with other nodes is reflected not only by the packet loss rate, but also by physical and link layer factors such as signal strength, data rate, and other parameters, which are not considered in existing trust models.

For example, an attacker or a selfish node may make use of the knowledge that the packet loss rate is the main parameter used in trust calculation (most current trust models choose this type of probability-based parameter). The attacker/ selfish node can obtain a normal or higher trust value, and, at the same time it can increase the delay time during forwarding data packets (for malicious purposes such as eavesdropping), decrease the throughputs, and intentionally choose close neighbours, while dropping or abandoning interactions from far away nodes. Compared with the selfish node, normal behaving nodes will forward the data packets with normal delay time, have normal throughputs, and communicate with all neighbours, either near or far. If the normal node's packet loss rate is higher than the selfish node's, even though the normal node behaves good in other parameters such delay and throughput, only using the packet loss rate as the deciding parameter may lead to a normal node's trust value being lower than that of an attacker.

Therefore, there is the conclusion that a trust scheme should consider multiple parameters, including those involved in the communications processes in order to prevent against such duplicity. To tackle this problem, MTFM determines the trust values based on multiple input parameters, not limited to only one factor – the probability-based parameter such as the probability of successful interactions or packet loss rate.

Conventionally a classical approach such as probabilistic estimation is used to process probability-based parameters. These parameters, such as the PLR generally have the form of *s/(s+f)*, where *s=number of successful interactions, f=number of failed interactions.*

However, many of the parameters in MANETs such as signal strength, delay, and throughput, are usually quantitative in their nature. Therefore, it is difficult to apply the probabilistic estimation methods to process these types of quantitative values. In MTFM, the use of Grey theory allows the comparison of different types of parameters so that we can incorporate both quantitative as well as qualitative (i.e. probabilistic) in the evaluation algorithms.

Based on RTS/CTS (Request To Send/Clear To Send) scheme in IEEE 802.11 MAC DCF (Distributed Coordination Function) (Razavi, Fleury, & Monaghan, 2007), the framework can collect more input parameters. For example, nodes could use ACK (acknowledgment frame) signals after RTS and CTS to present one successful/failed interaction and calculate packet loss rate (PLR), and can record end-to-end delay. What's more, the nodes can obtain the information about signal strength from other neighbour nodes, and data rate of the corresponding data link. For the simulations shown in this chapter, the RTS/CTS scheme is assumed to be in use. (If a wireless network without RTS/CTS scheme, the nodes can calculate the PLR by the ACK signals.)

Multiple observing factors about a node's behaviour can bring more useful information. In the framework of Figure 1, the nodes firstly need to collect the information via observing neighbours' actions. Based on the above, the framework chooses five input parameters, including packet loss rate, signal strength, data rate, end-to-end delay, and throughput. The selection of these multiple parameters is based on the consideration that a node' cooperations with other neighbour nodes can be reflected in the probability of successful interactions – packet loss rate, as well as the total count of successful interactions – throughput, along with quantifiable parameters such as the time for completing interactions – delay, the power when interacting with other nodes – signal strength, and the high/low channel speed affecting the throughput – data rate.

For multiple input parameters, Grey Theory can be used to proceed and calculate trust values. Let X be a grey relational set which is used as the evaluation index set, $X = \{ x_1, ..., x_m \}$, where x_j is an evaluation index. Here, it assumes that *X={packet loss rate, signal strength, data rate, delay, throughput}.*

During a time period t *(t=1,2,...T)*, from the view of a node that observes its neighbouring node k's behaviour and calculates its trust values, k's value of the evaluated index x_j is $a_{k,j}{}^t$ *(j=1,2,...,m)*. It can get node k's sample sequence $A_k{}^t = \{a_{k,j}{}^t\}$, $j=1,2,...,m$, and the sample matrix for all the neighbouring nodes at t, $A^t = [a_{k,j}{}^t]$, $j=1,2,...,m$, $k=1, 2,..., K$. Here defines the observing node has K neighbour nodes.

At period t, the best reference sequence is $G^t = (g_1{}^t, ..., g_m{}^t)$, while $g_j{}^t$ is the chosen best index from $\{a_{k,j}{}^t, k=1,2,..., K\}$. The best sequence is that, which chooses the lowest packet loss rate, lowest signal strength (balancing one node's power ability and the node's cooperation performance, discussed above), lowest delay, smallest date rates (considering the data forwarding speed limit in a data link) and highest throughputs (meaning more communications). We can obtain the Grey Relational Coefficient between node k's sample and the best reference sequence about x_j at period t as:

$$\theta_{k,j}^{\ t} = \frac{\min_k \left| a_{k,j}^{\ t} - g_j^{\ t} \right| + \rho \max_k \left| a_{k,j}^{\ t} - g_j^{\ t} \right|}{\left| a_{k,j}^{\ t} - g_j^{\ t} \right| + \rho \max_k \left| a_{k,j}^{\ t} - g_j^{\ t} \right|} \quad (1)$$

$\rho \in (0,1)$ is the distinguishing coefficient. Also we define the worst reference sequence $B^t = (b_1^{\ t}, ..., b_m^{\ t})$, while $b_j^{\ t}$ is the chosen worst index from $\{a_{k,j}^{\ t}, k=1,2,..., K\}$ which takes the values in opposition of the best one's. We can also obtain the Grey Relational Coefficient between node k's samples and worst reference sequence about x_j at period t as:

$$\phi_{k,j}^{\ t} = \frac{\min_k \left| a_{k,j}^{\ t} - b_j^{\ t} \right| + \rho \max_k \left| a_{k,j}^{\ t} - b_j^{\ t} \right|}{\left| a_{k,j}^{\ t} - b_j^{\ t} \right| + \rho \max_k \left| a_{k,j}^{\ t} - b_j^{\ t} \right|} \quad (2)$$

$\rho \in (0,1)$ is distinguishing coefficient. From (1) and (2), when normally setting $\rho = 1/2$, the value area of a grey relational coefficient is from 0.33 to 1. In order to make the grey relational coefficient to be in [0, 1], the values are converted by using the mapping $y = 1.5x - 0.5$ (x means the grey relational coefficient).

$$\theta_k^{\ t} = \sum_{j=1}^{m} h_j \theta_{k,j}^{\ t}, \quad \phi_k^{\ t} = \sum_{j=1}^{m} h_j \phi_{k,j}^{\ t}$$

$T_k^{\ t}$ is defined as the individual trust value of node k, which can also be viewed as the expectation value of node k, or the probability of node k's trust values being close to the best sequence. That is $1 - T_k^{\ t}$ as the probability of node k's trust values being close to the worst sequence.

Node k's trust value $T_k^{\ t}$, should minimize the uncertainties of belonging to both best and worst sequences. In other words, that is to decrease the fuzziness of node k's trust value $T_k^{\ t}$. Then, by using the least-square methods [Guo, et al., 2011], at period t, it has:

$$\min F(T_1^{\ t}, T_2^{\ t}, ..., T_n^{\ t}) = \min \sum_{k=1}^{n} \{ [(1 - T_k^{\ t})\theta_k^{\ t}]^2 + (T_k^{\ t}\phi_k^{\ t})^2 \}$$

Then let $\dfrac{\partial F}{\partial T_k^{\ t}} = 0$, the integrated expected value can be obtained at period t as node k's trust value:

$$T_k^{\ t} = \frac{1}{1 + \dfrac{(\phi_k^{\ t})^2}{(\theta_k^{\ t})^2}} \quad (3)$$

Few current trust models consider the different influences of different node relationships; generally, they set the weights of different nodes' opinions as fixed values, usually average values. This means that the important degrees of opinions about trust information from different types of neighbour nodes, are equal. In contrast, the approach here is to set the weights of trust relationships as changeable parameters in order to express the degree of trust of a node or nodes.

In addition, the trust assessment can be defined by using classes of grey clusters and a group of whitenization weight functions, which can describe one value's weights in different clusters, which can be viewed as the degree of how much the value belongs to a cluster (Liu & Lin, 2006). Defining three grey clusters, with d_1, d_2 and d_3 classes of trust, the corresponding whitening functions are $f_1(x), f_2(x)$ and $f_3(x)$, and the threshold values are $\sigma_1, \sigma_2, \sigma_3$. Three classes of grey clusters for MTFM are defined as shown in Table 1.

From Grey theory, the corresponding whitenization functions can be used to describe grey cluster classes, which are shown as follows:

$$f_1(x) = -x + 1, 0 \leq x \leq 1, \quad (4)$$

Table 1. Grey clusters

d1	Not quite trusted
d_2	Some trust
d_3	Quite trusted

$$f_2(x) = \begin{cases} 2x, x <= 0.5 \\ -2x + 2, x > 0.5 \end{cases}, \qquad (5)$$

$$f_3(x) = x, 0 \leq x \leq 1, \qquad (6)$$

The whitenization weight of a trust value T_{Bi} (node B's trust value evaluated by node i), which is calculated by *(3)*, belonging to the s class d_s is $f_s(T_{Bi})$, $s=1,2,3$. According to $max_s\{f_s(T_{Bi})\}$, MTFM can obtain the grey cluster class of node B based on T_{Bi}. The crossing points of three whitenization functions can indicate the detailed classification for the degrees of trust. If for $max_s\{f_s(T_{Bi})\}$, T_{Bi} is between $(\sigma_3+\sigma_1)/3$ and $2(\sigma_3+\sigma_1)/3$, the related grey cluster class is d_2 (some trust); if T_{Bi} of $max_s\{f_s(T_{Bi})\}$ is under $(\sigma_3+\sigma_1)/3$, the related grey cluster class is d_1, (not quite trusted); if T_{Bi} is above $2(\sigma_3+\sigma_1)/3$, the related grey cluster class is d_3, (quite trusted).

The total trust value of node B for node A is as follows:

$$T_{BA-total} = \frac{1}{2}(max_s\{f_s(T_{direct})\})T_{direct}$$
$$+ \frac{1}{2}\frac{2N_R}{2N_R + N_I}\sum_{N_R}\frac{w_i}{\sum w_i}(max_s\{f_s(T_{Bi})\})T_{Bi}$$
$$+ \frac{1}{2}\frac{N_I}{2N_R + N_I}\sum_{N_I}\frac{w_i}{\sum w_i}(max_s\{f_s(T_{Bi})\})T_{Bi}$$
$$\qquad (7)$$

The total trust value is calculated by three types of individual trust values, direct, recommendation and indirect values. T_{direct} can also be viewed as T_{BA}. Here, N_R means the number of recommendation nodes, while N_I means the number of indirect nodes. The N_R and N_I can express the effect levels of different trust relationships, to compose relationship weights. w_i (also named as w_{iA}) is the node weight of node i, which is set by the observing node A. T_{direct} can also be viewed as T_{BA}. From s for $max_s\{\sum_i[f_s(T_{Bi})]\}$, $T_{BA-total}$ can be known in the corresponding grey cluster class

d_s, then the total grey cluster class for *node B* for node A can also be obtained.

The network-average trust values node B is as follows:

$$T_{B-network-average} = \frac{1}{1 + N_R + N_I}\sum_{1+N_R+N_I}(max_s\{f_s(T_{Bi})\})T_{Bi}$$
$$\qquad (8)$$

Simulation Results and Analysis for Different Mobility Scenarios

MTFM presented in last section is proposed for mobile ad hoc networks. Therefore, the mobility of the wireless nodes and its influence on trust calculations is a key fact of any trust framework for MANETs. Different types of mobility are investigated to show the robustness of MTFM for various mobile scenarios.

The simulation chooses the Random waypoint model to mock/simulate the nodes' movements. The Random Waypoint model is a mobility model, which is often employed for mobility studies in mobile communication systems (Gerharz et al., 2012). This model is used to describe the movement pattern of mobile users/nodes, as well as how their velocity, acceleration and locations, change over time. It describes that mobile nodes move randomly and freely without restrictions. Specifically, the model sets all the destination, speed and direction randomly, transient phase and independently of other nodes' movements, (Klein, 2012).

The simulations use NS-2 to create a wireless mobile ad hoc network, using 802.11 standards. The DSDV routing protocol is used. The simulation sets 6 nodes in various scenarios, which the nodes have different status, static or mobile, shown as follows:

Scenario 1: All Nodes Static

In this scenario, shown in Figure 2, the simulation sets all the six nodes to be static. *Node 0* wants to get the trust value of *node 1* based on trust opinions from *node 0* and its neighbouring *nodes 2, 3, 4* and *5*. Each link from a *node i* to another *node j* sends a 10-second burst of Constant Bit Rate (CBR) type traffic, with selective data rate under 802.11 standards (5.5 Mbps, 2.0Mbps or 1.0Mbps). The size of each data packet is 512 Bytes. The parameters observed are: packet loss rate; received signal strength; delay; throughput; data rate. Initially all parameters have equal importance, $H=\{0.2,0.2,0.2,0.2,.0.2\}$. All nodes also have equal weights.

The purpose of Scenario 1 is to create a benchmark of static scenario that the trust values obtained can be used to compare with those values of other dynamic scenarios.

Scenario 2: Node 1 Mobile

The node movements in this scenario are set so that only *node 1* is mobile with the Random Waypoint model, while other nodes are static. The traffic and other parameters are the same as Scenario 1. The one node mobile scenario is that the observed node – *node 1* is a mobile one, to discover the changes of the trust values from *node 1*'s neighbour nodes, in a mobile scenario.

Scenario 3: Node 1 Static

In this scenario, the node movements are set so that only *node 1* is static, while other nodes are mobile. The traffic and other parameters are the same as Scenario 1. The 5-node mobile scenario is simulated to observe the changes of *node 1*'s trust values from its neighbour nodes.

Scenario 4: All Nodes Mobile

In this scenario, all the nodes are mobile, to obtain the trust values for all mobile nodes. The traffic and other parameters are the same as Scenario 1. This scenario set all nodes mobile, to observe *node 1*'s trust values.

All scenarios are simulated with NS-2 (version 2.30), under the Linux operating system (version Ubuntu 10.04). The calculations of individual and final trust values are realized by Perl programme language. The program flow diagram is shown in Figure 3.

In Scenario 1, a specified subject node like *node 0* wants to know the target node's (*node 1*) trust value, by considering the opinions from both the neighbour nodes and its own. Based on Equation *(3)*, MTFM calculates *node 1*'s individual trust value from *node 0*, named as T_{10}, which is the direct trust value of *node 1*. *Node 0* and *node 1* have common neighbouring nodes, *node 2* and *node 3*. T_{12} and T_{13} are the recommendation trust values for the subject node. *Nodes 4* and *5* are viewed as indirect neighbour nodes, due to only having interactions with *node 1*. *Node 0* can broadcast its request for node 1' trust values to other nodes in the network; if *node 4* and *5* receive the request, the indirect nodes can provide the trust evaluation information about *node 1* to *node 0*.

Thus MTFM obtains the three individual trust values (from *node 0, 2 and 3*) about *node 1*, over a period of 10 seconds. Here $\rho=0.5$, $H=\{0.2,0.2,0.2,0.2,0.2\}$, $N_R=2$, $N_I=0$, which means the indirect nodes *4, 5* are not included. All the initial node weight values w_{k0} are set to *1*. The direct trust value $T_{10}=0.8335$, while $T_{12}=0.2181$, and $T_{13}=0.5369$. From Equation *(4.7)*, and through the whitenization functions, the total value of *node 1* for *node 0* with 3 neighbour nodes is $T_{10-3nodes}=0.5143$, as shown in Figure 4.

When including the indirect trust values, MTFM calculates the trust values among 6 nodes, by considering several additional opinions. Here, $\rho=0.5$; $H=\{0.2,0.2,0.2,0.2,0.2\}$; $w_{k0}=1$, $N_R=2$, and $N_I=2$. It obtains $T_{10}=0.8335$, and $T_{12}=0.2181$, $T_{13}=0.5369$, $T_{14}=0.8410$, and $T_{15}=0.7066$. Using Equation *(4.7)*, *node 1*'s total trust value for *node 0* with 5 neighbour nodes $T_{10-5nodes}=0.5592$. Based on $max_s\{\sum_i[f_s(T_{1i})]\}=3.13614$, $s=3$, $i=0,2,3,4,5$,

Figure 2. Topology of Scenario 1

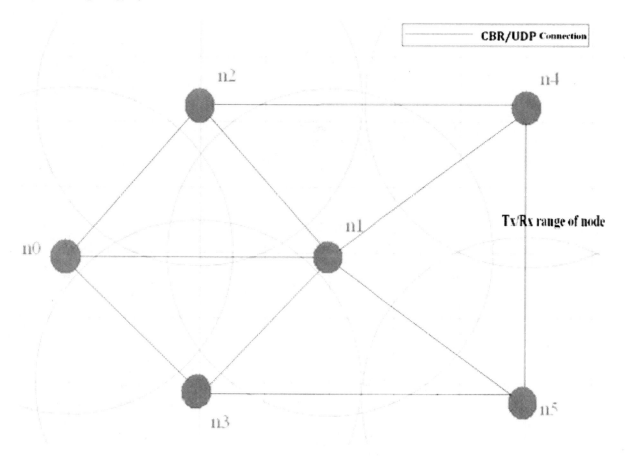

$(\Sigma_i[f_2(T_{1i})]=2.600294, \Sigma_i[f_1(T_{1i})]=1.86386)$, *node 1*'s grey cluster class is viewed as d_3.

Figure 4 shows the individual trust values of *node 1* from *node 0, 2, 3, 4, 5*, and the total values with 3 nodes and 5 nodes, the simple average value $T_{1\text{-simple average}}$ of $T_{10} \sim T_{15}$ and the network-average value $T_{1\text{-network-average}}$. Network-average value $T_{1\text{-network-average}}$ is calculated using Equation *(8)*.

From this figure, the results show that taking different relationship factors will affect the total value. If the simulation just considers the opinions of *nodes 0, 2, 3*, the result will be lower than the one including *nodes 0, 2, 3, 4, 5* because T_{15} is higher than T_{13}, and T_{14} is higher than T_{12}. Moreover, $T_{1\text{-simple average}}$ is higher than $T_{10\text{-3nodes}}$ and $T_{10\text{-5nodes}}$,

due to not including the relationship weights and whitenization weights.

A more complete range of trust values for various node mobility scenarios are now presented. These include the direct, recommendation and indirect trust values for *node 1*, which are given as $\{T_{10}\}$, $\{T_{12}, T_{13}\}$ and $\{T_{14}, T_{15}\}$ respectively. In addition, the total trust value calculated from all neighbour nodes (named as $T_{10\text{-5nodes}}$) and the network average trust value (termed $T_{1\text{-network-average}}$) are also shown for different mobile scenarios.

For various mobile scenarios (2, 3 and 4), 10 separate simulations were run with random waypoint paths for each scenario. Figure 5 shows the maximum, minimum, and average values for each trust metric, which are also shown in Figure

Figure 3. Program flow diagram

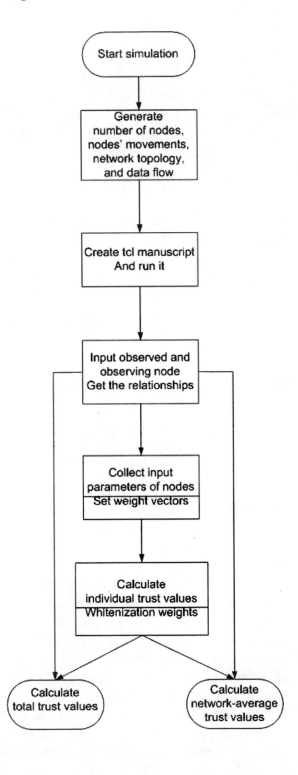

Figure 4. Trust values in the static scenario

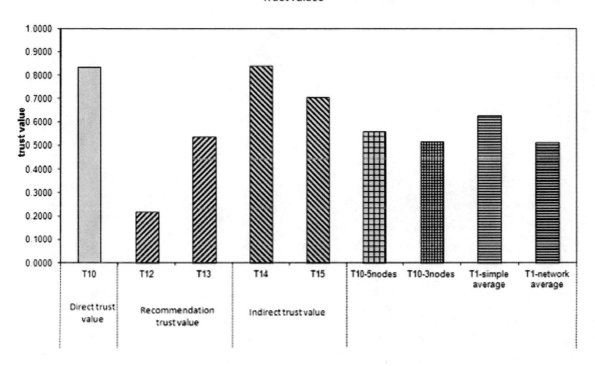

4 for the static scenario. It can be observed that the trust values obtained using the composite metrics ($T_{10\text{-}5nodes}$ and $T_{1\text{-}network\text{-}average}$) exhibit much less variation than the individual direct, recommendation and indirect trust values; moreover the complete trust value ($T_{10\text{-}5nodes}$) is almost identical to the static case, in Figure 5.

That means MTFM is quite insensitive to mobility, as a result of incorporating different nodes' individual trust values. This shows that MTFM for calculating the complete trust value is relatively insensitive to the mobility of neighbouring nodes, even though the individual direct, indirect and recommendation values are different from those in the all static scenario; the results also show that the simple average value exhibits a reasonably large degree of variation and so is more sensitive to the mobility of the observing

nodes in this scenario. This means MTFM is robust against different types of mobility.

The results indicate MTFM can be employed for mobile scenarios in MANETs, especially with the design of relationship weights, and whitenization functions. Figures 4 and 5 show the approach for total trust value and network-average trust value can mitigate the influence from different types of mobility.

THE MISBEHAVIOUR DETECTION FOR MTFM

The misbehaviour detection strategies of the multi-parameter trust framework for mobile ad hoc networks (MTFM) are presented in this section. This section introduces the detection strategies

Figure 5. Trust values in mobile scenarios

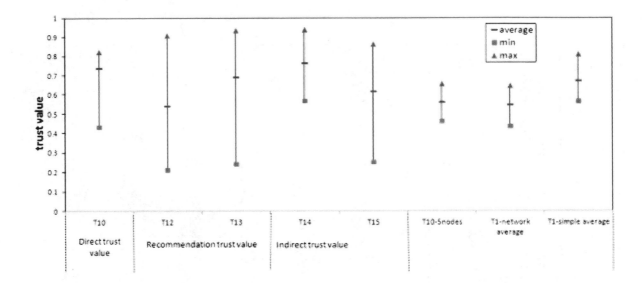

employing groups of several weight vectors for multiple parameters. In Section 6.1 and 6.2, the simulation results show that MTFM can detect single-parameter misbehaviours, and can also detect the particular parameter used in the strategy by the attacker or selfish node. Moreover, by using various weight vectors, MTFM can detect combined misbehaviours, shown in Section 6.3 and 6.4.

In Section 4, it is shown that Grey theory has been considered for the design of MTFM. Previous attempt is to employ more than one parameters with Grey theory have used fixed weights (usually with equal values) in trust evaluation (Fu et al., 2009). However a problem with this is that once attackers know which aspect is the most important factor in the system, or know that the system sets fixed weights for multiple factors, the malicious nodes can obtain high trust values by only behaving well in that specified aspect(s), while in fact they do not cooperate well with other normal nodes.

MTFM considers multiple and different types of parameters that cover various aspects of the physical and link layers to calculate the trust values, hence making it hard for a malicious node to replicate all of them. Moreover, it uses groups of weight vectors for multiple parameters, in order to obtain different trust values from different views; this can identify which detailed aspect of a node's behaviour is abnormal, compared with other neighbour nodes. With this idea, the proposed framework can detect selfish nodes' behaviour strategies.

Different weight vectors named as H (same as the weight vector H in Section 4) can be used to calculate individual trust values, and MTFM uses multiple groups of weight vectors from which it can calculate various trust values. These different values can help to highlight differences between abnormal and normal behaviours; therefore in order to detect the strategy that a selfish node employs, a range of vectors are used to identify the attempt to deceive the trust framework.

To determine the weight vectors for input parameters, this framework applies the Analytic Hierarchy Process (AHP) (Saaty, 2008). Comparing the impacts on the trust value of multiple parameters $X=\{packet\ loss\ rate,\ signal\ strength,\ data\ rate,\ delay,\ throughput\}$, the weights for the 5 parameters can be given by the AHP.

That is, for two parameters x_i and x_j from X, f_{ij} in the matrix $[F] = (f_{ij})_{n \times n}$ is presented as the ratio of x_i's impact to x_j's impact on the trust values. $[F]$ is the pairwise comparison judgement matrix between trust values and input parameters. If f_{ij} is the ratio of x_i's impact to x_j's impact, obviously it has $f_{ji=1/}f_{ij}$.

When setting the packet loss rate (PLR) as the most important parameter and other values also considered in the calculation, the intensity of importance for PLR compared with another parameter is 6, *strong plus*, from AHP (Saaty, 2008). It generates the matrix $[F]$:

$$[F] = \begin{bmatrix} 1 & 6 & 6 & 6 & 6 \\ 1/6 & 1 & 1 & 1 & 1 \\ 1/6 & 1 & 1 & 1 & 1 \\ 1/6 & 1 & 1 & 1 & 1 \\ 1/6 & 1 & 1 & 1 & 1 \end{bmatrix}$$

For the matrix $[F]$. the largest eigenvalue λ_{max} and corresponding eigenvector $[W_{max}] = [w_1, w_2, w_3, w_4, w_5]^T$ exist, and should have:

$$[F] \cdot [W_{max}] = \lambda_{max} [W_{max}]$$

That is:

$$\begin{bmatrix} 1 & 6 & 6 & 6 & 6 \\ 1/6 & 1 & 1 & 1 & 1 \\ 1/6 & 1 & 1 & 1 & 1 \\ 1/6 & 1 & 1 & 1 & 1 \\ 1/6 & 1 & 1 & 1 & 1 \end{bmatrix} \begin{bmatrix} w_1 \\ w_2 \\ w_3 \\ w_4 \\ w_5 \end{bmatrix} = \lambda_{max} \begin{bmatrix} w_1 \\ w_2 \\ w_3 \\ w_4 \\ w_5 \end{bmatrix} \quad (9)$$

From the Equation *(9)*, here it has:

$$\begin{cases} w_1 + 6(w_2 + w_3 + w_4 + w_5) = \lambda_{max} w_1 \\ 1/6 \cdot w_1 + (w_2 + w_3 + w_4 + w_5) = \lambda_{max} w_2 \\ 1/6 \cdot w_1 + (w_2 + w_3 + w_4 + w_5) = \lambda_{max} w_3 \quad (10) \\ 1/6 \cdot w_1 + (w_2 + w_3 + w_4 + w_5) = \lambda_{max} w_4 \\ 1/6 \cdot w_1 + (w_2 + w_3 + w_4 + w_5) = \lambda_{max} w_5 \end{cases}$$

Then from *(10)*, $w_1 = 6w_2$, $w_2 = w_3 = w_4 = w_5$, so $\lambda_{max} = 5$. The obtained eigenvector $[W_{max}]$ is equal to $\{0.6, 0.1, 0.1, 0.1, 0.1\}^T$. Thus the weight vector group H is $\{0.6, 0.1, 0.1, 0.1, 0.1\}$. In the AHP, if the *consistency proportion CR<0.1*, the consistency for the judgement matrix can be accepted (Saaty, 2008). Here it has:

$$CR = \frac{CI}{RI} \quad CI = \frac{\lambda_{max} - n}{n - 1}$$

CI is the *consistency check index*; *RI* is the *random index*. From (Alonso & Lamata, 2006), *RI=1.12* when *n=5*. Because $\lambda_{max} = 5$, obviously *CR<0.1*. Similarly, selecting other parameters to be the most important parameters, it can also obtain other weight vectors. For given the equal weight for each parameter, obviously *H* is $\{0.2, 0.2, 0.2, 0.2, 0.2\}$.

These vectors are presented as follows: $H=\{0.2,0.2,0.2,0.2,0.2\}$ all parameters have equal weight; $H=\{0.6,0.1,0.1,0.1,0.1\}$ emphasize packet loss rate; $H=\{0.1,0.6,0.1,0.1,0.1\}$ emphasize signal strength; $H=\{0.1,0.1,0.1,0.6,0.1\}$ emphasize delay; $H=\{0.1,0.1,0.1,0.1,0.6\}$ emphasize throughput; $H=\{0.1,0.1,0.6,0.1,0.1\}$ emphasize date rate.

The weight configuration is such that for 5 input parameters, we apply groups of 6 weight vectors: one vector group with equal weigh assigned to all input parameters, and 5 vectors each with one of the parameters having higher priority. From the above discussion, when the framework emphasizes one parameter, the weight of the most important parameter is given by the approximate value 0.6, other parameters with assigned equal weights of the left value *0.4 (=1-0.6),* based on the AHP method. By using this approach, the framework can not only detect general abnormal behaviour, but also identify which of the input parameters are more responsible for it, which will be illustrated in following parts.

Packet Loss Rate Misbehaviour

For a simple misbehaviour, a malicious node may directly deny some interactions with neighbour nodes for selfish purposes, which leads to an increase in its packet loss rates.

Taking a simulation from the all nodes mobile scenario in last section as an example, it here sets the malicious node to be *node 1*, and increases the packet loss rate from *node 0* by a certain level. By applying MTFM, the values of T_{10} will be affected, compared with those of *node 1* being normal in the simulation.

Figure 6 shows the trust values of T_{10} when using the following weight vector groups: (a) all parameters with equal weights, (b) emphasizing the packet loss rate, (c) emphasizing the signal strength, (d) delay time emphasized, (e) the throughput parameter emphasized, and (f) setting data rate as the most important parameter.

Generally, when the five parameters have equal weight values, the MTFM can find the difference in trust values between a normal node and a selfish one, shown in Figure 6(a).

Then, by using other weight vectors, it can be clearly seen that there is a very large gap between normal and selfish trust values, whenever PLR is set as the most important factor (weight value 0.6), as Figure 6(b) shown. This reveals that from the view of *node 0*, the observed node – *node 1* is likely to be behaving selfishly on the aspect of packet loss rate, due to the abnormal value in Figure 6(b). If a malicious node or an attacker just simply drops the data packets, it will get a low value. That means our solution can easily identify this type of misbehaviour.

Delay Misbehaviour

Sometimes, a node may be normal for communicating with neighbour nodes, while behaves malicious, by delaying or overhearing forwarding data packets. To do this misbehaviour, it needs more time to forward the packets.

Still using the same simulation as the example, it sets the malicious node – *node 1* maintains the packet loss rate at a normal level, but just increases its delay time, while cooperating with the observing node – *node 0*. Figure 7 shows the results obtained when using the following vectors the: *H={0.2,0.2,0.2,0.2,0.2}* for (a), *H={0.6,0.1,0.1,0.1,0.1}* for (b), while *H={0.1,0.6,0.1,0.1,0.1}* for (c), and *H={0.1,0.1,0.1,0.6,0.1}* for (d), *H={0.1,0.1,0.1,0.1,0.6}* for (e), *H={0.1,0.1,0.6,0.1,0.1}* for (f).

Generally, the difference of normal and malicious T_{10} trust values can be found, with setting equal weights for the five parameters, like Figure 7(a) shown.

When the delay is given the most important factor, a larger gap between normal and selfish trust values is presented in Figure 7(d), compared with those in other sub-graphs. It can tell that the observed node is likely to be behaving selfishly on the delay parameter, because of malicious behaviours in delay parameter. The misbehaviour with increasing delay is often linked with the eavesdropping attack, which an attacker tries to illegally analyze partners' data packets during forwarding, and thus needs more time.

By applying multiple parameters and weight vector groups, MTFM can detect more types of misbehaviour, not limited to the misbehaviour in PLR parameter. In contrast, the Beta distribution method only considers the probability of successful interactions. The misbehaviours in other parameters such as delay and throughput are not considered in such probabilistic estimation approach.

Figure 6. The trust values with PLR misbehaviour

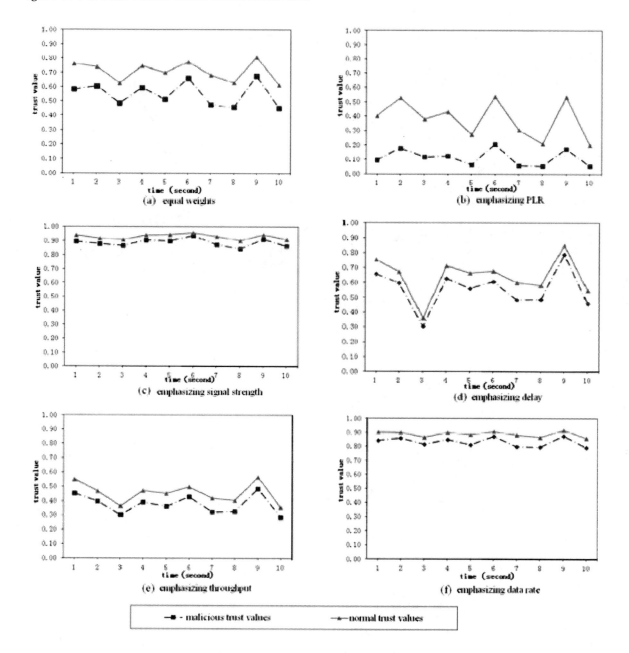

(a) equal weights

(b) emphasizing PLR

(c) emphasizing signal strength

(d) emphasizing delay

(e) emphasizing throughput

(f) emphasizing data rate

—■— - malicious trust values   —▲— normal trust values

Current trust framework approaches that select a single evaluation metric, use a count of successful/unsuccessful cooperating behaviours. Therefore the PDR or PLR (Packet Loss Rate) is usually chosen to express the probability of successful interactions in the calculation of trust values. (*PDR=1-PLR.*) By referring to the trust values obtained by Beta method, Figure 8 can show the difference between the new approach and classical probabilistic estimation method used to calculate trust values.

The trust values *t* by Beta distribution is calculated as the expectation value of *Beta(x, s, f)* (R. Li, Li, Liu, & Chen, 2007), which is *t=E(Beta(x,*

Figure 7. The trust values with delay misbehaviour

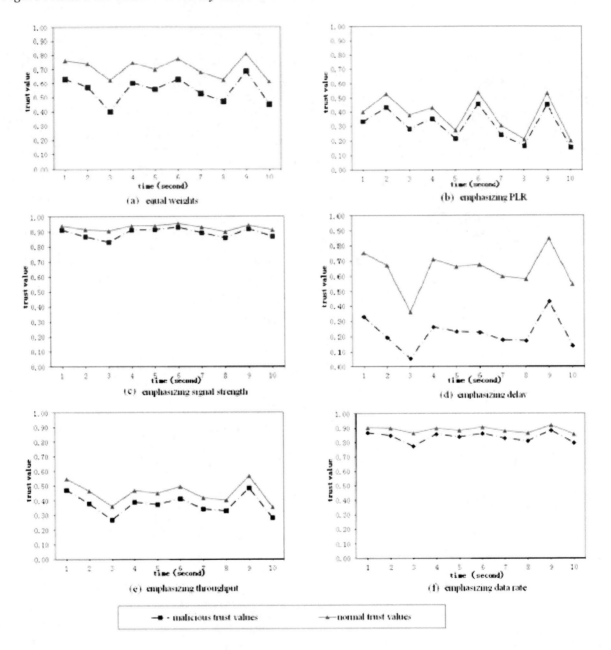

(a) equal weights

(b) emphasizing PLR

(c) emphasizing signal strength

(d) emphasizing delay

(e) emphasizing throughput

(f) emphasizing data rate

—■— malicious trust values   —▲— normal trust values

$s, f)) = s/(s+f)$. s and f are the number of successful interactions and the number of failed interactions (in the simulation, s and f mean the number of received packets and the number of dropped packets). The Beta trust value can be viewed as the packet delivery rate (PDR).

For example, *node 1* increases the delay time, while maintaining nearly same PLRs as before. With the MTFM, it is seen in Figure 8 that there is an obvious difference between the normal and malicious trust value (also shown as Figure 7(a)), compared with the trust values by Beta method

Figure 8. Comparison with Beta distribution method

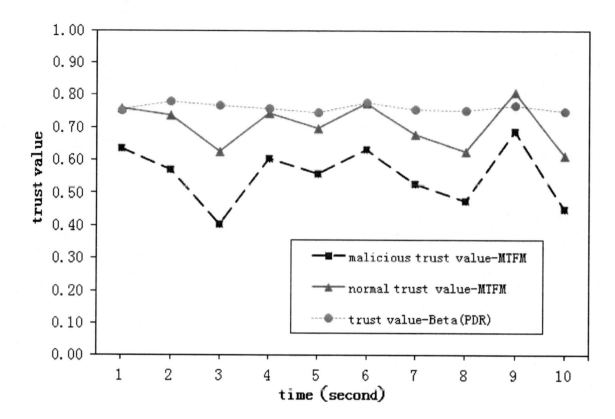

that do not show any significant changes. When a malicious node maintains the normal PLRs, those approaches that only employ the single probability-based parameter cannot detect other misbehaviours in other parameters.

Combined Throughput and Delay Misbehaviour

Still using the same example from all nodes mobile scenario, aiming at *node 0*, a malicious node (*node 1*) maintains the packet loss rate at a normal level, but increases its delay time, while reducing the throughputs. Figure 9 shows the results of T_{10}, with employing the weight vector groups.

It can be observed that the results for equal weighs have a very large distance between normal and selfish trust values, while Figure 9(d) displays a distinct difference with setting the delay time as the most important factor, also seen in Figure 9(e) for emphasizing throughput parameter. This reveals that the observed node is likely to be behaving selfishly both on delay and throughput, as the abnormal values in Figure 9(d) and (e).

Figure 10 also shows that there is an obvious difference between the normal and malicious trust value (same as Figure 9(a)), while Beta method cannot detect the difference. This is because such method based on probability estimation only considers the probability-based parameter.

Figure 9. The trust values for combined throughput and delay misbehaviours

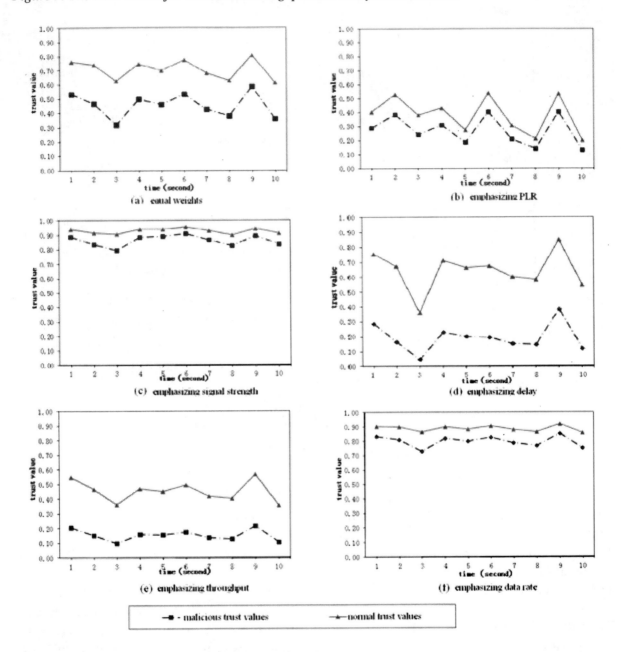

By employing several weight vectors, the system can help to find the difference of trust values between a normal node and a selfish one. Additionally, in the calculation of individual trust values, rather than just selecting PLR/PDR (as used in probabilistic methods), employing multiple parameters and processing these parameters with grey theory algorithms can provide a new aspect in the design of trust models. MTFM can give the trust values that include more information about nodes' behaviours, not only limited to the information about the probability-based parameters such as PLR.

Figure 10. Comparison between MTFM and Beta

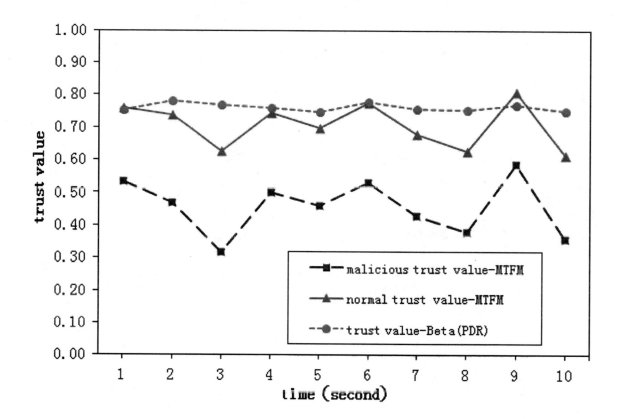

Misbehaviour in all Parameters

The MTFM can detect single misbehaviour and combined misbehaviours. Moreover, it can easily detect if the attacker or selfish node behaves malicious in all parameters. For different environments, the framework can choose different parameters (delete or add), to detect an adversary and misbehaviours.

For example (taking the simulation same as former sections), *node 1* increase its failed communications with other neighbours, which results in higher PLR; *node 1* also increases the delay time, and signal strength; *node 1* employs high date rate, while in fact deny to forwarding more data packets. In Figure 11, it clearly shows the bad node gets very low trust values from MTFM, not only in the Figure 11(a) that each parameter has equal weight, but also in other five pictures that emphasize single parameters.

In this section, the misbehaviour detection strategies of the proposed framework MTFM are presented. Distinctly, this detection described in this chapter employs groups of several weight vectors for multiple parameters through using the AHP. That brings a significant benefit, as the framework can not only detect selfish or malicious behaviour, but can also detect the particular parameter used in the strategy of the attacker or selfish node. The framework can also detect combined misbehaviours, showing larger differences between normal and selfish values. Simulation results are presented for the six nodes mobile scenario. This means the misbehaviour detection strategies of the framework shows robustness for mobility of nodes.

Figure 11. Misbehaviour in all parameters

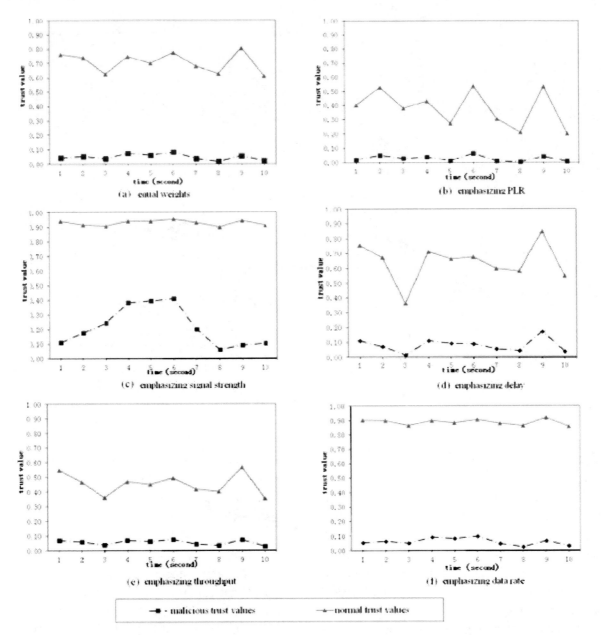

CONCLUSION

The original framework of MANET was designed without considering defensive mechanisms, thus many security schemes from different aspects have been proposed to protect the communicating information and nodes in MANETs. However, most of these schemes assume trusted third parties or centralized servers to issue digital certificates or cryptographic keys; there is currently a lacking of trust mechanisms. In recent years, a lot of researchers have studied in the area of trust metrics. Most existing trust models choose the classical approach of probability and statistics, to generate the trust values of nodes, and usually, only the packet loss rate or the probability of successful interactions is selected as the main parameter to describe the nodes' degrees of trust. However in fact, not only the packet loss rate can be used to indicate the nodes' behaviours, but also other physical factors can represent good or bad actions, such as delay time, throughput, and so on.

This chapter presents a multi-parameter trust framework for mobile ad hoc networks. MTFM focuses on employing multiple and different types of parameters of wireless nodes used in trust evaluation, not limited to the probability-based parameters. And the algorithms of MTFM are designed with Grey theory, to process the data with various units, and give an integrated value for a final decision. Thus, a key feature of the proposed framework is its use of multiple rather than a single parameter to decide the resulting trust value.

For a mobile ad hoc network, the mobility of the nodes in a trust grouping can also cause large variances in the trust values. That is, the mobility may have an adverse effect on the overall trust values calculated. In Section 5, simulation results conducted in an 802.11 based MANETs demonstrate that the proposed trust framework (MTFM) can maintain consistent total trust values in the presence of various types of mobility. MTFM can offer good robustness for mobile nodes as well as static nodes, which means good performance against nodes' mobility.

In Section 5, the misbehaviour detection strategies of MTFM are presented. Distinctly, the detection strategies employ groups of several weight vectors for multiple parameters, through using the Analytic Hierarchy Process (AHP). This brings a significant benefit as the framework can not only detect selfish or malicious behaviour, but can also detect the particular parameter(s) used in the strategy of the attacker or selfish node.

FUTURE RESEARCH DIRECTIONS

Having designed MTFM and the relevant algorithms for misbehaviour detection strategies, there is further research work, which could be expanded, based on the work presented in the chapter.

Firstly, the proposed framework could be examined within more wireless standards such as Bluetooth, and Zigbee, moreover for different types of wireless network topologies and routing protocols. That may require MTFM to be modified for those different scenarios

Secondly, MTFM currently applies a simple group of whitenization functions (triangle shape) for the classification with three degrees of trust. If the users want to describe more detailed categorization about the degrees of trust, the whitenization function groups can be modified with more complex shapes such trapezoid and curve shape.

Thirdly, the node weights in MTFM are fixed with equal values. With employing MTFM for a period, it is possible for the observing node(s) to give various values to its different neighbour nodes based on previous trust values. The algorithm about transferring trust values into node weights can be designed.

Fourthly, for various misbehaviours or attacks, MTFM may be required to add more functional blocks and adjusted, and modify different parameters, to detect more specific adversaries or misbehaviours. No security scheme is perfect, and none can claim to defend against all attacks. MTFM could be integrated with other existing trust models based on probabilistic estimation, Dempster-Shafer theory, information theory, and game theory, to have more robustness in identifying more attacks.

Fifthly, the proposed framework can be realized in the form of software or hardware, which can be equipped with the nodes in distributed environment. The efficacy of the framework can be tested in real environment. MTFM presented in this chapter can become an element in security systems in future, and even as a product of secure applications.

REFERENCES

Alfarez, A. R., & Stephen, H. (1997). A distributed trust model. In *Proceedings of the 1997 Workshop on New Security Paradigms - NSPW '97* (pp. 48-60). Cumbria, UK: NSPW.

Alonso, J. A., & Lamata, M. T. (2006). Consistency in the analytic hierarchy process: A new approach. *International Journal of Uncertainty. Fuzziness and Knowledge-Based Systems*, *14*(4), 445–459. doi:10.1142/S0218488506004114.

Aparicio-Navarro, F. J., Kyriakopoulos, K. G., & Parish, D. J. (2011). An on-line wireless attack detection system using multi-layer data fusion. In *Proceedings of the 2011 IEEE International Workshop on Measurements and Networking* (pp. 1-5). IEEE.

Aparicio-Navarro, F. J., Kyriakopoulos, K. G., & Parish, D. J. (2012). A multi-layer data fusion system for wi-fi attack detection using automatic belief assignment. In *Proceedings of the 2012 World Congress on Internet Security* [WorldCIS.]. *WORLD (Oakland, Calif.)*, CIS-2012, 45–50.

Blaze, M., Feigenbaum, J., & Keromytis, A. D. (1998). KeyNote: Trust management for public-key infrastructures. In B. Christianson, B. Crispo, W. S. Harbison, & M. Roe (Eds.), *Security protocols: 6th International Workshop* (LNCS), (Vol. 1550, pp. 59-63). Berlin, Germany: Springer.

Buchegger, S., & Boudec, J. L. (2005). Self-policing mobile ad-hoc networks by reputation system. *IEEE Communications Magazine*, *43*(7), 101–107. doi:10.1109/MCOM.2005.1470831.

Chang, C., Liu, C., & Wang, Y. (2009). A subjective trust model based on two-dimensional measurement. In *Proceedings of the 2009 International Conference on Computer Engineering and Technology* (pp. 37-41). Singapore: IEEE.

Chen, Y., Luo, J., & Ni, X. (2008). A fuzzy trust evaluation based access control in grid environment. In *Proceedings of the Third ChinaGrid Annual Conference, 2008, ChinaGrid'08* (pp. 190-196). ChinaGrid.

Cheshire, C., & Cook, K. S. (2004). The emergence of trust networks under uncertainty—Implications for internet interactions. *Analyse & Kritik*, *26*(1), 220–240.

Chu, Y., Feigenbaum, J., Lamacchi, B., Resnick, P., & Strauss, M. (1997). REFEREE: Trust management for web applications. *Journal of Computer Networks and ISDN Systems*, *29*(8-13), 953–964. doi:10.1016/S0169-7552(97)00009-3.

Corson, S., & Macker, J. (1999). *Mobile ad hoc networking (MANET): Routing protocol performance issues and evaluation considerations*. Retrieved March 9, 2012, from http://www.ietf.org/rfc/rfc2501.txt

Cover, T. M., & Thomas, J. A. (2006). *Elements of information theory*. Hoboken, NJ: John Wiley and Sons.

Damianou, N., Dulay, N., Lupu, E., & Sloman, M. (2001). The ponder policy specification language. In *Proceedings of the International Workshop on Policies for Distributed Systems and Networks, POLICY'01* (pp. 18-38). Bristol, UK: POLICY.

Deng, J. (1989). Introduction to grey system theory. *Journal of Grey System, 1*(1), 1–24.

Eschenauer, L., Gligor, V. D., & Baras, J. (2004). On trust establishment in mobile ad-hoc networks. In B. Christianson, B. Crispo, J. A. Malcolm, & M. Roe (Eds.), *Security protocols: 10th international workshop,* (pp. 47-66). New York: Springer.

Fu, C., Tang, F., Cui, Y., Liu, M., & Peng, B. (2009). Grey theory based nodes risk assessment in P2P networks. In *Proceedings of the 2009 IEEE International Symposium on Parallel and Distributed Processing with Applications* (pp. 479-483). IEEE.

Ganeriwal, S., Balzano, L. K., & Srivastava, M. B. (2008). Reputation-based framework for high integrity sensor networks. *ACM Transactions on Sensor Networks, 4*(3), 1–37. doi:10.1145/1362542.1362546.

Gerharz, M., Waal, C., Aschenbruck, N., Bothe, A., Camp, T., Ernst, R., & Walsh, C. (2012). *BonnMotion—A mobility scenario generation and analysis tool.* Retrieved 2012 from http://net.cs.uni-bonn.de/wg/cs/applications/bonnmotion/

Grandison, T., & Sloman, M. (2000). A survey of trust in internet applications. *IEEE Communications Surveys and Tutorials, 3*(4), 2–10. doi:10.1109/COMST.2000.5340804.

Grandison, T., & Sloman, M. (2002). Specifying and analysing trust for internet applications. In *Proceedings of the 2nd IFIP Conference on e-Commerce, e-Business, e- Government, I3e2002* (pp. 145-157). Lisbon, Portugal: IFIP.

Guo, J., Marshall, A., & Zhou, B. (2011). A trust management framework for detecting malicious and selfish behaviour in ad hoc wireless networks using fuzzy sets and grey theory. In *Proceedings of the 2011 IEEE 10th International Conference on Trust, Security and Privacy in Computing and Communications, TrustCom* (pp. 142-149). Changsha, China: IEEE.

Karami, M., & Fathian, M. (2009). A robust trust establishment framework using Dempster-Shafer theory for MANETs. In *Proceedings of Internet Technology and Secured Transactions, 2009, ICITST 2009* (pp. 1–7). London: ICITST.

Klein, A. (2012). *Random waypoint.* Retrieved 2012 from http://www.routingprotokollc.de/Routing/mobility_random_waypoint.htm

Konorski, J., & Orlikowski, R. (2009). Data-centric Dempster-Shafer theory-based selfishness thwarting via trust evaluation in MANETs and WSNs. In *Proceedings of the 2009 3rd International Conference on New Technologies, Mobility and Security, NTMS* (pp. 1-5). NTMS.

Li, H., & Singhal, M. (2007). Trust management in distributed systems. *Computer, 40*(2), 45–53. doi:10.1109/MC.2007.76.

Li, J., Li, R., & Kato, J. (2008). Future trust management framework for mobile ad hoc networks. *IEEE Communications Magazine, 46*(4), 108–114. doi:10.1109/MCOM.2008.4481349.

Li, R., Li, J., Liu, P., & Chen, H. (2007). An objective trust management framework for mobile ad hoc networks. In *Proceedings of the IEEE 65th Vehicular Technology Conference,* (pp. 56-60). IEEE.

Liu, S., & Lin, Y. (2006). *Grey information: Theory and practical applications.* London: Springer.

Ni, X., & Luo, J. (2008). A clustering analysis based trust model in grid environment supporting virtual organizations. In *Proceedings of the 22nd International Conference on Advanced Information Networking and Applications - Workshops (Aina Workshops 2008)* (pp. 100-105). Okinawa, Japan: Aina.

Poortinga, W., & Pidgeon, N. F. (2004). Trust, the asymmetry principle, and the role of prior beliefs. *Risk Analysis*, *24*(6), 1475–1486. doi:10.1111/j.0272-4332.2004.00543.x PMID:15660605.

Qin, Z., Jia, Z., & Chen, X. (2008). Fuzzy dynamic programming based trusted routing decision in mobile ad hoc networks. In *Proceedings of the Fifth IEEE International Symposium on Embedded Computing* (pp. 180-185). IEEE.

Razavi, R., Fleury, M., & Monaghan, S. (2007). Multimedia performance for IEEE.802.11 DCF RTS/CTS with varying traffic conditions. In Proceedings of 2007 European Wireless (pp. 1-5). IEEE.

Saaty, T. L. (2008). Decision making with the analytic hierarchy process. *International Journal of Services Sciences*, *1*(1), 83–98. doi:10.1504/IJSSCI.2008.017590.

Singh, R., Vatsa, M., Noore, A., & Singh, S. K. (2006). Dempster-Shafer theory based classifier fusion for improved fingerprint verification performance. In P. Kalra, & S. Peleg (Eds.), *Computer vision, graphics and image processing* (pp. 941–949). Berlin, Germany: Springer. doi:10.1007/11949619_84.

Song, Q., & Jamalipour, A. (2005). Network selection in an integrated wireless LAN and UMTS environment using mathematical modeling and computing techniques. *Journal of IEEE Wireless Communication*, *12*(3), 42–48. doi:10.1109/MWC.2005.1452853.

Stajano, F., & Anderson, R. J. (2000). The resurrecting duckling: Security issues for ad-hoc wireless networks. In *Proceedings of the 7th International Workshop on Security Protocols* (pp. 172-194). Cambridge, UK: IEEE.

Sun, Y. L., Han, Z., & Liu, K. J. R. (2008). Defense of trust management vulnerabilities in distributed networks. *IEEE Communications Magazine*, *46*(2), 112–119. doi:10.1109/MCOM.2008.4473092.

Sun, Y. L., Yu, W., Han, Z., & Ray Liu, K. J. (2006). Information theoretic framework of trust modeling and evaluation for ad hoc networks. *IEEE Journal on Selected Areas in Communications*, *24*(2), 305–317. doi:10.1109/JSAC.2005.861389.

Tao, L., Huang, D., & Hong, L. (2010). Research of subjective trust comprehensive evaluation model based on multi-element connection number. In *Proceedings of the 2nd International Conference on Information Science and Engineering 2010* (pp. 1433-1437). Hangzhou, China: IEEE.

Tuan, T. A. (2006). A game-theoretic analysis of trust management in P2P systems. In *Proceedings of the First International Conference on Communications and Electronics* (pp. 130-134). IEEE.

Winsborough, W. H., Seamons, K. E., & Jones, V. E. (1999). Automated trust negotiation. In *Proceedings of DARPA Information Survivability Conference and Exposition, DISCEX'00,* (pp. 88-102). DISCEX.

Zhang, S., Zou, Y., & Wang, B. (2009). A novel grid trust model based on fuzzy theory. In *Proceedings of the Third International Conference on Network and System Security* (pp. 203-207). IEEE.

ADDITIONAL READING

Cho, J., Swami, A., & Chen, I. (2011). A survey on trust management for mobile ad hoc networks. [IEEE.]. *IEEE Communications Surveys and Tutorials*, 562–582. doi:10.1109/SURV.2011.092110.00088.

Dunteman, G. H. (1989). *Principal component analysis*. Thousand Oakes, CA: Sage Publications.

Friedman, J. H., & Tukey, J. W. (1973). A projection pursuit algorithm for exploratory data analysis. *IEEE Transactions on Computers*, *C-23*(9), 881–890. doi:10.1109/T-C.1974.224051.

Fu, C., Huang, C., Zhang, Y., Han, L., & Peng, B. (2009). A risk assessment method based on grey relational projection in ad hoc networks. In *Proceedings of the 2009 International Conference on Multimedia Information Networking and Security* (pp. 370-373). IEEE.

Jøsang, A. (1997). Prospectives for modelling trust in information security. In *Proceedings of the Second Australasian Conference on Information Security and Privacy* (pp. 2-13). IEEE.

Jøsang, A. (1998). A subjective metric of authentication. In *Proceedings of European Symposium on Research in Computer Security* (pp. 329-344). IEEE.

Ye, J., Liu, M., & Fu, C. (2010). Trusted risk evaluation and attribute analysis in ad-hoc networks security mechanism based on projection pursuit principal component analysis. In *Proceedings of the 2010 IEEE/IFIP 8th International Conference on Embedded and Ubiquitous Computing (EUC)* (pp. 492-497). IEEE.

Zouridaki, C., Mark, B. L., Hejmo, M., & Thomas, R. K. (2005). A quantitative trust establishment framework for reliable data packet delivery in MANETs. In *Proceedings of the 3rd ACM Workshop on Security of Ad Hoc and Sensor Networks* (pp. 1-10). ACM.

Chapter 12
Trust Management and Modeling Techniques in Wireless Communications

Revathi Venkataraman
SRM University, India

M. Pushpalatha
SRM University, India

T. Rama Rao
SRM University, India

ABSTRACT

Trust management is an emerging technology to facilitate secure interactions between two communicating entities in distributed environments where the traditional security mechanisms are insufficient due to incomplete knowledge about the remote entities. With the development of ubiquitous computing and smart embedded systems, new challenges and threats come up in a heterogeneous environment. Trust management techniques that depend on a centralized server are not feasible in wireless peer-to-peer communication networks. Hence, the trust management and modeling strategies are becoming increasingly complex to cope with the system vulnerabilities in a distributed environment. The aim of this chapter is to have a thorough understanding of the trust formation process and the statistical techniques that are used at different stages of the trust computation process. The functional components of a trust management framework are identified and some of the existing statistical techniques used in different phases of the trust management framework are analyzed.

DOI: 10.4018/978-1-4666-4691-9.ch012

INTRODUCTION

In the recent years, trust is a topic of importance in many disciplines like computer science, wireless communications and Cognitive Sciences. Trust is defined as the belief over another person that he will behave according to an established pattern of rules. The multiagent system researchers introduced the concept of trust in computer science. These intelligent agents interact with each other and try to emulate the trust observed in human societies. Hence, trust has become an integral part of human lives and it was found to be an effective security mechanism for open environments like Internet. Considerable research has been done on modeling and managing trust and reputation in distributed systems

The definition of social trust was given by Diego Gambetta where trust is a particular level of subjective probability with which an agent will perform a particular action, independently of whether he is monitored or not. The notion of trust and reputation systems originate from the study of social sciences where the dynamics of trust in human societies are studied (Yu, Shen, Miao, Leung, & Niyato, 2010)(Abdul-Rahman & Hailes, 2000) (Misztal, 1995). Researchers in the field of distributed systems have shown that trust and reputation management schemes can be effectively used to improve security (English, Nixon, Terzis, McGettrick, & Lowe, 2002) and aid in decision-making process. Hence, trust based systems can be used as a comprehensive security tool in addition to cryptographic mechanisms. The properties of trust are discussed by many researchers (Josang & Ismail, 2002; Misztal, 1995). They are summarized as follows.

- **Trust is Useful in Uncertain Environments:** Here, the participating entities cooperate to achieve a common objective. In a predictable environment, every user will know each other's ac-

tions and there is no need to compute the trustworthiness of other entities. Trust is useful in situations where incomplete information is available at hand.

- **Trust is Context-Sensitive** (Abdul-Rahman & Hailes, 2000): An entity A trusts another entity B for a particular action X. Alternatively, A may not trust the entity B for another action Y. It depends on the subject's capability for a context.

- **Trust is Subjective (Ren, Li, Wan, Bao, Deng, & Kim, 2004; Josang A., 1998):** The formation of an opinion about someone's trustworthiness depends not only on the behaviors of the subject, but also on how these behaviors are perceived by the agent. It also depends on the expectation of the evaluating agent on the subject's performance.

- **Trust is Asymmetric** (Abdul-Rahman & Hailes, 1997; Ren, Li, Wan, Bao, Deng, & Kim, 2004): An agent's trust in a subject is based on the knowledge that it has about the subject. This knowledge may be acquired either through the agent's own observations, the recommendations from the agent's friends, or other means. The subject may not necessarily know the agent and therefore may not trust the agent in this case. Thus, an agent's trust in a subject may not be reciprocated.

- **Trust is Dynamic** (Ren, Li, Wan, Bao, Deng, & Kim, 2004): The agent's evaluation of a subject is continuous and hence, the trustworthiness changes over a period of time depending on the subject's behavior. This dynamic real time view of trust will result in a more flexible model that resembles the social trust relations in humans. The positive outcomes of interactions will increase the trust, while negative outcomes lower the trust of a neighboring entity.

- **Trust is Intransitive** (Gambetta, 2000): If there exists trust relationships between the nodes A;B and C in an ad hoc network such as A→B and B→C, then A→C is not implied. Since trust is highly subjective in nature and depends on one's own observations, it is also intransitive. Some of the researchers have also used conditional transitivity of trust depending on the applications that utilize the trust model.

The following are the different categories of trust

- **Centralized vs Decentralized Trust:** Each of the participating entities in MANET will evaluate the trustworthiness of an entity and send their evaluations to a central authority which will aggregate the values and compute the overall trust of a subject entity. Such centralized evaluations can be performed in a base station or a switching center where there is no shortage of resources. In a decentralized trust evaluation, every node is its own best judge for evaluating its peer. Each entity makes its own individual decision regarding the behavior of its neighbor.

- **Direct vs Indirect Trust:** The first-hand evidences obtained about the neighbor's behavioral patterns is collected and aggregated to form a direct trust. The indirect trust or recommendation trust refers to the propagation of the direct trust to other participating entities in the network. To what percentage, this recommendation trust should be considered is left to each entity.

- **Intensional vs Extensional Trust:** The uncertainties associated with trust computation are dealt with using in-network computation processes in intensional trust. These uncertainties are measured using formulas for partial aggregations and it is based on trust information available locally, at any instant of time. Such computations will be useful in protocols (eg; for routing decisions) where application level intervention is not required. In contrast, all data and partial opinions are collected at the initiator of the trust query for extensional trust. This type of trust computation will be suited for many application specific peer communications.

- **Subjective vs Objective Trust:** Trust computation is categorized as subjective and objective depending on the scenario under which the underlying trust model operates. Trust is perceived as subjective when it depends on every participating entity in the network and it varies from entity to entity. For example, a 'lenient' node may assign a higher trust value to its neighbor when compared to the trust value assigned by a conservative node in the network. Subjective trust gains importance when most of the trust computations rely on direct observations of the participating entities in the network. On the other hand, there may be a requirement to assign a global trust value to a participating entity in the network which is termed as Objective trust. In such cases, recommendation trust plays a major role in computing the trustworthiness of the evaluated entity.

Trust models have a wide variety of applications and the trust management strategies involve multiple perspectives with regard to the trust computation process. The context of trust depends on the application requirements that employ the trust models. The goal of this work is to identify the different phases in the development of a trust model and its suitability in wireless communication networks. It also provides a comprehensive survey on the rich literature in this important field of research.

TRUST MANAGEMENT IN WIRELESS NETWORKS

Wireless and Mobile networks comprise of small autonomous devices that are distributed spatially and co-operate among themselves to aid in information exchange. These devices are resource constrained in their energy, computational power, bandwidth, etc. In the presence of mobile and wireless devices, the network topology changes dynamically and hence, it will be difficult to make continuous observations about the neighbors. Hence, these wireless devices do not get enough opportunities to evaluate the trustworthiness of their neighbors. In addition, the absence of central monitoring resources in wireless ad hoc networks makes the trust evaluation process very difficult. Complete information about the malicious activities of the participating entities is not known to all the nodes in the network.

The related works on security and trust in MANETs have evolved rapidly in the last decade. With the proliferation of wireless devices, pervasive utility systems are deployed that cater to a wide range of services. This enables the user to access all the required information at anytime, anywhere. But, the potential cost involved is the uncertainty and risk factors associated with these services. The research on security and trust in wireless networks has resulted in development of many cryptographic and trust based approaches.

Secure Link State Protocol (SLSP) (Papadimitratos & Haas, 2003) is based on proactive ad hoc routing and the trust computations are also proactive. It uses digital signature and one-way hash chains to ensure link security updates. SLSP receives link state updates over the periodic Neighbor Lookup Protocol (NLP) where each node broadcasts a signed pairing between its IP address and its MAC address. If a node uses two MAC address for a same IP address, it is easily detected by NLP. SLSP prioritizes the nodes which give fewer link state updates. Masquerading attack is possible where an attacker can flood its victim's neighbors with link state updates that appear to originate at the victim. Even though the victim can detect this attack through the NLP's duplicate MAC address detection functionality, it cannot do anything about it.

A reactive ad hoc routing mechanism where the trust computations are also performed on-demand basis is the CONFIDANT(Buchegger & Boudec, 2002) protocol which detects and isolates misbehaving nodes and makes them unattractive for other nodes to communicate with. The trust model proposed in CONFIDANT originates from The Selfish gene (Dawkins, 1976). This concept proves that reciprocal altruism is beneficial for every ecological system. This triggers co-operation among nodes as there is instant gratification.

A generic mechanism based on pure reputation to enforce cooperation among nodes in an ad hoc network is suggested in CORE (Michiardi & Molva, 2002). Each ad hoc node tracks the collaboration between neighboring entities through reputation which are of three categories: subjective reputation, indirect reputation and functional reputation. A subjective reputation is the weighted mean of the observation's rating factors with more emphasis to past behaviors. Indirect reputations are the positive reputations reported by other mobile nodes which are the recommendation values. Functional reputation is computed by using many functions like forwarding function, packet delivery function, etc. and these are applied to a subjective or indirect reputation to arrive at a final value. The ambiguous collision problem and receiver collision problem are identified in CORE. False misbehavior can also be reported by some of the nodes in the network. Here, only positive reputations are exchanged and there is no way to express negative reputations.

A statistical trust model is proposed by Pirzada et al [(Pirzada, Datta, & McDonald, Incorporating trust and reputation in the DSR protocol for dependable routing, 2006)] for reactive routing protocols. The trust categories capture the misbehaviors in DSR and the underlying trust model incorporates mitigation techniques for dependable routing in DSR. The trust categories in the form of acknowledgments, packet precision, gratuitous route replies, blacklists and path salvaging are monitored and quantified in their statistical model. A monitoring node receives the status of successful transmission of a packet by link layer acknowledgments, passive acknowledgments and network layer acknowledgments. Packet precision refers to the accuracy of received data and routing packets. The gratuitous route replies in reactive routing protocols shows the benevolent behavior of nodes and hence, increases their trust rates. Blacklists are maintained in DSR protocol for exhibiting unidirectional behavior and hence, considered as a valued trust category to identify selfish nodes in the network. The correctness of a salvaged route by sending route error messages to the source is also considered as measure of trustworthiness of a co-operating node in the network. However, this mechanism suffers from receiver collision problem and ambiguous collision problem.

Some of the schemes that compute trust proactively over reactive ad hoc routing mechanisms are found in literature (Maltz, 1999) based on QoS-Guided route discovery. A node can specify a set of QoS metrics that has to be satisfied by a chosen path. If such a path to destination exists in route cache, the node chooses it. SQoS (Hu & Johnson, 2004) uses symmetric cryptographic primitives and hash chains for authentication and it is also suited for on demand ad hoc routing protocols. Even though QoS-guided routing guarantees bandwidth and latency requirements, other important factors like intermediate nodes willingness in the data transmission, computational complexity of the nodes, memory capacity and battery life are not taken into consideration in the route computation process.

PHASES IN THE TRUST COMPUTATION PROCESS

Representation of Trust

Trust is generally represented as a directed graph $G(V,E)$ whose vertices are the entities in a communication network. A weighted edge from a node i to a node j refers to the trustworthiness assigned by node i over node j. The trustworthiness of a neighboring node consists of two entities: the trust value and the confidence value. A snapshot of the aggregated trust values in a four node network is given in Figure 1.

Other representations of trust include continuous values in the range [0,1] and discrete values in the range [-1,1]. The probability and Beta distribution (Shaikh, Jameel, d' Auriol, Lee, Lee, & and Song, 2009; Chang & Kuo, 2009) are also used as a metric for trust. Another popularly used model(Li & Wu, 2010) is the representation of trust in the form of a triplet (b,d,u), b + d + u = 1 where b, d and u are belief, disbelief and uncertainty respectively. The functional blocks of a trust computation process are broadly identified as follows

- Evidence collection phase
- Computation of direct trust
- Computation of recommendation trust
- Trust estimation phase
- Trust propagation phase

Figure 1. Trust values in a four node network

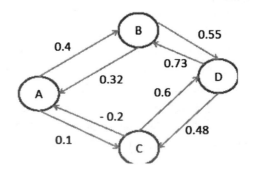

Depending on the requirements imposed by the trust applications, some of the phases may be eliminated. These phases closely interact to form an integrated trust framework as shown in Figure 2 for specific application environments.

Evidence Collection Phase

The evidence collection phase is an important and critical phase where every functional aspect of the neighboring node is captured in the form of trust metrics. The trust metrics are alternatively referred as trust categories in literature. Most of the literature in this area of research, have taken only the successful and failed interactions with the neighbors as the evidences. The need to include social trust and QoS trust in qualitative and quantitative form is proposed in (Cho, Swami, & Chen, 2005) . Social trust refers to few aspects of trust like sincerity and honesty of the participating nodes in the network. QoS trust may pertain to the energy levels, unselfishness in data transfer and other bandwidth related issues in multimedia applications like video quality, rate of data transfer, etc. The work in (Bao, Chen, Chang, & Cho, 2012) represents *intimacy* and *honesty* as social trust; *energy* and *unselfishness* as QoS trust. *Intimacy* refers to the duration of interaction experiences in time. *Honesty* measures the regularity of neighbor services and anomaly detection. *Energy* measures the competence of the neighboring entities whereas *unselfishness* represents the cooperativeness in routing and data transfer. These four trust metrics are represented as a real number in the range [0,1] and they are computed as shown in Equation 1.

$$T_{ij}^{X}(t) = (1\text{-}\alpha)\ T_{ij}^{X}(t\text{-}\Delta t) + \alpha\ T_{ij}^{X,direct}(t) \qquad (1)$$

where $T_{ij}^{X}(t)$ is the trust for a trust metric X assigned by node i towards an one-hop neighbor node j at time t, Δt is the trust update interval, α the trust decay parameter over time to expire old

trust observations and $T_{ij}^{X,direct}(t)$ is the direct trust observation at time t.

An earlier work (Pirzada, Datta, & McDonald, Incorporating trust and reputation in the DSR protocol for dependable routing, 2006) on trust management in wireless ad hoc routing illustrates the use of trust metrics like Packet Precision, Packet Acknowledgements, gratuitous route replies, etc for reactive routing protocols. These metrics are normalized before being considered for direct trust evaluations. For example, normalized route reply misbehavior is represented as shown in Equation 2.

$$R_{p} = \frac{R_{ps} - R_{pf}}{R_{ps} + R_{pf}} \qquad (2)$$

where R_{ps} is the number of successful route reply packets and R_{pf} is the number of failed route reply packets.

A non-exhaustive list of trust metrics in an ad hoc routing environment for wireless networks can be found in (Venkataraman, Pushpalatha, & Rama Rao, 2012) where the trust metrics are represented as ratios. The traditional intrusion detection techniques can be used to monitor abnormal activities in the neighborhood. These systems are capable of detecting every functional behavior of a neighboring node so that these behavioral aspects can be captured under the relevant trust categories. This is done by snooping or promiscuous listening of neighbor's transmission and reception. Although, it is very important to collect as many evidences as possible from this phase, the snooping capabilities in resource-constraint networks and battery life in heterogeneous networks comprising of small embedded sensor devices pose a great challenge.

Computation of Direct Trust

The individual trust metrics give a lot of insight into the functional anomalies of the neighboring peers in the communication system. However, some of the trust applications would desire to

Figure 2. Functional components in a typical trust management framework

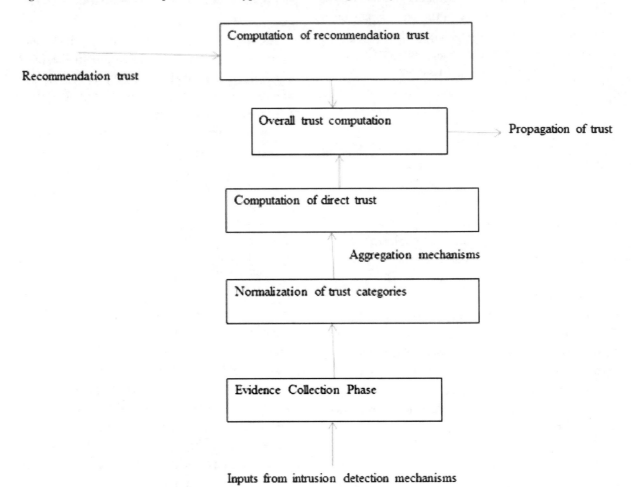

have an aggregated trust value of its communicating peers so as to aid in decision making processes. Hence, the trust metrics collected from the evidence collection phase are aggregated to yield a single trust value which indicates the overall trustworthiness of a neighboring node. This section surveys the aggregation mechanisms used in the computation of direct trust.

The work in (Pirzada, Datta, & McDonald, Incorporating trust and reputation in the DSR protocol for dependable routing, 2006) uses a weighted average mechanism wherein optimal situational weights are assigned to the trust categories depending on their utility and importance. For example, the direct trust value as computed by

node i for node j for four trust categories (metrics) is as shown in Equation 3.

$$T_{i,j} = \sum_{X=1}^{4} w_X T_{i,j}^X \qquad (3)$$

Where X represents the trust category and represents the weight or priority associated with the trust category X. The trust updates are done as discrete events. Since, the average computation tends to smoothen in the trust values, any recent abnormalities in the functional behaviors of the neighboring node will take a long time to get detected in this mechanism.

A scalable maturity-based trust model (Velloso, Laufer, Cunha, Duarte, & Pujolle, 2010) and the Markov-chain model (Chang & Kuo, 2009) computes the direct trust of its neighbors as a weighted sum of its own trust as shown in Equation 4. In these models, the trust categories that reflect the individual functional misbehavior of a neighboring node is not considered, even though a primitive mechanism considering the good and bad actions of the neighboring node is implemented in (Velloso, Laufer, Cunha, Duarte, & Pujolle, 2010).

$$T_{i,j} = \beta E_{i,j} + (1 - \beta) L_{i,j} \qquad (4)$$

Where $T_{i,j}$ is the direct trust computed by node i over node j, $E_{i,j}$ is the aggregated past trust experience, $L_{i,j}$ is the last trust value collected from the experience calculator and β is the factor to weight between the past and the latest trust experiences.

In the regression-based trust model (Venkataraman, Pushpalatha, & Rama Rao, 2012), the trust metrics from the evidence collection phase are stored as a single trust vector for each neighboring node. The trust metrics at different instants of time are represented as a stationery multivariate time series and Vector Auto-Regression (VAR) based trust model is used to estimate the trust in the next time interval as shown in Equation 5.

$$\hat{T}_{y(t)} = \alpha C_{y(t)} + \sum_{x=1}^{p} R_x T_{Y(t-x)} + \varepsilon \qquad (5)$$

Where $\hat{T}_{y(t)}$ is the estimated trust vector, $C_{y(t)}$ is the confidence vector, R_x is the regression coefficient matrix, p is the time lag and ε is the error vector. The confidence value plays an important role in remembering the past behavior of a neighboring node and this value depends on the length and frequency of association with the neighboring node. This model is suited for network environments where multiple attacks can be launched by the compromised peers.

The group-based trust management scheme (Shaikh, Jameel, d' Auriol, Lee, Lee, & and Song, 2009) uses sliding time window scheme to eliminate obsolete data. The time-based past interaction trust value of node y as computed by node x lies in the interval 0 to 100 is shown in Equation 6.

$$T_{x,y} = \left[100 \left(\frac{S_{x,y}}{S_{x,y} + U_{x,y}} \right) \left(1 - \frac{1}{S_{x,y} + 1} \right) \right] \qquad (6)$$

Where $S_{x,y}$ is the number of successful transactions, $U_{x,y}$ is the number of failed transactions. The expression $\left(1 - \frac{1}{S_{x,y} + 1} \right)$ would slowly rise to 1 with increase in the successful transactions. The expression $\left(\frac{S_{x,y}}{S_{x,y} + U_{x,y}} \right)$ indicates the percentage of successful interactions among total interactions. So, these expressions have a balancing effect so that few wrong interactions due to network traffic related problems can be tolerated.

Computation of Recommendation Trust

In many trust applications, it is desirable to have trust opinions of other nodes in the network with regard to the subject node under evaluation. The neighbor's recommendations are weighed based on their trust values. Recommendations from a good trustworthy neighbor can carry more weightage than recommendations from a less trustworthy neighbor. Another aspect to be taken into consideration is the trustworthiness of individual nodes along a recommendation path in multi-hop networks. This subsection describes the different mechanisms adopted in related literature for computation of recommendation trust.

In scalable maturity model (Velloso, Laufer, Cunha, Duarte, & Pujolle, 2010) the recommendations are defined as the weighted average of recommendations from a set of one-hop neighbors whose trust value is above a certain threshold. It is represented as shown in Equation 7.

$$R_a\left(b\right)=\frac{\sum_{i\epsilon K_a} T_a\left(i\right)M_i\left(b\right)X_i(b)}{\sum_{i\epsilon K_a} T_a\left(j\right)M_j\left(b\right)} \qquad (7)$$

Where $R_a\left(b\right)$ is the recommendation of node b as computed by node a, $T_a\left(i\right)$ refers to the trust level of the neighbors in the set K_a, $M_i\left(b\right)$ is the refers to the relationship maturity which is similar to the confidence values represented in (Baras G. T., 2006), $X_i(b)$ is the accuracy of the trust computation and it is represented as a random variable. A recommendation exchange protocol is used to exchange these recommendation trust values between the one-hop neighbors.

A similar recommendation trust evaluation is performed in group based scheme (Shaikh, Jameel, d' Auriol, Lee, Lee, & and Song, 2009) where recommendations from trustful neighbors are taken into account. In its general form, the recommendation trust is the sum of weighted trusted values of the recommender multiplied by the trust value as sent by the recommender.

In hierarchical trust management (Bao, Chen, Chang, & Cho, 2012), the one-hop neighbors alone act as recommenders and the recommendation trust computed by node i for node j which is not a neighbor is as shown in Equation 8.

$$\frac{\beta T_{i,k}\left(t\right)}{1+\beta T_{i,k}\left(t\right)}(T_{k,j}^{X,recom}\left(t\right)) \qquad (8)$$

where k is a one-hop neighbor and β is used to weigh indirect recommendations and normalize it relative to 1. This is used as a cover against good-mouthing and bad-mouthing attacks.

Estimation of Overall Trust

After computing the direct and recommendation trust values of an evaluating entity, it is desirable to have a single trustworthiness value by many trust applications to aid in decision making process. In the event of the subject node being an one-hop neighbor, both direct trust and recommendation trust values will be available. Generally, a weighing factor is introduced between these two trust categories depending on their utility and importance in a specific application scenario.

The work in hierarchical trust management (Bao, Chen, Chang, & Cho, 2012) aggregates the recommendations and past experiences through a term γ as shown in Equation 9. Here, N_i is a set comprising of one-hop neighbors and there alone act as recommenders.

$$T_{i,j}^X\left(t\right)=avg_{k\epsilon N_i}\left\{\left(1-\gamma\right)T_{ij}^X\left(t-\Delta t\right)+ {}^3 T_{k,j}^{X,recom}(t)\right\} \qquad (9)$$

A similar aggregation of direct and recommended trust observations is done in Markov-chain based model (Chang & Kuo, 2009). More composite factors are introduced in uncertainty modeling (Li & Wu, 2010) which is based on {belief, disbelief, uncertainty} model. The first-hand and second-hand opinions towards B are combined in node A as shown in Equation 10.

$$T_B^A =\phi_1.T_B^{A1st} + \phi_2.T_B^{A2nd}$$

where

$$T_B^A \epsilon\{b,d\}$$

and

$$u_B^A = 1 - b_B^A - d_B^A$$

$$\phi_1 = \frac{\gamma u_B^{A2nd}}{\left(1 - \gamma\right) . u_B^{A1st} + \gamma u_B^{A2nd} - 0.5 . u_B^{A1st} . u_B^{A2nd}}$$

$$\phi_2 = \frac{(1 - \gamma) u_B^{A1st}}{\left(1 - \gamma\right) . u_B^{A1st} + \gamma u_B^{A2nd} - 0.5 . u_B^{A1st} . u_B^{A2nd}}$$

(10)

When the value of $\gamma > 0.5$, the node relies on its own experience. The uncertainty factors are introduced in the equation where recommender's trust influences are higher or lower depending on the node's own uncertainty about the trust computation.

Trust Propagation

The overall computed trust is propagated to other neighbor nodes in the network either on demand basis or at regular trust update intervals using some standard recommendation exchange protocols. Generally, one-hop neighbors are considered for recommendation exchanges as inclusion of more entities may cause flooding of control messages.

The recommendation protocol in Scalable Maturity model (Velloso, Laufer, Cunha, Duarte, & Pujolle, 2010) comprises of three messages: Trust Request (TREQ) message, Trust Reply (TREP) message, and Trust Advertisement (TA) message. TREQ message is used to query other nodes regarding the trust of a target entity. If other nodes have the result, they respond with a TREP message containing the trust value of the target entity. Any changes in the trust values are periodically updated through TA messages. Apart from the trust values, the accuracy of target trust and the relationship maturity are also sent in the TREP message. These values are used by the querying node to compute the recommendation trust of the subject entity.

The uncertainties are reduced in (Li & Wu, 2010) where the trust information is disseminated proactively or reactively. Many schemes like Town Hall scheme, Travelling Preacher scheme and Hierarchical schemes are used for proactive dissemination of trust values. Reactive schemes include the assignment of a node as an ambassador and requirement of Certification Authorities for verification. Depending on the trust applications requirement and the utility of recommendation trust in communication systems, relevant exchange protocols are chosen.

Trust Applications

Trust is a multidisciplinary concept used in sociology, economics, psychology and autonomous networks. Mobile communications have a lot of requirements for trust models. And a very common and mandatory requirement in mobile and wireless communications is the security of the participating entities. Trust based solutions offer an excellent alternative to cryptographic security solutions which are categorized as hard security measures. Since the dynamically changing functionalities of a neighboring node cannot be detected by the traditional cryptographic mechanisms, trust based security models address the need to provide soft security.

Heterogeneous trusted networks are soon becoming a reality where the wireless nodes can be comprised of heterogeneous nodes like laptops, PDAs, sensor devices and other monitoring equipment with transceivers. The role of these nodes, their inherent capabilities like constraint resources and security play a major role in evaluating the trust associated with these nodes and the frequency of trust evaluations.

One of the upcoming important decision support tool for online services are trust and reputation systems. The trust systems are used by individual entities and they are used to derive local and subjective measures of trustworthiness for another entity. Hence, these trust based models are emerging as a comprehensive tool to aid in decision making process.

Trust in mobile vehicular systems is another fruitful research perspective and the architecture for vehicular ad hoc networks was proposed (Srinivasan, Nuggehalli, Chiasserini, & and Rao, 2003) which has a policy control model, a proactive trust model and a social network based system including the trust dynamics. In vehicular networks, None Line of Sight (NLOS) will interrupt direct communication among vehicles and prevent vehicles from properly monitoring their neighboring nodes. A trust evaluation model based on location information and verification in a NLOS condition is proposed (Golbeck, 2006). Vehicular network characteristics like vehicle mobility, driving nature and the obstacle may adversely disrupt the application services and exchange of critical messages like road safety and traffic congestion. In such a volatile environment, the trust dynamics vary frequently and the overall qualities of trust in decision making depends on the complex interactions and the identification of qualitative and quantitative trust metrics so that the composite trust can be evaluated and managed.

Cognitive wireless networks are fast becoming reality where intelligence is embedded into cognitive devices (Abumansoor & Boukerche, 2011). These networks depend on the current network conditions and past experiences and they reconfigure themselves to continuously changing network behaviors to improve survivability, QoS and scalability.

CONCLUSION

Trust networks are modeled based on subjective logic which is a belief reasoning strategy useful in situations involving uncertainty and incomplete information. Trust based system aid the users and organization in dealing with uncertainties, assessing the trustworthiness of remote communication entities in Internet. The functional phases involved

in the trust computation process are discussed. Some of the statistical techniques used in literature for different phases of trust modeling are analyzed. Trust being a multi-disciplinary area of research finds innumerous applications in various fields like computer science, information exchange, online web services, banking and e-business sites, etc.

Integration of trust based cognitive approaches to theoretical models in wireless security where the node can adapt itself to changing network behaviors like attack patterns, degree of maliciousness and node disconnection due to battery depletion, dynamic links and voluntary saving of energy resources is a interesting area of research to be pursued in future. The impact of network dynamics on trust is a prospective area of research. For example, the mobility of nodes in a wireless ad hoc network can strongly impact the trust propagations and other security mechanisms. Similarly, clear quantifiable relationship between the network dynamics like node mobility, link level transmissions, network density, etc. with the trust dynamics like trust prediction, evaluation and aggregation is yet to be analyzed. Trust in non-cooperative game theory is still an unexplored area of research.

REFERENCES

Abdul-Rahman, A., & Hailes, S. (1997). A distributed trust model. *Proceedings of of the ACM workshop on New security paradigms.*

Abdul-Rahman, A., & Hailes, S. (2000). Supporting trust in virtual communities. *HICSS 33.*

Abumansoor, O., & Boukerche, A. (2011). *Towards a secure trust model for vehicular ad hoc networks services.* IEEE Globecomm. doi:10.1109/GLOCOM.2011.6134243.

Bao, F., Chen, I.-R., Chang, M., & Cho, J.-H. (2012, June). Hierarchical Trust Management for Wireless Sensor Networks and its Applications to Trust-Based Routing and Intrusion Detection. *IEEE TRANSACTIONS ON NETWORK AND SERVICE MANAGEMENT*, 169-183.

Baras, G. T. (2006). On Trust Models and Trust Evaluation Metrics for Ad hoc Networks. *IEEE Journal on Selected Areas in Communications*, 24(2), 318–328. doi:10.1109/JSAC.2005.861390.

Baras, J. S., & Jiang, T. (2005). {Managing Trust in Self-Organized Mobile. *Ad Hoc Networks*.

Blaze, M., Feigenbaum, J., & Lacy., J. (1996). {Decentralized trust management}.

Blaze, M., Feigenbaum, J., Ioannidis, J., & Keromytis, A. (1999). *{The KeyNote Trust Management System}*. RFC 2704.

Boukerch, A., & Xu, L., & EL-Khatib, K. (2007). Trust-based security for wireless ad hoc and sensor networks. *Computer Communications*, 30, 2413–2427. doi:10.1016/j.comcom.2007.04.022.

Buchegger, S., & Boudec, J. (2002). Performance analysis of the CONFIDANT protocol: Cooperation of nodes - fairness in distributed ad-hoc networks. *IEEE/ACM Workshop on Mobile Ad Hoc Networking and Computing (MobiHoc)*.

Buchegger, S., & Boudec, J. L. (2003). *Coping with False Accusations in Misbehavior Reputation Systems for Mobile Ad-Hoc Networks}. EPFL IC/2003/31*. EPFL-DI-ICA.

Burbank, J. L., Chimento, P. F., Haberman, B. K., & Kasch, W. T. (2006). {Key Challenges of Military Tactical Networking and the Elusive Promise of MANET Technology}. *IEEE Communications Magazine*, 44(11), 39–45. doi:10.1109/COM-M.2006.248156.

Buttyan, L., & Hubaux, J.-P. (2007). *Security and Co-operation in wireless networks*. Cambridge University Press.

Buttya'n, L., & Vajda, I. (2004). {Towards Provable Security for Ad Hoc Routing Protocols}.

Chang, B.-J., & Kuo, S.-L. (2009). Markov chain trust model for trust-value analysis and key management in distributed multicast manets. *IEEE Transactions on Vehicular Technology*, 58(4), 1846–1863. doi:10.1109/TVT.2008.2005415.

Chlamtac, I., conti, M., & J.-N, L. J. (2003). {Mobile Ad hoc Networking: Imperatives and Challenges}. *Ad Hoc Networks, I*, 13–64. doi:10.1016/S1570-8705(03)00013-1.

Cho, J. H., Swami, A., & Chen, I. (2005). A context-aware trust-based security system for ad hoc networks. *First International Conference on Security and Privacy for Emerging Areas in Communication Networks-Workshop*.

Christianson, B., & Harbison, W. (1996). Why isn't trust transitive? Conti, M., & Glordano, S. (2007). {Multihop Ad hoc Networking: The Reality} *IEEE Communications Magazine, 45*, 88–95.

Conti, M., & Glordano, S. (2007). {Multihop Ad hoc Networking: The Theory}. *IEEE Communications Magazine, 45*, 78–86. doi:10.1109/MCOM.2007.343616.

Dawkins, R. (1976). *The Selfish Gene*. Oxford University Press.

English, C., Nixon, P., Terzis, S., McGettrick, A., & Lowe, H. (2002). Dynamic trust models for ubiquitous computing environments. *Workshop on Security in Ubiquitous Computing*.

Gambetta, D. (2000). *Trust: Making and Breaking Cooperative Relations*. Oxford: Blackwell.

Gambetta, D. (2000). *Trust: Making and Breaking Cooperative Relations*. Oxford Press.

Golbeck, J. (2006). *Computing with trust: Definition, properties, and algorithms*. Securecomm and Workshops-Security and Privacy for Emerging Areas in Communication Networks. doi:10.1109/SECCOMW.2006.359579.

Hu, Y., & Johnson, D. (2004). Securing quality-of-service route discovery in on-demand routing for ad hoc networks. *Proceedings of ACM SASN*.

Josang, A. (1998). *A subjective metric of authentication* (pp. 329–344). Lecture notes in Computer Science Springer-Verlag.

Josang, A. (2012). {Robustness of Trust and Reputation Systems: Does it Matter?}.

Josang, A., Azderska, T., & Marsh, S. (2012). {Trust Transitivity and Conditional Belief Reasoning}.

Josang, A., & Ismail, R. (2002). *The beta reputation system*. BCEC.

Josang, A., Ismail, R., & Boyd, C. (2007). A survey of trust and reputation systems for online service provision. *Decision Support Systems*, *43*, 26. doi:10.1016/j.dss.2005.05.019.

Kargl, F., Alfred, S. S., & Weber, M. (2005). {Secure Dynamic Source Routing}.

Karlof, C., Sastry, N., & Wagner, D. (2004). {TinySec: A link layer security architecture for wireless sensor networks}.

Li, F., & Wu, J. (2010). Uncertainty modeling and reduction in manets. *IEEE Transactions on Mobile Computing*, *9*(7), 1035–1048. doi:10.1109/TMC.2010.44.

Li, J., Li, R., & Kato, J. (2008). {Future Trust Management Framework for Mobile Ad hoc Networks}. *IEEE Communications Magazine*, *46*, 108–114. doi:10.1109/MCOM.2008.4481349.

Li, N., & Mitchell, J. (2003). {RT, A Role-based Trust-management Framework}.

Li, X., Lyu, M. R., & Liu, J. (2004). {A Trust Model Based Routing Protocol for Secure Ad Hoc Networks}.

Maltz, D. (1999). *Resource management in multihop ad hoc networks*. CMU School of computer Science Technical Report CMU-CS-00-150.

Michiardi, P., & Molva, R. (2002). *CORE: A collaborative reputation mechanism to enforce node cooperation in mobile ad-hoc networks*. IFIP-Communication and Multimedia Security Conference. doi:10.1007/978-0-387-35612-9_9.

Mishra, A. (2008). Security And Quality Of Service. In *Ad Hoc Wireless Networks*. New York: Cambridge University Press.

Misztal, B. (1995). *Trust in Modern Societies: The Search for the Bases of Social Order*. Polity press.

Moeller, S., Sridharan, A., Krishnamachari, B., & Ganawali, O. (2010). {Routing without routes: Backpressure Collection Protocol}.

Papadimitratos, P., & Haas, Z. J. (2002). {Secure Routing for Mobile Ad hoc. *Networks*.

Papadimitratos, P., & Haas, Z. J. (2003). Secure link state routing for mobile ad hoc networks. *IEEE Wksp. Security and Assurance in Ad hoc. Networks*.

Papadimitratos, P., & Haas, Z. J. (2006). {Secure Data Communication in Mobile Ad hoc Networks}. *IEEE Journal on Selected Areas in Communications*, *24*(2), 343–356. doi:10.1109/JSAC.2005.861392.

Patwardhan, A., Perich, F., Joshi, A., Finin, T., & Yesha, Y. (2005). {Active Collaborations for trustworthy data management in ad hoc networks}.

Patwardhan, A., Perich, F., Joshi, A., Finin, T., & Yesha, Y. (2006). {Querying in Packs: Trustworthy data management in ad hoc networks}. *Wireless Information Networks*, *13*(4), 263–274. doi:10.1007/s10776-006-0040-3.

Pirzada, A. A., Datta, A., & McDonald, C. (2006). Incorporating trust and reputation in the DSR protocol for dependable routing. *Elsevier Computer Communications, 29*(15), 2806–2821. doi:10.1016/j.comcom.2005.10.032.

Pirzada, A. A., & McDonald, C. (2006). Trust establishment in pure ad-hoc networks. *Wireless Personal Communications, 37*, 139–168. doi:10.1007/s11277-006-1574-5.

Pirzada, A. A., McDonald, C., & Datta, A. (2006). {Performance Comparison of Trust-based Reactive Routing Protocols}. *IEEE Transactions on Mobile Computing, 5*, 695–710. doi:10.1109/TMC.2006.83.

Ren, K., Li, T., Wan, Z., Bao, F., Deng, R., & Kim, K. (2004). Highly reliable trust establishment scheme in ad hoc networks. *Computer Networks, 45*(6), 687–699. doi:10.1016/j.comnet.2004.01.008.

Shaikh, R. A., Jameel, H., d'Auriol, B. J., Lee, H., Lee, S., & Song, Y.-J. (2009). Group-based trust management scheme for clustered wireless sensor networks. *IEEE Transactions on Parallel and Distributed Systems, 20*(11), 1698–1712. doi:10.1109/TPDS.2008.258.

Srinivasan, V., Nuggehalli, P., Chiasserini, C. F., & and Rao, R. R. (2003). Co-operation in wireless adhoc networks. *IEEE INFOCOMM*.

Velloso, P. B., Laufer, R. P., Cunha, D. d., Duarte, O. C., & Pujolle, G. (2010). Trust Management in Mobile Ad Hoc Networks Using a Scalable Maturity-Based Model. *IEEE TRANSACTIONS ON NETWORK AND SERVICE MANAGEMENT, 7*(3), 172–185. doi:10.1109/TNSM.2010.1009. I9P0339.

Venkataraman, R., Pushpalatha, M., & Rama Rao, T. (2012). Implementation of a Regression-based Trust Model in a Wireless Ad hoc Testbed. *Defence Science Journal, 62*(3), 167–173.

Wang, K., & Wu, M. (2010). Cooperative communications based on trust model for mobile ad hoc networks. *IET Information Security, 4*(2), 68–79. doi:10.1049/iet-ifs.2009.0056.

Yi, S., Naldurg, P., & R.Kravets. (2001). {A Security-Aware Routing Protocol for Wireless Ad Hoc Networks}.

Yoo, Y., & Agrawal, D. P. (2006). {Why Does It Pay To Be Selfish In A MANET?}. *IEEE Wireless Communications, 13*(6), 87–97. doi:10.1109/MWC.2006.275203.

Yu, H., Shen, Z., Miao, C., Leung, C., & Niyato, D. (2010). A survey of trust and reputation management systems in wireless communications. *Proceedings of the IEEE*, 1755-1772.

Zhou, L., & Haas, Z. J. (1999). {Securing Ad hoc Networks}. *IEEE Network, 13*, 24–30. doi:10.1109/65.806983.

Zhu, S., Setia, S., & Jajodia, S. (2003). {LEAP: Efficient security mechanisms for large-scale distributed sensor networks}.

ADDITIONAL READING

Abdul-Rahman, A., & Hailes, S. (1997). A distributed trust model. *Proceedings of of the ACM workshop on New security paradigms*.

Abdul-Rahman, A., & Hailes, S. (2000). Supporting trust in virtual communities. *HICSS 33*.

Abumansoor, O., & Boukerche, A. (2011). *Towards a secure trust model for vehicular ad hoc networks services*. IEEE Globecomm. doi:10.1109/GLOCOM.2011.6134243.

Anderson, R., & Stajano, F. (1999). {The Resurrecting Duckling}.

Bao, F., Chen, I.-R., Chang, M., & Cho, J.-H. (2012, June). Hierarchical Trust Management for Wireless Sensor Networks and its Applications to Trust-Based Routing and Intrusion Detection. *IEEE TRANSACTIONS ON NETWORK AND SERVICE MANAGEMENT*, 169-183.

Baras, G. T. (2006). On Trust Models and Trust Evaluation Metrics for Ad hoc Networks. *IEEE Journal on Selected Areas in Communications*, 24(2), 318–328. doi:10.1109/JSAC.2005.861390.

Baras, J. S., & Jiang, T. (2005). {Managing Trust in Self-Organized Mobile. *Ad Hoc Networks*.

Blaze, M., Feigenbaum, J., & Lacy., J. (1996). {Decentralized trust management}.

Blaze, M., Feigenbaum, J., Ioannidis, J., & Keromytis, A. (1999). *{The KeyNote Trust Management System}*. RFC 2704.

Boukerch, A., & Xu, L., & EL-Khatib, K. (2007). Trust-based security for wireless ad hoc and sensor networks. *Computer Communications*, 30, 2413–2427. doi:10.1016/j.comcom.2007.04.022.

Buchegger, S., & Boudec, J. (2002). Performance analysis of the CONFIDANT protocol: Cooperation of nodes - fairness in distributed ad-hoc networks. *IEEE/ACM Workshop on Mobile Ad Hoc Networking and Computing (MobiHoc)*.

Buchegger, S., & Boudec, J. L. (2003). *Coping with False Accusations in Misbehavior Reputation Systems for Mobile Ad-Hoc Networks}. EPFL IC/2003/31*. EPFL-DI-ICA.

Burbank, J. L., Chimento, P. F., Haberman, B. K., & Kasch, W. T. (2006). {Key Challenges of Military Tactical Networking and the Elusive Promise of MANET Technology}. *IEEE Communications Magazine*, 44(11), 39–45. doi:10.1109/COM-M.2006.248156.

Buttyan, L., & Hubaux, J.-P. (2007). *Security and Co-operation in wireless networks*. Cambridge University Press.

Buttya´n, L., & Vajda, I. (2004). {Towards Provable Security for Ad Hoc Routing Protocols}.

Chang, B.-J., & Kuo, S.-L. (2009). Markov chain trust model for trust-value analysis and key management in distributed multicast manets. *IEEE Transactions on Vehicular Technology*, 58(4), 1846–1863. doi:10.1109/TVT.2008.2005415.

Chlamtac, I., conti, M., & J.-N, L. J. (2003). {Mobile Ad hoc Networking: Imperatives and Challenges}. *Ad Hoc Networks, I*, 13–64. doi:10.1016/S1570-8705(03)00013-1.

Cho, J. H., Swami, A., & Chen, I. (2005). A context-aware trust-based security system for ad hoc networks. *First International Conference on Security and Privacy for Emerging Areas in Communication Networks-Workshop*.

Christianson, B., & Harbison, W. (1996). Why isn't trust transitive? Conti, M., & Glordano, S. (2007). {Multihop Ad hoc Networking: The Reality}. *IEEE Communications Magazine, 45*, 88–95.

Conti, M., & Glordano, S. (2007). {Multihop Ad hoc Networking: The Theory}. *IEEE Communications Magazine, 45*, 78–86. doi:10.1109/MCOM.2007.343616.

Dawkins, R. (1976). *The Selfish Gene*. Oxford University Press.

English, C., Nixon, P., Terzis, S., McGettrick, A., & Lowe, H. (2002). Dynamic trust models for ubiquitous computing environments. *Workshop on Security in Ubiquitous Computing*.

Gambetta, D. (2000). *Trust: Making and Breaking Cooperative Relations*. Oxford: Blackwell.

Gambetta, D. (2000). *Trust: Making and Breaking Cooperative Relations*. Oxford Press.

Golbeck, J. (2006). *Computing with trust: Definition, properties, and algorithms.* Securecomm and Workshops-Security and Privacy for Emerging Areas in Communication Networks. doi:10.1109/SECCOMW.2006.359579.

Hu, Y., & Johnson, D. (2004). Securing quality-of-service route discovery in on-demand routing for ad hoc networks. *Proceedings of ACM SASN.*

Josang, A. (1998). *A subjective metric of authentication* (pp. 329–344). Lecture notes in Computer Science Springer-Verlag.

Josang, A. (2012). {Robustness of Trust and Reputation Systems: Does it Matter?}.

Josang, A., Azderska, T., & Marsh, S. (2012). {Trust Transitivity and Conditional Belief Reasoning}.

Josang, A., & Ismail, R. (2002). *The beta reputation system.* BCEC.

Josang, A., Ismail, R., & Boyd, C. (2007) A survey of trust and reputation systems for online service provision. *Decision Support Systems, 43,* 26. doi:10.1016/j.dss.2005.05.019.

Kargl, F., Alfred, S. S., & Weber, M. (2005). {Secure Dynamic Source Routing}.

Karlof, C., Sastry, N., & Wagner, D. (2004). {TinySec: A link layer security architecture for wireless sensor networks}.

Li, F., & Wu, J. (2010). Uncertainty modeling and reduction in manets. *IEEE Transactions on Mobile Computing, 9*(7), 1035–1048. doi:10.1109/TMC.2010.44.

Li, J., Li, R., & Kato, J. (2008). {Future Trust Management Framework for Mobile Ad hoc Networks}. *IEEE Communications Magazine, 46,* 108–114. doi:10.1109/MCOM.2008.4481349.

Li, N., & Mitchell, J. (2003). {RT, A Role-based Trust-management Framework}.

Li, X., Lyu, M. R., & Liu, J. (2004). {A Trust Model Based Routing Protocol for Secure Ad Hoc Networks}.

Maltz, D. (1999). *Resource management in multi-hop ad hoc networks.* CMU School of computer Science Technical Report CMU-CS-00-150.

Michiardi, P., & Molva, R. (2002). *CORE: A collaborative reputation mechanism to enforce node cooperation in mobile ad-hoc networks.* IFIP-Communication and Multimedia Security Conference. doi:10.1007/978-0-387-35612-9_9.

Mishra, A. (2008). Security And Quality Of Service. In *Ad Hoc Wireless Networks.* New York: Cambridge University Press.

Misztal, B. (1995). *Trust in Modern Societies: The Search for the Bases of Social Order.* Polity press.

Moeller, S., Sridharan, A., Krishnamachari, B., & Ganawali, O. (2010). {Routing without routes: Backpressure Collection Protocol}.

Papadimitratos, P., & Haas, Z. J. (2002). {Secure Routing for Mobile Ad hoc. *Networks.*

Papadimitratos, P., & Haas, Z. J. (2003). Secure link state routing for mobile ad hoc networks. *IEEE Wksp. Security and Assurance in Ad hoc. Networks.*

Papadimitratos, P., & Haas, Z. J. (2006). {Secure Data Communication in Mobile Ad hoc Networks}. *IEEE Journal on Selected Areas in Communications, 24*(2), 343–356. doi:10.1109/JSAC.2005.861392.

Patwardhan, A., Perich, F., Joshi, A., Finin, T., & Yesha, Y. (2005). {Active Collaborations for trustworthy data management in ad hoc networks}.

Patwardhan, A., Perich, F., Joshi, A., Finin, T., & Yesha, Y. (2006). {Querying in Packs: Trustworthy data management in ad hoc networks}. *Wireless Information Networks, 13*(4), 263–274. doi:10.1007/s10776-006-0040-3.

Pirzada, A. A., Datta, A., & McDonald, C. (2006). Incorporating trust and reputation in the DSR protocol for dependable routing. *Elsevier Computer Communications*, *29*(15), 2806–2821. doi:10.1016/j.comcom.2005.10.032.

Pirzada, A. A., & McDonald, C. (2006). Trust establishment in pure ad-hoc networks. *Wireless Personal Communications*, *37*, 139–168. doi:10.1007/s11277-006-1574-5.

Pirzada, A. A., McDonald, C., & Datta, A. (2006). {Performance Comparison of Trust-based Reactive Routing Protocols}. *IEEE Transactions on Mobile Computing*, *5*, 695–710. doi:10.1109/TMC.2006.83.

Ren, K., Li, T., Wan, Z., Bao, F., Deng, R., & Kim, K. (2004). Highly reliable trust establishment scheme in ad hoc networks. *Computer Networks*, *45*(6), 687–699. doi:10.1016/j.comnet.2004.01.008.

Shaikh, R. A., Jameel, H., d'Auriol, B. J., Lee, H., Lee, S., & Song, Y.-J. (2009). Group-based trust management scheme for clustered wireless sensor networks. *IEEE Transactions on Parallel and Distributed Systems*, *20*(11), 1698–1712. doi:10.1109/TPDS.2008.258.

Srinivasan, V., Nuggehalli, P., Chiasserini, C. F., & and Rao, R. R. (2003). Co-operation in wireless adhoc networks. *IEEE INFOCOMM*.

Velloso, P. B., Laufer, R. P., Cunha, D. d., Duarte, O. C., & Pujolle, G. (2010). Trust Management in Mobile Ad Hoc Networks Using a Scalable Maturity-Based Model. *IEEE TRANSACTIONS ON NETWORK AND SERVICE MANAGEMENT*, *7*(3), 172–185. doi:10.1109/TNSM.2010.1009.I9P0339.

Venkataraman, R., Pushpalatha, M., & Rama Rao, T. (2012). Implementation of a Regression-based Trust Model in a Wireless Ad hoc Testbed. *Defence Science Journal*, *62*(3), 167–173.

Wang, K., & Wu, M. (2010). Cooperative communications based on trust model for mobile ad hoc networks. *IET Information Security*, *4*(2), 68–79. doi:10.1049/iet-ifs.2009.0056.

Yi, S., Naldurg, P., & R.Kravets. (2001). {A Security-Aware Routing Protocol for Wireless Ad Hoc Networks}.

Yoo, Y., & Agrawal, D. P. (2006). {Why Does It Pay To Be Selfish In A MANET?}. *IEEE Wireless Communications*, *13*(6), 87–97. doi:10.1109/MWC.2006.275203.

Yu, H., Shen, Z., Miao, C., Leung, C., & Niyato, D. (2010). A survey of trust and reputation management systems in wireless communications. *Proceedings of the IEEE*, 1755-1772.

Zhou, L., & Haas, Z. J. (1999). {Securing Ad hoc Networks}. *IEEE Network*, *13*, 24–30. doi:10.1109/65.806983.

Zhu, S., Setia, S., & Jajodia, S. (2003). {LEAP: Efficient security mechanisms for large-scale distributed sensor networks}.

KEY TERMS AND DEFINITIONS

Compromised Entities: Authorized logical entities in the network that are captured physically by adversaries.

Network Dynamics: It is the study of functional characteristics and behavior of a network with change in time.

Proactive Trust: Computations performed on a periodical basis where the results of the computations are used by the entities at a later instant of time

Reactive Trust: Computations performed on-demand basis when there is a need to compute the trustworthiness.

Social Trust: Functional characteristics and behaviors considered reliable as seen in human societies.

Trust Metrics: The functional behavior of the neighboring nodes in a network like sincerity in forwarding the data and routing information, gratuitous route replies, etc.

APPENDIX: REVIEW QUESTIONS

1. Name few cryptographic techniques used in security for wireless ad hoc networks
2. Differentiate hard and soft security.
3. Give an example scenario for the computation of intensional and extensional trust.
4. What are the QoS metrics related to trust?
5. List few trust metrics that can be used for proactive ad hoc routing environments.
6. What are the qualitative and quantitative trust metrics in mobile wireless networks?
7. Which topology would lead to a minimal trust computational overhead in mobile and wireless communication network? Justify your answer.
8. Name few security attacks that are (i) detected only by trust mechanisms (ii) cannot be detected by any trust mechanism.
9. Define Trust Dynamics.
10. What is the use of trust decay parameter? Discuss the pros and cons of having a fast decay and a slow decay trust metric.

Chapter 13
Privacy Protection in Vehicular Ad–Hoc Networks

Gongjun Yan
University of Southern Indiana, USA

Bhed Bahadur Bista
Iwate Prefectural University, Japan

Danda B. Rawat
Georgia Southern University, USA

Wu He
Old Dominion University, USA

Awny Alnusair
Indiana University – Kokomo, USA

ABSTRACT

The first main contribution of this chapter is to take a non-trivial step towards providing a robust and scalable solution to privacy protection in vehicular networks. To promote scalability and robustness the authors employ two strategies. First, they view vehicular networks as consisting of non-overlapping subnetworks, each local to a geographic area referred to as a cell. Each cell has a server that maintains a list of pseudonyms that are valid for use in the cell. Each pseudonym has two components: the cell's ID and a random number as host ID. Instead of issuing pseudonyms to vehicles proactively (as virtually all existing schemes do) the authors issue pseudonyms only to those vehicles that request them. This strategy is suggested by the fact that, in a typical scenario, only a fraction of the vehicles in an area will engage in communication with other vehicles and/or with the infrastructure and, therefore, do not need pseudonyms. The second main contribution is to model analytically the time-varying request for pseudonyms in a given cell. This is important for capacity planning purposes since it allows system managers to predict, by taking into account the time-varying attributes of the traffic, the probability that a given number of pseudonyms will be required at a certain time as well as the expected number of pseudonyms in use in a cell at a certain time. Empirical results obtained by detailed simulation confirm the accuracy of the authors' analytical predictions.

DOI: 10.4018/978-1-4666-4691-9.ch013

1. INTRODUCTION AND MOTIVATION

Recent statistics show that in 2008 there were over 238 million passenger cars and trucks in the US, a vehicular fleet that increases yearly by almost seven million new cars (US Department of Transporation, Research and Innovative Technology Association, 2011). In an effort to help their vehicles compete in the marketplace, car and truck manufacturers are offering more and more potent on-board devices, including powerful computers, a large array of sensors, radar devices, cameras, and wireless transceivers. These devices cater to a set of customers that expect their vehicles to provide a seamless extension of their home environment populated by sophisticated entertainment centers, access to Internet and other similar wants and needs (Arif et al., 2012; Wang, 2010). The powerful on-board devices support new applications, including location-specific services, on-line gaming, delivering multimedia content and various forms of mobile infotainment made possible by the emergence of vehicular networks (Li et al., 2005). In the near future, a vehicle will be capable of intelligent data-mining based on its owner's preferences (Wen et al., 2011), identifying favorite hotels, shopping malls, restaurants (e.g. Chinese restaurants featuring Szechuan-style cuisine) and, perhaps, a convenient parking lot (Yan et al., 2011). Knowing the driver's preferences, around lunchtime the vehicle will automatically send queries to the roadside infrastructure and other vehicles to find a list of Chinese restaurants nearby (Li et al., 2005; Wen et al., 2011).

The increased Internet presence that enables the above applications invites various forms of privacy attacks mounted by unscrupulous characters in order to identify the location of various parties that might be exploited for financial gains. One well-known such attack has for goal to establish that a family is away from their home so that a burglary can be perpetrated; yet another one has for goal to obtain compromising information that can later be used to blackmail the driver. Invariably,

these privacy attacks are mounted by exploiting the various forms of correlation that exist between the identity of a vehicle and that of its driver.

While a great deal of research has been devoted to information security in vehicular networks (Choi et al., 2006; Hubaux et al., 2004; Raya et al., 2006; Sun et al., 2010a, Yan et al., 2008; Yan et al., 2009a), far less attention has been given to privacy issues (Xie et al., 2010; Yan and Olariu, 2011). One of the reasons for this state of affairs is the mistaken idea that the privacy issues encountered in vehicular networks are similar to the ones experienced in cellular telephony and WiFi communications and, therefore, the same solutions can be applied. For example, it has been suggested that instead of radio communications, drivers use their cell phones to access the Internet. However, using a cell-phone while driving may not only be illegal, as it is currently in some states, it has also been identified as one of the principal causes of traffic accidents.

A more careful analysis reveals that many of the privacy challenges experienced in vehicular networks are either brought about or exacerbated by the increased on-line presence of drivers, the high mobility of the vehicular fleet as well as the short transmission requirements of the Dedicated Short Range Communications (DSRC) limiting transmission to between 300m and 1,000m (Yan and Olariu, 2011).

In summary, there are unique challenges to privacy protection in vehicular networks including (Yan et al., 2013; Arif et al., 2012):

- **High Vehicular Mobility:** This challenge renders the network connection inherently unstable and make pseudonyms difficult to manage and update (Yan and Olariu, 2011; Rawat et al., 2011). Therefore, the communication is not reliable;
- **Large and Fluctuating Population of Vehicles:** This challenge will make the scalability requirement of privacy solutions difficult to meet (Yan et al., 2012);

- **Traffic Flow Characteristics:** The vehicles in the network are bound by certain traffic flow parameters that are highly related to the geographical location differences;
- **Unmistakable Correlation Between a Vehicle and its Driver:** Tracking the driver often means tracking its vehicle and vice-versa.

1.1 Our Contributions

As mentioned, assigning pseudonyms to vehicles is a time-honored solution to providing privacy protection both in real-life and in vehicular networks (Huang et al., 2011). The major shortcoming of existing approaches is *scalability*. This is because the high rates of vehicular mobility combined with the short communication range of DSRC make the task of issuing, maintaining and revoking pseudonyms extremely difficult. The short-range vehicular communications rely on multihop routing which will involve multiple vehicles in the network. However, the more vehicles involved, the higher the potential for a privacy attack. The growing size of our vehicular fleet in conjunction with a steadily increasing Internet presence require privacy provisioning schemes to be both scalable and robust.

Considering the challenges outlined above, we take a non-trivial step towards protecting network layer and above privacy of vehicles. Our first main contribution is to provide a robust and scalable solution to privacy protection in vehicular networks. To promote scalability and robustness we employ a combination of two strategies:

- We view vehicular networks as consisting of non-overlapping subnetworks each local to a geographic area referred to as a *cell*. Depending on the topology and the nature of the area, these cells may be as large as few city blocks or, indeed, may comprise the entire downtown area of a smaller town. Each cell has a server that maintains a list of pseudonyms that are valid for use in the cell. Each pseudonym consists of the cell's ID and of a random host ID;
- Instead of issuing pseudonyms to vehicles proactively, as virtually all existing schemes do, we issue pseudonyms only to those vehicles that need them, and therefore request them. This strategy is suggested by accumulated empirical evidence suggesting that only a fraction of the vehicles in an area will engage in communication with other vehicles and/or with the infrastructure and, therefore, need pseudonyms. The others do not.

Our second main contribution is to model analytically the time-varying request for pseudonyms in a given cell. This is important for capacity planning purposes since it allows managers to predict stochastically the probability that a given number of pseudonyms will be required at a certain time as well as the expected number of pseudonyms in use in a cell at a certain time. Empirical results obtained by detailed simulation confirmed the accuracy of our analytical predictions.

Let us elaborate a bit to give the reader a better feel for what we do. Guided by the divide-and-conquer strategy, we partition the geographic area of interest into smaller entities that we call *cells*, where the size of a cell is dictated by the characteristic of the environment and will be discussed later. The municipality-wide vehicular network is partitioned into several subnetworks, each local to a cell. Each cell has its own pseudonym server that assigns, on demand, pseudonyms to the vehicles resident in the cell. To easily locate a network node, the address of a vehicle includes two parts: the cell ID and the pseudonym as a host ID. Pseudonym servers in various cells are connected by wired connection. Packets can be transmitted following the cell ID. Inside a cell, vehicles are located using their host IDs. This simple scheme helps scalability, robustness and the reliability of communication. If necessary, scalability can be enhanced by further dividing cells into microcells.

Vehicles that wish to communicate using the wireless channel need to request pseudonyms from the cell server prior to communicating with either the infrastructure or with other vehicles in the cell. However, it is worth noting that a vehicle does not need to request pseudonyms if it is merely receiving information from the network, such as listening to music, receiving traffic condition updates, etc.

The real identity of vehicle, either its host name, or its IP address, or both, will be hidden by the pseudonym. In this chapter, the identities of the vehicles are temporary and random numbers, the identity collector/attacker will not be able to track the vehicle by sniffing the network.

Operating similarly to the Dynamic Host Configuration Protocol (DHCP), the cell server needs to have an accurate estimate of number of pseudonyms, the probability and the expected number of pseudonym requests. Knowing dynamic information at any time, the server can maximize the utilization of resources (for example IP addresses as pseudonyms, bandwidth, etc.), as the resources are costly. But the difficulty lies in the time-varying nature of the pseudonym requests, mirroring the time-varying population of vehicles in the cell. One of our main contributions is to derive analytically the time-varying expected number of pseudonym requests in a given cell as a function of time. Empirical simulation results have confirmed the accuracy of our analytical derivations.

The remainder of this work is organized as follows: Section 2 reviews relevant results from the recent literature. Sections 3 and 4 introduce the system model assumed in the chapter as well as the privacy treat model whose effects we mitigate. They also discuss requirements of a privacy-preserving system. Section 5 presents the details of our privacy provisioning scheme. Further, Section 6 and 7 offers our analytical derivations both of the privacy scheme and of the stochastic model that we propose for pseudonym usage in a cell as a function of traffic intensity. Section 8 offers an empirical evaluation of our model using extensive numerical simulations. Finally, Section 9 offers concluding remarks and directions for future work.

2. STATE OF THE ART

The goal of this section is to review a number of approaches to preserving privacy in vehicular networks. The *mix zone* concept has been proposed recently for privacy protection (Le et al., 2011; Dahl et al., 2010; Palanisamy and Liu, 2011; Sun et al., 2010b). The mix zone is intended as a strategy to break the link between an old pseudonym and a new pseudonym assigned by the roadside infrastructure. Since the attackers can store past pseudonyms and link the new pseudonym to a vehicle that has been tracked, a mix zone can thwart attempts at tracking vehicles by mixing with other vehicles (Ribagorda-Garnacho, 2010; Sampigethaya et al., 2007). In spite of its novelty, the mix zone concept has not met with great success. One of the problems seems to be the synchronization of pseudonyms. If the traffic flow is high, there may have communication delay of synchronization of pseudonyms.

A *silent period* or *silent zone* is another solution to breaking the link between old and new pseudonyms (Dok et al., 2010; Song et al., 2009; Dahl et al., 2010). Group navigation can protect the privacy of several vehicles as a group and can decrease the overhead of pseudonym changes by individual vehicles (Studer et al., 2009; Sampigethaya et al., 2005; Guo et al., 2007). A group leader will normally be elected to represent the whole group. On the other hand, there are potential problems. The privacy of the group is highly dependent o the integrity of the group leader. If the group leader is compromised, the privacy of the whole group will temporally compromised.

Dok *et al.* (Dok et al., 2010) tried to merge the three strategies discussed above to provide better privacy protection. The mix zone is often selected as a place to assign pseudonyms. The group signature can allow vehicles in a group to use the same key to communicate (Studer et al., 2009; Sampigethaya et al., 2005; Guo et al., 2007). This is especially useful when the vehicles are in a mix zone or silent zone. Since the privacy information such as combination of identity, location and time can be stored and used to link the pseudonyms, adopting a random silent period can break the link between a pseudonym and the real identity of a vehicle.

The privacy analysis at an intersection has been discussed in (Dahl et al., 2010). By using a combination of public and private key encryption, the roadside infrastructure in charge of the intersection will assign keys to vehicles entering the intersection. A formal analysis of the transmission has been conducted by using ProVerif (Blanchet et al., 2008). RFID as a electronic device/tag has also been applied in privacy protection in vehicular networks (Arapinis et al., 2010; Brusò et al., 2010; Delaune et al., 2010).

Lu *et al.* (Lu et al., 2008) proposed a privacy preservation protocol in vehicular networks. The basic idea of the proposed method is to dynamically generate anonymous keys between the On-Board Units and the Roadside Units, which can provide fast anonymous authentication and privacy protection while minimizing the required storage for short-time anonymous keys. The authors proposed a filtering algorithm to prevent communication information from encrypting junk information (Lu et al., 2012b, Lu et al., 2012a). However, strictly speaking, the proposed methods are more of a security-preserving strategy than a privacy preservation method as the network identity (such as IP address, or network name) can still be used in tracking the identity of a driver. By contrast, our proposed method focus on network layer pseudonym protection that guarantees that the identity of the vehicles and drivers are both protected.

Lin *et al.* (Lin et al., 2011; Lu et al., 2010) proposed an interesting routing protocol which

preserves privacy. To help location-based routing protocol, they proposed a social-tier-assisted packet forwarding protocol by using some social spots, such as well-traversed shopping malls and busy intersections in a city. Without knowing the receiver's exact location information, a packet can be first forwarded and disseminated in the social tier. When the receiver visits one of social spots, it can successfully receive the packet. Vehicle can somehow preserve conditional privacy. However the method is at least two-hops communication and the delivery ratio, packet jitters and average delay are questionable. The method is also based on driver behavior. In many cases, drivers never visit social spots. Our proposed privacy-preserving scheme can overcome the potential problems raised by the social-related method. First, our scheme is reliable and independent of driver behavior and, second, the delivery ratio, packet jitters and average delay shown in simulation are greatly improved as the communication are one-hop.

3. SYSTEM MODEL

The main actors that we deal with in this chapter are the vehicles described in Subsection 3.1, the roadside infrastructure deployed by the municipality and/or third-party players to provide various services to the traveling public as discussed in Subsection 3.2 and the cell model which is the workhorse of our solution and will be discussed in Subsection 3.3.

3.1 The Vehicle Model

An important new concept in the automotive industry is *neighborhood awareness*. This allows a vehicle to know about the presence, location and even speed of neighboring vehicles. It is common-knowledge that present-day vehicles come equipped with powerful on-board resources. Specifically, we assume vehicles to be endowed with the following features (Yan et al., 2013; Arif et al., 2012):

- A GPS navigation system including a GPS receiver and GPS maps;
- A computer center, which will provide data processing, computing and storage;
- A wireless transceiver, using DSRC for fast communications;
- Public Key Infrastructure. We assume that the public key and private key of each vehicle and infrastructure are assigned and maintained by Certificate Authority (CA);
- A virus checker. However, virus protection is outside the scope of this chapter and will not be pursued further.

It is worth noting that the vehicle model adopted in this work is highly realistic and that, in fact, it is not uncommon to have all the assumed features in the high-end vehicular fleet. For example, Toyota Motor Corporation developed Pre-Crash Safety system (Toyota, 2007) which uses millimeter-wave radar to sense vehicles and obstacles on the road ahead back in 2002. Furthermore, GPS and computer center are popular vehicle accessories nowadays. To put things in perspective, and to illustrate the phenomenal technological advances that make their way into present-day vehicles, suffice it to mention that only a few short years back, a comparably-equipped vehicle used to be referred to as a "smart vehicles" (Hubaux et al., 2004; Yan et al., 2008).

3.2 Roadside Infrastructure Model

An important role in our scheme is played by the road side infrastructure deployed by the municipality to provide various services to the traveling public. While at present these services are minimal, we expect that in time they will develop to a full-blown roster of municipality and third-party services ranging from traffic updates to information about local events, parking availability, medical facilities, restaurants, and the like. The roadside infrastructure may be queried about road construction, congestion and can provide, on demand, travel estimates to various points on interest and up-to-the-minute parking lot availability.

The roadside unit has a powerful transceiver and the electronics needed to communicate with the vehicles in the cell. The down-link channel is of the broadcast type, the up-link channel (i.e. from the vehicles to the roadside unit) is contention-based. The roadside infrastructure of neighboring cells is connected by conventional high-bandwidth fiberglass cable.

Last, but certainly not least, the roadside infrastructure houses a pseudonym server that issues, on demand, pseudonyms to the vehicles currently in the cell.

3.3 Cell Model

The system discussed in this chapter assumes an urban environment. While we assume the downtown area of a large city, the same reasoning can be applied to a small town. The only difference is that in a small town, there might be only one cell or, indeed, a few cells, while in a larger urban setting the downtown area may be partitioned into several cells.

For reasons of efficiency, similar in nature to the ones motivating cellular telephony service providers, the city-wide vehicular network is partitioned into many smaller subnetworks, each local to a cell, as shown in Figure 1. The details of this partitioning will be discussed in Section 5.1.

Some of the advantages of the cell-based communication include:

- **Localized Communication:** This follows from the observation that drivers tend to be more interested in local information, such as traffic congestion, accidents, parking lot, or gas station, etc.;
- **Enabling Scalability:** No matter how far a destination is located, a vehicle can access it with help from the cell;
- **Customizing Security and Privacy Strategies:** Different cells can be deployed

Figure 1. Illustrating the partition of downtown Chicago into cells.(Yan et al., 2013; Arif et al., 2012)

with different security and privacy protocols. For example, users along a busy highway will want fast communication with least delay caused by encrypting and decrypting message (Yan et al., 2009b). A simpler cryptographic algorithm can be employed in this area.

4. THREAT MODEL AND REQUIREMENTS

During its residency in a cell, a vehicle may contact many other vehicles and the roadside infrastructure. Therefore, it is important to protect the privacy of vehicles by ensuring that their communication cannot be tracked. The privacy protector will not be able to protect privacy in the situation that vehicles may move out of scope of the protector or the protector will serve large amount of vehicles. Obviously, the privacy protection must be scalable because of the high mobility and large population of vehicles. The threat categories are:

- **Linking Pseudonyms:** The attackers can store the past identities (e.g. pseudonyms) of a vehicle and record the received new identities to link the past pseudonyms with the new pseudonyms (Yan et al., 2008);
- **Global Exploring:** The attackers can obtain full control of the network including roadside infrastructure, service servers, etc. The attackers therefore can explore any network infrastructure to track the identity of a vehicle;
- **Passive Eavesdropping:** The attackers can install a powerful radio receiver to passively eavesdrop the identity and location information of other vehicles nearby;
- **Spoofing User Identity:** The attackers pretend to be another user to obtain data and illegitimate advantages. One classic example is "man-in-the-middle attack" in which the attackers pretend to be Bob when communicating with Alice and pretend to be Alice when communicating with Bob. Both Alice an Bob will send decryptable messages to the attackers. Another similar example is "email address spoofing" in which the attackers fill with forged

return user's identity and create unreachability errors.

With the development of vehicle registration plate recognition, the attackers can track a vehicle by physically following the vehicle. The physical track is not able to prevent by simply use software method (Xi et al., 2007).

4.1 Requirements of a Privacy-Preserving Solution

Vehicular networks are complex systems with time-varying dynamics. While privacy protection in vehicular networks is our main concern in this chapter, there are other related, but equally important issues that any solution must consider. These issues translate into the following three requirements (Yan et al., 2013; Arif et al., 2012):

- **Hiding the real identity of vehicles in an effective way:** A vehicle's real identity must be replaced by a pseudonym which is a random number;
- **Routing packets in an efficient way:** It is helpful to think of the identity of a vehicle like something like an IP address of a network device in the TCP/IP protocol. The identity will be used to route packets and to locate the host;
- **Protecting the privacy of vehicles and their drivers in a scalable way:** Due to high vehicular mobility and a large number of vehicles on our roadways and streets, privacy-preserving strategies must be scalable and robust.

4.2 Level of Private Message

Based on the sensitivity, there are several levels of messages: Public, Personal, Private, Confidential and Private.

1. **For Public:** No sensitivity level is assigned to the message. This message can be transmitted to the whole network.
2. **For Personal:** The recipient will treat the message as personal information. The identity of the sender may or may not shown in the message. It is up to the sender to decide the appearance of the identity.
3. **For Private:** The recipient will treat the message as private information. No identities will be recovered.
4. **For Confidential and Private:** The recipient will treat the message as confidential and private information. No identities will be released and only the authenticated recipient can read this message.

5. OUR PRIVACY-PRESERVING SCHEME

Referring to Figure 1, our scheme partitions the geographic area of interest into non-overlapping cells. In turn, the municipality-wide vehicular network is partitioned into subnetworks, each local to a cell. Each subnetwork maintains a list of pseudonyms and assigns, on demand, a pseudonym to each vehicle in the cell. In principle, the pseudonym is valid for the duration of the residency in the cell. Each pseudonym is composed of two parts (Yan et al., 2013; Arif et al., 2012):

- **The ID of the Cell:** used as a geographic network prefix ID and mask ID that specifies the maximum number of vehicles presented in the cell;
- **The Pseudonym Assigned to a Vehicle:** used as a host ID which uniquely identifies the vehicle while in the cell. One example of the pseudonym is an IP address. With such a pseudonym, vehicles can route packets based on the network ID and receivers can be easily located inside a cell by host ID.

It is worth mentioning that the use of pseudonyms is not mandatory and the decision to use them or not is left with individual drivers who can opt to communicate without protection privacy. Cities, especially some busy districts, often broadcast information for example traffic congestion information, parking lot information, through FM radio or through the broadcast IP address. If a vehicle merely receives information passively, the vehicle does not have to request a pseudonym. It is only when the vehicle is about to send out requests or messages (for example, a direction to a specific address) that the vehicle needs to request a pseudonym. This is obvious if the pseudonym is an IP address. Bearing in mind the fact that pseudonym usage is not mandatory, we can assume that some vehicles will not request a pseudonym for the most part of their trip.

5.1 Cell Communication Enhances Privacy

In this subsection, we introduce cell communication which enhances privacy by reducing the linkage between the identity and location of vehicles. As we have already mentioned, in an urban scenario the whole vehicular network is partitioned into cells on the digital map, as shown in Figure 1. The digital maps with cell partitions are installed on vehicles, just as GPS navigator systems install digital maps with many other useful information such as gas stations, hotels, etc. The size of the cell is a system parameter and depends on a number of factors. For example, in the US the vehicles are assumed to use the DSRC protocol limiting the effective communication range to 1000m and so the cells must have edges of roughly 700 meters so that any two vehicles inside the cell can communicate with each other and with the pseudonym server regardless of their position within the cell. Thus, in a cell vehicles can directly communicate with the pseudonym server in one hop.

As illustrated in Figure 2, each cell has a transmission tower and a pseudonym server to provide privacy protection and wireless communication routing. Each vehicle can automatically find which cell the vehicle belongs to by checking the GPS location and the cell's map

In this chapter, we assume that a pseudonym uniquely identifies a vehicle, such as IP address, host-name in network. We briefly list the steps involved in requesting a pseudonym (Yan et al., 2013; Arif et al., 2012):

Figure 2. Each cell contains a trusted pseudonym server. GeoID is the unique identity of a cell while PseudoID is the unique identity of a vehicle inside the cell.(Yan et al., 2013; Arif et al., 2012).

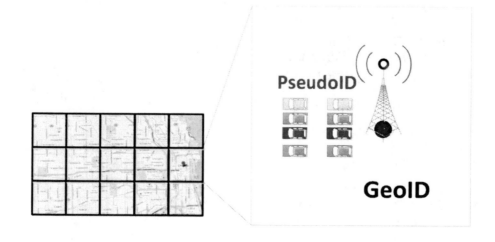

- The vehicle first encrypts a request by using the pseudonym server's public key. The request will also include a secret key (random number) that the vehicle will use to uncover new pseudonym. When the pseudonym server receives this request, the server will apply its private key to decrypt the message. In this step, the requesting vehicle will send its real identity. For security reasons, the pseudonym server will store an encrypted version of the real vehicular identity;

- The pseudonym server will authenticate the vehicle. If the vehicle is eligible to receive a new pseudonym, the pseudonym server then allocates an available random pseudonym to the vehicle. Having encrypted the new pseudonym with the secret key the pseudonym server then sends the encrypted message back to the vehicle. The pseudonym include a non-negative expiration time, i.e. a time-to-live (TTL);

- The vehicle applies the new pseudonym after decrypting and uncovering the new pseudonym. When the pseudonym expires, a new request has to be sent by the vehicle. In this chapter, we take the view that the TTL is set to infinity, that is, pseudonyms are valid to use during the entire residency in the cell. However, in general this need not be the case.

Based on the above discussion, it is reasonable to assume that the pseudonym servers will not be compromised and that the public key infrastructure (PKI) including public key and private key pairs cannot be cracked.

5.2 Pseudonyms Hide the Identity of Vehicles

The major goal of this subsection is to discuss how the real identity of a vehicle is hidden and how the requirements specified in Subsection 4.1 are

satisfied. As already mentioned, and as illustrated in Figure 3, the identity of a vehicle consists of two main parts: a cell(i.e. subnetwork) ID (GeoID prefix) and a host ID (Host ID). The subnetwork ID is shown as GeoID and the host ID is combined with subnetwork ID by adding the subnetwork ID to the host ID. The HostId is a random number generated and maintained by the cell pseudonym server. Therefore, the combination of the host ID and the subnetwork ID can also be thought of as a pseudonym.

To illustrate the previous discussion let us follow an example. Referring to Table 1, a vehicle ID is 64 bits, e.g. *0932.0968.0115.1300* (dot-hexdecimal notation). The subnetwork ID is specified by subnet mask, i.e. Geonet mask *FFFF.FFFF.FFFF.0* in table 1. Therefore, the GeoID prefix is obtained by a logical "AND" operation between the vehicle ID and the Geonet mask. The host ID is shown as *0000.0000.0000.1300*. The broadcasting address inside the cell will be *0932.0968.0115.FFFF* which can be obtained by replacing the host ID by all "1"s. It is clear that the network localization can use the GeoID prefix. Once the cell as a subnetwork has been identified, the Broadcast Address can be used to find the host vehicle.

Once a vehicle has obtained a pseudonym, it can use it to communicate with other vehicles and/or with the roadside infrastructure until it exits the cell or the pseudonym expires. As mentioned already, cell pseudonym servers are con-

Table 1. Identity pseudonyms: parameters and values.(Yan et al., 2013; Arif et al., 2012)

	Dot-HexDecimal notation
Vehicle ID	0932.0968.0115.1300
Geonet mask	FFFF.FFFF.FFFF.0000
GeoID prefix	0932.0968.0115.0000
Host ID	0000.0000.0000.1300
Broadcast Address	0932.0968.0115.FFFF

Figure 3. Illustrating the pseudonym structure. A 64 bits number is partitioned into two parts: GeoID which is the cell's ID and the PseudoMask which includes a subnetwork mask and a pseudonym ID which is a random number.(Yan et al., 2013; Arif et al., 2012).

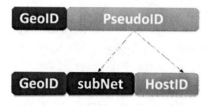

nected with each other by a wired network. Messages can be transmitted by following the network ID on wired networks. Inside a cell, the destination vehicle can be located by host ID. However, the network localization is very efficient since the size of a cell is small when compared to the whole network. Therefore, our method is both scalable and robust.

5.3 Dividing a Cell into Microcells to Improve Scalability

Seen from the perspective of a cell, the population of vehicles is fluctuating with time as vehicles constantly move in and out the cell. According to recent statistics published by the National Highway Traffic Safety Administration, we assume that the percentage of vehicles that will request pseudonym is about 24.5% of the population of vehicles in the cell (National Highway Traffic Safety Administration, 2012) although in our analytical derivations we take a more general view and let the probability that a vehicle requests a pseudonym be time-dependent.

When the request for pseudonyms reaches its peak, it may place a great deal of pressure on the pseudonym server. We present a method to improve scalability by dividing, on a per-need basis, a congested cell into microcells in a manner similar to that of cellular networks. A cell can be

divided into microcells, as shown in Figure 4. Each microcell has its own pseudonym server which has the same capability to process pseudonym requests, validation, and updates. The division to microcells can recursively proceed until the request rejection rate drops to zero.

5.4 Location Division Multiple Access (LDMA) to Reduce Collisions

Given that the number of vehicles in a cell can be large, the *broadcast storm* (Lu and Poellabauer, 2010) can be a potential problem that can greatly reduce the efficiency of communications. To mitigate the problem, we propose to use *Location Division Multiple Access* (LDMA), inspired by the classic Time Division Multiple Access (TDMA) protocol, to schedule the communications in order to reduce the number of wireless communication collisions. Like TDMA, data stream is divided into frames. Each frame is further divided into time slots. Each slot is assigned to a small region of a cell. Vehicles in the small region will share the same time slot. Therefore, the idea is to divide a cell into smaller sub-cells, i.e. the cell is divided into 8 slots, to reduce the wireless communication collision. Comparing with TDMA, LDMA only assigns time slots to a sub-cell, a smaller region to the original cell, instead of an individual user. For scalability, a sub-cell can be divided into finer granularity super-sub-cells and a time slots can be partitioned into smaller time fractions to

Figure 4. Illustrating the partition of a congested cell into microcells.(Yan et al., 2013; Arif et al., 2012).

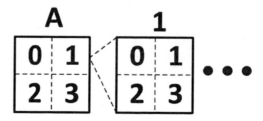

host super-sub-cells respectively. The structure of LDMA is illustrated in Figure 5.

5.5 Quiet Times Prevent the Tracking of ID and Location

To avoid tracking of vehicular ID and location, a silent zone will be adopted. The major function of the silent zone is to break the link between the old ID/location and the new ID/location. Therefore, it is natural to have the silent zones located at intersections because the semi-random mobility of vehicles can enhance the breakage of the correlation between the old ID and new ID. Inside the silent zone vehicles stop using their IDs. But this stoppage will not prevent vehicles from exchanging emergency messages. Only ID related applications will be temporally blocked. This is acceptable for most applications because the duration of the blockage will be only a few

seconds. When a vehicle exits the silent zone, it will start using the new ID. The vehicles that have no new ID will keep using their current (i.e. old) ID. (Figure 6)

5.6 Pseudonym Synchronization

A number of agencies can participate in generating pseudonyms. These agencies can be governmental transportation authorities, such as DMV or BMV. These governmental authorities are ideal agents to serve as pseudonym servers. Pseudonyms can also be issued by roadside infrastructure built by DMV/BMV and forced to be updated every expiration period even if the car is not on the road. The vehicular maintenance habits of drivers will not be changed and drivers will not be forced to perform other actions to get their vehicle certified and provided with a suitable set of pseudonyms.

Figure 5. Illustrating LDMA. Data stream is divided into frames. Each frame is divided into time slots. Each time slot is assigned to a sub-cell which is formed by partitioning a cell into 8 sub-cells. Vehicles in the cell slot can communicate only within its time slot.(Yan et al., 2013; Arif et al., 2012).

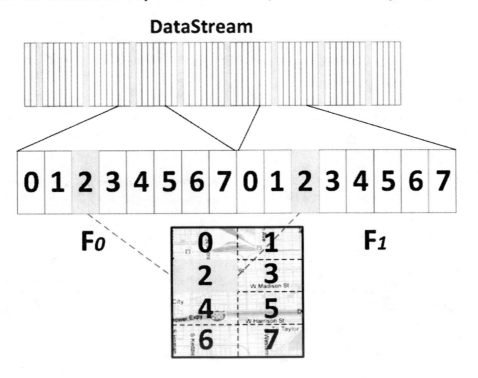

Figure 6. Illustrating the silent time $T_1 - T_0$ and silent zone. (Yan et al., 2013; Arif et al., 2012).

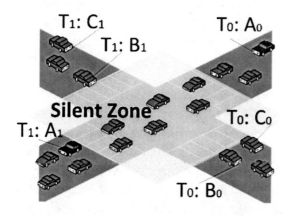

However, there are several problems associated with a central pseudonym authority, the single-point-of-failure concern being one of them. Yet another problem may be that the server IDs are not synchronized among cell servers. This problem will disable packet routing. To synchronize pseudonym servers, a possible solution is make a Pseudonym Server (PS) chain which includes several levels of PSs. Each local pseudonym server receives certificates and server IDs from the higher level servers. Each of them has a series of PSs. A tree structure can be organized as suggested by Figure 7.

Vehicle manufacturers can be the authorized to issue pseudonym as well. Manufacturers will receive permission and certificates from governmental transportation authorities and become a subdivision of PS. In addition, non-profit organizations can also act as authorized organizations. Similar to the vehicle manufacturer, non-profit organizations can obtain permission and certificates from governmental transportation authorities and become a subdivision of a PS.

At fabrication time, each vehicle will receive a pseudonym from the manufacturer or some governmental agency by using PKI encryption. Pseudonym assignment is on the basis of the unique ID and a certain expiration time. The pseudonym has to be periodically renewed at local pseudonym servers such as cell pseudonym servers, DMV/BMV pseudonym servers as sub-PSs.

5.7 Pseudonym Update and Expiration

There are three ways a pseudonym can expire. First, pseudonyms are time-sensitive. As mentioned before, each pseudonym is assigned a TTL value. When the TTL decreases to zero, the pseudonym expires and the vehicle will be automatically deregistered. A pseudonym is also associated with the issuing cell ID, i.e. GeoID shown in Figure 2.

Second, when a vehicle exits a cell and enters a new cell, the vehicle can requests a new pseudonym which will submit the old pseudonym as well. The pseudonym server in the new cell will identify the

Figure 7. Illustrating the Pseudonym Server (PS) tree structure which ensured that server IDs are synchronized.(Yan et al., 2013; Arif et al., 2012).

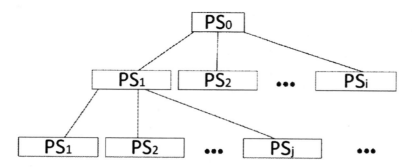

previous cell ID and TTL. If the TTL is still valid, a synchronizing message will be sent to the old cell to notify the old pseudonym server in the old cell. The old pseudonym server will deregister the vehicle that just entered the new cell.

Since each time of applying new pseudonym is not based on the full capacity of the pseudonym pool, we will need to estimate the size of the pseudonym pool. Assume that the expected number of pseudonyms is $E[X(t)]$ where $X(t)$ means the pseudonym server receives k requests at time t. Therefore, in order to accommodate the difference between theoretical predictions and the actual number of requests experienced by the cell, the size of the pseudonym pool may be taken to be $(1+\delta)E[X(t)]+1$ where $0<\delta<1$ is an application-dependent parameter that will have to be fine-tuned as empirical evidence accumulates.

5.8 Preventing Denial Of Service Attacks

As the pseudonym server is a single service provider in a cell, it can be subjected to Denial of Service (DoS) attacks which are relatively easy to mount and hard to prevent. The damage DoS can inflict includes resource depletion such as wasting computing, memory, storage, and network resources, service exception and starving, among many others. Our main strategies to mitigate the effects of DoS attacks are the following:

- **Location Authentication:** The senders of the pseudonym request must be inside the cell. The location authentication can detect the sender's location by using both GPS coordinates and signal strength. The location authentication can block most, if not all, the requests from outside the cell;
- **Filtering Pseudonym Requests:** The pseudonym server only provides pseudonym services. Any other type of requests will be rejected;

- **Request Throttling:** The pseudonym server only assigns a reasonable request quota to every street in the cell. If the quota of a street is exceeded, it would not use other street's quota.

6. PRIVACY ANALYSIS: MODEL 1

In this section, we present a model to analyze the cell. Suppose roads be partitioned into slots. Each slot can only hold exact one vehicle. Therefore, when a vehicle present at a place, the vehicle actually take one slot. Consider a single cell where the number of possible slots for vehicles is finite and the total number of slots is N. Denote by $X(t)$ the number of slots in use at time t. Then, our physical intuition is not violated by assuming that $\{X(t);t>0\}$ is a birth-death process. It also seems reasonable to assume that, the cars arrive at a rate of $\lambda(t)$, independent of the number of cars already in the traffic area, and if the traffic area contains k cars, then the departure rate is $k\mu(t)$, where $\mu(t)$ is a function of t.

The state space of this process is $S=\{0,1,\ldots,N\}$. For every positive integer k, $1 \leq k \leq N$, the event $X(t)=k$ occurs if the traffic area contains k cars at time t. We let $P_k(t)$ denote the probability that the event $X(t)=k$ occurs, that is

$$P_k(t) = P\{X(t) = K\}$$

To make the mathematical derivations more manageable, at this point we assume that $\lambda(t)=\lambda$ and $\mu(t)=\mu$. Thus, the transition rate matrix of this birth-death process is

$$Q = \begin{pmatrix} -\lambda & \lambda & \cdots & 0 & 0 \\ \mu & -\lambda+\mu & \cdots & 0 & 0 \\ 0 & 2\mu & 0 & 0 & \vdots \\ \vdots & \ddots & & \vdots & \vdots & 0 \\ 0 & \cdots & -[\lambda+(n-1)\mu] & (N-1) & \mu0 \\ 0 & \cdots & N\mu & -N\mu \end{pmatrix}$$

And the Fokker-Planck equation is as follows:

$$
\begin{cases}
\dfrac{dP_0(t)}{dt} = -\lambda P_0(t) + \mu P_1(t) \\
\dfrac{dP_j(t)}{dt} = \lambda p_{j-1}(t) - (\lambda + j\mu)P_j(t) + (j+1)\mu P_{j+1}(t) \\
\dfrac{dP_N(t)}{dt} = \lambda P_{N-1}(t) + N\mu P_N(t)
\end{cases}
$$

If the limit distribution $P = (P_0, P_1, P_N)$ exist, that is $P_j = \lim_{t \to \infty} P_{ij}(t)$ and it is independent of i, then we have $dP_j(t)/dt = 0$ as $t \to \infty$. Hence, in the above equation let $t \to \infty$ we have

$$
\begin{cases}
-\lambda P_0 + \mu P_1 = 0 \\
\lambda P_{j-1} - (\lambda + j\mu)P_j + (j+1)\mu P_{j+1} = 0 \\
\lambda P_{N-1} + N\mu P_N = 0
\end{cases}
$$

(1)

Let g, $g_j = \lambda P_{j-1} + j\mu P_j$ we have

$$
\lambda P_{j-1} - (\lambda + j\mu)P_j + (j+1)\mu P_j + 1
$$

$$
= \left[\lambda P_{j-1} - j\mu P_j\right] - \left[\lambda P_j - (j+1)\mu P_{j+1}\right]
$$

$$
= g_j - g_{j+1} = 0
$$

Hence $g_0 = 0$, and $g_j = g_{j+1}$, for $1 \leq j \leq N-1$. Now the equation system (1) can be written as

$$
\begin{cases}
P_1 = \dfrac{\lambda}{\mu} P_0 \\
P_j = \dfrac{\lambda}{j\mu} P_{j-1} = \dfrac{1}{j!}(\dfrac{\lambda}{\mu})^j P_0 \\
P_N = \dfrac{1}{N}(\dfrac{\lambda}{\mu})^N P_0
\end{cases}
$$

It is known that $\sum_{j=0}^{N} P_j = 1$, that is

$$
\left[\dfrac{\lambda}{\mu} + \dfrac{1}{2!}\left(\dfrac{\lambda}{\mu}\right)^2 + \dfrac{1}{N!}\left(\dfrac{\lambda}{\mu}\right)^N\right] P_0 = 1
$$

Hence, solve the above equations, we have

$$
P_j = \dfrac{\dfrac{1}{j!}(\dfrac{\lambda}{\mu})^j}{\sum_{i=0}^{N} \dfrac{1}{i!}(\dfrac{\lambda}{\mu})}
$$

7. PRIVACY ANALYSIS: MODEL 2

The main goal of this section is to offer a stochastic analysis of the privacy scheme discussed in the previous sections. The expected number of pseudonyms and the probability of a certain number of pseudonyms in a cell at any time are our main interests. The main reasons we need to model the expected number and probability of vehicles in a cell at time t include:

- **Reducing Security Risks:** If the pseudonym server includes a list of unused pseudonyms, attackers may take the unused pseudonyms and pretend that the pseudonym is legally assigned. If we can reduce the number of unused pseudonyms, the risk of security will be reduced as well;
- **Reducing Control Costs:** Compared with the strategy that a cell request N pseudonyms every time, the strategy that a cell requests the expected number pseudonyms will include far fewer pseudonyms and, consequently, the overhead of generating, transmitting, and processing will be correspondingly smaller;
- **Reducing Maintenance Costs:** We assume that pseudonyms cost money and that, while the pseudonym service is free to the public the municipality and/or other third party entities will have to pay for them. It is obvious, therefore, that request-

ing and maintaining a smaller number of pseudonyms, tailored to the expected number of vehicles in the cell, will be cheaper than maintaining the maximum number of pseudonyms.

7.1 Defining the Model

In this section, we define the stochastic model which will be used to derive the analytical close form. We take stochastic process to the process of pseudonym application and expiration. The stochastic model is defined as follows, shown in Figure 8:

1. We are interested on the pseudonym resources on the pseudonym server side. Therefore, we focus on the pseudonym server. Cars in cells mostly and passively receive information such as traffic congestion information from infrastructure. Cars will not need pseudonyms at this stage. When a driver wants to send requests or communicate with infrastructure/other cars, a vehicle will reactively request a pseudonym and start to communicate. In other words, cars request pseudonym in an on-demand way. The service server is the whole process of registering, validating, and unregistering pseudonyms for vehicles.

2. The pseudonym server will assign a pseudonym to the vehicle *only after* a vehicle request a pseudonym. Therefore, the *arrival rate of the stochastic process is defined as arrival rate of demands for pseudonyms from vehicles in a cell.*

3. A pseudonym will become expired either the TTL decreases to zero or the pseudonym server is notified by other pseudonym servers. Therefore, the *departure rate of the stochastic process is defined as expiring rate of pseudonyms.*

4. The *service time in the stochastic process is the duration of registering and unregistering the pseudonyms.*

5. Vehicles can be in the incoming traffic and become brand-new vehicle in the cell or the vehicle that has been parked the cell for a long time and get restarted.

It is important to point out that there exists some special cases that the model does not apply. One example is that phenomenal events in a cell, such as super bowl of football, air show, etc., will create exceptional arrival rate and departure rate comparing with normal traffic condition in that cell. The traffic in cells are extremely different to the normal traffic condition in regular days. However, thanks to predetermination of these events (schedules and locations are predefined), pseudonym servers in involving cells can be

Figure 8. Stochastic model. The arrival rate: arrival rate of demands for pseudonyms from vehicles in a cell. The departure rate: expiring rate of pseudonyms. (Yan et al., 2013; Arif et al., 2012).

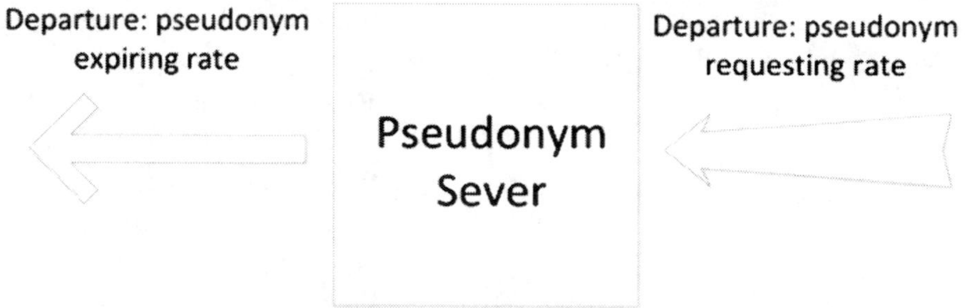

prepared for these phenomenal events. From the engineering perspective, we can request full capacity of pseudonyms and divide the involving cells into sub-cells or micro cells. Each of them has full capacity of pseudonyms. The cell's size can be decreased to a few hundred meters so that the server can feed each vehicle a pseudonym. Although it can be expensive, technically, it can be handleable.

7.2 Cell Size Analysis

We are interested in the following problem. Consider a cell with finite capacity N. At time $t=0$, the cell contains $n_0 \geq 0$ cars. After that, cars arrive and depart at time-dependent rates as described next. If the cell contains k, ($0 \leq k \leq N$), cars at time t, then the car arrival rate is

$$a_k(t) = \frac{N-K}{N} \lambda(t) \tag{2}$$

and the car departure rate $\beta_k(t)$ is

$$\beta_k(t) = k\mu(t) \tag{3}$$

where for all $t \geq 0$, $\lambda(t)$ and $\mu(t)$ are *integrable* on $[0,t]$. It is worth noting that both $a_k(t)$ and $\beta_k(t)$ are functions of both t and k. In particular, it may well be the case that for $t_1 \neq t_2$, $a_k(t_1) \neq a_k(t_2)$ and similarly for $\beta_k(t_1)$ and $\beta_k(t_2)$, giving mathematical expression to the fact that at different times of the day, say, the departure rate depends not only on the number of cars present in the cell but also on time-dependent factors.

Consider the counting process $\{X(t) \mid t \geq 0\}$ of continuous parameter t, where for every positive integer k, ($1 \leq k \leq N$), the event $\{X(t)=k\}$ occurs if the cell contains k cars at time t. We let $P_k(t)$ denote the probability that the event $\{X(t)=k\}$ occurs. In other words,

$$P_k(t) = \Pr\left[\{X(t) = k\}\right]$$

In addition to $P_k(t)$, of interest are the expected number $E[X(t)]$ and the variance $Var[X(t)]$ of the number of cars in the cell at time $t>0$, as well as the limiting behavior of these parameters as $t \rightarrow \infty$, whenever such a limit exists and/or makes sense.

7.3 Deriving a Closed Form for $P_k(t)$

To make the mathematical derivations more manageable, we set $P_k(t) = 0$ for $k<0$ and $k>N$. Thus, $P_k(t)$ is well defined for all integers $k \in (-\infty, \infty)$ and for all $t \geq 0$. In particular, the assumption about the cell containing n_0 cars at $t=0$ translates into $P_k(0) = 1$ if $k = n_0$ and 0 otherwise.

Let t, ($t \geq 0$), be arbitrary and let h be sufficiently small that in the time interval $[t,t+h]$ the probability of two or more arrivals or departures, or of a simultaneous arrival and departure, is $o(h)$. With h chosen as stated, the probability $P_k(t + h)$ that the cell contains k, ($0 \leq k \leq N$), cars at time $t+h$ has the following components:

$$P_k(t)\left[1 - h\frac{N-k}{N}\lambda(t) - kh\mu(t) + o(h)\right]$$

$$P_{k-1}(t)\left[1 - h\frac{N-k}{N}\lambda(t) - kh\mu(t) + o(h)\right]$$

$$P_{k+1}(t)\left[(k+1)h\mu(t) + o(h)\right]$$

Visibly: (See Box 1) with the initial condition $P_k(0) = 1$ for $k = n_0$ and 0 otherwise.

Let

$$G(z,t) = \sum_k P_k(t)z^k \tag{5}$$

Box 1.

$$P_k(t+h) = P_k(t)\left[1 - h\frac{N-k}{N}\lambda(t) - kh\mu(t)\right] + P_{k-1}(t)h\frac{N-k+1}{N}\lambda(t) + P_{k+1}(t)(k+1)h\mu(t) + o(h)$$

$$= P_k(t)\left[1 - h\frac{N-k}{N}\lambda(t)\right] + P_{k-1}(t)h\frac{N-k+1}{N}\lambda(t) + (k+1)h\mu(t) + o(h)$$

After transposing $P_k(t)$ and dividing by h we have:

$$\frac{P_k(t+h) - P_k(t)}{(t+h) - t} = \left[\frac{N-k}{N}\lambda(t) + k\mu(t)\right]P_k(t) + \frac{N-k+1}{N}\lambda(t)P_{k-1}(t) + P_{k+1}(t)\mu(t) + \frac{o(h)}{h}$$

Taking limits on both sides as $h \to 0$ yields the differential equation:

$$\frac{^0dP_k(t)}{^0dt} = -\left[\frac{N-k}{N}\lambda(t) + k\mu(t)\right]P_k(t) + \frac{N-k+1}{N}\lambda(t)P_{k-1}(t) + (k+1)\mu(t)P_{k+1}t \tag{4}$$

be the probability generating function of $P_k(t)$. Recall that since $P_k = 0$ for $k<0$ and $k>N$, there is no harm working with $k \in (-\infty, \infty)$. Upon multiplying (4) by z^k and upon summing over $k \in (-\infty, \infty)$ we obtain (see Box 2) with $G(z, 0) = z^n 0$ and auxiliary equations

$$\frac{^0dt}{1} = \frac{^0dz}{(z-1)\left[\dfrac{\lambda(t)}{N}z + \mu(t)\right]} = \frac{^0dG}{(z-1)\lambda(t)G} \tag{7}$$

After the change of variable $z - 1 = \cdot\dfrac{1}{y}$, the differential equation

$$\frac{^0dt}{1} = \frac{^0dz}{(z-1)\left[\dfrac{\lambda(t)}{N}z + \mu(t)\right]}$$

becomes

$$\frac{^0dy}{^0dt} + \left[\frac{\lambda(t)}{N} + \mu(t)\right]y = -\frac{\lambda(t)}{N} \tag{8}$$

Using standard techniques, equation (8) yields

$$e^{h(t)}y + \int_0^t \frac{\lambda(u)}{N} e^{h(u)0} du = cons \tan t$$

or, equivalently,

$$\frac{e^{h(t)}}{z-1} + \int_0^t \frac{\lambda(u)}{N} e^{h(u)0} du = c_1 \tag{9}$$

where c_1 is an arbitrary constant and the function $h : [0, \infty) \to [0, \infty$ is such that for all non-negative x,

$$h(x) = \int_0^x \left[\frac{\lambda(s)}{N} + \mu(s)\right]^0 ds \tag{10}$$

For later reference, we now state and prove the following technical result.

Box 2.

$$\frac{\partial G(z,t)}{\partial t} = \sum_k \frac{dP_k(t)}{dt} =$$

$$-\sum_k \left[\frac{N-k}{N}\lambda(t) + k\mu(t)\right]P_k(t)z^k + \lambda(t)\sum_k \frac{N-k+1}{N}P_{k-1}(t)z^k + \mu(t)\sum_k (k+1)P_{k+1}(t)z^k$$

$$= -\lambda(t)\sum_k \cdot P_k(t)z^k - z\mu(t)\sum_k \cdot kP_k(t)z^{k-1} + z\lambda(t)\sum_k P_{k-1}(t)z^{k-1} + \mu(t)\sum_k (k+1)P_{k+1}(t)z^k$$

$$= -\lambda(t)G(z,t) + \left[\frac{\lambda(t)}{N} - \mu(t)\right]z\frac{\partial G(z,t)}{\partial z} + \lambda(t)zG(z,t) - \frac{\lambda(t)}{N}z^2\frac{\partial G(z,t)}{\partial z} + \mu(t)\frac{\partial G(z,t)}{\partial z}$$

$$-(z-1)\left[\frac{\lambda(t)}{N}z + \mu(t)\right]\frac{\partial G(z,t)}{\partial z} + \lambda(t)(z-1)G(z,t)$$

Thus, we have obtained the partial differential equation

$$\frac{\partial G(z,t)}{\partial t} + (z-1)\left[\frac{\lambda(t)}{N} + \mu(t)\right]\frac{\partial G(z,t)}{\partial z} = \lambda(t)(z-1)G(z,t) \qquad (6)$$

$$c_1 = -1 + \frac{z}{z-1}e^{h(t)} - \int_0^t \mu(u)e^{h(u)0}du \qquad (11)$$

$$\int_0^t \left[\frac{\lambda(u)}{N} + \mu(u)\right]e^{h(u)0}du = e^{h(t)} - 1$$

By simple manipulations, (9) yields

which is implied by the Fundamental Theorem of Calculus. Thus (11) holds, as claimed.

Returning to the auxiliary equations (7), we observe that by selecting the multiplicands x_1, x_2, x_3 as

$$c_1 = \frac{e^{h(t)}}{z-1} + \int_0^t \frac{\lambda(u)}{N}e^{h(u)0}du$$

$$= \frac{e^{h(t)}}{z-1} + \int_0^t \left[\frac{\lambda(u)}{N} + \mu(u)\right]e^{h(u)0}du - \int_0^t \mu(u)e^{h(u)0}du$$

$$x_1 = -(z-G)\left[\frac{\lambda(t)}{N} + \mu(t)\right]$$

$$= \frac{e^{h(t)}}{z-1} + e^{h(t)} - 1 - \int_0^t \mu(u)e^{h(u)0}du$$

$$x_2 = G$$

$$= -1 + \frac{z}{z-1}e^{h(t)} - \int_0^t \mu(u)e^{h(u)0}du$$

$$x_3 = -\frac{z-1}{N}$$

the ratio

where we have used the fact that

$$R = \frac{x_1{}^0 dt + x_2{}^0 dz + x_3{}^0 dG}{x_1 + x_2(z-1)\left[-\frac{\lambda(t)}{N}z + \mu(t)\right] + x_3(z-1)\lambda(t)G}$$

$$= \frac{-\left[\frac{\lambda(t)}{N} + \mu(t)\right]^0 dt + \frac{{}^0 dz}{z-1} - \frac{{}^0 dG}{NG}}{0}$$

implying that

$$-\int_0^t \left[\frac{\lambda(u)}{N} + \mu(u)\right]^0 du + 1n(z-1) - 1nG\frac{1}{N} = Cons\tan t$$

which, in turn, yields

$$-ht + 1n\frac{z-1}{G(z,t)\frac{1}{n}} = cons\tan t$$

whereupon, by exponentiation, we obtain

$$\exp\left[-h(t) + 1n\frac{z-1}{G(z,t)\frac{1}{N}}\right] = \frac{z-1}{G(z,t)\frac{1}{N}}e^{-h(t)}$$

(12)

$$= c_2$$

(13)

for some constannt. c_2 The two constants c_1 and c_2 are related by

$$c_2 = \psi\left[c_1\right]$$

(14)

where Ψ is an arbitrary function.

As it turns out, (12), (14), along with condition $G(z,0) = z^n 0$ can be used to determine Ψ. For this purpose, we first find an explicit closed form for Ψ. It is easy to confirm that for an arbitrary real x,

$$\psi[x] = \frac{1}{x}\left[\frac{x}{x+1}\right]^{\frac{n_0}{N}}$$

(15)

Now, (9), (11), (12) and (15), combined, allow us to write (see Box 8)

$$G(z,t) = (z-1)^N e^{-Nh(t)}(1+c_1)^{n_0} c_1^{N-n_0}$$

$$= \left[e^{-h(t)}(z-1)(1+c_1)\right]^{n_0}\left[e^{-h(t)}(z-1)c_1\right]^{N-n_0}$$

$$= \left[z(1 - e^{-h(t)}\int_0^t \mu(u)e^{h(u)0}du) + e^{-h(t)}\int_0^t \mu(u)e^{h(u)0}du\right]^{n_0}$$

(16)

In spite of its complexity, (16) reveals a whole cell about the structure of the process $\{X(t)\,|\,t \geq 0\}$. To see this, observe that $G(z,t)$ is the product of the following two factors:

$$\left[z(1 - e^{-h(t)}\int_0^t \mu(u)e^{h(u)0}du) + e^{-ht}\int_0^t \mu(u)e^{h(u)0}du\right]^{n_0}$$

Box 8.

$$= \left[z(1 - e^{-h(t)}(1 + \int_0^t \mu(t)e^{h(u)0}du)) + e^{-h(t)}(1 + \int_0^t \mu(t)e^{h(u)0}du)\right]^{N-n_0}$$

(17)

which is the probability generating function of a binomial random variable with parameter n_0 and success probability

$$p(t) = 1 - e^{-h(t)} \int_0^t \mu(u)e^{h(u)0}du; \qquad (18)$$

$$\left[ze^{-h(t)} \int_0^t \frac{\lambda(u)}{N} e^{h(u)0}du + (1 - e^{-h(t)} \int_0^t \frac{\lambda(u)}{N} e^{h(u)0}du) \right]^{N-n_0}$$

which is the probability generating function of a binomial random variable with parameter $N - n_0$ and success probability

$$q(t) = e^{-h(t)} \int_0^t \frac{\lambda(u)}{N} e^{h(u)0}du \qquad (19)$$

Define two additional counting processes

- $\{R(t) \mid t \geq 0\}$ that keeps track of the number of the n_0 cars present at time $t=0$ that are still in the cell at time t; it is clear that the success probability

  $p(t) = 1 - e^{-h(t)} \int_0^t \mu(u)e^{h(u)0}du$ is precise-

  ly the probability that a generic such car is still in the cell at time t;

- $\{S(t) \mid t \geq 0\}$ that keeps track of the number of cars in the cell at time t that were not in the cell at time $t=0$; this is also a binomial process with parameters $N - n_0$ and success probability

$$e^{-h(t)} \int_0^t \frac{\lambda(u)}{N} e^{h(u)0}du$$

It is immediate that for all t, $R(t)$ and $S(t)$ are independent random variables. Further, the ex-

pression of $G(z,t)$ as a product implies that for all $t \geq 0$, $N(t)$ is the convolution of $R(t)$ and $R(t)$ and so

$$X(t) = R(t) + S(t). \qquad (20)$$

Next, we turn to the task of computing a closed form for the expected number, $E[X(t)]$, of cars in the cell at time t and its variance $Var[X(t)]$. Observe that by (20) and the linearity of expectation we can write the following equations (see Box 9-10).

$$E\big[X(t)\big] = E\big[R(t)\big] + E\big[S(t)\big]$$

$$= n_0 e^{-h(t)} + e^{-h(t)} \int_0^t \lambda(u)e^{h(u)0}du$$

$$= e^{-h(t)} \left[n_0 + \int_0^t \lambda(u)e^{h(u)0}du \right] \qquad (21)$$

Similarly, since as noted for every $t>0$, the random variables $R(t)$ and $S(t)$ are independent, and thus, uncorrelated, we can write

$$Var\big[X(t)\big] = Var\big[R(t)\big] + Var\big[S(t)\big]$$

$$= n_0 p(t)\big[1 - p(t)\big] + \Lambda(t)$$

$$= n_0 p(t)\big[1 - p(t)\big] + \frac{\int_0^1 \lambda(u)e \int_0^u \mu(s)^0 ds^0 du}{e \int_0^t \mu(u)^0 du}$$

$$= p(t)\left[n_0 \big[1 - p(t)\big] + \int_0^t \lambda(u)e \int_0^u \mu(s)^0 ds^0 du \right] \qquad (22)$$

Box 9.

$$= n_0(1 - e^{-h(t)} \int_0^t \mu(u)e^{h(u)0}du) + (N - n_0)e^{-h(t)} \int_0^t \frac{\lambda(u)}{N} e^{h(u)0}du$$

Box 10.

$$n_0 + Ne^{-h(t)} \int_0^t \frac{\lambda(u)}{N} e^{h(u)0}du - n_0e^{-h(t)} \int_0^t \left[\frac{\lambda(u)}{N} + \mu(u)\right]e^{h(u)0}du$$

7.4 Pseudonym Collision

Although we assume that the PSs and sub-PSs are generally synchronized, there may occasionally have situations (e.g. network congestion) that will cause the delays of updating pseudonyms. Thereafter, there will have a certain probability that the pseudonyms that are collided. We are interested to check the probability of the collision of pseudonyms in the worst cases. In each cell, the total number of pseudonyms is n in a pool. Each vehicle is given k pseudonyms from the cell CA. Given a vehicle a, define event c as another randomly selected vehicle b does not adopt any pseudonyms that the vehicle a does, i.e. no two vehicles share the same set of pseudonyms. We are interested in the probability $P(c)$.

$$P(c) = \frac{C_{n-k}^k}{C_k^n}$$

$$= \frac{(n-k)!^2}{n!(n-2k)!}$$

According to Stirling's approximation,

$$n! \approx \sqrt{2\pi(n^{n+0.5}e^{-n})}$$

We read

$$P(c) \approx \frac{(n-k)^{2n-2k+1}e^{-2n+2k}}{n^{n+0.5}e^{-n}(n-2k)^{n-2k+0.5}e^{-n+2k}}$$

$$= \frac{(1-\frac{k}{n})^{2(n-k+0.5)}}{(1-\frac{2k}{n})^{n-2k+0.5}}$$

When $x \to 0$, $1 - x \approx e^{-x}$. Since $n \gg k$, we write

$$= \frac{(1-\frac{k}{n})^{2(n-k+0.5)}}{(1-\frac{2k}{n})^{n-2k+0.5}}$$

8. SIMULATION RESULTS

In this section we evaluate the analytical results derived in Section 7.2 by comparing the theoretical predictions with numerical results. The numerical results were obtained by mathematically simulating the cell. We assume the capacity of the cell is fairly large (e.g., 1000), even though it is considered unbounded in the analytical derivations.

8.1 Simulation Setup

We assumed that, at the beginning of the simulation, i.e., at time $t=0$, there were $n_0 = 500$ vehicles in the cell. The vehicles were assumed to arrive into and and depart from the cell at certain time-varying rates. To evaluate the analytical results, we considered three scenarios, as described next:

- **Scenario 1:** the first set of results was designed for *constant* arrival rate and departure rates. For illustration purposes, we have chosen $\lambda=800$ and $\mu=2$;
- **Scenario 2:** the second set of results was designed for time-dependent arrival and departure rates but such that limit $\lim_{t \to \infty} \frac{\lambda(t)}{\mu(t)}$ does not exist;
- **Scenario 3:** the third set of results was designed for time-dependent arrival and departure rates such that limit $\lim_{t \to \infty} \frac{\lambda(t)}{\mu(t)}$ exists.

To set the stage for explaining our design decisions, imagine a typical long-term cell of a mid-size cell. A glance at the flight arrivals and departure schedule will convince us, first, that the flight arrival and departure rates are time-dependent stochastic phenomena; and, second, that flights depart and arrive on a 24-hour periodic schedule. It is, consequently, clear the car arrival and departure rates from the cell(s) will mirror fairly closely the flight departure and arrival rates. It follows that the car arrival and departure rates into/from the long-term cell and departure rates should also periodic functions of time.

While many periodic functions could possibly be employed, we have decided to adopt as generic arrival and departure rates

$$\lambda(t)=a+b\sin\Theta(t) \qquad (23)$$

and

$$\mu(t)=c+d\sin\Theta(t). \qquad (24)$$

where a, b, c, d are constants. Observe that b and d control the fluctuation of the arrival and departure rates, respectively. Indeed, from (23) it is clear that the larger b, the larger the fluctuation of $\lambda(t)$ as a function of time. Similarly for d. Having settled on this choice, there were two further problems that needed attention. The first was the most appropriate simulation granularity: after some trials we have decided that the most appropriate time unit model the car arrival and departure is one hour. With this is mind, for arbitrary $t \geq 0$, we have decided to take. $\Theta(t) = \frac{\pi t}{12}$

Assuming the average the number of pseudonyms of a mid-size cell to be between 400 and 500, we have chosen the constants $a=1300, b=500, c=3, d=1$. With this in mind, the arrival and departure rates used in Scenario 2 were

$$\lambda(t) = 1300 + 5\sin(\frac{\pi t}{12})$$

and the departure-rate of vehicles is

$$\mu(t) = 3 + 1\sin(\frac{\pi t}{12})$$

It is easy to confirm that, in this case, the limit $\lim_{t \to \infty} \frac{\lambda(t)}{\mu(t)}$ does not exist.

For Scenario 3, we adopted quasi-periodic time-dependent arrival and departure rates $\lambda(t)$ and $\mu(t)$, with a period close to 24 hours, in such a way that the limit $\lim_{t \to \infty} \frac{\lambda(t)}{\mu(t)}$ existed. Again many quasi-periodic functions could possibly be employed. But we have decided to adopt as generic arrival and departure rates as

$$\lambda(t) = 800 + 400\left[1 + 2\exp(-0.3t)\right]\sin(\frac{\pi t}{12})$$

and

$$\mu(t) = 2 + \left[1 + \exp(-0.2t)\right]\sin(\frac{\pi t}{12})$$

8.2 Detailed Discussion of Simulation Results

We begin by investigating the expected number $E[N(t)]$ of cars in the cell. The comparisons between the analytical results and the numerical results have been performed for the above three scenarios. For each scenario, we set the simulation time to 60 hours and we computed the expected number of existing vehicles at time t. Figure 9(a) shows $E[N(t)]$ plotted against time in Scenario 1 with arrival rate $\lambda=800$ and the departure rate $\mu=2$. We notice that $E[N(t)]$ stabilizes at $\frac{\lambda}{\mu} = 400$. In fact, even though the initial number of vehicles was 500, $E[N(t)]$ dropped sharply to 400 to within 3 hours into the simulation. This is because the vehicles initially existing have all left the cell in the first 3 hours. The cell becomes stabilized after that, due chiefly to the constant arrival and departure rates.

The effect of the initial conditions on $E[N(t)]$ is similar in Scenarios 2 and 3: due to the departure of the initially existing vehicles, the expected number of existing vehicles is dropping sharply as illustrated in Figures 9(b) and 9(c). However, once the effect of the initial conditions has worn off, Scenarios 2 and 3 are vastly different. As expected, in Scenario 2 we see a periodic fluctuation of the expected number of existing vehicles as shown in Figure 9(b). In addition,

Figure 9(b) clearly shows, as predicted by our analytical results, that $E[N(t)]$ is bounded by 400 and 450 after $t>3$. In the case of Scenario 3, Figure 9(c) shows, as expected, that in the long-run $E[N(t)]$ settles down to a constant value near the limit $\lim\limits_{t \to \infty} \dfrac{\lambda(t)}{\mu(t)}$. Before stabilization, fluctuating values are shown but fluctuation becomes weaker as t increases. The duration of the fluctuation actually depends on the exponential parameter. The exponential component of arrival rate in this result is $\exp(-0.3t)$ and the one of departure rate is $\exp(-0.2t)$. The bigger values of the exponential components are, the faster the system stabilizes.

Next, we turned our attention to evaluating $Var[N(t)]$ versus time. Three sets of comparisons (corresponding to the three scenarios discussed in Subsection 8.1) between the analytical results and the numerical results have been performed. For each of them, the simulation time t was 60 hours and, as before, the number of the initial existing vehicles is $n_0 = 500$. Figure 10(a) shows that in Scenario 1, $Var[N(t)]$ stabilizes to a constant value after fluctuation in the first few hours. Fluctuation in the first few hours is caused by the departure of the initially existing vehicles, explained earlier. As expected, the variance of the expected number of existing vehicles settles down to $\dfrac{\lambda}{\mu}$, i.e., 400 when $t>3$.

By contrast, Figure 10(b) captures the behavior of $Var[N(t)]$ in Scenario 2 where the limit $\lim\limits_{t \to \infty} \dfrac{\lambda(t)}{\mu(t)}$ does not exist. Just as predicted by our analytical derivations, Figure 10(b) shows that $Var[N(t)]$ fluctuates with a period of 24 hours. In addition, a noticeable variance range $[400, 450]$ can be read from Figure 10(b).

The situation is vastly different in Scenario 3 as illustrated in Figure 10(c). Here, $Var[N(t)]$ stabilizes at 400 after $t>25$ hours of simulation.

Figure 9. The expected the number of pseudonyms vs time.(Yan et al., 2013; Arif et al., 2012).

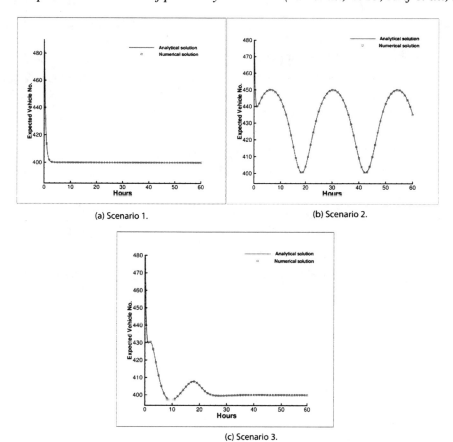

(a) Scenario 1.

(b) Scenario 2.

(c) Scenario 3.

The probability of the departure of initially existing vehicles and the exponential component in the arrival rate and departure rate can affect the pattern of the unstable fluctuation.

It is observed that the variance is stabilized at 400 for both Figure 10(a) and 10(c) and at a range [400, 450] in Figure 10(b). These values are rather large, considering that the expected number of existing vehicles $E[N(t)]$ is also 400. Therefore, we need to show the in spite of the large variance of $N(t)$, the probability that the number of vehicles in the cell is low is negligeable. We have decided to investigate, experimentally, $Pr[\{N(t)<400\}]$ and $Pr[\{N(t)<300\}]$. Three sets of comparisons (one for each scenario) have been performed. For each set of comparison, we adopt the same simulation settings as the previous ones and compute the probability values. Figure 11(a) shows the probability $Pr[\{N(t)<400\}]$ in the case of Scenario 1. The probability $Pr[\{N(t)<400\}]$ tends to 0.5 and $Pr[\{N(t)<300\}]$ tends to be 0 after an initial unstable fluctuation induced by the initial conditions. In Scenario 2, where both arrival rate and departure rates are periodical function of time and the limit $\lim_{t \to \infty} \dfrac{\lambda(t)}{\mu(t)}$ does not exist, we expect to see the periodical probability values. Figure 11(b) shows, as expected, that the probability $Pr[\{N(t)<400\}]$ is periodical and bounded by [0, 0.5]. The probability $Pr[\{N(t)<300\}]$ remains close to 0.

In the case of Scenario 3, Figure 11(c) shows that, as expected, the probability $Pr[\{N(t)<400\}]$ stabilizes at 0.5 after a certain fluctuation due mostly to the effect of initial conditions. The duration of the fluctuation is controlled by the initially existing vehicles and by exponential components in the arrival and departure rates.

In summary, the probability of the event that there are at least 300 vehicles in the cell is 100%. In other words, it is guaranteed that there are at least 300 vehicles existing in the cell at any time for our utilization.

To test the clustering of the probability mass around $E[N(t)]$, we have performed a three-dimensional plots of $P_k(t)$, i.e. $Pr[\{N(t)<k\}]$, time t and the number of existing vehicles k versus time. The goal was to find a direct view of rela-

tionships of the probability $P_k(t)$ at time t that there are k vehicles existing in the cell. We varied both time t and the number k of existing vehicles and calculate the probability values. Two cases have been investigated: Scenario 2 and Scenario 3. Figure 12 shows a shaded surface and as a contour plot of both cases. It clearly shows that in Scenario 2, the probability varies periodically with time t and k. By contrast, Figure 12(b) shows, as expected, that in Scenario 3 the probability eventually stabilizes after some initial fluctuation. To see better these trends, we also plotted the logarithm of the probability at various times t and

Figure 10. The variance of the the number of pseudonyms vs time. (Yan et al., 2013; Arif et al., 2012).

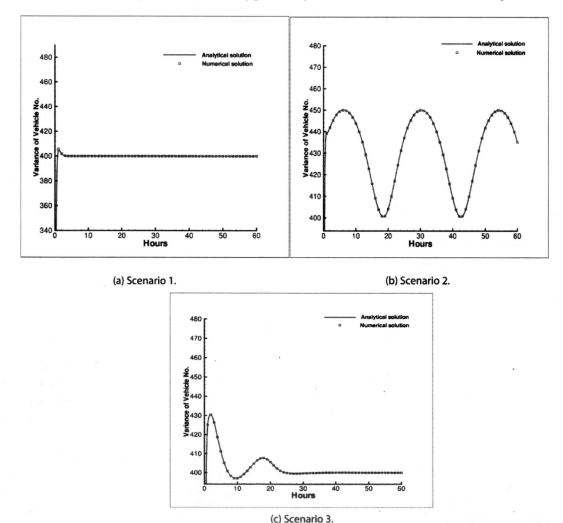

(a) Scenario 1.

(b) Scenario 2.

(c) Scenario 3.

the number of existing vehicles k. Figure 13(a) shows these results in the case of Scenario 2, while Figure 13(b) shows the logarithm of the probability at various times in the case of Scenario 3.

We are interested of the expected number of pseudonyms that the cell server will receive. The numerical results were obtained by mathematically simulating the cell. We assume the capacity of the cell is fairly large (e.g., 4000).We assumed that, at the beginning of the simulation, i.e., at time t=0, there were $n_0 = 500$ vehicles in the cell. The vehicles were assumed to arrive into and depart from the cell at certain time-varying rates. To evaluate the analytical results, we considered the following scenario: normal traffic conditions are designed with time-dependent arrival and departure rates but the limit $\lim\limits_{t \to \infty} \dfrac{\lambda(t)}{\mu(t)}$ does not exist.

To set the stage for explaining our design decisions, imagine a typical cell of a city. Obviously, traffic arrival and departure rates are time-dependent stochastic phenomena; and, second, the vehicles depart and arrive on a week periodic schedule for Scenario 1 and 2 according to the statistic data (Federal Highway Administration, 2012).

With this in mind, the arrival and departure rates used in this simulation scenario were

$\lambda(t)$=347.19+80.90*sin(0.8913t−2.8913)

and

$\mu(t)$=50.48+0.25sin(0.8913t−2.8913).

It is easy to confirm that, in this case, the limit $\lim\limits_{t \to \infty} \dfrac{\lambda(t)}{\mu(t)}$ does not exist.

8.3 Detailed Discussion of Simulation Results

The value of the initial conditions on P_j is small: the arrivals of the initially pseudonym requests will need a while to build up, as illustrated in Figures 14 and 15. However, once the effect of the initial conditions has worn off, simulation 1, 2 and 3 are stabilized. As expected, in simulations we see a periodic fluctuation of the probability P_j of pseudonym requests as shown in Figure 14, 15, and 16. In addition, Figure 14 clearly shows that P_j is bounded by 0 and 0.12. In the case of Scenario 2, Figure 15 shows, as expected, that the value of j significantly affect the value of P_j. Figure 16, compared with Figure 15, shows that the value of N does not significantly affect the value of P_j.

In addition, we were interested to investigate the relationship among three variables: N, t, and P_j. We varied the value of N from 10 to 500 and the value of t from 0 to 24 which stands for one day. The result, shown in Figure 17, clearly presents periodic fluctuation and stabilized the vales of P_j.

8.4 Network Simulation

We were interested to investigate the network performance of our proposed method. We first applied SUMO (Krajzewicz et al., 2002) to generate a mobility trace file and then fed the trace file to NS-2 (ns-, 2001) where the corresponding wireless network was simulated. We chose SUMO and NS-2.30 not only because they are publicly available, but also because they are both well maintained and well accepted in the research community. We assumed a 700m x 700m area of city streets to represent a cell, shown in Figure 18. The pseudonym server is placed at the center (350m, 350m) of the cell. Vehicles entered the

Figure 11. The probability Pr[N(t)].(Yan et al., 2013; Arif et al., 2012).

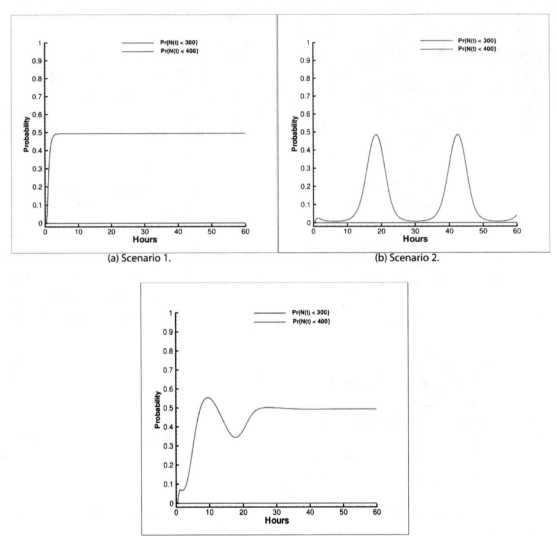

(a) Scenario 1. (b) Scenario 2.

(c) Scenario 3.

Figure 12. The number of existing vehicles k vs time t vs Pr[N(t)]. (Yan et al., 2013; Arif et al., 2012).

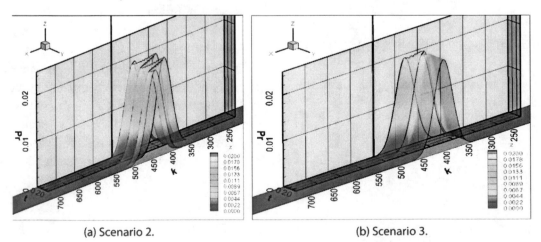

(a) Scenario 2. (b) Scenario 3.

Figure 13. The number of existing vehicles k vs time t vs lnPr[N(t)].(Yan et al., 2013; Arif et al., 2012).

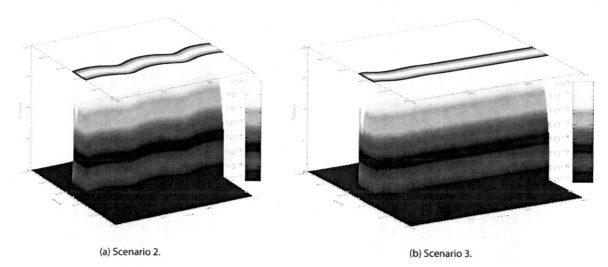

(a) Scenario 2.   (b) Scenario 3.

cell from the border streets and then randomly moved on streets in the cell.

We applied SUMO random traffic generator to choose a path between source and destination. We initially placed 150 vehicles. Vehicles make random turning decisions at each intersection. The speed limits on the streets range from 5 to 20 m/s (11-45 mile per hour), and the vehicles are constrained by the speed limit. Traffic lights are randomly simulated as well. At time t, a street can be green light or red. SUMO generates a mobility trace file that can be imported into NS-2. Then, NS-2 is executed and nodes in NS-2 follow the nodes in SUMO respectively. For the car following model, we used the Krauβ Model. Out of the initial 150 vehicles in the simulation, some of them are chosen (at random) as marked cars which will send pseudonym request randomly. The pseudonym server served as a data sink, i.e. service provider. There are 31 traffic flows, each corresponding to a street. Each traffic flow sends UDP packets (512 bytes for each packet).

We compared two scenarios. The first scenario sets the transmission range (TR) at 350m for each car, while the second scenario sets the transmission range as 700m for each car. The antenna height, the CSThresh and RXThresh values in NS-2 can

be configured to determine the communication range. Packets are routed from source to destination if there is no direct route. Each vehicle will buffer packets (in a finite queue) until a route has been found to the destination.

8.4.1 The Macroscopic Perspective

The average throughput of each street requests is of interest in network simulations. We varied the transmission range (TR) in three scenarios: 233 meters, 350 meters and 700 meters. For each scenario, we collected the throughput of each traffic flow and then computed the average throughput. Each traffic flow stands for an individual street. The result is shown in Figure 19. As expected, the throughput value of 700m TR is about 50% higher than for a TR of 350m. This is because cars in the scenario two can directly communicate with the pseudonym server but the cars in the scenario one will need to relay request to the pseudonym server when the direct connection is unavailable. It is interesting to notice that the throughput of 233m TR is similar to the one of 350m TR. This is because as long as relay is needed, two-hop communication does not make significant difference to three-hop communication. According

Figure 14. Result of simulation 1.(Yan et al., 2013; Arif et al., 2012).

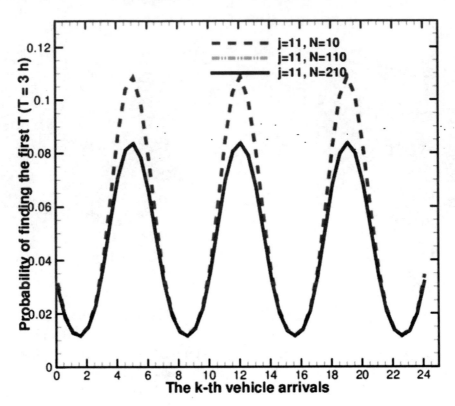

Figure 15. Result of simulation 2.(Yan et al., 2013; Arif et al., 2012).

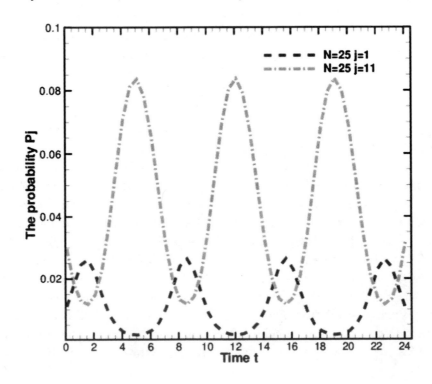

Figure 16. Result of simulation 3.(Yan et al., 2013; Arif et al., 2012).

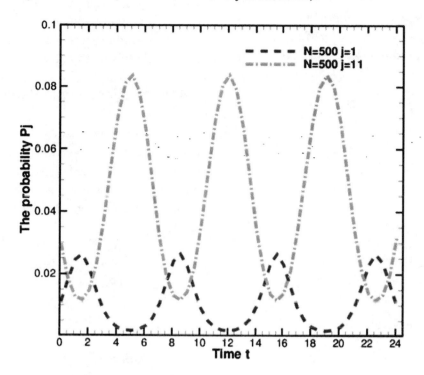

Figure 17. Result of simulation 4.(Yan et al., 2013; Arif et al., 2012).

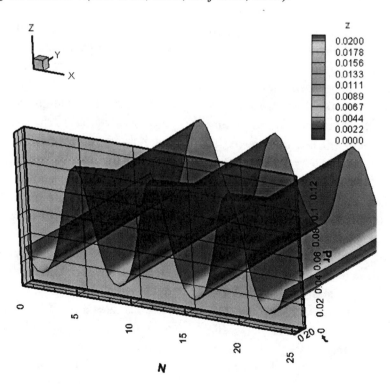

Figure 18. Illustrating our assumed map topology. The points (a,b,c,d,e) are the initial major entries of traffic. The green and red colored edges show the traffic lights at time t.(Yan et al., 2013; Arif et al., 2012).

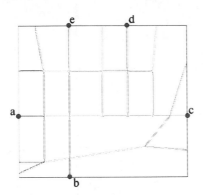

to Figure 19, the peak value of request, about 1.1 request per second, i.e. 3960 request per hour, closely matches the 4000 peak value.

We then computed the average loss rate of requests for every street and show the results in Figure 20. Figure 20 shows that the drop rate in the scenario one $TR=350m$ fluctuates from 0.2 to 0.9. This high loss rate in the worst case is because vehicles moving to the borders of the map need intermediate vehicle to relay packets and the relay vehicles are not always available. Once vehicles move to the center of the map, more routing paths are available, and the loss rate begins to decrease. Figure 20 shows that the case $TR=700m$ is better than the case $TR=350m$ and the case $TR=233m$ in terms of drop rate.

We were also interested in the request response delays. The packet response delays of each flow were collected and computed. The result is shown in Figure 21. As expected, the delay values of requests of the case $TR=233m$ and the case $TR=350m$ are slightly larger than the case $TR=700m$. The reason is obviously because of the unreliable vehicular networks communication. The more hops in communication, the bigger delay values

will be. In our proposed scheme, our assumption that the communication can directly reach to the cell shows both theoretical value and empirical meaning in this simulation.

8.4.2 The Microscopic Perspective

We also presented results from a microscopic perspective. One street was randomly selected to display more detailed network communication information. We investigated the jitter of requests in the selected street. The definition of jitter is as follows:

1. Jitter 1: $jitter(i+1)=jitter(i)+[|(R(i+1)-S(i+1))-(R(i)-S(i))|-jitter(i)]/16$
2. Jitter 2: $jitter(i+1)=jitter(i)+[|(R(i+1)-R(i))-(R(i)-R(i-1))|-jitter(i)]/16$

where $jitter(i)$ is the jitter value of packet 'i'; $S(i)$ is the time at which packet 'i' was transmitted from the sender; $R(i)$ is the time at which packet 'i' was received by the destination. The results of both Jitter 1 and 2 were collected and computed, as shown in Figures 22(a) and 22(b). As expected, the jitter values (both Jitter 1 and 2) shows that the jitter in scenarios $TR=233m$ and $TR=350m$ has a significantly larger amplitude and fluctuation than the one in scenario $TR=700m$. The reason lies in the mobility of vehicles. It is fairly interesting to note that the jitter values are higher at the middle of the day and the end of the day. For middle of day, more cars are on street and the wireless channels become more crowded and more likely to collide. So the jitter values increase. Towards the end of the day, the population of vehicles is greatly decreased. Vehicles in scenario one could fail to connect the pseudonym server because no intermediate cars can be used as communication relay nodes. Comparing Figure 22(a) and Figure 22(b), we note that jitter values will be different if the jitter is defined differently.

Figure 19. Throughput of server.(Yan et al., 2013; Arif et al., 2012).

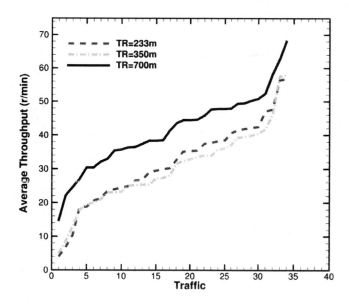

Figure 20. Drop rate of packets.(Yan et al., 2013; Arif et al., 2012).

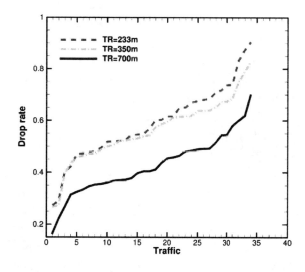

9. CONCLUDING REMARKS AND DIRECTIONS FOR FUTURE WORK

To accommodate increasing demand from the driving public, car and truck manufacturers are offering more and more sophisticated on-board devices, including powerful computers, a large array of sensors, radar devices, cameras, and wireless transceivers. The powerful on-board devices support new applications, including location-specific services, on-line gaming, delivering multimedia content and various forms of mobile infotainment made possible by the emergence, in the past decade, of vehicular networks. However,

Figure 21. Delay of requests.(Yan et al., 2013; Arif et al., 2012).

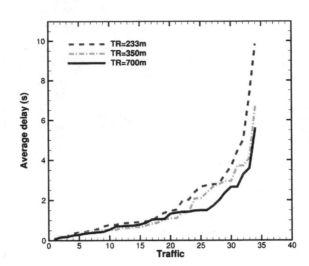

the increased Internet presence that enables the above applications invites various forms of privacy attacks. Invariably, these privacy attacks exploit the various forms of correlation that exist between the identity of a vehicle and that of its driver.

Virtually all published papers in the recent literature ignore the issues of scalability and robustness in the context of privacy protection. In this work we took a non-trivial step towards providing a robust and scalable solution to privacy protection in vehicular networks. To promote scalability and robustness we employ two strategies. First, we viewed vehicular networks as consisting of non-overlapping subnetworks each local to a geographic area referred to as a cell. Second, instead of issuing pseudonyms to vehicles proactively (as virtually all existing schemes do) we issue pseudonyms only to those vehicles that request them. This strategy is suggested by the fact that, in a typical scenario, only a fraction of the vehicles in an area will engage in communication with other vehicles and/or with the infrastructure and, therefore, do not need pseudonyms. Our second main contribution was to model analytically the time-varying request for pseudonyms in a given cell. This is important for capacity planning purposes since it allows managers to predict the probability that a given number of

pseudonyms will be required at a certain time as well as the expected number of pseudonyms in use in a cell at a certain time. Empirical results obtained by detailed simulation confirmed the accuracy of our analytical predictions.

It is important to point out that there are some special cases where our model does not apply. One example is that of special events in a cell, such as super-bowl of football game, air show, etc., will create exceptional arrival rates and departure rates when compared to normal traffic conditions in the cell. During these special events, the traffic patterns in the cell are very different from normal traffic conditions. However, since these events are planned for carefully and well ahead of time the pseudonym server can be prepared for the extra load imposed by these events. From an engineering perspective, we can request full capacity of pseudonyms and divide the involving cells into sub-cells or microcells. Each of them has full capacity of pseudonyms. The cell size can be decreased to a few hundred meters so that the server can feed each vehicle a pseudonym. Although it can be expensive, technically, it can be handled. However, while interesting and challenging in its own right, this aspect is well beyond the scope of the chapter and will be looked at in future work.

Figure 22. Jitters from a street.(Yan et al., 2013; Arif et al., 2012).

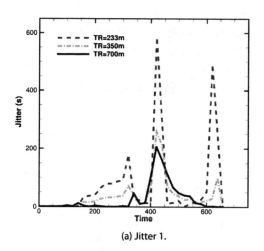

(a) Jitter 1.

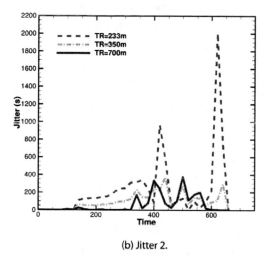

(b) Jitter 2.

As future work, we propose to combine the proposed privacy scheme with security and communication systems. In addition, the analytical model can be extended to more practical cases. For example some events such as football game will cause a large amount of vehicles parked in a cell and they will need to request pseudonyms at the same time when the game is over. Another example, vehicle accidents often result traffic arrival rate change. We will need to study how to work with the sudden traffic events.

REFERENCES

Arapinis, M., Chothia, T., Ritter, E., & Ryan, M. (2010). Analysing unlinkability and anonymity using the applied pi calculus. In *Proceedings of CSF*, (pp. 107–121). CSF.

Arif, S., Olariu, S., Wang, J., Yan, G., Yang, W., & Khalil, I. (2012). Datacenter at the airport: Reasoning about time-dependent parking lot occupancy. *IEEE Transactions on Parallel and Distributed Systems*, 99.

Blanchet, B., Abadi, M., & Fournet, C. (2008). Automated verification of selected equivalences for security protocols. *Journal of Logic and Algebraic Programming*, 75(1), 3–51. doi:10.1016/j.jlap.2007.06.002.

Brusò, M., Chatzikokolakis, K., & den Hartog, J. (2010). Formal verification of privacy for rfid systems. In *Proceedings of CSF*, (pp. 75–88). CSF.

Choi, J. Y., Golle, P., & Jakobsson, M. (2006). Tamper-evident digital signatures: Protecting certification authorities against malware. In *Proceedings of the IEEE International Symposium on Dependable, Autonomic and Secure Computing (DASC)*, (pp. 37–44). IEEE.

Dahl, M., Delaune, S., & Steel, G. (2010). Formal analysis of privacy for vehicular mix-zones. In *Proceedings of the 15th European Conference on Research in Computer Security* (ESORICS'10), (pp. 55–70). ESORICS.

Delaune, S., Kremer, S., & Ryan, M. (2010). Verifying privacy-type properties of electronic voting protocols: A taster. In *Towards Trustworthy Elections* (pp. 289–309). Academic Press. doi:10.1007/978-3-642-12980-3_18.

Dok, H., Fu, H., Echevarria, R., & Weerasinghe, H. (2010). Privacy issues of vehicular ad-hoc networks. *International Journal of Future Generation Communication and Networking*, 3(1), 17–32.

Federal Highway Administration. (2012). *Traffic congestion and reliability: Trends and advanced strategies for congestion mitigation.* Retrieved from http://www.ops.fhwa.dot.gov/congestion_report/chapter2.htm

Guo, J., Baugh, J. P., & Wang, S. (2007). A group signature based secure and privacy-preserving vehicular communication framework. In *Proceedings of the 2007 Mobile Networking for Vehicular Environments.* IEEE.

Huang, D., Misra, S., Xue, G., & Verma, M. (2011). Pacp: An efficient pseudonymous authentication based conditional privacy protocol for vanets. *IEEE Transactions on Intelligent Transportations*, *12*(3), 736–746. doi:10.1109/TITS.2011.2156790.

Hubaux, J.-P., Capkun, S., & Luo, J. (2004). The security and privacy of smart vehicles. *IEEE Security and Privacy Magazine*, *2*(3), 49–55. doi:10.1109/MSP.2004.26.

Krajzewicz, D., Hertkorn, G., Rössel, C., & Wagner, P. (2002). SUMO (simulation of urban mobility) — An open-source traffic simulation. In M. Al-Akaidi (Ed.), *MESM 2002, 4th Middle East Symposium on Simulation and Modelling*, (pp. 183–187). Erlangen, Germany: IEEE.

Le, Z., Ouyang, Y., Chen, G., & Makedon, F. (2011). Dynamic mix zone: Location data sanitizing in assisted environments. *Universal Access in the Information Society*, *10*(2), 195–205. doi:10.1007/s10209-010-0198-4.

Li, L., Song, J., Wang, F.-Y., Niehsen, W., & Zheng, N. (2005). New developments and research trends for intelligent vehicles. *IEEE Intelligent Systems*, *20*(4), 10–14. doi:10.1109/MIS.2005.73.

Lin, X., Lu, R., Liang, X., & Shen, X. (2011). Stap: A social-tier-assisted packet forwarding protocol for achieving receiver-location privacy preservation in vanets. In *Proceedings of the 30th IEEE International Conference on Computer Communications, Joint Conference of the IEEE Computer and Communications Societies*, (pp. 2147–2155). IEEE.

Lu, H., & Poellabauer, C. (2010). Balancing broadcast reliability and transmission range in vanets. *SIGMOBILE Mob. Comput. Commun. Rev.*, *14*(4), 25–27. doi:10.1145/1942268.1942278.

Lu, R., Lin, X., Liang, X., & Shen, X. S. (2012a). A dynamic privacy-preserving key management scheme for location-based services in vanets. *IEEE Transactions on Intelligent Transportation Systems*, *13*(1), 127–139. doi:10.1109/TITS.2011.2164068.

Lu, R., Lin, X., Luan, T., Liang, X., Li, X., Chen, L., & Shen, X. (2012b). Prefilter: An efficient privacy-preserving relay filtering scheme for delay tolerant networks. In *Proceedings of the 31th IEEE International Conference on Computer Communications, Joint Conference of the IEEE Computer and Communications Societies.* IEEE.

Lu, R., Lin, X., & Shen, X. (2010). Spring: A social-based privacy-preserving packet forwarding protocol for vehicular delay tolerant networks. In *Proceedings of the 29th IEEE International Conference on Computer Communications, Joint Conference of the IEEE Computer and Communications Societies*, (pp. 632–640). IEEE.

Lu, R., Lin, X., Zhu, H., Ho, P.-H., & Shen, X. (2008). Ecpp: Efficient conditional privacy preservation protocol for secure vehicular communications. In *Proceedings of 27th IEEE International Conference on Computer Communications, Joint Conference of the IEEE Computer and Communications Societies*, (pp. 1229–1237). IEEE.

National Highway Traffic Safety Administration. (2012). *An examination of driver distraction as recorded in NHTSA databases*. Retrieved from http://www-nrd.nhtsa.dot.gov/Pubs/811216.pdf

Ns. (2001). *The network simulator ns-2 (v2.1b8a)*. Retrieved from http://www.isi.edu/nsnam/ns/

Palanisamy, B., & Liu, L. (2011). Mobimix: Protecting location privacy with mix-zones over road networks. In *Proceedings of the 27th International Conference on Data Engineering (ICDE 2011)*, (pp. 494–505). Hannover, Germany: ICDE.

Rawat, D. B., Popescu, D., Gongjun, Y., & Olariu, S. (2011). Enhancing vanet performance by joint adaptation of transmission power and contention window size. *IEEE Transactions on Parallel and Distributed Systems*, 22(9), 1528–1535. doi:10.1109/TPDS.2011.41.

Raya, M., Papadimitratos, P., & Hubaux, J.-P. (2006). Securing vehicular communications. *IEEE Wireless Communications Magazine*, 8–15.

Ribagorda-Garnacho, A. (2010). Authentication and privacy in vehicular networks. *Journal of UPGRADE*, 11(1), 72–79.

Sampigethaya, K., Huang, L., Li, M., Poovendran, R., Matsuura, K., & Sezaki, K. (2005). Caravan: Providing location privacy for vanet. In Proceedings of Embedded Security in Cars. ESCAR.

Sampigethaya, K., Li, M., Huang, L., & Poovendran, R. (2007). Amoeba: Robust location privacy scheme for vanet. *IEEE Journal on Selected Areas in Communications*, 25(8), 1569–1589. doi:10.1109/JSAC.2007.071007.

Song, J., Wong, V. W. S., & Leung, V. C. M. (2009). Wireless location privacy protection in vehicular ad-hoc networks. *Mobile Networks and Applications*, 15(1), 160–171. doi:10.1007/s11036-009-0167-4.

Studer, A., Shi, E., Bai, F., & Perrig, A. (2009). Tacking together efficient authentication, revocation, and privacy in vanets. In *Proceedings of the 6th Annual IEEE Communications Society Conference on Sensor, Mesh and Ad Hoc Communications and Networks*, (pp. 484–492). IEEE.

Sun, J., Zhang, C., Zhang, Y., & Fang, Y. M. (2010a). An identity-based security system for user privacy in vehicular ad hoc networks. *IEEE Transactions on Parallel and Distributed Systems*, 21, 1227–1239. doi:10.1109/TPDS.2010.14.

Sun, Y., Su, X., Zhao, B., & Su, J. (2010b). Mix-zones deployment for location privacy preservation in vehicular communications. In *Proceedings of the 10th IEEE International Conference on Computer and Information Technology (CIT 2010)*, (pp. 2825–2830). West Yorkshire, UK: IEEE.

Toyota. (2007). *Pre-crash safety*. Retrieved from http://www.toyota.co.jp/en/about_toyota/in_the_world/pdf2007/safety.pdf

US Department of Transporation, Research and Innovative Technology Association. (2011). *National transportation statistics*. Retrieved from http://www.bts.gov/publications/national_transportation_statistics/

Wang, F.-Y. (2010). Parallel control and management for intelligent transportation systems: concepts, architectures, and applications. *IEEE Transactions on Intelligent Transportation Systems*, 11(3), 630–638. doi:10.1109/TITS.2010.2060218.

Wen, D., Yan, G., Zheng, N., Shen, L., & Li, L. (2011). Towards cognitive vehicles. *IEEE Intelligent Systems Magazine*, 26(3), 76–80. doi:10.1109/MIS.2011.54.

Xi, Y., Sha, K., Shi, W., Schwiebert, L., & Zhang, T. (2007). Enforcing privacy using symmetric random key-set in vehicular networks. In *Proceedings of the Eighth International Symposium on Autonomous Decentralized Systems*, (pp. 344–351). IEEE.

Xie, H., Kulik, L., & Tanin, E. (2010). Privacy-aware traffic monitoring. *IEEE Transactions on Intelligent Transportation Systems*, *11*(1), 61–70. doi:10.1109/TITS.2009.2028872.

Yan, G., & Olariu, S. (2011). A probabilistic analysis of link duration in vehicular ad hoc networks. *IEEE Transactions on Intelligent Transportation Systems*, *12*(4), 1227–1236. doi:10.1109/TITS.2011.2156406.

Yan, G., Olariu, S., & Popescu, D. (2012). *Notice: An architecture for the notification of traffic incidents*. IEEE Intelligent Transportation Systems Magazine.

Yan, G., Olariu, S., Wang, J., & Arif, S. (2013). Towards providing scalable and robust privacy in vehicular networks. *IEEE Transactions on Parallel and Distributed Systems*. doi:10.1109/TPDS.2013.142.

Yan, G., Olariu, S., & Weigle, M. (2009a). Providing location security in vehicular ad hoc networks. *IEEE Wireless Communications*, *16*(6), 48–55. doi:10.1109/MWC.2009.5361178.

Yan, G., Olariu, S., & Weigle, M. C. (2008). Providing VANET security through active position detection. *Computer Communications*, *31*(12), 2883–2897. doi:10.1016/j.comcom.2008.01.009.

Yan, G., Olariu, S., & Weigle, M. C. (2009b). Providing location security in vehicular ad-hoc networks. *IEEE Wireless Communications*, *16*(6), 48–55. doi:10.1109/MWC.2009.5361178.

Yan, G., Yang, W., Rawat, D. B., & Olariu, S. (2011). Smartparking: A secure and intelligent parking system. *IEEE Intelligent Transportation Systems Magazine*, *3*(1), 18–30. doi:10.1109/MITS.2011.940473.

Section 6
Wireless Sensor Networks

Chapter 14
Security Challenges in Wireless Sensor Network

Meenakshi Tripathi
Malaviya National Institute of Technology, India

M.S. Gaur
Malaviya National Institute of Technology, India

V.Laxmi
Malaviya National Institute of Technology, India

ABSTRACT

Wireless Sensor Networks are a subset of ad hoc networks. Their unique characteristics are smaller node size, high node density, unattended operation in remote areas. Dynamic topology and wireless communication make them vulnerable to numerous types of attacks. In addition to that, memory, processing, and energy constraint make it difficult to incorporate compute-intensive security solutions in these networks. Existing solutions for developing cost and energy efficient algorithms do not fit the security parameters for these resource constrained networks. As a result, these networks remain vulnerable to several types of attacks. This chapter presents a survey of various attacks at the different layers of WSN protocol stack, their detection, and countermeasures. Although every layer of the stack has its own security challenges, the network layer is most vulnerable to many security attacks because it provides an excellent basis for traffic monitoring activities, which helps the attacker form a strategy to perform the attack. The most common attacks on this layer are the Sybil attack, selective forwarding attack, wormhole attack, sinkhole attack, etc. This survey provides a comprehensive view of present attacking strategies to disrupt the normal functioning of WSN.

DOI: 10.4018/978-1-4666-4691-9.ch014

Figure 1. A typical Wireless Sensor Network

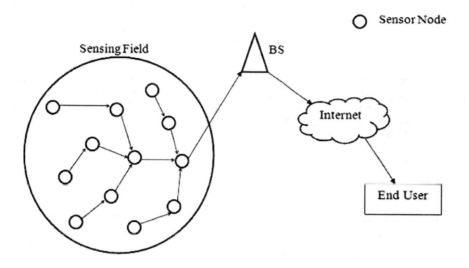

INTRODUCTION

In the 1980's when Defense Advanced Research Project Agency (DARPA) started its research on Distributed Sensor Network (DSN), the size of the sensors were large (i.e- shoe-box and up), which limited the potential application of these networks. Further in these DSNs the sensor nodes were using wired connectivity among them. Recent technological advancements have caused a significant shift in WSN (Matin and Islam, 2012; Wang and Balasingam, 2010) and nowadays, sensor nodes are much smaller in size (pack of cards or dust particle), distributed in nature and communicate with each other using wireless medium only. In a typical Wireless Sensor Network, sensor nodes sense the physical phenomenon, compute some result and transfer the result to the base station (BS), which is connected to the end user via internet (Akyildiz, Sankarasubramaniam, & Cayirci, 2002; Ahem, 2004; Elson & Estrin, 200) as shown in Figure 1.

The hardware component of a sensor node include one or more sensors to sense the physical phenomenon (e.g. Light, temperature, pressure, etc.), transceiver for wireless communication, a processing unit to convert sensed data into suitable

format for transmission, used to log the sensed data. Batteries act as power source. Figure 2 shows the schematic diagram of a sensor node.

WSN has been viewed as one of the most emerging technology for the 21'st century (Coy et al, 1999). Upcoming companies like Crossbow, Smart Dust Networks, Berkley etc. are also working hard in accelerating the commercialization of WSN by reducing the chip size (Coin size). Figure 3 shows the photographs of some modern sensor nodes.

The sensor node senses the required phenomena and sends the data to the base station or sink by a multihop infrastructure less architecture. The

Figure 2. Schematic diagram of a sensor node

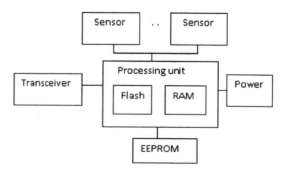

Figure 3. Current sensor node hardware. TelosB mote by Crossbow ("Telosb Mote", 2012), a coin-size mote by Smart Dust ("Smart Dust Mote", 2012) and Tmote Sky by Moteiv ("Tmote Sky", 2012)

sink may communicate to the end user via internet or satellite. Due to wireless nature of media all the security loopholes of any wireless network is inherent in sensor networks. Their unattended deployment in hostile environment and scarcity of resources makes them more vulnerable to physical attacks (Becher, Benenson & Dornseif, 2006). Their low cost allows user to deploy them in large amount but their limited processing capability, less storage and low power poses another challenge to use any of the existing security protocol of ad-hoc networks with them. Most of the researchers have tried to develop different security protocols for such resource constraint networks.

This chapter surveys various attacks and it's countermeasures based on protocol stack, in WSN.

The rest of the chapter is organized as follows: After discussing applications, challenges of WSN are presented followed by taxonomy of various attacks in WSN protocol stack. Next, we discuss security attacks and its countermeasures in the physical layer, followed by attacks and countermeasures at MAC layer. This is subsequently followed by a discussion on attacks and detection schemes in the network layer, transport layer and application layer. While enumerating various possible attacks, the chapter provides a detailed discussion on various existing security mechanisms and protocols to defend against and wherever possible prevent the possible attacks.

A number of future research issues and open problems are also mentioned before the chapter is finally concluded.

APPLICATIONS OF WIRELESS SENSOR NETWORKS

In general a WSN is deployed to perform a set of high-level information processing tasks such as detection, tracking, or classification. Performances of these tasks are measured on the basis of detection of false alarms, correctness of tracking and classification error. Applications of WSN (Chong and Kumar, 2003) are wide ranging. Some of the commercial and military applications include:

- Environmental monitoring (e.g. traffic, habitat, natural disaster, forest fire).
- Industrial sense and control applications (e.g. data logging, waste, machine health).
- Infrastructure protection (e.g. water distribution, structural health monitoring of bridges).
- Battlefield awareness (e.g. multi-target tracking, presence of enemy).
- Context-aware computing (e.g. smart homes, responsive environment).

CHALLENGES OF WIRELESS SENSOR NETWORKS

The unique characteristics of Wireless Sensor Networks make it difficult to implement security in it. Here, we are listing some of the challenges the researchers are facing while implementing security in these networks:

- **Wireless Communication:** Unreliable wireless communication channel may result in damaged packets or channel errors can even drop the whole packet. This may result in losing a packet which may contain security information e.g. a cryptographic key.

- **Resource Constraint Nature:** Sensor nodes have very low power and storage capability. All communications even passive listening have a significant impact on those reserves. So to maximize the lifetime of the network, several schemes have been developed to conserve the power at MAC layer (Demirkol & Ersoy, 2004; Zhao & Guibas, 2004). At the network layer it is critical to maximize the usefulness of every bit transmitted or received. Clearly, security mechanism should not only provide the security but also put special effort to conserve the energy of sensor nodes.

- **Unattended Operation:** Sensor networks can be deployed in hostile territory, where they can be subject to communication surveillance, node capture or can be compromised by adversaries. So security mechanisms must need to be designed so that these problems can be avoided (Walters, Liang, Shi, & Chaudhary, 2006) and they must be scalable enough to provide the protection against attacks irrespective of the size of the network.

- **Lack of Global Address Scheme:** Because of dense nature it is very difficult to employ any global addressing scheme of wired networks in WSNs. So traditional IP based security protocols may not be applied to them. An address free architecture is proposed (Elson et al., 2000) for these networks, where nodes or data are described by attributes rather than addresses. Any security solution must keep these things in mind.

- **Location Sensing:** A node's location can be used for geographic routing or for authentication purpose but whether absolute or relative it is not possible to detect the position of all the sensor nodes in the sensor network all the time and in most of the

cases sensor node's location may not be suitable for satellite determination equipment like GPS.

- **Multihop Routing:** Most sensor networks use multihop routing (in which if the source node is outside the destination node's wireless range, it needs to rely on intermediate hosts to relay its packets) for transferring data, from sensor nodes to sink for communication while most of the other wireless networks uses point to point communication (Gomez & Garcia-Macias, 2006). This increases the latency in the network thus making it difficult to achieve synchronization among sensor nodes which is must in most of the security protocols.

- **Data Aggregation:** It is the process of combining the data from various sources before it is being sent to the base station. Data aggregation is essential in WSN as it eliminates the redundancy of the data thus minimizes the number of transmissions and hence save the power. Many current data aggregation techniques does not concern about data efficiency, accuracy and privacy.

Due to these characteristics, security in wireless sensor networks is quite different than in any other kind of networks.

NECESSARY CONDITIONS FOR A SECURE WSN

Like any other ad-hoc networks, in WSN sensor nodes transfer the data among the various nodes in the wireless medium, which is vulnerable to various attacks. The necessary conditions to get a secure WSN cover both the conditions necessary for those of traditional ad-hoc network and of unique ad-hoc sensor network. They can be classified as primary and secondary conditions (Walters et. al., 2006).

The primary conditions are same as of traditional wireless networks:

Data Confidentiality

A sensor node should not leak its data to the neighbors. Data stored in it may be highly sensitive for applications like military services. Global information such as sensor node identities, security keys have to be protected from traffic analysis attack.

Data Integrity

Data integrity ensures that the data has not been tampered, altered or changed during the transmission. For example a malicious node may manipulate or add some furious data within a packet. This modified packet may leave the WSN in an unstable way.

Data Authentication

Data authentication allows receiver or sender to verify that the data is really sent by the claimed entity and is not a false packet. In general data authentication is achieved through symmetric and asymmetric key exchange mechanism. Adrian Perrig et al. (2002) proposed a key-chain distribution system for their μTESLA secure broadcast protocol in which asymmetric cryptography is achieved by delaying the disclosure of symmetric keys.

Data Availability

Availability ensures that the node is able to make use of its resources and can participate in network communication. For example unavailability of base station or cluster head will disrupt the entire working of WSN.

Authorization

Authorization is the process of granting access to the specific resource to an entity. In WSN only authorized sensor node should provide information to the network services.

Secondary conditions are unique for WSN only.

Data Freshness

Continuous monitoring applications like environment monitoring, where each sensor node transmits its data to the base station periodically, it is important that the base station gets fresh data periodically. Data reaching to the base station after certain threshold is not useful for analysis as it is stale. Data freshness ensures that the data is latest and has not been replayed. To ensure the freshness a nonce or any other time related counter can be added inside the packet.

Self Organization

In a WSN large number of sensor nodes may be deployed in heterogeneous and hostile environment. Self organizing capability allows all these sensor nodes to dynamically maintain organizational structure befitting the current purpose and situation without the need for human assistance. All the sensor nodes must be able to form an initial network via discovery mechanisms, establish needed end-to-end connections to end users, allow new nodes to be added and reconfigure when existing nodes fail, and to quickly evolve so as to achieve these functions via low power operation. A WSN must self-organize to support multihop routing as well as to conduct key management and building trust relation among sensors. If self-organization is lacking in any WSN, the effect of attack may be very damaging.

Time Synchronization

In any application of WSN that require coordination of locally sensed data and mobility like environmental monitoring, navigation data etc., all the sensor nodes must agree on a common time clock (Li and Rus, 2004). This common clock helps in processing and analyzing the data correctly, so that future behavior of the system can be predicted. For example, in the vehicle tracking application, each sensor may know the time when a vehicle is approaching. By matching the sensor location and sensing time, the sensor system may predict the vehicle moving direction and speed. Without a global agreement on time, the data from different sensors cannot be matched up. While implementing any security mechanism time synchronization is must.

Secure Localization

For applications like target detection and tracking, precision navigation, security surveillance etc. the proper knowledge of sensor nodes location is must. If the localization algorithm is not secured, any adversary can easily manipulate the location information of a node by reporting false signal strength, replaying signals etc. Zhang, Liu & Fang (2005) proposed a technique for secure localization based on TOA (Time Of Arrival). Trust Based Secure Localization (TBSL) has also been proposed (Zhang, He & Yang Zhang, 2011), to evaluate the trust of beacon nodes through detecting the identity and the behavior of such node and using the credible position information for localization.

THREAT MODELS IN WSN

Generally in WSN the number of nodes is very large so, it is impractical to monitor and protect each individual sensor node from physical or logical attack. Attacker may pose different types of security attacks to make the WSN system dysfunctional. Various classes of attacks are possible based on the nature or goal of the attacker. In this section we will describe the important classes.

Attacks Based On Resource Capability Of The Attacker

Attacker may use different type of devices having different power, storage, and transmission range capability. Based on this, attacker can be classified as *Mote-Class vs Laptop Class attacker.* Mote-class attacker may jam the radio links or steal the cryptography keys by using the devices having the same resources as of a sensor node in the network. While, Laptop class attacker will have more resources (e.g. a laptop) in terms of energy, processing power, transmission ranges as compared to nodes in the network. So they can easily perform some traffic injection or can get access to the low bandwidth and high latency communication channel.

Attacks Based On Location Of The Attacker

If the attacker is located outside the range of the WSN we call it as outsider attacker and if it lies within the range of WSN it is known as Insider attack. Outsider may perform attacks to consume the resources of the node, while insider may get access to cryptographic keys and lead to total disruption.

Attacks Based On Intervention Of The Attacker

If the attacker is only eavesdropping or stealing the information by monitoring the traffic of a WSN, it is a passive attacker. But, if an attacker can get a full control on a node by reprogramming it and can make it to act in an arbitrary way.

Attacks Based On Functionality Of The Attacker

- **Interruption:** This attack happens when a network component becomes unavailable or cannot be used. This is an attack on the availability of the system and it is used to launch Denial of Service (DoS) attacks.

- **Interception:** In this type of attack an attacker gets the access of the sensor node or data in it. Example of this type of attack is node capture attack. This attack means that there is a loss of privacy therefore it is an attack on confidentiality.

- **Modification:** When some malicious attacker not only gains access to a system but can make some changes in it, then this tempering is known as modification. It is an attack on the integrity of the network.

- **Fabrication:** If the attacker gains the access to the system and can inject false data into it, it is called fabrication and it threatens the authenticity of the network.

- **Message Replaying:** When an attacker captures the stream of messages between two nodes and replays it at a later time, it is known as message replaying attack. It is an attack on message freshness.

SECURITY THREATS BASED ON PROTOCOL STACK

The WSN protocol stack is much like the traditional protocol stack as described in Figure 4, which includes the following layers: Physical, Data Link, Network, Transport and Application. The WSN also manages the following management planes in order to function efficiently: Task, Mobility, Power Management, Quality of Service (QoS) and Security Management Planes.

These planes coordinate the power, movement, task distribution and security among the nodes and helps in reducing the power consumption of the network. The functionality of Power Management Plane is to minimize power consumption and nodes may go into off state to preserve energy. The Mobility Plane is responsible for detection and registering the movement of nodes so a data route to the sink is always maintained. The

Task Plane balances and schedules the sensing tasks assigned to the sensor field. For the real time data services QoS management plane deals with various QoS metrics like fault tolerance, error control, performance optimization etc. Security management plane is responsible for integrating various security modules such as encryption, authentication, and intrusion detection to manage, monitor and control the security of the network. Networking protocol developed for sensor network must address all five of these management planes. Due lack of proper implementation of all these planes along with the layered architecture, WSNs are vulnerable to various types of security threats. For each layer, there are some attacks and defensive mechanisms. In this Chapter we have explored the different existing attacks on different layers of WSN protocol stack along with their defenses and countermeasures.

Due to limited resources and deployment in unattended environment an attacker can easily perform the attack on various layers of protocol stack of WSN. Figure 5 gives taxonomy of security attacks on WSN protocol stack.

PHYSICAL LAYER

The most common way of communication between two sensor nodes is by using a radio. An attacker can use this radio to perform various kinds of attacks.

Jamming

In jamming, an attacker tries to prevent the reception of the signal at the nodes of Wireless Sensor Network by sending the signals at the frequency used by the nodes to communicate with each other. Attacker uses the same frequency signal but send the signal with high energy, which makes it difficult for other surrounding nodes to receive the messages from other nodes. Four generic jammer models have been proposed (Xu, Ma, Trappe,

Figure 4. The WSN protocol stack (Extended version of protocol stack of Figure 3 from (Akyildiz, Sankarasubramaniam, & Cayirci, 2002))

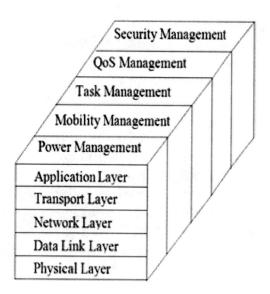

Figure 5. Taxonomy of security attacks in WSN

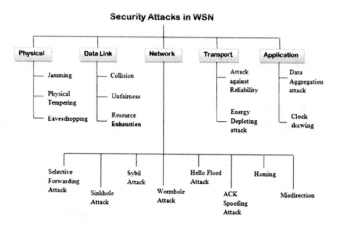

& Zhang, 2006): (1) The Constant Jammer, (2) The Deceptive Jammer, (3) The Random Jammer And (4) The Reactive jammer. A constant jammer emits a constant noise. A deceptive jammer either fabricates or replays valid signals. A random jammer sleeps for a random amount of time and jams for a random time after which it sleeps again. A reactive jammer listens for activity on the medium and sends out a random signal when activity is detected.

One usual solution for this can be, to use the signal which is of higher strength than the attacker's signal for communication in the sensor network but the attacker may have unlimited power or attacker knows the signal strength of the sensor nodes so this is not a good solution. Another solution is to change the frequency of the signal used by sensor nodes frequently, in this case even if the attacker knows one frequency it is difficult for him to follow the complete frequency pattern used in the network hence, it will be difficult for the attacker to disrupt the working of the network. But it is very costly solution in terms of resources and the complexity involved in the method. One can use Ultra Wide Band as a good solution for sensor network in which very small pulses are transmitted on a large frequency band simultaneously so it is difficult for the attacker to jam the communication. A technique called channel surfing (Xu, Trappe, & Zhang, 2008), was used to cope with interference whereby the sensor nodes in the network adapt their channel assignments to restore network connectivity even in the presence of interference.

Physical Tampering

Sensor node enclosures are not tamper resistant and mostly they are deployed in unattended environment so anybody can get physical access to a node and can damage the device. Physical attacks can be classified (Becher, Benenson, & Dornseif, 2006) based on the amount of information extracted by the attacker such as gaining the access to microcontroller or the flash memory or influencing sensor readings fully or partially etc. Skorobogatov (2005) classified the attacks on microcontroller into three categories: invasive, semi-invasive, and non-invasive attacks. Invasive attacks require access to a chip's internals, and some preparation on chip before the attack can begin. Semi-invasive attacks take much cheaper equipment and less time than invasive attacks, while non-invasive attacks are the easiest.

Some standard precautions are also suggested (Becher et al.,2004) to protect the sensor networks from physical tampering like disable the JTAG interface or protect the bootstrap loader password from attack. Uppuluri and Basu (2004) have proposed a tamper resistant-locks on the sensors which

ensure that if the sensors are attacked repeatedly than they destroy themselves so that their data cannot be accessed by the attacker.

EAVESDROPPING

All the communication between the sensor nodes and base station happens in the air so any attacker can easily detect the content of communication by using powerful resources and strong devices such as powerful receivers and well designed antennas. By doing this the attacker can extract the sensitive information of WSN and can reduce the data confidentiality. Researchers (Ruan, Jain, & Zhu, 2009) have developed a real-time eavesdropping system and built a component which can record the speech at one side of the network and can transmit it over the multi hop network so that on the other side after noise reduction attacker can receive the signal with sufficient power.

Location Privacy Protocol (Jian, Chen, Z. Zhang, & L. Zhang, 2007) was proposed so that in case of eavesdropping the attacker cannot derive the location of the receiver i.e. the base station of the network. Directional antenna (Hu & Evans, 2004; Yi, Pei, & Kalyanaraman, 2003) is another technique for access restriction. By confining the directions of the signal propagation, one can reduce the chances of adversaries accessing the communication channel.

DATA LINK LAYER

Data Link layer is responsible to provide channel access to various nodes of the WSN. One of the scheme to share the channel is CSMA (Carrier Sense Multiple Access), is most vulnerable to attacks. Wood & Stankovic (2003) have given a list of possible attacks on the link layer.

Packet Collision

An attacker transmit the packet at the same time when WSN nodes are sending the packet to each other, these packets collides with the packet sent by the sensor nodes, hence prevents the receiver nodes from receiving the packets or can cause some change in the content of the packet, even a small change in the packet would cause checksum mismatch at the receiver and hence the packet becomes invalid (Reindl,Nygard, & Xiaojiang, 2010).

Error correcting codes can be used to tolerate variable levels of corruption in the packet at the various levels but this also has some threshold on the level of corruption as well as require significant amount of processing. A cooperative collision detection method can be used by the nodes of the network, where the suspicious node could intentionally deny the access to the channel.

Exhaustion

A node can continuously either transmit or receive a packet causing battery exhaustion at both receiver and transmitter (Wood & Stankovic, 2003). For example, IEEE 802.11-based MAC protocols use Request To Send, Clear To send, and Data/Ack messages to reserve channel access and transmit data. The node could repeatedly request channel access with RTS, eliciting a CTS response from the targeted neighbor.

This kind of attack can be prevented by limiting the MAC admission control rate, in which the network can ignore excessive requests and prevents the unnecessary battery exhaustion.

Unfairness

Repeated application of exhaustion or collision based MAC layer attacks or an abusive use of cooperative MAC layer priority mechanisms, can lead into unfairness. This kind of attack is a partial DoS attack, but results in marginal performance degradation. For example, attacker may cause users

of a real-time MAC protocol to miss their deadlines (Wang, Attebury, & Ramamurthy, 2006).

One defense against this threat is to use small frames so that an individual node can capture the channel only for a short time. If the network typically transmits long messages, however, this approach increases framing overhead.

TinySec

TinySec (Karlof, Sastry, & Wagner, 2004) is a link-layer security mechanism that guarantees the authenticity, integrity and confidentiality of messages between neighboring nodes, while permitting in-network processing. It utilizes a single, symmetric key that is shared among a collection of sensor nodes. Before transmitting a packet, each node first encrypts the data and applies a Message Authentication Code (MAC), a cryptographically strong unforgeable hash to protect data integrity. The receiver verifies that the packet was not modified in transit using the MAC and then deciphers the message. TinySec works both in the TOSSIM simulator as well as on the Mica and Mica2 motes.

NETWORK LAYER

The main task of network layer is to route the data from sensor nodes to the sink (Perrig, Stankovic, & Wagner, 2004). Each node in a WSN may function as a router and forward packets for other peer nodes. The wireless channel is accessible to both legitimate nodes and malicious attackers. There is no well defined place where traffic monitoring or access control mechanisms can be deployed. So it's become difficult to define the boundary that separates the inside network from the outside. Various WSN routing protocols are available based on different metrics, such as such as least number of hops AODV (Perkins, Belding-Royer, & Das, 2003), DSR (Johnson & Maltz, 2001) minimal energy LEACH (Heinzelman, Chandrakasan, & Balakrishnan, 2001), TEEN (Manjeshwar &

Agrawal, 2001), SPEED (Hea Stankovica, Lub, & Abdelzahera, 2003), best link quality MintRoute (Woo, Tong, &Culler, 2003) etc. All these protocols are typically based on the assumption of a trusted and cooperative environment. As a result, a malicious attacker can readily become a router and disrupt network operations by intentionally disobeying the protocol specifications.

For WSNs attacks on network layer may fall into following categories (Karlof & Wagner, 2003; Padmavathi & Shanmugapriya, 2009):

- Selective Forwarding/Balckhole(Neglect and greed)
- Sinkhole Attack
- Sybil Attack
- Wormhole Attack
- HELLO FLOOD attack
- Acknowledgement Spoofing
- Homing
- Misdirection

Selective Forwarding

In this kind of attack malicious node may refuse to forward certain messages and simply drops them, ensuring that they are not propagated further. As shown in Figure 6 below the Attacker node is forwarding some of the packets coming to it while dropping others. There can be multiple variants of this attack: If attacker selectively drops the packets from a particular node or a group of node then we call it a Denial of Service (DoS) attack for that node or group of nodes. If it refuses to forward any packet passing through it, then we call it a Blackhole attack (Karlof et al., 2003). Another type of selective forwarding attack can add some delay to the packets passing through them, creating the confused routing information between sensor nodes. With this attack an attacker can disrupt a number of existing routing protocols such as TinyOS beaconing, Directed Diffusion (Intanagonwiwat, Govindan, Estrin, Heidemann, & Silva, 2003), GPSR (Karp & Kun, 2000) GEAR,

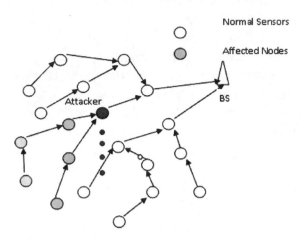

Figure 6. Selective forwarding attack in WSN

and clustered based protocols. This attack becomes easy if launched with sinkhole attack.

Karlof et al. (2003) suggested one way to mitigate this type of attack is, to use multipath routing. But with multipath routing the communication overhead increases as the number of paths increases in the network. Kaplantzis et al. (2007) have presented IDS to detect selective forwarding attack using Support Vector Machines (SVM) and sliding window. They have used one-class SVM classifier to classify the data and trained data generates the alarm when detect a selective forwarding attack. Their scheme cannot identify and revoke malicious nodes in network. Sharmila & Umamaheswari (2012) has proposed a new defensive mechanism against selective forwarding based on cumulative acknowledgement and energy of the node. Their scheme consist of cumulative acknowledgement packet between the check points of the forward path and the check point generates the trap message and is sent to the next node of the forwarding path. Upon receiving the cumulative acknowledgement packet and the trap message, the base station detects the exact malicious node in the forward path based on the negative acknowledgement. But the detection accuracy of this method was not 100 percent.

Sinkhole Attack

A sinkhole attack involves at least one attacker node that falsely advertises itself as having an extremely efficient route to a collection point in sensor network such as sink or base station. This can mislead the dynamic routing protocol in use, which then updates the entries in the sensor nodes so that all traffic on route to collection point will be misdirected toward the sinkhole. Figure 7 show an intruder in the sensor network has high communication and computation power, can create a high quality single hop route to the base station. Later on by sending this false routing information to other surrounding nodes in the network it can create a sinkhole (Lazos, Poovendran, Meadows, Syverson, & Changr, 2005; Ngai, Liu, & Lyu, 2007). As shown in Figure 4 wormhole can also be used to create this type of attack where the intruder as sinkhole forms the one part of the network and tunnels the messages to the other part of the network. Even a single sinkhole node in the network can affect the surrounding nodes and can dampen the network performance.

Karlof et al.(2003) have suggested one approach to avoid sinkholes using geographic pro-

Figure 7. (a) Sinkhole attack (b) Sinkhole attack using wormhole attack

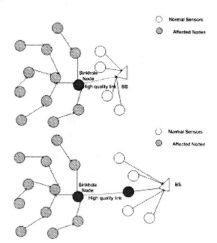

tocols. These protocols construct a topology on demand using only localized interactions and information and do not require any initiation from the base station. Because traffic is naturally routed towards the physical location of a base station, it is difficult to attract it elsewhere to create a sinkhole. Since this attack mainly depends on type of routing protocol used in the network so, various strategies have been proposed to detect it, depending upon the type of routing protocol used Sami, Wakeel, & Swailem (2007) have presented an algorithm in which on the basis of various parameters like packet ID, number of hop counts, delay, node power, HELLO messages, they find the presence of adversary node and later, they remove it from the active routing path so that a normal communication can happen between source and destination. For sinkhole detection Ngai et al (2007) finds a list of suspected nodes, and then carries out a network flow graph to identify a sinkhole attack by observing data missing from an attacked area. An IDS system have been developed by Krontiris, Dimitriou & Giannetsos (2007) in which the nodes simply monitor their neighborhood and collaborate with each other sharing valuable information that eventually leads to the successful detection of the attack. Their approach is specific to the MintRoute (Woo et al., 2003) routing protocol in sensor network. Choi et al. (2009) has proposed detection of sinkhole for LQI based routing. Their algorithm consists of two phases: network initialization phase and attack detection phase. Network initialization phase collects basic information for detection of sinkhole attack. General node collect minimum link cost between each neighborhood node. Detector nodes compute minimum path cost surrounding detector nodes as well as link cost with each neighborhood node. Detector node detects forgery of path cost in routing request message. After performing the above attack for all of its neighbors, the sinkhole node will eventually attract the traffic passing through the nodes. But their method requires lots of computation.

Sybil Attack

In sybil attack, a malicious device illegitimately fabricates multiple identities, behaving as if it were a larger number of nodes (instead of just one). A malicious device's additional identities are referred as sybil identities or sybil nodes. Douceur (2002) has first identified the problem of sybil attacks, in the context of peer-to-peer distributed systems. According to him in the absence of a logically centralized authority, sybil attacks are always possible, except under extreme and unrealistic assumptions about the resources available to attackers and the coordination among entities. Figure 8 demonstrates sybil attack where an adversary node 'M' is present with multiple identities. M appears as node 'F' for 'A', 'C' for 'B' and 'A' as to 'D' so when 'A' wants to communicate with F it sends the message to 'M' and now 'M' can perform any malicious task with the message. Sybil attack (Newsome, Shi, Song, & Perrig, 2004) can be differentiated as: *direct vs Indirect communication*, in direct communication legitimate sensor nodes directly communicate with the sybil nodes while in indirect communication, communication between legitimate nodes happens through malicious nodes. *Fabricated vs. stolen identities*, if the adversary creates new identities based on the format of identities used by legitimate nodes then they are called fabricated identities and if it uses the same identity used by any legitimate nodes then it is called stolen identity. *Simultaneous and non-simultaneous attack*, all the sybil identities will be active in the network at the same time in simultaneous attack while in non-simultaneous attack only some of the identities will be active in the network at a time though the attacker may generate large number of identities over a period of time.

Karlof et al (2003) suggested one solution to sybil attack using symmetric key cryptography. In their scheme every node shares a unique symmetric key with the base station. Each pair of nodes that wants to communicate then uses a

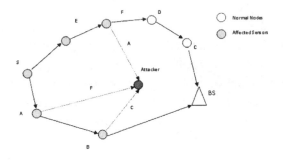

Figure 8. Sybil attack

Needham-Schroeder-like protocol to establish a shared key, via the base station. From this point, the two nodes can verify each other's identity by means of their established pairwise key but their approach is not scalable. Demirbas & Song (2006) have used RSSI from multiple receivers to detect the presence of attacker. The attacker detection based on the time difference of arrival (TDOA) between the source node and beacon nodes (Mi, Li, Zheng, & Chen, 2008) have also been proposed. The estimation of the TDOA of a message is done by Hyperbolic Position Location Solution (HPL) and then the TDOA ratio was associated with the senders ID. Once the same TDOA ratio with different ID is received, the receiver can identify about the sybil attack. Sharmila & Umamaheswari (2012) have proposed a scheme which forms the cluster in the network and based on the energy of the nodes they identify the sybil attacker using a three phase algorithm.

Wormhole Attack

In wormhole attack (Karlof et al., 2003; Hu, Perrig, & Johnson, 2006), a malicious node records packets in one location and with the help of another colluding node replays the packet at a distant part of the network. The colluding nodes can use communication techniques such as an out-of-band channel (a point-to-point link) or high power transmission (using directional antennas) to tunnel the packets. This tunneling enables the tunneled packet to arrive with fewer hops or lower delay than if the packet traversed a normal path. The arrival of packets with low delay or hop count attracts nearby traffic towards the malicious node, thus affecting routing. An example is shown in Figure 9, where Attacker1 and Attacker2 are the two end-points of the wormhole link. As the signals received on one end of the wormhole link are repeated at the other end, any transmission generated by a node in the neighborhood of Attacker1 will also be heard by any node in the neighborhood of Attacker2 and vice versa. The net effect is that all the nodes in left region assume that nodes in right region are their neighbors and vice versa.

Meghdadi, Ozdemir, & Guler (2011) have classified the wormhole attack as

- **Wormhole Using Out-of-Band Channel:** In which a high bandwidth out-of-bound channel is established between the two endpoints of the tunnel to create a wormhole link.
- **Wormhole Using Packet Encapsulation:** When received by one end point of the wormhole the packet gets encapsulated, to prevent nodes on the way from incrementing hop counts and when reaches to other end point packet is brought into its original form.
- **Wormhole Using High-Power Transmission Capability:** In this type of attack only one malicious node increases its chance to be in the routes established by normal nodes using high-power transmission.

- **Wormhole Using Packet Relay:** One malicious node replays packets between two far nodes and this way it creates fake neighbors.
- **Wormhole using Protocol Deviation:** The malicious node creates wormhole by forwarding packets without backing off unlike a legitimate node and thus, increases the possibility of wormhole path getting selected. Shari, & Leckie (2006) have also presented three variants of wormhole attack
- **Energy Depleting Wormhole Attack (EDWA), Indirect Black hole Attack (IBA), Targeted Energy Depleting Wormhole Attack (TEDWA):** In EDWA attacker reduces the network lifetime by forcing the nodes to deplete their energy in more broadcast operation. The indirect black hole attack is used to lure traffic into the vicinity of a specified node in order to create a DoS attack and deplete the energy of that node. TEDWA aims to deplete the energy of a particular node.

A defense mechanism against the wormhole attacks in WSN is called packet leashes (Hu, Perrig, & Johnson, 2003). Their solution consists of two types of leashes *Geographic Leashes and Temporal Leashes*. A geographic leash detects and prevents the wormhole attack by ensuring that the sender and the receiver are within a specified distance. To do that, each node must know its location and be timely synchronized

Figure 9. Wormhole attack

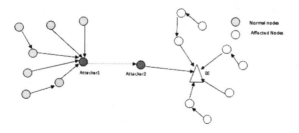

with other nodes. The other type of solution is a temporal leash. In this the packet's traveling time must be within a specified period of time and all nodes must be timely synchronized in terms of their clocks. When the sender starts sending the packets, it stores its sending time-stamp in the packet. Then, the receiver can compare its receiving time-stamp with the value in the packet. Therefore, the receiver will be able to detect if the packet traveled so fast according to a specified transmission time. Hani et al. have created a test bed called BANAID (Alzaid, Abanmi, Kanhere, & Chou, 2008) for detection and prevention of wormhole attack using the temporal leash. Tun & Maw, (2008) proposed a round trip time (RTT) and number of neighbors based wormhole detection mechanism. The identification of wormhole attack was based on the two faces. The first consideration is that the transmission time between two wormhole attack affected nodes is considerable higher than that between two normal neighbor nodes. The second detection mechanism is based on the fact that by introducing new links into the network, the adversary increases the number of neighbors of the nodes within its radius. Graff, Hegazy, Horton, & Nain, (2010) have introduced a distributed intrusion detection system by placing the intrusion detector nodes in the network. The intrusion detection system detects wormholes of length above a certain minimum value. Chen, Lou, Sun, & Wang (2010) proposed secure localization schemes against wormhole attacks in WSNs. To prevent the effect of wormhole, they proposed a distance-consistency-based secure location scheme which includes wormhole attack detection, valid location identification and self-localization. To achieve secure localization the concept of "conflicting-set" (Chen, Lou, & Wang, 2009) was proposed for each node so that the node can use all conflicting sets of its neighboring locators to filter out incorrect distance measurements of its neighboring locators. The limitation of this method is that it only works properly when the system has no packet loss. As

the attackers may drop the packets purposely, the packet loss is inevitable when the system is under a wormhole attack.

HELLO FLOOD Attack

Many protocols require nodes to broadcast HELLO packets to announce themselves to their neighbors. In HELLO FLOOD attack (Karlof et al., 2003), the attacker tries to convince all the other nodes to choose the attacker as a parent node using a powerful radio transmitter to bomb whole network with hello message announcing false neighbor status. A node receiving such messages may assume that it is within (normal) radio range of the sender (attacker). So legitimate nodes will attempt transmission to the attacking node, despite many are out of range.

If the attacker has the same reception capabilities, one way to avoid the HELLO FLOOD attacks is to verify the bi-directionality of local links (Karlof et al., 2003). When the adversary has powerful transmitter every node can authenticate each of its neighbors with an identity verification protocol using a trusted base station. Hamid, Rashid, & Hong (2006) described the defense against Lap-top class attacker (who can launch HELLO FLOOD attack) by introducing node to node authentication and multi-path routing using shared secret between sensor nodes. They have adopted a probabilistic key assignment protocol among sensor nodes and during communication, each node can calculate a pair wise key using these common secrets and hence improving the network resilience against security threats. Their defense mechanism can well tolerate the damage launched by the intruder. Khozium (2008) have proposed a probabilistic based approach, which forces few randomly selected nodes to report to base station about hello requests. The base station then further validates the legitimacy of request. On the basis of signal strength and client puzzles a method to detect HELLO FLOOD attack is proposed (Singh, Jain, & Singhai, 2010). They assume same signal strength for all sensor nodes in a radio range. Each node checks the signal strength of the received hello messages with respect to known radio range strength, if they are same then sender node is classified as a friend else sender is classified as a stranger. When a node is classified as a stranger, its validity is checked using some client puzzles. The difficulty of puzzle level is set using dynamic policy for each node in terms of number of hello messages sent. The more the number of hello message sent by a node, more will be the difficulty of the puzzles it has to solve.

Acknowledgement Spoofing

In the acknowledgement spoofing attack (Makri & Stamatiou, 2010), a malicious node may spoof link layer acknowledgments for the packets destined to a neighboring node which is dead or the packets lost due to the bad channel reliability, thus make the source node form a wrong routing decision based on the belief that the dead destination node is alive or the channel is reliable. Suppose there are 2 nodes A and B. Node A wants to send some data to B but node B is dead. A malicious node M overhears the message sent by node A and spoofs acknowledgement to node A at link layer and based on this spoofed acknowledgement A starts sending its's messages to base station through node M, now node M can drop some packets or can change the content of the packet.

Bendary et al.,(2011) have proposed a secure routing algorithm against acknowledgement spoofing attack, which is based on Directed Diffusion (Intanagonwiwat et al.,2003). It uses the TESLA (micro Timed, Efficient, Streaming, Loss-tolerant Authentication) broadcasting authentication algorithm in order to authenticate the acknowledgement messages sent from the sink to the source nodes for confirming the delivery of the data-event messages.

Homing

In a homing attack [19], the attacker looks at network traffic to deduce the geographic location of critical nodes, such as cluster heads or neighbors of the base station. The attacker can then physically disable these nodes. This leads to another type of black hole attack. This attack aims to block the traffic to the sink and to provide a better ground for lunching other attacks like data integrity or sniffing.

One approach to prevent this type of attack can be to restrict malicious node to join the network and for that network setup phase should be carried out in a secure way. Another approach is to hide the important nodes or to use encryption to conceal both message headers and its content.

Misdirection

Routing misdirection (Wood et al., 2003) is an attack whereby the intruder misdirects the incoming messages to other distant nodes to increase the latency, which prevents a few packets from reaching the base station. To remain unnoticed, the attacker keeps sending its own messages to its legitimate nodes.

One solution for hierarchical sensor network (Wood et al., 2003) is that parent node should verify that all routed packets from below have been originated legitimately by their children only. Abdullah, Hua, & Alsharabi (2008) have proposed a local administrative function algorithm which is efficient to establish a secure link layer communication. Local administrative function guarantees integrity between sender and receiver at anytime with the help of a hash function.

TRANSPORT LAYER

An efficient transport layer should provide reliable message delivery and congestion control with minimal overhead and retransmission. Attacks against WSN transport layer protocols come in two flavors: attacks against reliability and energy depleting attacks.

Attack Against Reliability

A reliable transport protocol must be able to guarantee that every packet loss is detected and that lost packets can be retransmitted until they reach their destination. Thus, an attack against reliability (Buttyan & Laszlo Csik, 2010) is considered to be successful, if either a packet loss remains undetected, or the attacker can permanently deny the delivery of a packet. In general, ACK-based schemes are vulnerable to attacks against reliability. The protocol which uses ACK assumes, that an arbitrary fragment which was acknowledged explicitly or implicitly, can be deleted from the system as it arrived to its destination. Since an attacker can forge and insert fake ACKs for fragments that are actually lost, fragments can be lost permanently.

Garuda (Park et. al., 2004), a transport layer protocol, was proposed to avoid the above attack in which, every 3rd node is a CORE node, serving as a local and designated loss recovery server. Nodes use implicit multiple NACKs to recollect missing fragments, where the NACK is the sequence number of the last message ID the node has received so far.

Energy Depleting Attacks

An attacker forces the sensor nodes to perform energy intensive operations, in order to deplete their batteries, and thus, to decrease the lifetime of the network. In WSNs, the overall energy consumption of a sensor node is highly proportional to the number of the packets transmitted by the node. Therefore, an energy depleting attacker (Buttyan & Laszlo Csik, 2010) may try to force the sensor nodes to unnecessarily re-transmit packets or packet fragments. In general, an injected fake NACK forces the nodes to unnecessarily re-

transmit a fragment. For multiple NACK schemes one packet can provoke the retransmission of multiple fragments, which multiplies the impact of the attack.

A security extension to DTSN Distributed Transport for Sensor Networks (Marchi,Grilo,& Nunes,2007) is proposed (Buttyan &Csik,2011). In which they have used symmetric key cryptographic techniques to authenticate ACK and NACK packets. Acknowledgment or negative acknowledgment information helps node to verify that packet in its cache is the valid data packet referred to by the ACK or NACK. On the basis of this information intermediate node can decide whether to delete packet from the cache (in case of an ACK) or to re-transmit it. This method ensures reliability and reduces unnecessary retransmission.

APPLICATION LAYER

Application layer is responsible for managing or processing or aggregating the data and verifying its correctness. In Wireless Sensor Network, data aggregation is a vital primitive enabling efficient data queries. An aggregator device collects data from sensor nodes and produces an aggregated result of it which is then sent to the sink or end-user, thus reducing the communication cost of the query. Since only aggregated data has to travel from aggregator to sink.

Data Aggregation Distortion

In sensor network certain nodes are, called aggregators, which collect the raw information from the sensors, process it locally, and send aggregated reply to the base station. In this attack (Xing, Srinivasan, Rivera, Li, & Cheng, 2010) attacker may maliciously modify the data to be aggregated, and make the final aggregation results computed by the base stations distorted. For example, an aggregator node could claim that all the nodes downstream from it reported a very large value. In this way, the compromise of just a few aggregator nodes could have an unbounded effect on the correctness of the data returned by a sensor network.

Przydatek, Perrig, & Song (2003) used random sampling mechanism and proposed a aggregate-commit-prove framework, which enable the user to verify that the answer given by the aggregators is a good approximation of the true value even when the aggregators and/or a fraction of the sensor nodes may be corrupted.

Clock Skewing

This kind of attack happens in application where sensor nodes need to maintain a clock to remain synchronized. The attacker (Xing, Srinivasan, Rivera, Li, & Cheng, 2010) can desynchronize the various sensors by disseminating false timing information. Once nodes adjust their clocks based on the wrong information, they will be out of synchronization with the other sensors of the network.

To detect this kind of attack the Secure Pairwise Synchronization Protocol (SPS) have been proposed (Ganeriwal, Capkun, Hanand & Srivastava, 2005). It is designed to be run by two nodes that reside within each other's communication ranges. The message integrity and authenticity are ensured through the use of Message Authentication Codes (MAC) and a key K shared between those two nodes. This prevents external attacker from successfully modifying any values in the synchronization pulse or in the acknowledgement packet. These nodes also use a random nonce during handshake to protect the protocol from replay attacks.

Table 1 describes the threats and defense mechanism against threat according to the protocol stack of WSN.

OPEN RESEARCH ISSUES

From our survey we have found several unresolved research issues in the Wireless Sensor Network, these are:

- **Security Protocols for the Mobile Wireless Sensor Networks** (Stavrou, Pitsillides,Hadjichristofi, & Hadjicostis,2010): Most of the work in terms of security has been done only for static sensor networks. New protocols including mobile nodes, mobile base station has yet to be developed. Because flow of the data will be quite different in case of heterogeneous mobile Wireless Sensor Network.

- **Intelligent Attack Detection Mechanism:** Instead of checking all the nodes for the possibility of attack, if attack detection mechanism checks only for those nodes which are having higher probability of being attacked then overall network resources can be saved.

- **Security vs QoS:** Most of the security protocols degrade the performance of the network so new security protocols that can maintain the balance between the QoS and security need to be developed. T. Pazynyuk, Li, Oreku, & Pan (2008) have integrated QoS to increase the security on applications running in WSNs.

- **Protection of Base Station:** In any sensor network base station holds lots of responsibilities like it aggregates data reported by sensors, manages and monitors all the sensor nodes, disseminates queries requested by users and at times also provides security service to routing protocols so the failure of BS will lead to the collapse of the whole sensor network. Hence, security measures for base station is considered to be a most urgent and significant issue. Cao et al.(2006) have presented reputation

Table 1. Layer wise attacks and defense mechanism

Layer	Threat	Defense Mechanism
Physical	Jamming	Use of ultra-wide band, Channel surfing, Spread- spectrum
	Physical Tampering	Disable JTAG interface, Protect bootstrap loader password Tamper resistant locks
	Eavesdropping	Location privacy protocol, use of directional antennas
Data Link	Packet Collision	Error correcting codes, collision detection methods
	Exhaustion	Limit the MAC admission control rate
	Unfairness	Use of small frames
Network	Selective Forwarding	Multipath routing, cumulative acknowledgement
	Sinkhole	Geographic protocols, neighboring node collaboration
	Sybil Attack	Cryptography, RSSI based techniques, TDOA based techniques
	Wormhole Attack	Packet leashes, RTT and neighbor number based techniques
	HELLO FLOOD attack	Authentication and multipath routing, client puzzles
	Acknowledgement Spoofing	Sender and receiver authentication
	Homing	Header and packet encryption
	Misdirection	Hashing with security keys
Transport	Attack against reliability	Use of NACK based protocol
	Energy depleting attack	Use of ACK based protocol with cryptography
Application	Data aggregation distortion	Random sampling mechanism
	Clock skewing	Use of Message Authentication Code (MAC) and cryptography

based client puzzle scheme to protect Base Station against DoS attack but still a lot more research is to be done in this area.

- **Security Aspect for Global Sensor Networks:** Aberer, Hauswirth, & Salehi (2006) have presented the concept of global sensor network which consist of interconnection of various heterogeneous sensor networks. They have considered the adaptivity, scalability and portability as its main features but security is still missing. So one has to develop protocols to secure sensor in global sensor networks.

- **Combination of Attacks:** Although we have surveyed the various attacks separately but an attacker can perform combination of attacks such as Sybil attack can be done in combination with wormhole attack so the algorithms need to be developed to handle these combination of attacks as well.

- **Cross-Layer Security:** In our survey we have reviewed that most of the security solutions ensure security at a particular layer for example link layer security ensures data integrity and data freshness but does not address any security for physical layer. Cross-layer security solutions (Gawdan, Chow, Zia and Gawdan, 2011) enable different layers of the communication stack to share state information or to coordinate their actions. Researchers have to put more efforts in finding out cross layer security solutions.

CONCLUSION

Wireless Sensor Networks are being used in many commercial and military applications. These networks are the easy target of attackers due to its popularity and inefficient security mechanism at elementary level. Attackers try to hamper or falsify the WSN generated information for their own benefit. Several solutions are available in literature to mitigate the effect of attacks and to enhance the protection metrics. This chapter presents a survey of various types of attacks on WSN protocol stack. The attack characteristics of every attack have been discussed along with their detection and countermeasures. In addition, the current research issues in these networks have been included to give a new direction to WSN security researchers.

REFERENCES

Abdullah, M. Y., Hua, G. W., & Alsharabi, N. (2008). Wireless sensor networks misdirection attacker challenges and solutions. In *Proceedings of the International Conference on Information and Automation*. Zhang Jia Jie City, China: IEEE Press.

Aberer, K., Hauswirth, M., & Salehi, A. (2006). *Global sensor networks* (Technical report LSIR-REPORT-2006-001). Lausanne, Switzerland: School of Computer and Communication Sciences. Retrieved from http://lsirpeople.epfl.ch/salehi/papers/LSIR-REPORT-2006-001.pdf

Akyildiz, I. F., Su W., Sankarasubramaniam, Y., & Cayirci, E. (2002). Wireless sensor networks: A survey. *Computer Networks, 38*, 393–422. doi:10.1.1.5.2442

Alzaid, H., Abanmi, S., Kanhere, S., & Chou, C. T. (2008). BANAID: A sensor network test-bed for wormhole attacks. In *Proceedings of SET-MAPE Research and Development Stream of the AUSCERT 2008 Conference*. The University of Queensland St. Lucia.

Becher, A., Benenson, Z., & Dornseif, M. (2006). Tampering with motes: Real-world physical attacks on wireless sensor networks. In *Security in pervasive computing* (pp. 104–118). Berlin: Springer-Verlag. doi:10.1007/11734666_9.

Buttyan, L., & Csik, L. (2010). Security analysis of reliable transport layer protocols for wireless sensor networks. In *Proceedings of IEEE Workshop on Sensor Networks and Systems for Pervasive Computing (PerSeNS)*. Mannheim, Germany: IEEE. doi:10.1.1.153.9959

Buttyan, L., & Csik, L. (2011). A secure distributed transport protocol for wireless sensor networks. In *Proceedings of IEEE International Confenrence onCommunications (ICC)*. Kyoto, Japan: IEEE Press.

Cao, Z., Zhou, X., Xu, M., Chen, Z., Hu, J., & Tang, L. (2006). Enhancing base station security against DoS attacks in wireless sensor networks. In *Proceedings of IEEE WICOM'06*. Wuha, China: IEEE Press.

Chen, H., Lou, W., Sun, X., & Wang, Z. (2010). A secure localization approach against wormhole attacks using distance consistency. *EURASIP Journal on Wireless Communication and Networking, 22*–32. Retrieved from dl.acm.org/citation.cfm?id=1740705

Chen, H., Lou, W., & Wang, Z. (2009). Conflicting-set-based wormhole attack resistant localization in wireless sensor networks. In D. Zhang, M. Portmann, A.-H. Tan, & J. Indulska (Eds.), Proceedings of Ubiqitous Intelligence and Computing: 6th International Conference, UIC 2009, (Vol. 5585, pp. 296-309). Berlin, Germany: Springer.

Choi, B. G., Cho, E. J., Kim, J. H., Hong, C. S., & Kim, J. H. (2009). A sinkhole attack detection mechanism for lqi based mesh routing in WSN. In *Proceedings of 23rd International Conference on Information Networking*. Chiang Mai, Thailand: IEEE Press.

Demirbas, M., & Song, Y. (2006). An RSSI-based scheme for Sybil attack detection in wireless sensor networks. In *Proceedings of the International Symposium on World of Wireless, Mobile and Multimedia Networks* (pp. 570–575). Buffalo, NY. doi:10.1.1.87.304

Demirkol, I., Ersoy, C., & Alagoz, F. (2004). MAC protocols for wireless sensor networks: A survey. *IEEE Communications Magazine, 44*(4), 115–121. doi:10.1109/MCOM.2006.1632658.

Douceur, J. R. (March, 2002). The Sybil attack. In *Proceedings of the Workshop on Peer-to-Peer Systems (IPTPS02)*. Cambridge, MA. doi:10.1.1.17.1073

El-Bendary, N., Hassanien, A. E., Sedano, J., Soliman, O. S., & Ghali, N. I. (2011). TESLA-based secure routing protocol for wireless sensor networks. In *Proceedings of First ACM International Workshop on Security and Privacy Preserving in e-Societies*. Baabda, Lebanon: ACM.

Elson, J., & Estrin, D. (2000). *An address-free architecture for dynamic sensor networks* (Technical Report 724). University of Southern California, Computer Science Department. doi:10.1.1.42.9521

Ganeriwal, S., Capkun, S., Hanand, C., & Srivastava, M. B. (2005). Secure time synchronization service for sensor networks. In *Proceedings of 4th ACM Workshop on Wireless Security*. doi:10.1.1.85.8733

Gawdan, I. S., & Chow, C. Z, T. A., & Gawdan, Q. I. (2011). Cross-layer based security solutions for wireless sensor networks. *International Journal of the Physical Sciences, 6*(17), 4245-4254. Retrieved from www.academicjournals.org/IJPS/

Graaf, R., Hegazy, I., Horton, J., & Safavi-Nain, R. (2010). Distributed detection of wormhole attacks in wireless sensor networks. In J. Zheng, S. Mao, S. F. Midkiff, & H. Zhu (Eds.), *Ad Hoc Networks: First International Conference, ADHOCNETS 2009*, (pp. 208-222). Berlin, Germany: Springer.

Hamid, A., Mamun-Or-Rashid, M., & Hong, C. S. (2006). Defense against lap-top class attacker in wireless sensor network. In *Proceedings of International Conference on Advanced Communications Technology*. Gangwon-Do, Korea. doi:10.1.1.99.6579

Hea, T., Stankovica, J. A., Lub, C., & Abdelzahera, T. (2003). SPEED: A stateless protocol for real-time communication in sensor networks. In *Proceedings of the 23rd International Conference on Distributed Computing Systems (ICDCS)*. Providence, RI. doi:10.1.1.12.1662

Heinzelman, W., Chandrakasan, A., & Balakrishnan, H. (2000). *Energy-efficient communication protocols for wireless microsensor networks*. Paper presented at Hawaiian International Conference on Systems Science. Washington, DC. doi:10.1.1.112.3914

Hu, L., & Evans, D. (2004). Using directional antennas to prevent wormhole attacks. In Proceedings of Network and Distributed System Security Symposium (NDSS). San Diego, CA. doi:10.1.1.135.7144

Hu, Y. C., Perrig, A., & Johnson, D. B. (2003). Packet leashes: A defense against wormhole attacks in wireless networks. In *Proceedings of Twenty-Second Annual Joint Conference of the IEEE Computer and Communications.* doi:10.1.1.113.4100

Hu, Y. C., Perrig, A., & Johnson, D. B. (2006). Wormhole attacks in wireless networks. *IEEE Journal on Selected Areas in Communication, 24*(2), 370-381. doi:10.1.1.117.698

Intanagonwiwat, C., Govindan, R., Estrin, D., Heidemann, J., & Silva, F. (2003). Directed diffusion for wireless sensor networking. *IEEE/ACM Transactions on Networking, 11*(1), 2-18. doi:10.1.1.1.3918

Jian, Y., Chen, S., Zhang, Z., & Zhang, L. (2007). Protecting receiver location privacy in wireless sensor networks. In *Proceedings of INFOCOM.* IEEE Computer Science Society Press.

Johnson, D. B., & Maltz, A. D. (2001). DSR: The dynamic source routing protocol for multi-hop wireless ad hoc networks. *Discovery, 5*(1), 1-25. doi:10.1.1.115.3829

Kaplantzis, S., Shilton, A., Mani, A., & Sekerciolu, Y. A. (2007). Detecting selective forwarding attacks in wireless sensor networks using support vector machines. In *Proceedings of the 3rd International Symposium on Intelligent Sensors, Sensor Networks and Information Processing.* Melbourne, Australia: IEEE Computer Science Society Press.

Karlof, C., Sastry, N., & Wagner, D. (2004). Tinysec— A link layer security architecture for wireless sensor networks. In *Proceedings of 2nd International Conference on Embedded Networked Sensor Systems.* New York. doi:10.1145/1031495.1031515

Karlof, C., & Wagner, D. (2003). Secure routing in wireless sensor networks: Attacks and countermeasures. *Elsevier's AdHoc Networks Journal, 1*(2-3), 293-315. Retreived from www.journals.elsevier.com/ad-hoc-networks

Karp, B., & Kun, H. T. (2000). GPSR: Greedy perimeter stateless routing for wireless networks. In *Proceedings of the 6th Annual International Conference on Mobile Computing and Networking.* Boston, MA. doi: 10.1145/345910.345953

Khozium, M. O. (2008). Hello flood counter measure for wireless sensor networks. *International Journal of Computer Science and Security, 2*(3), 57–65. Retrieved from www.cscjournals.org/description.php?Jcode=IJCSS.

Krontiris, I., Dimitriou, T., Thanassis, G., & Mpasoukos, M. (2007). Intrusion detection of sinkhole attacks in wireless sensor networks. In Proceedings of the 3rd International Conference on Algorithmic Aspects of Wireless Sensor Networks. Wroclaw, Poland. doi:0.1.1.105.3047

Lazos, L., Poovendran, R., Meadows, C., Syverson, P., & Changr, L. W. (2005). Preventing wormhole attacks on wireless ad hoc networks: A graph theoretic approach. In *Proceedings of the Wireless Communication and Networking Conference WCNC 05.* New Orleans, LA. doi:10.1.1.76.7850

Li, Q., & Rus, D. (2006). Global clock synchronization in sensor networks. *IEEE Transactions on Computers, 55*(2), 214–226. Retrieved from www.computer.org/portal/web/tc doi:10.1109/TC.2006.25.

Makri, E., & Stamatiou, Y. C. (2010). Key management techniques for wireless sensor networks: Practical and theoretical considerations. In A. K. Pathan (Ed.), *Security of self-organizing networks— MANET, WSN, WMN, VANET* (pp. 317–345). Boca Raton, FL: CRC Press. doi:10.1201/EBK1439819197-18.

Manjeshwar, E., & Agrawal, D. P. (2001). TEEN: A routing protocol for enhanced efficiency in wireless sensor networks. In *Proceedings of the 15th International Parallel and Distributed Processing Symposium (IPDPS)*. San Francisco, CA. doi:10.1109/IPDPS.2001.925197

Marchi, B., Grilo, A., & Nunes, M. (2007). DTSN— Distributed transport for sensor networks. In *Proceedings of the IEEE Symposium on Computers and Communications*. Aveiro, Portugal. doi:10.1.1.80.4025

Meghdadi, M., Ozdemir, S., & Guler, I. (2011). A survey of wormhole-based attacks and their countermeasures in wireless sensor networks. *IETE Technical Review, 28*(2), 89–102. doi:10.4103/0256-4602.78089.

Newsome, J., Shi, E., Song, D., & Perrig, A. (2004). The Sybil attack in sensor networks: Analysis and defenses. In *Proceedings of the 3rd International Symposium on Information Processing in Sensor Networks*. San Francisco, CA. doi:10.1.1.3.1233

Ngai, E. C. H., Liu, J., & Lyu, M. R. (2007). An efficient intruder detection algorithm against sinkhole attacks in wireless sensor networks. *Computer Communications, 30*(11), 2354–2364. doi: doi:10.1016/j.comcom.2007.04.025.

Padmavathi, G., & Shanmugapriya, D. (2009). A survey of attacks, security mechanisms and challenges in wireless sensor networks. *International Journal of Computer Security, 4*(1), 117–125.

Pazynyuk, T., Li, J., Oreku, G. S., & Pa, L. (2008). QoS as means of providing WSNs security. In *Proceedings of the Seventh International Conference on Networking*. Cancun, Mexico. doi:10.1109/ICN.2008.22

Perkins, C., Belding-Royer, M. E., & Das, S. R. (2003). Ad hoc on-demand distance vector (aodv) routing. *RFC 202*. Retrieved November 2012 from http://moment.cs.ucsb.edu/pub/draft-perkins-manet-aodvbis-00.txt

Perrig, A., Stankovic, J., & Wagner, D. (2004). Security in wireless sensor networks. *Communications of the ACM, 47*(6), 53-57. doi:10.1.1.4.9059

Perrig, A., Zewczyk, R., Tygar, J. D., Wen, V., & Culler, D. E. (2002). Spins: Security protocols for sensor networks. *ACM Journal of Wireless Networks, 8*(5), 521-534. Retrieved from http://link.springer.com/journal/11276

Przydatek, B., Perrig, A., & Song, D. (2003). SIA: Secure information aggregation in sensor networks. *Journal of Computer Security, 15*(1), 69–102. Retrieved from dl.acm.org/citation.cfm?id=1370616.

Reindl, P., Nygard, K., & Du, X. (2010). Defending malicious collision attacks in wireless sensor networks. In *Proceedings of the IEEE/IFIP 8th International Conference on Embedded and Ubiquitous Computing*. Hong Kong, China: IEEE Press.

Ruan, G., Jain, S., & Zhu, S. (2009). *SensorEar: A sensor network based eavesdropping system*. Paper presented the 8th IEEE International Symposium on Reliable Distributed System. New York. doi:10.1.1.210.9177

Sami, D., Al-Wakeel, S., & Al-Swailem, A. (2007). PRSA: A path redundancy based security algorithm for wireless sensor networks. In *Proceedings of the Wireless Communication and Networking Conference (WCNC 2007)*. Hong Kong, China: ACM Press.

Sharif, W., & Leckie, C. (2006). New variants of wormhole attacks for sensor networks. In *Proceedings of the Australian Telecommunication Networks and Applications Conference*. Melbourn, Australia. doi:10.1.1.122.2838

Sharmila, S., & Umamaheswari, G. (2012). Defensive mechanisms of selective forward attack in wireless sensor networks. [Retreived from http://research.ijcaonline.org/]. *International Journal of Computers and Applications, 39*(4), 46–52. doi:10.5120/4812-7048.

Singh, V. P., Jain, S., & Singhai, J. (2010). Hello flood attack and its countermeasures in wireless sensor networks. *International Journal of Computer Science, 7*(11), 23–28. Retrieved from www.ijarcs.info/.

Smart Dust Mote. (n.d.). Retrieved December 2012 from http://robotics.eecs.berkeley.edu/~pister/SmartDust/

Stavrou, E., Pitsillides, A., Hadjichristofi, G., & Hadjicostis, C. (2010). Security in future mobile sensor networks: Issues and challenges. In *Proceedings of the International Conference on Security and Cryptography (SECRYPT)*. Athens, Greece: Springer.

Telosb Mote. (n.d.). Retrieved December 2012 from http://www.willow.co.uk/telosb_datasheet.pdf

Tmote Sky. (n.d.). Retrieved December 2012 from www.snm.ethz.ch/Projects/TmoteSky

Tun, Z., & Maw, A. II. (2008). Wormhole attack detection in wireless sensor networks. *World Academy of Science. Engineering and Technology, 28*(2), 545–551.

Uppuluri, P., & Basu, S. (2004). Lase: Layered approach for sensor security and efficiency. In *Proceedings of the IEEE International Conference on Parallel Processing Workshops*. doi:10.1109/ICPPW.2004.1328038

Walters, J. P., Liang, Z., Shi, W., & Chaudhary, V. (2006). Wireless sensor network security—A survey. In Security in Distributed, Grid, and Pervasive Computing, (pp. 208-222). Boca Raton, FL: Auerbach Publications, CRC Press. doi:10.1.1.77.3003

Wang, Y., Attebury, G., & Ramamurthy, B. (2006). A survey of security issues in wireless sensor networks. *IEEE Communications Surveys and Tutorials, 8*, 2-23. doi:10.1.1.133.6857

Woo, A., Tong, T., & Culler, D. (2003). Taming the underlying challenges of reliable multihop routing in sensor networks. In *Proceedings of the 1st International Conference on Embedded Networked Sensor Systems*. New York. doi:10.1.1.1.5480

Wood, A., & Stankovic, J. A. (2002). Denial of service in sensor networks. *IEEE Computer, 35*(10), 54–62. doi:10.1109/MC.2002.1039518.

Xing, K., Srinivasan, S. S. R., Rivera, M. J., Li, J., & Cheng, X. (2010). Attacks and countermeasures in sensor networks: A survey. In S. C.-H. Huang, D. MacCallum, & D.-Z. Du (Eds.), *Network security* (pp. 251–272). New York: Springer. doi:10.1007/978-0-387-73821-5_11.

Xu, W., Ma, K., Trappe, W., & Zhang, Y. (2006). Jamming sensor networks: Attack and defense strategies. *IEEE Network, 20*(3), 41–47. doi:10.1109/MNET.2006.1637931.

Xu, W., Trappe, W., & Zhang, Y. (2008). Defending wireless sensor networks from radio interference through channel adaptation. *ACM Transactions on Sensor Networks, 4*(4), 1–34. doi:10.1145/1387663.1387664.

Yi, S., Pei, Y., & Kalyanaraman, S. (2003). On the capacity improvement of ad hoc wireless networks using directional antennas. In *Proceedings of the 4th ACM International Symposium on Mobile Ad Hoc Networking & Computing*. New York: ACM Press.

Zhang, Y., Liu, W., & Fang, Y. (2005). Secure localization in wireless sensor networks. In *Proceedings of the IEEE Military Communications Conference* (Milcom'05). Atlantic City, NJ: IEEE Press.

Zhao, F., & Guibas, F. (2004). *Wireless sensor networks: An information processing approach.* Burlington, MA: Morgan Kaufmann.

ADDITIONAL READING

Du, X., & Chen, H. H. (2008). Security in wireless sensor networks. *IEEE Wireless Communications*, *5*(4), 60–66. doi: doi:10.1109/MWC.2008.4599222.

Li, C. T. (2012). Security of wireless sensor network: Current status and key issues. In H. D. Chinh, & Y. K. Tan (Eds.), *Smart wireless sensor network* (pp. 299–337). InTech Open Science.

Malik, M. Y. (2012). An outline of security in wireless sensor networks: Threats, countermeasures and implementations. In N. Zaman, K. Ragab, & A. Abdullah (Eds.), *Wireless sensor networks and energy efficiency: Protocols, routing and management* (pp. 507–527). Hershey, PA: IGI Global. doi:10.4018/978-1-4666-0101-7.ch024.

Patil, H. K., & Szygenda, S. A. (2012). *Security for wireless sensor networks using identity-based cryptography*. Boca Raton, FL: Auerbach Publications, CRC Press. doi:10.1201/b13080.

Sen, J. (2013). Security in wireless sensor networks. In S. Khan, A. K. K. Pathan & N. A. Alrajeh (Eds.), Wireless sensor networks: Current status and future trends (pp. 407-460). Boca Raton, FL: CRC Press, Taylor and Francis group. Retrieved from http://www.crcpress.com

KEY TERMS AND DEFINITIONS

Adhoc Network: A system of network elements that combine to form a network requiring little or no planning.

Adversary: A malicious entity that opposes the normal operation of the system.

Aggregation: Is any process in which information is gathered and expressed in a summary form.

Attack: To begin to affect harmfully.

Collision: The result of simultaneous data packet transmission between two or more network devices.

Cluster: Group of nodes working together closely to improve the performance.

Eavesdropping: The act of secretly listening to the private conversation of others without their consent.

Exhaustion: The action or state of using something up or of being used up completely.

Global Address: The predefined address that is used as an address for all users of that network.

Intrusion Detection System: A software that detects an attack on the system.

Localization: A determination of the place where something is.

Mote: A sensor node.

Multihop: Communication between two end nodes through a number of intermediate nodes whose function is to relay information from one point to another.

Network: A system that enables users to exchange information over long distances by connecting with each other through a system of routers, servers, switches, and the like.

Protocol: Defines rules and conventions for communication between network devices.

Protocol Stack: A particular software implementation of a computer network protocol suite.

QoS: A broad collection of networking technologies and techniques that provide guarantees on the ability of a network to deliver predictable results.

Reliability: The probability that system will perform its intended functions and operations in a given environment, without experiencing failures.

Security: Protecting the system from unwanted users.

Sensor Node: A node in a wireless sensor network that is capable of performing some processing, gathering sensory information and communicating with other connected nodes in the network.

Sink/ Base Station: Component of WSN with much more computational, energy and communication resources and act as a gateway between sensor nodes and the end user.

Spoofing: Hiding one's identity or faking the identity of another user to deceive the system.

Threat: Refers to anything that has the potential to cause serious harm to the system.

WSN/DSN: A network of sensor nodes that can sense the environment and communicate the gathered information through the wireless link to the sink.

Chapter 15
Voting Median Base Algorithm for Measurement Approximation of Wireless Sensor Network Performance

Nazar Elfadil
Fahad Bin Sultan University, Saudi Arabia

Yaqoob J. Al-Raisi
The Research Council of the Sultanate of Oman, Sultanate of Oman

ABSTRACT

The success of Wireless Sensor Network application monitoring relies on the accuracy and reliability of its nodes operation. Unfortunately, operation deviations of these nodes appear as regular occurrences not isolated events as in traditional networks. This is due to their special characteristics that reduce network manufacturing and deployment costs and maintain the nodes immunity against internal and external conditions. The goal of this chapter is to propose a real-time, distributed, passive, and low resources usage performance-monitoring algorithm that monitors Wireless Sensor Network functionality and isolates the detected deviated nodes from norm operation. Simulation and empirical experiments showed that the proposed algorithm has a slight processing and storage overhead. It is important to mention that these experiments showed that the proposed algorithm has a high reliability in tracking and isolating network nodes problems.

INTRODUCTION

Sensor networks are considered to be one of the most motivating research areas since it has strong effect on the technological developments. What make them popular are their abilities to fit into a smaller volume with some good features such as the low production costs with a more power. In addition to this, sensors can be implemented in any environment with harsh conditions to transmit data to the base station regularly. It is not worthy that Sound Surveillance System (SOSUS) is the

DOI: 10.4018/978-1-4666-4691-9.ch015

first obvious sensor networks application (Chong & Kumar 2003). This system with assistance of acoustic sensors was used in the Cold War to track Soviet submarines. However, around 1980, Defense Advanced Research Projects Agency (DARPA) created Distributed Sensor Networks (DSN) program. While Wireless Sensor Networks (WSNs) are generally classified into two categories; namely: (1) Infrastructure-base, and (2) ad-hoc wireless networks. Wireless ad-hoc networks can be further classified into several categories based on their applications; namely: (a) Mobile ad-hoc networks, (b) Wireless sensor networks, (c) wireless mesh networks, and (d) hybrid wireless networks (Piyush et al. 2012), (Akyildiz, & Wang 2005), and (Hande & Erosy 2010).

Wireless Sensor Network (WSN) is expected to be a new revolutionary technology in the manner of the internet due to its characteristics that allow them to have disposal, small size, and unattended maintenance-free nodes. These characteristics arise because the WSNs designers and manufacturers target a cheap system at a fixed performance not as in the traditional network to improve the performance and hold the price constant over the time. This strategy helps to reduce the overall network resources usage. On the other hand, these characteristics, along with the usage of wireless communication, the event-driven nature of the operating system, the harsh environment the nodes work in and the limited usage of fault-tolerant/diagnosis tools, reduce node immunity against internal and external interference, such as software bugs. This reduction increases the probability of deviating network nodes operation from their norm; decreases network overall functionality and degrade network collected data reliability even when the network protocols robustness increases such that it combats against worst-case scenarios. For example, in some practical deployments, such as (Ramanathan et al. 2006), (Tolle et al. 2005), and (Zhao 2004), an analysis of network collected data showed a reduction in their quality and quantity to an amount of 49% and 55%, respectively.

Nevertheless, these analyses showed that these reductions might cause in some cases a failure of the WSN monitoring.

These deviations occur because of two types of errors; i.e. systematic and transient (Eiman & Badri 2003). The systematic type arises because of hardware faults; such as calibration, reduction in the operating power level, and change in the operating condition. It affects the operation continuously until the problem is solved. The transient arises due to temporary external/internal conditions, such as random environment effects, software bugs and channel interference. This type deviates the operation until the effect disappears.

These two deviation types affect the quality and the quantity of the collected data in network (Nasir 2002), and (Laura 2007). They directly affect individual sensor node measurements and drift them by a constant value; i.e. biased error; change the difference between sensor measurement and the actual value; i.e. drift error; and remain sensor measurements constant regardless of changes in the actual value; i.e. complete failure error. In addition, they directly affect network packets communication and drop them. The indirect effect happens when the deviations affect network collaboration function and reduce network performance in terms of the collected data reliability and increase the use of the network resources.

Tracking and detecting the above discussed deviations in WSN is not flexible as in traditional network because of the factors that affect the monitoring analysis and degrade its efficiency such as the:

- Limited finite energy and communication resources,
- Unavailability of a dominant protocol or algorithm that is suitable to work in all applications,
- Unavailability of global measurement variables due to the use of distributed control protocols that reduce the consumption of network resources,

- Network's adaptive nature to frequent changes in connectivity, link failure and node status,
- Imbalance in network traffic as a result of different data characteristics in terms of monitored phenomenon changes, reporting rate duration and the number of sinks in the network,
- Tolerance to data changes and losses as a result of redundancy,
- Collaboration functions used in different tasks to increase the accuracy of collected data and reduce the usage of node resources,
- Direct interaction of nodes with the environment that increases noise level and increases the probability of node failure,

Performance techniques are similar to diagnosis techniques but without iteration tests and screw pack techniques. Unfortunately there is little literature and research on systematic measurement and monitoring in wireless sensor networks. Yonggang (2004) studied the effect of low network level and impact on network stability and network processing. He studied the effect of the environment conditions, traffic load, network dynamic, collaboration behavior, and constraint recourse on packet delivery performance using empirical experiments and simulations. Although packet delivery is important in wireless communication and can predict network performance, it can give wrong indications of network performance level due to collaboration behavior, and measurement redundancy which makes a network able to tolerate a certain degree of changes. Also, Zhao proposed an energy map aggregation based approach that sends messages recording significant energy level drops to the sink. Although energy consumption is very important in WSNs and all network levels affected by it, several researchers such as (Szewczyk 2004) showed in their analysis that there can be a sudden drop in node and network functionality which is not possible to detect by measuring voltage level. This drop causes network instability due to sudden route change, and more energy consumption due to usage of non-optimal routes to the destination.

The goal of this paper is to propose Voting Median Based Algorithm (VMBA) for approximate measurement and monitoring Wireless Sensor Network that takes into consideration the above network challenges and reduces their impact on the proposed monitoring tool efficiency. It is worth to mention that, the use of voting for obtaining highly reliable data from multiple unreliable versions was first suggested in the mid 1950s (Behrooz 1994). In addition to this voting is considered to be essential for unreliable systems which use multi computation paradigm. Much research has been carried on the implementation and effectiveness of voting schemes. Although most of them concentrated on the simple majority voting approach (Behrooz 1994). However, voting could be reliable because of many factors; to mention some: (1) It reasonable availability, (2) Its simple statements contains a clear correctness proofs and (3) Simple implementation (Sushil & Mutchler 1987), and (Paris 1986). Mainly this is considered to be a passive voting algorithm that can detect faults that may affect the quality and quantity of the collective data of WSN. This process could be achieved in four modules; listening and filtering, data analysis and threshold test, decision and confidence control and warning packet exchange. In this section, some definitions followed by the VMBA functional algorithm will be shown (Raisi & Elfadil 2010), and (Raisi & Elfadil 2009).

The proposed algorithm works in real-time bases to reduce the required memory and in a distributed scheme so that it will be scalable for any size of network. Moreover, it passively extracts its metrics from network application, low and high network levels by utilizing the overhearing that exists in the neighborhood, as a result of the wireless communication medium. The proposed algorithm reduces its analyses complexity; memory storage and required learning time by calculating the collected parameters uncertainty depending on an interval that relies on the power dissipation model of the monitored phenomenon. This interval gives the imprecision of neighborhood nodes operation and any uncertainty in the monitored phenomenon.

The proposed VMBA algorithm performance was tested under different simulation and empirical experiments scenarios and was approve as uses a slight processing and storage overhead. This insures its easy implementation on the existing constraints resources platform. In addition, these experiments showed the high reliability of the proposed algorithm in tracking and isolating nodes problems in network and nodes levels. This comes with a high resilience to both high neighbors' packet loss and random measurements deviations. Unfortunately, this also comes with some limitations due to the simple passive analysis method adapted in the algorithm.

The results outcome from these conducted experiments are divided are into two parts. This paper 'part one' deals with our approach node power consumption and its impact on the network lifetime, the proposed algorithm spatial-temporary events tracking, the proposed algorithm detection of neighborhood reliability. Finally, it discusses some of the proposed algorithm limitations detected in the experiments. The second part of the paper deals with the proposed algorithm detection at network and node levels, the proposed algorithm released warning messages and the impact of threshold value in algorithm detection and warning messages release. The rest of the paper layout is as follows: Section two discusses related work; section three then provides an explanation of the algorithm different module function. The fourth section discusses some of important experiment results of algorithm resources usage and their impact on network lifetime. Finally, the paper ends with a conclusion, limitations and suggestions for future work.

RELATED WORK

Although the researchers' analysis of several real WSN deployments expected there to be an improvement of the deployed network's functionality of up to 51% if a real-time monitoring/measuring tool was used (Ramanathan 2006), the special characteristics of WSNs, discussed above, lessen the functionality of these tools, reduce their efficiency and increase their impact on network lifetime. As a result, the researchers proposed several methods, such as a tradeoff between the algorithm's detection accuracy, its response time and resource usage, to reduce the impact of such tools on monitored network. This was achieved by selecting the algorithm's parameters, controlling the required packet exchange, and controlling the level of complexity of the analysis.

The researchers selected the algorithm's parameters so that the required extraction resources could have a low impact on the network's lifetime. This was done by using common parameters that are available at low or high network levels and attribute them to network status. For example, at low network levels, they tracked packet losses between neighbor nodes and related them to network congestion, environmental effects, node battery depletion, and other hardware problems, as discussed in (Ramanathan et al. 2005). While at high network levels, they tracked the changes of node measurements and share them to sensor node software/hardware problems, as discussed in (Eiman & Badri 2003). Moreover, some of them were extracted at particular parameters that would track certain goals designed in the network, such as power consumption (Zhao 2004), node coverage and connectivity Vuran et al. 2004.

Also, they control the rate of exchange of the algorithm's parameters in order to reduce the impact of monitoring tool on the network's lifetime. Some of them continuously use techniques to collect parameters and analyze them centrally, such as (Zhao 2004); others distribute these analyses to reduce the number of exchanged packets and the reply time, as discussed in (Jaikaeo 2001). The third group uses predicted models that exchange the packets if there is a large discrepancy between the actual and the predicted values, such as in (Raquel 2003).

Finally, these researchers reduce the impact of the algorithm on the network's lifetime by controlling the complexity of the algorithm's analysis and the resources it uses. This is achieved by generating the residual of the monitored parameters in terms of physical or analytical redundancy (Nasir 2002) and (Laura 2007). Physical redundancy generates an estimate of the actual value of a quantity based on the available redundant information; this is accomplished either by statistical methods (such as descriptive or inferential statistics), or by data fusion. The main advantage of this type of redundancy is that it is relatively easy to implement and provide a high degree of certainty; its reliability relies on the accuracy of the collected measurements. Analytical redundancy methods, on the other hand, provide values other than direct measurements from the parameters and variables of interest using a process model such as a Kalman filter, parity relations, Principal Component Analysis (PCA), and Artificial Neural Networks (ANN). These methods are not easy to implement and they depend on the reliability of the process model.

All the above methods for extracting, exchanging and analysis were gathered together to ensure the reliability of data collected in the network by using four main techniques: data cleaning, fault-tolerance, diagnosis, and performance measurement. Data cleaning techniques work at a high network level and consider reading impacts from a deviated sensor on multi-sensor aggregation/fusion such as in (Jung 2004) and (Caimu & Cauligi 2004). Such research proposed several methods that isolate deviated readings by tracking or predicting correlation between neighbor nodes measurements. The proposed methods that adapt statistical methods in their analysis did not consider the impact of the packet loss which reduces its

detection accuracy and the others that adapt the analytical method in their analysis used complex methods or models that need a high resource usage to detect and predict sensor measurements. In addition, these techniques rectify deviated data after detecting them without checking their cause and their impact on network functionality.

Fault-tolerance techniques are important in embedded networks where it is difficult to access them physically. The advantage of these techniques is their ability to address all network levels; such as circuit level, logical level, memory level, program level and system level. But due to WSNs scare recourses these techniques have a limited usage. In general WSNs fault-tolerant techniques detect faults in fusion and aggregation operation, network deployment and collaboration, coverage and connectivity, energy consumption, energy event fault tolerance, reporting rate, network detection, and many others (Indranil et al. 2001), (Clouqueur 2004), (Vuran et al. 2004), Song & Edward 2004), (Ding et al. 2005), (Bhaskar & Iyengar 2004), (Koushanfar et al. 2003), and (Luo & Huang 2006). Faults are detected using logical decision predicates computed in individual sensors, faulty node detection, or event region and event boundary detection. These methods detect metrics either at high or low network level without relating them to each other and without checking their impact on network functionality. The main problem of these techniques is the impact of deviation on network functionality and collected data accuracy before it is detected and isolated. This is because the techniques operate when there is an effect on functionality that the network cannot tolerate with it and need to readjust itself to solve it.

Diagnosis techniques use active or proactive monitoring to trace, visualize, simulate and debug historical network log files in real and non real time as discussed in (Jaikaeo 2001). These techniques are used to detect faults at high or low network levels after testing their cause. For example Nithya in (Yonggang 2004), proposed a debugging system that debugs low network level statistical changes by drawing correlations between seemingly unrelated, distributed events and produces graphs that highlight those correlations. Most of these diagnosis techniques are complex and use iteration tests for their detection. This is because they assume a minimal cost associated with continuously transmitting of debug information to centralized or distributed monitor nodes and send/receive test packets to confirm the detection of a fault.

Finally, performance techniques are similar to diagnosis techniques but without iteration tests. Unfortunately, there is little literature and research on systematic measurement and monitoring in wireless sensor networks. Zhao in (Zhao 2004) studied the effect of low network level and its impact on network stability and network processing. He studied the effect of the environment conditions, traffic load, network dynamic, collaboration behavior, and constraint recourse on packet delivery performance using empirical experiments and simulations. Although packet delivery is important in wireless communication and can predict network performance, it can give wrong indications of network performance level due to collaboration behavior, and measurement redundancy which makes a network able to tolerate a certain degree of changes. Also, Zhao proposed an energy map aggregation based approach that sends messages recording significant energy level drops to the sink. Although energy consumption is very important in WSNs and all network levels affected by it, several researchers such as (Szewczyk 2004), showed in their analysis, that there can be a sudden drop in node and network functionality which is not possible to detect by measuring voltage level. This sudden drop causes network instability due to sudden route change, and more energy consumption due to usage of non-optimal routes to the destination.

Although the above discussed methods and tools help in monitoring and measuring WSN functionality, their limits are more than expected, especially at large network scale. As consequence,

this paper was motivated by such drawbacks and limitations. The main contribution will be to find a real-time monitoring tool that efficiently detects the degradation of WSN performance before it happens, isolates the detected deviated nodes and uses low network resources.

ALGORITHM APPROACH

The range of simulation/empirical experiments that were conducted, and different researches which were discussed in related work section, demonstrates the goal of the proposed algorithm, the algorithm needs to be divided into four modules; namely: (A) listening and filtering, (B) data analysis and threshold tests, (C) decision confidence control, and (D) warning packet exchange. This is because the main resource usages that affect the lifetime of the monitored network and the detection confidence of the algorithm come from the:

- Algorithm's collected parameters and the method used to collect them from the monitored network;
- Complexity of the analysis method used;
- Uncertainty level of the algorithm's analysis;
- Algorithm's packet exchange.

As a result, controlling individually each of the factors listed above ensures a reduction in the effect of the proposed algorithm on the network's lifetime and increases the algorithm's detection confidence. The proposed algorithm designed such that it works in a distributed manner to ensure the scalability at any large-size network. It collects its metrics online from network application low and high network levels to ensure the reduction of the required overhead usage; such as memory and processing. VMBA algorithm relies in its analysis on a simple voting technique that calculates the median of network protocols parameters. It provides an operation interval for neighborhood nodes operation that depends on network designed goals to quantify the uncertainty in the monitored phenomenon and nodes operation. This simple analysis reduces the complexity of the algorithm and makes it without a need for learning time like most of the uncertainty models. In addition, the algorithm relates the two network levels parameters to test the impact of the change on collected data reliability and network functionality. This is done by checking the percentage of deviated nodes from neighborhood median operation and the level of their weighted residual.

Listening and Filtering Module

The first module is considered to be the most important item in the algorithm because other algorithm modules analysis depends on its collected parameters. The module integrated in network application flow process such that it reuses the same application protocols parameters, and their used memory. This reduce the VBMA algorithm required resources usage for metrics calculation, follow the application process such that it is not affected by used power save techniques and there will not be a need for a special synchronization timer for its functionality.

The module starts its functionality by waiting for a period of time after the application triggers a report of sensor. This time period is controlled by the period between the two measurements and/or the sleeping node period. In addition, it depends on the network's data delivery period, node functionality in the network collaboration function, and node location. Any un-received measurements within this assigned period are considered to be a loss. If more than one measurement packet is received from a neighbor during this period, the monitoring node will take the first at that time interval. After that, the module examines all neighborhood available measurements to determine whether they fall in the range of normal sensor operation (i.e. depend on sensor nodes characteristics and collaboration as

discussed in (Ricardo 2007)). Measurements that are out of this range filter and the counter of node deviation increment; as shown in the pseudo-code in Appendix B and its notation definitions in Appendix A. This measurement filtering prevents the node from wasting resources on obvious deviated measurements.

After that the module constructs neighbor readings tables; i.e. depends on the application requirements. Finally, the median of available measurements is calculated and the available measurements and calculated median sent to algorithm module 2.

The proposed algorithm uses statistical method for its uncertainty analysis to estimate phenomenon readings because it is the lowest resources usage method compared to the fusion and the analytical methods. It uses median because it's robust to noise and error borne where it tolerates to small error in a large fraction of measurements, small calibration error or noise and tolerates large error in small fraction of measurements such as it tolerate with 50% error. Wagner in (Wagner 2004) showed that median error is low, its resilience is if and its break point; i.e. the point at which the method calculation will be affected; is 50% of nodes; where n denotes the total number of nodes, k denote the number of error nodes and the standard deviations of nodes measurements. In addition, the proposed algorithm uses divide-and-conquer method for measurement sort in order to reduce analysis growth of the function to (Cormen 2004).

Data Analysis and Threshold Test Module

The second module starts its function after receiving the calculated median value and time instant neighbors collected measurements from module 1. It calculates the difference between the last stored calculated neighborhood median and the new received calculated median to validate the accuracy of the new calculated median value. If the difference is larger than a threshold that represents the maximum expected change in the measured phenomenon within that period of monitoring time, the module increment neighborhood accuracy degradation counters and replaces the new calculated median with the stored median value; as shown in Appendix C. Else, the old stored median value replaced by the new value. (This is done to reduce the affect of the high neighbor packets losses on median calculation). After that, the module evaluates the measurements received from module 1 at that time instance by comparing their residual difference from the median with a threshold value that relies on the power dissipation model of the monitored phenomenon. If any of the calculated residual is greater than the threshold value, the module increment deviation detection counters of that node. Else, the algorithm is going to stop its function up to the new request from module 1.

The algorithm uses this threshold to accommodate the uncertainty in wireless sensor node operation. This threshold works as interval that contains the expected correct operation value and represents the imprecision of expected correct operation. This required some knowledge of the monitored phenomenon, the specification of used sensor node, and network designed goals between neighbor nodes taken from the deployed network designed goals; as discussed in (Caimu & Cauligi 2004).

The used method allows the proposed algorithm to follow a straightforward approach that calculates any faulty deviations in sensor node operation, which reduces the required analysis complexity, required memory storage and with it there will be no learning time interval that all prediction models have. This is because the approach assumes that true measurements of a phenomenon's characteristics, following a Gaussian pdf, centre on a calculated median of neighborhood readings with variation that controlled by the correlation between the neighbor nodes at the end of monitoring node sensing range (The assumption is based on the fact that the change within node

sensor range is governed by deployed network designed goals and the imprecision of sensor node). Any external impact or monitored phenomenon characteristic change will affect all neighbors at the same time but to a different degree depending on its location from the nodes and the position of the nodes from each other. If this effect exceeds the designed goal between neighbor nodes, the deployment goal fails and the network should reconfigure itself again to achieve it.

The second module also tests the effect of any loss on the reliability of the collected data by calculating the degree of distortion in the neighborhood data that has occurred because of its effect on the collected data accuracy and network functionality. This is done by calculating the ratio of the number of healthy readings to the total number readings as shown in Appendix C step 8.

Decision and Confidence Control Module

The third module of the proposed algorithm is concerned with a decision-making framework to analyze the detected changes in the operation of neighbor nodes and network functionality. This is done at the proposed algorithm by monitoring window method and collected data validity method. In monitoring window method, the algorithm detection control by varying the period of monitoring window and its detection threshold; i.e. similar to what discussed in (Hempstead 2007). While in collected data validation method the algorithm detection controlled by changing the allowed range of sensed regions; i.e. similar to what discussed in (Nasir 2002); degree of neighbor measurement closeness or conflict, and redundancy of measurements. Both methods of configuration settings depend on the characteristics of network application and its tolerance to changes (as discussed in (Laura 2007))); the required algorithm response time and the required accuracy of collected data. The function of this module is shown in Appendix D. Else, the module initializes the counters.

Warning Packet Exchange Module

When module four receives a send request, it checks its neighbors warning exchange memory to ensure that none of the neighbor nodes have reported the same fault in that monitoring window period. If none of the neighbors has a report, it sends a message or it cancels the request. In addition, this module tests warning messages received from its neighbors with statistics from module three. If the suspected node flags up a counter indication smaller than a threshold, (i.e. below the 30% set for the experiments), a message will be released indicating 'NO_EVIDENCE_OF_ FAULT'. On the other hand; if the threshold is higher or equal to the threshold, then the node cancels any similar warning message request from module three during that monitoring period. This is to ensure the reliability of the warning message detection and to correct any incorrect detection that may occur because of the loss or other network circumstances. Moreover, module four reduces the algorithm warning packets released by checking if any of its neighbors sent the same message at that time interval. If it has been sent, the algorithm will discard module three requests as shown in Appendix E part 3, and to reduce algorithm positive detection when the algorithm detect 'NO_EVIDENCE_OF_FAULT' messages more than one time at that time interval of the same reported fault, it will drop send warning message to the sink. This will save the multi-hop routing message consumption and reduce it to consumption of neighbor broad cast at neighborhood.

EXPERIMENTAL RESULTS

The researchers used various empirical and simulation experiments scenarios to evaluate the multiple aspects of the proposed algorithm and test its efficiency. Also, these experiments tested algorithm analysis resilience to network dynamic and the high packet losses, its adaptability and responsiveness to different network conditions and its scalability. At this stage, the paper discusses some of the important results on algorithm resources usage, algorithm spatial-temporary events tracking and algorithm neighborhood reliability detection.

Algorithm Resources Usage and Power Consumption

Several simulation experiments conducted in MATLAB and PowerTossim (Intel Lab 2007) test the proposed algorithm resources usage in different random network deployment sizes with different scenarios of faults rate, packet loss, and random measurement deviations. The outcomes of these experiments evaluated based on two metrics. The first algorithm concern is measuring the impact of VMBA algorithm on node lifetime. This is approach used the average extra CPU power consumption metric, which is the difference between CPU power consumption of the TinyOS 'Surge' application with and without algorithm use under the same network and nodes arrangements. This metric estimates the increase in CPU computation when the algorithm used. The second metrics was the average node lifetime reduction, which is the average decrease of node lifetime for both algorithm best and worst case (that is Best when none of the nodes having faulty deviation and worst when 50% of readings above predefined algorithm threshold). This metric point out the proposed algorithm influence on node lifetime.

The conducted experiments on PowerTossim showed a little increase in node power consumption when the TinyOS 'Surge' application node programmed with the proposed algorithm. The experiments included neighbors ranging from 2 to 16 single hop communicate with the sink each of 50 meter transceiver range and a Mode 1 Mote duty cycle; i.e. 1% to 99% operation. This detected increase raised as a result of the extra CPU consumption; as shown in Figure 6; and the power used to release algorithm warning packets after detecting the fault; as shown in Figure 2. The

PowerTossim simulations showed that the average CPU power consumption increase was in the rage of 4.4±1.5 mJ with a maximum 5.9 mJ (that is 0.8% added to CPU consumption). In addition, these simulations showed a varying of CPU power consumption along with the change of the number of neighbor nodes where it was at the maximum when the number of nodes at neighborhood was fewer than four nodes; as shown in Figure 1. This is because of the increase in node wakeup period as the number of neighbor's increases. This makes the consumed CPU power almost negligible when compared with other at the same period, such as processing and storing received packets. More-over, this low consumption in CPU is due the start of algorithm process when only deviation from neighborhood estimated value detected.

When the same PowerTossim power consumption model used to calculate the impact of the proposed algorithm released warning messages on network lifetime in MATLAB code based experiments of the same network scenarios, the experiments results showed that at the worst case (that is when the number of faulty node is 50% and all warning messages reached to algorithm stop sending condition), the maximum impact of the proposed algorithm affects the original expected network lifetime before algorithm imple-

Figure 1. CPU Power Consumption between Codes with and without the Algorithm in the 'Surge' Application

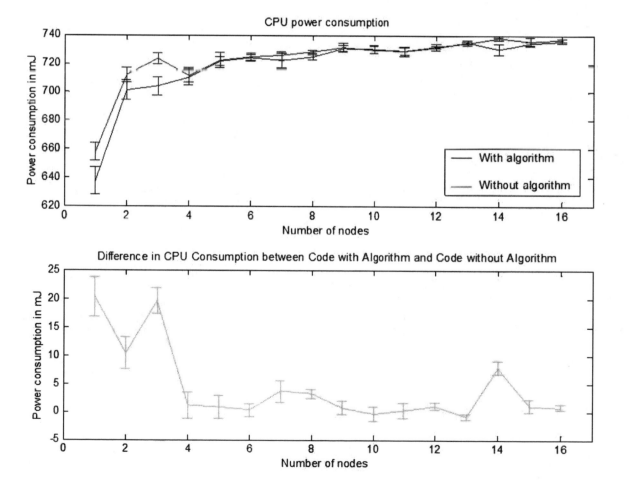

mentation by 0.03 days (out off 224 days); which is equal to 0.01% of network lifetime as shown in Figure 2.

Algorithm Spatial-Temporal Events Tracking

To evaluate the performance of algorithm spatial-temporal events analysis and tracking, and test the effect of removing the confirmed deviated node on the accuracy algorithm analysis, real world data sets were used; i.e. Intel Lab data set (David et al. 2001). The data set consist of temperature,

humidity and light intensity measurements, and was collected by 54 sensor nodes deployed in the Intel lab from February 28th until April 5th 2004 for 720 hours with a scheduled communication approach used with a waking period of four seconds and a 13% duty cycle. The data set had a lot of missing data, noise, and failed sensors, especially when the battery levels were low at the end of the experiment. This is due to the deployment goal of this experiment which was concerned to test the behavior of a sensor network with different conditions of battery power depletion, traffic generation, and multi-hop aspects.

Figure 2. Maximum Packet Transmissions and the Expected Node Lifetime with Temporary and Permanent Neighbor Faults

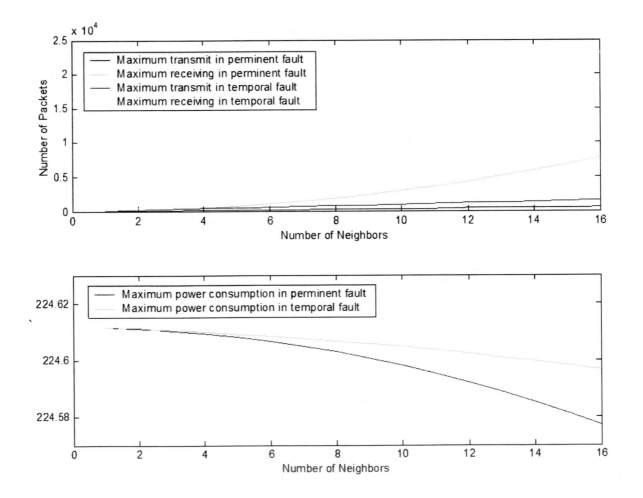

Four metrics were chosen to analyze the results of the experiments. The first metric is the residual value of deviated neighbors, which is the difference between the neighborhood median and the data at a given time instance. This metric computes the diversity level of individual readings from other neighborhood nodes. In addition, it shows the behavior of the fault. The second metric was the weight residual metrics: i.e. the difference between a reading and the median calculated at a time instance multiplied by the ratio of similar correlated readings compared to the total number of readings at the same time instance. This metric shows the weight of each deviation on the neigh-borhood node collected data. The third metric was network performance, which is the ratio of healthy readings as opposed to the total number of nodes in the neighborhood. This metric computes the effect of the losses on the network's functionality.

Figure 3 shows the functionality of the network when the Intel Lab experiment data sets employed MATLAB as a tool in simulating the proposed algorithm functionality on node 1 (as monitoring node), without removing suspected nodes. The figure shows fluctuation in the accuracy of the collected data accuracy and the network's performance as a result of the residual impact of deviated data on the neighborhood data accuracy,

Figure 3. Simulation of VBMA function at Intel data set without Isolation of Faulty Nodes

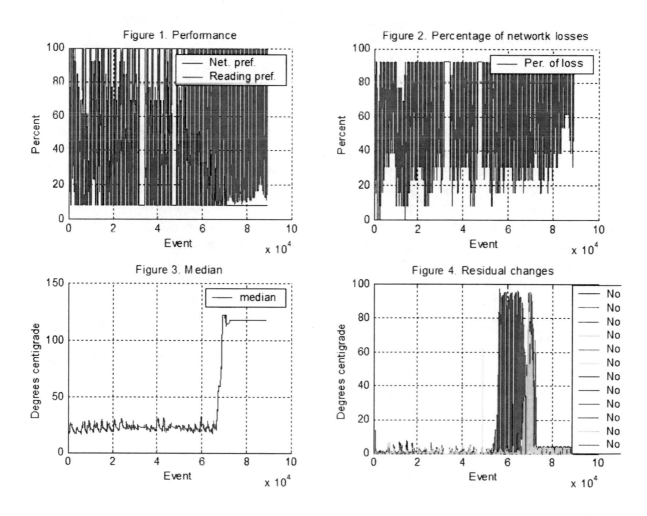

as shown in Figures 3.1 and 3.4. This fluctuation continues up to the time where it becomes very heavy due to the effect of losses and the preponderance of unhealthy readings that become the majority; as shown in Figure 3.1. Afterwards, this heavy fluctuation becomes constant when the number of permanently deviated nodes is greater than the healthy nodes at the end of the experiment (i.e. from event 680000 upwards). Normally, this heavy fluctuation does not occur in WSNs due to the redundancy that schedules the function of nodes, which makes the probability of failure occurring at the same time low. Even if this happens, it can be detected by the dramatic change in data accuracy and the increase in the weighted residual which moves up to a constant level for a long period.

The figure also shows that even there is heavy fluctuation in neighbor readings accuracy due to losses. The calculated median that the algorithm depends on in its analysis does not deviate from the correct phenomenon value until permanently faulty nodes become the majority (as shown in Figure 3.3). This is due to fact that, the algorithm beside its median calculation to time interval neighborhood measurements compares the difference between the new calculated median and the old stored median values with the application's permitted degree of change that depend on the measured phenomenon characteristics. This is used as a filter to remove median values. That is value obviously deviate from the normal as a result of the loss impact of neighborhood packet.

Figure 4 illustrates the proposed algorithm's calculation of the weighted residual for individual node measurements with respect to the neighborhood median. If this figure is compared with Figure 3.4, almost the same changes in detection can be seen but with different residual values; these depend on the number of deviated readings at each time interval.

If the algorithm is allowed to isolate faulty deviated nodes in a specified monitoring window, the neighborhood's performance is improved but with any new deviated node making a higher impact, as shown in Figure 5. This happens because of the increase in the impact of the residual on the collected data as a result of reducing the number of data samples at each time interval. On the other hand, not removing the deviated reading affects the accuracy of the collected data for the period it occurs, as shown in Figure3.

The above experiments were repeated so that the analysis could be carried out on Node 2 acting as the monitoring node. Table 1 shows the detection interval and the number of messages sent by Nodes 1 and 2 before isolating faulty nodes. As can be seen from the table, some of the nodes detected faulty nodes at the same event while others detected them at different times. The table shows that more algorithm warning messages were sent by Node 2. This was as a result of the different neighbor packet losses each node faced.

Algorithm Detection

Since there is no ground truth for the measured phenomenon, statistical methods were used to check the algorithm's detection of the location of faults. This was done by using the Box-Whisker method [38] (i.e. a box plot) which quantifies changes in the measurements of neighbor sensor nodes. With this method, the box represents the middle of the data while the median is the line around it at a range known as the inter quartile range. The analysis shows that 97% of the faults detected by the proposed algorithm lie within the same outlier regions as those detected by the Box-Whisker method. The algorithm detected 108133 changes of value for all nodes, and conformed 83891 to be faulty deviations for a data set with 65% loss. Other 3% were measurements deviations which happened at the same time instance and have the same residual weight.

Figure 4. VMBA Algorithm Detection with Weighted Residual Changes

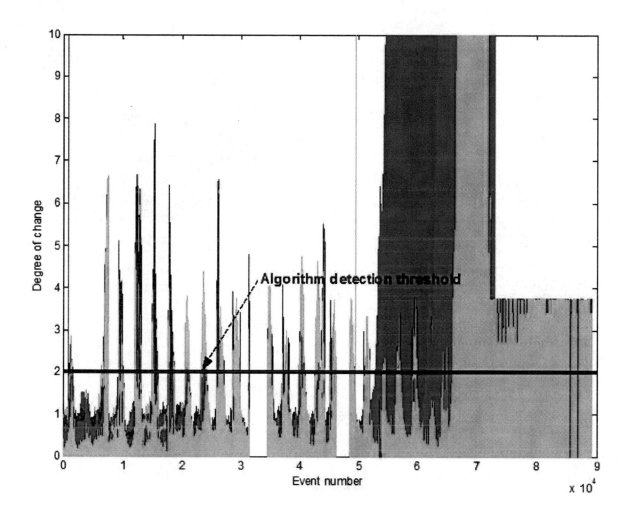

Algorithm Detection of Neighbor-Hood Reliability

The proposed algorithm combine in its analysis the two network levels parameters to analyze events not only gives the impact of the two levels on network performance and data reliability but increase the confidence of the algorithm detection. It detects neighborhood malfunctions by testing the affect of losses on the calculated neighborhood median, as shown in Figure 6(for node 1 analysis neighborhood temperature measurements of Intel data set [39]). When a change detected between two consecutive median calculations that is larger

than the expected change in the phenomenon, the algorithm detects neighborhood's functionality malfunctions. This change causes communication and application protocols in the network to recalculate their tables often and change data gathering points that change data collection accuracy, and communication paths. Such frequent changes cause instability in the network. If this instability detected for a specified period, the algorithm sends a message to point out a neighborhood problem. In addition, the relation between high and low network levels predicts the impact on neighborhood Intel data set collected data accuracy as shown in Figure 7. The figure shows the simulation of

Figure 5. Simulation of VBMA function at Intel data set without Isolation of Faulty Nodes

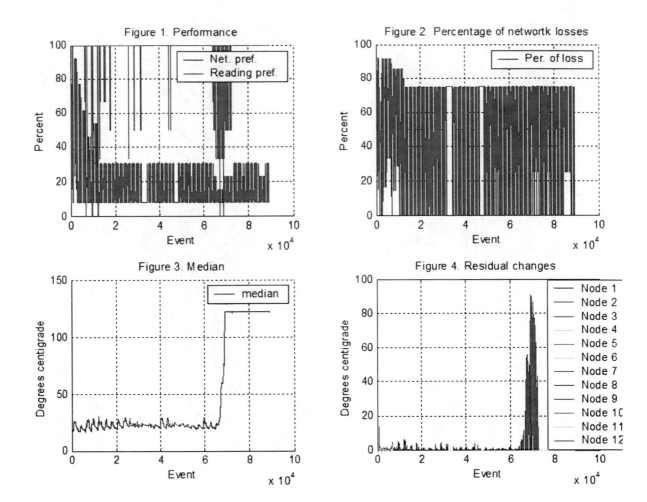

Impact of Packet Losses on Algorithm Detection

Figure 8 illustrates the effect of increasing the percentage of packet losses on the proposed algorithm's detection with 20% of faulty deviated nodes. (The experiments for this data set employed MATLAB as a tool in simulation scenarios using 1000 sensor nodes randomly distributed over 1000 square meters, each of them with a 50 meter transceiver range). The figure shows that,

the same data set and the impact of the losses on degrading neighborhood collected data reliability.

as losses increased, the algorithm's detection decreased linearly and reached 40% at 60% loss. This occurred along with a gradual increase in the algorithm's positive detection which reached 20% with 60% losses. If a monitoring window of a sample size of 10 and a 6 sample threshold was used, the positive detection would be reduced to almost 0%.

Detection of Deviated Faulty Nodes

Figure 9 illustrates the effect of the increased percentages of faulty deviated nodes on the proposed algorithm's detection per event in 100 runs with

Figure 6. Neighborhood Calculated Median Value Between Events 60000 and 67000 at Intel Lab Data Set.

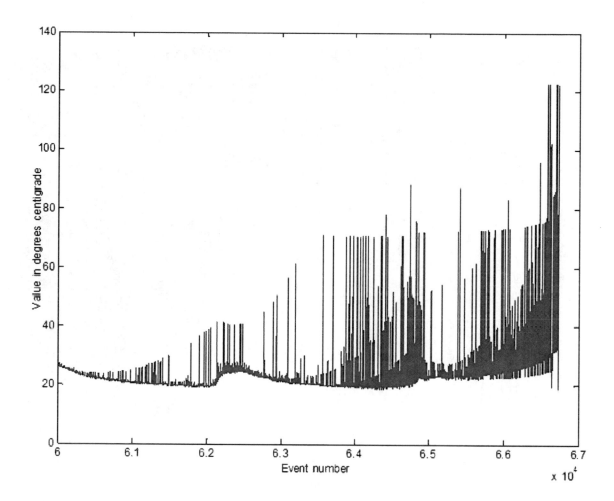

1,000 nodes had a 50 meter transceiver range; these are randomly deployed over the 1,000 square meters with 0.1% packet losses, 0.1% deviated node measurements, and 0.1% dead nodes. The figure shows that, as the percentage of deviated faulty nodes increases the proposed algorithm's detection of faulty nodes decreases exponentially and reaches around 20% when faulty deviated nodes reach a level of 80%. The algorithm's positive false detection increases linearly as the number of deviated faulty nodes increases, reaching around 80% when 80% of the network's nodes are faulty.

Table 1. Event number of removed detected faulty nodes

	1	3	4	33	35	37	39
Node1	--	66240	60960	15840	53760	62880	66720
Times	--	17	15	15	37	20	18
Node2	--	66240	60960	18240	24000	24000	66720
Times	--	13	6	29	21	16	24

Figure 7. Neighborhood Collected data reliability at Intel Lab data set experiment

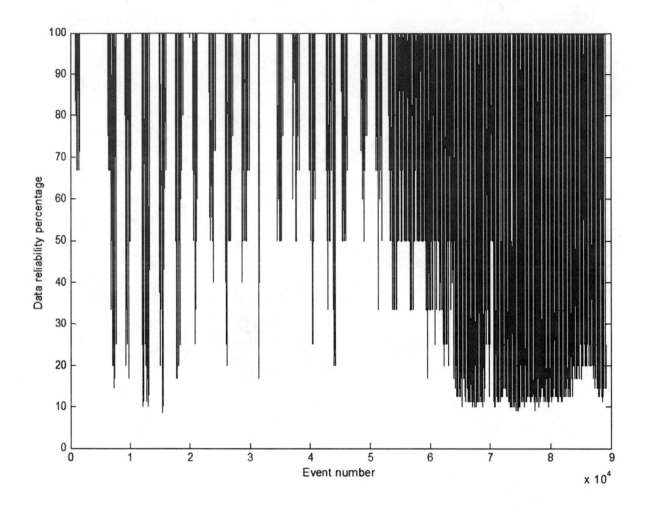

LIMITATIONS OF THE ALGORITHM

The proposed algorithm uses passive voting analysis and assumes that readings different from the majority constitute a change due to either a fault in a sensor node, the depletion of a sensor battery, a calibration problem, or a coverage problem. Because of this simple method, the algorithm functionality and its detection confidence relies on the number of neighbors, the number of deviated neighbor readings at each time interval, loss percentages and the degree of measurement deviation from the others. The number of neighbor nodes is very important since it is concerned with the confidence of algorithm detection. The conducted experiments showed that as the number of received measurements from neighborhood increased, the algorithm detection error percentage decrease.

Moreover, these experiments showed that detection error value depends on the ratio of unhealthy neighbors to the total number of neighbors. If this ratio is more than 50% then the algorithm calculated median may drift from the real neighborhood phenomenon measurements. This drift is sensitive to packet losses spatially if the losses make the faulty deviated nodes the majority at that monitoring time interval. This drawback was solved by adding historical readings from the last

Figure 8. The Algorithm Detection of Faulty Deviated Nodes with different Data Loss Percentages, 0.1% Packet Loss and 0.1% Dead Nodes.

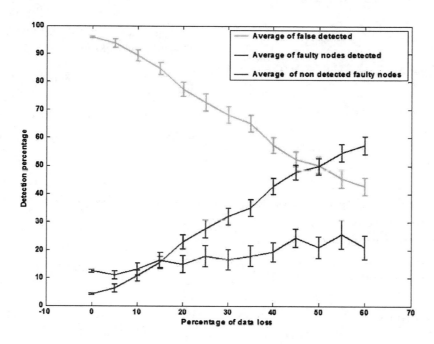

Figure 9. The Algorithm Detection versus the Percentage of Faulty Nodes.

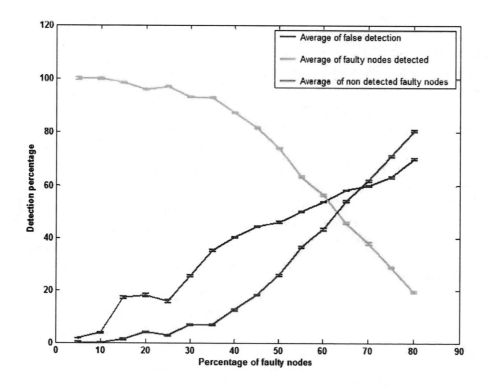

medium calculation and comparing this with the new median and with a threshold of allowable phenomenon changes.

CONCLUSION AND FUTURE WORK

The algorithm proposed in this paper enables each sensor node in a sensor network to detect the Wireless Sensor Network's performance in a distributed manner. It sends a warning packet to the sink reporting any detection of degradation in nodes or neighborhood. This is done by tracking the changes in the status of the nodes and compares them with an estimated norm value of the neighborhood.

Simulation experiments showed that 97% of faults detected by the Box-Whisker method were detected by the algorithm. These experiments showed a similar level of detection of deviations by neighbor nodes that used the algorithm, with slight changes in detection time due to losses that each node faced in receiving its neighbors' measurements.

Although the experiments showed a good level of detection for the proposed algorithm and limited impact on network lifetime, there are some limitations due to the simple adapted method that may degrade the algorithm performance especially at small size networks or very high packet loss. Numerous aspects can be considered in the future in order to extend this work and improve the algorithm's functionality, such as checking the impact of the mobility of sensor nodes on the algorithm's functionality. Also, we are planning to use the influence diagram to replace the existence window and data validity tests and check the algorithm's time response and the level of deviation affect on the network functionality.

REFERENCES

Chong, C.-Y., & Kumar, S. P. (2003). Sensor networks: Evolution, opportunities, and challenges. *Proceedings of the IEEE, 91*(8).

Charan, P., Paulu, R., Kumar, M., & Jaiswal, A. (2012). A survey on the performance optimization in wireless sensor networks using cross layer approach. *Journal of Scientific and Research Publications, 2*(5), 1–6.

Akyildiz, I. F., & Wang, X. (2005). A survey on WMNs. *IEEE Communications Magazine.*

Alemdar, H., & Erosy, C. (2010). Wireless sensor networks for healthcare: A survey. *Journal Elsevier-Computer Networks, 54*(1), 2688–2710. doi:10.1016/j.comnet.2010.05.003.

Ramanathan, N., Schoellhammer, T., Estrin, D., Hansen, M., Harmon, T., Kohler, E., & Srivastava, M. (2006). *The final frontier: Embedding networked sensors in the soil (CENS Technical Report #68).* Los Angeles, CA: Center for Embedded Networked Sensing, UCLA.

Tolle, J., Polastre, J., Szewczyk, R., Culler, D., Turner, N., & Tu, K. … Hong, W. (2005). A macro-scope in the redwoods. In *Proceedings of ACM Conference on Embedded Networked Sensor Systems (SenSys'05)* (pp. 51-63). ACM.

Yonggang, Z. (2004). *Measurement and monitoring in wireless sensor networks*. (PhD Thesis). Computer Science Department, University of Southern California, Los Angeles, CA.

Elnahrawy, E., & Nath, B. (2003). Cleaning and querying noisy sensors. In *Proceedings of the First ACM Conference on Embedded Networked Sensor Systems (SenSys'03)* (pp. 78-87). ACM.

Mehranbod, N. (2002). *A probabilistic approach for sensor fault detection and identification*. (Doctoral Thesis). Drexel University, Philadelphia, PA.

Balzano, L. K. (2007). *Addressing fault and calibration in wireless sensor networks.* (Master Thesis). University of California, Los Angeles, CA.

Zhao, Y. (2004). *Measurement and monitoring in wireless sensor networks.* (PhD Thesis). Computer Science Department, University of Southern California, Los Angeles, CA.

Szewczyk, R., Mainwaring, A., Polastre, J., Anderson, J., & Culler, D. (2004). An analysis of a large scale habitat monitoring application. In *Proceedings of the 2nd International Conference on Embedded Networked Sensor Systems* (pp. 214-226). New York: ACM Press.

Parhami, B. (1994). Voting algorithms. *IEEE Transactions on Reliability, 43*(4), 617–629. doi:10.1109/24.370218.

Jajodia, S., & Mutchler, D. (1987). Enhancements to the voting algorithm. In *Proceedings of the 13th VLDB Conference* (pp. 399-406). VLDB.

Paris, J.-F. (1986). Voting with witnesses: A consistency scheme for replicated files. In *Proceedings of the 6th International Conference on Distributed Computing Systems* (pp. 606-612). Cambridge, UK: IEEE.

AL-Raisi. N. E. (2010). A novel approach for monitoring wireless sensor network performance by tracking node operational deviation. In *Proceedings of IEEE-ISCC2010* (pp. 113-119). IEEE.

AL-Raisi. N. E. (2009). Wireless sensor networks performance measurements and monitoring. In Proceeding of Symposia and Workshops on Ubiquitous, Autonomic and Trusted Computing (pp. 286-291). Brisbane, Australia: IEEE.

Ramanathan, N., Chang, K., Kapur, R., Girod, L., Kohler, E., & Estrin, D. (2005). Sympathy for the sensor network debugger. In *Proceeding of the 3rd ACM Conf. Embedded Networked Sensor Systems* (pp. 255-267). ACM.

Vuran, M. C., Akan, O. B., & Akyildiz, I. F. (2004). Spatio-temporal correlation: Theory and applications for wireless sensor networks. *Computer Networks Journal, 45*(1), 245–261. doi:10.1016/j.comnet.2004.03.007.

Jaikaeo, C., Srisathapornphat, C., & Shen, C.-C. (2001). Diagnosis of sensor networks. In *Proceeding of ICC- IEEE International Conference* (pp. 1627-1632). IEEE.

Mini, R. A. F., Machado, M. V., Loureiro, A. A. F., & Nath, B. (2003). Prediction-based energy map for wireless sensor networks. In *Proceedings of the Simpsio Brasilerio De Redes De Computadores* (pp. 165-169). IEEE.

Wen, Y.-J., Agogino, A., & Goebel, K. (2004). Fuzzy validation and fusion for wireless sensor networks. In *Proceeding of ASME International Mechanical Engineering Congress and RD&D Expo (IMECE2004).* Anaheim, CA: ASME.

Tang, C., & Raghavendra, C. S. (2004). Correlation analysis and applications in wireless micro sensor networks. In *Proceeding of Mobile and Ubiquitous Systems: Networking and Services (MOBIQUITOUS 2004)* (pp. 184-193). MOBIQUITOUS.

Gupta, I., van Renesse, R., & Birman, K. P. (2001). Scalable fault-tolerant aggregation in large process groups. In *Proceeding of the 2001 International Conference on Dependable Systems and Networks* (pp. 433-442). IEEE.

Clouqueur, T., Saluja, K. K., & Ramanathan, P. (2004). Fault tolerance in collaborative sensor networks for target detection. *IEEE Transactions on Computers, 53*(1), 320–333. doi:10.1109/TC.2004.1261838.

Han, S., & Chan, E. (2004). Continuous residual energy monitoring in wireless sensor networks. In *Proceeding of International Symposium on Parallel and Distributed Processing and Applications* (pp. 169-177). IEEE.

Ding, M., Chen, D., Xing, K., & Cheng, X. (2005). Localized fault-tolerant event boundary detection in sensor networks. In *Proceeding of IEEE INFOCOM* (pp. 902–913). IEEE.

Krishnamachari, B., & Iyengar, S. (2004). Distributed Bayesian algorithms for fault-tolerant event region detection in wireless sensor networks. *IEEE Transactions on Computers, 53*, 421–250. doi:10.1109/TC.2004.1261832.

Koushanfar, F., Potkonjak, M., & Sangiovanni-Vincentelli, A. (2003). On-line fault detection of sensor measurements. *Proceedings of the IEEE, 2*, 974–979.

Luo, X., Dong, M., & Huang, Y. (2006). On distributed fault-tolerant detection in wireless sensor networks. *IEEE Transactions on Computers, 55*, 58–70. doi:10.1109/TC.2006.13.

Gutierrez-Osuna, R. (2007). *Sensor characteristics*. Retrieved from http://courses.cs.tamu.edu/rgutier/ceg499_s02/l2.pdf

Wagner, D. (2004). Resilient aggregation in sensor networks. In *Proceedings of the Security of Ad Hoc and Sensor Networks* (pp. 78-87). New York: ACM Press.

Cormen, T. H., Leiserson, C. E., Rivest, R. L., & Stein, C. (2004). *Introduction to algorithms* (2nd ed.). New York: McGraw-Hill.

Shnayder, V., Hempstead, M., Chen, B.-R., & Welsh, M. (2007). *Power TOSSIM: Efficient power simulation for TinyOS applications* (Report No. CS263). Retrieved from http://www.eecs.harvard.edu/~shnayder/ptossim/

Intel Lab. (2007). *Intel lab experiment data set*. Retrieved from http://berkeley.intel-research.net/labdata/

Hand, D., Mannila, H., & Smyth, P. (2001). *Principles of data mining*. Cambridge, MA: The MIT Press.

APPENDIX A: DEFINITIONS OF THE NOTATIONS USED IN THE ALGORITHM PSEUDO-CODE

1. Monitoring node use VBAM algorithm.
2. T: waiting time.
3. k: Number of neighbors.
4. N(): Set of neighbor.
5. Measurement of node j received by monitoring node i.
6. Loss counter of node j (by monitoring node i).
7. Minimum and maximum limits of the sensor node measurements.
8. Deviation detection counter of node j by monitoring node i.
9. median value at node i.
10. Old median value.
11. Maximum expected phenomenon variation.
12. Median deviation counter at monitoring node i.
13. Deviation of node j.
14. Uncorrelated readings counter.
15. Coverage problem counter of node j monitored by node i.
16. Neighborhood malfunctions counter.
17. Thresholds of median, coverage, distortion and monitoring window respectively.
18. Median of neighborhood loss .

APPENDIX B: LISTENING AND FILTERING MODULE PSEUDO-CODE

1. Each sense the phenomenon and wait for time T to receive N() readings
2. IF t > T THEN
3. For each not received increment ;
4. IF > >
5. Remove from data set and increment
6. Calculate of the available data set

APPENDIX C: DATA ANALYSIS AND THRESHOLD TEST MODULE PSEUDO-CODE

1. IF | - | >
2. Increment and let = = | - |
3. IF > and | - | <
4. Increment
5. ELSE increment
6. IF > 40%
7. Increment
8. IF * >
9. Increment

APPENDIX D: DECISION CONFIDENCE CONTROL MODULE PSEUDO-CODE

1. Calculate
2. IF > 60%
3. Send to module 4 a request to send an inefficient power consumption warning message
4. IF >
5. Send to module 4 a request to send a neighborhood malfunction due to losses warning message
6. IF >
7. Send to module 4 a request to send to detecting node j a coverage problem message
8. IF distortion > & median of > 60%
9. Send to module 4 a request to send a degrade detection in network functionality message
10. IF >
11. Send to module 4 a request to send a detection of node j malfunction message

APPENDIX E: WARNING PACKET EXCHANGE MODULE PSEUDO-CODE

1. Receiving neighbor warning
   a. Check received warning with the same module 3 counter of reported node.
   b. IF module 3 counter < 30%
   c. Release 'NO_EVEDENCE_OF_FAULT' message
   d. ELSE flag the stop sending of the same message from the node at this monitoring time.
2. Receiving module 3 request
   a. Test stop flag of received request warning
   b. IF flag = 1 discard message
   c. IF send message repeated 3 times send 'FAULT_MESSAGE_STOP' message and flag stop fault counter.
   d. ELSE send the requested message by module 3.
3. Testing warning packet release
   a. IF detected fault returns to normal reset the same fault counters, send 'FAULT_CLEAR' message and recalculate protocol tables.
   b. IF step 2 and 3-a alternate for the same fault three times in a predefined monitoring window, the module send s an 'TOPOLOGY_UNSTABLE' message to report the detection and flags a permanent fault counter to stop reporting the same fault.
   c. If 'NO_EVIDENCE_OF_FAULT' at the neighborhood exceeds 1, then drop the warning message intend to send to the sink.
4. By the end of the predefined period reset all counters.

Section 7
Cloud and Mobile Communications

Chapter 16
Mobile Cloud Computing and Its Security and Privacy Challenges

Hassan Takabi
University of Pittsburgh, USA

Saman Taghavi Zargar
University of Pittsburgh, USA

James B. D. Joshi
University of Pittsburgh, USA

ABSTRACT

Mobile cloud computing has grown out of two hot technology trends, mobility and cloud. The emergence of cloud computing and its extension into the mobile domain creates the potential for a global, interconnected mobile cloud computing environment that will allow the entire mobile ecosystem to enrich their services across multiple networks. We can utilize significant optimization and increased operating power offered by cloud computing to enable seamless and transparent use of cloud resources to extend the capability of resource constrained mobile devices. However, in order to realize mobile cloud computing, we need to develop mechanisms to achieve interoperability among heterogeneous and distributed devices. We need solutions to discover best available resources in the cloud servers based on the user demands and approaches to deliver desired resources and services efficiently and in a timely fashion to the mobile terminals. Furthermore, while mobile cloud computing has tremendous potential to enable the mobile terminals to have access to powerful and reliable computing resources anywhere and anytime, we must consider several issues including privacy and security, and reliability in realizing mobile cloud computing. In this chapter, the authors first explore the architectural components required to realize a mobile cloud computing infrastructure. They then discuss mobile cloud computing features with their unique privacy and security implications. They present unique issues of mobile cloud computing that exacerbate privacy and security challenges. They also discuss various approaches to address these challenges and explore the future work needed to provide a trustworthy mobile cloud computing environment.

DOI: 10.4018/978-1-4666-4691-9.ch016

INTRODUCTION

The growth and use of handheld, wireless mobile devices with the goal of "information at your fingertips anywhere, anytime" has fundamentally changed our lives (Catteddu & Hogben 2009). A large percent of the world's population now has access to mobile phones and incredibly fast mobile networks give users ubiquitous connectivity (Bruening & Treacy 2009). At the end of 2009, there were four billion mobile phones and that number is projected to grow to 6 billion by 2013 (Bertino, Paci & Ferrini 2009). Nowadays, new devices like the iPhone and Android smartphones are providing users with a lot of applications and services.

However, it has long been recognized that mobile terminals, such as thin clients, mobile devices, PDAs, tablets and WiFi sensors are always poor in computational resources such as processor speed, memory size, and disk capacity (Catteddu & Hogben 2009). While the hardware continues to evolve and improve, they will always be resource-poor relative to static hardware. On the other hand, cloud computing has become the new approach of delivering services. It has raised significant interest in both academia and industry and essentially aims to incorporate the evolutionary development of many existing computing approaches and technologies such as distributed services, applications, information and infrastructure consisting of pools of computers, networks, information and storage resources (Ko, Ahn & Shehab 2009). To alleviate the problems of a mobile terminal, it should get resources from an external source and one of such sources is cloud computing platforms (Bertino, Paci & Ferrini 2009). We need to find ways to increase computing performance without investing in a new infrastructure and use available computing resources more efficiently. In fact, hardware is currently under-utilized and it is believed that adequate software platforms can be developed to provide a set of new services to users (Joshi et al.

2004). Cloud computing is considered a good way to extend or augment the capabilities of resource constrained devices.

The emergence of cloud computing and its extension into the mobile domain creates the potential for a global, interconnected mobile cloud that will allow content providers, developers, mobile marketers and enterprises to access valuable network and billing capabilities across multiple networks. Mobile cloud services can make it easy for the entire mobile ecosystem to enrich their services with mobility—whether these applications run on a mobile device, on the Web, in a software-as-a-service cloud, on the desktop or on an enterprise server (Blaze et al. 2009). Mobile cloud computing has grown out of these two hot technology trends, mobile computing and cloud computing. Using the significant resource optimization and increased operating power that cloud computing offers, we could enable seamless and transparent use of cloud resources to augment the capabilities of resource constrained mobile terminals and provide them the ability of high performance computing (Bertino, Paci & Ferrini 2009). In mobile cloud computing, we should enable the mobile terminals to have access to powerful and reliable computing resources anywhere and anytime by building a virtual computing environment between the front-end mobile terminals and the back-end cloud-based servers. By doing so, we can enable new service models, where resources are seamlessly utilized at the time and location that are best suited to the needs of the current workload, while at the same time optimizing business objectives such as minimizing cost and maintaining service quality levels (Ko, Ahn & Shehab 2009). Moreover, using the mobile cloud instead of proprietary resource management schemes improves the portability and scalability of applications and services within organizations that employ mobile computing infrastructures. Mobile cloud computing should support various customers to use appropriate mobile objects in infrastructure, platform and application levels. It should provide the mobile terminals the ability to conveniently and seamlessly use remote applications, so they would not be required to install so many applications.

Mobile cloud computing is still in its infancy and there is no single agreed upon definition so far and different researchers have various definitions. Some define mobile cloud computing as "the availability of cloud computing services in a mobile ecosystem. This incorporates many elements, including consumer, enterprise, femtocells, transcoding, end-to-end security, home gateways, and mobile broadband-enabled services" (Bruening & Treacy 2009). Cisco defines mobile cloud computing as "mobile services and apps delivered from a centralized (and perhaps virtualized) data center to a mobile device such as a smartphone" (Catteddu & Hogben 2009). Yankee Group defines it as "a federated point of entry enabling access to the full range of capabilities inherent in the mobile network platform" (Blaze et al. 2009).

However, in order to realize mobile cloud computing, we need to come up with mechanisms to achieve interoperability among heterogeneous and distributed devices. We need to cogitate on the design and the desired structure of the underlying infrastructure. We need solutions to discover best available resources in nearby cloud servers based on the needs of the users and approaches to deliver needed resources and services efficiently and in a timely manner to the mobile terminals.

As is for the cloud, it is critical to the success of the mobile cloud that we understand its security and privacy risks and develop efficient and effective solutions to deal with them. Security and privacy concerns are key to the slow adoption of cloud computing, as indicated by several surveys (Ko, Ahn & Shehab 2009; Chen, Paxson & Katz 2010). In the mobile cloud environment, such concerns are expected to be much increased because of the threats coming from two domains. Hence, without appropriate security and privacy solutions mobile computing could become a huge failure.

In this chapter, we first explore the architectural components required to realize a mobile cloud computing infrastructure. We will review some of the efforts that are being done to realize mobile cloud computing at different delivery models. We then discuss mobile cloud computing features with their unique privacy and security implications. Understanding the security risks in mobile cloud computing and developing efficient and effective solutions are critical for its success. So, we look at potential privacy and security challenges by analyzing the unique issues of mobile cloud computing that exacerbate these challenges. We also discuss various approaches to address these challenges and explore research directions needed to provide a trustworthy mobile cloud computing environment.

MOBILE CLOUD COMPUTING

Mobile Cloud Computing aims to overcome limitations of the mobile terminals (e.g. mobile devices, WiFi sensors, etc.); mainly lack of resources for computation (i.e. processing power, and data storage), communication (i.e. limited data rates for 3G and even 4G), and power (i.e. battery life). Towards that, various schemes have been proposed in the literature to tackle one or more of these challenges. In this section, we first classify Mobile Cloud Computing schemes that have been proposed to date into two main categories and explore their unique features. Then, we enumerate and discuss various proposed schemes for each of these two categories.

Mobile cloud computing can be classified into two main categories as follows:

1. **Cloud of Mobile Devices as a (Cloud) Service:** These schemes leverage the resources of mobile devices (e.g. processing power, memory capacity, network connectivity) to enable collaborative data-intensive computing and communication among the

cloud of mobile devices. This category of mobile cloud computing is very suitable when there is no or weak connectivity to the Internet and main cloud providers. Furthermore, some of the proposed approaches that lie in this category allow for migration of entire or parts of the applications to the neighboring mobile devices; hence, they are cost-efficient since they eliminate the data charges, particularly in roaming scenarios.

2. **Cloud Computing Services/Resources Available For Mobile Devices/Users:** Based on how these schemes exploit cloud computing services/resources, they can be further classified into two categories as follows:

   a. **Extending Conventional Cloud Services as Supplemental Capabilities:** These schemes focus on extending available cloud services (e.g. IaaS, SaaS) to mobile devices. In other words, this category of schemes are augmenting the capabilities of mobile devices with the support of cloud computing (e.g. Jupiter (Guo et al. 2011), CloneCloud (Chun et al. 2011), Mobile photo sharing (Vartiainen & Väänänen-Vainio-Mattila 2010)).

   b. **Exclusive Services:** Schemes in this category are aimed at exploiting some of the interesting features of the mobile devices, including context enabled features such as: camera, voice/audio, mobility characteristics (e.g., location, presence), etc., to create unique, cloud-delivered service offerings (e.g., location-based services, bar-code scanning, real-time translation).

3. **Cloud of Mobile Devices as a (Cloud) Service:** Although today's computational, communication, and storage capabilities of mobile devices are continuously increasing and they are becoming as powerful as conventional desktop computers with mobile broadband access of several Mbit/s, most of these resources are underutilized. Recently, researchers have proposed various schemes in order to leverage the resources of mobile devices to enable variety of collaborative services among the cloud of mobile devices; some of the major schemes include the following:

   a. **Virtual Private Mobile Network (VPMN)** (Baliga et al. 2011): This scheme proposes architecture for a virtual mobile network infrastructure that exploits novel virtualization approaches to dynamically create private, resource isolated, customizable, and end-to-end mobile networks on a common physical mobile network (Baliga et al. 2011). Basically, this scheme considers network resources as flexible pool of assets which can be dynamically utilized as needed. VPMN is based on Long Term Evolution (LTE) (Sesia, Toufik & Baker 2011) and Evolved Packet Core (EPC) (Olsson et al. 2009) mobile technologies. VPMN aims to enable new service abstractions where these services need to interact closely with the network or customize the network behavior.

   b. **Pocket Cloudlets** (Koukoumidis et al. 2011): This architecture leverages the large quantity in Non-Volatile Memory (NVM) capacities of mobile devices to alleviate the battery life and latency challenges that mobile users are facing while accessing cloud services. A Pocket cloudlet provides a cloud service cache architecture that exists in the mobile device's NVM and utilizes both single and community access models in order to maximize its hit rate; subsequently it reduces total service latency and energy consumption. Pocket cloudlets can also help improve the mobile users' access to cloud services in three ways:

i. Mobile users' latency and power scarcity will be eliminated since all or part of information they need exists on the phone.

ii. Personalizing mobile users' services according to their behavior and usage patterns will be easier since most of the interactions between mobile users and services occur on the mobile devices.

iii. Mobile users' privacy could be protected since all the personalized information and services reside on the phone.

4. **Embracing Network as a Service** (Gutierrez & Ventura 2010): *Gutierrez et al.* in (Gutierrez & Ventura 2010) propose Network as a Service (NaaS) as new market driven application for the Next Generation Network (NGN). They propose deploying mobile cloud by telecommunication industries in order to offer network capabilities/resources (e.g. presence, location, and payment) to 3rd party application service providers through standardized gateways. They emphasized the use of Open Mobile Alliance – Policy Evaluation, Enforcement and Management (OMA PEEM) for resource exposure in order to cover NaaS concept.

5. **Mobile Cloud Computing for Data-Intensive Applications** (Teo & Narasimhan 2011): The main idea behind the proposed implementation in (Teo & Narasimhan 2011) is to enable collaborative data-intensive computing across a cloud of mobile devices instead of migrating those computation tasks to the cloud using global cellular networks. Most of the processing resources of mobile devices are under-utilized. Hence, by using local wireless networks, mobile devices can communicate and collaborate with each other

to transfer their data-intensive computation jobs to their local peers by consuming less bandwidth of the global cellular networks. In order to reach the aforementioned goals, Hyrax (Marinelli 2009), a system based on Hadoop (The Apache Hadoop Project 2011) framework on mobile devices, was introduced by Marinelli to share data and computation among a cloud of mobile devices. Hyrax was deployed on a networked collection of Android smartphones. Initial implementation of Hyrax has been shown to be inappropriate for wide-scale deployment on the mobile devices of common users (The Apache Hadoop Project 2011). Hence, *Teo et al.* in (Teo & Narasimhan 2011) have proposed improvements to Hyrax's implementation to support communication and collaboration among network of mobile devices to enable migration of their data intensive jobs among their local peers. They have also developed a relevant mobile multimedia share and search application to evaluate the performance of their approach and to identify possible directions for their future work.

6. **Mobile Process as a Service (MPaaS)** (Zaplata & Lamersdorf 2010): This scheme incorporates mobile process as a service to enable the execution of mobile processes when there is no available central Process as a Service (PaaS) server. MPaaS shares mobile and immobile process engines based on the concept of context-based cooperation. MPaaS involves three stages to run mobile processes. First, if the process could be executed locally by the application on the mobile device, that device will take care of the process. Second, if there is no local application available on the mobile device to run the mobile process, device can search for the available service provided by other mobile devices in its vicinity and migrate its mobile processes to those devices upon

availability. Finally, if a mobile device cannot find the required services on its direct vicinity, a process can be migrated to another remote device within the vicinity in order to find required services. The main implementation challenge for this service is the necessity and willingness to cooperate by a huge number of participants. Larger the number of the participants, the more the profit for the MPaaS providers will be and thus the more willingness to share resources.

a. **Virtual Cloud Computing Provider for Mobile Devices** (Huerta-Canepa & Lee 2010): This scheme presents a preliminary framework to implement virtual Ad-hoc mobile cloud computing providers among the mobile devices in the vicinity in order to offload the computationally intensive applications without connecting to infrastructure-based cloud providers.

b. **Accessing Mpeg-7 Based Multimedia Services Through Other Mobile Devices** (Cao et al. 2009): As another example of employing capabilities of a cloud of mobile devices as a service, *Cao et al.* in (Cao et al. 2009) proposed a middleware that allows mobile devices to access a collection of multimedia services provided by other mobile devices. Moreover, mobile devices could for instance host other services (e.g. web service) that could be accessed by other mobile devices, thus exposing their computing capabilities to the other mobile peers in an ad-hoc cloud.

7. **Cloud Computing Services/Resources Available for Mobile Devices/Users:** Exploiting Cloud computing resources/services at the mobile devices makes them thin clients that run various light mobile applications and that transfer their computational overhead to the Cloud. By transferring the computational overhead to the cloud, the battery lives of the mobile devices get extended. For instance, *openmobster* (Openmobster 2010) is an open source project that provides architecture to exploit cloud resources/services available for the mobile devices/users. *Openmobster* project describes various essential services that the mobile cloud clients as well as the cloud servers require for supporting cloud computing for mobile devices. As we mentioned earlier, schemes that have been proposed in this category to date are classified based on how they exploit cloud computing services/resources into two categories; some of the major schemes in each of these categories are as follows:

a. **Extending Conventional Cloud Services as Supplemental Capabilities**

   i. **Mobile Agent Based Open Cloud Computing Federation (MABOCCF)** (Zhang & Zhang 2009): MABOCCF proposes a combination of benefits from Mobile Agents and cloud computing towards realizing the Open Cloud Computing Federation (OCCF). A mobile agent is a piece of software with its data that can migrate from one environment to another, with its data intact, and still be capable of performing computations appropriately in the new environment. Mobile agents can be used to realize portability and interoperability between multiple heterogeneous Cloud Computing platforms.

   ii. **Jupiter** (Guo et al. 2011): Jupiter is a recently proposed framework that aims to provide transparent augmentation of smartphone capabilities with the support of cloud computing. Furthermore, by exploiting the virtual machine technology, Jupiter claims that it can launch desktop applications on smartphones. One of the main implementation challenges for Jupiter to provide aforementioned services is its connection dependency. In order to mitigate Jupiter's connection dependency, caching has been added to Jupiter's implementation through a transparent mobile file system (e.g. TransFS). Employing TransFS, both application's configurations and data could be stored at the server-side and accessed transparently through TransFS. Jupiter takes advantage of the enormous storage capability of the cloud to provide near infinite storage for mobile phones. Jupiter is on its early stage and more experimental evaluations need to be done to understand its effectiveness..

iii. **CloneCloud** (Chun et al. 2011), **Calling the Cloud** (Giurgiu et al. 2009), **and MAUI** (Cuervo et al. 2010): Executing cloud applications on mobile phones as a heterogeneous and continuously changing environment with limited resources is a challenging problem. In order to address this problem, cloud applications may need to be dynamically partitioned and some of their components can be remotely executed. Hence, an application's overall performance can be improved by delegating part of the application to be executed remotely on a resourceful cloud infrastructure. *CloneCloud* partitions mobile applications that are running in the application-level virtual machine of the mobile devices into different parts at runtime. Then, these partitioned executables can be transferred seamlessly from mobile devices onto cloned replicas of the device operating in a computational cloud. Finally, the results from the augmented execution are gathered upon completion. *CloneCloud* exploits a combination of static analysis and dynamic profiling to partition applications automatically at a fine granularity while optimizing execution time, energy usage, financial cost, and security for a target computation and communication environment. *CloneCloud* gives its mobile users an illusion that they have powerful devices that can run various complex applications without offloading the execution of any part of those applications to elsewhere.

Calling the cloud is based on an application middleware that automatically distributes various layers of an application between the mobile device and a server (e.g. resource in a cloud) while optimizing several parameters such as latency, data transfer, cost, etc. There is a distributed module management at the core of *Calling the cloud* approach that dynamically and automatically decides which application modules and when they should be offloaded, considering the optimal performance or the minimal cost of the overall application.

In the same way, *MAUI* enables fine-grained offloading of the mobile code modules to the cloud while maximizing devices' battery life. During the programming, developers indicate which methods could be offloaded for remote execution. Various execution patterns of migrate-able methods could be profiled for better prediction of future invocations and to better decide what methods should be offloaded. Then, an optimization problem with the profiling information, network connectivity measurements, bandwidth, and latency estimations as input parameters is periodically solved to decide which methods and when should they be offloaded. *MAUI* provides a fine grained offloading mechanism at the single method level compared to Calling the cloud where offloading occurs at the whole software modules granularity.

iv. **Mobile Cloud for Assistive Healthcare (MoCAsH)** (Hoang & Chen 2010): One of the important areas that novel technologies such as mobile cloud computing are applicable is assistive healthcare systems to deal with emerging services such as collaborative consultation, distant monitoring, and electronic health records. MoCAsH is an infrastructure developed for assistive healthcare by inheriting the cloud computing advantages. MoCAsH embraces important features of mobile sensing, active sensor records, and collaborative planning by deploying intelligent mobile agents, context-aware

middleware, and collaborative protocol for efficient resource sharing and planning. MoCAsH deploys selective and federated P2P cloud in order to protect data, preserve data ownership, and strengthen aspects of security. Furthermore, it solves various quality-of-service issues related to critical responses and energy consumption.

b. **Exclusive Services**

i. **Next Generation Mobile Applications Using Representative State Transfer (Rest)Ful Web-Services and Cloud Computing** (Christensen 2009): Smart mobile devices are mostly context aware which enables number of new specific applications such as location-based services that exploit location as a context, social proximity applications that exploit spatial contexts (e.g. position, proximity, and path) and etc. *Christensen et al.* propose to combine smart mobile devices, the context provided by enabled sensors on these devices, and cloud computing with RESTful web-services to define new applications or services for mobile users (Christensen 2009). Cloud computing provides required resources (e.g. storage, processing capabilities) to create applications/services that exceed the capabilities of traditional mobile devices.

ii. **Collaborative Speech Recognition with Mobile Cloud** (Chang & Hung 2011): *Chang et al.* present an approach to design collaborative mobile cloud applications that could dynamically transfer the workload to efficiently take advantage of the resources in the cloud. They present the system architecture, the principle for partitioning applications, the method for offloading computation, and the control policy for data access. They use speech recognition application as an exclusive cloud service to present their experimental results.

In this section, we have classified and overviewed several mobile cloud computing schemes that have been proposed so far. Other mobile cloud computing schemes exist in the literature that could be covered as well, but the aim of this section was to provide the readers with an overview of the various possible mobile cloud computing schemes. Mobile cloud computing has been proposed to enable offloading of the computation and storage demands of mobile applications into the cloud without interrupting users' interactivity, restricting potential mobile applications or increasing users' waiting time (i.e. latency). Furthermore, mobile cloud computing schemes should be adaptive to the environmental changes and provide mobile users with the optimized performance in a cost-efficient way considering different metrics (e.g. program modules' execution time, resource consumption, battery level, security or bandwidth). In doing so, various decisions should be made based on the calculated optimized solution such as: how to partition the application code in to various modules, where to run each module (i.e. locally/remotely), what should be the data transfer rate, etc.

As a conclusion to this section we note that none of the existing schemes fully meets the aforementioned requirements of mobile cloud computing. Mobile applications that are running on the *cloud of mobile devices* and on the *mobile devices using cloud computing services/resources* are the two main types of mobile cloud applications. The former is using capabilities of mobile devices, but its integration with the cloud is limited. The latter does not sufficiently employ available computing and storage resources on the mobile device and have potential interactivity problems. Hence, we believe that mobile cloud computing and its applications need to more focus on schemes that can dynamically and optimally separate the responsibilities (e.g. computation, storage) between mobile devices and the cloud components. These schemes mostly lie in between two aforementioned classified application types. Mobile cloud computing, we believe, is going to be the challenging research area for several upcoming years with the range of challenging problems.

SECURITY AND PRIVACY ISSUES OF MOBILE CLOUD

Several surveys of potential cloud adopters indicate that security and privacy are the number one concern delaying its adoption (Catteddu & Hogben 2009). A mobile cloud is not an exception and despite the enormous opportunity and value it offers, without appropriate security and privacy solutions it could become a huge failure. Critical to the success of the mobile cloud is to understand its security and privacy risks and develop efficient and effective solutions to deal with them. In the following, we articulate the key security and privacy challenges that mobile cloud computing raises.

Identity and Access Management (IAM): By using cloud services users easily can access their personal information and it is also available to various services across the Internet. We need to have an identity management mechanism for authenticating users and services based on credentials and characteristics (Bruening & Treacy 2009).

The concepts behind IAM used in traditional computing are fundamentally different from those of a cloud environment. One key issue in cloud concerning IAM is the interoperability issues that could result from using different identity tokens and different identity negotiation protocols. An IAM system should be able to accommodate protection of private and sensitive information related to users and processes. While users interact with a front end service, this service may need to ensure that his/her identity is protected from other services that it interacts with (Bruening & Treacy 2009; Bertino, Paci, & Ferrini 2009). Segregation of customer's identity and authentication information is a crucial component, especially in a multitenant cloud environment.

Heterogeneity and diversity of services, and the domains' diverse access requirements in cloud computing environments would require fine-grained access control policies (Takabi, Joshi, & Ahn 2010b). In particular, access control services should be flexible enough to capture dynamic, context or attribute/credential based access requirements, and facilitate enforcement of the principle of least privilege. Such access control services may need to integrate privacy protection requirements expressed through complex rules. It is important that the access control system employed in mobile clouds is easily managed and its privilege distribution is administered efficiently.

Mobile Network Security Vulnerabilities: One of the interesting features of smartphones is the number of ways in which users can access them. In addition to accessing through a cellular network, most are also accessible via Wi-Fi and Bluetooth, and some are accessible by infrared and radio-frequency identification (RFID). The cellular network (3G or 4G) enables access to phone services, of course, and Internet services as well as Short Messaging Service (SMS) communications. The other interfaces (Wi-Fi, Bluetooth, infrared, and RFID) are used primarily for data exchange. From a security perspective, all interfaces have the potential to expose sensitive information and possibly receive malicious data.

Privacy Management and Data Protection: Many customers are not comfortable storing their data and applications on systems that reside outside of their physical on-premise data centers where they do not have control over them (Shin & Ahn 2005). This may be the single most fear that cloud clients may have. The organization hosting the network service may collect potentially sensitive data from various users. It is vital that users understand the privacy implications of such a service and be able to enforce limitations on what data is transmitted to the provider. Mobile cloud service providers must assure their customers and provide a high degree of transparency into their operations and privacy assurance. Privacy protection mechanisms need to be potentially embedded in all the security solutions. Another important issue in mobile cloud is the ability of "tracking" of individuals through location-based navigation data offloaded to the cloud which adds to privacy complications. From provider's point of view, a privacy breach could have potentially devastating effects and risk damaging its brand and revenue potential. A mobile cloud requires a neutral third party to provide a diverse set of offerings, as well as immediate remedies and protections should a privacy issue arise.

A related issue is data provenance; increasingly, it is becoming important to know who created a piece of data, who modified it and how, etc. This issue is more significant in mobile cloud as data may move among various mobile devices. Provenance information could be used for various purposes such as traceback, auditing, history based access control, etc. Balancing between data provenance and privacy is a significant challenge in clouds where physical perimeter is abandoned.

Encryption and Key Management: One of the core mechanisms that mobile cloud should use for data protection is strong encryption with key management. The resources are protected using encryption while access to protected resources is enabled by key management. Issues like encrypting data in transit over networks, encrypting data at rest and encrypting data on backup media should be taken into account. Considering the possibility of exotic attacks in mobile cloud computing environments, we need to further explore solutions for encrypting dynamic data, including data residing in memory. More work is needed to overcome barriers to adoption of robust key management schemes. There are several key management challenges within mobile cloud such as secure key stores, access to key stores, key backup and recoverability that should be handled in an appropriate way. The resource limitations in mobile devices further make the overall key management and secure protocols to support mobile cloud services more difficult.

Risk Management: Risk management, in general includes the methods and processes used to evaluate risks and opportunities related to the achievement of objectives. In mobile cloud environment, there are many variables, values and risks that may affect the decision whether an organization should adopt a cloud service. The organization should weigh those variables to decide whether the mobile cloud service is an appropriate solution for achieving its goals. Basically, mobile cloud services and security should be seen as supply chain security issues meaning that the service provider relationships and dependencies should be examined and assessed to the extent possible. The device mobility aspects further extend the attack surface and add to the risks that already exist in cloud environments.

Physical Security: The basic types of physical threats to mobile devices are lending, loss, and theft. Lending a mobile device to a family member or friend may seem harmless but does raise the possibility of enabling that person to access data or applications to which that person is not authorized. There is also the possibility of enabling access to an Internet site that might pose a danger to the smartphone, e.g., by downloading malware. Mobile devices that are lost or stolen raise the issue of misuse of data on the device as well as misuse of the device itself. Mobile devices typically feature a pin-based or password-based lockout capability. However, this feature is often not used by owners. Even when the lockout feature is enabled, though, there are ways to subvert the lockout.

Malware: Smartphones are sophisticated and fully featured computers, and hence are receiving the growing attention of malware creators. Security vendors have marketed mobile specific versions of antivirus software. However, as the complexity of mobile platforms and threats increase, we argue that mobile antivirus solutions will look more like their desktop variants. The functionality required to detect sophisticated malware can have significant power and resource overheads – which critical resources on mobile devices. The mobile cloud offers one solution to this threat (malware) that is not available to smartphones in general. Authorized software can be stored in and distributed from the cloud. When malware is detected or suspected, the smartphone software can be restored from trusted backups in the cloud.

Intrusion Detection and Prevention: As we discussed earlier, smartphones' increasing popularity attracts attackers in attacking such platforms by exploiting various vulnerabilities of smartphones (e.g. Malware, Mobile network security vulnerabilities, etc.). For instance, latest smartphone security study in (Catteddu & Hogben 2009) discusses Trojans used for stealing sensitive information that are talked through smartphones by exploiting voice-recognition algorithms. Other than invading privacy and security of the smartphone users, such security threats could generate coordinated large-scale attacks on the communication infrastructures of smartphones by forming botnets.

There are several on-device and network-based intrusion detection and response approaches already proposed in the literature to address smartphone security challenges (2, 4). Most of the previously proposed on-device solutions (e.g.

lightweight intrusion detection on the smartphones (Taylor et al. 2011)) are impractical due to several limitations (e.g. memory, computational resources, and battery power) (Cloud Security Alliance 2011). Moreover, most of the proposed solutions detect malwares or misbehaving users based on the signatures that they download from a central database. Hence, this adds another limitation which is the lack of large amount of storage on the mobile device to store signatures. Furthermore, signatures based detection could be easily evaded by introducing zero-day attacks. Network-based solutions address the resource limitations of on-device solutions but due to lack of knowledge and feedback from the smartphone's internal behavior, their accuracy and performance can be significantly affected. The very next necessary step after attack detection is automated attack response and recovery which is not addressed by neither of the previously proposed on-device nor network-based solutions (1). Addressing aforementioned challenges is necessary in order to facilitate next generation of smartphones with a powerful intrusion detection and prevention mechanism.

SECURITY AND PRIVACY APPROACHES FOR MOBILE CLOUD

Here, we discuss various approaches to cope with the previously mentioned challenges, existing solutions, and the work needed to provide a trustworthy mobile cloud computing environment.

Authentication and Identity Management: The user-centric identity management has recently received attention for handling private and critical identity attributes (Takabi, Joshi, & Ahn 2010a). In this approach, identifiers or attributes help identify and define a user and individuals are allowed to have multiple identifiers. Such an approach lets users control their digital identities and takes away the complexity of IDM from the enterprises, thereby allowing them to focus on their own functions. Research problems may arise

in developing IDM solutions. For example, how to provide the individual with the convenience of secure single sign-on to multiple distinct entities? How to enable the individual to give fine-grained permission for the sharing of specific personal identities between such entities when it is to their advantage to do so? In other words, how do we know what identity information to share when two users meet?

Researchers are currently pursuing other federated IDM solutions that might benefit cloud environments. IDM services in the cloud should be able to be integrated with an enterprise's existing IDM framework. In some cases, it's important to have privacy-preserving protocols to verify various identity attributes by using, for example, zero-knowledge proof-based techniques. These techniques, which use pseudonyms and accommodate multiple identities to protect users' privacy, can further help build a desired user-centric federated IDM for clouds. IDM solutions can also be extended with delegation capabilities to address identification and authentication issues in composed services.

Access Control: In the multi-tenant mobile cloud environment, besides the traditional security mechanisms, one also needs to consider additional potential security risks introduced by mobile users who share the same application instances and resources with others. In such an environment, data access control isolation is one of the most critically security issues that need to be addressed. Data access control and information isolation can be integrated through a cryptography based solution to prevent a user from getting privileges to access resources belonging to other tenants. There are generally two kinds of access control isolation patterns: implicit filter and explicit permission. They can be extended and generalized to realize the access control isolation of other resources through proper designs of the filter and permission mechanisms. In *implicit filter based access control isolation pattern*, when one tenant requests to access shared resources, a common platform level account is delegated to handle this request. The delegated account is shared by all tenants and has the privileges to access resources of all the tenants. However, the key aspect of this mechanism is to implicitly compose a tenant-oriented filter that will be used to prevent one user from tapping into resources of other tenants. This can be achieved by using a cryptography-based solution, i.e., group key management based solutions to secure information flow. In *explicit permissions based access control isolation pattern*, access privileges for the resources are explicitly pre-assigned to the corresponding tenant accounts by using the Access Control List (ACL) mechanism. Therefore, there is no need to leverage an additional common delegated account across tenants.

Privacy Management and Data Protection: Data in the cloud typically resides in a shared environment, but the data owner should have full control over who has the right to use the data and what they are allowed to do with it once they gain access (49). To provide this data control in the cloud, a standard based heterogeneous data-centric security approach is an essential element that shifts data protection from systems and applications. In this approach, documents must be self-describing and defending regardless of their environments. Cryptographic approaches and usage policy rules must be considered. When someone wants to access data, the system should check its policy rules and reveal it only if the policies are satisfied. Existing cryptographic techniques can be utilized for data security, but privacy protection and outsourced computation need significant attention—both are relatively new research directions.

Encryption and Key Management: Existing key management solutions usually consider the key management and Identity Management (IDM) as different issues. Attribute based key management (ABKM) is an extended version of identity-based cryptography that integrates key management and IDM to simplify key management. In ABKM, all the attributes are considered to belong to an entity

as its public key. Each attribute can be considered as a public key component, and each of the attributes is also paired with a private key component. The private key, which in turn is formed by multiple private key components, is distributed from a trusted authority. ABKM is basically an extended version of identity-based cryptography, in which the identity can be considered multiple descriptive attributes and the attributes can be used to represent descriptive policies through logical operators such as "AND" and "OR". Compared to traditional PKI based key management solutions where a user's private key is only known to the public owner, using ABKM, the trusted authority generates private key components for each user according to his/her public attributes. This approach delivers a major benefit of the use of ABKM, in that the private key can be generated for descriptive terms or statements instead of using a large random number (e.g., RSA). The descriptive terms can be used to specify data access control policies, which is very efficient in terms of security policy management.

Physical security: Developers can add an extra layer of application and data-level security when critical data is controlled by their software. Certainly not all applications access critical data, but developers of those that do can enhance the security of their applications by building in access control. Developers can also be cognizant of where data is stored on a smartphone. Subscriber identity module (SIM) cards typically hold subscriber and contact data and text messages. These cards can easily be removed from many devices and read by anyone. Developers should not store any data on a SIM card that does not need to be stored there. The mobile cloud also offers some degree of protection against data loss resulting from a lost or stolen smartphone. Backups or synchronization of data with the cloud should be enabled by developers, mandated by business policy, and consciously pursued by users.

Malware: To address the growing concern of mobile device threats, conserve scarce mobile resources and improve detection of modern threats, we can move mobile antivirus functionality to an off-device in-cloud network service. By moving the detection capabilities to a network service, we gain numerous benefits including increased detection coverage, less complex mobile software, and reduced resource consumption. CloudAV is an in-cloud antivirus system that can be extended for the mobile cloud environment. Extending the benefits of the CloudAV platform requires that an agent be deployed on a mobile platform. This mobile agent interfaces with the CloudAV network service. The CloudAV network service is also extended with a mobile-specific behavioral detection engine. The behavioral engine runs candidate applications in a virtualized operating environment hosted in the network service and monitors the application's system calls and inter-process communication for malicious behavior. The security services hosted in the network service are not limited to antivirus functionality and in-cloud platform can enable a range of different security services such as SMS spam filtering, phishing detection and centralized blacklists. Although we aim at securing mobile devices and send out files to cloud for malware detection, there is no guarantee that those files uploaded will be kept absolutely secret. Especially in the cases of systems sending out an entire file for processing, any leakage of the file contents may lead to a larger damage. This is one of the concerns that we must consider seriously. Some of these issues include concerns about privacy and data ownership and security. Some of these concerns are especially relevant to mobile devices.

Intrusion Detection and Prevention (IDP): On-device IDP systems for smartphones have been previously proposed in the literature like the one in (Joshi et al. 2004) which extracts features that describe the state of the device and exploit those features for anomaly detection. As we mentioned earlier, the main challenge for on-device mobile IDP systems is the resource limitations of smartphones in order to run a complex IDP system on them. Hence, to address those limita-

tions and in order to provide mobile cloud users with a holistic intrusion detection and prevention system, mobile cloud-based IDP has been recently introduced (5, 6, 1). Mobile cloud-based IDP aims to detect and respond to the attacks by exploiting the resources in the cloud and by collaborating with other mobile peers. In other words, mobile cloud-based IDP systems must be able to run both on-device and off-device (i.e. migrated to the cloud). For instance, in case there is no or insufficient Internet connectivity, on-device IDP system is necessary. Furthermore, future mobile cloud-based IDP could facilitate both the detection and response processes with the collaborative and distributed capabilities to effectively detect and respond to the intruders in a distributed fashion and by collaborating with their peers. Employing collaborative and distributed mobile cloud-based IDP, mobile devices could share their knowledge about detecting malicious activities with their peers in order to effectively detect and response to the intruders (Taghavi Zargar, Takabi, & Joshi 2011; Taghavi Zargar & Joshi 2010, Taghavi Zargar, Joshi, & Tipper 2013).

Moreover, a distributed environment, which a mobile cloud-based IDS provides, raises some new security challenges (e.g. privacy, location dependency) that should be solved for the mobile cloud environment. Location of the mobile device is an important factor in detecting and responding to various intrusions. For instance, mobile devices in some locations may be more prone to Bluetooth attacks or other threats that are specific to a given location. In order to handle these security challenges, the paper propose a location-aware mobile Intrusion Prevention System (mIPS) architecture, which exploits a distributed execution environment where processor intensive services can be outsourced to the cloud providers. mIPS allows mobile devices to query the location threat profiles in a privacy-preserving way (Zhang & Joshi 2009). With regards to privacy, the approach proposed in (Blaze et al. 2009) constructs the privacy policy into the intrusion detection and prevention rules by defining a privacy-preserving rule language. Their privacy-preserving rule language pseudonymises the payload and other sensitive information.

Data Centric Security Model: The Data Centric Security Model (DCSM) is an emerging security model that offers reasonable approaches to securing the mobile cloud (50). It offers an approach to protecting data by associating it with one of a variety of levels and then enacting access control to each level. The data levels or categories can be set up arbitrarily, but typically they group data according to the level of damage that would occur if the data is accessed by someone with malicious intent. Most businesses use data that can be differentially categorized. For example, one company database might include customer data (Social Security Number, credit card data), corporate data (mergers and acquisitions, financials), and intellectual property (source code, pricing). Categorizing data is often a function of business requirements and regulations. The US Health Insurance Portability and Accountability Act (HIPAA) security regulation is one example of government-mandated data security. After categories are established, access control rules can be written and enforced. In this case, the mobile cloud conceivably can enhance enforcement of access control rules. For example, a user's access to a particular category of data might require that the user's mobile device report its geo-location as somewhere in the United States, otherwise access is denied.

Data Loss Prevention: Data Loss Prevention (DLP) is a methodology that attempts not only to deter data loss but also to detect data that is at risk of being lost or misused. DLP approaches deal with data in motion, data at rest, and data in use. Data in motion refers to monitoring of traffic on the network to identify content being sent across specific communications channels for the purpose of determining the suitability of that channel for the data. A mismatch between data and channel could indicate a potential security threat. Data at rest involves scanning storage and other content repositories to identify where sensitive content is located. If the container isn't authorized for that data, then a corrective action is indicated. Data in use means monitoring data as users interact with it. If a user attempts to transfer sensitive data to an unauthorized device, the user can be alerted, or the action can be blocked. This emerging technology of DLP affords a good opportunity for developers and researchers. Good threat signature identification will be an ongoing problem as new types of threats emerge. Threat detection rules and security policy enforcement are needed. Also, implementation is a fertile area for growth. For example, DLP-bots — small applications that run on smartphones and tablets — might be one vehicle for deploying DLP in the mobile cloud.

FUTURE RESEARCH DIRECTIONS

One possible research trend in mobile cloud computing is to incorporate hypervisors into smartphones. This development is intended to simplify smartphone management problems. It also has potential to simplify security management. Another research trend is the growth of what is known as the *Internet of Things*. The growth in the variety of mobile devices that can interact with the cloud will undoubtedly bring new security concerns as well.

As we mentioned before, the mobile devices can be lost or stolen. A research challenge is how to prevent malicious attackers from using the mobile devices. Intuitively, biometrics based identification techniques on the mobile devices such as voice recognition, fingerprints, etc., can be used as a second authentication method to protect the mobile devices. However, biometrics enabled devices will increase the device cost, and protecting the biometrics' information of a mobile user becomes another issue. Thus, the research question is that can we use mobile cloud to protect user's data, even if the mobile devices are lost or compromised?

CONCLUSION

The emergence of cloud computing and its extension into the mobile domain creates the potential for a global, interconnected mobile cloud computing environment that will allow the entire mobile ecosystem to enrich their services across multiple networks. However, in order to realize mobile cloud computing, we need to develop mechanisms to achieve secure interoperability among heterogeneous and distributed devices. We need solutions to discover best available resources in cloud servers based on the needs of the users and approaches to deliver desired resources and services efficiently and in a timely manner to the mobile terminals. In this chapter, we have explored the architectural components required to realize a mobile cloud computing infrastructure. We note that none of the existing schemes fully meets the requirements of mobile cloud computing. We anticipate that in future, mobile cloud computing and its applications will focus more on schemes that are dynamically and optimally separating their responsibilities (e.g. computation, storage) between mobile devices and the cloud. Mobile cloud computing is a challenging research area with the range of various problems in the field of communication and information to be solved.

Furthermore, while mobile cloud computing has tremendous potential to enable the mobile terminals to have access to powerful and reliable computing resources anywhere and anytime, we must consider several issues including privacy and security, and reliability in realizing mobile cloud computing. We have presented unique security and privacy challenges of mobile cloud computing and discussed various approaches to address these challenges. Finally, we have discussed some research directions and the future work needed to provide a trustworthy mobile cloud computing environment.

ACKNOWLEDGMENT

This research has been supported by Cisco systems' research award, the US National Science Foundation award IIS-0545912, and US National Science Foundation award CCF-0720737.

REFERENCES

Baliga, A., Chen, X., Coskun, B., Reyes, G., Lee, S., Mathur, S., & van der Merwe, J. E. (2011). VPMN: Virtual private mobile network towards mobility-as-a-service. In L. Cox & E. de Lara (Eds.), *Proceedings of the 2nd International Workshop on Mobile Cloud Computing and Services (MCS '11)* (pp. 7-12). Bethesda, MD: ACM Press.

Bertino, E., Paci, F., & Ferrini, R. (2009). Privacy-preserving digital identity management for cloud computing. *IEEE Computer Society Data Engineering Bulletin*, *1*(32), 1–4.

Blaze, M., Kannan, S., Lee, I., Sokolsky, O., Smith, J. M., Keromytis, A. D., & Lee, W. (2009). Dynamic trust management. *IEEE Computer*, *42*(2), 44–51. doi:10.1109/MC.2009.51.

Bruening, P. J., & Treacy, B. C. (2009). *Cloud computing: Privacy, security challenges. Privacy & Security Law Report*. Washington, DC: The Bureau of National Affairs, Inc..

Cao, Y., Jarke, M., Klamma, R., Mendoza, O., & Srirama, S. (2009). Mobile access to MPEG-7 based multimedia services. In *Proceedings of the 10th International Conference on Mobile Data Management: Systems, Services and Middleware* (pp. 102-111). Taipei, Taiwan: IEEE Press.

Catteddu, D., & Hogben, G. (2009). Cloud computing: Benefits, risks and recommendations for information security. *European Network and Information Security Agency (ENISA) Report*. Retrieved August 10, 2011, from http://www.enisa.europa.eu/act/rm/files/deliverables/cloud-computing-risk-assessment/at_download/fullReport

Chang, Y. S., & Hung, S. H. (2011). Developing collaborative applications with mobile cloud—A case study of speech recognition. *Journal of Internet Services and Information Security*, *1*(1), 18–36.

Chen, Y., Paxson, V., & Katz, R. H. (2010). *What's new about cloud computing security?* (Technical Report No. UCB/EECS-2010-5). EECS Department, University of California at Berkeley. Retrieved August 10, 2011, from http://www.eecs.berkeley.edu/Pubs/TechRpts/2010/EECS-2010-5.html

Christensen, J. H. (2009). Using RESTful web-services and cloud computing to create next generation mobile applications. In *Proceedings of the 24th ACM SIGPLAN Conference Companion on Object Oriented Programming Systems Languages and Applications (OOPSLA '09)*. New York: ACM Press.

Chun, B. G., Ihm, S., Maniatis, P., Naik, M., & Patti, A. (2011). CloneCloud: Elastic execution between mobile device and cloud. In *Proceedings of the 6th European Conference on Computer Systems (EuroSys 2011)* (pp. 301-314). Salzburg, Austria: ACM Press.

Cloud Security Alliance. (2011). *Security guidance for critical areas of focus in cloud computing*. Retrieved August 10, 2011, from http://cloudsecurityalliance.org/csaguide.pdf

Cuervo, E., Balasubramanian, A., Cho, D. K., Wolman, A., Saroiu, S., Chandra, R., & Bahl, P. (2010). MAUI: Making smartphones last longer with code offload. In *Proceedings of the 8th International Conference on Mobile Systems, Applications, and Services (ACM MobiSys '10)* (pp. 49-62). San Francisco, CA: ACM Press.

Giurgiu, I., Riva, O., Juric, D., Krivulev, I., & Alonso, G. (2009). Calling the cloud: Enabling mobile phones as interfaces to cloud applications. In *Proceedings of the 10th ACM/IFIP/USENIX International Conference on Middleware (Middleware '09)*. New York: Springer-Verlag.

Guo, Y., Zhang, L., Kong, J., Sun, J., Feng, T., & Chen, X. (2011). Jupiter: Transparent augmentation of smartphone capabilities through cloud computing. In P. Druschel (Ed.), *Proceedings of the 3rd ACM SOSP Workshop on Networking, Systems, and Applications on Mobile Handhelds (MobiHeld '11)* (pp. 1-6). Cascais, Portugal: ACM Press.

Gutierrez, M. A. F., & Ventura, N. (2010). Mobile cloud computing: Embracing network as a service. In *Proceedings of the Southern Africa Telecommunication Networks and Applications Conference (SATNAC'10)*. SATNAC.

Hoang, D. B., & Chen, L. (2010). Mobile cloud for assistive healthcare (MoCAsH). In *Proceedings of the IEEE Asia-Pacific Services Computing Conference (APSCC '10)* (pp. 325-332). Washington, DC: IEEE Press.

Huerta-Canepa, G., & Lee, D. (2010). A virtual cloud computing provider for mobile devices. In *Proceedings of the 1st ACM Workshop on Mobile Cloud Computing & Services Social Networks and Beyond (MCS '10)* (pp. 1-5). San Francisco, CA: ACM Press.

Joshi, J. B. D., Bhatti, R., Bertino, E., & Ghafoor, A. (2004). Access control language for multi domain environments. *IEEE Internet Computing*, 8(6), 40–50. doi:10.1109/MIC.2004.53.

Ko, M., Ahn, G. J., & Shehab, M. (2009). Privacy enhanced user-centric identity management. In G. Fettweis (Ed.), *Proceedings of the IEEE International Conference on Communications* (pp. 1-5). Dresden, Germany: IEEE Press.

Koukoumidis, E., Lymberopoulos, D., Strauss, K., Liu, J., & Burger, D. (2011). Pocket cloudlets. *SIGPLAN Not.*, 47(4), 171–184. doi:10.1145/2248487.1950387.

Marinelli, E. E. (2009). *Hyrax: Cloud computing on mobile devices using MapReduce*. (Unpublished master thesis). Carnegie Mellon University, Pittsburgh, PA.

Mell, P., & Grance, T. (2011). *The NIST definition of cloud computing* (NIST Special Publication 800-145 [Draft]). Retrieved August 10, 2011, from http://csrc.nist.gov/publications/drafts/800-145/Draft-SP-800-145_cloud-definition.pdf

Olsson, M., Sultana, S., Rommer, S., Frid, L., & Mulligan, C. (2009). *SAE and the evolved packet core driving the mobile broadband revolution*. Elsevier.

Openmobster. (2010). Retrieved August 10, 2011, from http://code.google.com/p/openmobster/

Sesia, S., Toufik, I., & Baker, M. (2011). *LTE—The UMTS long term evolution—From theory to practice* (2nd ed.). New York: John Wiley & Sons. doi:10.1002/9780470978504.

Shin, D., & Ahn, G. J. (2005). Role-based privilege and trust management. *Computer Systems Science and Engineering, 20*(6).

Subramanyan, R., Wong, E., & Yang, H. I. (Eds.). (2010). *Proceedings of the 34th annual IEEE computer software and applications conference workshops (COMPSACW 2010)* (pp. 393-398). Seoul, South Korea: IEEE Press.

Taghavi Zargar, S., & Joshi, J. B. D. (2010). A collaborative approach to facilitate intrusion detection and response against DDoS attacks. In K. Aberer, & J. B. D. Joshi (Eds.), *Proceedings of the 6th International Conference on Collaborative Computing: Networking, Applications and Worksharing (CollaborateCom2010)*. Chicago, IL: IEEE Press.

Taghavi Zargar, S., Joshi, J. B. D., & Tipper, D. (2013). A survey of defense mechanisms against distributed denial of service (DDoS) flooding attacks. *IEEE Communications Surveys and Tutorials*, (99): 1–24. doi:10.1109/SURV.2013.031413.00127.

Taghavi Zargar, S., Takabi, H., & Joshi, J. B. D. (2011). DCDIDP: A distributed, collaborative, and data-driven intrusion detection and prevention framework for cloud computing environments. In D. Georgakopoulos & J. B. D. Joshi (Eds.), *Proceedings of the 7th International Conference on Collaborative Computing: Networking, Applications and Worksharing (CollaborateCom2011)*. Orlando, FL: IEEE Press.

Takabi, H., & Joshi, J. B. D. (2012a). Semantic based policy management for cloud computing environments. *International Journal of Cloud Computing, 1*(2), 2012.

Takabi, H., & Joshi, J. B. D. (2012b). Toward a semantic based policy management framework for interoperable cloud environments. In *Proceedings of the International IBM Cloud Academy Conference (ICA CON 2012)*. IBM.

Takabi, H., & Joshi, J. B. D. (2012c). Policy management in cloud computing environment: Challenges and approaches. In D. G. Rosado, D. Mellado, E. Fernandez-Medina, & M. Piattini (Eds.), *Security Engineering for Cloud Computing: Approaches and Tools*. Hershey, PA: IGI Global. doi:10.4018/978-1-4666-2125-1.ch010.

Takabi, H., Joshi, J. B. D., & Ahn, G. J. (2010a). SecureCloud: Towards a comprehensive security framework for cloud computing environments. In S. I. Ahamed, D. H. Bae, S. Cha, C. K. Chang (Eds.), *Proceedings of the Computer Software and Applications Conference Workshops (COMPSACW)*, (pp. 393-398). COMPSACW.

Takabi, H., Joshi, J. B. D., & Ahn, G. J. (2010b). Security and privacy challenges in cloud computing environments. *IEEE Security and Privacy*, 8(6), 24–31. doi:10.1109/MSP.2010.186.

Takabi, H., Joshi, J. B. D., & Ahn, G. J. (2013). Security and privacy in cloud computing: Towards a comprehensive framework. In X. Yang, & L. Liu (Eds.), *Principles, methods and service-oriented approaches for cloud computing*. Hershey, PA: IGI Global. doi:10.4018/978-1-4666-2854-0.ch007.

Taylor, S., Young, A., Kumar, N., & Macaulay, J. (2011). The mobile cloud: When two explosive markets collide. *Cisco IBSG*. Retrieved August 10, 2011, from http://www.cisco.com/web/about/ac79/docs/sp/Mobile-Cloud-Overview-POV.pdf

The Apache Hadoop Project. (n.d.). Retrieved August 10, 2011, from http://hadoop.apache.org

Vartiainen, E., & Väänänen-Vainio-Mattila, K. (2010). User experience of mobile photo sharing in the cloud. In C. Mascolo & E. O'Neill (Eds.), *Proceedings of the 9th International Conference on Mobile and Ubiquitous Multimedia (MUM '10)* (pp. 1-10). Limassol, Cyprus: ACM Press.

Zaplata, S., & Lamersdorf, W. (2010). Towards mobile process as a service. In *Proceedings of the ACM Symposium on Applied Computing (SAC '10)*. New York: ACM Press.

Zhang, Y., & Joshi, J. B. D. (2009). Access control and trust management for emerging multidomain environments. In S. Upadhyaya, & R. O. Rao (Eds.), *Annals of Emerging Research in Information Assurance, Security and Privacy Services*. London: Emerald Group Publishing Limited.

Zhang, Z., & Zhang, X. (2009). Realization of open cloud computing federation based on mobile agent. In *Proceedings of the IEEE International Conference on Intelligent Computing and Intelligent Systems (ICIS '09)* (Vol. 3, pp. 642-646). IEEE.

ADDITIONAL READING

Ahmed, M., Xiang, Y., & Ali, S. (2010). Above the trust and security in cloud computing: A notion towards innovation. In *Proceedings of the IEEE/IFIP 8th International Conference on Embedded and Ubiquitous Computing (EUC)* (pp. 723-730). IEEE.

Almorsy, M., Grundy, J., & Ibrahim, A. S. (2011). Collaboration-based cloud computing security management framework. In *Proceedings of the 4th IEEE International Conference on Cloud Computing (CLOUD)* (pp. 364-371). IEEE.

Basescu, C., Carpen-Amarie, A., Leordeanu, C., Costan, A., & Antoniu, G. (2011). Managing data access on clouds: A generic framework for enforcing security policies. In *Proceedings of the IEEE International Conference on Advanced Information Networking and Applications (AINA '11)*. IEEE.

Bernstein, D., & Vij, D. (2010). Intercloud security considerations. In *Proceedings of the IEEE Second International Conference on Cloud Computing Technology and Science (CloudCom)* (pp. 537-544). IEEE.

Celesti, A., Tusa, F., Villari, M., & Puliafito, A. (2010). Security and cloud computing: InterCloud identity management infrastructure. In *Proceedings of the 19th IEEE International Workshop on Enabling Technologies: Infrastructures for Collaborative Enterprises (WETICE)* (pp. 263-265). IEEE.

Christodorescu, M., Sailer, R., Schales, D. L., Sgandurra, D., & Zamboni, D. (2009). Cloud security is not (just) virtualization security. In *Proceedings of the ACM Workshop on Cloud Computing Security (CCSW '09)* (pp. 97-102). ACM.

Deng, M., Petkovic, M., Nalin, M., & Baroni, I. (2011). A home healthcare system in the cloud—Addressing security and privacy challenges. In *Proceedings of the IEEE International Conference on Cloud Computing (CLOUD)* (pp. 549-556). IEEE.

Di Modica, G., & Tomarchio, O. (2011). Semantic security policy matching in service oriented architectures. In D. S. Milojicic & M. Kirchburg (Eds.), *Proceedings of the 2011 IEEE World Congress on Services* (pp. 399-405). Washington, DC: IEEE Press.

Dowell, S., Barreto, A., Michael, J. B., & Shing, M.-T. (2011). Cloud to cloud interoperability. In I. Ray (Ed.), *Proceedings of the 6th International Conference on System of Systems Engineering (SoSE)* (pp. 49-58). Tahoe City, CA: ACM Press.

Echeverria, V., Liebrock, L. M., & Shin, D. (2010). Permission management system: Permission as a service in cloud computing. In S. I. Ahamed, D. H. Bae, S. Cha, C. K. Chang, R. Subramanyan, W. Wong, & H. I. Yang (Eds.), *Proceedings of the 34th Annual Computer Software and Applications Conference Workshops (COMPSACW '10)* (pp. 371-375). Seoul, South Korea: IEEE Press.

Grobauer, B., Walloschek, T., & Stocker, E. (2011). Understanding cloud computing vulnerabilities. *IEEE Security and Privacy, 9*(2), 50–57. doi:10.1109/MSP.2010.115.

Gruschka, N., & Jensen, M. (2010). Attack surfaces: A taxonomy for attacks on cloud services. In *Proceedings of the IEEE 3rd International Conference on Cloud Computing (CLOUD)* (pp. 276-279). IEEE.

Hu, Y. J., Wu, W. N., & Yang, J. J. (2011). Semantics-enabled policies for information sharing and protection in the cloud. In A. Datta, R. Rogers, & S. Shulman (Eds.), *Proceedings of the 3rd International Conference on Social Informatics (SocInfo'11)* (pp. 49-58). Singapore: SocInfo.

Itani, W., Kayssi, A., & Chehab, A. (2009). Privacy as a service: Privacy-aware data storage and processing in cloud computing architectures. In *Proceedings of the 8th IEEE International Conference on Dependable, Autonomic and Secure Computing (DASC '09)* (pp. 711-716). IEEE.

Jaeger, T., & Schiffman, J. (2011). Outlook: Cloudy with a chance of security challenges and improvements. *IEEE Security and Privacy, 8*(1), 77–80. doi:10.1109/MSP.2010.45.

Jansen, W. A. (2011). Cloud hooks: Security and privacy issues in cloud computing. In *Proceedings of the 44th Hawaii International Conference on System Sciences (HICSS)* (pp. 1-10). IEEE.

Jasti, A., Shah, P., Nagaraj, R., & Pendse, R. (2010). Security in multi-tenancy cloud. In *Proceedings of the IEEE International Carnahan Conference on Security Technology (ICCST)* (pp. 35-41). IEEE.

Jensen, M., Schäge, S., & Schwenk, J. (2010). Towards an anonymous access control and accountability scheme for cloud computing. In W. Chou & A. M. Goscinski (Eds.), *Proceedings of the 3rd International Conference on Cloud Computing (Cloud '10)* (pp. 540-541). Miami, FL: IEEE Press.

Jensen, M., Schwenk, J., Bohli, J. M., Gruschka, N., & Iacono, L. L. (2011). Security prospects through cloud computing by adopting multiple clouds. In *Proceedings of the IEEE 4th International Conference on Cloud Computing (CLOUD)* (pp. 565-572). IEEE.

Jia, W., Zhu, H., Cao, Z., Wei, L., & Lin, X. (2011). SDSM: A secure data service mechanism in mobile cloud computing. In *Proceedings of the IEEE Conference on Computer Communications Workshops* (pp. 1060-1065). IEEE.

Jing, X., & Jian-Jun, Z. (2010). A brief survey on the security model of cloud computing. In *Proceedings of the 9th International Symposium on Distributed Computing and Applications to Business, Engineering and Science (DCABES '10).* DCABES.

Jung, Y., & Chung, M. (2010). Adaptive security management model in the cloud computing environment. In *Proceedings of the 12th International Conference on Advanced Communication Technology (ICACT)* (Vol. 2, pp. 1664-1669). ICACT.

Kim, A., McDermott, J., & Kang, M. (2010). Security and architectural issues for national security cloud computing. In *Proceedings of the IEEE 30th International Conference on Distributed Computing Systems Workshops (ICDCSW)* (pp. 21-25). IEEE.

Klein, A., Mannweiler, C., Schneider, J., & Schotten, H. D. (2010). Access schemes for mobile cloud computing. In *Proceedings of the 11th International Conference on Mobile Data Management (MDM '10)* (pp. 387-392). Washington, DC: IEEE Press.

Kretzschmar, M., Golling, M., & Hanigk, S. (2011). Security management areas in the intercloud. In *Proceedings of the IEEE International Conference on Cloud Computing (CLOUD)* (pp. 762-763). IEEE.

Lakshman, T. K., & Thuijs, X. (2011). Enhancing enterprise field productivity via cross platform mobile cloud apps. In *Proceedings of the Second International Workshop on Mobile Cloud Computing and Services (MCS '11)* (pp. 27-32). MCS.

Li, J., Zhao, G., Chen, X., Xie, D., Rong, C., & Li, W. ... Tang, Y. (2010). Fine-grained data access control systems with user accountability in cloud computing. In G. Zhao & J. Qiu (Eds.), *Proceedings of the Second International Conference on Cloud Computing Technology and Science (CloudCom '10)* (pp. 89-96). Indianapolis, IN: IEEE Press.

Li, Y., Shi, Y., Guo, Y., & Ma, W. (2010). Multi-tenancy based access control in cloud. In Y. He (Ed.), In *Proceedings of the 2010 International Conference on Computational Intelligence and Software Engineering (CiSE)* (pp. 1-4). Wuhan, China: IEEE Press.

Liu, J., Wan, Z., & Gu, M. (2011). Hierarchical attribute-set based encryption for scalable, flexible and fine-grained access control in cloud computing. In F. Bao & J. Weng (Eds.), *Proceedings of the 7th International Conference on Information Security Practice and Experience (SPEC'11)* (pp. 98-107). China: Springer.

Lv, H., & Hu, Y. (2011). Analysis and research about cloud computing security protect policy. In *Proceedings of the International Conference on Intelligence Science and Information Engineering (ISIE)* (pp. 214-216). ISIE.

Na, S. H., Park, J. Y., & Huh, E. N. (2010). Personal cloud computing security framework. In *Prceedings of the IEEE Asia-Pacific Services Computing Conference (APSCC)* (pp. 671-675). IEEE.

Nagin, K., Hadas, D., Dubitzky, Z., Glikson, A., Loy, I., Rochwerger, B., & Schour, L. (2011). Intercloud mobility of virtual machines. In *Proceedings of the 4th Annual International Conference on Systems and Storage (SYSTOR '11)*. SYSTOR.

Nguyen, T. D., Gondree, M. A., Shifflett, D. J., Khosalim, J., Levin, T. E., & Irvine, C. E. (2010). A cloud-oriented cross-domain security architecture. In *Proceedings of the Military Communications Conference (MILCOM'10)* (pp. 441-447). IEEE.

Pearson, S., & Benameur, A. (2010). Privacy, security and trust issues arising from cloud computing. In *Proceedings of the IEEE Second International Conference on Cloud Computing Technology and Science (CloudCom)* (pp. 693-702). IEEE.

Popa, L., Yu, M., Ko, S. Y., Ratnasamy, S., & Stoica, I. (2010). CloudPolice: Taking access control out of the network. In *Proceedings of the 9th ACM SIGCOMM Workshop on Hot Topics in Networks (Hotnets-IX)*. New York: ACM Press.

Prasad, P., Ojha, B., Shahi, R. R., Lal, R., Vaish, A., & Goel, U. (2011). 3 dimensional security in cloud computing. In *Proceedings of the 3rd International Conference on Computer Research and Development (ICCRD)* (pp. 198-201). ICCRD.

Prasadreddy, P. V. G. D., Rao, T. S., & Venkat, S. P. (2011). A threat free architecture for privacy assurance in cloud computing. In *Proceedings of the IEEE World Congress on Services (SERVICES)* (pp. 564-568). IEEE.

Preiya, V. S., & Pavithra, R., & Joshi. (2011, May-June). Secure role based data access control in cloud computing. *International Journal of Computer Trends and Technology*.

Sabahi, F. (2011). Cloud computing security threats and responses. In *Proceedings of the 3rd IEEE International Conference on Communication Software and Networks (ICCSN)* (pp. 245-249). IEEE.

Sandhu, R., Boppana, R., Krishnan, R., Reich, J., Wolff, T., & Zachry, J. (2010). Towards a discipline of mission-aware cloud computing. In *Proceedings of the ACM Workshop on Cloud Computing Security* (CCSW '10). ACM.

Santos, N., Gummadi, K. P., & Rodrigues, R. (2009). Towards trusted cloud computing. In *Proceedings of the Conference on Hot Topics in Cloud Computing (HotCloud'09)*. Berkeley, CA: USENIX Association.

Sasaki, T., Nakae, M., & Ogawa, R. (2010). Content oriented virtual domains for secure information sharing across organizations. In *Proceedings of the ACM Workshop on Cloud Computing Security* (CCSW '10). ACM.

Sengupta, S., Kaulgud, V., & Sharma, V. S. (2011). Cloud computing security—Trends and research directions. In Y. He (Ed.), *Proceedings of the 2011 IEEE World Congress on Services* (pp. 524-531). Washington, DC: IEEE Press.

Srivastava, P., Singh, S., Pinto, A. A., Verma, S., Chaurasiya, V. K., & Gupta, R. (2011). An architecture based on proactive model for security in cloud computing. In *Proceedings of the International Conference on Recent Trends in Information Technology (ICRTIT)* (pp. 661-666). ICRTIT.

Takabi, H., & Joshi, J. B. D. (2010). StateMiner: An efficient similarity-based approach for optimal mining of role hierarchy. In B. Carminati (Ed.), *Proceedings of the 15th ACM Symposium on Access Control Models and Technologies* (pp. 55-64). Pittsburgh, PA: ACM Press.

Takabi, H., Kim, M., Joshi, J. B. D., & Spring, M. B. (2009). An architecture for specification and enforcement of temporal access control constraints using OWL. In E. Damiani, S. Proctor, & A. Singal (Eds.), *Proceedings of the 2009 ACM Workshop on Secure Web Services* (pp. 21-28). Chicago, IL: ACM Press.

Tchifilionova, V. (2010). Security and privacy implications of cloud computing: Lost in the cloud. In *Proceedings of the IFIP WG 11.4 International Conference on Open Research Problems in Network Security* (pp. 149-158). IFIP.

Tsai, W. T., & Shao, Q. (2011). Role-based access-control using reference ontology in clouds. In *Proceedings of the 10th International Symposium on Autonomous Decentralized Systems (ISADS)* (pp. 121-128). ISADS.

Verma, A., & Kaushal, S. (2011). Cloud computing security issues and challenges: A survey. *ACM Transactions on Information and System Security, 193*(4), 445–454.

Wang, G., Liu, Q., & Wu, J. (2010). Hierarchical attribute-based encryption for fine-grained access control in cloud storage services. In *Proceedings of the 17th ACM Conference on Computer and Communications Security (CCS '10)* (pp. 735-737).

Wu, R., Ahn, G. J., Hu, H., & Singhal, M. (2010). Information flow control in cloud computing. In K. Aberer & J. B. D. Joshi (Eds.), *Proceedings of the 6th International Conference on Collaborative Computing: Networking, Applications and Worksharing (CollaborateCom2010)*. Chicago, IL: IEEE Press.

Yildiz, M., Abawajy, J., Ercan, T., & Bernoth, A. (2009). A layered security approach for cloud computing infrastructure. In *Proceedings of the 10th International Symposium on Pervasive Systems, Algorithms, and Networks (ISPAN)* (pp. 763-767). ISPAN.

Yu, S., Wang, C., Ren, K., & Lou, W. (2010). Achieving secure, scalable, and fine-grained data access control in cloud computing. In M. C. Chuah, R. Cohen, & G. Xue (Eds.), *Proceedings of the 29th Conference on Information Communications (Infocom'10)* (pp. 1-9). San Diego, CA: IEEE Press.

Zhao, G., Rong, C., Jaatun, M. G., & Sandnes, F. E. (2010). Deployment models: Towards eliminating security concerns from cloud computing. In *Proceedings of the International Conference on High Performance Computing and Simulation (HPCS)* (pp. 189-195). IEEE.

KEY TERMS AND DEFINITIONS

Cloud Computing: Cloud computing is a model for enabling ubiquitous, convenient, on-demand network access to a shared pool of configurable computing resources (e.g., networks, servers, storage, applications, and services) that can be rapidly provisioned and released with minimal management effort or service provider interaction.

Cloud Service Provider: Cloud service provider is an entity that offers one or more Cloud based services that are used by Cloud users.

Mobile Computing: Mobile computing is capability of using computing power without being constrained to a pre-defined location and/or connection to a network. It involves ad-hoc and infrastructure networks as well as communication properties, and protocols, mobile devices and mobile software dealing with requirements of mobile applications.

Mobile Cloud Computing: Mobile cloud computing is the combination of cloud computing and mobile computing to bring benefits for mobile users, network operators, as well as cloud service providers. In mobile cloud computing, we should enable the mobile terminals to have access to powerful and reliable computing resources anywhere and anytime by building a virtual computing environment between the front-end mobile terminals and the back-end cloud servers. Mobile cloud computing can involve other mobile devices and/or servers accessed via the Internet. Applications are run on a remote server and then sent to the user.

Cloudlet: Cloudlet is a related notion to mobile cloud computing and has been viewed in different ways but its goal is to move the cloud closer to the mobile user. A cloudlet is a trusted, resource-rich computer or cluster of computers that is well-connected to the Internet and is available for use by nearby mobile devices.

Access Control: Access control systems provide the essential services of authorization that determines what actions a subject is allowed to do on an object. In access control systems, subjects are the entities that perform actions and objects are the entities representing resources on which the action is performed.

Data Centric Security Model: The Data Centric Security Model (DCSM) is an emerging security model that offers reasonable approaches to securing the mobile cloud. It offers an approach to protecting data by associating it with one of a variety of levels and then enacting access control to each level.

APPENDIX: REVIEW QUESTIONS

1. What are the two main types of mobile applications? Briefly explain each of them and enumerate some of their differences.
2. What are some of the main goals of the mobile cloud computing?
3. What is a cloudlet and what type of mobile cloud it belongs to?
4. What is Mobile Process as a Service (MPaaS)? Explain its advantages and disadvantages.
5. What are the three main security challenges of mobile cloud computing if you get to choose among the challenges explained on this chapter?
6. How can we address the malware in the mobile cloud computing environments as an ever-growing security challenge?
7. Explain implicit filter based access control isolation and compare it with explicit permissions based access control isolation pattern.
8. What are the key management challenges within mobile cloud and how we can address them?
9. Explain how the data centric security model (DCSM) can be used in mobile cloud computing?
10. What is the best way to deploy data loss prevention (DLP) in the mobile cloud?

Chapter 17
State of the Art for Near Field Communication:
Security and Privacy Within the Field

Maria Moloney
Escher Group Ltd, Ireland

ABSTRACT

This chapter provides an overview of Near Field Communication (NFC) technology. It first introduces the technology and gives a brief history. It examines what the technology is and how it works. It looks at the various operation modes and hardware architectures available for the technology. This is followed by some examples in use of the technology today, in particular NFC in use in mobile payment environment. The chapter then focuses on NFC technology from the perspective of security and privacy of personal information when using the technology. Finally, the chapter looks at the security and privacy challenges that are currently faced by the technology and suggests some possible solutions to these challenges.

INTRODUCTION

For years now pervasive computing researchers have investigated ways of connecting the virtual world of the Internet with the physical world in which we live (Want, 2011). Near field communication (NFC) has been heralded as the standard that might make this vision a reality (Want, 2011). By connecting the physical with the virtual, objects, people and places can be linked with online content. Naturally, there are advantages and disadvantages to this linkage, some of which will be discussed in this chapter. But one of the central advantages is that this linkage can provide useful

DOI: 10.4018/978-1-4666-4691-9.ch017

related information that can be amalgamated and displayed in various formats. The most interesting potential of NFC technology is observed when it is used in conjunction with mobile devices. NFC mobile phones or smart phones function as contactless cards which are used to leverage the existing contactless infrastructure used by smart cards (Agrawal & Bhuraria, 2012). On top of this, NFC smart phones leverage the Internet and multimedia capabilities to create many innovative services, which have been demonstrated as having a transformational impact across disciplines like electronic payments and retailing, public transportation and even healthcare (Agrawal & Bhuraria, 2012).

Points for virtual coupons or loyalty cards can be collected with an NFC smart phone from company advertising posters found in magazines or located in any public place. These virtual coupons or points can be redeemed in store to receive discounts or special offers. For example, a coffee store advertising a 10% discount available from their advertising posters can be scanned and used the next time the consumer enters the coffee store.

NFC enabled smart phones can increase technology ease of use for consumers in many ways. An example of this ease of use can be understood by imagining a scene where a person going to the movies has an NFC smart phone and waves it in front of a poster for the desired movie on his way into the cinema. The tickets are automatically bought and loaded onto the smart phone, eliminating the need for cash and the time needed to queue for tickets. Similar scenarios can be envisioned when using public transport or boarding a plane. Mobile check-in for flights using an NFC enabled device can facilitate consumers boarding flights with one simple swipe of their NFC smart phone.

To some, these scenarios may still seem like science fiction but such scenarios could potentially be in operation in the very near future.

In order to better understand this technology and how it has evolved relatively quickly into stuff of science fiction, a brief description and history of the technology is now outlined.

NFC is a Radio Frequency (RF) technology for short-range communication that exchanges data between a reader, such as a phone or sensor, and a target, such as another reader or a microchip embedded in a device. NFC devices can receive and transmit data at the same time. The specification details of NFC can be found in ISO 18092 (Information technology - Telecommunications and information exchange between systems — Near Field Communication — Interface and Protocol (NFCIP-1), 2004). It is a follow-on technology from Radio Frequency Identification (RFID). The history of RFID can be traced back to the Second World War, where the Royal Air force tagged their planes with suitcase-sized devices to establish a friend-foe detection system. The first commercial release of the technology came in the 1960's in the form of a 1 bit RFID for securing goods in shops, which is still widely used. In the 1990's RFID became more common for use in admission control systems and toll road systems (Roberti). NFC devices can indeed function as a passive RFID tag but they can also function as smart contactless cards and a smart medium to exchange data between various devices.

In 2002, NFC was developed by NXP Semiconductors and Sony. In general, because NFC is an evolution of RFID and smartcard technology (Vazquez-Briseno, Hirata, Sanchez-Lopez, Jimenez-Garcia, Navarro-Cota, & Nieto-Hipolito, 2012), it is compatible with most existing RFID and contactless smartcard systems, but its architecture is different in principle. While RFID and contactless smartcards have a reader/tag structure, an NFC device can be both reader and transmitter. An NFC Data Exchange Format (NDEF) was specified to ensure RFID tags and contactless smartcards are compatible with NFC applications. A key characteristic of NFC is that its wireless communication interface usually has a working distance limit of about 10cm.

In 2004, the NFC forum was founded by Philips, Nokia and Sony. The NFC Forum informs users on how to access content and services in an intuitive way in order to facilitate secure digital commerce and connectivity in which consumers can access and pay for physical and digital services anywhere, at any time, using any device. The forum aims to advance the use of NFC technology by developing standards-based specifications that ensure interoperability between devices and services, encouraging the development of products using NFC Forum specifications, educating the market globally about NFC technology, and ensuring that products claiming NFC capabilities comply with NFC Forum specifications (Preuss, 2009).

The move towards installing NFC technology into mobile devices is already underway (NFC Forum, 2008). By adding the functions of a mobile phone to those of a contactless NFC card, a new intelligent device or an "NFC Mobile Phone," was defined. This newly defined device is an intelligent mobile network-enabled device that can connect with other NFC devices in close proximity. This unique combination of both mobile and NFC technology enables users to enjoy innovative services. Users can access myriad NFC services in their daily lives by having an all-in-one personal device that provides them with a highly personalized and interactive environment (NFC Forum, 2008). A specific use for NFC devices was pioneered in Japan and has since been introduced to the US market, which enables a suitably equipped mobile phone or tablet to act as either an NFC payment card or payment terminal or both (Anderson, 2012). An interesting example of this technology is the Google Wallet, which is discussed in more detail at a later stage in this chapter. Figure 1 gives various examples of how an NFC mobile phone can be used:

For any device to be NFC enabled it has to have an NFC or smart tag built into it. These NFC tags have an antenna attached to them. This antenna enables the devices to exchange information between themselves. NFC communicates via *magnetic field induction*. This is where both loop antennas of each NFC device are located within proximity of each other. An air-core transformer is then created. A functioning air core transformer can be created easily by simply placing the antennas very close to one another. NFC devices are unique in that they are capable of changing their mode of operation. These various operation modes are now described in detail.

NFC OPERATION MODES

The NFC interface operates in several modes. The modes are decided by whether a device can create its own RF field or whether it retrieves power from the RF field generated by another device. If the device generates its own RF field it is called an *active* device, if it does not, it is called a *passive* device. Active devices usually have a power supply; passive devices, such as contactless smart cards, usually do not. The way data is transmitted from device A to device B indicates whether the transmitting device is in active or passive mode (Breitfuss, 2006).

Three different communication modes for NFC devices are possible, 1) peer to peer mode, 2) reader/writer mode, and 3) card emulation mode (Kerschberger, 2011).

Peer-to-Peer

Peer to peer mode enables communication between two NFC devices. This mode enables a link-level communication between two NFC devices. The device which starts the communication is called the *initiator* the other is called the *target*. Device A sends a message to device B and device B sends a reply. Device B cannot send any data to device A without first receiving data from device A. This protocol, which handles the initiator and target configuration in peer to peer mode ensures a smooth establishment of communication, and is called the *Logical Link Control Protocol* (LLCP).

Figure 1. Potential uses of NFC mobile phones, taken from (NFC Forum, 2008)

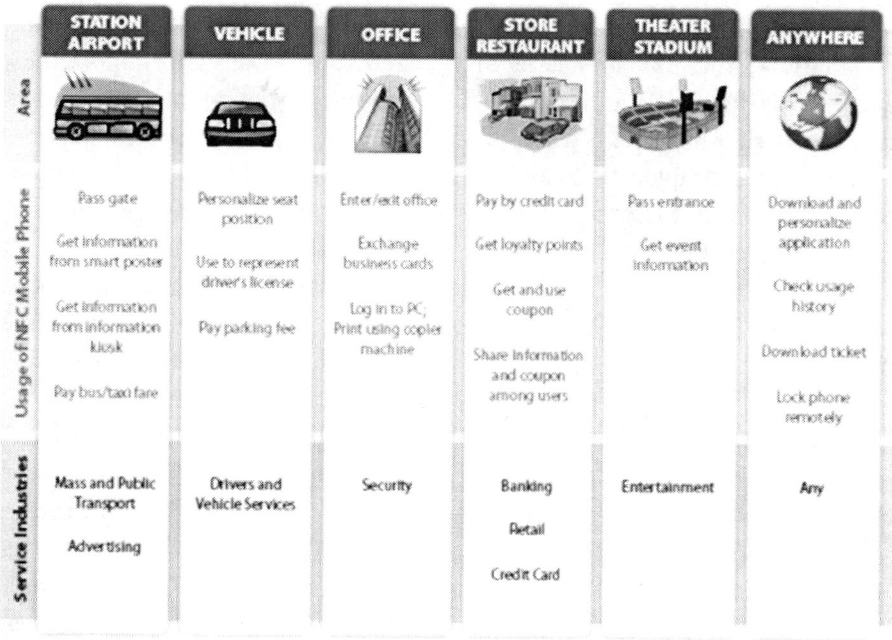

The main difference of this mode is the difference in energy consumption of the initiator and the target. In the active communication mode, the power required for generating the RF field is shared by initiator and target, whereas in passive communication mode the initiator has to supply the power required for the field generation (Kerschberger, 2011).

Read/Writer Mode

The second mode is the reader/writer mode, which allows the NFC devices to communicate with NFC forum tags. These tags are typically passive components. Thus, this mode is also known as passive mode and allows just one way communication from the passive NFC tag to the NFC device. The NFC tag can simply send out the signal to the NFC device but it cannot receive any signal. The tags can be placed in posters or other places and by touching the tag with the NFC device, the stored information is transmitted to the device. They can contain either information, such as Internet addresses or perform actions on the device, such as connecting to a wireless network (Kerschberger, 2011).

Card Emulation Mode

The third and final mode that an NFC device can have is the optional card emulation mode. This mode is used when the NFC device works as a smart card or RFID card. It allows the NFC device to communicate with well known RFID readers and smart card readers. The device, therefore, can emulate one or more RFID smartcard(s) and act as an access card or a rail card. This mode can also be specially configured to send messages that will enable the NFC device to act as a contactless card (Agrawal & Bhuraria, 2012). With this mode it is possible to use the existing contactless infrastructure such as for payment or admission control.

The emulation of the smartcard[1] can be done either in the application layer or in a so called *Secure Element*. A Secure Element is a device, similar to a real smartcard that uses an interface to the NFC device to transfer its data. In combination with the reader/writer mode, it is possible to implement a similar but simpler mode to the peer to peer mode, which with the correct hardware implementation makes it possible to use the NFC device when it is switched off or is short of energy (Google.com, 2012). Figure 2 shows the three operation modes for NFC.

Multiple NFC Devices

NFC communication is not limited to a simple pair of devices. In fact, one initiator device can talk to multiple target devices. In such a scenario, all target devices are enabled at the same time, but before sending a message, the initiator device selects a receiving device. The message is then ignored by all non selected target devices. Only the selected target device is allowed to reply to the received data. It is not possible to send data to more than one device at the same time, i.e. broadcasting messages are not supported.

NFC STANDARDS

Of these three modes, card emulation and reader emulation modes are supported by the Application Programming Interface (API) that is used by current contactless communication networks and that is defined in the proximity card standards. The contactless communication API is a Java specification led by Nokia and defined under the Java Community Process as JSR-257. It defines a set of APIs for proximity, contactless-based communication. NFC is both a send and receive technology and operates in the globally available unlicensed radio frequency of 13.56 MHz (ISM band) (Agrawal & Bhuraria, 2012). Figure 3 below shows the flow of the message from/to the NFC enabled smart phone in all three modes of communication. Depending on the usage, the application in the NFC device decides which mode of communication is to be used (Agrawal & Bhuraria, 2012).

NFC is an open platform technology and is standardised in the ECMA-340 and ISO/IEC 18092 sets of standards. These standards specify the modulation schemes, the coding, the transfer speeds and the frame formats for the RF interface of NFC smart phones and devices. They also

Figure 2. NFC operation modes, taken from (Lazarri, 2008)

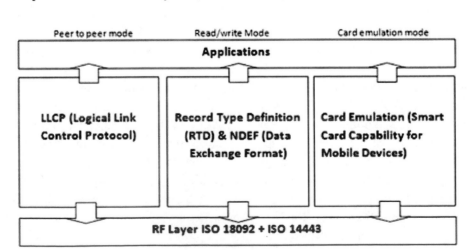

Figure 3. NFC Mobile Devices - Modes of Operation adapted from (Agrawal & Bhuraria, 2012)

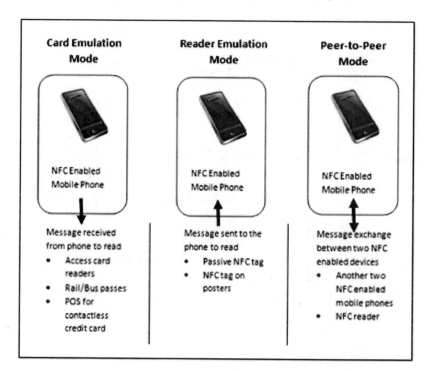

outline the schemes for initialisation and the conditions for controlling data collision during the initialisation process for both passive and active modes of the NFC device. Transport protocol definitions, including data protocol activation and data exchange methods are also defined in these standards.

HARDWARE ARCHITECTURE

Hardware architecture comprises a system's physical components and their interrelationships. The main components of the NFC hardware architecture are (Kerschberger, 2011):

1. **The Host-Controller:** Application Execution Environment (AEE), the environment where the application rests, such as the mobile phone;

2. **The Secure Element:** Trusted Execution Environment (TEE), the secure environment where sensitive information such as debit card data is stored within the host controller;

3. **The NFC-Controller:** Contactless Frontend (CLF), the link between the host and NFC, with an interface to the Secure Element;

4. **NFC-Antenna:** Simply put this is simply loops of wire, occupying as much surface area as the device allows.

The two central components from the list above are now discussed, that of the secure element and the NFC controller. Figure 4 shows the NFC elements within a mobile device.

The NFC Controller

The NFC-Controller is the link between the air interface[2], the host-controller and the secure element.

415

Figure 4. A description of the NFC related elements in mobile devices, adapted from (Jan Kremer Consulting Services, 2010)

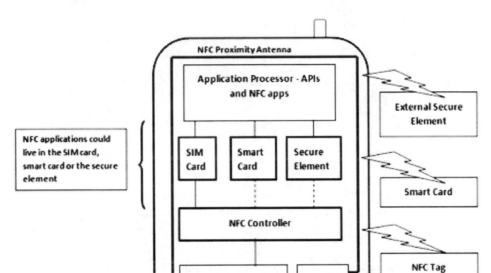

The Host-Controller is most likely a mobile device like a mobile phone, or a smart car key. There are various interfaces between the host controller and the NFC controller such as the serial peripheral interface (SPI), and universal serial bus (USB). For the communication with the secure element there are typically smartcard interfaces, the NFC wired interface or the single wire protocol in use. The controller works as a modulator/demodulator between the analogue air interface and other digital interfaces. The NFC-controllers have integrated microcontrollers, which implement the low level services, so the exchange with the host controller is limited to the application data and some control commands.

The Secure Element

On most mobile devices, such as mobile phones, there is no way to store secure data directly. For most NFC applications, i.e. payment and authentication solutions, secure storage systems are essential. For sensitive data, the storage needs to be resistant to manipulation and it must be able to execute cryptographic functions and to execute security-relevant software. Smartcards usually implement these requirements (Kerschberger, 2011). To implement such secure elements, there are different possibilities, each with its own advantages and disadvantages (Google.com, 2012):

1. **Software Without Secure Hardware:** Software is the most flexible and independent solution, but software could not be optimally secured without the hardware as there is always the possibility that the unsecured hardware is manipulated.

2. **Device Integrated Hardware:** This is the most host dependent, but most reliable solution. The secure element is either a part of the host or is built in as its own chip. The communication with the element and the NFC-Controller works like a smartcard or over the NFC Wired Interface. The biggest disadvantage of this solution is, if the user changes the device, the provider of the secure

service has to remove the data from the old device and to put it on the new one.

3. **Changeable Hardware:** In most cases, this would be the best compromise between reliability, usability and costs. Because a hardware interface is needed to plug in the removable secure element, the production costs of the host device are higher. Such removable devices could be a Secure Memory Card (SMC), which combines the secure smartcard functions with a usual memory card function, or a Universal Integrated Circuit Card (UICC); for example in a mobile phone this is the Subscriber Identity Module (SIM) card. On actual SIM cards there is only one out of 8 connectors free for use, so the Single Wire Protocol was introduced by European Telecommunication Standards Institute (ETSI). While the SMC is usually owned by the user, which allows him/her to change his/her data independently, the SIM card of a mobile phone is owned by the network provider and, thus, the network provider must cooperate with the secure service provider.

An NFC system implementing a Secure Element is often abbreviated as *Secure NFC*, this is misleading because only the data stored on the secure element is secured, not the whole NFC communication (Breitfuss, 2006). Figure 5 shows possible solutions for the location of the Secure Element.

NFC DATA FORMATS

To ensure compatibility between all the NFC and RFID devices, the data exchange formats used in both NFC and RFID were standardized.

The NFC Forum Tags

These tags are an important part of NFC technology. They implement the passive storage devices such as smart-posters, and other areas where small amounts of data can be stored and transferred to active NFC devices. Data can be retrieved from these passive tags by touching it with an NFC device. For example, the live area of the poster can be used as a touch point for the active NFC device. The stored data on the NFC tag may contain any form of data, but common applications are for storing URLs from where the NFC device may find further information. In view of this only small amounts of data are usually possible.

The NFC Data Exchange Format

The NFC Data Exchange Format (NDEF) (NFC Data Exchange Format (NDEF) - Technical Specification, 2006) defines a message encapsulation to provide communication between two NFC devices or an NFC device and an NFC Forum Tag. Because of this, data management in NFC devices is simplified. It guarantees a consistent format for data exchange in NFC applications (Kerschberger, 2011).

NFC Record Type Definition

The NFC record type definition defines the principal semantics of the record types and each type has is its own specification. To give other organizations the possibility to specify their own types independently from the NFC Forum there is a classification in NFC Forum External Types and NFC Forum Well-Known Types. The NFC Forum well-known types are standardized by the technical specifications of the NFC Forum, which provide the guideline for processing and representing the data. They are:

Figure 5. Possible secure element solutions

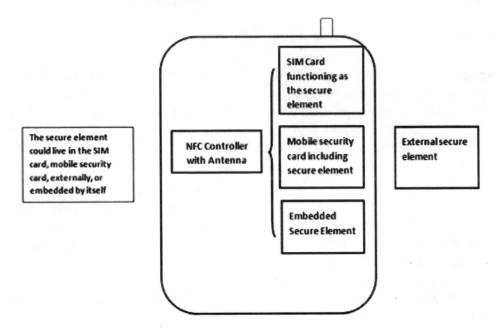

- **Text Record Type:** This contains simple Text, and no specific application is assigned.
- **URI Record Type:** This contains a Uniform Resource Identifier (URI), which could be e-mail, web addresses, telephone numbers or other identification codes.
- **Smart Poster Record Type:** This is an extension of the URI Record Type; it provides extra information about the URI such as icons or recommended actions.
- **Generic Control Record Type:** This provides a structure for any control activity.
- **Signature Record Type:** This contains a signature, which is provided to certify the correctness of the data.
- **Connection Handover:** This provides handover of an NFC connection to another communication technology with higher data throughput (e.g. Bluetooth).

Pairing Bluetooth with NFC

NFC technology works in a similar manner to Bluetooth technology in the manner that the two technologies rely on close-range and secure transmission of data. However, NFC is faster to connect two active devices together but Bluetooth transmits further than NFC. Nokia is the only manufacturer so far that has taken advantage of pairing Bluetooth and NFC. Nokia's recent Bluetooth devices, like the Luna headset and Play 360 external speaker, can be paired with an NFC equipped Nokia phone with a simple tap of the devices. this sidesteps the old Bluetooth pairing process that often required users to find hidden menu settings, execute searches for the device, and enter PIN codes. Pairing Bluetooth and NFC by tapping on the phone to setup a connection is known as Wireless Nirvana.

APPLICATIONS OF NFC

NFC has numerous applications as referred to in the introduction to this chapter. It can be used in many diverse devices; examples of such devices include smart phones, PDAs, laptops, PCs and games consoles. NFC can also be used in many diverse industries. A recent report by ABI Research predicts that the transportation and ticketing industries will be the first market to benefit from the convergence of NFC technology with the smart phone. Twenty-six percent of all NFC enabled smart phones are forecast to house at least one contactless ticketing application by 2017 (Epstein, 2012). This will enable transport authorities to offer additional added value services such as route planners, delay bulletins, time tables, as well as retail and loyalty applications. Companies will be able to offer advertising applications that offer own brand or partner brands special offers and discounts. Local businesses and government agencies can set up a platform with a set of applications that offer additional solutions to generate new revenue streams. The rest of this section outlines a few of these industries that are due to benefit from the convergence.

The Mobile Ticketing Industry

A mobile ticketing service based on NFC technology offers numerous benefits for end users compared to previous solutions such as smart card based ticketing. Unlike smart cards, mobile phones have other uses besides ticketing, so the user is less likely to forget their mobile phone than a smart card with a single use. Similarly, integrating mobile ticketing in smart phones means that users no longer have to carry multiple smart cards with them, each having a single use. By giving the end user the ability to purchase tickets with their smart phone, users no longer have to travel to find a service centre or a ticket machine in order to top up a smart card. Mobile ticketing also eliminates the need to carry cash in order to

purchase a ticket. The user can automate purchases so that their travel account is automatically topped up when it reaches a certain threshold. Unlike with a smart card, the user can also review the status of their tickets and account from their mobile phone. This way they can check the remaining value on their account and decide when to top up. Users can also display information about previous travel if they desire to do so (Juntunen, Luukkainen, & Tuunainen, 2010).

The Transportation Industry

NFC devices can also be used as tickets, boarding passes and for loyalty points when travelling. Travellers can touch their phones to an NFC reader device when they board a train or any other mode of transport to purchase a one-way trip and then touch the device again when dismounting the mode of transport to create a round trip ticket.

In 2012, the US Patent and Trademark Office granted Apple a patent for a service that lets travellers use their mobile phone to both buy an airline ticket and pass more smoothly and speedily through an airport on their day of travel (Clarke, 2012).

The US patent entitled a "System and method for transportation check-in", which is usually referred to as the iTravel patent, describes an unmanned, automated airport ticketing and baggage counter kiosk and introduces the concept of an automated security checking process where users of the application can process themselves through the security clearance system and check themselves in at the boarding gate.

Apple demonstrated part of this potential service during their announcement in June 2012 of its Passbook mobile wallet service. This service is due to arrive with iOS 6. The iTravel patent was filed in September 2008 and first published in April 2010. It was one of a suite of NFC and mobile wallet-related patents which were published on behalf of Apple that month:

- The 'iPay, iBuy and iCoupons' patents describe a comprehensive mobile payments, mobile commerce and mobile marketing business based around an NFC-enabled iPhone.
- An NFC-based mobile payments service lets consumers make payments to merchants and other consumers via a credit or debit card, directly from their bank account or using credit stored in their iTunes account.
- An NFC-based concert, entertainment and sports venue ticketing application that includes exclusive bonus features for users of Apple's service.
- An NFC-enabled iPod, games controller, TV and iPhone.

The Payments Industry

NFC devices can be used in contactless payment systems, similar to those currently used in credit cards and electronic ticket smartcards, and allow mobile payment to replace or supplement these systems. Most NFC smart phones can be used at existing point of service (POS) contactless machines. A report released in October 2012 by ABI Research predicted that investment in NFC mobile payment systems would break the $100 billion mark by 2017. The report predicts that payments using the contactless payment technology would reach $4 billion in 2012 and would balloon to $191 billion annually after 2017. In the United States, Google's "Google Wallet" remains the most widespread NFC mobile payment solution (Epstein, 2012).

NFC and Google Wallet

Google Wallet is a software app for NFC Android phones that supports NFC payments and enables other phone apps to interface to the payment system. It allows consumers to store credit card and store loyalty card information in a virtual wallet

and then use an NFC-enabled device at terminals that accept MasterCard or PayPass transactions.

Such NFC phones contain a Secure Element (SE), a smartcard chip mounted in a tamper-resistant package with an NFC chip and antenna. A bank can load a payment card into the SE chip in the form of a signed Java card applet; the user can then select it using the phone's screen and use it to pay, whether by tapping it against a payment terminal in a physical store, or by an online transaction [5]. The wallet and its associated infrastructure deal with tedious and time consuming problems for the user, such as provisioning the phone with the right cards, revoking them should the phone be lost or stolen, and logging transactions to resolve disputes.

The 2012 London Olympic Games and NFC

A limited edition of Samsung's Galaxy S3 mobile handset, the official phone of the 2012 London Olympic Games, was loaded with Visa's mobile payment application, Visa payWave, and given to athletes and selected trial users at the Olympic games in 2012 (Davis, 2012). These users were then able to buy items by waving the NFC enabled handsets in front of any of the 140,000 NFC readers installed in taxis and shops across the UK in preparation for the Olympic Games. The NFC readers were even installed in the Olympic Park itself.

The selected athletes and trial users that were issued with the Samsung Galaxy S III NFC phones used their devices to make an average of fifteen transactions each during the London 2012 Olympics (Clarke, Visa releases Olympics NFC and contactless usage statistics, 2012). The use of contactless payments at the Olympics, where only Visa cards or cash could be used to make a purchase, also boosted overall usage of NFC devices in the UK in the following ways:

- In the 10 weeks leading up to and including the Games, the number of contactless transactions in the UK doubled.
- There were six times the number of contactless transactions during Games time as there were during the same period in 2011.
- During the Games the Olympic venues accounted for 15% of contactless transactions in the UK.
- Contactless payments at Olympic venues over the Games period represented 10% of all on-site Visa transactions and 20% of all on-site Visa transactions under £20.
- At some venues, such as Horse Guards Parade, one in four of all Visa transactions below £20 were made using contactless technology.
- Today, one in five Visa cards in the UK includes contactless technology. Visa believe that this transaction figure demonstrates consumer enthusiasm for using the technology when it is made more easily available.
- Overall, there are now more than 40 million NFC contactless Visa cards across Europe, 24 million of which are in the UK. By the end of 2012, that number is expected to rise to 50 million contactless NFC Visa cards across Europe.
- NFC contactless Visa cards can now be used at over 120,000 contactless terminals in the UK and more than 378,000 around Europe (Clarke, Visa releases Olympics NFC and contactless usage statistics, 2012).

The London 2012 Olympic and Paralympics Games offered a unique opportunity to demonstrate the value and potential of NFC contactless payments (Clarke, Visa releases Olympics NFC and contactless usage statistics, 2012). Indeed a lot of banks, financial institutions and telecom companies recognise that NFC is the future of payments technology (Agrawal & Bhuraria, 2012).

Advertising and NFC

NFC enables devices can be used to read the tag on other NFC devices to get information. By adding NFC tags to poster and magazine advertisements, a person can read the tags with an NFC smart phone and act immediately. For example users of NFC smart phones can read an advertisement from a taxi service containing NFC tags and use a smart phone to electronically read the advertisement to find the location of the nearest taxi rank or to call a taxi to their location.

As the number of NFC-equipped handsets grows, the technology becomes an attractive way for advertisers to bridge the offline print world with the online digital world and boost consumer engagement. The UK's first NFC print magazine advert ran in subscriber issuers of December 2012's Marie Claire magazine. The advertisements have been placed by Nuffield Health. NFC smart phone owners were able to tap a tag on the page to get a free two-day gym membership pass. Those without an NFC phone were able to get the offer via SMS or by visiting Nuffield's website (Clarke, 2012).

The Marie Claire magazine employed the NFC advertising technology to ensure ease of use for their readers. Advertising campaigns are only successful if they manage to get time-poor consumers to act on the message contained within the advert before the moment of interest is lost. They believe that customers will embrace NFC technology because it is a way of receiving instant rewards. The magazine also believes that by using such technology in their advertising campaigns they have found an instant, intuitive way to promote on-the-spot response (Clarke, 2012).

NFC SAFETY AND SECURITY CHALLENGES

As discussed, however, in the introduction to this chapter, NFC technology faces some challenges.

Figure 6. The UK's first NFC advertisement run in Marie Claire Magazine, December 2012

One such challenge is data security when using NFC technology. Another challenge of this technology is dealing with a situation where an NFC smart phone is lost or stolen or even when an NFC smart phone needs to be replaced. Whenever a user changes an NFC smart phone, they will have to ensure that all personal information and payments applications are securely transferred from one mobile phone to the other. In cases where the smart phone is lost or stolen the user will have to report the loss to the various difference banks that have stored transaction information on the device. A request for payment application deactivation or blocking will need to be implemented. When the account is deactivated on the host system, the card or phone will no longer be able to receive any authorisation.

This section discusses the safety and security measures available for NFC. Initially, it looks at general security and privacy within the NFC field. This is followed by a discussion of security with an NFC mobile payment scheme and uses the Google Wallet as an example.

General NFC Safety and Security

For a communication system, *safety can be defined as the provision of a guaranteed transfer of the data and in the event of a disturbance that there is a safe state where no catastrophic consequences can occur.* Security for a communication system is *the prevention of unauthorized access and unauthorized manipulation of data.* Security is categorized into three principles (CIA for short):

- *Confidentiality* is the principle whereby only those with sufficient privileges and a demonstrated need may access certain information. When unauthorised individuals or systems can view information, confidentiality is breached.
- *Integrity* is the principle of ensuring information is maintained in a complete and uncorrupted state. The integrity of information is threatened when it is exposed to corruption, damage, destruction, or other disruption of its authentic state. Corruption

can occur while information is being entered, stored or transmitted.

- *Availability* is the principle that allows entities to access information in a usable format without interference or obstruction. An entity may be a person or another computer system. Availability does not imply that the information is accessible to any user; rather, it means availability to authorised users.

Figure 7 outlines how security is created using the principles of confidentiality, integrity and availability. There are many ways to break the security of a system. The majority of attacks fall under four threat headings:

- **Spying**: Unauthorised access to information;
- **Deception**: Deceive through wrong information;
- **Denial of Service (DOS)**: Compromise the availability of the NFC system;
- **Protection of Privacy**: Ensuring all sensitive information transferred and stored within the NFC system is protected.

All types of wireless communication are vulnerable to these threats. It is easy to listen into a wireless channel and the intended signal can easily be disturbed by other signals. The problem with radio transmission is that malicious users can access the communication channel undetected. Without any protection, it is possible to pick up messages, alter information in live communication and store messages with the intention to replay them with the same or altered content at a later time (Kortvedt, 2009). To overcome the threats, the system needs to implement authentication, integrity checks, confidentiality and replay protection. The level of security needed is defined by the application itself. Whenever money is involved, an application will attract potential malicious users. Private content sharing on the other hand may not require the same level of security. MasterCard and VISA are big actors in this arena and various equipment vendors implement different security solutions in this field. Some of the work of these companies is public, but specific technical specifications are kept within the companies and their trusted partners. The passive communication mode seems like a good solution for transfer of sensitive data, as this mode seems harder to eavesdrop upon compared to the active communication mode (Kortvedt, 2009).

Three key elements within NFC security are discussed here, namely, attacks: over the air

Figure 7. Creating security in a system

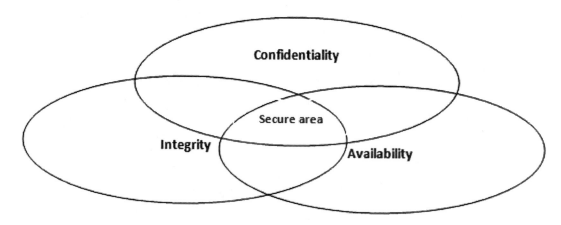

interface of NFC, via the NFC tag, and/or via the NFC device (Kerschberger, 2011).

Attacks Over the Air Interface

As a result of the air interface being contactless, attacks can be performed without physical access. That means that there are many possibilities for the attacker to conceal his attacks. Known attacks to the air interface are:

High distance read: the attacker modifies an NFC device to increase its range so he can read tags from a safe distance. This is not easy, however. The attacker has to increase the energy of the high frequency field, use an optimised antenna and handle the increasing noise in the communication.

Jamming: here a sender blocks the NFC system by sending a disturbance signal on its frequency. This sender must be either placed near the NFC system or use appropriate antennas and power rates. This attack compromises the availability of the NFC system.

Denial of service: as there could be more than one NFC device/tag in range, an anti-collision algorithm has to be performed to select the individual device, with which to communicate. The attacker generates collisions/answers for every possible device address and simulates the existence of a high amount of devices in range of the reader. The reader will now try to reach each of the simulated devices to disable them and communicate with the desired device. But in the case that the reader can never reach the simulated devices, the desired communication is blocked. This attack compromises the availability of an NFC system.

Man in the middle: in this attack two parties are tricked into a three party communication, without their knowledge. Instead of directly communicating with each other they communicate through a third participant, who intercepts the messages between the other two. Thus, he is able to modify data before sending it to the original receiver. An authentication system would not help, because the attacker can also intercept and set up one secure channel to the first party and a second secure channel to the second one. This attack compromises the confidentiality and integrity of an NFC system.

- **Eavesdropping:** Since NFC systems communicate over an open, accessible medium (air) with electromagnetic waves, eavesdropping is a logical attack. Because the receiver of the attacker does not need the power of the active part of the communication for answering, he is able to amplify weak signals received over a distance up to 30 - 40cm (Kortvedt, 2009; Kfir & Wool, Picking Virtual Pockets using Relay Attacks on Contactless, 2005). In (Kortvedt, 2009) it is demonstrated that producing such eavesdropping equipment can be done at relatively low coast. This attack compromises the confidentiality of an NFC system (Kerschberger, 2011).
- **Relay Attack:** In this attack the invader uses another communication channel (relay) as an intermediary to increase the

Figure 8. Man in the middle setup

Figure 9. Relay attack on NFC devices, taken from (Weiss, 2010)

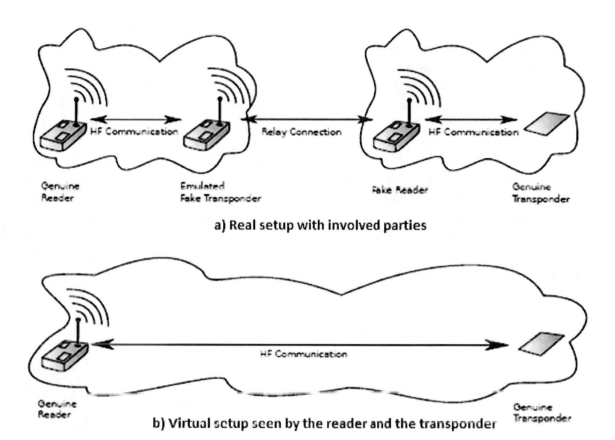

a) Real setup with involved parties

b) Virtual setup seen by the reader and the transponder

range. The attacker needs no physical access to the device, but only an antenna and the relay in reading range. The other, perhaps more conspicuous, devices could be far away. This attack would compromise the secrecy of an NFC system.

- **Data Modification:** The attacker utilizes modulation of the signal to provide the receiver a valid but manipulated message. The feasibility of this attack depends highly on the coding mechanism for the modulation, and the data cannot be changed arbitrary but only to dominant states. This attack compromises the integrity of an NFC system.

- **Data Insertion:** If the answering device needs a long time for its answer, the attacker could insert a message into the communication. This would be only successful if the transmission is finished, before the answering device starts with its answer. Otherwise the message would be corrupted. This attack compromises the integrity of an NFC system.

Attacks on the NFC Tag

The attacks that can be performed on the NFC tag are as follows:

- **Destroy:** This is the simplest attack which could be used. Afterwards the tag is not able to communicate any longer with an NFC device. It could be destroyed mechanically, for example by cutting the connection to its antenna. Another way to destroy the tag is an overpowered electrical field on the tag's working frequency, so that the electrical components would overload. Destroying the electrical circuits of the tag could also be done by placing the tag into a microwave oven. This attack would compromise the availability of an NFC system.

- **Remove:** In this attack, the tag is removed from the carrier object. The motivation for this could be a thief, who wants to smuggle the carrier object through the security checks without recognition. This attack would compromise the availability of an NFC system.

- **Shield:** This attack is only temporary and it could be done by placing the tag inside a metal box or a wrapping it in tinfoil. The inductive coupling is disturbed by high losses caused by eddy current induction inside the metal. This method could be used, for example, to pass automated toll checkpoints without recognition. The tag is not destroyed permanently. This attack would compromise the availability of an NFC system.

- **Clone:** In this attack the original tag is read and an exact copy is created. The complexity of this attack depends on the tag. A read-only tag which stores only a simple numeric ID can be cloned very easily. There are also simple solutions possible where the ID can be changed. The reader can not decide if it is the original or the cloned tag. If some kind of certification is used, this attack would get more complex. This attack compromises the secrecy of an NFC system.

- **Falsify/Replace:** This attack overwrites the data of a tag or physically replaces it. Overwriting can be done easily if the original tag is a writeable tag without any security measures (or these measures are broken). The aim of this attack is to falsify the original tag, e.g. for phishing purposes. This attack compromises the integrity of an NFC system.

- **Tracking:** If a tag always uses the same unique ID for anti-collision (or is a simple read only tag with a numeric ID) an attacker could track the tag easily. If the tag is always carried by the user, his movements could be tracked. This attack compromises the secrecy of an NFC system.

Attacks on the NFC Device

An NFC device is often a complex and powerful device such as a mobile phone. Such devices are valuable to attackers and, thus, there is a high risk of attack. An example of an attack on the device is hacking into an application which uses the NFC interface. Attacks on NFC devices are performed either with the knowledge of the user i.e. the user is the attacker, or without the user's knowledge i.e. the hacker accesses the device through an internet connection.

Security Measures Against Attacks in NFC

Since NFC devices have become popular for payment and ticketing solutions, security has become a high priority. Most of the attacks listed above can be prevented by using authentication and encryption methods (Kerschberger, 2011). MIFARE technologies[3], which are manufactured by NXP Semiconductors, have introduced ISO/IEC 14443 compliant solutions with support for 3DES, AES, RSA encryption protocols (Kortvedt, 2009). Their first attempt to implement security was Crypto-1, an NXP proprietary stream cipher with 48 bit key made for MIFARE Classic. Because of low cost and good reliability, this version has been heavily deployed in electronic wallet, public transportation and ticketing applications. Several publications during 2007 and 2008 describe how to break this cipher, one of them with a secret key recovery time down to 40 ms on a laptop (Kortvedt, 2009). The latest solutions from both MIFARE and FeliCa are approved at minimum Common Criteria (CC) assurance level EAL4, and the hardware of MIFARE SmartMX has passed EAL5+ evaluation. CC is standardized in ISO/IEC 15408, which is a certification standard for IT security. EAL4 is the highest EAL-level which is expected to be economically feasible while implementing the security in an existing product line. EAL5 is applicable for systems requiring high level of independently assured security in a planned development. The design process is rigorous, but should keep the cost related to security specialists at a reasonable level. In their RC-S860 chip, FeliCa has implemented mutual authentication using 3DES and data encryption by a transaction key generated in the authentication procedure. FeliCa claims in the product description that the features make forgery and card fraud nearly impossible (Kortvedt, 2009).

A more challenging attack to perform is the *Man in the Middle attack*. For this to occur, three devices have to be in a single range in order to disturb each other. To get a stable working communication, the attacker in the middle has to shield the connection between the other two devices. This results in an attack if one of the parties is removed and replaced. Such an attack could be prevented by the use of authentication through a common, independent, trusted certification provider (Breitfuss, 2006).

Experiments show that a passive eavesdropping attack can occur up to a distance of 30 - 40cm, which limits the possibilities for an attacker to hide either himself or his equipment (Kfir & Wool, Picking Virtual Pockets using Relay Attacks on Contactless Smartcard, 2005). However, in certain situations like a crowded underground train at rush hour, the attacking equipment can be placed in a bag to avoid suspicion and the owners of the NFC devices would, thus, be unaware that their device is being surreptitiously read from a passerby. To avoid this type of attack, the host device would need an application, which asks for permission, i.e. by entering a PIN code, before granting access to the data. As there are cases where the NFC function should also work even when the host device is short of energy or is switched off, there should also be the possibility to disable the NFC function. A simple mechanical switch would solve this requirement. Switching off the NFC functionality would then prevent an attacker from skimming the NFC data while walking by (Madlmayr, Langer, Kantner, & Scharinger, 2008).

SAFETY AND SECURITY IN NFC MOBILE PAYMENT SYSTEMS

It has been predicted that mobile wallets will, in future, be the mediator between the payment mechanism of a mobile device and the apps (being) downloaded on that mobile device seeking payment. The reason for this is to avoid untrustworthy apps having access to payment information of users. In the absence of a wallet app, rogue or subversive apps could phish the user by requesting him/her to enter their pin in exchange for payment of a game costing, let us say, €2.50, while actually initiating payment for a much larger transaction in the background. By providing a trustworthy logging mechanism and user interface, the wallet can create a payment platform that supports secure innovation [6].

Governance over an NFC payments system is a challenge as the system usually involves hundreds and thousands of vendors, banks and merchants, each one wishing to cut costs and customise their own systems, both of which can seriously undermine security. When a serious security breach actually does occur nobody wants to take responsibility or pay the costs. Additionally, as users sign up to the system, it invariably involves more and more stakeholders and becomes increasingly more complex, making governance even harder.

Another challenge for NFC payment systems is that crimes that were difficult to achieve on traditional chip and pin devices, suddenly become feasible. Take for example the following scenario outlined in [6], which explains that at present, it is possible to connect a false chip and pin terminal remotely to a false chip and pin card, so that when the victim buys coffee from a vending machine upon which the false terminal has been fixed, a crook can steal money from an ATM hundreds of miles away using the false card. With conventional chip and pin systems, this requires specialist equipment, so it has not been industrialised at any scale. But once mobile phones contain NFC technology, a criminal can program one phone to act as a false terminal, and another to act as a false card. An attack that once required serious engineering is now just a software application. Unfortunately, crimes can be pirated just as easily as music. Once a card cloning scam gets into widespread use, the question arises as to who is capable of stopping it, and how [6].

The strategic risk for companies investing in NFC technology for mobile payments is that of an attack that makes fraud so easy that the mobile platform or channel that they are developing becomes unviable. A nightmare scenario for Google wallet engineers, for example, is that malware on a mobile phone might take over the device so comprehensively that a remote software attack becomes possible. If malware can infect a phone to such an extent that large amount of money can be defrauded, while it sits quietly in the user's pocket, then its viability as a mobile payments platform is threatened. Hardware security devices such as the Secure Element are designed to reduce such risks, but it is always possible that design error or governance failure could lead to such a catastrophe [6].

LATEST NFC TECHNOLOGY DEVELOPMENTS

Opinions on the future for NFC technology vary depending on the source of the information. After the success of the 2012 London Olympic user trial, Visa Europe intends to put mobile contactless payment schemes into consumers' hands and introduce digital wallets on a mass scale in 2013. They predict there will be 40 mobile contactless payments issuers in Europe in 2013.

NFC in the Enterprise

NFC is currently being tested by a variety of organizations who want to use smartphones as next-generation access cards, which would be an ideal use of the technology in the enterprise. In fact, in the fall of 2011, BlackBerry-maker Research In Motion and HID Global, a provider of secure physical access cards and readers, announced that some of RIM's new BlackBerrys would be equipped with HID Global's iCLASS digital credentials.

The NFC BlackBerry Bold and Curve models are compatible with HID Global's iCLASS readers, which are widely used to enable physical access systems in buildings, as well as serve as student ID readers and track employee time-clock check-ins and attendance.

Employees could also use NFC-enabled smartphones and other devices to access staff parking areas or cafeterias and pay for services. NFC tags could be placed inside meeting or conference rooms, and attendees could tap their compatible devices to silence them or to turn on Wi-Fi (Sacco, 2012).

NFC in Government

NFC also represents countless opportunities for governments to improve public services and enhance transit systems, among other things. Some cities and urban areas are already using NFC to better serve their citizens and improve quality of life. NFC technology could let commuters pay for their commutes to work with their mobile devices. Commuters who drive to work could access parking lots and pay for parking with their smartphones. And city residents could get access to public facilities, such as swimming pools or libraries, with a tap of a smart phone

France's Association "Francais Du Sans Contact Mobile" (AFSCM), or Association for Mobile Contactless in France, has already implemented NFC-based services. And in Europe, France ranks among the top countries based on the number of citizens with NFC-enable phones, according to the group. AFSCM expected 2.5 million French citizens to have NFC devices by the end of 2012. The French "Cityzi" service lets users in certain French locales to quickly scan their smart devices to access train stations and tap their devices against NFC tags placed in a variety of locations to get maps or other information on products or services (Sacco, 2012).

The Future of Security in NFC

According to a report on NFCWorld website in September 2012, a NFC and contactless technology specialist has developed a way to turn NFC phones into "secured antennas" that can securely pull down sensitive data stored in the cloud and present it to a POS terminal or a contactless door lock, without the need to include an NFC secure element in the phone (Clarke, 2012). According to the report, a cloud-based approach to managing sensitive data used to make secure NFC transactions holds a wide range of advantages over the use of a secure element within an NFC phone. However, the speed of current generation mobile data services may mean that it could be up to two to three years before the concept becomes a commercial reality.

A cloud-based secure element is a new concept that works on the principle that sensitive data is stored in the cloud rather than locally on the mobile phone. When the user conducts a transaction, the data is pulled from a remote virtual secure element in the cloud in encrypted format and pulled via the mobile phone to a point-of-sale terminal (Clarke, 2012). The approach has a number of fundamental advantages over current generation solutions:

- Current secure elements need to be large enough to store an unknown quantity of applications that the user may wish to add to their NFC phone as required. They also need to provide high grade security to meet the requirements of organisations like EMVCo for storing card data. This makes the secure element expensive. This cost could be eliminated or significantly reduced with a cloud-based approach. A much smaller and cheaper secure element could be used, which would only handle user and device authentication rather than storing data. Or a secure element could be avoided altogether by using a trusted zone within the main processor of NFC smart phone.
- The cloud secure element would make it much simpler for secure service providers to implement NFC services, since there would be no need to integrate provisioning to a secure element on the phone itself.
- There would be no limit to the number of applications that an NFC phone could access, since these would live in the cloud on a secure server emulating a physical secure element.
- Consumers would be able to access all their applications from all their devices, since they would all be stored in one place on the cloud and could then be used on any of the individual's NFC-enabled mobile phones, laptops or tablets.
- Since the system is fully online, fraud detection would be instant.

- NFC controller chips could be simpler and, therefore, both smaller and cheaper since they would not need to be able to handle the same range of functions.
- NFC phones would not need a dedicated mobile wallet in which information on services available is stored. Since the virtual secure element is stored in the cloud, users would be able to access and modify their mobile wallet services via a standard web browser. This would also reduce the need for secure service providers to develop different applications for different types of mobile phone.
- The solution addresses an emerging issue of how to safely pass on an NFC phone to a new user or to send it safely in for repair without risking that sensitive data could be accessed by a third party, since card and other secret data would no longer be stored on the device itself.
- The solution would meet the requirements for 'card present' transactions since, like current generation secure element solutions, the NFC phone would appear to the POS device to be a standard chip card. There would also be no need for specific upgrades to hardware or software.
- A single NFC phone could be linked to multiple virtual secure elements, allowing any organisation to own its own secure element.

A key issue for gaining adoption of this cloud based secure element will be the ability to conduct transactions quickly enough and to provide very strong authentication of both the user and their mobile devices (Clarke, 2012).

NFC in Universities, Device-to-Device Sharing, and Collaboration

NFC can also be used as a short-range technology to beam files and other content between devices that are close to each other. The functionality could be great for collaboration in corporate environments and universities when sharing documents or for multiplayer gaming. The popular NFC-enabled Samsung Galaxy S III, and a number of additional new NFC Android phones use a feature called Android Beam to send data back and forth between compatible devices via NFC (Sacco, 2012).

Zynga, a virtual poker game for Android, uses NFC-based Android Beam to let users tap their smart phones or tablets together to play live multiplayer online poker (Sacco, 2012).

CONCLUSION

In this chapter a review of near field technology was conducted. Specific aspects of the technology were chosen for the review, namely, introducing the technology, the various operation modes of the technology, its hardware architecture, data formats and the security built around the technology to prevent breaches. Various novel applications for using NFC technology were described, namely uses in the mobile ticketing, transportation, advertising, and electronic payments industries. A pilot study of use in the Olympic games 2012 was also described. The chapter went on to discuss current potential security attacks that can be launched on the NFC technology and the measures taken to prevent these attacks. Finally, future developments within the NFC technology field are outlined and innovative ideas on how NFC technology can be used in various other domains such as academic and practical industry domains are described, these domains included uses for both enterprise and government.

REFERENCES

Agrawal, P., & Bhuraria, S. (2012). Near field communication. *SETLab Briefings, 10*(1), 67–76.

Anderson, R. (2012). Risk and privacy implications of consumer payment innovation. In *Proceedings of the Consumer Payment Innovation in the Connected Age Conference*. Kansas City, KS: IEEE.

Breitfuss, E. H. (2006). Security in near field communications. In *Proceedings of the Workshop on RFID Security*. Graz, Austria: IEEE.

Clarke, S. (2012a, July 11). *Apple awarded patent for mobile airline ticketing and travel service*. Retrieved January 28, 2013, from http://www.nfcworld.com/2012/07/11/316784/apple-awarded-patent-for-mobile-airline-ticketing-and-travel-service/

Clarke, S. (2012b, September 25). *Inside secure to offer cloud-based NFC secure element solution*. Retrieved January 28, 2013, from http://www.nfc-world.com/2012/09/25/318059/inside-secure-to-offer-cloud-based-nfc-secure-element-solution/

Clarke, S. (2012c, November 7). *Marie Claire magazine runs NFC print advertisement*. Retrieved January 28, 2013, from http://www.nfcworld.com/2012/11/07/320956/marie-claire-magazine-runs-nfc-print-advertisement/

Clarke, S. (2012d, September 19). *Visa releases Olympics NFC and contactless usage statistics*. Retrieved January 28, 2013, from NFC http://www.nfcworld.com/2012/09/19/317958/visa-releases-olympics-nfc-and-contactless-usage-statistics/

Davis, J. (2012, July 12). *Olympics*. Retrieved January 28, 2013, from http://www.nfcworld.com/2012/07/12/316820/hands-on-with-the-visa-olympics-nfc-phone/

Epstein, Z. (2012, October 19). *With or without apple, NFC mobile payment market to hit $100 billion*. Retrieved January 28, 2013, from http://bgr.com/2012/10/19/nfc-mobile-payments-growth-abi/

Forum, N. F. C. (2008). *Essentials for successful NFC mobile ecosystems*. Retrieved April 26, 2012, from http://www.nfc-forum.org/resources/white_papers/NFC_Forum_Mobile_NFC_Ecosystem_White_Paper.pdf

Google.com. (2012). *How it works: Use-it-instore*. Retrieved May 10, 2012, from http://www.google.com/wallet/how-it-works.html#in-store

International Organisation for Standardisation. (2004). *Information technology—Telecommunications and information exchange between systems—Near field communication—Interface and protocol (NFCIP-1)*. Retrieved March 29, 2012, from http://www.iso.org/iso/catalogue_detail.htm?csnumber=38578

Jan Kremer Consulting Services. (2010). *NFC near field communication white paper*. Retrieved April 26, 2012, from http://jkremer.com/White%20Papers/Near%20Field%20Communication%20White%20Paper%20JKCS.pdf

Juntunen, A., Luukkainen, S., & Tuunainen, V. K. (2010). Deploying NFC technology for mobile ticketing services—Identification of critical business model issues. In *Proceedings of the Ninth International Conference on Mobile Business* (pp. 82-90). Athens, Greece: IEEE.

Kerschberger, M. (2011). *Near field communication A survey of safety and security measures*. Retrieved March 29, 2012, from https://www.auto.tuwien.ac.at/bib/pdf_TR/TR0156.pdf

Kfir, Z., & Wool, A. (2005). Picking virtual pockets using relay attacks on contactless. In *Proceedings of the First International Conference on Security and Privacy for Emerging Areas in Communications Networks (SECURECOMM'05)* (pp. 47-58). Washington, DC: IEEE Computer Society.

Lazarri, T. D. (2008). *Near field communication.* Retrieved April 26, 2012, from http://www.slideshare.net/tdelazzari/near-field-communication-presentation

Madlmayr, G., Langer, J., Kantner, C., & Scharinger, J. (2008). NFC devices: Security and privacy. In *Proceedings of the Third International Conference on Availability, Reliability and Security, 2008, (ARES 08)* (pp. 642-647). Barcelona, Spain: ARES.

NFC Forum Technical Specifications. (2006). *NFC data exchange format (NDEF)—Technical specification.* Retrieved March 29, 2012, from http://www.nfc-forum.org/specs/spec_list/

Preuss, P. (2009). *NFC forum: NFC use cases.* Retrieved May 10, 2012, from: http://www.nfc-forum.org/events/oulu_spotlight/Forum_and_Use_Cases.pdf

Roberti, M. (n.d.). *The history of RFID technology.* Retrieved March 29, 2012, from http://www.rfidjournal.com/article/view/1338/1

Sacco, A. (2012, August 14). *NFC not just for mobile payments: Six future uses.* Retrieved January 28, 2013, from http://www.cio.com/article/713618/NFC_Not_Just_for_Mobile_Payments_Six_Future_Uses?page=2&taxonomyId=3045

Smart Card. (2012). *Wikipedia.* Retrieved May 10, 2012, from http://en.wikipedia.org/wiki/SmartCard

Vazquez-Briseno, M., Hirata, F. I., Sanchez-Lopez, J. d., Jimenez-Garcia, E., Navarro-Cota, C., & Nieto-Hipolito, J. I. (2012). Using RFID/NFC and QR-code in mobile phones to link the physical and the digital world. In I. Deliyannis (Ed.), *Interactive Multimedia.* Janeza Trdine, Croatia: InTech. doi:10.5772/37447.

Want, R. (2011). Near field communication. *Pervasive Computing, 10,* 4–7. doi:10.1109/MPRV.2011.55.

Weiss, M. (2010). *Performing relay attacks on ISO 14443 contactless smart cards using NFC mobile equipment.* Retrieved April 26, 2012, from http://www.sec.in.tum.de/assets/studentwork/finished/Weiss2010.pdf

KEY TERMS AND DEFINITIONS

Air Interface: In mobile or wireless communication, the air interface is the radio-based communication link between the mobile station and the active base station. In GSM/UMTS, the various UTRA standards are air interfaces, and are also (but not exclusively) referred to as "access modes".

Application Programming Interface (API): This is a protocol that is intended to be used as an interface by software components to communicate with each other. An API is a library that may include specification for routines, data structures, object classes, and variables.

Bluetooth Technology: Bluetooth is a wireless technology standard for exchanging data over short distances (using short-wavelength radio transmissions in the ISM band from 2400–2480 MHz) from fixed and mobile devices, creating personal area networks (PANs) with high levels of security.

Mobile Payments: this can also be referred to as mobile money, mobile money transfer, and mobile wallet. These terms generally refer to payment services operated under financial regulation and performed from or via a mobile device. Instead of paying with cash, check, or credit cards, a consumer can use a mobile phone to pay for a wide range of services and digital or hard goods.

Near field Communication(NFC): Near field communication is a set of standards for smart phones and mobile devices that is used to establish radio communication between each device by bringing them into close proximity with each other, usually within no more than a few centimetres.

Open Platform Technology: In computing, an open platform technology describes a software system which is based on open standards, such as published and fully documented external application programming interfaces (APIs) that allow using the software to function in other ways than the original programmer intended, without requiring modification of the source code. Using these interfaces, a third party could integrate with the platform to add functionality. The opposite is a closed platform.

Peer-to-Peer (P2P): Peer-to-peer (P2P) is a form of computing or networking that has a distributed application architecture. It has this type of architecture to enable the partitioning of tasks or work loads between peers. Peers are equally privileged participants in the application, hence the term 'peer to peer' each member of the network is equal. This network of equal participants forms a peer-to-peer network of nodes.

Phishing: This is the fraudulent practice of sending e-mails purporting to be from legitimate companies and making the "false" email address look as believable as possible, in order to induce individuals to reveal personal information, such as credit-card numbers, online.

Read/Writer Mode: When a device is in this mode, other devices can read its contents and write new content to it. Regarding NFC devices in this mode it usually means the device is passive and only functions as an information tag which can be overwritten with new information.

ENDNOTES

[1] A smart card is any pocket-sized card with embedded integrated circuits. It is usually made of plastic and contains volatile memory and microprocessor components. Smart cards may also provide strong security authentication for single sign-on (SSO) within large organizations. Its benefits include the provision of identification, authentication, data storage and application processing (Wikipedia.com, 2012).

[2] In mobile or wireless communication, the air interface is the radio-based communication link between the mobile station and the active base station.

[3] MIFARE is the NXP Semiconductors-owned trademark of a series of chips widely used in contactless smart cards and proximity cards.

Chapter 18
Modeling and Verification of Cooperation Incentive Mechanisms in User–Centric Wireless Communications

Alessandro Aldini
University of Urbino "Carlo Bo", Italy

Alessandro Bogliolo
University of Urbino "Carlo Bo", Italy

ABSTRACT

User-centric wireless networks are characterized by a community-scale objective aiming at the shared provision of user-generated services and contents. This may be contrasted by the reticence of individuals to share the limited resources of mobile devices. Hence, cooperation incentives play a key role to promote prosocial decisions and to isolate selfish nodes and cheating behaviors. In particular, trust-based incentives and remuneration are used to induce collaborative behaviors in Wi-Fi communities. Typically, these mechanisms are based on reputation infrastructures and virtual currency systems, the application of which should not hinder the normal operation of the network. In this chapter, the authors present an approach to the combined use of indirect rewards deriving from trust-based incentives and direct rewards deriving from remuneration. The effectiveness and efficiency of such an approach in the setting of user-centric wireless networks is verified by conducting a formal study of the benefits of the joint application of these rewards and of the related impact upon performance.

DOI: 10.4018/978-1-4666-4691-9.ch018

INTRODUCTION

The recent trends in autonomic wireless architectures are giving rise to community-scale initiatives with the purpose to guarantee broader connectivity and to share user-provided contents, applications, and services. For this kind of architectures, called *user-centric networks* (UCNs, for short), cooperation incentives play an essential role to stimulate users to share services (including access to public networks) and resources (including bandwidth, computational power, and storage space) in spite of possibly selfish and cheating participants hindering the functioning of the entire system. In particular, reputation (either inherent in the social dimension or based on trust-management infrastructures) and remuneration (based either on fiat money or on virtual currency) emerged as two complementary incentive mechanisms to increase motivation and to discourage and isolate selfishness, cheats, and mistrust.

On one hand, reputation not only represents an intrinsic incentive to cooperate deriving spontaneously from social interactions, but it is also adopted as an extrinsic enabling condition for taking part in the community, refer to Jøsang et al. (2007) for a survey. Reputation is the result of prosocial behaviors and gives a perception of the public trustworthiness of a community member. Reputation-based decisions are supported by trust management systems, which give explicit quantitative estimations to the subjective reliance on the character, integrity, ability, and honesty of each community member.

On the other hand, reputation may not be perceived as a sufficient incentive to take prosocial decisions, especially in the setting of wireless communities, which very often are highly dynamic because of the short-term membership of a significant part of the community. As a consequence, users may not be adequately motivated to maintain and support a reliable and stable trust system. Moreover, in a situation such as this, reputation fails to guarantee reciprocity, which is a property describing the evolution of cooperative behaviors influenced by the probability of future mutual interactions. In other words, the lack of conditions favoring mutual exchanges of resources and services does not stimulate the willingness to cooperate. For these reasons, monetization represents an alternative way of estimating the value of prosocial decisions that does not rely on reciprocity and overcomes the limitations of barter. Monetization is supported in online communities by virtual currency, see, e.g., Greengard (2011). Virtual currency represents a form of credit-based remuneration replacing the role of real money, thus bypassing all the issues related to strong security requirements, taxation, and mistrust, which may impair the functioning and applicability of payment mechanisms in wireless networks.

Combining trust-based and credit-based rewards is an appealing approach that has received attention in the last years, as it gives the opportunity of taking advantage of the complementary strengths of the two incentive mechanisms while overcoming their weaknesses. Based on these observations, the general cooperation framework for wireless UCNs we present combines the application of trust management and virtual currency mechanisms. According to this general model, the main driving principles adopted to join the cooperation incentives establish that:

- Trust is used to affect individual decisions and opportunities;
- Trust cannot be traded for virtual currency or money;
- Virtual currency is a commodity money mainly used to facilitate cooperation among community members;
- Virtual currency can be traded for fiat money at the only purpose of allowing the community to benefit from external services and to provide services to non-member end-users.

These modeling assumptions guide the definition of a general four-step cooperation model in which the typical phases of any cooperation, namely service request, negotiation, transaction, and feedback, are made explicit. In the setting of each phase, both indirect and direct rewards are exploited, separately or in a combined way, in order to apply the principles above and to provide the motivations needed to strengthen the cooperative attitude of the community members.

The study of the effects of the integration of indirect and direct rewards requires the analysis of several orthogonal aspects. First of all, in spite of the fact that reputation cannot be traded for virtual money explicitly, the intertwining of both trust-based and credit-based incentives emphasizes the need for evaluating the consequences of mutual dependences among these two different rewards. As an example, it is worth investigating whether making the service cost dependent on the trust towards the buyer (or, analogously, making reputation of the seller influenced by the cost of the offered service) is beneficial for all the actors involved in the cooperation infrastructure.

Similarly, even if the effectiveness of the combined use of both rewards is demonstrated, it is worth estimating the tradeoff between the use of these mechanisms and other issues that are fundamental in the setting of wireless communications, like the constraints upon resource usage and quality of experience. In fact, both incentive mechanisms might hinder the normal operation of the network, thus ultimately impairing performance. This can be due both to the communication overhead of trust management and payment systems, and to the interference between individual motivations and resource management strategies. For instance, due to these reasons, the virtual currency mechanisms used in the setting of wireless networks are typically implemented by means of soft, lightweight security solutions, which do not rely on pervasive control systems, thus exposing the community to dishonest behaviors that shall be contrasted by the use of cooperation incentives aiming at isolating cheats and mistrust.

In general, orthogonal problems of different nature come into play, ranging from social to economical issues, and from performance to trustworthiness aspects. All of them require tradeoff analyses involving completely different quantitative values, including earning estimations, trust metrics, and performance measures. The complexity of such a scenario makes the modeling and verification of mixed cooperation infrastructures hard in practice. For these reasons, formal verification techniques can provide a beneficial support to a complete analysis (based on theoretical means) that would not be exhaustive and practical through empirical experiments.

The application of formal approaches in this setting includes game-theoretic analytical studies and probabilistic/stochastic model and equivalence checking, which in the last years revealed to be a valid support to the mathematical analysis of applications for wireless communications, see, e.g., papers by Acquaviva et al. (2004), Srivastava et al. (2005), Li and Shen (2011), Aldini and Bogliolo (2012b). The main advantage of formal methods is given by the support of mathematically rigorous techniques and tools for the design and verification of complex systems with orthogonal requirements, which are characterized by variables ranging over completely different domains (like, e.g., time, probabilities, credit-based rewards, and trust-based rewards). More precisely, formal specifications are mathematical models (e.g., sets of equations, automata, labeled transition systems), formal verifications are based on well-formed statements (e.g., mathematical functions, logic formulas, instances of equivalence relations), and automatic checks rely on analysis algorithms (e.g., optimization algorithms, equivalence checking, model checking). In order to model and verify our cooperation framework, we employ a formalism inspired by Kripke structures and we apply probabilistic/stochastic model checking, see, e.g., the tutorial book by Clarke et al. (2001) for a survey. Such an approach is supported by the use of the software tool PRISM, see Forejt et al. (2011), which we employ to pursue the following objectives:

- Establishing measurable metrics (related, e.g., to expected earnings and security risks) that allow us to obtain a complete perception of the attitude to cooperate;
- Exploring and evaluating cooperation strategies, modeling choices, and design parameters that affect not only the metrics above, but also the quality of service experienced by each user.

The analysis results are used to emphasize the way in which the main aspects affecting the functioning of cooperative UCNs in wireless environments must be combined in order to guarantee the success of such networks.

Summarizing, the objective of this chapter is twofold. On one hand, we present a general model of cooperation joining both trust-based and credit-based incentives in the specific context of communities with Wi-Fi enabled devices capable of establishing ad-hoc connections. On the other hand, we explore the effective use of probabilistic and stochastic model checking techniques for the comparative and sensitivity analysis of the effects of mixed cooperation incentives in wireless UCNs.

The rest of the chapter is organized as follows. After a discussion on related work and comparisons, in the following section we recall some features of trust and virtual currency systems, by emphasizing the way in which they can be combined together. Then, a general cooperation framework for Wi-Fi communities is presented, by illustrating the underlying model and by discussing the tradeoff existing among trust, remuneration, and performance. Afterwards, we advocate the use of formal methods for the modeling and analysis of the cooperation framework. In particular, we present the results of model checking based verification giving an estimation of the tradeoffs

considered above. The contribution of this chapter represents a revised extension of material presented by Bogliolo et al. (2012) and by Aldini and Bogliolo (2012a and 2012b).

Related Work

The first computational model of trust has been proposed in the seminal work by Marsh (1994), while its application in the challenging setting of distributed and mobile environments, where a prominent role is played by uncertainty and incompleteness of trust values, goes back to Eschenauer et al. (2002). In this setting, we refer to Cho et al. (2011) for a survey on trust management for mobile ad-hoc networks. In the specific framework of UCNs, reputation may act as an incentive as long as it represents an enabling condition for taking part in the community and obtaining services, including broader connectivity access and resource sharing, see, e.g., Wei et al. (2011). In general, whenever the trust framework is distributed, the absence of centralized trusted authorities makes it difficult protecting users from attacks, supporting lightweight trust computation mechanisms, and evolving timely with respect to reputation variations. For details about these properties, we refer to Liu and Issarny (2004) and to Suryanarayana and Taylo (2004). Two representative examples of distributed trust frameworks are the Bayesian approach proposed by Quercia et al. (2006) and the work by Theodorakopoulos and Baras (2006), which is based on the formal theory of semirings.

As far as remuneration is concerned, it is well-established that direct rewards are necessary to leverage the "propensity to truck, barter and exchange one thing for another", as emphasized historically by Adam Smith (1776). In the setting of virtual currency systems, it is worth distinguishing between centralized and distributed schemes, the main difference being the adoption of a trusted third party acting as an online/offline bank. In particular, in the setting of distributed payment systems, several cryptography based schemes have been proposed that deal with typical attacks, like double spending or forgery, and with nontrivial requirements, like traceability and anonimity. Among them, we mention, e.g., proposals by Buttyan and Hubaux (2001), Yang and Garcia-Molina (2003), Camenisch et al. (2005), Wei et al. (2005), Osipkov et al. (2007), and Nakamoto (2009).

The use of cooperation incentives based on virtual currency is particularly appealing in UCNs in which reputation may not be perceived as a sufficient motivation to share services and resources. For instance, in the setting of wireless communities, the frequent renewal of the set of active nodes and the short-term participation of members in the community may impair the reliability of the reputation infrastructure, thus favoring selfishness and cheating behaviors. Hence, the combination of indirect and direct rewards in the incentive mechanisms is very attractive, as confirmed by several pioneering approaches proposed in the literature. For instance, Seigneur et al. (2002) suggest to use trust values directly as digital money, Fernandes et al. (2004) introduce economical incentives to encourage the provision of accurate feedback influencing trust, which represents the main virtuous mechanism enabling a reliable reputation infrastructure, while Yang et al. (2007) as well as Zhang et al. (2007) employ trust to give prioritized access to services, similarly as proposed in our framework. In particular, the file sharing system by Yang et al. (2007) is designed to give downloading preferences to users with high reputation, while the incentive mechanism by Zhang et al. (2007) allocates services to consumers depending on their reputation and submitted bid. However, with respect to our approach, these systems do not relate directly the computation of trust-based and credit-based rewards.

COOPERATION INCENTIVES

The application of trust management and virtual currency is a key feature for the success of cooperation models in UCNs. Trust systems provide indirect rewards encouraging resource sharing (and discouraging selfish behaviors) in the framework of a reliable reputation infrastructure. Virtual currency systems provide direct rewards, which usually overcome the weaknesses of reputation-based incentives. In this section, we specify in detail some assumptions concerning these systems that are needed to present our cooperation framework.

Trust and Reputation

While trust represents a subjective firm reliance on the character, integrity, and ability of someone or something, reputation can be viewed as the public *trustworthiness* of a community member as perceived by the other participants in the community. Such a trustworthiness derives from the aggregation of individual trust values computed by several different members for the same subject. The objective of trust metrics is favoring ethical community norms ensuring the minimum level of mutual confidence that is needed to set up a working cooperation infrastructure. As a consequence, even if reputation is not directly related to any form of earnings (in particular, it cannot be traded for money), a trusted member is more likely to be involved in remunerative tasks.

In our framework, as far as the modeling issues are concerned, we assume that trust is represented as a discrete metric, refer to Jøsang (2007) for a survey on discrete trust-based systems. In particular, the trust value T of a user i towards another user j is computed according to a formula abstracted as follows:

$$T = \alpha \cdot trust + (1 - \alpha) \cdot recs \qquad (1)$$

where $\alpha \in [0,1]$ is a risk factor, *trust* is the trust metric deriving from previous direct interactions between i and j (the initial value of this metric is equal to the dispositional trust, *dt*, of i towards unknown users), and *recs* is the average of the trust metrics towards j recommended by other users. Without loss of generality, we assume that each user may ask recommendations to n users representing the average number of neighbors in the network. This means that the complexity of the communication overhead will be evaluated as a function of n.

In general, trust-based policies establish that j can obtain access to a given service offered by i whenever T is at least equal to the service trust threshold set by i, call it st, which represents the minimum amount of trust that is needed to apply with success for the service request.

Virtual Currency

The role of credit-based rewards as an incentive instrument is particularly important whenever the community is highly dynamic, people do not know each other in person, and the trading relations are not continuous. Moreover, remuneration provides guarantee of reciprocity, according to which the evolution of (and the attitute to) cooperative behaviors strongly depends on the likelihood of mutual interactions. Hence, it is quite expected that virtual currency has emerged in online communities as a mechanism to buy and sell virtual goods, thus supporting monetization and the quantification of the value of sharing services and resources.

In order to strengthen the relation between trust-based and credit-based incentives, we adopt a service cost model in which trust is perceived as an incentive to pay less. Using a cost function that somehow depends on trust is fundamental to make the incentive mechanism work, as demonstrated by Aldini and Bogliolo (2012b) and by Li and Shen (2011). In particular, the trust value T of i towards j must contribute to determine the value of the cost variable C used by i to set the price for the service delivered to j. Other important parameters influencing C are the minimum price that is applied regardless of the trust level, C_{min}, the maximum price asked to serve untrusted

users, C_{max}, and the trust threshold above which the minimum price is applied, T_{th}.

As an example, a simple formula proposed by Bogliolo et al. (2012) that includes all these parameters is the following one:

$$C(T) = \begin{cases} C_{min} + \dfrac{C_{max} - C_{min}}{T_{th}} \cdot (T_{th} - T) & T < T_{th} \\ C_{min} & T \geq T_{th} \end{cases} \quad (2)$$

Here we do not go into the details of the specific payment system that is adopted, as it is independent of the general cooperation framework that we present. However, whenever performance comes into play, its role must be evaluated carefully, as we emphasize in the analysis section.

COOPERATION FRAMEWORK

In the following, we present a general model of cooperation merging indirect and direct rewards, by emphasizing the possible effects of the incentive mechanisms used to implement the cooperation infrastructure. In particular, we investigate the mutual dependences between the incentive mechanisms and their impact upon performance. As we will see, several strategies are discussed that can be adopted to obtain a balanced tradeoff.

A General Model of Cooperation

The general cooperation process we consider consists of the following four phases in which trust management and virtual currency are combined to merge indirect and direct rewards.

1. **Request:** A user, called *requester*, issues a service request to a user called *requestee*. The selection of one of the requestees offering the desired service is either nondeterministic or governed by reputation-based and/

or cost-based principles. Whenever guided by quantitative principles, the choice can be either prioritized or probabilistic. In the former case, precedence is given on the basis of the adopted principle and of the requestee availability to negotiate. If the principle is not sufficient to discriminate among several requestees, then the selection of one of them is random. In the latter case, the probabilities governing the choice are weighted with respect to the adopted principle. For instance, if the principle of interest is reputation, then the estimation used to parameterize the choice is given by the application of Equation 1.

2. **Negotiation:** If the requester is trustworthy enough to access the required service and the requestee is available to cooperate, the two parties reach an agreement in terms of quality of service and price to pay. In particular, trust and cost models are combined to strengthen the relation between trustworthiness and remuneration, as shown, e.g., in the case of Equation 2.

3. **Transaction:** Both the service and the related payment are provided. These two operations are not conditioned to each other. Instead, requester and requestee are bound to the negotiated terms. The violation of the agreement by one of the parties does not authorize the other to do as much. This lack of control is needed to obtain lightweight transactions, while the risk of abuses should be mitigated by the small granularity of transactions and by the combined use of indirect/direct incentives, as we will verify formally in the next sections.

4. **Feedback:** The requester evaluates the transaction result by comparing the negotiated quality of service with the perceived quality of experience and by taking into account the service cost. Similarly, the requestee provides a feedback about the behavior of the requester. These evaluations are fundamental

to adjust trust and to make the reputation system reliable.

A few comments are in order in the case of the credit-based remuneration mechanism. Credits are assigned to the UCNs members whenever they join the community and can be spent (resp., earned) by buying (resp., selling) services. Basically, credits should be exchangeable (for real money) in order to make the UCN be part of the Internet value chain in such a way that community members can cooperate with nodes that are outside the community. However, trading credits for money, called monetization, is a process that requires some form of control in order to avoid the typical problems of exchange systems, like speculation and selfishness. To this aim, monetization is limited by imposing that only earned credits can be monetized, while traded credits cannot.

Trading the Cooperation Incentives

The combination of indirect and direct rewards contrasts selfish and cheating behaviors by means of mechanisms that imply some tradeoff. Other aspects of cooperation that are not concerned with the incentive mechanisms can be involved, such as performance, in a way that may thwart the efforts payed to maintain the cooperation infrastructure. For each phase of the general cooperation model, we now discuss how to trade trust, remuneration, and performance.

In the first phase, whenever the choice is guided by reputation, the requester computes the trust value towards each candidate requestee according with Equation 1. Such a computation has an impact upon performance. Indeed, recalling that n represents the average number of neighbors in the network, Equation 1 requires in the worst-case scenario the transmission of n requests and n^2 recommendations, as each contacted neighbor would communicate his/her personal trust towards all the other users. Both the requester and the recommenders can adopt strategies to reduce such an overhead.

Firstly, the requester can set $\alpha = 1$, thus avoiding any recommendation request and using only his/her direct experience for the computation of the trust value. In general, strategies ignoring recommendations impair the ability to reveal dishonest behaviors, so that they should be considered very carefully; we refer to Marmol and Perez (2009) for a survey. Alternatively, the requester can use only recommendations spontaneously sent by other users. While the former strategy favors performance with respect to the reliability of the computed reputation, the latter strategy is aimed at trading the two aspects. Secondly, each recommender can decide to reply to a recommendation request according to a probabilistic choice guided by parameter β, so that the complexity would become $O(n + \beta \cdot n^2)$.

On the other hand, the way in which reputation is used to govern the selection of a requestee is another aspect that may impair system performance. In particular, if the requester adopts a prioritized choice that privileges the most trustworthy requestee, which is proved to be the strategy that maximizes the incentive to be cooperative, then the requestees with highest reputation would become a bottleneck. In other words, this strategy contrasts any load balancing principle, which is at the basis of typical mechanisms used to ensure best effort performance. This side effect can be mitigated by using a probabilistic choice model, where reputations play the role of probabilistic weights.

Whenever the choice is governed by cost, the requester polls the system for the best offer. Hence, in the worst-case scenario the complexity is $O(n + n)$, as basically n is the number of offers obtained in response to the poll. Similarly as observed in the reputation-based case, such an overhead can be reduced by:

- Avoiding completely cost-based choices, thus eliminating the overhead;

- Using only offers spontaneously sent by requestees that periodically advertise their services;
- Sending offers according to a probabilistic choice guided by parameter β, thus reducing by such a factor the communication overhead.

If the offers sent by the requestees are computed as a function of the trustworthiness of the requester, an additional overhead is due to the estimation of trust, as imposed, e.g., by Equation 2 (we postpone the analysis of this overhead to the following discussion about negotiation). Moreover, the role of price in the choice model deserves the same considerations about load balancing surveyed above in the case of reputation.

Finally, notice that reputation-based and cost-based principles can be combined in the choice process, in which case the complexity and the side effects of the two incentive strategies would sum up.

After the selection performed in the request phase, it may be the case that the chosen requestee is not ready to negotiate, for example because of a temporary non-cooperative attitude or because of the saturation of the available resources. In the second case, we can envision at least two different strategies for the requester. Firstly, the requester can accept to be queued, because the adopted choice policy (reputation of the requestee or offered price) is considered to be more important than performance for the expected service. Secondly, the requester can decide to look for the subsequent requestee in the choice list, because the request is considered to be urgent. In such a case, it could be reasonable to provide an immediate negative feedback, the effect of which would be a decrease of the reputation of the unavailable requestee, so that future requests of the same service would be probably issued to other requestees. Notice that such a negative reputation feedback does not represent the result of the evaluation of any transaction between the two parties, as commonly required by classical trust management systems. However, it is compatible with usual load balancing principles.

As far as trust-based incentives are concerned, the requestee is expected to compute the trust towards the requester, in order to decide whether to offer the service and, if so, to negotiate the price according to a cost function that possibly depends on trust, as in the case of Equation 2. The computation of the trust value T requires gathering recommendations about the requester, with a complexity linearly dependent on n. Once again, such an overhead can be reduced by avoiding recommendations at all ($\alpha = 1$), by using only recommendations previously received without issuing any new request, or by allowing neighboring nodes to reply to recommendation requests according to a probabilistic choice model.

As far as cost-based incentives are concerned, the service cost can be either fixed or dependent on trust. In the latter case, negotiation must follow the mechanism described above to compute the trust value T.

Service delivery and related payment are the constituting operations of the third phase, during which we observe the effects of the payment system upon performance. Existing solutions can be either centralized, involving online or offline interactions with a trusted third party playing the role of a bank, or distributed, relying on the exchange of information to protect from cheating. Therefore, depending on their nature, these systems may either involve several message exchanges of strong cryptographic protocols, or adopt soft security mechanisms with a lightweight impact upon performance. Discussing the technical merits of the alternative solutions and the tradeoff between performance and security is beyond the scope of this work. However, here we emphasize an obvious relation between Equation 2 and performance in the case of reputation-based incentives. Indeed, whenever the requestee sets $C_{min} = 0$ and the requester is trustworthy enough, the overhead due to the payment is null. The immediate consequences

of such a strategy are a beneficial impact upon performance and a negative impact upon earnings from the viewpoint of the requestee. On the other hand, on the long run we observe another positive effect, namely the reputation increase due to the recommendations provided by the trustworthy requesters that interact with the requestee, which therefore would be chosen also by new incoming community members, thus enabling a virtuous mechanism positively affecting the earnings.

In the fourth phase, both the requester and the requestee are expected to evaluate the result of the transaction. On one hand, the requestee decides whether the trust towards the requester is to be adjusted, e.g., by evaluating the promptness of the payment or the way in which the offered resources have been used. On the other hand, the requester evaluates the perceived quality of experience and compares it with negotiated service cost and quality of service. The feedback is then used to adjust the reputation of the requestee, thus triggering the virtuous mechanism needed by the cooperation infrastructure. In order to strengthen the relation between reputation and performance, additional positive/negative reputation variations may be considered in case of performance results that are above/under predefined thresholds. Finally, this phase imposes some communication overhead only if the feedback is broadcast either deterministically, with complexity $O(n)$, or probabilistically with parameter β, with complexity $O(\beta \cdot n)$, in order to inform the neighbors about the reputation variation.

VERIFICATION OF THE COOPERATION FRAMEWORK

Formal verification techniques are widely used to conduct mathematical analysis of the properties of wireless networks. Among the several different approaches, we mention:

- Game theory, used, e.g., by Li and Shen (2011) and by Srivastava et al. (2005);
- Model checking, like in papers by Aldini and Bogliolo (2012b), Gallina et al. (2012), and Fruth (2011);
- Equivalence checking and numerical analysis of Markov chains, as shown by Martalò et al. (2009) and Acquaviva et al. (2005).

Among the properties we mention energy consumption, service throughput, resource usage, and, finally, effectiveness of the cooperation incentives. In particular, both the contributions by Li and Shen (2011) and by Aldini and Bogliolo (2012b) demonstrate that the integration of trust-based and cost-based strategies optimizes the effect of the cooperation incentives. The latter approach is based on the application of the model checker PRISM, for a tutorial survey of which we refer to the papers by Kwiatkowska et al. (2007) and Forejt et al. (2011).

The modeling language of PRISM is a state-based mathematical formalism inspired by the Reactive Modules introduced by Alur and Henzinger (1999), from which different types of non-deterministic, probabilistic, and temporal models can be derived, including discrete-time Markov chains (DTMCs), continuous-time Markov chains (CTMCs), timed automata, and Markov decision processes (MDPs), which are Markov processes including nondeterministic behaviors. We refer the interested reader to Stewart (1994), Alur and Dill (1994), and Segala (1995) for a survey on these formal models and related analysis techniques. The language of PRISM for specifying properties to verify by means of model checking techniques is a temporal logic subsuming both probabilistic computation tree logic (PCTL) and linear time logic (LTL), which are expressive enough to specify both state-based and path-based properties, and include both probabilistic and reward operators, in the same style of ideas formalized by Baier and Katoen (2008). In practice, through the software

tool PRISM it is possible to model systems that exhibit temporal/probabilistic behaviors and to model check properties that describe quantities of very different nature, including time, trust, or money.

In this section, we show how to apply PRISM for the modeling and analysis of the cooperation framework surveyed above. In particular, we consider three dimensions of the analysis:

- Security, which is a pillar condition underlying the functioning of trust- and credit-based mechanisms;
- Socio-economic aspects, which give a perception of the efficiency of the cooperation incentives;
- Tradeoff of the previous properties with performance, which is necessary to determine the applicability in real wireless networks.

Modeling Assumptions

In the network scenario we envision each node acts either as requester or as requestee. All of them are involved in the exchange of one type of service. As discussed in previous sections, we assume discrete trust values, which range in the interval [0,10], such that $null = 0$, $low = 2$, $med = 5$, $high = 8$, and finally $top = 10$. With respect to the four phases of the general cooperation model, we consider the following basic assumptions.

In the request phase, the selection of a requestee is guided by reputation of the requestees and is not based on recommendations. Hence, reputation of the candidate requestees is computed by taking $\alpha = 1$. Initially, the reputation is *low* for every requestee.

During the negotiation phase, if the chosen requestee is not available, then the request is issued to the subsequent requestee in the choice list. Unavailable requestees are not punished by decreasing their reputation. As far as the parameters used by the requestee are concerned, we assume that the risk factor α ranges over the set {0.5, 0.8, 1} and the service trust threshold *st* over the set {*low, med, high*}. The dispositional trust *dt* is chosen to be equal to the service trust threshold *st* in order to make it possible for a new requester to start negotiating services with the requestees. As far as the cost function is concerned, the default values are $C_{min} = 0$, $C_{max} = 10$, and $T_{th} = high$.

For the transaction phase, we assume that the service can be paid or not by the requester, either nondeterministically or probabilistically with parameter $p \in [0,1]$, namely the requester pays the obtained service with probability *p*.

Finally, as far as the feedback phase is concerned, we assume that whenever the service is satisfactory, the reputation of the requestee as perceived by the requester is increased by 1. No feedback is spontaneously broadcast by the requester. On the other hand, the trust of the requestee towards the requester increases by a factor 1 whenever the service is paid, while it decreases by a factor *k*, the domain of which is given by the set {1, 2, ∞}, whenever the requester does not pay for the delivered service (∞ stands for the immediate assignment of the value *null* to the trust value). Feedback is broadcast spontaneously by the requestee to the other nodes in the network.

Modeling with PRISM

In order to exemplify the capabilities of formal modeling paradigms like that supported by PRISM, in the following we present part of the model of a simple requester. A model is described through a state-based language in which the main concepts are the modules, describing the behavior of system components, and the local variables associated with the modules. The local state of a module is represented by the values of its local variables. A module description starts with its name declaration:

```
module Requester
```

followed by the definition of the local variables:

```
x: [0..n] init 0;
ns: [0..N] init 0;
...
```

For instance, the requester component can be in one of n local states (with n being an integer constant), modeled through the local variable x, such that x=0 denotes the initial state. The local variable ns denotes the number of requested services, the maximum value of which is given by constant N.

Then, the behavior of a module is given by a set of guarded commands specifying variable updates. For the sake of simplicity, we assume that the requested service can be offered by two different requestees. Initially, the requester is expected to select a requestee, chosen nondeterministically. Therefore, the first commands of our simple example are as follows:

```
[ ] x=0 & ns<N -> (x'=11);
[ ] x=0 & ns<N -> (x'=21);
[ ] x=0 & ns=N -> (x'=1);
[ ] x=1 -> true;
```

where a pair of brackets denotes the start of the command, the symbol -> separates the guards from the update, and the primed name x' represents the new value taken by the local variable x, while all the other local variables remain unchanged. Keyword true denotes that all the module variables remain unchanged. In our example, when x has value 0 and ns has value less than N, either the update x'=11 or the update x'=21 is applied. Such a choice is nondeterministic.

In the following, we describe the commands guarded by condition x=11, modeling the case in which the requester has chosen the first requestee (in an orthogonal way condition x=21 describes the case concerning the second requestee). Then, such a requestee is expected either to accept the request and deliver the service, or to refuse the request. In the former case, the requester shall decide to pay or not for the obtained service. The commands of the requester module expressing such a behavior are as follows:

```
[accept] x=11 -> (x'=12) & (ns'= ns+1);
[refuse] x=11 -> (x'=13) & (ns'= ns+1);
[pay] x=12 -> (x'=0);
[nopay] x=12 -> (x'=0);
[ ] x=13 -> (x'=0);
...
endmodule
```

Notice that in some cases the brackets marking the start of the command include a label, which expresses an action name on which the module is expected to synchronize with another module, in the same style of many process algebraic languages, see, e.g., Aldini et al. (2010). In our example, when x has value 11 and the first requestee is ready to execute a command labeled with the action name accept, then the updates x'=12 and ns'=ns+1 are executed. In this case, the requester decides nondeterministically to synchronize with the first requestee either through action pay or through action nopay, after which the module goes back to its initial state. The module specification terminates with the keyword endmodule. It is also worth noticing that PRISM allows for controlled forms of action, variable, and module renaming that prevent from code duplication, thus facilitating the specification, e.g., of systems made of several different requesters and/or requestees.

Now, let us consider an enriched version of the requester module in which the nondeterminism is replaced by probabilistic choices. In particular, as far as the selection of the requestee is concerned, we assume that the choice is weighted by the reputation of the requestees. Hence, in the requester module we add two more local variables, one for

each requestee, storing the reputation value as presented:

```
rep1: [0..top] init low;
rep2: [0..top] init low;
```

Then we change the selection as follows:

```
[ ] x=0 -> (rep1/totrep):(x'=11)
         + (rep2/totrep):(x'=21);
```

where the syntactic expression p1:(c1) + p2:(c2) indicates that command c1 is executed with probability p1, while command c2 is executed with probability p2, such that p1+p2=1. Parameter totrep represents the overall reputation of the requestees, which is necessary to compute the relative weights, and is defined in PRISM as the result of the following expression:

```
formula totrep = (rep1+rep2)
               = 0 ? 1: (rep1+rop2);
```

which is a conditional expression taking the value (rep1+rep2) if such a value is different from 0 and value 1 otherwise.

Analogously, the other source of nondeterminism in the requester module, which is the payment related choice, is changed as follows:

```
[accept] x=11 -> p:(x'=12) + (1-p):(x'=13);
[refuse] x=11 -> (x'=14);
[pay] x=12 -> (x'=0) & (rep' = min(rep+1,top));
[nopay] x=13 -> (x'=0) & (rep' = min(rep+1,top));
[ ] x=14 -> (x'=0);
```

Notice that constant p represents the parameter governing probabilistically the choice between the honest and cheating behaviors, while the reputation of the first requestee is increased whenever the service request is accepted.

All the modules surveyed above subsume a discrete model of time in which the execution of a command takes one tick of time. In particular, the former version with nondeterministic behaviors subsumes an MDP, while the latter (without nondeterminism) a DTMC. Modeling stochastic time, thus specifying the behavior of a CTMC, is obtained in similar style to a DTMC, the main difference being that commands are labeled with positive-valued rates of exponential distributions rather than probabilities.

For instance, the selection of the requestee in the case of reputation-based prioritized model of choice is as follows in Box 5.

```
[ ] (x=0) & (rep1>=rep2) -> tau: (x'=11);
[ ] (x=0) & (rep2>=rep1) -> tau: (x'=21);
```

where tau is a real constant previously defined as follows:

```
const double tau = 1;
```

which represents the rate of the exponential distribution modeling stochastically the passage of time whenever the transition from state x=0 to state x=11 (or x=21) is executed. If multiple transitions are enabled at the same time (e.g., this occurs in the example above when the two requestees have equal reputations), then a race condition occurs, establishing that the fastest transition wins. We refer the interested reader to Hillston (1996), Kwiatkowska et al. (2007), or Aldini et al. (2010) for a formal treatment of stochastic time.

Finally, it is worth commenting on the modeling of properties. The property specification language of PRISM extends classical logics, like LTL and CTL, with their probabilistic and stochastic versions, like CSL (Continuous Stochastic Logic), which is an extension of Probabilistic CTL for CTMCs. Here, we stress the features that allow cost-based properties to be specified. This is done through an approach based on reward structures. A reward is a value associated with a certain state- or transition-based condition. For instance, the reward structure denoting the cost due by the requester to the first requestee for each service delivery is as follows:

```
rewards "cost1"
[pay] true: formula;
endrewards
```

which says that pay–labelled transitions from states enabling the guard true acquire a reward equal to the value of the expression *formula*, which here abstractedly denotes Equation 2. Then, as an example, the property specifying the total earning for the first requestee that is accumulated until t time units have elapsed, is as follows:

```
R{"cost1"} = ? [ C<=t ]
```

The operator C<=t is used to reason about the transient-state behavior of a system. Similarly, steady-state based analysis is possible through the S operator for expressing the behavior in the long-run, that is at the equilibrium.

Model Checking Security

Trust systems represent soft security solutions that overcome the strong resource constraints of classical security mechanisms that are not compatible with the limitations of wireless networks. The related exposure to cheating behaviors is contrasted by the adoption of cooperation incentives, the effectiveness of which represents a fundamental aspect to analyze.

The first property we consider is a security condition establishing such an effectiveness with respect to possible cheating requesters, which may exploit the lightweight transaction mechanism to obtain services without paying for them. As discussed in previous sections, access to services is governed by reputation, so that a dishonest requester, sooner or later, should become untrusted by any requestee. Hence, we are interested in evaluating the following property:

Property 1: What is the maximum number of services (out of *N* requests) that can be obtained by a requester without honouring the payment?

We analyze this property in a scenario with a single, possibly cheating requester and three different requestees. The requester chooses non-deterministically the strategy to adopt during the request phase and is able to observe the configuration parameters of all the requestees. Therefore, the requester can be viewed as an adversary aiming at determining the strategy maximizing the number of unpaid services, thus revealing the worst case from the viewpoint of the requestees. Formally, the semantics of the model turns out to be an MDP on which *Property 1* is evaluated by solving the nondeterminism in all possible ways. Therefore, the model checker returns the result for the best adversary strategy.

For the sake of completeness, we also report the formal specification of this property in PRISM, which is defined through the following "reachability reward" property:

```
R{"nopayed"}max = ? [ F (x=1) ]
```

computing the maximum reward, as described by the reward structure "nopayed", that is accumulated along paths until the condition (x=1) holds (notice that F represents the *eventually* operator of LTL). We recall that (x=1) holds whenever *N* requests have been submitted (see the nondeterministic model of the previous section). The reward structure "nopayed" is then defined as follows:

```
rewards "nopayed"
[nopay1] true: 1;
[nopay2] true: 1;
[nopay3] true: 1;
endrewards
```

When model checking *Property 1*, the parameters under analysis for the requestees are α and *st* (that affect the service access conditions), and *k* (influencing the feedback computation). In Figure 1, we report the results concerning 12 (out of 27) combinations of the three parameters, which have been analyzed by Aldini and Bogliolo (2012b). The horizontal axis denotes the total number of requests, ranging from 1 to 25, while the vertical axis reports the maximum number of unpaid services. The chosen pictures confirm the general perception that the success of the cheating strategy is inversely proportional to the factor *k* and to the service trust threshold *st*. A value of parameter α tending to 1 makes the cooperation work if and only if the dispositional trust is not less than the service trust threshold, while values equal to (or below) 0.5 expose the system to a typical attack of a requester cheating only one requestee, which gives too much weight to the positive recommendations provided by the other requestees.

In general, by observing the obtained results, two limiting profiles emerge that characterize opposite attitudes of the requestee. On one hand, we have a *risky* profile, for which the unpaid services increase linearly and most of the served requests risk to remain unpaid. On the other hand, we have a *cautious* profile, for which the number of unpaid services is essentially constant. These two profiles give a clear and precise perception of the requestee attitude to take prosocial decisions in a potentially hostile environment. In the rest of the experiments, we assume that risky requestees are represented by configuration $\alpha = 0.5$, *st* = low, and *k* = 1, that is: the same importance is given to direct experience and external recommendations, the minimum trust required to apply for the service is *low*, and the reaction to undesired behaviors is as mild as possible. Cautious requestees are represented by configuration $\alpha = 0.8$, *st* = med, and k = ∞, that is: direct experience has a prominent role, the minimum trust required to apply for the service is *med*, and the reaction to undesired behaviors is as punishing as possible.

Whenever the profile is not specified, configuration $\alpha = 0.8$, $st = low$, and $k = 1$ is taken as default.

While *Property 1* reveals the effectiveness of the trust-based incentives against the worst adversary, it is also meaningful to observe the system evolution on average. To this aim, we eliminate any form of nondeterminism by assuming that the requester adopts the prioritized model of choice and that the service payment is honoured probabilistically with parameter p. As a consequence, the semantics of the model turns out to be a DTMC, on which both steady-state and transient-state analyses can be conducted.

On one hand, the steady-state analysis reveals the success of the cooperation mechanism on the long run. In particular, at the equilibrium it turns out that for each $p < 1$ the requester becomes untrusted with probability 1 by every requestee. On the other hand, the transient analysis is useful to reveal the convergence speed towards such a positive result. Hence, the next property to study is as follows:

Property 2: What is the probability for a cheating requester of being untrusted by each requestee after N requests?

The analysis is conducted by varying parameter p and by assuming $N \in \{10, 25, 50, 100\}$. The three scenarios illustrated in Figure 2 are as follows, respectively:

1. Three risky requestees;
2. Three requestees among which one is risky and one is cautious, while the default configuration is adopted for the third one;
3. Three cautious requestees.

All the curves tend rapidly to 1 for $p < 0.5$ and converge to zero as p tends to 1. In particular, it is worth observing that in the case of 3 cautious requestees and for $N \geq 25$, the curves approximate a step function, meaning that a cheating requester is almost immediately untrusted by each requestee.

Model Checking the Tradeoff Among Cooperation Incentives

While in the previous section we have considered the effectiveness of the trust-based system as a soft security mechanism, in this section we show how to analyze its efficiency from social and economic perspectives. To this aim, we consider the following three properties:

Property 3: What is the number of requests accepted by each requestee?
Property 4: What is the total expected earning for each requestee?
Property 5: What is the average earning per accepted request?

These properties are used to compare the two main requestee profiles in a scenario with 50 requests, one requester following the prioritized model of choice, one risky requestee, one cautious requestee, and one default requestee. The performance results illustrated in Figure 3 are expressed as a function of parameter p. The curves emphasize the following results.

Firstly, the number of services accepted by the risky requestee is higher than that concerning the cautious requestee. The difference is due to the more permissive conditions applied by the risky requestee, among which the most influencing one is the assumption $k = 1$. In fact, by setting $k = \infty$ also for the risky requestee, its curve would collapse with that of the cautious requestee. It is worth observing that in case of honest requester (i.e., $p = 1$), the profile of the requestees does not play any role, so that the requests are equally distributed among them, because they are assigned with the same initial reputation.

Secondly, as p increases, the total expected earnings of the risky requestee become much higher than those of the cautious one. The difference can be interpreted as a reward for taking more risk.

Figure 1. Security analysis: verification of Property 1 for different configurations of parameters α/st/k

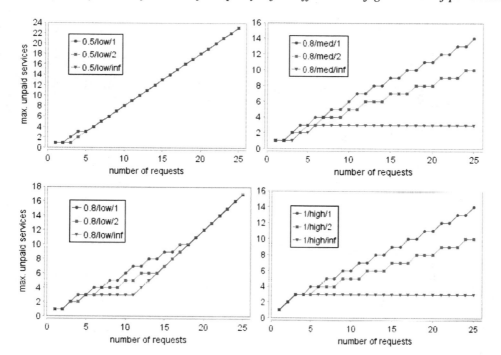

Thirdly, the average expected reward/cost per service grows with the value of *p* up to a maximum point beyond which the expected reward/cost decreases because of the effect of the trust-based discount applied to trustworthy requesters. Such a maximum point is reached earlier by the risky requestee, thus motivating the better performance of the cautious requestee for $p \in [0.6;0.9]$. We also observe that in such an interval the trust value of the requester becomes stably high from the viewpoint of the risky requestee, as emphasized by the corresponding total earnings curve. For *p* ≥ 0.95, the result is better for the risky requestee, because the requester becomes trustworthy also from the viewpoint of the cautious requestee, with a positive impact upon the number of services such a requestee accepts.

In general, the combined effect of cost function and trust management works as an incentive to adopt a risky prosocial behavior. On the other hand, it is obvious that the requester obtains more

services at a lower average cost whenever adopting a honest behavior.

Extended results can be obtained by conducting a sensitivity analysis, the objective of which is to reveal the impact of each configuration parameter. For instance, just to cite some examples, we emphasize that:

- The value of parameter C_{min} affects the earnings without influencing the shape of the reward/cost curves.
- The performance results concerning number of accepted services and total earnings improve as *k* decreases, thus enforcing the role of *k* as a measure of the tolerance to cheating behaviors. As a side effect, the average earnings decrease, because small negative variations of the trust value due to a small value of *k* contribute to keep low the cost per service. Whenever the requester is always honest, parameter *k* does not play any role.

Figure 2. Security analysis: verification of Property 2

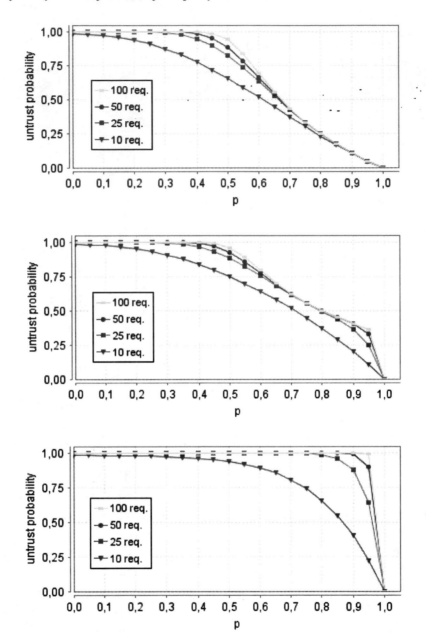

- A role similar to that of parameter k is played also by the dispositional trust and by the service trust threshold.

Another important tradeoff concerns the relation between the socio-economic aspects surveyed above and each behavior affecting the reputation of the requestees.

For instance, the prioritized model of choice adopted by the requester works as a very convincing incentive to maintain a high reputation value for those requestees interested in the economic results. This is confirmed by a series of experi-

Figure 3. Socio-economic analysis: verification of Property 3 to 5

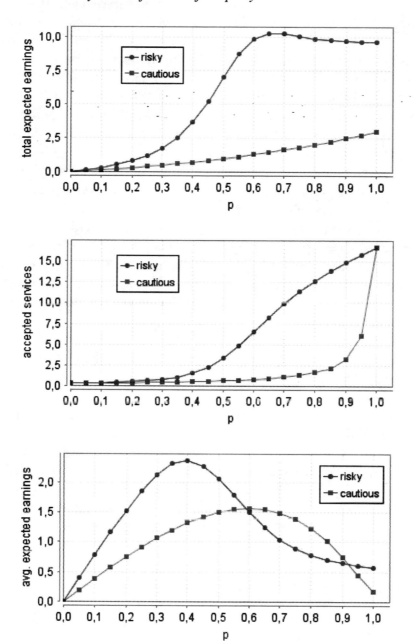

ments showing that whenever the initial reputation (deriving, e.g., from past interactions) is not the same for each requestee, all the requests, regardless of the requestee profile, are directed to the requestees with highest reputation. On the other hand, a smooth distribution of the requests among the requestees is obtained if the choice model adopted in the request phase is probabilistic rather than prioritized. Such a situation is illustrated in Figure 4, showing that a cautious requestee with initial *low* reputation is not prevented from serving some requests even in the presence of a risky requestee with initial *high* reputation, while this would not happen in the case of the prioritized choice model.

The role of reputation is exacerbated when taking requestees with a very scarce attitude to cooperation, which are characterized by configurations in which $dt < st$. In other words, such requestees do not accept any request from unknown users unless a sufficiently high number of good recommendations is provided. Hence, the startup for these requestees, which we call paranoid, strongly depends on the presence of other, more collaborative requestees in the network. Because of this attitude, paranoid requestees are always outperformed by the other requestees and, in most cases, they are not even able to receive any service request.

Finally, in order to verify more deeply the relation between feedback and reputation, it is worth investigating the impact of possibly negative evaluations provided by the requester. This may happen, e.g., when the requestee fails to respect the negotiated quality of service. Such a situation is analyzed through the following property.

Property 6: How does reputation impact the number of accepted requests in the case of fallible services?

As emphasized when discussing the tradeoff between cooperation incentives, another source of negative feedback could derive from the non-cooperative behavior of the chosen requestee, which may refuse to negotiate. In this case, a negative feedback of the requester can be useful to balance the network performance. The related property is specified as follows.

Property 7: How does reputation vary in the case of non-cooperative requestees?

For both properties, as expected, the analysis conducted by Aldini and Bogliolo (2012b) emphasizes that negative evaluations of the services delivered by the requestee impair reputation and, as a consequence, the economic outcome for the requestee.

Model Checking Performance

The analysis of the system behavior is not complete if classical performance properties like, e.g., system throughput, are not considered. This kind of analysis is also useful to validate with respect to orthogonal perspectives the efficiency of the cooperation incentives that, in the previous sections, have been faced from security, social, and economic viewpoints. To this aim, it is worth

Figure 4. Socio-economic analysis: verification of Property 3 with probabilistic choice of the requestee

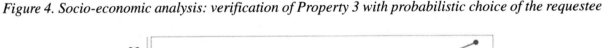
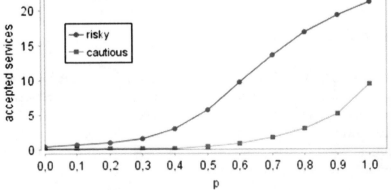

considering a version of the model specification including information about the temporal behavior of the system. More precisely, temporal delays are represented as rates of exponentially timed distributions, so that the underlying semantics turns out to become a CTMC, on which stochastic model checking and numerical analysis techniques can be applied to evaluate performance metrics.

Without loss of generality, we assume that the basic time unit is represented by the rate associated with the transmission delay of a message over the community network. The time needed by internal computations is considered to be negligible except for the virtual currency mechanism used to formalize the payment in the third phase. As emphasized, e.g., in real systems like that proposed by Wei et al. (2005), even scalable and lightweight payment solutions impose a non-negligible overhead due to extra communications and computational efforts to check cryptographic signatures. Hence, we first assume that the ratio r between the basic time unit and the time needed to complete a payment is chosen to be 1:5.

With these assumptions in view, in the following we consider two honest requesters competing for the service offered by two honest requestees with equal initial reputations. The performance metric under analysis is the number of services delivered per time unit, which is estimated in two different cases:

- On the long run (steady state analysis, denoted by Σ);
- By t=100 time units (transient state analysis, denoted by $T_{<100}$).

While the steady state analysis gives a perception of the system behavior at the equilibrium, the transient state analysis is particularly useful for evaluating dynamic situations in which the frequent renewals of users/requests keep the system from having a stable behavior.

We illustrate such a kind of analysis by comparing from the performance standpoint the

model described above with respect to four variants implementing different strategies that can be adopted in the negotiation phase. The first two variants take into account parameters α and C_{min}, under the control of the requestee, which are changed as follows with respect to the default case considered so far:

1. $\alpha = 1$;
2. $C_{min} > 0$.

The other two variants concern the strategy adopted by the requester:

3. Reputation is decreased if the requestee is busy and the request is issued to another requestee;
4. Reputation is not decreased if the requestee is busy and the request is queued (busy waiting).

Since the objective is comparing the effects of different modeling assumptions, in Table 1 we report the relative performance gain/loss for each of the four variants with respect to the performance obtained by the basic model.

The result obtained in case A suggests to trade the security risks of the condition $\alpha = 1$ with the major performance that such a choice implies. For instance, the requestee could dynamically set $\alpha = 1$ for those requesters that become sufficiently trustworthy (with respect to a given trust threshold) by virtue of previous direct interactions. Similarly, the performance loss in case B is the price to pay for the avidity of the requestee, which imposes a cost also to highly trustworthy requesters. In case C the difference is negligible (less than 0.1%) for both types of analysis, while in case D we observe a small performance loss at the steady state and a more significant decay for transient state analysis. On one hand, at the steady state the strategies influencing the reputation variation do not affect significantly the performance behavior, because on the long run reputations tend to equilibrium values. On the other hand, in the case of transient state analysis, the observed results depend on the modeling assumptions, according to which the two requestees have the same initial reputation. Hence, it is interesting to extend the analysis by studying how different combinations of the initial reputations affect the results of the transient state analysis for both cases C and D, as presented in Table 2. Similarly as shown above, we repeat the same experiment by changing the distribution of the initial reputations of the two requestees.

While the first row refers to the same scenario surveyed in the previous table (in which the two requestees have equal initial reputations), in the second (resp., third) row we assume that the value of the initial reputation of one requestee is twice (resp., 3 times) the corresponding value of the other requestee. As a result, the higher the reputation difference is, the bigger the impact upon the performance gain/loss. In other words, increasing the difference between the initial reputations exacerbates the effects of the reputation based strategies.

In order to evaluate the impact of heavy virtual currency systems–this may be the case of, e.g., fully distributed systems like that proposed by Nakamoto (2009)–in Table 3 we show the results obtained in the case $r = 1:10$.

Cases A and C are not reported as they offer results analogous to the previous ones, the main reason being that they are not related to the payment system. The most interesting case is B, for which the performance loss is very high. The reason is that in the other cases the condition $C_{min} = 0$ mitigates the negative performance of the virtual currency mechanism, especially at the steady state. Analogously, the performance decay

in case D is higher than that observed in the previous experiment. This is due to the busy waiting phase, which suffers from the major overhead of the payment system.

CONCLUSION AND FUTURE RESEARCH

The application of cooperation incentives is fundamental for the success of user-centric wireless networks, the functioning of which depends on the willingness of users to share resources and services. In particular, the joint use of reputation infrastructures and virtual currency provides orthogonal incentives to adopt cooperative behaviors. While joint strategies envisioned to emphasize the role of reputation stimulate the attitude to honest and prosocial behaviors, the impact of such strategies upon performance must be evaluated carefully, as it turns out that there exists a tradeoff between cooperation incentives and performance.

In the presentation of the four-phase general cooperation model, we have emphasized the overhead and the possible improvements concerned with each cooperation strategy. The theoretical analysis supported by the software tool PRISM has been useful to estimate all the tradeoffs involving security, social, economic, and performance aspects, thus revealing to what extent each of them can be optimized without jeopardizing the others. The perspectives provided by this analysis are under discussion for being adopted by the ULOOP Consortium (2010-2013).

In general, the verification of the combined use of orthogonal cooperation incentive strategies is not an easy task whenever several different re-

Table 1. Performance gain/loss (with r = 1:5)

	A	B	C	D
Σ	+ 49.9%	− 45.5%	-	− 2.5%
$T_{<100}$	+ 50.3%	− 40.0%	-	− 10.4%

Table 2. Transient-state performance gain/loss for different distributions of the initial reputations

Reputation ratio	C	D
1:1	-	− 10.4%
1:2	+ 3.4%	− 13.2%
1:3	+ 7.3%	− 18.3%

Table 3. Performance gain/loss (with r = 1:10)

	B	D
Σ	− 62.5%	− 6.5%
$T_{<100}$	− 53.8%	− 16.2%

quirements of very different nature come into play. The application of formal methods supported by automated verification tools helps to investigate all the tradeoffs resulting from such combinations and the related results shall be used to guide the implementation of cooperation infrastructures for wireless networks.

We think that the approach proposed in this chapter emphasizes the importance of emerging trends towards the analysis of the tradeoff among orthogonal aspects, which in the specific field of wireless communications is not limited to the cooperation problem, but includes also the optimized usage of limited resources, safety and fault tolerance, availability and reliability of service, soft security issues, privacy, and quality of experience. Hence, as a future direction, we advocate the use of a general methodology based on formal techniques for the verification of the balanced tradeoff among all these aspects.

ACKNOWLEDGMENT

The research leading to these results has received funding from the EU IST Seventh Framework Programme ([FP7/2007-2013]) under grant agreement number 257418, project ULOOP User-centric Wireless Local Loop.

REFERENCES

Acquaviva, A., Aldini, A., Bernardo, M., Bogliolo, A., Bontà, E., & Lattanzi, E. (2004). Assessing the impact of dynamic power management on the functionality and the performance of battery-powered appliances. In *Proceedings of the 5th International Conference on Dependable Systems and Networks (DSN'04)—Performance and Dependability Symposium*, (pp. 731-740). IEEE CS Press.

Aldini, A., Bernardo, M., & Corradini, F. (2010). *A process algebraic approach to software architecture design*. New York: Springer. doi:10.1007/978-1-84800-223-4.

Aldini, A., & Bogliolo, A. (2012a). *Trading performance and cooperation incentives in user-centric networks*. Paper presented at the International Workshop on Quantitative Aspects in Security Assurance. Pisa, Italy.

Aldini, A., & Bogliolo, A. (2012b). Model checking of trust-based user-centric cooperative networks. In *Proceedings of AFIN 2012: The Fourth International Conference on Advances in Future Internet* (pp. 32-41). IARIA.

Alur, R., & Dill, D. (1994). A theory of timed automata. *Theoretical Computer Science, 126*, 183–235. doi:10.1016/0304-3975(94)90010-8.

Alur, R., & Henzinger, T. (1999). Reactive modules. *Formal Methods in System Design, 15*, 7–48. doi:10.1023/A:1008739929481.

Baier, C., & Katoen, J.-P. (2008). *Principles of model checking*. Cambridge, MA: MIT Press.

Bogliolo, A., Polidori, P., Aldini, A., Moreira, W., Mendes, P., Yildiz, M., & Seigneur, J.-M. (2012). Virtual currency and reputation-based cooperation incentives in user-centric networks. In *Proceedings of the International Wireless Communications and Mobile Computing Conference (IWCMC)* (pp. 895-900). Washington, DC: IEEE CS Press.

Buttyan, L., & Hubaux, J.-P. (2001). *Nuglets: A virtual currency to simulate cooperation in self-organized ad hoc networks* (Technical Report DSC/2001/001). Lausanne, Switzerland: Swiss Federal Institute of Technology.

Camenisch, J., Hohenberger, S., & Lysyanskaya, A. (2005). Compact e-cash. In *Proceedings of EUROCRYPT*, (LNCS), (vol. 3494, pp. 302-321). New York: Springer.

Cho, J.-H., Swami, A., & Chen, I.-R. (2011). A survey on trust management for mobile ad hoc networks. [New York: IEEE CS Press.]. *Communications Surveys & Tutorials*, *13*(4), 562–583. doi:10.1109/SURV.2011.092110.00088.

Clarke, E., Grumberg, O., & Peled, D. (2001). *Model checking*. Cambridge, MA: MIT Press.

Eschenauer, L., Gligor, V., & Baras, J. (2002). On trust establishment in mobile ad hoc networks. In *Proceedings on the Security Protocols Workshop*, (LNCS), (vol. 2845, pp. 47-66). New York: Springer.

Fernandes, A., Kotsovinos, E., Ostring, S., & Dragovic, B. (2004). Pinocchio: Incentives for honest participation in distributed trust management. In iTrust, (LNCS), (vol. 2995, pp. 63-77). New York: Springer.

Forejt, V., Kwiatkowska, M., Norman, G., & Parker, D. (2011). Automated verification techniques for probabilistic systems. In M. Bernardo & V. Issarny (Eds.), *Formal methods for eternal networked software systems (SFM'11)*, (LNCS), (vol. 6659, pp. 53-113). New York: Springer.

Fruth, M. (2011). *Formal methods for the analysis of wireless network protocols*. (Ph.D. thesis). Oxford University, Oxford, UK.

Gallina, L., Han, T., Kwiatkowska, M., Marin, A., Rossi, S., & Spanò, A. (2012). Automatic energy-aware performance analysis of mobile ad-hoc networks. In *Proceedings of the IFIP Wireless Days Conference (WD'12)*. IFIP.

Greengard, S. (2011). Social games, virtual goods. *Communications of the ACM*, *54*(4), 19–22. doi:10.1145/1924421.1924429.

Hillston, J. (1996). *A compositional approach to performance modelling*. Cambridge, UK: Cambridge University Press. doi:10.1017/CBO9780511569951.

Jøsang, A. (2007). Trust and reputation systems. In A. Aldini & R. Gorrieri (Eds.), *Foundations of security analysis and design IV (FOSAD'07)*, (LNCS), (vol. 4677, pp. 209-245). New York: Springer.

Jøsang, A., Ismail, R., & Boyd, C. (2007). A survey of trust and reputation systems for online service provision. *Decision Support Systems*, *43*(2), 618–644. doi:10.1016/j.dss.2005.05.019.

Kwiatkowska, M., Norman, G., & Parker, D. (2007). Stochastic model checking. In M. Bernardo & J. Hillston (Eds.), *Formal methods for performance evaluation (SFM'07)*, (LNCS), (vol. 4486, pp. 220-270). New York: Springer.

Li, Z., & Shen, H. (2011). *Game-theoretic analysis of cooperation incentive strategies in mobile ad hoc networks*. Transactions on Mobile Computing.

Liu, J., & Issarny, V. (2004). Enhanced reputation mechanism for mobile ad hoc networks. In *Proceedings to the 2nd International Conference on Trust Management*, (LNCS), (vol. 2995, pp. 48-62). New York: Springer.

Marmol, F. G., & Perez, G. M. (2009). Security threats scenarios in trust and reputation models for distributed systems. *Computers & Security*, *28*, 545–556. doi:10.1016/j.cose.2009.05.005.

Marsh, S. (1994). *Formalising trust as a computational concept*. (PhD Thesis). Department of Mathematics and Computer Science, University of Stirling, Stirling, UK.

Martalò, M., Busanelli, S., & Ferrari, G. (2009). Markov chain-based performance analysis of multihop IEEE 802.15.4 wireless networks. *Performance Evaluation, 66*(12), 722–741. doi:10.1016/j.peva.2009.08.011.

Nakamoto, S. (2009). *Bitcoin: A peer-to-peer electronic cash system* (Technical Report). Retrieved from http://www.bitcoin.org

Osipkov, I., Vasserman, E., Hopper, N., & Kim, Y. (2007). Combating double-spending using cooperative P2P systems. In *Proceedings of the 27th International Conference on Distributed Computing Systems, ICDCS'07*. Washington DC: IEEE CS Press.

Quercia, D., Hailes, S., & Capra, L. (2006). B-trust: Bayesian trust framework for pervasive computing. In *Trust Management: Proceedings of the 4th International Conference iTrust,* (LNCS), (pp. 298-312). New York: Springer.

Segala, R. (1995). *Modeling and verification of randomized distributed real-time systems*. (Ph.D. thesis). Laboratory for Computer Science, MIT, Cambridge, MA.

Seigneur, J.-M., Abendroth, J., & Jensen, C. D. (2002). Bank accounting and ubiquitous brokering of trustos. In *Proceedings of the 7th Cabernet Radicals Workshop*. Cabernet.

Smith, A. (1776). *An inquiry into the nature and causes of the wealth of nations*. London: Strahan and Cadell.

Srivastava, V., Neel, J., MacKenzie, A., Menon, R., DaSilva, L., Hicks, J., & Gilles, R. (2005). Using game theory to analyze wireless ad hoc networks. *Communications Surveys and Tutorials, 7*(4), 46–56. doi:10.1109/COMST.2005.1593279.

Stewart, W. J. (1994). *Introduction to the numerical solution of Markov chains*. Princeton, NJ: Princeton University Press.

Suryanarayana, G., & Taylo, R. N. (2004). *A survey of trust management and resource discovery technologies in peer-to-peer applications* (Technical Report UCI-ISR-04-6). Los Angeles, CA: University of California.

Theodorakopoulos, G., & Baras, J. (2006). On trust models and trust evaluation metrics for ad hoc networks. *Journal on Selected Areas in Communications, 24*(2), 318–328. doi:10.1109/JSAC.2005.861390.

ULOOP Consortium. (2013). *EU IST FP7 ULOOP: User-centric wireless local loop*. Retrieved from http://uloop.eu

Wei, K., Chen, Y.-F., Smith, A., & Vo, B. (2005). *WhoPay: A scalable and anonymous payment system for peer-to-peer environments* (Technical Report No. UCB/CSD-5-1386). University of California at Berkeley, Berkeley, CA.

Wei, L., Zhu, H., Cao, Z., & Shen, X. (2011). MobiID: A user-centric and social aware reputation based incentive scheme for delay/disruption tolerant networks. In *Proceedings of the International Conference on Ad Hoc Networks and Wireless,* (LNCS), (vol. 6811, pp. 177-190). New York: Springer.

Yang, B., & Garcia-Molina, H. (2003). PPay: Micropayments for peer-to-peer systems. In *Proceedings of the ACM Conference on Computer and Communications Security (CCS'03)* (pp. 300-310). New York: ACM Press.

Yang, M., Feng, Q., Dai, Y., & Zhang, Z. (2007). A multi-dimensional reputation system combined with trust and incentive mechanisms in P2P file sharing systems. In *Proceedings of the Distributed Computing Systems Workshops*. Washington, DC: IEEE CS Press.

Zhang, Y., Lin, L., & Huai, J. (2007). Balancing trust and incentive in peer-to-peer collaborative system. *Journal of Network Security, 5*, 73–81.

ADDITIONAL READING

Abrams, Z., McGrew, R., & Plotkin, S. (2005). A non-manipulable trust system based on Eigen-Trust. *ACM SIGecom Exchanges*, *5*(4), 21–30. doi:10.1145/1120717.1120721.

Aldini, A., & Bernardo, M. (2007). Mixing logics and rewards for the component-oriented specification of performance measures. *Theoretical Computer Science*, *382*, 3–23. doi:10.1016/j.tcs.2007.05.006.

Anderson, R., Manifavas, C., & Sutherland, C. (1996). Netcard—A practical electronic cash system. In *Proceedings of the Fourth Cambridge Workshop on Security Protocols*. IEEE.

Aringhieri, R., Damiani, E., De Capitani Di Vimercati, S., Paraboschi, S., & Samarati, P. (2006). Fuzzy techniques for trust and reputation management in anonymous peer-to-peer systems. *Journal of the American Society for Information Science and Technology*, *57*(4), 528–537. doi:10.1002/asi.20307.

Aziz, A., Sanwal, K., Singhal, V., & Brayton, R. (2000). Model checking continuous time Markov chains. *ACM Transactions on Computational Logic*, *1*(1), 162–170. doi:10.1145/343369.343402.

Bachmann, R., & Zaheer, A. (2006). *Handbook of trust research*. Cheltenham, UK: Edward Elgar Publishing.

Baier, C., Haverkort, B. R., Hermanns, H., & Katoen, J.-P. (2000). Model checking continuous-time Markov chains by transient analysis. In *Computer Aided Verification, (LNCS)* (Vol. 1855, pp. 358–372). New York: Springer. doi:10.1007/10722167_28.

Baier, C., Haverkort, B. R., Hermanns, H., & Katoen, J.-P. (2000). On the logical characterisation of performability properties. In *Automata, Languages, and Programming, (LNCS)* (Vol. 1853, pp. 780–792). New York: Springer. doi:10.1007/3-540-45022-X_65.

Cahill, V., Gray, E., Seigneur, J.-M., Jensen, C. D., Chen, Y., Shand, B., & Nielson, M. (2003). Using trust for secure collaboration in uncertain environments. *Pervasive Computing*, *2*(3), 52–61. doi:10.1109/MPRV.2003.1228527.

Carbone, M., Nielsen, M., & Sassone, V. (2003). A formal model for trust in dynamic networks. In *Proceedings of the 1st IEEE International Conference on Software Engineering and Formal Methods* (pp. 54-63). Washington, DC: IEEE CS Press.

Castelfranchi, C., & Falcone, R. (2001). Social trust: A cognitive approach. In *Trust and deception in virtual societies* (pp. 55–90). Kluwer Academic. doi:10.1007/978-94-017-3614-5.

Christianson, B., & Harbison, W. S. (1996). Why isn't trust transitive? In *Proceedings of the Security Protocols International Workshop*. University of Cambridge.

Clarke, E., Emerson, E., & Sistla, A. (1986). Automatic verification of finite-state concurrent systems using temporal logic specications. *ACM Transactions on Programming Languages and Systems*, *8*, 244–263. doi:10.1145/5397.5399.

Cohen, B. (2003). Incentives build robustness in BitTorrent. In Proceedings of P2P-Econ. P2P-Econ.

Feldman, M., Lai, K., & Zhang, L. (2005). A price-anticipating resource allocation mechanism for distributed shared clusters. In *Proceedings of the ACM E-Commerce Conference* (pp. 127-136). ACM.

Feller, W. (1968). *An introduction to probability theory and its applications*. New York: John Wiley & Sons.

Hardin, G. (1968). The tragedy of the commons. *Science*, *162*, 1243–1248. doi:10.1126/science.162.3859.1243 PMID:5699198.

Howard, R. A. (1971). Dynamic probabilistic systems: Vol. 1. *Markov models*. New York: John Wiley & Sons.

Jøsang, A. (2007). Probabilistic logic under uncertainty. In *Proceedings of Computing: The Australian Theory Symposium (CATS2007)* (Vol. 65). CRPIT.

Jøsang, A., & Lo Presti, S. (2004). Analyzing the relationship between risk and trust. In *Proceedings of the 2nd International Conference on Trust Management (iTrust'04)*, (LNCS), (pp. 135-145). New York: Springer.

Kim, T. K., & Seo, H. S. (2008). A trust model using fuzzy logic in wireless sensor network. *World Academy of Science. Engineering and Technology, 42*, 63–66.

Krukow, K., & Nielsen, M. (2006). From simulations to theorems: A position paper on research in the field of computational trust. In *Proceedings of the Workshop of Formal Aspects of Security and Trust (FAST 2006)*. FAST.

Kwiatkowska, M., Norman, G., & Parker, D. (2010). Advances and challenges of probabilistic model checking. In *Proceedings of the 48th Annual Allerton Conference on Communication, Control and Computing* (pp. 1691-1698). Washington, DC: IEEE CS Press.

Kwiatkowska, M., Norman, G., & Parker, D. (2011). PRISM 4.0: Verification of probabilistic real-time systems. In *Proceedings of the 23rd International Conference on Computer Aided Verification (CAV'11)*, (LNCS), (vol. 6806, pp. 585-591). New York: Springer.

Kwiatkowska, M., Parker, D., & Simaitis, A. (2013). Strategic analysis of trust models for user-centric networks. In *Proceedings of the 1st International Workshop on Strategic Reasoning (SR'13)*, (pp. 53-60). SR.

Levien, R. (2004). *Attack resistant trust metrics*. (PhD thesis). University of California at Berkeley, Berkeley, CA.

Lipton, R. J., & Ostrovsky, R. (1998). Micropayments via efficient coin-flipping. In Financial cryptography.

Ma, T. B., Lee, S. C. M., Lui, J. C. S., & Yau, D. K. Y. (2004). A game theoretic approach to provide incentive and service differentiation in P2P networks. In The ACM SIGMETRICS/PERFORMANCE (pp. 189-198). ACM.

Marmol, F. G., & Perez, G. M. (2011). Providing trust in wireless sensor networks using a bio-inspired technique. *Journal of Telecommunication Systems, 46*(2), 163–180. doi:10.1007/s11235-010-9281-7.

Marti, S. (2005). *Trust and reputation in peer-to-peer networks*. (PhD Thesis). Stanford University, Palo Alto, CA.

McMillan, K. L. (1993). *Symbolic model checking*. Dordrecht, The Netherlands: Kluwer Academic. doi:10.1007/978-1-4615-3190-6.

Micali, S., & Rivest, R. L. (2002). Micropayments revisited. In *Proceedings of CT-RSA*. CT-RSA.

Oualha, N., & Roudier, Y. (2006). *Cooperation incentive schemes* (Research Report RR-06-176). Eurecom.

Patel, J., Teacy, W. T., Jennings, N., & Luck, M. (2005). A probabilistic trust model for handling inaccurate reputation sources. In *Proceedings of the 3rd International Conference on Trust Management*, (LNCS), (vol. 3477, pp. 193-209). New York: Springer.

Ranganathan, K., Ripeanu, M., Sarin, A., & Foster, I. (2003). To share or not to share: An analysis of incentives to contribute in collaborative file sharing environments. In *Proceedings of the Workshop on Economics of Peer to Peer Systems* (pp. 13-18). IEEE.

Resnick, P., & Zeckhauser, R. (2002). Trust among strangers in internet transactions: Empirical analysis of Ebay's reputation system. In *The Economics of the Internet and E-Commerce*. London: Elsevier. doi:10.1016/S0278-0984(02)11030-3.

Sabater, J., & Sierra, C. (2002). Reputation and social network analysis in multi-agent systems. In *Proceedings of the First International Joint Conference on Autonomous Agents & Multiagent Systems (AAMAS)*. AAMAS.

Sabater, J., & Sierra, C. (2005). Review on computational trust and reputation models. *Artificial Intelligence Review*, *24*(1), 33–60. doi:10.1007/s10462-004-0041-5.

Seigneur, J.-M., & Jensen, C. (2004). Trading privacy for trust. In *Proceedings of the 2nd International Conference on Trust Management*, (LNCS), (vol. 2995, pp. 93-107). New York: Springer.

Srivatsa, M., Xiong, L., & Liu, L. (2005). TrustGuard: Countering vulnerabilities in reputation management for decentralized overlay networks. In *Proceedings of the 14th International Conference on World Wide Web* (pp. 422-431). IEEE.

Xiong, L., & Liu, L. (2004). Peertrust: Supporting reputation-based trust for peer-to-peer electronic communities. *IEEE Transactions on Knowledge and Data Engineering*, *16*, 843–857. doi:10.1109/TKDE.2004.1318566.

KEY TERMS AND DEFINITIONS

Cooperation Incentive: Distributed networks and systems require trust among entities and fairness of the respective contributions. Incentives to cooperate respond to these concerns and provide means to encourage collaboration and participation. Incentives can be intrinsic (e.g., social attitude to be involved in a community) or explicit (e.g., economical remuneration).

Markov Chain: It is a finite- (or countable-) state labeled transition system describing a random process characterized by the memoryless property, meaning that the next state depends only on the current state and not on the previous history that preceded the current state. The random state changes (i.e., the transitions) can model discrete steps from the viewpoint of the passage of time, in which case we talk about discrete-time Markov chains. Alternatively, rather than firing transitions at each discrete time step, we can make the system stay in the current state for some random amount of time, in which case we talk about continous-time Markov chains. The probability distributions modeling such a random amount of time are exponential as this kind of distribution satisfies the memoryless property. Whenever the system behavior is partly random and partly under the control of an external scheduler, then we talk about Markov Decision Processes.

Model Checking: It is an automatic technique for the design and verification of finite-state concurrent systems. The advantages over traditional approaches like testing and simulation are the formal base and the efficiency of the verification algorithms, which facilitate the application of model checking to several classes of systems, ranging from hardware controllers to communication protocols and software architectures.

Reputation: While trust is a subjective phenomenon based on personal experience, the concept of reputation can be viewed as a collective estimation of the trustworthiness about a certain entity deriving from referrals, recommendations, or ratings provided by other entities in the same community.

Temporal Logic: It is a logical formalism for describing sequences of transitions between states in a state-transition system, like a Markov chain or a finite-state automaton. The characterizing feature of temporal logics is the presence of modal operators that are used to express formally statements like "something will *eventually* happen", or "something cannot happen *until* a certain condition holds", or "something is *always* true". These operators can be combined with classical logical connectives to form the base for logics like Linear Temporal Logic (LTL) and Computation Tree Logic (CTL).

Trust System: In information technology, a trust system manages in a symbolic and computational way the notion of social trust arising from human interactions. The symbolic representation can be given in terms of credentials, while the computational trust derives from metrics resulting from automated decision-making processes.

Virtual Currency: It is also called virtual money to emphasize its use, which is devoted to the purchase of virtual goods in the framework of online communities, online gaming, and social networks. Usually, virtual currency is specific within each community and, analogously, the value of the purchased virtual goods is intangible outside the community.

APPENDIX: REVIEW QUESTIONS

1. What is soft security? [Hint: refer to Jøsang (2007)].
    a. Soft security is a lightweight cryptographic algorithm for protecting the real time transmission of multimedia over the Internet.
    b. Soft security is the collaborative enforcement of, and adherence to common ethical norms by participants in a community.
    c. Soft security is a set of relaxed security constraints.
    d. Soft security is a paradigm for the specification of security policies and the estimation of trust metrics.

2. Trust is:
    a. a transitive relation.
    b. the overall quality of an entity as perceived by community members in general.
    c. the result of a recommendation provided by the neighbouring nodes of a network.
    d. a directional relation between two parties denoting the reliability of one of the two parties as perceived by the other party with respect to a specific domain of actions.

3. Trust management cannot help to protect a community against:
    a. malicious nodes providing bad services whenever selected by specific users as service providers.
    b. a malicious collective made of colluding nodes influencing the reputation of a single user.
    c. a man-in-the-middle attack aiming at altering recommendations and feedback.
    d. the use of weak passwords and criptographic keys to protect sensitive data.

4. A property that a payment system for peer-to-peer environments cannot ensure is [Hint: refer to Wei et al. (2005)]:
    a. security of each coin, the value of which cannot be tampered with.
    b. anonimity of the payer and of the payee.
    c. trust towards the payer.
    d. transferability of coins, that is a earned coin can be spent without banking it.

5. Incentives to provide a reliable feedback:
    a. are not useful as trust management does not rely on feedback.
    b. can help to strengthen the quality of recommendations.
    c. are paid in terms of credit earnings.
    d. are given in terms of lower access cost to services.

6. Consider the piece of code [ ] x=0 -> (0.5):(x'=1) + (0.5):(x'=0);
    a. it subsumes a nondeterministic choice.
    b. it does not update variable x.
    c. it requires synchronization with an external module.
    d. either it updates x or it leaves x unchanged with equal probabilities.

7. Consider the logical formula R{"transmit"}max = ? [F (ack=true)]
    a. it computes the maximum number of states satisfying the boolean condition (ack=true).
    b. it computes the maximum probability of reaching a state satisfying the boolean condition (ack=true).
    c. it computes the maximum reward called transmit that is accumulated until a state satisfying the boolean condition (ack=true) is reached.
    d. it computes the maximum reward called transmit that is earned in states satisfying the boolean condition (ack=true).

8.   Transient state model checking with time limit t<100 can be applied to compute:
    a.   the truth value of a given formula on the long run.
    b.   the probability for a given state of being the current state at the instant of time t=101.
    c.   the minimum reward accumulated by the temporal limit t=100.
    d.   the number of paths that satisfy a given formula before 100 time units.

Answers: 1) a. 2) d. 3) d. 4) c. 5) b. 6) d. 7) c. 8) c.

Section 8
Wireless Network Management and Analysis

Chapter 19
Seamless Mobility Management:
A Need for Next Generation All-IP Wireless Networks

Sulata Mitra
Bengal Engineering and Science University, India

ABSTRACT

The next generation wireless networks will be heterogeneous wireless environments because of the coexistence of a large variety of wireless access technologies. The different networks have different architectures and protocols. So it is difficult for a user to roam from one radio system to another which can be solved by using the Internet protocol as a common interconnection protocol as it needs no assumptions about the characteristics of the underlying technologies. An all-IP wireless network is an IP-based wireless access system that makes wireless networks more robust, scalable, and cost effective. The nodes in such a network are mobile nodes as they change their location and point of attachment to the Internet frequently. The mobility management is an important research issue in an all-IP wireless network for providing seamless roaming facility to mobile nodes from one wireless system to another. The dynamic resource management is also required in this environment to ensure sufficient resource in the selected route for transmission or reception of the data packets during seamless roaming of the mobile nodes. This chapter is aimed at the researchers and the policy makers making them aware of the different means of mobility management and resource management for mobile nodes in all-IP wireless networks.

DOI: 10.4018/978-1-4666-4691-9.ch019

INTRODUCTION

In next generation wireless network, mobile users are capable of connecting to the core network through various heterogeneous wireless access networks, such as cellular network, wireless metropolitan area network, wireless local area network and ad hoc network. The next generation wireless network is expected to provide high bandwidth connectivity with guaranteed quality of service (QoS) to mobile users in a seamless manner; however, this desired function demands seamless coordination of the heterogeneous radio access network technologies. The integration of heterogeneous networks and technologies is a challenging problem mainly because of the following issues:

- **Access Technologies:** Different networks apply different radio technologies for the air interface.
- **Network Architectures and Protocols**: Different networks have different architectures and protocols for transport and routing, resource and mobility management.
- **Service Demands:** Mobile users demand different services with different resource and quality of service requirements.

To cope up with these heterogeneities a common interconnection protocol which makes no assumptions about the characteristics of the underlying technologies is required. The Internet protocol (IP) provides a universal network layer protocol for wireless packet networks, and is viewed as an attractive candidate to play the same role in wireless systems. An all-IP wireless network, i.e. IP-based wireless access and fixed core, could make wireless networks more robust, scalable and cost effective. It will also enable the applications and software technologies developed for wires IP networks to be used over wireless networks. An IP-enabled mobile device supporting multiple air interfaces could roam seamlessly among different wireless systems if IP is adopted as the common network layer protocol.

In the integrated scenario of radio access technologies, mobile terminals are allowed to seamlessly switch among various access networks and to be served at lower cost with better QoS. Although individual radio resource management schemes may work optimally within their respective radio access networks, they may not perform efficiently in next generation wireless network if different radio resource management schemes are not managed properly. Hence a major issue is how to jointly utilize the resources of the different radio access technologies in an efficient manner while achieving the desired QoS. Moreover wireless networks struggle with limited radio resources which intensifies the need for efficient resource management. The goal of efficient resource management is to achieve maximum radio resource utilization while providing a desired level of QoS to users.

Hence integration and interoperation of heterogeneous resource management mechanisms is of parameter importance for seamless roaming. Two schemes are elaborated in this chapter. Scheme_I (Mitra, 2008) is a dynamic mobility management scheme whereas Scheme_II (Mitra, 2008) is a dynamic resource management scheme in all-IP wireless network. Both the schemes consider an integrated architecture as shown in Figure 1. It is an integration of cellular network and wireless local area network (WLAN) to exploit the seamless roaming support of cellular network and high data rate of WLAN. WLAN found its application as a low cost high speed solution to cover the hot spot like Internet cafe, office building, apartment building etc., to solve the wideband data access problem and to utilize the existing infrastructure which helps to reduce the implementation cost of the network. On the other hand, cellular network has the excellence of wide coverage, seamless roaming support and better QoS.

The integration of cellular network and WLAN form a heterogeneous wireless networks environment in Figure 1. The global mobility agent (GMA)

Figure 1. Integrated architecture

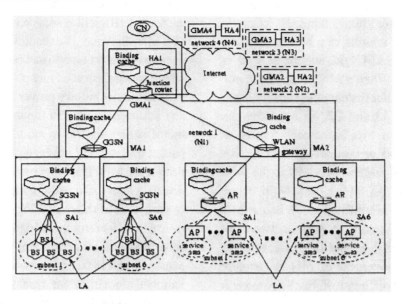

is the integration point of cellular network and WLAN. Each wireless network is considered as an individual domain having mobility agent (MA) at the root level, subnet agent (SA) at the intermediate level and local agent (LA) at the leaf level. MA1 is the mobility agent of cellular domain and MA2 is the mobility agent of WLAN domain. The MA is gateway general packet radio system (GPRS) support node (GGSN) for cellular network and gateway for WLAN. The SA is serving GPRS support node (SGSN) for cellular network and access router (AR) for WLAN. The LA is base station (BS) for cellular network and access point (AP) for WLAN. GMAs are MIPv6 nodes having 128 bit IP address. The home agent (HA) is a router located in the home network of a MN. It acts on behalf of the MN from the home link. M_1 is a MN in the coverage area of the LA B. A MN moves through different networks with seamless connectivity. A MN notifies it's HA on its home link after leaving its home link and entering into a new network. In Figure 1 HA1 is the home agent in network 1 (N1). The correspondent node (CN) is a node that can communicate with a MN through Internet.

Both the schemes consider the IP address of the various components (MA, SA, LA, MN) of a network in the dotted decimal format. The network 1 is identified as N1. GMA1 in N1 has IP address N1.0.0.0.0. The cellular (WLAN) domain is identified as MA1 (MA2). The IP address of MA1 (MA2) in N1 is N1.MA1.0.0.0 (N1.MA2.0.0.0). In N1 under the control of domain MA1, each SGSN say S, each BS say B and each MN say M has IP address N1.MA1.S.0.0, N1.MA1.S.B.0 and N1.MA1.S.B.M respectively whereas under the control of domain MA2, each AR say S2, each AP say B3 and each MN say M has IP address N1.MA2.S2.0.0, N1.MA2.S2.B3.0 and N1.MA2. S2.B3.M respectively. LCoA is the local care of address (CoA) of MN in the form LA_id.MN_id, where LA_id is LA identification and MN_id is MN identification. In case a MN moves from one LA to other LA under the coverage area of the same SA LA_id part of its LCoA changes. Such a movement of MN is formally known as intra subnet handoff. SCoA is the subnet care of address of a MN in the form SA_id.LA_id.MN_id, where SA_id is SA identification. In case a MN moves from one SA to other SA under the coverage area of the same MA both SA_id and

LA_id change. Such a movement of MN is formally known as inter subnet handoff. RCoA is the regional care of address of a MN in the form MA_id.SA_id.LA_id.MN_id, where MA_id is MA identification. When a MN moves from one MA to other MA under the coverage area of same GMA MA_id, SA_id and LA_id need change. Such a movement of MN is formally known as inter domain handoff or vertical handoff. GCoA is the global care of address of a MN in the form of GMA_id.MA_id.SA_id.LA_id.MN_id, where GMA_id is GMA identification. When a MN moves from one network to other network all GMA_id, MA_id, SA_id and LA_id need to be changed. Such a movement of MN is formally known as inter network handoff. Each component of a network maintains a binding cache (BC) to store the CoA of the MNs within its coverage area.

Scheme_I supports seamless roaming facility of MNs in all-IP wireless network. It assigns an IP address to a MN during its initial registration phase in the network. The MN is able to roam across any other network without any interruption in transmission or reception and without any change in future IP address during handoff. No handoff registration is required from a MN which helps to reduce the overhead in terms of power consumption of the mobile unit, location update cost, delay, and packet loss. Moreover, two separate interfaces are not required at a MN to access the cellular and WLAN domain which helps to reduce the complexity of the mobile unit. It selects a route after receiving any transmission or reception request from a MN assuming that all the components of the network (GMA, MA, SA, LA) has sufficient resource to establish the route. But during seamless roaming a MN must be able to transmit or receive packets without any packet loss and considerable delay. Moreover the transmission or reception of the packets of a MN must be over within its battery power life time. It needs the selection of an optimal route having sufficient resource for satisfying such QoS requirement of the MNs. So Scheme_I is extended in Scheme_II in which

dynamic resource management is considered for ensuring sufficient resource in the selected route of a MN. Scheme_II executes route selection algorithm to select an optimal route for a MN using which transmission or reception of the packets is over within its battery power life time. In case of any additional delay in the existing route, route modification algorithm modifies it to reduce the packet loss and the wastage of battery power life time of the MN. The route modification algorithm selects a new route using which the transmission or reception of the remaining packets of a MN is over within its remaining battery power life time. A vertical handoff controller (VHC) is maintained at each GMA to trigger network initiated vertical handoff algorithm for transferring an existing route from one domain to another domain in case the power consumption of the domain having the existing route crosses a threshold. This algorithm balances the effective load among the two domains. It triggers vertical handoff dynamically depending upon the network condition. As the effective load of the two domains remain balanced by this algorithm, the average value of the delay, cost, packet loss and throughput of the network remain almost constant. Both the schemes consider the transmission or reception of two classes of traffic (voice and data) having identical priority.

BACKGROUND

Several integration architectures have been proposed so far. A radio resource management architecture and algorithms for integrated radio access technologies are proposed in (Chiron, 2008; Cui, 2009). The proposed architecture can be categorized as network-centric, user-centric and hybrid architectures. The proposed integrated inter-system architecture in (Christian, 2008) guarantees seamless roaming and service continuity. It enables the integration and interworking of current wireless systems. It also supports user mobility management while roaming among access networks. A cooperative framework based on distributed joint radio resource management is proposed in (Hamed, 2011). The concept of producer-consumer interaction in a market place is emphasized in (Hamed, 2011) to satisfy the requirement of operators and users. The joint radio resource management architecture in (Ibrahim, 2009) provides efficient resource management in heterogeneous access network. By jointly managing system resources, resource managers of all networks are capable of achieving optimum resource allocation in both centralized and distributed manner. But no specific user requirements are stressed in the proposed scheme.

A dynamic QoS based bandwidth allocation is proposed in (Esmailpour, 2011) to support heterogeneous traffic with different QoS requirements in worldwide interoperability for microwave access networks (WiMAX). The allocated bandwidth is dynamically adjusted for ongoing and new arrival connections based on traffic characteristics and service demand for maximizing the system capacity. A distributed multi-service resource allocation algorithm for constant bit rate and variable bit rate services in a heterogeneous wireless access environment is presented in (Ismail, 2012). The utility function of each individual access system is defined and the utility maximization problem is solved optimally for resource allocation in a distributed manner. A novel economic model of radio resource allocation for both code-division multiple-access network and wireless local area network are considered in (Pei, 2010). The problem of radio resource allocation for both networks is formulated as the network welfare maximization issue. A joint access control strategy is designed for achieving efficient resource sharing and load balancing. A utility-based bandwidth allocation algorithm is proposed in (Luo, 2009). It considers the utility fairness within the wireless access networks and among different access networks.

The utility optimization of individual access networks and the problem of joint network performance optimization are considered in the previous works for achieving cooperative service providing scenario. But though the competition among the service providers is considered, the QoS requirements of users and the competition of users within the access network are not fully considered.

Unlike the previous schemes the schemes in the proposed chapter minimize the delay and packet loss during transmission or reception of the packets by a MN while roaming. It ensures sufficient resource in the selected route for a MN during its seamless roaming so that the transmission or reception of the packets is over within the stipulated time. It helps to reduce the frequency of vertical handoff and hence the possibility of packet loss due to handoff.

DESCRIPTION OF SCHEMES

Scheme_I: Dynamic Mobility Management Scheme

It is a dynamic mobility management scheme (Mitra, 2008) for next generation all-IP wireless network. The mobility management of ith MN (MN_id=M_i) is considered for discussion in this section.

Mobility Management

Let M_i is in the coverage area of LA identified as B which is in the coverage area of SA say S, MA say MA1 and GMA say GMA1 in the network N1. A route is selected from M_i to CN (CN to M_i) after receiving a transmission (reception) request from M_i. The route of transmission (reception) is M_i->B->S->MA1->GMA1 (GMA1->MA1->S->B->M_i). The identification of the selected route is assumed as identical to MN_id. So the selected route is identified as M_i. GMA1, MA1, S, B are the nodes associated with the route M_i. All the nodes associated with the selected route stores the route identification number (r_id) M_i in memory. S, MA1, GMA1 and HA bind new LCoA ($B.M_i$), SCoA ($S.B.M_i$), RCoA ($MA1.S.B.M_i$) and GCoA ($GMA1.MA1.S.B.M_i$) of M_i respectively in BC. HA sends the binding update of M_i to CN so that CN can send the packets of M_i directly to GMA1 and GMA1 delivers the packets of M_i at its original destination address within N1.

Now let M_i enters into the coverage area of a new LA identified as B1 after handoff. B1 sends M_i as the route identification number to its parent SA (P_{SA}). P_{SA} searches its memory for the route identification number M_i among the existing routes. If found P_{SA} is the SA which is associated with the existing route M_i and so it is identical to S (parent of B). So M_i enters into the LA B1 after handoff from the LA B. As both B and B1 are under the coverage area of the same SA S the handoff of M_i is intra subnet type and the transmission of the route identification (r_id) number from B1 to P_{SA} is considered as the transmission of intra subnet message. S modifies the existing route as M_i->B1->S->MA1->GMA1->CN (CN->GMA1->MA1->S->B1->M_i) (i.e. B1 is under the coverage area of SA S which is in the network N1 and domain MA1) and the route is identified as M_i. As the handoff is intra subnet type so the LA_id changes and S binds new LCoA ($B1.M_i$) of M_i in BC.

Otherwise P_{SA} is not associated with the existing route M_i and so it is a new SA say S1. S1 sends M_i as route identification number to its parent MA (P_{MA}). P_{MA} searches its memory for the route identification number M_i among the existing routes. If found P_{MA} is the MA which is associated with the existing route M_i and so it is identical to MA1 (parent of S). So M_i enters into the LA B1 which is under the coverage area of SA S1, MA MA1 and GMA GMA1 after handoff from LA B. As both B and B1 are under the coverage area of the same MA but different SA, the handoff of M_i is inter subnet type and the transmission of the route identification number from B1 to P_{MA} through S1 is considered as the transmission of inter subnet message. MA1 modifies the existing

route as M_i->B1->S1->MA1->GMA1->CN (CN->GMA1->MA1->S1->B1->M_i) (i.e. B1 is under the coverage area of SA S1 which is in the network N1 and domain MA1) and the route is identified as M_i. As handoff is inter subnet type so both LA_id and SA_id change. S1 and MA1 bind new LCoA ($B1.M_i$) and SCoA ($S1.B1.M_i$) of M_i in BC.

Otherwise P_{MA} is not associated with the existing route M_i and so it is a new MA MA2. MA2 sends M_i as route identification number to its parent GMA (P_{GMA}). P_{GMA} searches its memory for the route identification number M_i among the existing routes. If found P_{GMA} is the GMA which is associated with the existing route M_i and so it is identical to GMA1 (parent of MA1). So M_i enters into the LA B1 which is under the coverage area of SA S1, MA MA2 and GMA GMA1. As both B and B1 are under the coverage area of the same GMA but different MA, the handoff of M_i is inter domain type and the transmission of the route identification number from B1 to P_{GMA} through S1 and MA2 is considered as the transmission of inter domain message. GMA1 modifies the existing route as M_i->B1->S1->MA2->GMA1->CN (CN->GMA1->MA2->S1->B1->M_i) (i.e. B1 is under the coverage area of SA S1 which is in the network N1 and domain MA2) and the route is identified as M_i. As the handoff is inter domain type so the LA_id, SA_id and MA_id need change. S1, MA2 and GMA1 bind new LCoA ($B1.M_i$), SCoA ($S1.B1.M_i$) and RCoA ($MA2.S1.B1.M_i$) of M_i in BC.

Otherwise, P_{GMA} is not associated with the existing route M_i and so it is a new GMA say GMA2 (Figure 1) in network 2 (N2). So B1 is in the coverage area of SA S1 MA MA2 and GMA GMA2. As B and B1 are under the coverage area of different network, the handoff of M_i is inter network type. GMA2 sends a message to M_i through MA2, S1 and B1. In response M_i sends a message containing the encrypted version of encryption/decryption key to HA through B1, S1, MA2, GMA2. In case of valid encryption/decryption key, HA sends a positive acknowledgement to GMA2, GMA2 sends a positive acknowledgement to B1 through MA2 and S1. GMA2 also stores the encrypted message of M_i in memory to verify its authentication in case of any future inter domain handoff of M_i. GMA2 sends GMA2.MA2.S1.B1. M_i as GCoA of M_i to HA. A route is established as $M_i{-}{>}B1{-}{>}S1{-}{>}MA2{-}{>}GMA2{-}{>}CN$ $(CN{-}{>}GMA2{-}{>}MA2{-}{>}S1{-}{>}B1{-}{>}M_i)$ and the route is identified as M_i. As the handoff is inter network type so all LA_id, SA_id, MA_id and GMA_id need to be changed. S1, MA2, GMA2 and HA bind new LCoA (B1.M_i), SCoA (S1.B1.M_i), RCoA (MA2.S1.B1.M_i) and GCoA (GMA2.MA2.S1.B1.M_i) of M_i in BC. HA sends the binding update of M_i to CN.

Theoretical Analysis

In this section the expression for location update cost (LUC), handoff latency, and packet loss per traffic class are presented.

LUC per Network per Second

The LUC per network per second is the summation of the LUC due to intra subnet, inter subnet, and inter domain handoff. The LUC for each type of handoff in a network is the product of the length of wireless message (wire_mess) requires to exchange in bits and cost per bit. The length of wire_mess in bits for each type of handoff in a network is shown in a tabular form (*Table 1*).

In case of 100000 MNs, the number of bits require to represent a MN (MN_BIT) is 17. So the number of bits per intra subnet handoff message (NO_OF_BIT$_{intra\_mess}$), inter subnet handoff message (NO_OF_BIT$_{inter\_mess}$) and inter domain handoff message (NO_OF_BIT$_{domain\_mess}$) are 17, 34, and 51 respectively.

Now MA crossing rate (R_D) is the ratio of SA crossing rate (R_S) to the number of SAs per MA (NO_OF_SA$_{MA}$) and SA crossing rate is the ratio of LA crossing rate (R_L) to the number of LAs per

Table 1. Length of wire_mess in bits for each type of handoff

Type of handoff	Number of bits in wire_mess
Intra subnet	MN_BIT (new LA->old SA i.e. B1->S)
Inter subnet	2*MN_BIT (new LA->new SA->old MA i.e. B1->S1->MA1)
Inter domain	3*MN_BIT (new LA->new SA->new MA->old GMA i.e. B1->S1->MA2->GMA1)

SA (NO_OF_LA$_{SA}$). So $R_D = R_S/NO\_OF\_SA_{MA}$, $R_S = R_L/NO\_OF\_LA_{SA}$. The total number of handoff per second is $R_L + R_S + R_D$ and LUC per second is

$$[(R_L * NO\_OF\_BIT_{intra\_mess}) + (R_S * NO\_OF\_BIT_{inter\_mess}) + (R_D * NO\_OF\_BIT_{domain\_mess})] * cost/bit \tag{1}$$

Dolay in Handoff per Network per Second

The delay per network per second is the summation of the delay due to intra subnet, inter subnet, and inter domain handoff. The delay for each type of handoff in a network is the product of the length of wire_mess requires to exchange in bits and time per bit.

$$Delay = [(R_L * NO\_OF\_BIT_{intra\_mess}) + (R_S * NO\_OF\_BIT_{inter\_mess}) + (R_D * NO\_OF\_BIT_{domain\_mess})] * time/bit. \tag{2}$$

Considering wireless network data rate as 30 kbps (http://www.computerworld.com/mobiletopics/mobile/technology/story/0,10801,87486,00. html http://www.ee.latrobe.edu.au/mf/EL-E52PMC/Lectures/PMC-06.ppt)

$$Delay = [(R_L * NO\_OF\_BIT_{intra\_mess}) + (R_S * NO\_OF\_BIT_{inter\_mess}) + (R_D * NO\_OF\_BIT_{domain\_mess})]/30\,msec$$

Packet Loss per Handoff

The time required to sense intra subnet handoff by SA (intra_sub_time) is $(NO\_OF\_BIT_{intra\_mess})/30$ msec, inter subnet handoff by MA (inter_sub_time) is $(NO\_OF\_BIT_{inter\_mess})/30$ msec and inter domain handoff by GMA (inter_domain_time) is $(NO\_OF\_BIT_{domain\_mess})/30$ msec.

The transmission time of a voice (data) packet is the ratio of the length of voice (data) packet in bits to time/bit. So it is $L_{vo}/30$ $(L_d/30)$ msec, where L_{vo} is the length of voice packet and L_d is the length of data packet.

The loss of voice (data) packet per intra subnet, inter subnet and inter domain handoff are loss_voice$_{intra\_sub}$ (loss_data$_{intra\_sub}$), loss_voice$_{inter\_sub}$ (loss_data$_{inter\_sub}$) and loss_voice$_{inter\_domain}$ (loss_data$_{inter\_domain}$) respectively. So

$$loss\_voice_{intra\_sub}=(NO\_OF\_BIT_{intra\_mess}/L_{vo}). \quad (3)$$

$$loss\_voice_{inter\_sub}=(NO\_OF\_BIT_{inter\_mess}/L_{vo}) \quad (4)$$

$$loss\_voice_{inter\_domain}=(NO\_OF\_BIT_{domain\_mess}/L_{vo}). \quad (5)$$

$$loss\_data_{intra\_sub}=(NO\_OF\_BIT_{intra\_mess}/L_d) \quad (6)$$

$$loss\_data_{inter\_sub}=(NO\_OF\_BIT_{inter\_mess}/L_d) \quad (7)$$

$$loss\_data_{inter\_domain}=(NO\_OF\_BIT_{domain\_mess}/L_d). \quad (8)$$

Packet Loss per Network per Second Due to Handoff

Loss of packets in bits per network per second due to handoff may be calculated as the product of packet flow rate (PFR) and delay. The loss of voice (data) packets due to delay in handoff is loss$_{voice}$ (loss$_{data}$). It is calculated as the ratio of the product of PFR and delay to the length of voice (data) packet in bits.

$$So\ loss_{voice}=(PFR*Delay)/L_{vo} \quad (9)$$

$$loss_{data}=(PFR*Delay)/L_d \quad (10)$$

Performance Analysis

In this section the performance of Scheme_I is evaluated numerically.

In the proposed scheme NO_OF_SA$_{MA}$ and NO_OF_LA$_{SA}$ are assumed as 10-30. R_L is assumed as 10. L_{vo} is in the range 560-640 bits and L_d is in the range 8000-12000 bits. The cost/bit is assumed as 1 unit. The number of MNs per domain is assumed as 100000 and PFR varies from 5-15 kbps.

LUC and Delay per network per second are calculated using Equation (1) and Equation (2) respectively for different values of NO_OF_SA$_{MA}$, NO_OF_LA$_{SA}$, R_S, and R_D. The results are shown in Table 2 for R_L=10.

LUC and Delay per network per second is shown in Table 3 for NO_OF_SA$_{MA}$=20, R_S var-

Table 2. LUC and Delay per network per second

NO_OF_SA$_{MA}$	NO_OF_LA$_{SA}$	R_S	R_D	LUC	Delay
10	20	0.5	0.05	189.55	6.3183
20	20	0.5	0.025	188.275	6.2758
30	20	0.5	0.0166	187.85	6.2616
10	10	1	0.1	209.1	6.97
10	20	0.5	0.05	189.55	6.3183
10	30	0.3333	0.0333	183.03	6.101

Table 3. LUC and Delay per network per second

R_S	R_L	R_D	LUC	Delay
1	20	0.05	376.55	12.551
2	40	0.1	753.1	25.103
3	60	0.15	1129.65	37.655
4	80	0.2	1506.2	50.206
5	100	0.25	1882.75	62.758
6	120	0.3	2259.3	75.31
7	140	0.35	2635.85	87.8616
8	160	0.4	3012.4	100.413
9	180	0.45	3388.95	112.965
10	200	0.5	3765.5	125.516

ies from 1 – 10, and $NO\_OF\_LA_{SA}$=20. LUC and Delay per network per second is also shown in Table 4 for R_L=20, $NO\_OF\_LA_{SA}$=20, R_S=1, and $NO\_OF\_SA_{MA}$ varies from 5 – 50.

Packet loss per traffic class per handoff is calculated using Equation (3) to (8) for $NO\_OF\_BIT_{intra\_mess}$=17, L_{vo}=600 bits, L_d=9600 bits. $NO\_OF\_BIT_{inter\_mess}$=34, and $NO\_OF\_BIT_{domain\_mess}$=51. The results are shown in Table 5.

The loss of voice and data packet per network per second is calculated using Equation (9) and

Table 4. LUC and Delay per network per second

$NO\_OF\_SA_{MA}$	R_D	LUC	Delay
5	0.2	384.2	12.806
10	0.1	379.1	12.636
15	0.066	377.4	12.58
20	0.05	376.55	12.551
25	0.04	376.04	12.534
30	0.0333	375.7	12.523
35	0.0285	375.46	12.515
40	0.025	375.275	12.509
45	0.0222	375.133	12.504
50	0.02	375	12.5

Table 5. Packet loss per traffic class per handoff

$loss\_voice_{intra\_sub}$	0.028
$loss\_voice_{inter\_sub}$	0.056
$loss\_voice_{inter\_domain}$	0.085
$loss\_data_{intra\_sub}$	0.0018
$loss\_data_{inter\_sub}$	0.0035
$loss\_data_{inter\_domain}$	0.0053

Equation (10) respectively assuming L_{vo}=600 bits and L_d=9600 bits. The computation is performed for different values of PFR and Delay. The results are shown in Table 6 for voice packet loss and Table 7 for data packet loss respectively.

From Table 2 it can be observed that when $NO\_OF\_SA_{MA}$ increases with constant $NO\_OF\_LA_{SA}$, R_D reduces and hence LUC as well as Delay reduces. But when $NO\_OF\_LA_{SA}$ increases with constant $NO\_OF\_SA_{MA}$, both R_S and R_D reduce which causes more reduction in LUC as well as delay.

From Table 3 it can be observed that when R_S increases with constant $NO\_OF\_SA_{MA}$ and $NO\_OF\_LA_{SA}$, R_L and R_D increase which causes increase in LUC and Delay.

From Table 4 it can be observed that when $NO\_OF\_SA_{MA}$ increases with constant R_L and $NO\_OF\_LA_{SA}$, R_D reduces which causes decrease in LUC and Delay.

From Table 5 it can be observed that the loss of voice (data) packet for each intra subnet, inter subnet, and inter domain handoff is a fraction of one packet. To avoid packet loss during handoff of M_i, SA for intra subnet, MA for inter subnet, and GMA for inter domain handoff retransmits the last packet of M_i to CN in case of transmission and

Table 6. Voice packet loss per network per second

Delay	PFR=5	PFR=10	PFR=15
6.101	0.0508	0.1016	0.1525
6.2616	0.0521	0.1043	0.1565
6.2758	0.0522	0.1045	0.1568
6.3183	0.0526	0.1053	0.1579
6.97	0.0580	0.1161	0.1742

Table 7. Data packet loss per network per second

Delay	PFR=5	PFR=10	PFR=15
6.101	0.00317	0.00635	0.00953
6.2616	0.003261	0.00652	0.00978
6.2758	0.003268	0.00653	0.00980
6.3183	0.00329	0.00658	0.00987
6.97	0.00363	0.00726	0.01089

to M_i in case of reception. To avoid packet loss in case of transmission during inter network handoff of M_i, LA stores the packets transmitted by M_i in a buffer after detecting M_i as a new MN within its coverage area and sends those packets to CN after establishing the route. In case of reception, M_i sends the sequence number (SN) of the last received packet to HA so that CN can send the rest of the packets of M_i starting from SN+1 directly to the new GMA after establishing the route.

From Table 6 and Table 7 it can be observed that the loss of voice (data) packets per network per second increases with Delay and PFR.

The performance of the proposed scheme is compared with the schemes described in (Chakraborty, 2004; Dommety, 2001; Montavont, 2002; Johnson, 2001; Soliman, 2001; Misra, 2005) on the basis of LUC as well as packet loss and is summarized in Table 8.

Scheme_II: Dynamic Resource Management Scheme

It is a dynamic resource management scheme (Mitra, 2008) for next generation all-IP wireless network. It selects an optimal route after receiving a route request message (Route request message) from a MN. A MN sends this message to its current LA for transmission or reception of its packets.

The selection of optimal route depends upon the availability of resource at various nodes associated with the route. If more than one MN send route request message to the same LA in WLAN domain simultaneously, LA arranges the MNs in the descending order of their amount of data in a queue (MN_QUEUE$_{rrm}$) and triggers route selection algorithm for the MN having lot of data due to low cost, high speed and high bandwidth of WLAN domain. Such consideration helps to minimize the frequency of vertical handoff from WLAN domain to cellular domain.

If more than one MN send route request message to the same LA in cellular domain simultaneously, LA arranges the MNs in the ascending order of their amount of data in MN_QUEUE$_{rrm}$ and triggers route selection algorithm for the MN having little amount of data due to high cost and low bandwidth of cellular domain.

It modifies an existing route after receiving a MN initiated message from a MN. A MN sends this message to its current LA when its remaining battery power life time becomes equal to a threshold. If more than one MN send MN initiated message to the same LA in WLAN or cellular domain simultaneously, LA arranges the MNs in the ascending order of their remaining battery power life time in a queue (MN_QUEUE$_{mim}$) and

Table 8. Comparison of Scheme_I and other schemes

Reference	PFR	Packet Loss
(Chakraborty, 2004)	0.1-30	0-20 kbytes
(Dommety, 2001;Montavont, 2002)	0.1-30	0-170 kbytes
Scheme_I	1-30	1.27104-43.5624 bits
Reference	**SA per MA**	**LUC (units)**
(Chakraborty, 2004)	5-50	2000
(Dommety, 2001;Montavont, 2002)	5-50	50000
Scheme_I	5-50	375-384.2
Reference	R_s	**LUC (units)**
(Johnson, 2001)	1-10	1500000-7000000
(Soliman, 2001)	1-10	1000000-1200000
(Misra, 2005)	1-10	1000000-1100000
Scheme_I	1-10	376.55-3765.5

triggers route modification algorithm for MN having minimum battery power life time.

The priority of MN initiated message is assumed as higher than the priority of route request message in order to complete an ongoing transmission before initiating a new transmission. Figure 2 shows the existing route in each domain of network N1.

Each node in Figure 2 maintains a list (NODE_LIST) of records in memory. Each record in NODE_LIST contains 5 attributes as Route, route identification (r_id), number of packets (n_pac), packet size (p_sz), data rate (d_r). The NODE_LIST maintains by node 0 in Figure 2 is shown in Table 9.

As the routes specified in row R1, R2, R3, R4, R5 of Table 9 pass through node 1 in Figure 2, NODE_LIST at node 1 is identical to the rows R1, R2, R3, R4 and R5 of Table 9.

As the routes specified in row R6, R7 of Table 9 pass through node 2 in Figure 2, NODE_LIST at node 2 is identical to the rows R6 and R7 of Table 9.

As the routes specified in row R1, R2, R3 of Table 9 pass through node 11 in Figure 2, NODE_LIST at node 11 is identical to the rows R1, R2 and R3 of Table 9.

As the routes specified in row R4, R5 of Table 9 pass through node 12 in Figure 2, NODE_LIST at node 12 is identical to the rows R4 and R5 of Table 9.

Figure 2. Existing routes in each domain

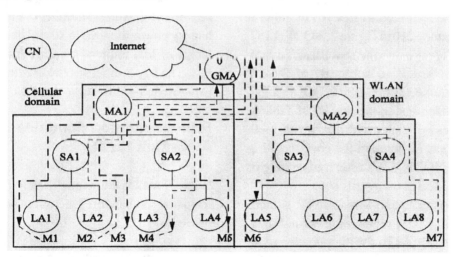

Table 9. NODE_LIST at node 0 in Figure 2

Row	Route	r_id	n_pac	p_sz	d_r
R1	0->1->11->110->M1	M_1	TP_1	P_1	d_1
R2	M2->111->11->1->0	M_2	TP_2	P_2	d_2
R3	0->1->11->111->M3	M_3	TP_3	P_3	d_3
R4	M4->120->12->1->0	M_4	TP_4	P_4	d_4
R5	0->1->12->121->M5	M_5	TP_5	P_5	d_5
R6	0->2->21->210->M6	M_6	TP_6	P_6	d_6
R7	M7->221->22->2->0	M_7	TP_7	P_7	d_F

As the route specified in row R6 of Table 9 passes through node 21 in Figure 2, NODE_LIST at node 21 is identical to the row R6 of Table 9.

As the route specified in row R7of Table 9 passes through node 22 in Figure 2, NODE_LIST at node 22 is identical to the row R7 of Table 9.

As the route specified in row R1of Table 9 passes through node 110 in Figure 2, NODE_LIST at node 110 is identical to the row R1 of Table 9.

As the routes specified in row R2, R3 of Table 9 pass through node 111 in Figure 2, NODE_LIST at node 111 is identical to the rows R2 and R3 of Table 9.

As the route specified in row R4 of Table 9 passes through node 120 in Figure 2, NODE_LIST at node 120 is identical to the row R4 of Table 9.

As the route specified in row R5 of Table 9 passes through node 121 in Figure 2, NODE_LIST at node 121 is identical to the row R5 of Table 9.

As the route specified in row R6 of Table 9 passes through node 210 in Figure 2, NODE_LIST at node 210 is identical to the row R6 of Table 9.

As the route specified in row R7 of Table 9 passes through node 221 in Figure 2, NODE_LIST at node 221 is identical to the row R7 of Table 9.

All the nodes associated with a particular route modify the n_pac attribute in the corresponding record in their NODE_LIST after transmitting or receiving each packet using this route.

Let M_1 in Figure 2 wants to receive TP_1 number of packets from CN. It sends route request message to its current LA (B) for the selection of an optimal route. The route request message of M_1 contains 4 tuple as MN_id (MN_id=M_1), p_sz=P_1, n_pac=TP_1 and d_r=d_1. In case of 100000 MNs, the number of bits requires to represent MN_id is 17. So the number of bits requires to represent M_1 is 17. The requested packet size of each MN is assumed as 600 bits for voice and 9600 bits for data. So the maximum number of bits requires to represent packet size is 10 for voice and 14 for data. The requested data rate of each MN can be one of the values from the set (64 kbps, 128 kbps, 256 kbps). So the maximum possible data rate is 256 kbps and the number of bits requires to represent data rate is 8. So the length of route request message (rrm_bit$_1$) is $35+\log_2 TP_1$ bits for voice packet and $39+\log_2 TP_1$ bits for data packet. The LA B selects an optimal route which passes through the nodes GMA1 (GMA_id=0), MA1 (MA_id=1), S (SA_id=11) and B (LA_id=110) in the network N1 using route selection algorithm as shown in Figure 2. The route is identified (r_id) as M_1.

Let M_1 receives N_1 number of packets using the selected route and then finds that its remaining battery power life time becomes equal to a threshold. So M_1 sends MN initiated message for the reception of TP_1-N_1 number of packets to its current LA (B). The MN initiated message of M_1 contains remaining battery power life time information. In the proposed scheme the initial battery power life time (life_time) is considered as 0.6×10^6 sec. So the maximum number of bits to represent battery power life time is 20 and hence for M_1 the length of MN initiated message (mim_bit$_1$) is 20 bits. The LA B modifies the existing route of M_1 using route modification algorithm.

Route Selection (Modification) Algorithm for M_1

B calls route selection (modification) algorithm by triggering no handoff function to select (modify) the route.

- **Condition for Route Selection (Modification):** The condition for selecting the route M_1 is desire_BW$_1 \leq$f_BW and $D\_q_1+d_{avg\_1}+r\_s\_time_1+r\_d\_time_1 \leq$life_time. The condition for modifying the route M_1 is desire_BW$_1 \leq$f_BW and $D\_q_1+d_{avg\_1}+r\_m\_time_1+r\_d\_time_1 \leq r_1$.

desire_BW$_1$ is the desired bandwidth of M_1 to receive TP_1 number of packets in case of route selection and TP_1-N_1 number of packets in case of route modification. It is computed as $d_1/2$ by the concept of sampling theorem.

f_BW is the free bandwidth at LA that executes the algorithm.

D_q_1 is the waiting delay of M_1 in MN_QUEUE$_{rrm}$ (MN_QUEUE$_{mim}$) after sending route request message (MN initiated message).

d_{avg_1} is the average delay of the route M_1 due to network congestion if any.

$r\_s\_time_1$ is the selection time of route M_1.

$r\_d\_time_1$ is the duration time of the route M_1 to complete the reception of TP_1 number of packets in case of route selection and TP_1-N_1 number of packets in case of route modification. It is computed as $(TP_1*P_1)/d_1$ in case of route selection and $(TP_1-N_1)*P_1/d_1$ in case of route modification.

$r\_m\_time_1$ is the modification time of the route M_1.

r_1 is the remaining battery power life time of M_1.

- **No Handoff Function:** This function searches NODE_LIST of B to compute f_BW at B. It also computes desire_BW$_1$. This function verifies the condition of route selection (modification) at B. If the condition is true, it sends route request message (MN initiated message) of M_1 to GMA1 through S and MA1 to select (modify) the route CN->GMA1->MA1->S->B->M_1. The r_s1 (u_i1) function is used for inserting (modifying) the record of the route M_1 in NODE_LIST maintained by all the nodes associated with the selected (modified) route. All the nodes associated with the selected (modified) route compute $r\_d\_time_1$.

- **r_s1 Function:** After selecting the route M_1 the nodes GMA1, MA1, S and B insert record in their NODE_LIST as Route=CN->GMA1->MA1->S->B->M_1, r_id=M_1, p_sz=P_1, n_pac=TP_1 and d_r=d_1. S binds LCoA as B.M_1, MA1 binds SCoA as S.B.M_1, GMA1 binds RCoA as MA1.S.B.M_1 and HA binds GCoA as

GMA1.MA1.S.B.M_1 of M_1 in BC (Mitra, 2008) till $r\_d\_time_1$.

- **u_i1 Function:** After establishing the modified route M_1, the nodes GMA1, MA1, S and B modify the record of M_1 in their NODE_LIST by replacing n_pac=TP_1 by n_pac=TP_1-N_1 and by replacing r_id by the identification of the modified route. S binds LCoA as B.M_1, MA1 binds SCoA as S.B.M_1, GMA1 binds RCoA as MA1.S.B.M_1 and HA binds GCoA as GMA1.MA1.S.B.M_1 of M_1 in BC /9mitra, 2008) till $r\_d\_time_1$.

Otherwise no handoff function at B sends route request message (MN initiated message) of M_1 to S for triggering intra subnet handoff function to select (modify) the route.

- **Intra Subnet Handoff Function:** It searches NODE_LIST of S to compute f_BW at all the LAs under its coverage area. It also computes desire_BW$_1$. It verifies the condition of route selection (modification) at all the LAs under S. If the condition is true it creates a set of routes between S and selected LA(s) wherein the condition is satisfied. It computes the power consumption of all the created routes and finds the optimal route having minimum power consumption. Let this optimal selected (modified) route of M_1 passes through LA say B1 under S. The intra subnet handoff function at S initiates intra subnet handoff of M_1 from B to B1 under S so that M_1 can utilize the selected (modified) route for reception of its packets. In case of route selection S sends route request message of M_1 to GMA1 through MA1 and to B1 to select the route CN->GMA1->MA1->S->B1->M_1. In case of route modification S sends route request message of M_1 to B1 and LCoA as B1.M_1 of M_1 to GMA1 through MA1 to establish the modified route CN->GMA1->MA1->S->B1->M_1. The r_s2 (u_i2) function is used for inserting (modifying) the record of the route M_1 in NODE_LIST maintained by all the nodes associated with the selected (modified) route. All the nodes associated with the selected route compute $r\_d\_time_1$.

- **r_s2 Function:** After selecting the route M_1 the nodes GMA1, MA1, S and B1 insert record in their NODE_LIST as Route=CN->GMA1->MA1->S->B1->M_1, r_id=M_1, p_sz=P_1, n_pac=TP_1 and d_r=d_1. S binds LCoA as B1.M_1, MA1 binds SCoA as S.B1.M_1, GMA1 binds RCoA as MA1.S.B1.M_1 and HA binds GCoA as GMA1.MA1.S.B1.M_1 in BC till $r\_d\_time_1$.

- **u_i2 Function:** After establishing the modified route M_1, B1 inserts and GMA1, MA1, S modify the record of M_1 in their NODE_LIST as Route=CN->GMA1->MA1->S->B1->M_1, r_id=M_1, p_sz=P_1, n_pac=TP_1-N_1, d_r=d_1. S modifies LCoA as B1.M_1, MA1 modifies SCoA as S.B1.M_1 and GMA1 modifies RCoA MA1.S.B1.M_1 of M_1 in BC till $r\_d\_time_1$.

Otherwise intra subnet handoff function at S sends route request message (MN initiated message) of M_1 to MA1 for triggering inter subnet handoff function to select (modify) the route.

- **Inter Subnet Handoff Function:** This function searches NODE_LIST of MA1 to compute f_BW at all the LAs under its coverage area. It also computes desire_BW_1. It verifies the condition of route selection (modification) at all the LAs under MA. If condition is true it creates a set of routes between MA1, parent SA(s) of the selected LA(s) wherein the condition is satisfied and selected LA(s). It computes the power consumption of all the created routes and finds optimal route having minimum pow-

er consumption. Let this optimal selected (modified) route of M_1 passes through LA say B2 under S1. The inter subnet handoff function at MA1 initiates inter subnet handoff of M_1 from S to S1 under MA1 so that M_1 can utilize the selected (modified) route for reception of its packets. In case of route selection MA1 sends route request message of M_1 to B2 through S1 to select the route CN->GMA1->S1->B2->M_1. In case of route modification MA1 sends route request message of M_1 to B2 through S1 and SCoA as S1.B2.M_1 of M_1 to GMA1 to establish the modified route CN->GMA1->MA1->S1->B2->M_1.The r_s3 (u_i3) function is used for inserting (modifying) the record of the route M_1 in NODE_LIST maintained by all the nodes associated with the selected (modified) route. All the nodes associated with the route compute $r\_d\_time_1$.

- **r_s3 Function:** GMA1, MA1, S1 and B2 insert record in their NODE_LIST as Route=CN->GMA1->MA1->S1->B2->M_1, r_id=M_1, p_sz=P_1, n_pac=TP_1 and d_r=d_1. S1 binds LCoA as B2.M_1, MA1 binds SCoA as S1.B2.M_1, GMA1 binds RCoA as MA1.S1.B2.M_1 and HA binds GCoA as GMA1.MA1.S1.B2.M_1 in BC till $r\_d\_time_1$.

- **u_i3 Function:** S1, B2 insert and GMA1, MA1 modify record of M_1 in their NODE_LIST as Route= CN->GMA1->MA1->S1->B2->M_1, r_id=M_1, p_sz=P_1, n_pac=TP_1-N_1, d_r=d_1. S1 binds LCoA as B2.M_1, MA1 modifies SCoA as S1.B2.M_1 and GMA1 modifies RCoA as MA1.S1.B2.M_1 of M_1 in BC till $r\_d\_time_1$.

Otherwise MA1 sends route request message (MN initiated message) of M_1 to GMA1 for triggering inter domain handoff function to select (modify) the route.

- **Inter Domain Handoff Function:** This function searches NODE_LIST of GMA1 to compute f_BW at all the LAs under the coverage area of MA2. It also computes desire_BW$_1$. It verifies the condition of route selection (modification) at all the LAs under MA2. If condition is true it creates a set of routes between GMA1, MA2, parent SA(s) of the selected LA(s) wherein the condition is satisfied and selected LA(s). It computes power consumption of all the created routes and finds optimal route having minimum power consumption. Let this optimal selected (modified) route of M$_1$ passes through LA say B3 under S2 in domain MA2. The inter domain handoff function at GMA1 initiates inter domain handoff of M$_1$ from MA1 to MA2 under GMA1 so that M$_1$ can utilize the selected (modified) route for reception of its packets. GMA1 sends route request message of M$_1$ to MA2, S2 and B3 to select (modify) the route CN->GMA1->MA2->S2->B3->M$_1$. The r_s4 (u_i4) function is used for inserting (modifying) the record of the route M$_1$ in NODE_LIST maintained by all the nodes associated with the selected (modified) route.

- **r_s4 function:** GMA1, MA2, S2 and B3 insert record in their NODE_LIST as Route=CN->GMA1->MA2->S2->B3->M$_1$, r_id=M$_1$, p_sz=P$_1$, n_pac=TP$_1$ and d_r=d$_1$. S2 binds LCoA as B3.M$_1$, MA2 binds SCoA as S2.B3.M$_1$, GMA1 binds RCoA as MA2.S2.B3.M$_1$ and HA binds GCoA as GMA1.MA2.S2.B3.M$_1$ in BC till r_d_time$_1$.

- **u_i4 function:** MA2, S2, B3 insert and GMA1 modifies the record of M$_1$ in their NODE_LIST as Route=CN->GMA1->MA2->S2->B3->M$_1$, r_id=M$_1$, p_sz=P$_1$, n_pac=TP$_1$-N$_1$ and d_r=d$_1$. S2 binds LCoA as B3.M$_1$, MA2 binds SCoA

as S2.B3.M$_1$ and GMA1 modifies RCoA as MA2.S2.B3.M$_1$ of M$_1$ in BC till r_d_time$_1$.

Otherwise in case of route selection algorithm GMA1 increases call block counter by 1. GMA1 computes the call blocking probability of the network as the ratio of the call block counter and the total service request counter. GMA1 increases the total service request counter by 1 after receiving each route request message from MN. In case of route modification algorithm GMA1 computes the number of packet drop and packet dropping probability of M$_1$ as TP$_1$-N$_1$ and (TP$_1$-N$_1$)/TP$_1$ respectively. The packet dropping probability of the network is

$$(\sum_{i=1}^{U}(\text{TP}_i - \text{N}_i)) / \sum_{i=1}^{U}(\text{TP}_i),$$

where U is the number of MNs in the network, TP$_i$ is the total number of packets with i[th] MN (M$_i$), TP$_i$-N$_i$ is the number of drop of packets of M$_i$.

- **Network Initiated Vertical Handoff Algorithm:** If the power consumption of a domain crosses a threshold (P[th]), VHC triggers vertical handoff algorithm to maintain the effective load of each domain in a network very close to its threshold (E[th]). P[th] is assumed as 0.6 watt in case of download and 1 watt in case of upload. E[th] is assumed as the average of the total load in WLAN and cellular domain.

The MNs having a little data for transmission or reception and long idle period are suitable for cellular domain. Though the power consumption of the network interface card (NIC) in the mobile unit for upload in cellular domain is almost two times than that of WLAN domain still it is suitable because using lesser bandwidth of cellular domain MNs can transmit or receive only a small amount of data. On the other hand the WLAN domain is suitable for MNs having lot of data due to its high speed, high bandwidth and low cost which helps to complete transmission or reception in the same domain which in turn reduces the frequency of vertical handoff. The power consumption of the NIC in the mobile unit in case of idle mode is almost 9 times higher in WLAN domain in comparison to cellular domain. So it would be more advantageous to activate the cellular domain for mobility management (Mitra, 2008) as energy efficient interface in case of idle MN. The proposed algorithm triggers vertical handoff for MNs having a little data for transmission or reception and long idle period from WLAN domain to cellular domain whereas triggers vertical handoff for MNs having lot of data for transmission or reception from cellular domain to WLAN domain.

The kth route is selected as a new route after vertical handoff by the algorithm for M_1 provided the condition such as desire_$BW_1 \leq$ f_BW of LA associated with k^{th} route and d_{avg_k}+r_t_time$_1$+r_d_time$_1 \leq r_1$ is satisfied. In this case r_d_time$_1$ is the time requires for completing the reception of rest of the packets of M_1 using k^{th} route and r_t_time$_1$ is the transfer time of route M_1 from one domain to another domain.

In case of vertical handoff from cellular domain to WLAN domain the proposed algorithm schedules the transmission or reception of the MNs in cellular domain in the descending order of their amount of data to be sent or received. Let M_1 is scheduled first. The algorithm searches NODE_LIST of MA2 to compute the f_BW at all the LAs under the coverage area of MA2. It also computes desire_BW_1. It verifies the condition of route selection at all the LAs under MA2 and selects LA(s) wherein the condition is satisfied. It also creates a set of routes between GMA1, MA2, parent SA(s) of the selected LA(s) and selected LA(s). It computes power consumption of all the created routes and finds optimal route having minimum power consumption. Let this optimal selected route of M_1 passes through LA

say B5 under S3 in domain MA2. The algorithm initiates vertical handoff of M_1 to WLAN domain, sends route request message of M_1 to B5 through MA2 and S3. VHC at GMA1 (VHC$_1$) informs the nodes associated with the route selected for vertical handoff to delete the record of M_1 from their NODE_LIST. MA2, S3, B5 insert and GMA1 modifies the record of M_1 in their NODE_LIST. S3 binds LCoA as B5.M_1, MA2 binds SCoA as S3.B5.M_1, and GMA1 modifies RCoA as MA2. S3.B5.M_1 of M_1 in BC till r_d_time$_1$. The algorithm repeats these steps for other scheduled MNs till the effective load of cellular domain reduces to very close of its threshold and power consumption of cellular domain goes below its threshold.

In case of vertical handoff from WLAN domain to cellular domain, the proposed algorithm schedules the transmission or reception of MNs in WLAN domain in the ascending order of their amount of data to be sent or received. Let M_1 is scheduled first. The algorithm searches the NODE_LIST of MA1 to compute the f_BW at all the LAs under the coverage area of MA1. It also computes desire_BW_1. It verifies the condition of route selection at all the LAs under MA1 and selects LA(s) wherein the condition is satisfied. It also creates a set of routes between GMA1, MA1, parent SA(s) of the selected LA(s) and selected LA(s). It computes power consumption of all the created routes and finds optimal route having minimum power consumption. Let this optimal selected route of M_1 passes through LA say B4 under S1 in domain MA1. The algorithm initiates vertical handoff of M_1 to cellular domain, sends route request message of M_1 to B4 through MA1 and S1. VHC$_1$ informs the nodes associated with the route selected for vertical handoff to delete the record of M_1 from their NODE_LIST. MA1, S1, B4 insert and GMA1 modifies the record of M_1 in their NODE_LIST. S1 binds LCoA as B4.M_1, MA1 binds SCoA as S1.B4.M_1 and GMA1 modifies RCoA as MA1.S1.B4.M_1 of M_1 in BC till r_d_time$_1$. VHC$_1$ also identifies MNs having long idle period and initiates vertical handoff from

WLAN domain to cellular domain for mobility management (Mitra, 2008) of such MNs. The algorithm repeats these steps for other MNs till the effective load of WLAN domain reduces to very close of its threshold and power consumption of WLAN domain goes below its threshold.

Theoretical Analysis

In this section the performance of dynamic resource management scheme is analyzed numerically.

- **Computation of f_BW at LA and Power Consumption of a Route:** Each node determines LAs under its coverage area, computes f_BW at all these LAs and power consumption of all the routes passing through these LAs. The f_BW of a particular LA is computed by subtracting the sum of desire_BW of all the existing route passing through that LA from its available bandwidth. Data rate per LA in cellular domain in case of uplink is 153.6 kbps, so available uplink bandwidth is 76.8 KHz. Data rate per LA in cellular domain in case of downlink is 2.4 Mbps, so available downlink bandwidth is 1.2 MHz. Data rate per LA in WLAN domain is 11 Mbps, so available bandwidth is 5.5 MHz.

For example, in row R1 of TABLE-9 LA_id is 110 as specified in the route. This route is downlink in cellular domain. So f_BW of 110 is 1.2 MHz-$d_1/2$ where 1.2 MHz is the available downlink bandwidth in cellular domain and $d_1/2$ is desire_BW to maintain reception of M_1.

The power consumption of a route can be computed as the product of consumption rate and route duration time. The consumption rate (C) is the ratio of initial battery power of a MN to life time. It is assumed as 5 mJ/sec. So the power consumption of the route in row R1 of TABLE-9 is $C*r\_d\_time_1$.

- **Computation of d_{avg_1}:** After selecting the route M_1 and after starting reception using it, each node associated with this route maintains two counter N_1 and $count_1$. At any instant of time N_1 indicates how many packets have already been received and $count_1$ indicates how much time is elapsed to receive N_1 number of packets. Now time requires to receive N_1 number of packets (TRN_1) is $(N_1*P_1)/d_1$ sec. d_{avg_1} is the difference of $count_1$ and TRN_1 in second. The same set of nodes may be associated with multiple routes. For example, the nodes 0, 1, 11, 111 are associated with route M_2 and M_3 (TABLE-9). So the average delay for transmission or reception using the route M_2 (d_{avg_2}) or M_3 (d_{avg_3}) is $(d_{avg\_2}+d_{avg\_3})/2$ seconds.

- **Computation of r_1 for M_1:** M_1 computes r_1 dynamically during reception of its packets as follows:

Time requires to receive N_1 number of packets by M_1 $(time_1)$ using the route M_1 is the sum of $TRN_1, r\_s\_time_1, D\_q_1$ and d_{avg_1} in sec. So $time_1 = [(N_1*P_1)/d_1] + r\_s\_time_1 + D\_q_1 + d_{avg\_1}$.

$r_1 =$ life_time-$time_1$ sec

Like all other nodes associated with the route M_1, M_1 computes d_{avg_1} and $r\_s\_time_1$ respectively. Knowing D_q_1, d_{avg_1} and $r\_s\_time_1$, M_1 computes $time_1$ and r_1. M_1 also computes the threshold value of r_1 (r_{1_th}) as $(TP_1-N_1)*P_1/d_1+d_{avg\_1}$ sec. If r_1 is equal to r_{1_th}, M_1 sends MN initiated message mentioning r_1 to its current LA for the reception of TP_1-N_1 number of packets. The LA runs route modification algorithm.

- **Computation of Effective Load of a Domain:** VHC_1 computes effective load experienced by each domain. The effective load of a domain is the product of traffic load of that domain and the percentage of total route request that will go to that domain. The traffic load of a domain is computed as the ratio of arrival rate and departure rate of service request. In the present work both the arrival rate and departure rate of service request in a domain is considered as poisson distribution.

VHC_1 computes the percentage of total request that will go to a particular domain as the ratio of the number of service request to that domain to the sum of the service request of both the domain. For example in TABLE-9 the routes corresponding to the rows R1, R2, R3, R4 and R5 pass through domain 1 whereas routes corresponding to the rows R6 and R7 pass through domain 2. So the percentage of total service request reach to the domain 1 is (5/7*100) and domain 2 is (2/7*100).

- **Computation of $r\_s\_time_1$:** This is the time requires for the selection of the route M_1 to receive TP_1 number of packets of M_1. It depends upon the number of bits ($r\_s\_bit_1$) in wireless message (route request message) requires to exchange among various nodes for selecting this route. $r\_s\_time_1$ is the product of $r\_s\_bit_1$ and time/bit.

If the route M_1 is selected using no handoff function and r_s1 function, the number of wireless message exchange is 5 (as M_1->B->S->MA1->GMA1->CN). So $r\_s\_bit_1$=rrm_bit$_1$*5.

If the route M_1 is selected using intra subnet handoff function and r_s2 function, the number of wireless message exchange is 6 (as M_1->B->S->MA1->GMA1->CN and S->B1). So $r\_s\_bit_1$=rrm_bit$_1$*6.

If the route M_1 is selected using inter subnet handoff function and r_s3 function, the number of wireless message exchange is 7 (as M_1->B->S->MA1->GMA1->CN and MA1->S1->B2). So $r\_s\_bit_1$=rrm_bit$_1$*7.

If the route is established using inter domain handoff function and r_s4 function, the number of wireless message exchange is 8 (as M_1->B->S->MA1->GMA1->MA2->S2->B3, GMA1->CN). So $r\_s\_bit_1$=rrm_bit$_1$*8.

Finally $r\_s\_time_1$=$r\_s\_bit_1$*time/bit in sec.

Considering wireless network data rate as 30 kbps (http://www.computerworld.com/mobiletopics/mobile/technology/story/0,10801,87486,00.html

http://www.ee.latrobe.edu.au/mf/ELE52PMC/Lectures/PMC-06.ppt)

$r\_s\_time_1$=$r\_s\_bit_1$/30000 sec.

- **Computation of $r\_m\_time_1$:** This is the time requires for modifying the existing route M_1 for reception of (TP_1-N_1) number of packets of M_1. It depends upon the number of bits ($r\_m\_bit_1$) in wireless message (MN initiated message, route request message, care of address) requires to exchange among various nodes for modifying this route. It is the product of $r\_m\_bit_1$ and time/bit.

If the route M_1 is modified using no handoff function and u_i1 function, $r\_m\_bit_1$=$r\_nh\_bit_1$. The number of wireless message exchange is as follows:

M_1->B->S->MA1->GMA1 (sends r_1).

So $r\_m\_bit_1$=$r\_nh\_bit_1$=4*mim_bit$_1$.

VHC_1 senses one no handoff of M_1 during reception of its packets.

If the route M_1 is modified using intra subnet handoff function and u_i2 function, $r\_m\_bit_1$=$r\_intra\_bit_1$. The number of wireless message exchange is as follows:

M_1->B->S (sends r_1).

S->B1 (sends route request message).

S->MA1->GMA1 (sends LCoA as LA_id.MN_id).

So $r\_m\_bit_1=r\_intra\_bit_1=(2*mim\_bit_1+rrm\_bit_1+2*\log_2(NO\_OF\_LA_{SA})+2*17)$. VHC_1 senses one intra subnet handoff of M_1 during reception of its packets.

If the route M_1 is modified using inter subnet handoff function and u_i3 function, $r\_m\_bit_1=r\_inter\_bit_1$. The number of wireless message exchange is as follows:

M_1->B->S->MA1 (sends r_1).

MA1->S1->B2 (sends route request message).

MA1->GMA1 (sends SCoA as SA_id.LA_id.MN_id).

So

$r\_m\_bit_1=r\_inter\_bit_1=$

$(3*mim\_bit_1+2*rrm\_bit_1+$

$\log_2(NO\_OF\_SA_{MA})+$

$\log_2(NO\_OF\_LA_{SA})+17)$.

VHC_1 senses one inter subnet handoff of M_1 during reception of its packets.

If the route is modified using inter domain handoff function and u_i4 function, $r\_m\_bit_1=r\_uv\_bit_1$. The number of wireless message exchange is as follows:

M_1->B->S->MA1->GMA1 (sends r_1).

GMA1->MA2->S2->B3 (sends route request message).

So $r\_m\_bit_1=r\_uv\_bit_1=4*mim\_bit_1+3*rrm\_bit_1$. VHC_1 senses one inter domain handoff of M_1 during reception of its packets.

Finally $r\_m\_time_1=r\_m\_bit_1/30000$ sec.

- **Computation of $r\_t\_time_1$:** This is the time requires for transferring the existing route M_1 from one domain to other domain due to network initiated vertical handoff. It depends upon the number of bits ($r\_nv\_bit_1$) in wireless message (route request message as the route is selected in a new domain) requires to exchange among various nodes for transferring this route from one domain to other domain. It is the product of $r\_nv\_bit_1$ and time/bit. The number of wireless message exchange in case of network initiated vertical handoff is 3 (as VHC_1->MA->SA->LA). So $r\_nv\_bit_1=rrm\_bit_1*3$. Finally $r\_t\_time_1=r\_nv\_bit_1/30000$ sec. In case of route transfer VHC_1 senses one network initiated vertical handoff of M_1 during reception of its packets.

- **Computation of Average Cost ($Cost_n$) and Average Delay ($Delay_n$) of Network:** $Cost_n$ ($Delay_n$) is the ratio of the sum of cost (delay) to maintain all the routes (R_n) in the network and R_n. The cost to maintain the route M_1 ($Cost_1$) in the network is the product of the number of bits requires to exchange and cost/bit. Now the number of bits requires to exchange (bit_{1C}) is the sum of the number of bits requires for selecting this route, number of bits that M_1 receives using this route, number of bits requires for modifying this route and number of bits requires for transferring this route.

Let VHC_1 senses the number of various handoff of M_1 during reception of its TP_1 number of packets as follows:

no_u_1=number of no handoff
$intra\_u_1$=number of intra subnet handoff
$inter\_u_1$=number of inter subnet handoff
v_u_1=number of inter domain handoff
v_n_1=number of network initiated vertical handoff

The number of bits requires to exchange for modifying the route M_1 is the sum of $no\_u_1*r\_nh\_bit_1$, $intra\_u_1*r\_intra\_bit_1$, $inter\_u_1*r\_inter\_bit_1$ and $v\_u_1*r\_uv\_bit_1$. So

$bit_{iC} =$

$r\_s\_bit_1+TP_1*P_1+$

$(no\_u_1*r\_nh\_bit_1+intra\_u_1*r\_intra\_bit_1+inter\_u_1*$

$r\_inter\_bit_1+v\_u_1*r\_uv\_bit_1)+v\_n_1*r\_nv\_bit_1.$

$Cost_1 = bit_{iC}*cost/bit,$

where cost/bit is assumed as 1 unit for WLAN domain and 2 unit for cellular domain.

$$Cost_n = \frac{\sum_{i=1}^{Rn}(Cost_i)}{Rn} unit,$$

where $Cost_i$ is the cost to maintain the route M_i.

The delay to maintain the route M_1 ($Delay_1$) is the sum of the time requires to exchange message among nodes, d_{avg_1} and D_q_1. Now the time requires to exchange message among nodes is the product of the number of bits requires to exchange and time/bit. Now the number of bits requires to exchange (bit_{1D}) is

$r\_s\_bit_1+$

$(no\_u_1*r\_nh\_bit_1+intra\_u_1*r\_intra\_bit_1+$

$inter\_u_1*r\_inter\_bit_1+v\_u_1*r\_uv\_bit_1)+$

$v\_n_1*r\_nv\_bit_1.$

$Delay_1 = bit_{1D}*time/bit + D\_q_1+d_{avg\_1} sec.$

$Delay_n =$

$$(\sum_{i=1}^{Rn}Delay_i) / R_n msec,$$

where $Delay_i$ is the delay to maintain the route M_i.

- **Computation of Average Power Consumption of Network (PC_n):** VHC_1 computes the power consumption of a domain as the sum of power consumption to maintain upload and download using the routes in that domain. PC_n is the ratio of the sum of power consumption of the two domains and R_n. So $PC_n=$ ($\sum_{i=1}^{Rc}(PC_i) + \sum_{j=1}^{Rw}(PC_j))/R_n$ mw, where R_c is the number of routes in cellular domain, R_w is the number of routes in WLAN domain. PC_i is the power consumption of the route M_i in cellular domain and PC_j is the power consumption of the route M_j in WLAN domain.
- **Computation of average throughput of network (T_n):** The time requires to complete the reception of TP_1 number of packets of M_1 (τ_1) is $(TP_1*P_1)/d_1 + d_{avg\_1}$. The throughput in the route M_1 (TH_1) is TP_1/τ_1 in packets/min. So $T_n =$ ($\sum_{i=1}^{Rc}(TH_i) + \sum_{j=1}^{Rw}(TH_j))/R_n$ packets/min, where TH_i is the throughput of the route M_i in cellular domain and TH_j is the throughput of the route M_j in WLAN domain.

Simulation Results

In this section the simulation results of Scheme_II are considered for discussion. The total simulation time is 300 sec.

The power consumption of a domain depends upon the power consumption to maintain transmission or reception using the routes in that domain. It also depends upon the available bandwidth of the domain. High bandwidth reduces the power consumption of a route as well as the average power consumption of the domain. Figure 3 shows the plot of power consumption in cellular domain and WLAN domain during upload and download. It can be observed from Figure 3 that the power consumption of cellular domain crosses its threshold at simulation time 40 and 110 during upload whereas at simulation time 60 and 120 during download. The network initiated vertical handoff algorithm triggers vertical handoff from cellular domain to WLAN domain at the simulation time 40, 60, 110 and 120. After each vertical handoff the power consumption of cellular domain reduces and of WLAN domain increases. But the slope of increase in WLAN domain is lesser due to its high bandwidth. The power consumption of WLAN domain crosses its threshold at simulation time 85 and 135 during upload whereas at simulation time 95 during download. The network initiated vertical handoff algorithm triggers vertical handoff from WLAN domain to cellular domain at simulation time 85, 95 and 135. After each vertical handoff the power consumption of WLAN domain decreases and of cellular domain increases.

Figure 4 and Figure 5 show the plot of $Delay_n$ and T_n vs. simulation time.

The congestion of the network increases with simulation time which causes an increase in $Delay_n$. But still T_n increases slowly with simulation time due to high bandwidth of WLAN domain.

After each vertical handoff the value of bit_i increases due to additional $r\_nv\_bit_i$, which increases $Delay_n$ and $Cost_n$. The network initiated vertical handoff balances the effective load among the two domain. Moreover the high bandwidth of WLAN domain reduces $Delay_n$ and increases T_n more in case of vertical handoff from cellular domain to WLAN domain whereas low bandwidth

Figure 3. Power consumption vs. simulation time

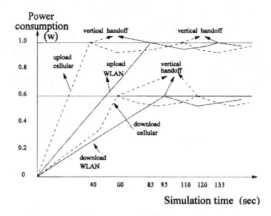

Figure 4. Average network delay vs. simulation time

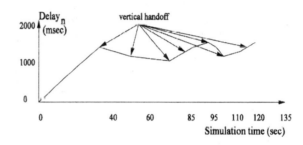

Figure 5. Throughput vs. simulation time

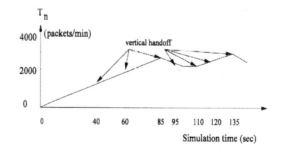

of cellular domain increases $Delay_n$ and reduces T_n in case of vertical handoff from WLAN domain to cellular domain. As a result $Delay_n$ lies within a range of 1100-1700 msec and T_n lies within a range of 2500-3500 packets/min.

$Cost_n$ reduces in case of vertical handoff from cellular domain to WLAN domain due to low cost of WLAN domain and increases in case of vertical handoff from WLAN domain to cellular domain due to high cost of cellular domain. So the nature of the plot of $Cost_n$ vs. simulation time is identical to Figure 4 and it lies within the range 10000 unit to 15000 unit as observed during simulation.

The performance of the proposed scheme is compared with the scheme (Sharma, 2007) on the basis of throughput and is presented in Table 10. The packet size is assumed as 10 KB.

FUTURE RESEARCH DIRECTIONS

In the next generation wireless network, a user may roam over a series of networks during his global travel. Internet browsing "on-the-move", video conferencing and file transfer are some of the new expected services in near future. Moreover the QoS requirement of different users is different. The user should be able to select the best interface for a particular application. This is a challenging task especially in heterogeneous networks environments where QoS parameter changes their values rapidly. The switching among interfaces should cause minimal disruption to on-going communication sessions. Such switching mechanism needs to be very fast as real-time application can only tolerate delays in the range of milliseconds.

Moreover due to high speed Internet and multimedia applications, future wireless communication are expected to support multimedia traffic such as voice, video, text with a variety of QoS requirements and make efficient use of radio resource. Such kind of traffic requires high level of QoS guarantees. Hence simulation work of both the schemes may be done to report on the

performance of the proposed algorithm when applied to a link carrying multimedia traffic.

A clean architecture should be designed where mobility management and resource management are separated so that changes in one should not affect the other.

CONCLUSION

In this chapter a mobility management scheme is proposed in Scheme_I and a resource management scheme is proposed in Scheme_II for all-IP wireless network. To conclude the chapter Scheme_I can be extended by capturing the current traffic flow conditions and balances its contradictory QoS requirements for QoS sensitive multimedia services. The performance of Scheme_II is evaluated considering only the data class of traffic. It can be extended by evaluating its performance in presence of other traffic classes in the environment.

REFERENCES

Chakraborty, M., Misra, I. S., Saha, D., & Mukherjee, A. (2004). A novel fat handover technique for TLMM: Three level mobility for next generation wireless IP-based networks. In *Proceedings of INDICON*. IDICON.

Chiron, P., Njedjon, E., Seite, P., Gosse, K., Melin, E., & Roux, P. (2008). Architectures for IP-based network-assisted mobility management across heterogeneous networks. *IEEE Wireless Communications*, *15*, 18–25. doi:10.1109/MWC.2008.4492974.

Christian, M., & Samuel, P. (2008). An architecture for seamless mobility support in IP-based next-generation wireless networks. *IEEE Transactions on Vehicular Technology*, *57*, 1209–1225. doi:10.1109/TVT.2007.906366.

Table 10. Comparison with existing schemes

Reference	Simulation time (sec)	Throughput (kbps)
(Sharma, 2007)	0-250	4
Scheme_II	0-300	2664

Cui, Y., Xue, Y. B., Shang, H. Y., Sha, X., & Ding, Z. (2009). A novel scheme access architecture for joint radio resource management in heterogeneous networks. []. Guangzhou, China: IEEE.]. *Proceedings of the International Forum on Information Technology and Applications, 1*, 24–27.

Dommety, G., Yegin, A., Perkins, C., El-Malki, K., & Khalil, M. (2001). *Fast handovers mobile IPv6*. IETF draft, draft-ietf-mobileipfast-mipv6-03.txt.

Esmailpour, A., & Nasser, N. (2011). Dynamic QoS-based bandwidth allocation framework for broadband wireless networks. *IEEE Transactions on Vehicular Technology, 60*, 2690–2700. doi:10.1109/TVT.2011.2158674.

Hamed, S., Mojtaba, M. S., & Siavash, K. (2011). Cooperative joint radio resource management in heterogeneous networks. In *Proceedings of the International Symposium on Computer Networks and Distributed Systems*, (pp. 111-115). Tehran, Iran: IEEE.

Ibrahim, M., Khawam, K., & Tohme, S. (2009). Network centric joint radio resource policy in heterogeneous WiMAX/UMTS networks for streaming and elastic traffic. In *Proceedings of the IEEE Wireless Communications and Networking Conference*, (pp. 1-6). Budapest, Hungary: IEEE.

Ismail, M., & Zhuang, W. H. (2012). A distributed multi-service resource allocation algorithm in heterogeneous wireless access medium. *IEEE Journal on Selected Areas in Communications, 30*, 425–432. doi:10.1109/JSAC.2012.120222.

Johnson, D., & Perkins, C. (2001). *Mobility support in IPv6*. IETF draft, draft-ietf-mobileip-ipv6-15.txt.

Luo, C. Q. Ji. H., & Li, Y. (2009). Utility-based multi-service bandwidth allocation in the 4G heterogeneous wireless access networks. In *Proceedings of the IEEE Wireless Communications and Networking Conference*, (pp. 1-5). Budapest, Hungary: IEEE.

Misra, I. S., Dey, S., & Saha, D. (2005). *TLMIPv6: A next generation three layer mobile IPv6 mobility management architecture*. WWC.

Mitra, S. (2008). Dynamic mobility management for next generation all-IP wireless network. In *Proceedings of the International Conference on Communication Systems and Networks* (Vol. 1, pp. 165-170). AsiaCSN.

Mitra, S. (2008). Dynamic resource management in next generation all-IP wireless network. []. IEEE.]. *Proceedings of IEEE INDICON, 1*, 165–170.

Montavont, N., & Noel, T. (2002). Handover management for mobile nodes in IPv6 network. *IEEE Communications Magazine*, 38–43. doi:10.1109/MCOM.2002.1024413.

Pei, X. B., Jiang, T., Qu, D. M., Guangxi, Z., & Jian, L. (2010). Radio resource management and access control mechanism based on a novel economic model in heterogeneous wireless networks. *IEEE Transactions on Vehicular Technology, 59*, 3047–3056. doi:10.1109/TVT.2010.2049039.

Sharma, S., Baek, I., Dodia, Y., & Chiueh, T.-C. (2007). Omnicon: A mobile IP-based vertical handoff system for wireless LAN and GPRS links. *Software, Practice & Experience, 1*(37), 779–798. doi:10.1002/spe.790.

Soliman, H., Castelluccia, C., Malki, K., & Bellier, L. (2001). *Hierarchical MIPv6 mobility management*. IETF, draft-soliman-mobileip-hmipv6-05.txt.

ADDITIONAL READING

Chen, L.-J., Yang, G., Sun, T., Sanadidi, M. Y., & Gerla, M. (2004). Adaptive video streaming in vertical handoff: A case study. In *Proceedings of the First Annual International Conference on Mobile and Ubiquitous Systems: Networking and Services (MobiQuitous'04)*. Retrieved from http://nrlweb.cs.ucla.edu/publication/download/269/getPDF.pdf

Ekiz, N., Salih, T., Kucukoner, S., & Fidanboylu, K. (2007). An overview of handoff techniques in cellular networks. World Academy of Science, Engineering and Technology, (6), 591 – 594.

Furht, B. (1996). *Multimedia tools and applications*. Norwell, MA: Kluwer Academic Publisher. Retrieved from http://cntic03.hit.bme.hu/meres/ATMFAQ/d19.htm

Kassar, M., Kervella, B., & Pujolle, G. (2008). An overview of vertical handover decision strategies in heterogeneous wireless networks. *International Journal of Computer Communications*, (31), 2607 – 2620.

Li, J., Wong, W. E., & Guo, W. (2004). Case study of a multimedia wireless system. In *Proceedings of the 2004 IEEE International Conference on Multimedia and Expo, 2004*. Retrieved from http://ieeexplore.ieee.org/xpls/abs_all.jsp?arnumber=1394609

Liu, B., Wang, J., & Li, J. (2009). A joint vertical handover technique for heterogeneous wireless networks. In Proceedings of Computer Science & Education. ICCSE.

Park, H., Lee, H. H., & Chan, H. A. (2013). Gateway service for integration of heterogeneous networks using different interworking solutions. In *Proceedings of Advanced Communication Technology*. ICACT.

Ralf, S., & Klara, N. (2004). *Multimedia applications*. New York: Springer.

Sakshat Virtual Labs. (2013). *Hand off in mobile communication*. Retrieved from http://iitd.vlab.co.in/?sub=65&brch=179&sim=1293&cnt=1

Song, W., Zhuang, W., & Saleh, A. (2007). Interworking of 3G cellular networks and wireless LANs. *International Journal of Wireless and Mobile Computing*, 4(2), 237–247. doi:10.1504/IJWMC.2007.016718.

Tutorialspoint. (n.d.). *WiMAX—Reference network model*. Retrieved from http://www.tutorialspoint.com/wimax/wimax_network_model.htm

Washington University in St. Louis. (n.d.). *Ad hoc networks: Characteristics*. Retrieved from http://www.cse.wustl.edu/~jain/cse574-10/ftp/j_ladh/sld003.htm

Yan, X., Sekercioglu, A., & Narayanan, S. (2010). A survey of vertical handover decision algorithms in fourth generation heterogeneous wireless networks. *International Journal of Computer Networks*, (54), 1848 – 1863.

KEY TERMS AND DEFINITIONS

Cellular Network: A cellular network is a mobile network that provides services by using a large number of base stations with limited power, each covering only a limited area. This area is called a cell. The limited power makes it possible to re-use the same frequency a few cells away from the base station without causing interference. In this way a geographic large area can be covered with only a limited set of frequencies. A cellular network is a very efficient manner of using the scarce frequency resources. The size of a cell can vary according to the number of users that have to be served in a certain area and the amount of traffic per user. If there is much traffic in an area the cell size will be smaller than in rural areas.

Handoff Management: It is the process by which a mobile node keeps its connection active when it moves from one access point to another. There are three stages in a handoff process. First, the initiation of handoff is triggered by either the mobile device, or a network agent, or the changing network conditions. The second stage is for a new connection generation, where the network must find new resources for the handoff connection and perform any additional routing operations. Finally, data-flow control needs to maintain the delivery of the data from the old connection path to the new connection path according to the agreed-upon QoS guarantees.

Internet Protocol (IP): It is used for communicating data from one computer to another on the Internet. It is a principal communication protocol for relaying data across network boundaries.

IP Address: It is a unique numeric identifier. It is needed by every device which is connected to the Internet. It helps to manage the shared common resource for ensuring continuous growth and stability of the Internet.

Next Generation Wireless Systems: In recent years, mobile wireless technology has gained tremendous popularity due to its ability to provide ubiquitous information access to users on the move. However, presently, there is no single wireless network technology that is capable of simultaneously providing a low latency, a high bandwidth, and wide area data service to a large number of mobile users. Next generation wireless systems typically constitute different types of access technologies. A mobile device with multiple wireless network interfaces can access these networks as it moves between different network environments. The heterogeneity that will characterize future wireless systems instigates the development of intelligent and efficient handoff management mechanisms that can provide seamless roaming capability to end-users moving between several different access networks.

Quality of Service: It is the ability to provide different priority to different applications, users, or data flows, or to guarantee a certain level of performance to a data flow. For example, a required bit rate, delay, jitter, packet dropping probability and/or bit error rate may be guaranteed. Quality of service guarantees are important if the network capacity is insufficient for example in cellular data communication. The fixed bit rate and minimum delay are the required quality of service for the real-time streaming multimedia applications.

Seamless Roaming: Phone coverage can be a regular problem for people constantly on the move. This is especially true for traveling business people who take frequent flights or drives across states or even internationally. The wide variety of different data networks can make the use of mobile applications on phones difficult or impossible. Seamless roaming is a term used to describe technology that helps to solve this problem. It allows a user to move from one area to another without any interruption.

Vertical Handoff: Vertical handoff refers to a network node changing the type of connectivity it uses to access a supporting infrastructure. When a computing device could connect to the Internet via two different network technologies, it is automatically connected to the available network. This shuffling or changing from one network to the other is the vertical handover.

Vertical Handover: Enables the exploitation of higher bandwidth and lower costs for networks like wide local area networks. It also provides extended coverage for cellular networks. For example: a suitably equipped laptop might be able to use both a high speed wireless LAN and a cellular technology for Internet access. Wireless LAN connections generally provide higher speeds, while cellular technologies generally provide more ubiquitous coverage. Thus the laptop user might want to use a wireless LAN connection whenever one is available, and to 'fall over' to a cellular connection when the wireless LAN is unavailable. Vertical handovers refer to the automatic fall

489

over from one technology to another in order to maintain communication. This is different from a 'horizontal handover' between different wireless access points that use the same technology in that a vertical handover involves changing the data link layer technology used to access the network.

Wireless Local Area Network (WLAN): In WLAN a mobile user can connect to a local area network through a wireless connection. It links two or more devices using some wireless distribution method (typically spread-spectrum), and usually providing a connection through an access point to the wider Internet. This gives users the mobility to move around within a local coverage area and still be connected to the network. Wireless LANs have become popular in the home due to ease of installation, and in commercial complexes offering wireless access to their customers.

APPENDIX

Review Questions

1. What is wireless metropolitan area network?
2. What are the basic characteristics of ad hoc network?
3. How next generation wireless network differs from current wireless network?
4. Define the features of microwave access networks (WiMAX).
5. What is handoff?
6. Define intra subnet, inter subnet, and inter domain handoff.
7. Why multimedia traffic is important for next generation wireless network?
8. Discuss about the various characteristics of CBR, VBR, ABR traffic.
9. Why WLAN domain is suitable for MNs having lot of data?
10. Why cellular domain is suitable for MNs having little data for transmission or reception and long idle period?
11. How data rate and bandwidth are related with each other?
12. Define speed and data rate, bandwidth and capacity.

Chapter 20
900MHz Spectrum Refarming Analysis for UMTS900 Deployment

Chitra Singh Budhathoki Magar
ZTE India, India

ABSTRACT

Refarming means re-arrangement of the traditionally allotted spectrum for a technology/application/ service and carving out a part of the spectrum for technology/application/service with higher value. The refarming concept can be used for 3G network deployment in 2G bands or for 4G network deployment in 2G/3G bands. Relative to the UMTS core band (2100MHz), in the 900MHz band radio signal propagation loss is lower. Fewer base stations can be deployed in 900MHz band to achieve the same coverage. Especially in the rural areas, villages, etc., covering limited areas, the UMTS900 band coverage advantages are more obvious. The lower carrier frequency penetration capability becomes much stronger. It reduces the loss while penetrating the wall. This chapter aims to focus on the global UMTS900 refarming status, key advantages of UMTS900 refarming, major challenges of transitioning to UMTS900, technical feasibility of GSM/UMTS co-existence band, and UMTS900 frequency refarming case study in sandwich mode. ECC interference analysis and simulation results are provided for study on co-existence of GSM900 and UMTS900. In the later part of the chapter a detailed case study on 900MHz refarming on sandwich mode is provided with system simulation, frequency planning, capacity migration, and deployment strategy.

DOI: 10.4018/978-1-4666-4691-9.ch020

INTRODUCTION

900 MHz spectrum band has been historically used for providing second generation mobile services using GSM technology. Given the limitation of the 2100MHz spectrum band, the growing number of UMTS customers and the expiration of certain GSM licenses, the mobile telecommunications community is looking for potentially refarm the GSM900 MHz band for UMTS. UMTS900 satisfies the requirement for deep coverage in urban areas and address the problem of indoor coverage, weak coverage and blind area coverage. It is a highly cost effective solution for providing UMTS services in suburban and rural areas.

Deploying the UMTS network on the 900MHz band is widely used in many scenarios. Reduction of spectrum available to GSM mobiles should be carefully planned if capacity and quality is to be maintained. For network planning and optimization, the main challenges of 900 MHz refarming are frequency reallocation strategy, interference analysis and capacity migration. The reallocation strategy for existing 900MHz spectrum should be designed to reduce interference between GSM and UMTS. Interference between GSM and UMTS should be mitigated by use of separation requirements. Capacity migration strategy for GSM900 users should be mainly aimed at migrating existing users smoothly through traffic balance and avoid worsening the user perception of the live network. Capacity, quality, coverage for GSM only mobiles need to be maintained by the remaining GSM900 and GSM1800 layers.

BACKGROUND

The International Telecommunications Union (ITU) has originally allocated 900MHz band for GSM and 2100MHz band for UMTS operations. GSM900 and EGSM operate on 880-915/925-960 MHz and a total of 2 * 35MHz. UMTS 2100 operates on 1920 - 1980 MHz / 2110 -2170 MHz,

and a total of 2 * 60MHz. Most operators have GSM900 network in this band cannot be further allocated or provide complete 5MHz spectrum to UMTS network. At the same time, the existing GSM900 network has already accumulated large number of the subscribers, which is an important source of profits for the operators.

The main interest for some European operators to deploy UMTS in the 900 MHz band is the better coverage compared to UMTS at 2100 MHz, especially to provide coverage for rural areas. UMTS900 offers a considerably more cost efficient solution for operators to offer UMTS services in rural areas with low population density. GSM/UMTS900 frequency refarming is one of the inevitable future solutions for low cost GSM/UMTS co-existence, ensure the overall capacity of the network and to balance and enhance the quality of the network.

Since 3G technologies have better capabilities and greater efficiency than GSM, refarming of GSM900 spectrum will generate more value for operators and consumers. For existing GSM900 network operators, refarming of 900M frequency band and introduction of UMTS network carries certain significance for its frequency refarming again for a smooth transition to LTE in the future.

Worldwide UMTS900 Spectrum Refarming Status

As of May 9, 2013, globally 68 countries and regions permits or considering UMTS900 system deployment. 69 UMTS900 networks have been commercially launched in 47 countries and more than 21 UMTS900 networks are planned, getting tested or getting deployed by May 9, 2013. List of countries where UMTS900 networks is already launched is shown below (Until May 9, 2013) in Table 1 and List of countries where UMTS900 is commercially launched, planned or under deployment (Until May 9, 2013, data resource from GSA report) is shown in Table 2, Table 3, and Table 4.

Table 1. List of countries where UMTS900 networks are already launched (Until May 9, 2013)

69 commercial UMTS900 networks in 47 countries		© GSA May 9, 2013
Country	Operator	Service launch
Finland	Elisa	November 2007
Estonia	Elisa	January 2008
Thailand	AIS	May 2008
Australia	Optus	May 2008
Belgium	Mobistar	May 2008
Belgium	Proximus	July 2008
New Zealand	Vodafone	July 2008
Finland	DNA	October 2008
Iceland	Siminn	October 2008
Venezuela	Digitel	March 2009
Finland	TeliaSonera	June 2009
France	Orange	Q2 2009
Croatia	Tele2	July 2009
Australia	VHA	August 2009
France	SFR	September 2009
Faroe Islands	Faroese Telecom	November 2009
Armenia	Orange	November 2009
Latvia	LMT	November 2009
Poland	Aero2	November 2009
Ghana	MTN	December 2009
Hong Kong	CSL Limited	January 2010
Dominican Rep	Orange	February 2010
South Africa	MTN	March 2010
Tanzania	Rural Telco	March 2010
Romania	Vodafone	April 2010
Estonia	EMT	June 2010
Bulgaria	Vivacom	June 2010
Malaysia	Maxis	June 2010
Saudi Arabia	Mobily	2010
Saudi Arabia	Zain	2010
Slovenia	Tusmobil	July 2010
Greenland	TELE	August 2010
South Africa	Cell C	September 2010
Poland	P4 (Play mobile)	January 2011
Estonia	Tele2	March 2011
UK	O2	March 2011
Qatar	Vodafone	March 2011
Kazakhstan	Tele2	April 2011
Papua New Guinea	Digicel	May 2011
Sweden	3	May 2011
Hong Kong	3	June 2011
Norway	Netcom	August 2011

69 commercial UMTS900 networks in 47 countries		© GSA May 9, 2013
Country	Operator	Service launch
New Caledonia	OPT	August 2011
Saudi Arabia	STC	2011
New Zealand	2degrees	September 2011
Spain	Vodafone	September 2011
Slovenia	Si.mobil	October 2011
Spain	Movistar	October 2011
Germany	E-Plus	December 2011
Poland	Polkomtel Plus	December 2011
Mozambique	Mcel	2012
Philippines	Globe	2012
Spain	Orange	2012
Russia	Megafon	January 2012
Russia	MTS	January 2012
Russia	Vimpelcom	January 2012
Hungary	Vodafone	March 2012
Paraguay	Vox/Copaco	May 2012
Switzerland	Sunrise	May 2012
Japan	Softbank Mobile	July 2012
Tunisia	Tunisiana	July 2012
UK	Vodafone	July 2012
Macedonia	VIP	August 2012
Greece	Vodafone	October 2012
Indonesia	Indosat	October 2012
Singapore	Starhub	November 2012
Benin	MTN	November 2012
France	Bouygues Tel	2013
France	Free Mobile	2013

Link Budget Coverage Cell Radius/ Area of UMTS2100, UMTS900 and GSM900

From Table 5 we can find out there is 8dB uplink and downlink frequency transformation to 2.1GHz and overall 5.5dB coverage improvement in rural areas. In Urban areas, there is 11dB uplink and downlink frequency transformation to 2.1GHz and overall 8.5dB coverage improvement. 1dB feeder cable losses improvement can be found in downlink of 900MHz.

When the cell radius is reduced to half 4 times more base stations required to be deployed in the network which means the number of base stations required to provide the same coverage will be increased by 4 times. From Figure 1 and 2 we can find out the number of base station will be reduced significantly when the network is deployed in UMTS90 rather than UMTS2100. A UMTS network can be constructed in the GSM900 frequency band at a lower cost with better coverage than a UMTS2100 network.

Table 2. List of countries where UMTS900 networks is commercially launched, planned, testing or under deployment (Until May 9, 2013)

Country	UMTS900 operator	Network status	Network status
Armenia	Orange		Launched
Australia	Optus		Launched
Australia	VHA		Launched
Belgium	Mobistar		Launched
Belgium	Proximus		Launched
Benin	MTN		Launched
Bosnia and Herzegovina	BH Telecom	In deployment	
Bulgaria	Vivacom		Launched
Bulgaria	Globul	Testing	
Croatia	Tele2		Launched
Denmark	3(Hi3G)	In deployment	
Dominican Republic	Orange Dominicana		Launched
Egypt	Vodafone	In deployment	
Estonia	Elisa		Launched
Estonia	EMT		Launched
Estonia	Tele2		Launched
Faroe Islands	Faroese Telecom		Launched
Finland	DNA		Launched
Finland	Elisa		Launched
Finland	TeliaSonera		Launched
France	Bouygues Telecom		Launched
France	Free Mobile		Launched
France	Orange		Launched
France	SFR		Launched
Germany	E-Plus		Launched
Ghana	MTN		Launched
Greece	Cosmote	Testing	
Greece	Vodafone		Launched
Greenland	TELE		Launched
Hong Kong	CSL Limited		Launched
Hong Kong	3 HK		Launched
Hungary	Vodafone		Launched
Iceland	Siminn		Launched
Indonesia	Indosat		Launched
Italy	3 Italia (H3G)	Testing	
Italy	TIM	In deployment	
Italy	Vodafone	Testing	

Table 3. List of countries where UMTS900 networks is commercially launched, planned, testing or under deployment (Until May 9, 2013) continued

Country	UMTS900operator	Network status	Network status
Japan	Softbank		Launched
Kazakhstan	Tele2		Launched
Kuwait	Wataniya Telecom	In deployment	
Latvia	LMT		Launched
Macedonia	VIP		Launched
Malaysia	Maxis		Launched
Malaysia	Celcom	In deployment	
Mozambique	Mcel		Launched
Netherlands	T Mobile NL	In deployment	
New Caledonia	OPT		Launched
New Zealand	2degrees		Launched
New Zealand	Vodafone		Launched
Norway	Netcom		Launched
Norway	TeleNor	Planned	
Papua New Guinea	Digicel		Launched
Paraguay	Vox-Copaco		Launched
Poland	Aero2		Launched
Poland	Orange	In deployment	
Poland	TMobile	In deployment	
Poland	P4(Play)		Launched
Poland	Polkomtel Plus		Launched
Portugal	Vodafone	In deployment	
Qatar	Vodafone		Launched
Romania	Cosmote	Planned	
Romania	Orange	In deployment	
Romania	Vodafone		Launched
Russia	Megafon		Launched
Russia	MTS		Launched
Russia	Vimpelcom		Launched
Saudi Arabia	Mobily		Launched
Saudi Arabia	STC		Launched
Saudi Arabia	Zain		Launched
Singapore	Starhub		Launched
Slovenia	Si.mobil		Launched
Slovenia	Tusmobil		Launched
South Africa	Cell C		Launched
South Africa	MTN		Launched
South Africa	Vodacom	Testing	
Spain	Movistar		Launched
Spain	Orange		Launched
Spain	Vodafone		Launched

Table 4. List of countries where UMTS900 networks is commercially launched, planned, testing or under deployment (Until May 9, 2013) continued

Country	UMTS900operator	Network status	Network status
Sweden	3(Hi3G)		Launched
Switzerland	Orange	In deployment	
Switzerland	Sunrise		Launched
Tanzania	Rural Telco		Launched
Thailand	AIS		Launched
The Philippines	Globe		Launched
Tunisia	Tunisiana		Launched
Ukraine	Beeline	Planned	
Ukraine	MTS	Planned	
UK	o2		Launched
UK	Vodafone		Launched
Venezuela	Digitel		Launched

Table 5. Link budget of UMTS2100,UMTS900, GSM900

UPLINK	UMTS2100 60k CS	UMTS900 64k CS	UMTS900 Voice	GSM900 Voice
Max power UE(dBm)	21	21	21	33
Combiner loss(dB)				
Eb/No	4	4	6	
Noise density(dBm HZ)	-174	-174	-174	
Node B Noise Factor(dB)	3	3	3	
Service Bit Rate(kbps)	64	64	12.2	
Node B BTS sensitivity(dBm)	-118.9	-118.9	-124.1	-111.5
Difference(TX-RX)	139.9	139.9	145.1	144.5
Feeder losses(dB)	0	0	0	0
SHO Gain UL(dB)	2	2	2	0
Interference margin for rural(dB)	2	2	2	0
UE Antenna Gain(dBi)	-3	-3	-3	-3
Node B Antenna Gain(dBi)	18	15.5	15.5	15.5
Body loss(dB)	0	0	3	3
LNG Fading Margin(dB)	7.5	7.5	7.5	7.5
Fast Fading Margin(dB)	1.5	1.5	1.5	1.5
Sum UL System Gains	13.5	11	11	11
Service specifics margins	7.5	7.5	10.5	10.5
Total Margin (Gains Losses)	6	3.5	0.5	0.5
UL path loss(dB)	145.9	143.4	145.6	145
Frequency Transform 2.1GHZ		8	8	8
UL path loss(dB)+Fre.trans.		151.4	153.6	153
Path loss gain compared to UMTS2100		5.5	7.7	7.1

DOWNLINK	UMTS2100 64k CS	UMTS900 64k CS	UMTS900 Voice	GSM900 Voice
Max power Node B BTS(dBm)	36	36	33	47
Combiner loss(dB)	0	0	0	4
Eb/No	6	6	8	
Noise density(dBm HZ)	-174	-174	-174	
UE Noise Factor(dB)	7.5	10.5	10.5	
Service Bit Rate(kbps)	64	64	12.2	
UE sensitivity(dBm)	-112.4	-109.4	-114.6	-104
Difference(TX-RX)	148.4	145.4	147.6	147
Feeder losses(dB)	3	2	2	2
SHO Gain UL(dB)	2	2	2	0
Interference margin for rural(dB)	2	2	2	0
UE Antenna Gain(dBi)	-3	-3	-3	-3
Node B Antenna Gain(dBi)	18	15.5	15.5	15.5
Body loss(dB)	0	0	3	3
LNG Fading Margin(dB)	7.5	7.5	7.5	7.5
Fast Fading Margin(dB)	1.5	1.5	1.5	1.5
Sum UL System Gains	10.5	9	9	9
Service specifics margins	7.5	7.5	10.5	10.5
Total Margin (Gains Losses)	3	1.5	1.5	1.5
DL path loss(dB)	151.4	146.9	146.1	145.5
Frequency Transform 2.1GHZ		8	8	8
DL path loss(dB)+Fre.trans.		154.9	154.1	153.5
Path loss gain compared to UMTS2100		3.5	2.7	2.1

Figure 1. Cell radius comparison of UMTS900 (voice/video), GSM900 voice and UMTS2100 video in Rural areas

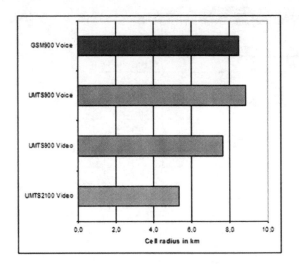

Figure 2. Cell area comparison of UMTS900 (voice/video), GSM900 voice and UMTS2100 video in Rural areas

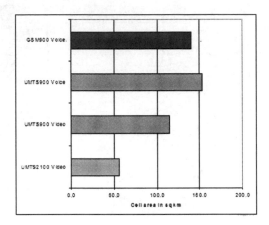

Key Advantages of UMTS900

Since there is lower propagation loss and stronger penetration capability, UMTS900 network compared to UMTS2100 network can provide better coverage performance and reduce the construction cost. Firstly, according to radio wave propagation features, radio signals are transmitted farther at a lower carrier frequency and allow one site to cover a wider area. This makes UMTS900 an excellent wide coverage solution. Therefore investment of mobile network goes down as wider coverage per site means fewer sites.

Especially in the villages, covering the restricted area, the UMTS900 band coverage advantages will become more obvious. In the urban areas, outdoor base station can provide in-depth coverage of the building, reducing the indoor building site construction, thus saving the cost of indoor- building network construction and maintenance costs.

According to the GSMA (GSM Association) report, UMTS 900 compared with UMTS 2100 coverage range of each base station can be increased by 44% (in urban areas) and 119% (rural areas). UK telecoms regulator Ofcom's comparative data is shown in the following Table 6.

Table 6. Impact of frequency on base station densities

Base stations per km²	UMTS 900	UMTS 1800	UMTS 2100
Suburban	0.017	0.027	0.037
Remote/rural	0.008	0.013	0.018

Source: Ofcom mobile liberalisation consultation

According to Nokia Siemens Networks (2008a) ("NSN"), WCDMA frequency refarming white Paper, with comparison to UMTS2100, in UMTS900 network the number of base stations can be reduced by 65%; TCO (total cost of ownership) can be reduced by 40%. TCO will be lower in the rural environment and can be reduced by 60% in five years. In typical suburban environment, comparing different band GSM and WCDMA base station coverage (voice and 1 Mbps data services), WCDMA900 using GSM900 same base station coverage can provide 1Mbps rate, as shown in the Figure 3 below.

Secondly, the UMTS900 network is better for indoor coverage and has better network coverage

Figure 3. Voice and 1Mbps data rate comparison of GSM and WCDMA

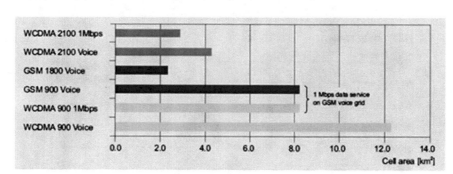

Figure 4. Data rates achieved by networks with the same number of sites and different spectrum bands, as seen from a range of indoor locations

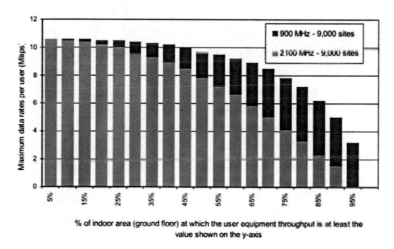

performance. Low-frequency carrier signals suffer less loss when penetrating building walls. Thus, with a UMTS900 network quality of service (QoS) is improved and better user experience. Since fewer base stations are required for UMTS900 roll-out than UMTS2100, the customer experience is better due to fewer hand-overs. Over 70% of phone calls are now made indoors and UMTS900 can help to improve the Quality of Services (QoS). By providing better indoor coverage, UMTS900 network can enhance the quality of service and subscriber's network experience.

Figure 4 below, shows the comparison of data achieved by networks with the same number of sites and different spectrum. From the Figure 4 we can see that UMTS 900 network provides higher data rates than a UMTS 2100 network in most indoor locations. For the last 20% of locations at which either network provides service, the UMTS 2100 customers get less than half the speed available for UTMS 900 customers, or practically no service at all (below 0.1 Mbps), while UMTS 900 customers still get good data rates (3 to 7 Mbps).

Compared with UMTS2100, UMTS900 outdoor propagation loss is decreased by 6-12dB, indoor penetration and propagation loss is lowered by 0-8dB. HSPA900 shows better performance improvement than HSPA210. HSPA2100 and HSPA900 performance comparison at different indoor penetration loss is shown in Figure 5 below.

Figure 5. HSPA data rates comparison for different frequencies under differ indoor penetration loss

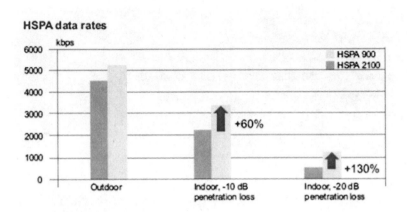

Thirdly, GSM900 and UMTS900 signal has almost similar propagation characteristics, therefore, when constructing UMTS900 network, UMTS900 can share infrastructures, antennas and feeders etc with existing GSM900 sites. This can reduces new network equipment, deployment costs, infrastructure costs, as well as reduces the maintenance costs. Shared antenna between GSM900 and UMTS900 is shown in Figure 6.

900 MHz Refarming Challenges

The introduction of UMTS900 into existing GSM spectrum involves their partial occupation of existing GSM 900 MHz frequencies. It raises both technical and regulatory issues. In the technical or engineering context it poses risks of a degradation of quality and an increase in number of dropped voice calls of GSM subscribers if the allocation of frequencies made between UMTS and GSM networks is not reasonable. In the regulatory and competitive context, the issue is one of policies that affect how increasingly precious spectrum below 1 GHz. It includes current 900 MHz allocations as well as future or in a very few countries recently allocated new digital dividend spectrum, should be made available to (or even redistributed among) competing mobile operators.

Figure 6. GSM/UMTS shared antenna system

The major challenges for refarming 900MHz spectrum and deployment of UMTS900 networks are as follows:

- Since GSM networks still carry large amounts of voice and data traffic, releasing GSM spectrum for UMTS900 services raises various issues for operators. Existing GSM capacity and quality need to be maintained despite using 5MHz of spectrum allocations in 900MHz for a single UMTS carrier. Traffic should be migrated from GSM to UMTS and cost will be increased during the migration, i.e. replacement of devices, decommissioning, hardware upgrades, labor costs etc.

- In many regions spectrum is still allocated in terms of technology. For regulatory liberalizing GSM spectrum raises a number of challenges. Various issues to be considered by regulators such as should operators that have been allocated with 900 MHz spectrum for GSM retain it after it is liberalized, or are there market or competition reasons to release some of that spectrum for other operators. Reasonable timescales for clearing / releasing the GSM spectrum for other operators.

- As service providers require 5MHz of paired spectrum for UMTS networks, obtaining sufficient spectrum at 900 MHz is a big challenge.

- Service providers need to contend with interference issues due to spectrum crowding. Managing and minimizing interference between existing GSM and UMTS systems will be one of the major challenge faced during the refarming and deployment of UMTS900 networks.

- Some existing GSM providers may choose to migrate from GSM with enhanced (E)-EDGE, before moving to UMTS technology. This will delay reaching sufficient traffic density to achieve in operational efficiency for UMTS900 networks.

- Availability of handsets that are compatible with both technologies in 900MHz and able to switch seamlessly between 900MHz and 2100Mhz.

TECHNICAL FEASIBILITY FROM NETWORK PERSPECTIVE

GSM/UMTS Frequency Allocation Mode

GSM900 and UMTS900 frequency allocation has two modes: a) Uncoordinated case b) Coordinated/sandwich mode, as shown in the Figure 7 and 8.

1. **Uncoordinated Case:** In uncoordinated case as shown in Figure 7, UMTS sub-band is located in the edge of the existing spectrum of the operators and is likely to be adjacent with other GSM operator frequencies. f1 ie carrier spacing/ centre frequency interval between same UMTS and the GSM system operator can be configured according to the product support minimum interval capability. There should be larger carrier spacing f2 between UMTS and center frequency of the other operators. As the RF performance of GSM of the other operators is unknown,

Figure 7. Uncoordinated case

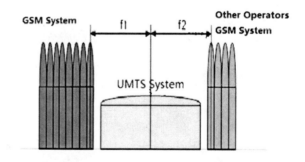

Figure 8. Coordinated/Sandwich Mode

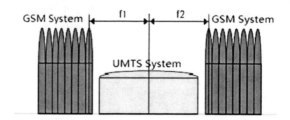

it may cause interference in the UMTS system, particularly when the edge GSM channel is used for BCCH (Broadcast Control Channel) or PDCH is (Packet Data Channel). As these channels do not use the power control, they may bring more interference to UMTS system in the future.

If the adjacent spectrum of other operator is UMTS compared to GSM, carrier spacing f2 can be smaller. UMTS system uses fast power control and the interference can be reduced.

2. **Coordinated /Sandwich Mode:** In coordinated/Sandwich mode as shown in Figure 8, UMTS sub-band is located between the GSM spectrum of the same operator, i.e. on both sides are the GSM spectrum of the same operator. Therefore, carrier spacing/centre frequency interval f1 and f2 between UMTS system and the GSM system can be configured as per minimum carrier spacing capability of the product. Thus, compared

to uncoordinated case, more GSM carriers may be configured in sandwich mode. Moreover, it is not required to reconsider or adjust frequency guard interval between edge frequency and other operator spectrum.

Interference in GSM/UMTS Co-Existence and Simulation Results

Research of 3GPP, ECC and other related institutions shows that UMTS900 more susceptible to interference from the GSM900 system. When GSM900 and the UMTS900 adjacent channel center frequency interval is less than the spacing recommended by 3GPP of 2.8MHz, recommended by the 2.8MHz, need to consider whether the actual deployed network equipment performance meets the requirements, especially the GSM900 transmitter (including base station and terminal) ACLR (adjacent channel power leakage ratio) indicator and UMTS900 receiver ACS (adjacent channel selectivity) indicator. Otherwise, the adjacent

Figure 9. Interference in GSM/UMTS co-existence

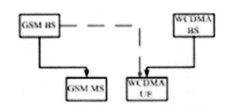
UMTS DL capacity loss due to GSM interference

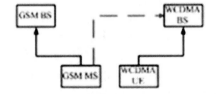
UMTS UL capacity loss due to GSM interference

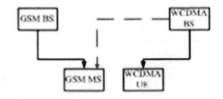
GSM DL outage due to UMTS interference

GSM UL outage due to UMTS interference

channel interference will reduce the UMTS900 the system capacity. 4 cases of GSM and UMTS interference in GSM/UMTS coexistence are given in Figure 9.

Simulation Results and Analysis

3GPP, ECC and other bodies, has capacity loss simulation results only for the frequency interval of 2.8M, but also provides the capacity loss with the variation of ACIR(adjacent channel interference ratio). Based on the ACIR values under differ frequency interval (carrier spacing) respective capacity loss can be derived. Generally while allocating GSM/UMTS frequency it is recommended GSM macro cell frequencies are adjacent UMTS frequencies, but GSM microcell frequencies will not be adjacent to UMTS frequencies, thus it only provides specific GSM macro cell frequencies and UMTS adjacent frequencies data. The summary of simulation assumptions for GSM/UMTS coexistence is given in Table 7.

Figure 10 provides the simulation result of UMTS DL as a victim the UMTS downlink capacity loss (%) due to interference from GSM downlink as function of ACIR between UMTS carrier and the nearest GSM carrier. It shows that, at ACIR=30.5 dB, the UMTS downlink capacity

loss due to interference from GSM downlink is smaller than 1.5%.

Figure 11 provides the simulation results for the case of UMTS UL as victim, the UMTS UL capacity loss (%) due to interference from GSM uplink as function of ACIR between UMTS carrier and the nearest GSM carrier. Taking the average results at the point of ACIR=43.1DB, the UMTS uplink capacity loss due to interference from GSM uplink is expected to be smaller than 5%.

The Figure 12 gives the simulation results (5 simulation curves) of UMTS DL as victim for the co-existence scenario 2, the UMTS downlink capacity loss due to interference from the GSM downlink as function of ACIR between UMTS carrier and the nearest GSM carrier. At the operating point of ACIR=30.5 dB, the UMTS downlink capacity loss is below 1.2%.

The Figure 13 provides the simulation results (4 simulation curves) for the case of UMTS UL as victim, the UMTS UL capacity loss (%) due to interference from GSM uplink as function of ACIR between UMTS carrier and the nearest GSM carrier. 19. As shown in Figure 13, all of the 4 simulation curves indicate that the UMTS uplink capacity loss due to interference from GSM MS at ACIR=43.1 dB is smaller than 3%.

Table 7. UMTS capacity loss when GSM/UMTS central frequency separation of 2.8MHz

UMTS(macro)-GSM(macro)		Different operators		Same operator	
Urban Cell radius 250m	DL capacity loss	< 1.5%	Scenario 1	--	
	UL capacity loss	< 5%		--	
Rural Cell radius 2500m	DL capacity loss	< 1.2%	Scenario 2	< 1%	Scenario 3
	UL capacity loss	< 3%		ignore	
Simulation conditions	1. GSM/UMTS central carrier spacing 2.8M 2. Frequency allocation mode: 1,2 Uncoordinated case: 3 Sandwich mode 3. UL ACIR=43.1dB; DL ACIR=30.5dB 4. Simulation scenario: (1) DL: GSM only BCCH channel;UL:GSM Maximum load, all timeslots are in use; (2) GSM doesn't use hopping; (3) GSM/UMTS co-existence relations: 1,2 GSM base station is located in the edge of the UMTS cell, 3 GSM/UMTS co-site.				

Figure 10. UMTS DL capacity loss due to GSM interference, scenario 1

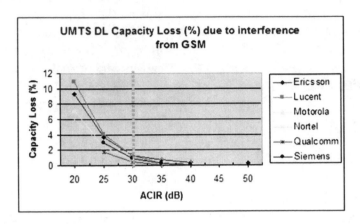

Figure 11. UMTS UL capacity loss due to GSM interference, scenario 1

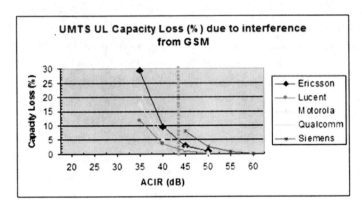

Figure 12. UMTS DL capacity loss due to GSM interference, scenario 2

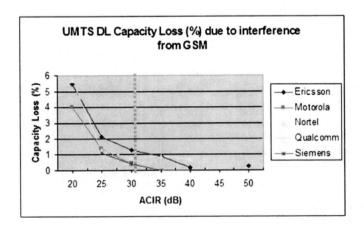

Figure 13. UMTS UL capacity loss due to GSM interference, scenario 2

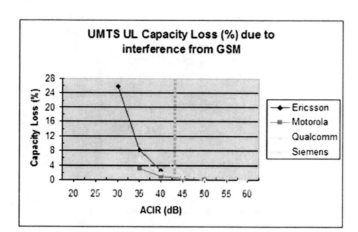

Figure 14. UMTS DL capacity due to GSM interference, scenario 3

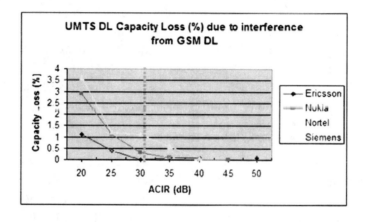

Figure 14 provides simulation assumptions where two simulation cases (UMTS DL and UL as victim) were studied for this co-existence scenario 3. Four simulation curves of simulation results of UMTS DL as victim are plotted in Figure 14, the UMTS downlink capacity loss due to interference from GSM downlink as function of ACIR between UMTS carrier and the nearest GSM carrier. It is shown in Figure 14 that at the operating point of ACIR=30.5 dB, the UMTS downlink capacity loss is below 1%.

The simulation results for the case of UMTS UL as victim, th e UMTS UL capacity loss (%) due to interference from GSM uplink as function of ACIR between UMTS carrier and the nearest GSM carrier, are given in Figure 15. Three simulation results/curves of UMTS uplink capacity loss due to interference from GSM uplink for the scenario 3 are plotted in figure15. As shown in the Figure 15, at ACIR=43.1 dB, the UMTS uplink capacity loss is very small, it is negligible.

Figure 15. UMTS UL capacity due to GSM interference, scenario 3

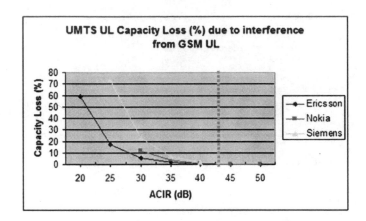

UMTS900 REFARMING A CASE STUDY ON SANDWICH MODE

A certain operator has GSM network operating on 6.2MHz of 900 MHz spectrum and 4.4 MHz spectrum will be available on 1800 MHz Band. It is preparing for deployment of UMTS900 as 2100MHz spectrum for UMTS was not allocated to this particular operator. Detailed study on interference analysis and technical feasibility between GSM/UMTS system was done and solution for UMTS900 refarming based on spectrum availability is presented as an example.

Sandwich mode is selected to avoid or to minimize the interference between GSM and UMTS system. 900MHz refarming solutions support a minimum bandwidth of 2.4MHz in urban areas and 2.2MHz in rural. In the initial phase I, carrier spacing of 2.2MHz between GSM900

and UMTS900 is used. It requires 4.2MHz to be freed from GSM900 and allocated to UMTS900, GSM900 will continue to use remaining 2MHz spectrum. 4.4MHz in 1800MHz will be used to absorb the existing GSM network capacity demands. GSM and UMTS will be co-located and the UMTS frequencies will be surrounded by the GSM frequencies of the same operator as shown in Figure 16.

Gradually, subscriber will be migrated from GSM900 to UMTS900 in phase II as shown in Figure 17. 2.2 MHz carrier spacing is recommended only as temporary solution, as long as the UMTS900 traffic demand is low and all possibilities of tighten the GSM reuse are exhausted. Accompanying with UMTS subscribers growth, in phase II, carrier spacing of 2.4MHz between GSM and UMTS900 will be deployed. It requires 4.6MHz to be freed from GSM900 and allocated

Figure 16. Phase I 2.2MHz and Phase II 2.4 carrier spacing between GSM and UMTS

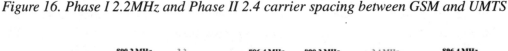
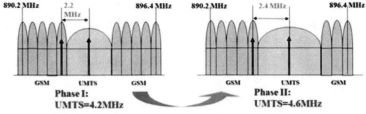

Figure 17. Phase I and phase II GSM/UMTS deployment plan and subscriber migration

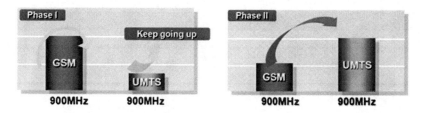

to UMTS900, GSM900 will continue to use 1.6MHz of remaining spectrum. Operator will continue to use 4.4MHz in 1800MHz to absorb the existing GSM network capacity demands. 15% of the existing users will be migrated to UMTS network. GSM and UMTS will be co-located and the UMTS frequencies will be surrounded by the GSM frequencies of the same operator UMTS900 bandwidth will be increase to 4.6MHz in the second phase as shown in Figure 16.

GSM/UMTS900 System Simulation Analysis

Simulation results for carrier spacing is 2.2, 2.4 and 2.6MHz and UMTS carrier of 4.2, 4.6 and 5MHz

System analysis and simulations for different carrier spacing scenarios are done to calculate UMTS UL carrier loss. As per 3GPP the threshold for co-existence is that the UMTS UL/DL capacity loss due to interference from GSM UL/DL should not be bigger than 5%. The simulation results show that a lower carrier spacing decreases the capacity performance of UMTS900. The simulation results from Figure 18 and 19 shows that for carrier spacing of 2.6 MHz and UMTS carrier 5MHz, UMTS UL capacity loss is less than 0.5%, for carrier spacing of 2.4 MHz and UMTS carrier 4.6MHz, UMTS UL capacity loss is less than 1.2%, for carrier spacing of 2.2 MHz and UMTS carrier 4.2MHz, UMTS UL capacity loss is less than 2.5%.

Figure 18. UMTS UL capacity loss due to interference from GSM

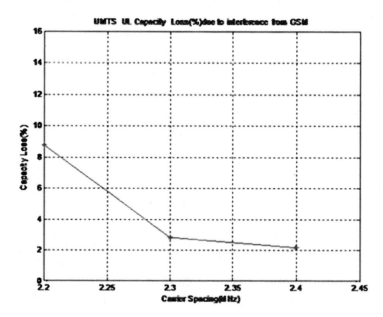

Figure 19. UMTS capacity loss (%) for various carrier spacing scenarios

Carrier Spacing (MHz)	UMTS Carrier (MHz)	UMTS UL Capacity Loss
2.2	4.2	<2.5%
2.4	4.6	<1.2%
2.6	5	<0.5%

Frequency Planning and Capacity Migration Strategy

Frequency hopping has a great impact on the network quality, especially if the load of the frequency hopping is too high. More compact frequency reuse technology was adopted. In the first phase, 4.2MHz UMTS900 in sandwich mode will be surrounded by GSM of same operators and co-location of GSM and UMTS. GSM will adopt frequency hopping. GSM BCCH frequencies separated far from UMTS frequencies and Non-BCCH GSM frequencies will be used near to UMTS frequencies as shown in Figure 20. It is recommended that the maximum load of frequency hopping in TCH (traffic channel) should not be greater than 50%.

If the frequency reuse in the live network is loose, under the pre-condition of certain C/I performance, a more compact frequency reuse pattern can be considered. For example if the BCCH reuse pattern is 5X3, we can consider changing to 4X3, similarly if TCH reuse pattern is 1X3, we can consider changing to 1X1. The BCCH band and PDCH band should be as far as possible from UMTS to minimize the interference of UMTS900 and the GSM system. Frequency re-planning strategy for GSM using remaining 2MHz of 900 MHz spectrum and available 4.4MHz in 1800MHz spectrum is carefully studied. To match the existing GSM 900MHz network coverage the number if sites required to be added is calculated.

The following principles are adopted to insure the smooth migration of original subscribers.

1. Improving GSM900 network capacity without degrading the service quality.
2. Migrating GSM900 traffic to GSM1800 and traffic balance between GSM900 and GSM1800.
3. Migrating GSM900 traffic to UMTS and traffic balance between GSM and UMTS.

The capacity of GSM system mainly depends on the amount of spectrum resources allocated. Given the same network quality, the more resources an operator has, the more TRXs can be configured and the more subscribers the network can support. After 900 MHz refarming a part of GSM900 is reduced and the maximum sites configuration is

Figure 20. GSM900 and UMTS900 refarming

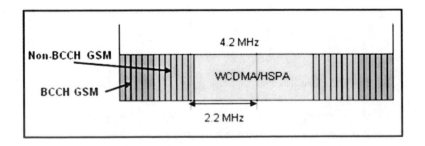

Figure 21. GSM subscribers remains stable in a period of time

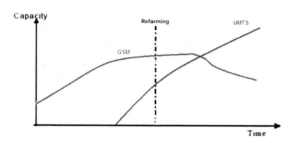

Figure 22. GSM subscribers remains keeps increasing in a period of time

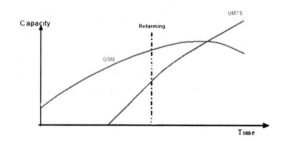

reduced, ie the number of subscribers a network can support is decreased. Therefore, the number of subscribers absorbed by the GSM900 network will decline significantly.

Especially in urban areas, VIP areas and hot-spots with higher configuration without necessary traffic balance after GSM900 capacity reduction, service quality failure will lead to rise of wide-spread customer complaints. If 1800 MHz is available, traffic balance can relieve the traffic load of GSM900 to some extent. However, the coverage of 900MHz differs from that of 1800MHz, so 1800MHz cannot efficiently absorb users on the outer layer of 900MHz.

As 1800MHz is available traffic balance within GSM system between two frequency bands was considered first. GSM1800 is fully used to absorb the traffic and relieve the traffic load of GSM900 Network. It is a most common practice to select dual-band network for capacity migration involved in frequency refarming. It is usually applicable for markets where GSM is and will be dominant for a period of time as shown in Figure 21 and 22. To absorb the traffic as much as possible, besides network parameter setting, we should guarantee continuous good coverage of GSM1800. Optimization of GSM1800 network should be done on first priority. Balance between capacity and coverage should be considered while expanding the GSM1800 capacity. GSM900 network traffic congestion due to GSM1800 coverage shrinkage should be avoided. Network parameter setting for

GSM900 and GSM1800 traffic balance, 2-3G inter operation parameters setting will not be elaborated in this chapter.

FUTURE RESEARCH DIRECTIONS

With the arrival of mobile broadband era, wireless network traffic will grow in an explosive rate of a 500 times. Demand for wireless data and Internet services are expected to grow exponentially, both in advanced and emerging markets in the near future. The traditional GSM voice users will no longer be satisfied with the speed of data access. Therefore, how to cope with increasing demand for mobile data services? How to protect the network investment of the equipment and deployment, smooth evolution to UMTS, have further LTE? Global mobile operators are looking for solutions.

On the other hand, the frequency resources are very limited and non inexhaustible. As user's demand of the frequency resource continues to grow, frequency resources limitation is increasingly prominent. In addition, the high auction fee paid for used frequency resources and huge investment of high frequency resources brings high-cost operating pressure to the network operators. Therefore, for network operators reasonable planning and effective use of the frequency resources has becomes very critical.

As mobile operators tread the 4G path they will be forced to focus on using their existing 2G and 3G spectrum resources in different ways and with different combinations. At the same time, operators will be struggling for new spectrum allocations to meet increasing network coverage and capacity demands dictated by the mobile internet. Spectrum refarming relates to allowing operators to use their existing spectrum on a technology neutral basis. Allowing neutrality at 900MHz will not automatically involve spectrum assignment or reallocation in the band. Refarming will indeed offer the opportunity for the band reorganization as necessary. GSM/UMTS900 refarming and GSM/LTE1800 refarming solution will provide the best answer in the future.

CONCLUSION

The following conclusions can be made from the study of UMTS900 refarming and analysis on simulation results of various GSM/UMTS co-existence scenarios:

- It is recommended to use 2.8MHz carrier spacing between GSM900 and UMTS900 of different operators in uncoordinated case.
- It is recommended 5MHz carrier spacing between two UMTS900 of different operators in uncoordinated case.
- It is recommended 2.8MHz – 2.2MHz carrier spacing between GSM900 and UMTS900 of same operators in coordinated/ sandwich mode.
- 900MHz refarming solutions support a minimum bandwidth of 2.4MHz in urban areas and 2.2MHz in rural.
- The Coverage area of UMTS900 is 3 to 5 times larger compared to coverage area of UMTS2100.
- The indoor coverage of UMTS900 is 10 to 20 db better than the indoor coverage of UMTS2100.

- The HSPA throughput of UMTS900 at cell edge is more than doubled compared to UMTS2100 at cell edge.
- RF system characteristics assumed for UMTS900 are suitable and sufficient for UMTS900 to be deployed in rural environments in co-existence with GSM at cell ranges of 5000 m in coordinated operation.

REFERENCES

ECC REPORT 82. (2006). *Comparability study for UMTS operating within the GSM 900 and GSM 1800 frequency bands*. 3GPP. TS45.005 (Rel-5), GSM/EDGE Radio Access Network, Radio Transmission and Reception. 3GPP.

GSA UMTS900 Global Status Report. (2013, May). *GSM/3G market/technology update*. Global Mobile Suppliers Association.

Hadden, A. (2008, December). UMTS900 market overview. In *Proceedings of the UMTS900 Workshop*. UMTS.

Lin, L. C. (2010, February). Get ready for 900MHz Refarming. *Huawei Communicate, 54*.

Nagpal, A., Sanders, L., & Dobsonm, J. (2010). *Liberalising 2G spectrum and GSM refarming*. Analysys Mason Limited.

Nokia Siemens Networks. (2008a). *WCDMA frequency refarming: A leap forward towards ubiquitous mobile broadband coverage*. Nokia.

Nokia Siemens Networks. (2008b). *Extending 3G coverage with cost-efficient WCDMA frequency refarming*. Nokia.

Nokia Siemens Networks. (2008c). WCDMA frequency refarming overview. In *Proceedings of the Mobile World Congress*. Nokia.

Prieur, E. (2009, September). Developing a fully inclusive mobile broadband strategy: Bring mobile broadband to remote and rural areas. In Proceedings of Mobile Broadband World. IEEE.

GSA Report. (2008, September). *UMTS900—A case study*. Global Mobile Suppliers Association.

GSA Report. (2009, June). *UMTS900—A case study optus*. Global Mobile Suppliers Association.

Vanghi, V., Saglam, M., & Jindi, J. (2007). Frequency coordination between UMTS and GSM systems at 900 MHz. In *Proceedings of the IEEE 18th International Symposium*. IEEE.

Vieira, R. D., Paiva, R. C. D., Hulkkonen, J., Jarvela, R., Iida, R. F., & Saily, M. … Niemela, K. (2010). GSM evolution importance in refarming 900 MHz band. In *Proceedings of the 2010 IEEE 72nd Vehicular Technology Conference*. IEEE.

KEY TERMS AND DEFINITIONS

Carrier Spacing: Carrier spacing is a term used in radio frequency planning. It describes the frequency difference between adjacent allocations in a frequency plan.

Cell Radius: Cell radius is a term used to describe the geographical limit of reliable transmissions from a particular focused transmission beam of a mobile cellular base station or Point to Multi point radio system.

DL: DL (Downlink), where information are sent from base station to mobile station.

ECC: ECC refers to Electronic Communications Committee. The ECC considers and develops policies on electronic communications activities in European context, taking account of European and international legislations and regulations.

EDGE: Enhanced Data rates for GSM Evolution (EDGE) is a digital mobile phone technology that allows improved data transmission rates as a backward-compatible extension of GSM. EDGE is considered a pre-3G radio technology and is part of ITU's 3G definition.

GSM: GSM (Global system for Mobile Communications) is a standard second generation (2G) protocol developed by European Telecommunications Standards Institute. Second generation of mobile telephony systems uses digital encoding. 2G networks support voice, limited data communications.

GSM1800: GSM1800 is a term used to describe GSM used in the 1800 MHz frequency band.

GSM900: GSM900 is a term used to describe GSM used in the 900 MHz frequency band.

Interference: Interference is the effect of unwanted signals upon the reception of a wanted signal in a radio system, resulting in degradation of performance, misinterpretation or loss of information compared with that which would have been received in the absence of the unwanted signal.

Link Budget: Link budget is a careful accounting of all the gains and losses from the transmitter, through the medium (considering propagation loss, feeder jumper cables loss etc) to the receiver in a telecommunication system.

LTE: Long term evolution (LTE) marketed as 4G LTE, is a standard for wireless communication of high-speed data for mobile phones and data terminals. It is based on the GSM/EDGE and UMTS/HSPA network technologies, increasing the capacity and speed using a different radio interface together with core network improvements.

Propagation: Propagation means the transmission of radio waves. Propagation characteristics depend on frequency and are affected by the environmental conditions, such as terrain and atmospheric conditions, encountered on the path.

Refarming: Refarming means re-arrangement of existing spectrum and carving out a part of the spectrum for services with higher value. The users of the existing spectrum are forced out, although they may be compensated in some manner. The frequency bands are assigned to communications services that yield greater economic or social benefit.

Simulation: Simulation is an approach which can be used to model large complex stochastic systems for forecasting or performance measurement purposes. Simulation models in the telecommunication field are used to solve a wide variety of problems at different decision making levels.

UL: UL (Uplink), where information are sent from mobile station to the base station.

UMTS: UMTS (The universal Mobile Telecommunications system) is a third generation (3G) mobile cellular system for networks based on the GSM standard developed and maintained by 3GPP. Third generation of mobile telephony systems provide higher data speeds and supports multi-media applications such as full-motion video, video conferencing and internet access.

UMTS2100: UMTS2100 is a term used to describe UMTS used in the 2100 MHz frequency band.

UMTS900: UMTS900 is a term used to describe UMTS used in the 900 MHz frequency band.

Compilation of References

Aad, I., Hubaux, J. P., & Knightly, E. W. (2008). Impact of denial of service attacks on ad hoc networks. *IEEE/ACM Transactions on Networking, 16*(4), 791–802. doi:10.1109/TNET.2007.904002.

Abdalla, G. M. T., Abu-rgheff, M. A., & Senouci, S. M. (2007). *Current trends in vehicular ad hoc networks*. Paper presented at the UBIROADS Workshop. New York, NY.

Abdallah, Y., Latif, M. A., Youssef, M., Sultan, A., & El Gamal, H. (2011). Keys through ARQ: Theory and practice. *IEEE Transactions on Information Forensics and Security, 6*(3), 737–751. doi:10.1109/TIFS.2011.2123093.

Abdulkawi, A., Saleh, T. S., Khattab, S., & Farag, I. (2012). Anti-jamming defense in wireless networks using channel hopping and error correcting code. In *Proceedings of the 8th International Conference on Informatics and Systems (INFOS)* (pp. 12-17). INFOS.

Abdullah, M. Y., Hua, G. W., & Alsharabi, N. (2008). Wireless sensor networks misdirection attacker challenges and solutions. In *Proceedings of the International Conference on Information and Automation*. Zhang Jia Jie City, China: IEEE Press.

Abdul-Rahman, A., & Hailes, S. (1997). A distributed trust model. *Proceedings of of the ACM workshop on New security paradigms*.

Abdul-Rahman, A., & Hailes, S. (2000). Supporting trust in virtual communities. *HICSS 33.*

Aberer, K., Hauswirth, M., & Salehi, A. (2006). *Global sensor networks* (Technical report LSIR-REPORT-2006-001). Lausanne, Switzerland: School of Computer and Communication Sciences. Retrieved from http://lsirpeople.epfl.ch/salehi/papers/LSIR-REPORT-2006-001.pdf

Abumansoor, O., & Boukerche, A. (2011). A cooperative multi-hop location verification for non line of sight (NLOS) in VANET. In *Proceedings of the IEEE Wireless Communications and Networking Conference (WCNC)* (pp. 773-778). IEEE.

Abumansoor, O., & Boukerche, A. (2011). *Towards a secure trust model for vehicular ad hoc networks services.* IEEE Globecomm. doi:10.1109/GLOCOM.2011.6134243.

Abumansoor, O., & Boukerche, A. (2012). A secure cooperative approach for nonline-of-sight location verification in VANET. *IEEE Transactions on Vehicular Technology, 61*(1), 275–285. doi:10.1109/TVT.2011.2174465.

Acquaviva, A., Aldini, A., Bernardo, M., Bogliolo, A., Bontà, E., & Lattanzi, E. (2004). Assessing the impact of dynamic power management on the functionality and the performance of battery-powered appliances. In *Proceedings of the 5th International Conference on Dependable Systems and Networks (DSN'04)—Performance and Dependability Symposium*, (pp. 731-740). IEEE CS Press.

Acs, G., Buttyan, L., & Vajda, I. (2006). Provably secure on-demand source routing in mobile ad hoc networks. *IEEE Transactions on Mobile Computing, 5*(11), 1533–1546. doi:10.1109/TMC.2006.170.

Adigun, A., Amar Bensaber, B., & Biskri, I. (2012). Proof of concept of a security based on lifetime of communication's pseudonyms for the VANETs. In *Proceedings of the Second ACM International Symposium on Design and Analysis of Intelligent Vehicular Networks and Applications* (pp. 111-114). ACM.

Adjih, C., Clausen, T., Jacquet, P., Laouiti, A., Muhlethaler, P., & Raffo, D. (2003). Securing the OLSR protocol. In *Proceedings of Med-Hoc-Net* (pp. 25–27). IEEE.

Advanced, L. T. E. (n.d.). *Wikipedia*. Retrieved April 20, 2013, from http://en.wikipedia.org/wiki/LTE_Advanced

Agrawal, P., Ghosh, R. K., & Das, S. K. (2008). Cooperative black and gray hole attacks in mobile ad hoc networks. In *Proceedings of the 2nd International Conference on Ubiquitous Information Management and Communication* (pp. 310-314). ACM.

Agrawal, A., Rezki, Z., Khisti, A., & Alouini, M. (2011). Noncoherent capacity of secret-key agreement with public discussion. *IEEE Transactions on Information Forensics and Security, 6*(3), 565–574. doi:10.1109/TIFS.2011.2158999.

Agrawal, P., & Bhuraria, S. (2012). Near field communication. *SETLab Briefings, 10*(1), 67–76.

Ahlswede, R., & Csiszar, I. (1993). Common randomness in information theory and cryptography—Part I: Secret sharing. *IEEE Transactions on Information Theory, 39*(4), 1121–1132. doi:10.1109/18.243431.

Akhlaq, M., Aslam, B., Alserhani, F., Awan, I. U., & Mellor, J. (2009). Empowered certification authority in VANETs. In *Proceedings of the International Conference on Advanced Information Networking and Applications Workshops* (pp. 181-186). IEEE.

Akyildiz, I. F., Su W., Sankarasubramaniam, Y., & Cayirci, E. (2002). Wireless sensor networks: A survey. *Computer Networks, 38*, 393–422. doi:10.1.1.5.2442

Akyildiz, I. F., Lee, W. Y., Vuran, M. C., & Mohanty, S. (2006). NeXt generation/dynamic spectrum access/cognitive radio wireless networks: A survey. *Computer Networks, 50*(13), 2127–2159. doi:10.1016/j.comnet.2006.05.001.

Akyildiz, I. F., & Vuran, M. C. (2010). *Wireless sensor networks*. New York: John Wiley & Sons. doi:10.1002/9780470515181.

Akyildiz, I. F., & Wang, X. (2005). A survey on WMNs. *IEEE Communications Magazine*.

Aldini, A., & Bogliolo, A. (2012a). *Trading performance and cooperation incentives in user-centric networks*. Paper presented at the International Workshop on Quantitative Aspects in Security Assurance. Pisa, Italy.

Aldini, A., & Bogliolo, A. (2012b). Model checking of trust-based user-centric cooperative networks. In *Proceedings of AFIN 2012: The Fourth International Conference on Advances in Future Internet* (pp. 32-41). IARIA.

Aldini, A., Bernardo, M., & Corradini, F. (2010). *A process algebraic approach to software architecture design*. New York: Springer. doi:10.1007/978-1-84800-223-4.

Alemdar, H., & Erosy, C. (2010). Wireless sensor networks for healthcare: A survey. *Journal Elsevier-Computer Networks, 54*(1), 2688–2710. doi:10.1016/j.comnet.2010.05.003.

Alfarez, A. R., & Stephen, H. (1997). A distributed trust model. In *Proceedings of the 1997 Workshop on New Security Paradigms - NSPW '97* (pp. 48-60). Cumbria, UK: NSPW.

Almeida, J., Shintre, S., Boban, M., & Barros, J. (2011). A dynamic key distribution protocol for PKI-based VANETs. In *Proceedings of the IEEE/IFIP Wireless Days (WD)* (pp. 1-3). Niagara Falls, Canada: IEEE.

Alonso, J. A., & Lamata, M. T. (2006). Consistency in the analytic hierarchy process: A new approach. *International Journal of Uncertainty. Fuzziness and Knowledge-Based Systems, 14*(4), 445–459. doi:10.1142/S0218488506004114.

AL-Raisi. N. E. (2009). Wireless sensor networks performance measurements and monitoring. In Proceeding of Symposia and Workshops on Ubiquitous, Autonomic and Trusted Computing (pp. 286-291). Brisbane, Australia: IEEE.

AL-Raisi. N. E. (2010). A novel approach for monitoring wireless sensor network performance by tracking node operational deviation. In *Proceedings of IEEE-ISCC2010* (pp. 113-119). IEEE.

Alshaer, H., & Elmirghani, J. J. M. (2009). Road safety based on efficient vehicular communications. In *Proceedings of the IEEE Intelligent Vehicle Symposium*. XI'an, China: IEEE.

Alshaer, H., & Horlait, E. (2004). Emerging client-server and ad-hoc approach in inter-vehicle communication platform. In *Proceedings of the IEEE VTC-Fall*. Los Angeles, CA: IEEE.

Alshaer, H., & Horlait, E. (2005). An optimized adaptive broadcast scheme for inter-vehicle communication. In *Proceedings of the IEEE VTC-Spring*. Stockholm, Sweden: IEEE.

Alshaer, H., Ernst, T., & Fortelle, A. D. L. (2012). A QoS architecture for provisioning high quality in intelligent transportation services. In *Proceedings of the 13th IEEE/IFIP Network Operations and Management Symposium (NOMS)* (pp. 595-598). IEEE.

Alshaer, H., Ernst, T., & Fortelle, A. D. L. (2012). An integrated architecture for multi-homed vehicle-to-infrastructure communications. In *Proceedings of 1the 3th IEEE/IFIP Network Operations and Management Symposium (NOMS)* (pp. 1042-1047). IEEE.

Al-Shurman, M., Yoo, S. M., & Park, S. (2004). Black hole attack in mobile ad hoc networks. In *Proceedings of the 42nd Annual Southeast Regional Conference* (pp. 96-97). ACM.

Alur, R., & Dill, D. (1994). A theory of timed automata. *Theoretical Computer Science, 126*, 183–235. doi:10.1016/0304-3975(94)90010-8.

Alur, R., & Henzinger, T. (1999). Reactive modules. *Formal Methods in System Design, 15*, 7–48. doi:10.1023/A:1008739929481.

Alves, H., Souza, R., Debbah, M., & Bennis, M. (2012). Performance of transmit antenna selection physical layer security schemes. *IEEE Signal Processing Letters, 19*(6), 372–375. doi:10.1109/LSP.2012.2195490.

Alzaid, H., Abanmi, S., Kanhere, S., & Chou, C. T. (2008). BANAID: A sensor network test-bed for wormhole attacks. In *Proceedings of SETMAPE Research and Development Stream of the AUSCERT 2008 Conference*. The University of Queensland St. Lucia.

Anderson, R. (2012). Risk and privacy implications of consumer payment innovation. In *Proceedings of the Consumer Payment Innovation in the Connected Age Conference*. Kansas City, KS: IEEE.

Anderson, R., & Stajano, F. (1999). {The Resurrecting Duckling}.

Anderson, R., Chan, H., & Perrig, A. (2004). Key infection: Smart trust for smart dust. In *Proceedings of the 12th IEEE International Conference on Network Protocols,* (pp. 206-215). IEEE.

Anita, E. M., & Vasudevan, V. (2010). Black hole attack prevention in multicast routing protocols for mobile ad hoc networks using certificate chaining. *International Journal of Computers and Applications, 1*(12), 21–22.

Anjum, F., & Mouchtaris, P. (2007). *Security for wireless ad hoc networks*. New York: Wiley-Interscience. doi:10.1002/0470118474.

Aono, T., Higuchi, K., Ohira, T., Komiyama, B., & Sasaoka, H. (2005). Wireless secret key generation exploiting reactance-domain scalar response of multipath fading channels. *IEEE Transactions on Antennas and Propagation, 53*, 3776–3784. doi:10.1109/TAP.2005.858853.

Aparicio-Navarro, F. J., Kyriakopoulos, K. G., & Parish, D. J. (2011). An on-line wireless attack detection system using multi-layer data fusion. In *Proceedings of the 2011 IEEE International Workshop on Measurements and Networking* (pp. 1-5). IEEE.

Aparicio-Navarro, F. J., Kyriakopoulos, K. G., & Parish, D. J. (2012). A multi-layer data fusion system for wi-fi attack detection using automatic belief assignment. In *Proceedings of the 2012 World Congress on Internet Security*[WorldCIS.]. WORLD (Oakland, Calif.), CIS-2012, 45–50.

Awerbuch, B., Curtmola, R., Holmer, D., Rubens, H., & Nita-Rotaru, C. (2005). On the survivability of routing protocols in ad hoc wireless networks. In *Proceedings of the First International Conference on Security and Privacy for Emerging Areas in Communications Networks,* (pp. 327-338). IEEE.

Awerbuch, B., Holmer, D., Nita-Rotaru, C., & Rubens, H. (2002). An on-demand secure routing protocol resilient to byzantine failures. In *Proceedings of the 1st ACM Workshop on Wireless Security* (pp. 21-30). ACM.

Awerbuch, B., Curtmola, R., Holmer, D., Nita-Rotaru, C., & Rubens, H. (2008). ODSBR: An on-demand secure Byzantine resilient routing protocol for wireless ad hoc networks. *ACM Transactions on Information and System Security, 10*(4), 6. doi:10.1145/1284680.1341892.

Aziz, B., Nourdine, E., & Mohamed, E. K. (2008). A recent survey on key management schemes in manet. In *Proceedings of the 3rd International Conference on Information and Communication Technologies: From Theory to Applications,* (pp. 1-6). IEEE.

Baccelli, E., Jacquet, P., & Rodolakis, G. (2008). IEEE 802.11p: Towards an international standard for wireless access in vehicular environments. In *Proceedings of the Vehicular Technology Conference (VTC) Spring* (pp. 2036-2040). Singapore: IEEE.

Backhauling X2. (n.d.). Retrieved April 20, 2013, from http://cbnl.com/sites/all/files/userfiles/files/Backhauling-X2_0.pdf

Baier, C., & Katoen, J.-P. (2008). *Principles of model checking*. Cambridge, MA: MIT Press.

Balakrishnan, V., Varadharajan, V., & Tupakula, U. K. (2006). Fellowship: Defense against flooding and packet drop attacks in MANET. In *Proceedings of the Network Operations and Management Symposium,* (pp. 1-4). IEEE.

Baliga, A., Chen, X., Coskun, B., Reyes, G., Lee, S., Mathur, S., & van der Merwe, J. E. (2011). VPMN: Virtual private mobile network towards mobility-as-a-service. In L. Cox & E. de Lara (Eds.), *Proceedings of the 2nd International Workshop on Mobile Cloud Computing and Services (MCS '11)* (pp. 7-12). Bethesda, MD: ACM Press.

Balzano, L. K. (2007). *Addressing fault and calibration in wireless sensor networks*. (Master Thesis). University of California, Los Angeles, CA.

Bao, F., Chen, I.-R., Chang, M., & Cho, J.-H. (2012, June). Hierarchical Trust Management for Wireless Sensor Networks and its Applications to Trust-Based Routing and Intrusion Detection. *IEEE TRANSACTIONS ON NETWORK AND SERVICE MANAGEMENT*, 169-183.

Baracca, P., Laurenti, N., & Tomasin, S. (2012). Physical layer authentication over MIMO fading wiretap channels. *IEEE Transactions on Wireless Communications, 11*(7), 2564–2573. doi:10.1109/TWC.2012.051512.111481.

Baras, G. T. (2006). On Trust Models and Trust Evaluation Metrics for Ad hoc Networks. *IEEE Journal on Selected Areas in Communications, 24*(2), 318–328. doi:10.1109/JSAC.2005.861390.

Baras, J. S., & Jiang, T. (2005). {Managing Trust in Self-Organized Mobile. *Ad Hoc Networks*.

Barbeau, M. (2005). WiMAX/802.16 threat analysis. In *Proceedings of the 1st ACM International Workshop on Quality of Service & Security in Wireless and Mobile Networks* (pp. 8-15). New York: ACM.

Barbeau, M., & Laurendeau, C. (2007). Analysis of threats to WiMAX/802.16 decurity. In C. Xhang, & H. H. Chen (Eds.), *Mobile WiMAX: Toward broadband wireless metropolitan area networks*. Boca Raton, FL: Taylor and Francis CRC Press.

Barna, C., Shtern, M., Smit, M., Tzerpos, V., & Litoiu, M. (2012). Model-based adaptive dos attack mitigation. In *Proceedings of the ICSE Workshop on Software Engineering for Adaptive and Self-Managing Systems (SEAMS)* (pp. 119-128). ICSE.

Barros, J., & Rodrigues, M. R. D. (2006). Secrecy capacity of wireless channels. In *Proceedings of the 2006 IEEE International Symposium on Information Theory,* (pp. 356-360). Seattle, WA: IEEE.

Barros, J., & Rodrigues, M. R. D. (2006). Secrecy capacity of wireless channels. *In Proceedings of the IEEE International Symposium on Information Theory*, (pp. 356–360). Seattle, WA: IEEE.

Bashar, S., Ding, Z., & Xiao, C. (2012). On secrecy rate analysis of MIMO wiretap channels driven by finite-alphabet input. *IEEE Transactions on Communications, 60*(12), 3816–3825. doi:10.1109/TCOMM.2012.091212.110199.

Bassily, R., & Ulukus, S. (2012). Secure communication in multiple relay networks through decode-and-forward strategies. *Journal of Communications and Networks, 14*(4), 352–363.

Becher, A., Benenson, Z., & Dornseif, M. (2006). Tampering with motes: Real-world physical attacks on wireless sensor networks. In *Security in pervasive computing* (pp. 104–118). Berlin: Springer-Verlag. doi:10.1007/11734666_9.

Benjamin, R. (1990). Security considerations in communications systems and networks. *IEEE Proceedings I: Communications, Speech and Vision, 137*(2), 61-72.

Bennett, C., Brassard, G., Crepeau, C., & Maurer, U. (1995). Generalized privacy amplification. *IEEE Transactions on Information Theory, 41*(6), 1915–1923. doi:10.1109/18.476316.

Bertino, E., Paci, F., & Ferrini, R. (2009). Privacy-preserving digital identity management for cloud computing. *IEEE Computer Society Data Engineering Bulletin, 1*(32), 1–4.

Bhargava, S., & Agrawal, D. P. (2001). Security enhancements in AODV protocol for wireless ad hoc networks. In *Proceedings of the Vehicular Technology Conference,* (Vol. 4, pp. 2143-2147). IEEE.

Bisheng, L., Yiping, Z., & Shiyong, Z. (2007). *Probabilistic isolation of malicious vehicles in pseudonym changing VANETs.* Paper presented at the Computer and Information Technology, 2007. New York, NY.

Biswas, K., & Ali, M. L. (2007, March). Security threats in mobile ad hoc network. *Department of Interaction and System Design School of Engineering,* 9-26.

Blaze, M., Feigenbaum, J., & Keromytis, A. D. (1998). KeyNote: Trust management for public-key infrastructures. In B. Christianson, B. Crispo, W. S. Harbison, & M. Roe (Eds.), *Security protocols: 6th International Workshop* (LNCS), (Vol. 1550, pp. 59-63). Berlin, Germany: Springer.

Blaze, M., Feigenbaum, J., & Lacy., J. (1996). {Decentralized trust management}.

Blaze, M., Feigenbaum, J., Ioannidis, J., & Keromytis, A. (1999). *{The KeyNote Trust Management System}.* RFC 2704.

Blaze, M., Kannan, S., Lee, I., Sokolsky, O., Smith, J. M., Keromytis, A. D., & Lee, W. (2009). Dynamic trust management. *IEEE Computer, 42*(2), 44–51. doi:10.1109/MC.2009.51.

Blazevic, L., Le Boudec, J. Y., & Giordano, S. (2005). A location-based routing method for mobile ad hoc networks. *IEEE Transactions on Mobile Computing, 4*(2), 97–110. doi:10.1109/TMC.2005.16.

Bloch, M., Thangaraj, A., McLaughlin, S., & Merolla, J.-M. (2006). LDPC-based secret key agreement over the Gaussian wiretap channel. In *Proceedings of the 2006 IEEE International Symposium on Information Theory* (pp. 1179-1183). IEEE.

Bloch, M., Barros, J., Rodrigues, M. R. D., & McLaughlin, S. W. (2008). Wireless information- Theoretic security. *IEEE Transactions on Information Theory, 54,* 2515–2534. doi:10.1109/TIT.2008.921908.

Bloch, M., Barros, J., Rodrigues, M. R. D., & McLaughlin, S. W. (2008). Wireless information-theoretic security. *IEEE Transactions on Information Theory, 54*(6), 2515–2534. doi:10.1109/TIT.2008.921908.

Bloch, M., Debbah, M., Liang, Y., Oohama, Y., & Thangaraj, A. (2012). Special issue on physical-layer security. *Journal of Communications and Networks, 14*(4), 349–351.

Blum, J. J., Eskandarian, A., & Hoffman, L. J. (2004). Challenges of intervehicle ad hoc networks. *IEEE Transactions on Intelligent Transportation Systems, 5*(4), 347–351. doi:10.1109/TITS.2004.838218.

Bogliolo, A., Polidori, P., Aldini, A., Moreira, W., Mendes, P., Yildiz, M., & Seigneur, J.-M. (2012). Virtual currency and reputation-based cooperation incentives in user-centric networks. In *Proceedings of the International Wireless Communications and Mobile Computing Conference (IWCMC)* (pp. 895-900). Washington, DC: IEEE CS Press.

Bonnmotion. (n.d.). Retrieved from http://net.cs.uni-bonn.de/wg/cs/applications/-bonnmotion/

Borisov, N., Goldberg, I., & Wagner, D. (2001). Intercepting mobile communications: The insecurity of 802.11. In *Proceedings of the 7th Annual International Conference on Mobile Computing and Networking* (pp. 180-189). ACM.

Bose, S., Bharathimurugan, S., & Kannan, A. (2007). Multi-layer integrated anomaly intrusion detection system for mobile adhoc networks. In *Proceedings of the International Conference on Signal Processing, Communications and Networking,* (pp. 360-365). IEEE.

Boukerch, A., & Xu, L., & EL-Khatib, K. (2007). Trust-based security for wireless ad hoc and sensor networks. *Computer Communications, 30,* 2413–2427. doi:10.1016/j.comcom.2007.04.022.

Boukerche, A., & Ren, Y. (2008). The design of a secure key management system for mobile ad hoc networks. In *Proceedings of the 33rd IEEE Conference on Local Computer Networks,* (pp. 320-327). IEEE.

Boyd, C., & Mathuria, A. (2003). *Protocols for authentication and key establishment.* New York: Springer. doi:10.1007/978-3-662-09527-0.

Brassard, G., & Salvail, L. (1994). Secret-key reconciliation by public discussion. In *Proceedings of the Workshop on the Theory and Application of Cryptographic Techniques on Advances in Cryptology* (pp. 410–423). Secaucus, NJ: Springer-Verlag. Retrieved from http://dl.acm.org/citation.cfm?id=188307.188368

Breitfuss, E. H. (2006). Security in near field communications. In *Proceedings of the Workshop on RFID Security.* Graz, Austria: IEEE.

Briesemeister, L., & Hommel, G. (2000). Role-based multicast in highly mobile but sparsely connected and hoc networks. In *Proceedings of the IEEE/ACM Workshop on MobiHoc,* (pp. 45-50). IEEE/ACM.

Bruening, P. J., & Treacy, B. C. (2009). *Cloud computing: Privacy, security challenges. Privacy & Security Law Report.* Washington, DC: The Bureau of National Affairs, Inc..

Buchegger, S., & Boudec, J. (2002). Performance analysis of the CONFIDANT protocol: Cooperation of nodes - fairness in distributed ad-hoc networks. *IEEE/ACM Workshop on Mobile Ad Hoc Networking and Computing (MobiHoc).*

Buchegger, S., & Le Boudec, J. Y. (2002a). Nodes bearing grudges: Towards routing security, fairness, and robustness in mobile ad hoc networks. In *Proceedings of the 10th Euromicro Workshop on Parallel, Distributed and Network-Based Processing* (pp. 403-410). IEEE.

Buchegger, S., & Le Boudec, J. Y. (2002b). Performance analysis of the CONFIDANT protocol. In *Proceedings of the 3rd ACM International Symposium on Mobile Ad Hoc Networking & Computing* (pp. 226-236). ACM.

Buchegger, S., & Boudec, J. L. (2003). *Coping with False Accusations in Misbehavior Reputation Systems for Mobile Ad-Hoc Networks}. EPFL IC/2003/31.* EPFL-DI-ICA.

Buchegger, S., & Boudec, J. L. (2005). Self-policing mobile ad-hoc networks by reputation system. *IEEE Communications Magazine, 43*(7), 101–107. doi:10.1109/MCOM.2005.1470831.

Buchegger, S., & Buddec, J. L. (2001). *The selfish node: Increasing routing security in mobile ad hoc network (IBM Research Report: RR 3354).* IBM.

Buchegger, S., & Le Boudee, J. Y. (2005). Self-policing mobile ad hoc networks by reputation systems. *IEEE Communications Magazine, 43*(7), 101–107. doi:10.1109/MCOM.2005.1470831.

Burbank, J. (2008). Security in cognitive radio networks: The required evolution in approaches to wireless network security. In *Proceedings of the 3rd International Conference on Cognitive Radio Oriented Wireless Networks and Communications* (CROWNCOM 2008) (pp. 1-7). CROWNCOM.

Burbank, J. L., Chimento, P. F., Haberman, B. K., & Kasch, W. T. (2006). {Key Challenges of Military Tactical Networking and the Elusive Promise of MANET Technology}. *IEEE Communications Magazine, 44*(11), 39–45. doi:10.1109/COM-M.2006.248156.

Burg, A. (2003). Ad hoc network specific attacks. In *Seminar on ad hoc networking: Concepts, applications, and security.* Technische Universität München.

Burnett, S., & Paine, S. (2001). *The RSA security's official guide to cryptography.* New York: McGraw-Hill, Inc..

Buttya´n, L., & Vajda, I. (2004). {Towards Provable Security for Ad Hoc Routing Protocols}.

Buttyan, L., & Csik, L. (2010). Security analysis of reliable transport layer protocols for wireless sensor networks. In *Proceedings of IEEE Workshop on Sensor Networks and Systems for Pervasive Computing (PerSeNS).* Mannheim, Germany: IEEE. doi:10.1.1.153.9959

Buttyan, L., & Csik, L. (2011). A secure distributed transport protocol for wireless sensor networks. In *Proceedings of IEEE International Confenrence on Communications (ICC).* Kyoto, Japan: IEEE Press.

Buttyan, L., & Hubaux, J.-P. (2001). *Nuglets: A virtual currency to simulate cooperation in self-organized ad hoc networks* (Technical Report DSC/2001/001). Lausanne, Switzerland: Swiss Federal Institute of Technology.

Buttyan, L., & Hubaux, J.-P. (2007). *Security and Co-operation in wireless networks*. Cambridge University Press.

Caballero, E. J. (2006). Vulnerabilities of intrusion detection systems in mobile ad-hoc networks—The routing problem. In *Proceedings of TKK T-110.5290 Seminar on Network Security* (pp. 1-2). TKK.

Camenisch, J., Hohenberger, S., & Lysyanskaya, A. (2005). Compact e-cash. In *Proceedings of EUROCRYPT*, (LNCS), (vol. 3494, pp. 302-321). New York: Springer.

Cao, Y., Jarke, M., Klamma, R., Mendoza, O., & Srirama, S. (2009). Mobile access to MPEG-7 based multimedia services. In *Proceedings of the 10th International Conference on Mobile Data Management: Systems, Services and Middleware* (pp. 102-111). Taipei, Taiwan: IEEE Press.

Cao, Z., Kong, J., Lee, U., Gerla, M., & Chen, Z. (2008). Proof-of-relevance: Filtering false data via authentic consensus in vehicle ad-hoc networks. In *Proceedings of the IEEE Conference on Computer Communications Workshops* (pp. 1-6). IEEE.

Cao, Z., Zhou, X., Xu, M., Chen, Z., Hu, J., & Tang, L. (2006). Enhancing base station security against DoS attacks in wireless sensor networks. In *Proceedings of IEEE WICOM'06*. Wuha, China: IEEE Press.

Čapkun, S., Buttyán, L., & Hubaux, J. P. (2003b). SEC-TOR: Secure tracking of node encounters in multi-hop wireless networks. In *Proceedings of the 1st ACM Workshop on Security of Ad Hoc and Sensor Networks* (pp. 21-32). ACM.

Capkun, S., Buttyán, L., & Hubaux, J. P. (2003a). Self-organized public-key management for mobile ad hoc networks. *IEEE Transactions on Mobile Computing*, 2(1), 52–64. doi:10.1109/TMC.2003.1195151.

Capkun, S., Hubaux, J. P., & Buttyan, L. (2006). Mobility helps peer-to-peer security. *IEEE Transactions on Mobile Computing*, 5(1), 43–51. doi:10.1109/TMC.2006.12.

Catteddu, D., & Hogben, G. (2009). Cloud computing: Benefits, risks and recommendations for information security. *European Network and Information Security Agency (ENISA) Report*. Retrieved August 10, 2011, from http://www.enisa.europa.eu/act/rm/files/deliverables/cloud-computing-risk-assessment/at_download/fullReport

CBC-MAC. (n.d.). *Wikipedia*. Retrieved April 20, 2013, from http://en.wikipedia.org/wiki/CBC-MAC

Celine, B. (2009). *Contribution to securing the routing in ad hoc networks*. (PhD thesis). Limoges University, Limoges, France.

Cepheli, Ö., & Karabulut, K. G. (2013). *Efficient PHY layer security in MIMO-OFDM: Spatiotemporal selective artificial noise*. Paper presented at the Fourth International Workshop on Data Security and Privacy in wireless networks. Madrid, Spain.

Chaddoud, G., & Martin, K. (2006). Distributed certificate authority in cluster-based ad hoc networks. In *Proceedings of the Wireless Communications and Networking Conference* (Vol. 2, pp. 682-688). IEEE.

Chakraborty, M., Misra, I. S., Saha, D., & Mukherjee, A. (2004). A novel fat handover technique for TLMM: Three level mobility for next generation wireless IP-based networks. In *Proceedings of INDICON*. IDICON.

Chan, A. F. (2004). Distributed symmetric key management for mobile ad hoc networks. In *Proceedings of INFOCOM 2004 Twenty-Third Annual Joint Conference of the IEEE Computer and Communications Societies* (Vol. 4, pp. 2414-2424). IEEE.

Chang, C., Liu, C., & Wang, Y. (2009). A subjective trust model based on two-dimensional measurement. In *Proceedings of the 2009 International Conference on Computer Engineering and Technology* (pp. 37-41). Singapore: IEEE.

Chang, Q., Zhang, Y. P., & Qin, L. L. (2010). A node authentication protocol based on ECC in WSN. In *Proceedings of the International Conference on Computer Design and Applications (ICCDA)* (pp. 606-609). ICCDA.

Chang, B.-J., & Kuo, S.-L. (2009). Markov chain trust model for trust-value analysis and key management in distributed multicast manets. *IEEE Transactions on Vehicular Technology*, *58*(4), 1846–1863. doi:10.1109/TVT.2008.2005415.

Chang, Y. S., & Hung, S. H. (2011). Developing collaborative applications with mobile cloud—A case study of speech recognition. *Journal of Internet Services and Information Security*, *1*(1), 18–36.

Chapkin, S., Bako, B., Kargl, F., & Schoch, E. (2006). Location tracking attack in ad hoc networks based on topology information. In *Proceedings of the 2006 IEEE International Conference on Mobile Adhoc and Sensor Systems (MASS)* (pp. 870-875). IEEE.

Charan, P., Paulu, R., Kumar, M., & Jaiswal, A. (2012). A survey on the performance optimization in wireless sensor networks using cross layer approach. *Journal of Scientific and Research Publications*, *2*(5), 1–6.

Chartrand, G., & Zhang, P. (2005). *Introduction to graph theory*. Singapore: McGraw Higher Education.

Chen, H., Lou, W., & Wang, Z. (2009). Conflicting-set-based wormhole attack resistant localization in wireless sensor networks. In D. Zhang, M. Portmann, A.-H. Tan, & J. Indulska (Eds.), Proceedings of Ubiqitous Intelligence and Computing: 6th International Conference, UIC 2009, (Vol. 5585, pp. 296-309). Berlin, Germany: Springer.

Chen, H., Lou, W., Sun, X., & Wang, Z. (2010). A secure localization approach against wormhole attacks using distance consistency. *EURASIP Journal on Wireless Communication and Networking*, 22–32. Retrieved from dl.acm.org/citation.cfm?id=1740705

Chen, Y., Luo, J., & Ni, X. (2008). A fuzzy trust evaluation based access control in grid environment. In *Proceedings of the Third ChinaGrid Annual Conference, 2008, ChinaGrid'08* (pp. 190-196). ChinaGrid.

Chen, Y., Paxson, V., & Katz, R. H. (2010). *What's new about cloud computing security?* (Technical Report No. UCB/EECS-2010-5). EECS Department, University of California at Berkeley. Retrieved August 10, 2011, from http://www.eecs.berkeley.edu/Pubs/TechRpts/2010/EECS-2010-5.html

Chen, C., & Jensen, M. (2011). Secret key establishment using temporally and spatially correlated wireless channel coefficients. *IEEE Transactions on Mobile Computing*, *10*(2), 205–215. doi:10.1109/TMC.2010.114.

Cheng, L., & Panichpapiboon, S. (2012). Effects of inter-vehicle spacing distributions on connectivity of VANET: A case study from measured highway traffic. *IEEE Communications Magazine*, *50*(10), 90–97. doi:10.1109/MCOM.2012.6316781.

Chen, Y., Yang, J., Trappe, W., & Martin, R. (2010). Detecting and localizing identity-based attacks in wireless and sensor networks. *IEEE Transactions on Vehicular Technology*, *59*(5), 2418–2434. doi:10.1109/TVT.2010.2044904.

Chen, Z., & Nan, X. H. (2006). *CPK identity authentication*. Beijing, China: National Defence Industry Press.

Cheshire, C., & Cook, K. S. (2004). The emergence of trust networks under uncertainty—Implications for internet interactions. *Analyse & Kritik*, *26*(1), 220–240.

Chin, W.-L., Tseng, C.-L., Tsai, C.-S., Kao, W.-C., & Kao, C.-W. (2012). Channel-based detection of primary user emulation attacks in cognitive radios. In *Proceedings of the 2012 IEEE 75th Vehicular Technology Conference (VTC Spring)* (pp. 1-5). IEEE.

Chiron, P., Njedjon, E., Seite, P., Gosse, K., Melin, E., & Roux, P. (2008). Architectures for IP-based network-assisted mobility management across heterogeneous networks. *IEEE Wireless Communications*, *15*, 18–25. doi:10.1109/MWC.2008.4492974.

Chlamtac, I., conti, M., & J.-N, L. J. (2003). {Mobile Ad hoc Networking: Imperatives and Challenges}. *Ad Hoc Networks*, *1*, 13–64. doi:10.1016/S1570-8705(03)00013-1.

Cho, J. H., Swami, A., & Chen, I. (2005). A context-aware trust-based security system for ad hoc networks. *First International Conference on Security and Privacy for Emerging Areas in Communication Networks-Workshop*.

Choi, B. G., Cho, E. J., Kim, J. H., Hong, C. S., & Kim, J. H. (2009). A sinkhole attack detection mechanism for lqi based mesh routing in WSN. In *Proceedings of 23rd International Conference on Information Networking*. Chiang Mai, Thailand: IEEE Press.

Choi, S., Kim, D. Y., Lee, D. H., & Jung, J. I. (2008). WAP: Wormhole attack prevention algorithm in mobile ad hoc networks. In *Proceedings of the IEEE International Conference on Sensor Networks, Ubiquitous and Trustworthy Computing,* (pp. 343-348). IEEE.

Cho, J.-H., Swami, A., & Chen, I.-R. (2011). A survey on trust management for mobile ad hoc networks.[New York: IEEE CS Press.]. *Communications Surveys & Tutorials, 13*(4), 562–583. doi:10.1109/SURV.2011.092110.00088.

Chong, C.-Y., & Kumar, S. P. (2003). Sensor networks: Evolution, opportunities, and challenges. *Proceedings of the IEEE, 91*(8).

Christensen, J. H. (2009). Using RESTful web-services and cloud computing to create next generation mobile applications. In *Proceedings of the 24th ACM SIGPLAN Conference Companion on Object Oriented Programming Systems Languages and Applications (OOPSLA '09).* New York: ACM Press.

Christian, M., & Samuel, P. (2008). An architecture for seamless mobility support in IP-based next-generation wireless networks. *IEEE Transactions on Vehicular Technology, 57*, 1209–1225. doi:10.1109/TVT.2007.906366.

Christianson, B., & Harbison, W. (1996). Why isn't trust transitive? Conti, M., & Glordano, S. (2007). {Multihop Ad hoc Networking: The Reality}. *IEEE Communications Magazine, 45*, 88–95.

Chun, B. G., Ihm, S., Maniatis, P., Naik, M., & Patti, A. (2011). CloneCloud: Elastic execution between mobile device and cloud. In *Proceedings of the 6th European Conference on Computer Systems (EuroSys 2011)* (pp. 301-314). Salzburg, Austria: ACM Press.

Chu, Y., Feigenbaum, J., Lamacchi, B., Resnick, P., & Strauss, M. (1997). REFEREE: Trust management for web applications. *Journal of Computer Networks and ISDN Systems, 29*(8-13), 953–964. doi:10.1016/S0169-7552(97)00009-3.

Clancy, T. C. (2005). *Security review of the light-weight access point protocol draft-ohara-capwap-lwapp-02.*

Clarke, S. (2012a, July 11). *Apple awarded patent for mobile airline ticketing and travel service.* Retrieved January 28, 2013, from http://www.nfcworld.com/2012/07/11/316784/apple-awarded-patent-for-mobile-airline-ticketing-and-travel-service/

Clarke, S. (2012b, September 25). *Inside secure to offer cloud-based NFC secure element solution.* Retrieved January 28, 2013, from http://www.nfcworld.com/2012/09/25/318059/inside-secure-to-offer-cloud-based-nfc-secure-element-solution/

Clarke, S. (2012c, November 7). *Marie Claire magazine runs NFC print advertisement.* Retrieved January 28, 2013, from http://www.nfcworld.com/2012/11/07/320956/maric-claire-magazine-runs-nfc-print-advertisement/

Clarke, S. (2012d, September 19). *Visa releases Olympics NFC and contactless usage statistics.* Retrieved January 28, 2013, from NFC http://www.nfcworld.com/2012/09/19/317958/visa-releases-olympics-nfc-and-contactless-usage-statistics/

Clarke, E., Grumberg, O., & Peled, D. (2001). *Model checking.* Cambridge, MA: MIT Press.

Clausen, T., & Jacquet, P. (n.d.). *Optimized link state routing protocol.* Retrieved from http://tools.ietf.org/id/draft-ietf-manet-olsr-11.txt

Cloud Security Alliance. (2011). *Security guidance for critical areas of focus in cloud computing.* Retrieved August 10, 2011, from http://cloudsecurityalliance.org/csaguide.pdf

Clouqueur, T., Saluja, K. K., & Ramanathan, P. (2004). Fault tolerance in collaborative sensor networks for target detection. *IEEE Transactions on Computers, 53*(1), 320–333. doi:10.1109/TC.2004.1261838.

Condie, T., Kacholia, V., Sankararaman, S., Hellerstein, J., & Maniatis, P. (2006). Induced churn as shelter from routing-table poisoning. In *Proceedings of the 13th Annual Network and Distributed System Security Symposium (NDSS'06).* NDSS.

Conti, M., & Glordano, S. (2007). {Multihop Ad hoc Networking: The Theory}. *IEEE Communications Magazine, 45*, 78–86. doi:10.1109/MCOM.2007.343616.

Cormen, T. H., Leiserson, C. E., Rivest, R. L., & Stein, C. (2004). *Introduction to algorithms* (2nd ed.). New York: McGraw-Hill.

Corson, S., & Macker, J. (1999). *Mobile ad hoc networking (MANET): Routing protocol performance issues and evaluation considerations.* Retrieved March 9, 2012, from http://www.ietf.org/rfc/rfc2501.txt

Counter, C. T. R. (n.d.). *Wikipedia.* Retrieved April 20, 2013, from http://en.wikipedia.org/wiki/Block_cipher_modes_of _operation#Counter_.28CTR.29

Courtois, N. T., & Meier, W. (2003). Algebraic attacks on stream ciphers with linear feedback. In *Proceedings of the 22nd International Conference on Theory and Applications of Cryptographic Techniques* (pp. 345–359). Berlin, Germany: Springer-Verlag. Retrieved from http://dl.acm.org/citation.cfm?id=1766171.1766200

Cover, T. M., & Thomas, J. A. (2006). *Elements of information theory.* Hoboken, NJ: John Wiley and Sons.

Crepeau, C., Davis, C. R., & Maheswaran, M. (2007). A secure MANET routing protocol with resilience against Byzantine behaviours of malicious or selfish nodes. In *Proceedings of the 21st International Conference on Advanced Information Networking and Applications Workshops,* (Vol. 2, pp. 19-26). IEEE.

Csiszár, I., & Korner, J. (1978). Broadcast channels with confidential messages. *IEEE Transactions on Information Theory, 24,* 339–348. doi:10.1109/TIT.1978.1055892.

Csiszar, I., & Narayan, P. (2008). Secrecy capacities for multiterminal channel models. *IEEE Transactions on Information Theory, 54*(6), 2437–2452. doi:10.1109/TIT.2008.921705.

Cuervo, E., Balasubramanian, A., Cho, D. K., Wolman, A., Saroiu, S., Chandra, R., & Bahl, P. (2010). MAUI: Making smartphones last longer with code offload. In *Proceedings of the 8th International Conference on Mobile Systems, Applications, and Services (ACM MobiSys '10)* (pp. 49-62). San Francisco, CA: ACM Press.

Cui, K., Wang, J., Zhang, H.-F., Luo, C.-L., Jin, G., & Chen, T.-Y. (2013). A real-time design based on FPGA for expeditious error reconciliation in QKD system. *IEEE Transactions on Information Forensics and Security, 8*(1), 184–190. doi:10.1109/TIFS.2012.2228855.

Cui, Y., Xue, Y. B., Shang, H. Y., Sha, X., & Ding, Z. (2009). A novel scheme access architecture for joint radio resource management in heterogeneous networks. []. Guangzhou, China: IEEE.]. *Proceedings of the International Forum on Information Technology and Applications, 1,* 24–27.

Cuppens, F., Cuppens-Boulahia, N., Nuon, S., & Ramard, T. (2007). Property based intrusion detection to secure OLSR. In *Proceeding of the Third International Conference on Wireless and Mobile Communications.* Washington, DC: IEEE Computer Society.

Curtmola, R., & Nita-Rotaru, C. (2007). BSMR: Byzantine-resilient secure multicast routing in multi-hop wireless networks. In *Proceedings of the 4th Annual IEEE Communications Society Conference on Sensor, Mesh and Ad Hoc Communications and Networks,* (pp. 263-272). IEEE.

Da Silva, E., Dos Santos, A., Albini, L. C. P., & Lima, M. (2008). Identity-based key management in mobile ad hoc networks: Techniques and applications. *IEEE Wireless Communications, 15*(5), 46–52. doi:10.1109/MWC.2008.4653131.

Daeinabi, A., & Rahbar, A. G. (2011). Detection of malicious vehicles through monitoring in vehicular ad-hoc networks. *Multimedia Tools and Applications,* , 1–14.

Damianou, N., Dulay, N., Lupu, E., & Sloman, M. (2001). The ponder policy specification language. In *Proceedings of the International Workshop on Policies for Distributed Systems and Networks, POLICY'01* (pp. 18-38). Bristol, UK: POLICY.

Data Encryption Standard. (n.d.). *Wikipedia.* Retrieved April 20, 2013, from http://en.wikipedia.org/wiki/Data_Encryption_ Standard

Davis, J. (2012, July 12). *Olympics.* Retrieved January 28, 2013, from http://www.nfcworld.com/2012/07/12/316820/hands-on-with-the-visa-olympics-nfc-phone/

Dawkins, R. (1976). *The Selfish Gene.* Oxford University Press.

Daza, V., Herranz, J.; Morillo, P., & Ràfols, C. (2007). Cryptographic techniques for mobile ad-hoc networks. *Computer Networks, 51*(18), 4938–4950. doi:10.1016/j.comnet.2007.08.002.

Dekleva, S., Shim, J. P., Varshney, U., & Knoerzer, G. (2007). Evolution and emerging issues in mobile wireless networks. *Communications of the ACM–Smart Business Networks*, *50*(6), 38–43.

Demirbas, M., & Song, Y. (2006). An RSSI-based scheme for Sybil attack detection in wireless sensor networks. In *Proceedings of the International Symposium on World of Wireless, Mobile and Multimedia Networks* (pp. 570–575). Buffalo, NY. doi:10.1.1.87.304

Demirkol, I., Ersoy, C., & Alagoz, F. (2004). MAC protocols for wireless sensor networks: A survey. *IEEE Communications Magazine*, *44*(4), 115–121. doi:10.1109/MCOM.2006.1632658.

Deng, H., Li, W., & Agrawal, D. P. (2002). Routing security in wireless ad hoc networks. *IEEE Communications Magazine*, *40*(10), 70–75. doi:10.1109/MCOM.2002.1039859.

Deng, H., Li, W., & Agrawal, D. P. (2002). Routing security in wireless ad hoc networks. *IEEE Communications Magazine*, *40*(10), 70–75. doi:10.1109/MCOM.2002.1039859.

Deng, J. (1989). Introduction to grey system theory. *Journal of Grey System*, *1*(1), 1–24.

Denko, M. K. (2005). Detection and prevention of denial of service (DoS) attacks in mobile ad hoc networks using reputation-based incentive scheme. *Journal of Systemics. Cybernetics and Informatics*, *3*(4), 1–9.

Desai, M., & Manjunath, D. (2002). On the connectivity in finite ad-hoc networks. *IEEE Communications Letters*, *6*(10), 437–439. doi:10.1109/LCOMM.2002.804241.

Diffie, W., & Hellman, M. (1976). New directions in cryptography. *IEEE Transactions on Information Theory*, *22*(6), 644–654. doi:10.1109/TIT.1976.1055638.

Diffie, W., & Hellman, M. (1976). New directions in cryptography. *IEEE Transactions on Information Theory*, *22*(6), 644–654. doi:10.1109/TIT.1976.1055638.

Ding, M., Chen, D., Xing, K., & Cheng, X. (2005). Localized fault-tolerant event boundary detection in sensor networks. In *Proceeding of IEEE INFOCOM* (pp. 902–913). IEEE.

Dommety, G., Yegin, A., Perkins, C., El-Malki, K., & Khalil, M. (2001). *Fast handovers mobile IPv6*. IETF draft, draft-ietf-mobileipfast-mipv6-03.txt.

Don, D. A., Pandit, V., & Agrawal, D. P. (2012). Multivariate symmetric polynomial based group key management for vehicular ad hoc networks. In *Proceedings of the IEEE International Conference on Communications (ICC)*. IEEE.

Dong, L., Han, Z., Petropulu, A. P., & Poor, H. V. (2008). Secure wireless communications via cooperation. In *Proceedings of the 46th Annual Allerton Conference on Communications, Control, Computing* (pp. 1132–1138). Monticello, IL: Allerton.

Dong, L., Han, Z., Petropulu, A. P., & Poor, H. V. (2009). Amplify-and-forward based cooperation for secure wireless communications. In *Proceedings of IEEE International Conference on Acoustics, Speech, and Signal Processing* (pp. 2613–2616). Taipei, Taiwan: IEEE.

Dong, Y., Sui, A. F., Yiu, S. M., Li, V. O., & Hui, L. C. (2007). Providing distributed certificate authority service in cluster-based mobile ad hoc networks. *Computer Communications*, *30*(11), 2442–2452. doi:10.1016/j.comcom.2007.04.011.

Dotzer, F., Fischer, L., & Magiera, P. (2005). VARS: A vehicle ad hoc network reputation system. In *Proceedings of the 6th IEEE International Symposium World Wireless Mobile Multimedia Networks* (Vol. 1, pp. 454-456). IEEE.

Douceur, J. R. (2002). The sybil attack. In *Revised papers from the first international workshop on peer-to-peer systems* (pp. 251-260). London, UK: Springer-Verlag. Retrieved from http://dl.acm.org/citation.cfm?id=646334.687813

Douceur, J. R. (March, 2002). The Sybil attack. In *Proceedings of the Workshop on Peer-to-Peer Systems (IPTPS02)*. Cambridge, MA. doi:10.1.1.17.1073

Douceur, J. (2002). The Sybil attack. *Peer-to-Peer Systems*, *1*, 251–260. doi:10.1007/3-540-45748-8_24.

Douceur, J. R. (2002). The Sybil attack. In *Peer-to-peer systems* (pp. 251–260). Berlin, Germany: Springer. doi:10.1007/3-540-45748-8_24.

Du, W., Deng, J., Han, Y. S., Chen, S., & Varshney, P. K. (2004). A key management scheme for wireless sensor networks using deployment knowledge. In *Proceedings of IEEE Infocom* (pp. 1–8). Hong Kong: IEEE.

ECC REPORT 82. (2006). *Comparability study for UMTS operating within the GSM 900 and GSM 1800 frequency bands*. 3GPP. TS45.005 (Rel-5), GSM/EDGE Radio Access Network, Radio Transmission and Reception. 3GPP.

ECMA International. (2013). *ECMA international*. Retrieved May 5, 2013, from http://www.ecma-international.org

Ekrem, E., & Ulukus, S. (2009). Cooperative secrecy in wireless communications. In R. Liu, & W. Trappe (Eds.), *Securing wireless communications at the physical layer*. New York: Springer-Verlag.

Ekrem, E., & Ulukus, S. (2011). The secrecy capacity region of the Gaussian MIMO multi-receiver wiretap channel. *IEEE Transactions on Information Theory*, *57*(4), 2083–2114. doi:10.1109/TIT.2011.2111750.

Ekrem, E., & Ulukus, S. (2012). Capacity-equivocation region of the Gaussian MIMO wiretap channel. *IEEE Transactions on Information Theory*, *58*(9), 5699–5710. doi:10.1109/TIT.2012.2204534.

El Hajj Shehadeh, Y., Alfandi, O., & Hogrefe, D. (2012). Towards robust key extraction from multipath wireless channels. *Journal of Communications and Networks*, *14*(4), 385–395.

El-Bendary, N., Hassanien, A. E., Sedano, J., Soliman, O. S., & Ghali, N. I. (2011). TESLA-based secure routing protocol for wireless sensor networks. In *Proceedings of First ACM International Workshop on Security and Privacy Preserving in e-Societies*. Baabda, Lebanon: ACM.

Elizabeth, N. E., Radha, S., Priyadarshini, S., Jayasree, S., & Swathi, K. N. (2012). SRT-secure routing using trust levels in MANETs. *European Journal of Scientific Research*, *75*(3).

Elnahrawy, E., & Nath, B. (2003). Cleaning and querying noisy sensors. In *Proceedings of the First ACM Conference on Embedded Networked Sensor Systems (SenSys'03)* (pp. 78-87). ACM.

Elson, J., & Estrin, D. (2000). *An address-free architecture for dynamic sensor networks* (Technical Report 724). University of Southern California, Computer Science Department. doi:10.1.1.42.9521

English, C., Nixon, P., Terzis, S., McGettrick, A., & Lowe, H. (2002). Dynamic trust models for ubiquitous computing environments. *Workshop on Security in Ubiquitous Computing*.

Epstein, Z. (2012, October 19). *With or without apple, NFC mobile payment market to hit $100 billion*. Retrieved January 28, 2013, from http://bgr.com/2012/10/19/nfc-mobile-payments-growth-abi/

Erceg, V., Greenstein, L. J., Tjandra, S. Y., & Parkoff, S. R. (1999). An empirically based path loss model for wireless channels in suburban environments. *IEEE Journal on Selected Areas in Communications*, *17*(7), 1205–1211. doi:10.1109/49.778178.

Eriksson, J., Krishnamurthy, S. V., & Faloutsos, M. (2006). Truelink: A practical countermeasure to the wormhole attack in wireless networks. In *Proceedings of the 2006 14th IEEE International Conference on Network Protocols*, (pp. 75-84). IEEE.

Eschenauer, L., & Gligor, V. D. (2002). A key-management scheme for distributed sensor networks. In *Proceedings of the 9th ACM Conference on Computer and Communications Security* (pp. 41-47). ACM.

Eschenauer, L., Gligor, V. D., & Baras, J. (2004). On trust establishment in mobile ad-hoc networks. In B. Christianson, B. Crispo, J. A. Malcolm, & M. Roe (Eds.), *Security protocols: 10th international workshop*, (pp. 47-66). New York: Springer.

Esmailpour, A., & Nasser, N. (2011). Dynamic QoS-based bandwidth allocation framework for broadband wireless networks. *IEEE Transactions on Vehicular Technology*, *60*, 2690–2700. doi:10.1109/TVT.2011.2158674.

Etesami, J., & Henkel, W. (2012). LDPC code construction for wireless physical-layer key reconciliation. In *Proceedings of the 2012 1st IEEE International Conference on Communications in China (ICCC)* (pp. 208-213). ICCC.

Extensible Authentication Protocol (EAP). (2013). *Wikipedia*. Retrieved April 20, 2013, from http://en.wikipedia.org/wiki/Extensible_Authentication_Protocol

Fahad, T., Djenouri, D., & Askwith, R. (2007). On detecting packets droppers in manet: A novel low cost approach. In *Proceedings of the Third International Symposium on Information Assurance and Security*, (pp. 56-64). IEEE.

Fakoorian, S. A. A., & Swindlehurst, A. L. (2011). MIMO interference channel with confidential messages: Achievable secrecy rates and precoder design. *IEEE Transactions on Information Forensics and Security, 6*(3), 640–649. doi:10.1109/TIFS.2011.2156788.

Fernandes, A., Kotsovinos, E., Ostring, S., & Dragovic, B. (2004). Pinocchio: Incentives for honest participation in distributed trust management. In iTrust, (LNCS), (vol. 2995, pp. 63-77). New York: Springer.

Ferrag M. A., & Nafa M. (2011). Securing the OLSR routing protocol for ad hoc networks detecting and avoiding wormhole attack. *Journal of Selected Areas in Telecommunications*, 51-58.

Ferrag, M. A. (2012, November 3). *Study of attacks in ad hoc networks*. Saarbrücken, Germany: LAP LAMBERT Academic Publishing.

Ferrag, M. A., Nafa, M., & Ghanmi, S. (2013). A new security mechanism for ad-hoc on-demand distance vector in mobile ad hoc social networks. In *Proceedings of the 7th Workshop on Wireless and Mobile Ad-Hoc Networks (WMAN 2013) in Conjunction with the Conference on Networked Systems NetSys/KIVS*. Stuttgart, Germany. WMAN.

Fok, M. P., Wang, Z., Deng, Y., & Prucnal, P. R. (2011). Optical layer security in fiber-optic networks. *IEEE Transactions on Information Forensics and Security, 6*(3), 725–736. doi:10.1109/TIFS.2011.2141990.

Ford, R., Carvalho, M., Allen, W. H., & Ham, F. (2009). Adaptive security for MANETs via biology. In *Proceedings of the 2nd Cyberspace Research Workshop*. IEEE.

Forejt, V., Kwiatkowska, M., Norman, G., & Parker, D. (2011). Automated verification techniques for probabilistic systems. In M. Bernardo & V. Issarny (Eds.), *Formal methods for eternal networked software systems (SFM'11)*, (LNCS), (vol. 6659, pp. 53-113). New York: Springer.

Forum, N. F. C. (2008). *Essentials for successful NFC mobile ecosystems*. Retrieved April 26, 2012, from http://www.nfc-forum.org/resources/white_papers/NFC_Forum_Mobile_NFC_Ecosystem_White_Paper.pdf

Fraleigh, C., Tobagi, F., & Diot, C. (2003). Provisioning IP backbone networks to support latency sensitive traffic. In *Proceedings of IEEE Infocom*. IEEE.

Franklin, M., & Boneh, D. (2001). Identity based encryption from weil pairing.[Berlin: Springer Verlag.]. *Proceedings of CRYPTO, 2001*, 213–239.

Fruth, M. (2011). *Formal methods for the analysis of wireless network protocols*. (Ph.D. thesis). Oxford University, Oxford, UK.

Fu, C., Tang, F., Cui, Y., Liu, M., & Peng, B. (2009). Grey theory based nodes risk assessment in P2P networks. In *Proceedings of the 2009 IEEE International Symposium on Parallel and Distributed Processing with Applications* (pp. 479-483). IEEE.

Gallina, L., Han, T., Kwiatkowska, M., Marin, A., Rossi, S., & Spanò, A. (2012). Automatic energy-aware performance analysis of mobile ad-hoc networks. In *Proceedings of the IFIP Wireless Days Conference (WD'12)*. IFIP.

Gambetta, D. (2000). *Trust: Making and Breaking Cooperative Relations*. Oxford Press.

Ganeriwal, S., Capkun, S., Hanand, C., & Srivastava, M. B. (2005). Secure time synchronization service for sensor networks. In *Proceedings of 4th ACM Workshop on Wireless Security*. doi:10.1.1.85.8733

Ganeriwal, S., Balzano, L. K., & Srivastava, M. B. (2008). Reputation-based framework for high integrity sensor networks. *ACM Transactions on Sensor Networks, 4*(3), 1–37. doi:10.1145/1362542.1362546.

Gawdan, I. S., & Chow, C. Z, T. A., & Gawdan, Q. I. (2011). Cross-layer based security solutions for wireless sensor networks. *International Journal of the Physical Sciences, 6*(17), 4245-4254. Retrieved from www.academicjournals.org/IJPS/

Gerhards-Padilla, E., Aschenbruck, N., Martini, P., Jahnke, M., & Tolle, J. (2007). Detecting black hole attacks in tactical MANETs using topology graphs. In *Proceedings of the 32nd IEEE Conference on Local Computer Networks*, (pp. 1043-1052). IEEE.

Gerharz, M., Waal, C., Aschenbruck, N., Bothe, A., Camp, T., Ernst, R., & Walsh, C. (2012). *BonnMotion—A mobility scenario generation and analysis tool*. Retrieved 2012 from http://net.cs.uni-bonn.de/wg/cs/applications/bonnmotion/

Ghaffari, A. (2006). Vulnerability and security of mobile ad hoc networks. In *Proceedings of the 6th WSEAS International Conference on Simulation, Modelling and Optimization* (pp. 124-129). World Scientific and Engineering Academy and Society (WSEAS).

Gharan, O. S., Fashandi, S., & Khandani, A. K. (2010). Diversity-rate trade-off in erasure networks. In *Proceedings of the IEEE Infocom* (pp. 1-9). San Diego, CA: IEEE.

Ghonge, M. M., Jawandhiya, P. M., & Ali, D. M. (2011). *Countermeasures of network layer attacks in MANETs.* IJCA.

Ghosh, A., Wolter, D. R., Andrews, J. G., & Chen, R. (2005). Broadband wireless access with WiMax/802.16: Current performance benchmarks and future potential. *IEEE Communications Magazine, 43*(2), 129–136. doi:10.1109/MCOM.2005.1391513.

Ghosh, M., Varghese, A., Gupta, A., Kherani, A. A., & Muthaiah, S. N. (2010). Detecting misbehaviors in VANET with integrated root-cause analysis. *Ad Hoc Networks, 8*(7), 778–790. doi:10.1016/j.adhoc.2010.02.008.

Giurgiu, I., Riva, O., Juric, D., Krivulev, I., & Alonso, G. (2009). Calling the cloud: Enabling mobile phones as interfaces to cloud applications. In *Proceedings of the 10th ACM/IFIP/USENIX International Conference on Middleware (Middleware '09)*. New York: Springer-Verlag.

Goel, S., Aggarwal, V., Yener, A., & Calderbank, A. (2011). The effect of eavesdroppers on network connectivity: A secrecy graph approach. *IEEE Transactions on Information Forensics and Security, 6*(3), 712–724. doi:10.1109/TIFS.2011.2148714.

Goel, S., & Negi, R. (2008, June). Guaranteeing secrecy using artificial noise. *IEEE Transactions on Wireless Communications, 7*(6), 2180–2189. doi:10.1109/TWC.2008.060848.

Golbeck, J. (2006). *Computing with trust: Definition, properties, and algorithms.* Securecomm and Workshops-Security and Privacy for Emerging Areas in Communication Networks. doi:10.1109/SECCOMW.2006.359579.

Goldsmith, A. (2005). *Wireless communications.* Cambridge, UK: Cambridge University Press. doi:10.1017/CBO9780511841224.

Golle, P., Greene, D. H., & Staddon, J. (2004). Detecting and correcting malicious data in VANETs. In *Proceedings of the 1st ACM International Workshop Vehicular Ad-Hoc Network* (pp. 29-37). ACM.

Golle, P., Greene, D., & Staddon, J. (2004). Detecting and correcting malicious data in VANETs. In *Proceedings of the ACM International Workshop on Vehicular Ad Hoc Networks* (pp. 29-37). ACM.

Gong, W., You, Z., Chen, D., Zhao, X., Gu, M., & Lam, K. Y. (2010). Trust based routing for misbehavior detection in ad hoc networks. *Journal of Networks, 5*(5), 551–558. doi:10.4304/jnw.5.5.551-558.

Google. com. (2012). *How it works: Use-it-instore.* Retrieved May 10, 2012, from http://www.google.com/wallet/how-it-works.html#in-store

Gordon, R. L., & Dawoud, D. S. (2009). Direct and indirect trust establishment in ad hoc networks by certificate distribution and verification. In *Proceedings of the 1st International Conference on Wireless Communication, Vehicular Technology, Information Theory and Aerospace & Electronic Systems Technology,* (pp. 624-629). IEEE.

Graaf, R., Hegazy, I., Horton, J., & Safavi-Nain, R. (2010). Distributed detection of wormhole attacks in wireless sensor networks. In J. Zheng, S. Mao, S. F. Midkiff, & H. Zhu (Eds.), *Ad Hoc Networks: First International Conference, ADHOCNETS 2009,* (pp. 208-222). Berlin, Germany: Springer.

Gracelin, S. R., Edna, E. N., & Radha, S. (2010). A novel method for detection and elimination of modification attack and TTL attack in NTP based routing algorithm. In *Proceedings of the 2010 International Conference on Recent Trends in Information, Telecommunication and Computing (ITC)* (pp. 60-64). IEEE.

Grandison, T., & Sloman, M. (2002). Specifying and analysing trust for internet applications. In *Proceedings of the 2nd IFIP Conference on e-Commerce, e-Business, e-Government, I3e2002* (pp. 145-157). Lisbon, Portugal: IFIP.

Grandison, T., & Sloman, M. (2000). A survey of trust in internet applications. *IEEE Communications Surveys and Tutorials, 3*(4), 2–10. doi:10.1109/COMST.2000.5340804.

Greengard, S. (2011). Social games, virtual goods. *Communications of the ACM*, *54*(4), 19–22. doi:10.1145/1924421.1924429.

GSA Report. (2008, September). *UMTS900—A case study*. Global Mobile Suppliers Association.

GSA Report. (2009, June). *UMTS900—A case study optus*. Global Mobile Suppliers Association.

GSA UMTS900 Global Status Report. (2013, May). *GSM/3G market/technology update*. Global Mobile Suppliers Association.

Guang, L., Assi, C., & Benslimane, A. (2006). Interlayer attacks in mobile ad hoc networks. In *Proceedings of the Second International Conference on Mobile Ad-Hoc and Sensor Networks (MSN 2006)*, (pp. 436-448). New York: Springer.

Guidelines for LTE Backhaul Traffic Estimation (LTE BTE). (n.d.). Retrieved April 20, 2013, from http://www.ngmn.org/uploads/media/NGMN_Whitepaper_Guideline_for_LTE_Backhaul_Traffic_Estimation.pdf

Gunasekaran, R., & Uthariaraj, V. R. (2009). Prevention of denial of service attacks and performance enhancement in mobile adhoc networks. In *Proceedings of the First International Communication Systems and Networks and Workshops*, (pp. 1-6). IEEE.

Guo, J., Marshall, A., & Zhou, B. (2011). A trust management framework for detecting malicious and selfish behaviour in ad hoc wireless networks using fuzzy sets and grey theory. In *Proceedings of the 2011 IEEE 10th International Conference on Trust, Security and Privacy in Computing and Communications, TrustCom* (pp. 142-149). Changsha, China: IEEE.

Guo, Y., Zhang, L., Kong, J., Sun, J., Feng, T., & Chen, X. (2011). Jupiter: Transparent augmentation of smartphone capabilities through cloud computing. In P. Druschel (Ed.), *Proceedings of the 3rd ACM SOSP Workshop on Networking, Systems, and Applications on Mobile Handhelds (MobiHeld '11)* (pp. 1-6). Cascais, Portugal: ACM Press.

Guo, Y., & Perreau, S. (2010). Detect DDoS flooding attacks in mobile ad hoc networks. *International Journal of Security and Networks*, *5*(4), 259–269. doi:10.1504/IJSN.2010.037666.

Gupta, I., van Renesse, R., & Birman, K. P. (2001). Scalable fault-tolerant aggregation in large process groups. In *Proceeding of the 2001 International Conference on Dependable Systems and Networks* (pp. 433-442). IEEE.

Gupte, S., & Singhal, M. (2003). Secure routing in mobile wireless ad hoc networks. *Ad Hoc Networks*, *1*(1), 151–174. doi:10.1016/S1570-8705(03)00017-9.

Gutierrez, M. A. F., & Ventura, N. (2010). Mobile cloud computing: Embracing network as a service. In *Proceedings of the Southern Africa Telecommunication Networks and Applications Conference (SATNAC'10)*. SATNAC.

Gutierrez-Osuna, R. (2007). *Sensor characteristics*. Retrieved from http://courses.cs.tamu.edu/rgutier/ceg499_s02/l2.pdf

Haas, J. J., Hu, Y. C., & Laberteaux, K. P. (2009). Design and analysis of a lightweight certificate revocation mechanism for VANET. In *Proceedings of the ACM International Workshop on Vehicular Internetworking* (pp. 89-98). ACM.

Hadden, A. (2008, December). UMTS900 market overview. In *Proceedings of the UMTS900 Workshop*. UMTS

Haenggi, M. (2005). On distances in uniformly random networks. *IEEE Transactions on Information Theory*, *51*(10), 3584–3684. doi:10.1109/TIT.2005.855610.

Haggerty, J., Shi, Q., & Merabti, M. (2005). Early detection and prevention of denial-of-service attacks: A novel mechanism with propagated traced-back attack blocking. *IEEE Journal on Selected Areas in Communications*, *23*(10), 1994–2002. doi:10.1109/JSAC.2005.854123.

Hamblen, M. (2008, May 14). *WiMax vs. long term evolution: Let the battle begin*. Retrieved April 20, 2013, from http://www.computerworld.com/s/article/9085202/WiMax_vs._Long_Term_Evolution_Let_the_battle_begin

Hamed, S., Mojtaba, M. S., & Siavash, K. (2011). Cooperative joint radio resource management in heterogeneous networks. In *Proceedings of the International Symposium on Computer Networks and Distributed Systems*, (pp. 111-115). Tehran, Iran: IEEE.

Hamid, A., Mamun-Or-Rashid, M., & Hong, C. S. (2006). Defense against lap-top class attacker in wireless sensor network. In *Proceedings of International Conference on Advanced Communications Technology*. Gangwon-Do, Korea. doi:10.1.1.99.6579

Han, S., & Chan, E. (2004). Continuous residual energy monitoring in wireless sensor networks. In *Proceeding of International Symposium on Parallel and Distributed Processing and Applications* (pp. 169-177). IEEE.

Hand, D., Mannila, H., & Smyth, P. (2001). *Principles of data mining*. Cambridge, MA: The MIT Press.

Harrison, W., Almeida, J., McLaughlin, S., & Barros, J. (2011, September). Coding for cryptographic security enhancement using stopping sets. *IEEE Transactions on Information Forensics and Security, 6*(3), 575–584. doi:10.1109/TIFS.2011.2145371.

Hartenstein, H., & Laberteaux, K. P. (2008). A tutorial survey on vehicular ad hoc networks. *IEEE Communications Magazine*, , 164–171. doi:10.1109/MCOM.2008.4539481.

Hassan, A. A., Stark, W. E., Hershey, J. E., & Chennakeshu, S. (1996). Cryptographic key agreement for mobile radio. *Digital Signal Processing, 6*(4), 207–212. doi:10.1006/dspr.1996.0023.

Hayashi, M. (2011). Exponential decreasing rate of leaked information in universal random privacy amplification. *IEEE Transactions on Information Theory, 57*(6), 3989–4001. doi:10.1109/TIT.2011.2110950.

Haykin, S. (2005). Cognitive radio: Brain-empowered wireless communications. *IEEE Journal on Selected Areas in Communications, 23*(2), 201–220. doi:10.1109/JSAC.2004.839380.

Hea, T., Stankovica, J. A., Lub, C., & Abdelzahera, T. (2003). SPEED: A stateless protocol for real-time communication in sensor networks. In *Proceedings of the 23rd International Conference on Distributed Computing Systems (ICDCS)*. Providence, RI. doi:10.1.1.12.1662

Hegland, A. M., Winjum, E., Mjolsnes, S. F., Rong, C., Kure, O., & Spilling, P. (2006). A survey of key management in ad hoc networks. *IEEE Communications Surveys and Tutorials, 8*(3), 48–66. doi:10.1109/COMST.2006.253271.

Heinzelman, W., Chandrakasan, A., & Balakrishnan, H. (2000). *Energy-efficient communication protocols for wireless microsensor networks*. Paper presented at Hawaiian International Conference on Systems Science. Washington, DC. doi:10.1.1.112.3914

Hershey, J. E., Hassan, A. A., & Yarlagadda, R. (1995). Unconventional cryptographic keying variable management. *IEEE Transactions on Communications, 43*, 3–6. doi:10.1109/26.385951.

Hillston, J. (1996). *A compositional approach to performance modelling*. Cambridge, UK: Cambridge University Press. doi:10.1017/CBO9780511569951.

Hoang, D. B., & Chen, L. (2010). Mobile cloud for assistive healthcare (MoCAsH). In *Proceedings of the IEEE Asia-Pacific Services Computing Conference (APSCC '10)* (pp. 325-332). Washington, DC: IEEE Press.

Hortos, W. S. (2009). Unsupervised algorithms for intrusion detection and identification in wireless ad hoc sensor networks. In SPIE Defense, Security, and Sensing (pp. 73520J-73520J). International Society for Optics and Photonics.

Hossain, I., & Mahmud, S. (2006). *Group key management for secure multicasting in remote software upload to future vehicles*. Warrendale, PA: Society of Automotive Engineers. doi:10.4271/2006-01-1584.

Hsieh, H. Y., & Sivakumar, R. (2002). Transport over wireless networks. Handbook of Wireless Networks and Mobile Computing, 289.

Hsin, C. F., & Liu, M. (2002). A distributed monitoring mechanism for wireless sensor networks. In *Proceedings of the 1st ACM workshop on Wireless security* (pp. 57-66). ACM.

Hu, L., & Evans, D. (2004). Using directional antennas to prevent wormhole attacks. In *Network and Distributed System Security Symposium (NDSS)*. NDSS.

Hu, Y. C., Perrig, A., & Johnson, D. B. (2003). Packet leashes: A defense against wormhole attacks in wireless networks. In *Proceedings of Twenty-Second Annual Joint Conference of the IEEE Computer and Communications*. doi:10.1.1.113.4100

Hu, Y. C., Perrig, A., & Johnson, D. B. (2003). Rushing attacks and defense in wireless ad hoc network routing protocols. In *Proceedings of the 2nd ACM Workshop on Wireless Security*. ACM.

Hu, Y. C., Perrig, A., & Johnson, D. B. (2006). Wormhole attacks in wireless networks. *IEEE Journal on Selected Areas in Communication, 24*(2), 370-381. doi:10.1.1.117.698

Hu, Y., & Johnson, D. (2004). Securing quality-of-service route discovery in on-demand routing for ad hoc networks. *Proceedings of ACM SASN.*

Huang, Y. A., Fan, W., Lee, W., & Yu, P. S. (2003). Cross-feature analysis for detecting ad-hoc routing anomalies. In *Proceedings of the 23rd International Conference on Distributed Computing Systems, 2003* (pp. 478-487). IEEE.

Huang, Y., & Lee, W. (2000). A cooperative intrusion detection system for ad hoc networks. In *Proceedings of the 1st ACM Workshop on security of Ad Hoc and Sensor Networks*. Fairfax, VA: ACM.

Huang, Y., & Lee, W. (2004). Attack analysis and detection for ad hoc routing protocols. In *Proceedings of the 7th International Symposium on Recent Advances in Intrusion Detection (RAID)* (Vol. 3224, pp. 125-145). New York: Springer.

Huang, Y., & Palomar, D. P. (2010). Rank-constrained separable semidefinite programming with applications to optimal beamforming. *IEEE Transactions on Signal Processing, 58*(2), 664–678. doi:10.1109/TSP.2009.2031732.

Huang, Z. (2011). *On reputation and data-centric misbehavior detection mechanisms for VANETs (Technical report)*. Ottawa, Canada: University of Ottawa.

Hubaux, J. P., Buttyán, L., & Capkun, S. (2001). The quest for security in mobile ad hoc networks. In *Proceedings of the 2nd ACM International Symposium on Mobile Ad Hoc Networking & Computing* (pp. 146-155). ACM.

Huerta-Canepa, G., & Lee, D. (2010). A virtual cloud computing provider for mobile devices. In *Proceedings of the 1st ACM Workshop on Mobile Cloud Computing & Services Social Networks and Beyond (MCS '10)* (pp. 1-5). San Francisco, CA: ACM Press.

Hu, Y. C., Johnson, D. B., & Perrig, A. (2003b). SEAD: Secure efficient distance vector routing for mobile wireless ad hoc networks. *Ad Hoc Networks, 1*(1), 175–192. doi:10.1016/S1570-8705(03)00019-2.

Hu, Y. C., Perrig, A., & Johnson, D. B. (2003a). Packet leashes: A defense against wormhole attacks in wireless networks.[IEEE.]. *Proceedings of INFOCOM, 2003*, 1976–1986.

Hu, Y. C., Perrig, A., & Johnson, D. B. (2005). Ariadne: A secure on-demand routing protocol for ad hoc networks. *Wireless Networks, 11*(1-2), 21–38. doi:10.1007/s11276-004-4744-y.

Hu, Y. C., Perrig, A., & Johnson, D. B. (2006). Wormhole attacks in wireless networks. *IEEE Journal on Selected Areas in Communications, 24*(2), 370–380. doi:10.1109/JSAC.2005.861394.

Ibrahim, M., Khawam, K., & Tohme, S. (2009). Network centric joint radio resource policy in heterogeneous WiMAX/UMTS networks for streaming and elastic traffic. In *Proceedings of the IEEE Wireless Communications and Networking Conference*, (pp. 1-6). Budapest, Hungary: IEEE.

IEEE 802.16e. (2013). Retrieved from http://grouper.ieee.org/groups/802/16/tge/ on April 20, 2013

IEEE LAN/MAN Standards Committee (IEEE L/M SC). (2002). *IEEE standard for local and metropolitan area networks: Overview and architecture*. Retrieved April 20, 2013, from http://standards.ieee.org/getieee802/download/802-2001.pdf

IEEE Trial-Use Standard for Wireless Access in Vehicular Environments—Security Services for Applications and Management Messages. (2006). *IEEE Std 1609.2-2006*, 0. doi: 10.1109/IEEESTD.2006.243731

Ilyas, M. (2010). *The handbook of ad hoc wireless networks*. Boca Raton, FL: CRC Press.

Intanagonwiwat, C., Govindan, R., Estrin, D., Heidemann, J., & Silva, F. (2003). Directed diffusion for wireless sensor networking. *IEEE/ACM Transactions on Networking, 11*(1), 2-18. doi:10.1.1.1.3918

Intel Lab. (2007). *Intel lab experiment data set*. Retrieved from http://berkeley.intel-research.net/labdata/

International Organisation for Standardisation. (2004). *Information technology—Telecommunications and information exchange between systems—Near field communication—Interface and protocol (NFCIP-1)*. Retrieved March 29, 2012, from http://www.iso.org/iso/catalogue_detail.htm?csnumber=38578

Isaka, M., & Kawata, S. (2011). Signal sets for secret key agreement with public discussion based on Gaussian and fading channels. *IEEE Transactions on Information Forensics and Security, 6*(3), 523–531. doi:10.1109/TIFS.2011.2131132.

Islam, N., & Shaikh, Z. A. (2013). Security issues in mobile ad hoc network. In *Wireless Networks and Security* (pp. 49–80). Berlin, Germany: Springer Verlag. doi:10.1007/978-3-642-36169-2_2.

Ismail, M., & Zhuang, W. H. (2012). A distributed multi-service resource allocation algorithm in heterogeneous wireless access medium. *IEEE Journal on Selected Areas in Communications, 30*, 425–432. doi:10.1109/JSAC.2012.120222.

ISO/IEC 7498-1. (1994). *Information processing systems, open systems interconnection (OSI) reference model, the basic model*. ITU-T Recommendation X.200.

ITU-R M.2135. (2008). *Guidelines for evaluation of radio interface technologies for IMT-advanced*. Geneva, Switzerland: ITU Rep. ITU-R M.2135.

ITU-R M.2135-1. (2009). *Guidelines for evaluation of radio interface technologies for IMT-advanced*. Geneva, Switzerland: ITU Rep. ITU-R M.2135-1.

Jacoby, G. A., & Davis, N. J. (2007). Mobile host-based intrusion detection and attack identification. *IEEE Wireless Communications, 14*(4), 53–60. doi:10.1109/MWC.2007.4300984.

JaeHyu. K., & Song, J. (2012). A pre-authentication method for secure communications in vehicular ad hoc network. In *Proceedings of the 8th International Conference on Wireless Communications, Networking and Mobile Computing (WiCOM)* (pp. 1- 6). WiCOM.

Jaikaeo, C., Srisathapornphat, C., & Shen, C.-C. (2001). Diagnosis of sensor networks. In *Proceeding of ICC-IEEE International Conference* (pp. 1627-1632). IEEE.

Jain, S., & Jain, S. (2010). Detection and prevention of wormhole attack in mobile ad-hoc networks. *International Journal of Computer Theory and Engineering, 2*(1).

Jajodia, S., & Mutchler, D. (1987). Enhancements to the voting algorithm. In *Proceedings of the 13th VLDB Conference* (pp. 399-406). VLDB.

Jakobsson, M., Wetzel, S., & Yener, B. (2003). Stealth attacks on ad-hoc wireless networks. In *Proceedings of the 58th Vehicular Technology Conference,* (Vol. 3, pp. 2103-2111). IEEE.

Jan Kremer Consulting Services. (2010). *NFC near field communication white paper*. Retrieved April 26, 2012, from http://jkremer.com/White%20Papers/Near%20Field%20Communication%20White%20Paper%20JKCS.pdf

Jeon, H., Hwang, D., Choi, J., Lee, H., & Ha, J. (2011). Secure type-based multiple access. *IEEE Transactions on Information Forensics and Security, 6*(3), 763–774. doi:10.1109/TIFS.2011.2158312.

Jian, Y., Chen, S., Zhang, Z., & Zhang, L. (2007). Protecting receiver location privacy in wireless sensor networks. In *Proceedings of INFOCOM*. IEEE Computer Science Society Press.

Joerer, S., Sommer, C., & Dressler, F. (2012). Toward reproducability and comparability of IVC simulation studies: A literature survey. *IEEE Communications Magazine, 50*(10), 82–88. doi:10.1109/MCOM.2012.6316780.

John, S. P., & Samuel, P. (2011). A predictive clustering technique for effective key management in mobile ad hoc networks. *Information Security Journal: A Global Perspective, 20*(4-5), 250-260.

Johnson, D. B., & Maltz, A. D. (2001). DSR: The dynamic source routing protocol for multi-hop wireless ad hoc networks. *Discovery, 5*(1), 1-25. doi:10.1.1.115.3829

Johnson, D., & Perkins, C. (2001). *Mobility support in IPv6*. IETF draft, draft-ietf-mobileip-ipv6-15.txt.

Johnson, D. B., & Maltz, D. A. (1996). *Dynamic source routing in ad hoc wireless networks*. Dordrecht, The Netherlands: Kluwer. doi:10.1007/978-0-585-29603-6_5.

Johnston, D., & Walker, J. (2004). Overview of IEEE 802.16 security. *IEEE Security & Privacy*, 2(3), 40–48. doi:10.1109/MSP.2004.20.

Jorgensen, M. L., Yanakiev, B. R., Kirkelund, F. E., Popovski, P., Yomo, H., & Larsen, T. (2007). Shout to secure: Physical-layer wireless security with known interference. In *Proceedings of IEEE GLOBECOM* (pp. 33–38). Washington, DC: IEEE.

Jøsang, A. (2007). Trust and reputation systems. In A. Aldini & R. Gorrieri (Eds.), *Foundations of security analysis and design IV (FOSAD'07)*, (LNCS), (vol. 4677, pp. 209-245). New York: Springer.

Josang, A. (2012). {Robustness of Trust and Reputation Systems: Does it Matter?}.

Josang, A., Azderska, T., & Marsh, S. (2012). {Trust Transitivity and Conditional Belief Reasoning}.

Josang, A. (1998). *A subjective metric of authentication* (pp. 329–344). Lecture notes in Computer ScienceSpringer-Verlag.

Josang, A., & Ismail, R. (2002). *The beta reputation system BCEC*.

Jøsang, A., Ismail, R., & Boyd, C. (2007). A survey of trust and reputation systems for online service provision. *Decision Support Systems*, 43(2), 618–644. doi:10.1016/j.dss.2005.05.019.

Joseph, J. F. C., Das, A., Seet, B. C., & Lee, B. S. (2007). Cross layer versus single layer approaches for intrusion detection in MANETs. In *Proceedings of the 15th IEEE International Conference on Networks*, (pp. 194-199). IEEE.

Joseph, J. F. C., Das, A., Seet, B. C., & Lee, B. S. (2008). CRADS: Integrated cross layer approach for detecting routing attacks in MANETs. In *Proceedings of the Wireless Communications and Networking Conference*, (pp. 1525-1530). IEEE.

Joshi, J. B. D., Bhatti, R., Bertino, E., & Ghafoor, A. (2004). Access control language for multi domain environments. *IEEE Internet Computing*, 8(6), 40–50. doi:10.1109/MIC.2004.53.

Juels, A. (2006). RFID security and privacy: A research survey. *IEEE Journal on Selected Areas in Communications*, 24(2), 381–394. doi:10.1109/JSAC.2005.861395.

Juntunen, A., Luukkainen, S., & Tuunainen, V. K. (2010). Deploying NFC technology for mobile ticketing services—Identification of critical business model issues. In *Proceedings of the Ninth International Conference on Mobile Business* (pp. 82-90). Athens, Greece: IEEE.

Kahate, A. (2003). *Cryptography and network security* (2nd ed.). New York: Tata McGraw-Hill.

Kannhavong, B., Nakayama, H., Nemoto, Y., Kato, N., & Jamalipour, A. (2007). A survey of routing attacks in mobile ad hoc networks. *IEEE Wireless Communications*, 14(5), 85–91. doi:10.1109/MWC.2007.4396947.

Kapil, A., & Rana, S. (2009). Identity-based key management in MANETs using public key cryptography. *International Journal of Security*, 3(1), 1.

Kaplantzis, S., Shilton, A., Mani, A., & Sekerciolu, Y. A. (2007). Detecting selective forwarding attacks in wireless sensor networks using support vector machines. In *Proceedings of the 3rd International Symposium on Intelligent Sensors, Sensor Networks and Information Processing*. Melbourne, Australia: IEEE Computer Science Society Press.

Karabatis, G., & Aleroud, A. (2012). Discovering unknown cyber attacks using contextual misuse and anomaly detection. *Science Journal*, 1(3), 106–120.

Karami, M., & Fathian, M. (2009). A robust trust establishment framework using Dempster-Shafer theory for MANETs. In *Proceedings of Internet Technology and Secured Transactions, 2009, ICITST 2009* (pp. 1–7). London: ICITST.

Karas, D. S., Karagiannidis, G. K., & Schober, R. (2011). Neural network based PHY-layer key exchange for wireless communications. In *Proceedings of the IEEE 22nd International Symposium on Personal Indoor and Mobile Radio Communications (PIMRC)* (pp. 1233-1238). IEEE.

Kargl, F., Alfred, S. S., & Weber, M. (2005). {Secure Dynamic Source Routing}.

Karlof, C., & Wagner, D. (2003). Secure routing in wireless sensor networks: Attacks and countermeasures. *Elsevier's AdHoc Networks Journal, 1*(2-3), 293-315. Retreived from www.journals.elsevier.com/ad-hoc-networks

Karlof, C., Sastry, N., & Wagner, D. (2004). {TinySec: A link layer security architecture for wireless sensor networks}.

Karlof, C., & Wagner, D. (2003). Secure routing in wireless sensor networks: Attacks and countermeasures. *Ad Hoc Networks, 1*(2), 293–315. doi:10.1016/S1570-8705(03)00008-8.

Karp, B., & Kun, H. T. (2000). GPSR: Greedy perimeter stateless routing for wireless networks. In *Proceedings of the 6th Annual International Conference on Mobile Computing and Networking*. Boston, MA. doi: 10.1145/345910.345953

Karygiannis, T., & Owens, L. (2002). Wireless network security. *NIST Special Publication, 800*, 48.

Kaufman, C., Perlman, R., & Speciner, M. (2002). *Network security: Private communication in a public world*. Upper Saddle River, NJ: Prentice Hall Press.

Kerschberger, M. (2011). *Near field communication A survey of safety and security measures*. Retrieved March 29, 2012, from https://www.auto.tuwien.ac.at/bib/pdf_TR/TR0156.pdf

Kesting, K., Treiber, M., & Helbing, D. (2010). Connectivity statistics of store-and-forward intervehicle communication. *IEEE Transactions on Intelligent Transportation Systems, 11*(1), 172–181. doi:10.1109/TITS.2009.2037924.

Kfir, Z., & Wool, A. (2005). Picking virtual pockets using relay attacks on contactless. In *Proceedings of the First International Conference on Security and Privacy for Emerging Areas in Communications Networks (SE-CURECOMM'05)* (pp. 47-58). Washington, DC: IEEE Computer Society.

Khalili, A., Katz, J., & Arbaugh, W. A. (2003). Toward secure key distribution in truly ad-hoc networks. In *Proceedings of the 2003 Symposium on Applications and the Internet Workshops, 2003* (pp. 342-346). IEEE.

Khalil, I., & Bagchi, S. (2011). Stealthy attacks in wireless ad hoc networks: Detection and countermeasure. *IEEE Transactions on Mobile Computing, 10*(8), 1096–1112. doi:10.1109/TMC.2010.249.

Khan, M. A., & Hasan, A. (2008). Pseudo random number based authentication to counter denial of service attacks on 802.11. In *Proceedings of the 5th IFIP International Conference on Wireless and Optical Communications Networks,* (pp. 1-5). IEEE.

Khisti, A., & Wornell, G. W. (2007). Secure transmission with multiple antennas: The MIMOME channel. *IEEE Transactions of Information Theory*. Retrieved from http://arxiv.org/abs/0708.4219

Khisti, A., Diggavi, S. N., & Wornell, G. W. (2011). Secret-key agreement with channel state information at the transmitter. *IEEE Transactions on Information Forensics and Security, 6*(3), 672–681. doi:10.1109/TIFS.2011.2151188.

Khisti, A., Diggavi, S. N., & Wornell, G. W. (2012). Secret-key generation using correlated sources and channels. *IEEE Transactions on Information Theory, 58*(2), 652–670. doi:10.1109/TIT.2011.2173629.

Khisti, A., & Wornell, G. (2010). Secure transmission with multiple antennas— Part II: The MIMOME wiretap channel. *IEEE Transactions on Information Theory, 56*(11), 5515–5532. doi:10.1109/TIT.2010.2068852.

Khozium, M. O. (2008). Hello flood counter measure for wireless sensor networks. *International Journal of Computer Science and Security, 2*(3), 57–65. Retrieved from www.cscjournals.org/description.php?Jcode=IJCSS.

Kim, T. H. J., Studer, A., Dubey, R., Zhang, X., Perrig, A., & Bai, F. … Iyer, A. (2010). VANET alert endorsement using multi-source filters. In *Proceedings of the ACM International Workshop on Vehicular Internetworking* (pp. 51-60). ACM.

Kim, Y., Sankhla, V., & Helmy, A. (2004). Efficient traceback of DoS attacks using small worlds in MANET. In *Proceedings of the Vehicular Technology Conference,* (Vol. 6, pp. 3979-3983). IEEE.

Kim, J., Ikhlef, A., & Schober, R. (2012). Combined relay selection and cooperative beamforming for physical layer security. *Journal of Communications and Networks*, *14*(4), 364–373.

Klein, A. (2012). *Random waypoint*. Retrieved 2012 from http://www.routingprotokolle.de/Routing/mobility_random_waypoint.htm

Klinc, D., Ha, J., McLaughlin, S., Barros, J., & Kwak, B.-J. (2011). LDPC codes for the Gaussian wiretap channel. *IEEE Transactions on Information Forensics and Security*, *6*(3), 532–540. doi:10.1109/TIFS.2011.2134093.

Ko, M., Ahn, G. J., & Shehab, M. (2009). Privacy enhanced user-centric identity management. In G. Fettweis (Ed.), *Proceedings of the IEEE International Conference on Communications* (pp. 1-5). Dresden, Germany: IEEE Press.

Kobayashi, M., Piantanida, P., Yang, S., & Shamai, S. (2011). On the secrecy degrees of freedom of the multiantenna block fading wiretap channels. *IEEE Transactions on Information Forensics and Security*, *6*(3), 703–711. doi:10.1109/TIFS.2011.2159376.

Kocher, P. C. (1998). On certificate revocation and validation. In *Financial Cryptography* (pp. 172–177). Berlin, Germany: Springer Verlag. doi:10.1007/BFb0055481.

Komninos, N., Vergados, D., & Douligeris, C. (2006). Layered security design for mobile ad hoc networks. *Computers & Security*, *25*(2), 121–130. doi:10.1016/j.cose.2005.09.005.

Konorski, J., & Orlikowski, R. (2009). Data-centric Dempster-Shafer theory-based selfishness thwarting via trust evaluation in MANETs and WSNs. In *Proceedings of the 2009 3rd International Conference on New Technologies, Mobility and Security, NTMS* (pp. 1-5). NTMS.

Konstantinou, E. (2011). Efficient cluster-based group key agreement protocols for wireless ad hoc networks. *Journal of Network and Computer Applications*, *34*(1), 384–393. doi:10.1016/j.jnca.2010.05.001.

Koukoumidis, E., Lymberopoulos, D., Strauss, K., Liu, J., & Burger, D. (2011). Pocket cloudlets. *SIGPLAN Not.*, *47*(4), 171–184. doi:10.1145/2248487.1950387.

Koushanfar, F., Potkonjak, M., & Sangiovanni-Vincentelli, A. (2003). On-line fault detection of sensor measurements. *Proceedings of the IEEE*, *2*, 974–979.

Krawczyk, H., Bellare, M., & Canetti, R. (1997). *HMAC: Keyed-hashing for message authentication*. Retrieved from http://www.ietf.org/rfc/rfc2104.txt

Krishnamachari, B., & Iyengar, S. (2004). Distributed Bayesian algorithms for fault-tolerant event region detection in wireless sensor networks. *IEEE Transactions on Computers*, *53*, 421–250. doi:10.1109/TC.2004.1261832.

Krontiris, I., Dimitriou, T., Thanassis, G., & Mpasoukos, M. (2007). Intrusion detection of sinkhole attacks in wireless sensor networks. In Proceedings of the 3rd International Conference on Algorithmic Aspects of Wireless Sensor Networks. Wroclaw, Poland. doi:0.1.1.105.3047

Kulasekaran, S., & Ramkumar, M. (2011). APALLS: A secure MANET routing protocol. *Mobile Ad Hoc Networks: Applications*.

Kurita, S., Komoriya, K., & Uda, R. (2012). Privacy protection on transfer system of automated teller machine from brute force attack. In *Proceedings of the 26th International Conference on Advanced Information Networking and Applications Workshops (WAINA)* (pp. 72-77). WAINA.

Kurosawa, S., Nakayama, H., Kato, N., Jamalipour, A., & Nemoto, Y. (2007). Detecting blackhole attack on AODV-based mobile ad hoc networks by dynamic learning method. *International Journal of Network Security*, *5*(3), 338–346.

Kwiatkowska, M., Norman, G., & Parker, D. (2007). Stochastic model checking. In M. Bernardo & J. Hillston (Eds.), *Formal methods for performance evaluation (SFM'07)*, (LNCS), (vol. 4486, pp. 220-270). New York: Springer.

Kyösti, P, Meinilä, J, Hentilä, L., Zhao, X., Jämsä, T., Schneider, C.,... Rautiainen, T. (2008). *WINNER II channel models*. IST-4-027756, WINNER II D1.1.2, v1.2.

Kyasanur, P., & Vaidya, N. (2003). Detection and handling of MAC layer misbehavior in wireless networks. In *Proceedings of the International Conference on Dependable Systems and Networks* (pp. 22-25). IEEE.

Kyasanur, P., & Vaidya, N. H. (2002). Handling MAC layer misbehavior in wireless networks. In *Proceedings of MOBICOM'02*. Atlanta, GA: ACM.

Lai, L., Liang, Y., & Du, W. (2012). Cooperative key generation in wireless networks. *IEEE Journal on Selected Areas in Communications, 30*(8), 1578–1588. doi:10.1109/JSAC.2012.120924.

Lai, L., Liang, Y., & Du, W. (2012). Cooperative key generation in wireless networks. *IEEE Journal on Selected Areas in Communications, 30*(8), 1578–1588. doi:10.1109/JSAC.2012.120924.

Lai, L., Liang, Y., & Poor, H. V. (2012). A unified framework for key agreement over wireless fading channels. *IEEE Transactions on Information Forensics and Security, 7*(2), 480–490. doi:10.1109/TIFS.2011.2180527.

Lazarri, T. D. (2008). *Near field communication*. Retrieved April 26, 2012, from http://www.slideshare.net/tdelazzari/near-field-communication-presentation

Lazos, L., Poovendran, R., Meadows, C., Syverson, P., & Changr, L. W. (2005). Preventing wormhole attacks on wireless ad hoc networks: A graph theoretic approach. In *Proceedings of the Wireless Communication and Networking Conference WCNC 05*. New Orleans, LA. doi:10.1.1.76.7850

Leavitt, N. (2011, June). Mobile security: Finally a serious problem? *Computer, 44*(6), 11–14. doi:10.1109/MC.2011.184.

Lee, E.-K., Gerla, M., & Oh, S. Y. (2012). Physical layer security in wireless smart grid. *IEEE Communications Magazine, 50*(8), 46–52. doi:10.1109/MCOM.2012.6257526.

Lee, W. C. (2006). *Wireless and cellular telecommunications*. New York: McGraw-Hill.

Lei, J., Han, Z., Vaazquez-Castro, M., & Hjorungnes, A. (2011). Multibeam satcom systems design with physical layer security. In *Proceedings of the 2011 IEEE International Conference on Ultra-Wideband (ICUWB)* (pp. 555-559). IEEE.

Lei, J., Han, Z., Vazquez-Castro, M., & Hjorungnes, A. (2011). Secure satellite communication systems design with individual secrecy rate constraints. *IEEE Transactions on Information Forensics and Security, 6*(3), 661–671. doi:10.1109/TIFS.2011.2148716.

Li, N., & Mitchell, J. (2003). {RT, A Role-based Trust-management Framework}.

Li, R., Li, J., Liu, P., & Chen, H. (2007). An objective trust management framework for mobile ad hoc networks. In *Proceedings of the IEEE 65th Vehicular Technology Conference,* (pp. 56-60). IEEE.

Li, X., Lyu, M. R., & Liu, J. (2004). {A Trust Model Based Routing Protocol for Secure Ad Hoc Networks}.

Li, Z., Trappe, W., & Yates, R. (2007). Secret communication via multiantenna transmission. In *Proceedings of 41st CISS* (pp. 905–910). Baltimore, MD: CISS.

Liang, Y., Poor, H. V., & Shamai (Shitz), S. (2009). Information theoretic security. *Found. Trends Commun. Inf. Theory, 5*(4-5), 355-580. Retrieved from http://dx.doi.org/10.1561/0100000036

Liang, Y., Poor, H. V., & Shamai, S. (2008). Secure communication over fading channels. *IEEE Transactions on Information Theory, 54*(6), 2470–2492. doi:10.1109/TIT.2008.921678.

Liang, Y., Poor, H., & Ying, L. (2011, September). Secure communications over wireless broadcast networks: Stability and utility maximization. *IEEE Transactions on Information Forensics and Security, 6*(3), 682–692. doi:10.1109/TIFS.2011.2158311.

Liao, W. C., Chang, T. H., Ma, W. K., & Chi, C. Y. (2010). Joint transmit beamforming and artificial noise design for QoS discrimination in wireless downlink. In *Proceedings of the 2010 IEEE International Conference on Acoustics Speech and Signal Processing,* (pp. 2562-2565). IEEE.

Li, F., & Wu, J. (2010). Uncertainty modeling and reduction in manets. *IEEE Transactions on Mobile Computing, 9*(7), 1035–1048. doi:10.1109/TMC.2010.44.

Li, H., & Singhal, M. (2007). Trust management in distributed systems. *Computer, 40*(2), 45–53. doi:10.1109/MC.2007.76.

Li, J., Li, R., & Kato, J. (2008). {Future Trust Management Framework for Mobile Ad hoc Networks}. *IEEE Communications Magazine, 46*, 108–114. doi:10.1109/MCOM.2008.4481349.

Li, J., & Petropulu, A. P. (2011, September). Ergodic secrecy rate for multiple-antenna wiretap channels with Rician fading. *IEEE Transactions on Information Forensics and Security, 6*(3), 861–867. doi:10.1109/TIFS.2011.2158538.

Li, J., Petropulu, A. P., & Weber, S. (2011). On cooperative relaying schemes for wireless physical layer security. *IEEE Transactions on Signal Processing, 59*(10), 4985–4997. doi:10.1109/TSP.2011.2159598.

Limmanee, A., & Henkel, W. (2010). Secure physical-layer key generation protocol and key encoding in wireless communications. In *Proceedings of the 2010 IEEE GLOBECOM workshops (GC WKSHPS)* (pp. 94-98). IEEE.

Lin, L. C. (2010, February). Get ready for 900MHz Refarming. *Huawei Communicate, 54*.

Lin, X., Sun, X., Ho, P. H., & Shen, X. (2007). GSIS: A secure and privacy-preserving protocol for vehicular communications. *IEEE Transactions on Vehicular Technology, 56*(6), 3442–3456. doi:10.1109/TVT.2007.906878.

Li, Q., & Rus, D. (2006). Global clock synchronization in sensor networks. *IEEE Transactions on Computers, 55*(2), 214–226. Retrieved from www.computer.org/portal/web/tc doi:10.1109/TC.2006.25.

Liu, B., Zhong, Y., & Zhang, S. (2007). Probabilistic isolation of malicious vehicles in pseudonym changing VANETs. In *Proceedings of International Conference on Computer and Information Technology* (pp. 967-972). IEEE.

Liu, J., & Issarny, V. (2004). Enhanced reputation mechanism for mobile ad hoc networks. In *Proceedings to the 2nd International Conference on Trust Management,* (LNCS), (vol. 2995, pp. 48-62). New York: Springer.

Liu, R., Liu, T., Poor, H., & Shamai, S. (2010). Multiple-input multiple-output Gaussian broadcast channels with confidential messages. *IEEE Transactions on Information Theory, 56*(9), 4215–4227. doi:10.1109/TIT.2010.2054593.

Liu, S., & Lin, Y. (2006). *Grey information: Theory and practical applications*. London: Springer.

Li, W., Ghogho, M., Chen, B., & Xiong, C. (2012). Secure communication via sending artificial noise by the receiver: Outage secrecy capacity/region analysis. *IEEE Communications Letters, 16*(10), 1628–1631. doi:10.1109/LCOMM.2012.081612.121344.

Li, Z., & Shen, H. (2011). *Game-theoretic analysis of cooperation incentive strategies in mobile ad hoc networks*. Transactions on Mobile Computing.

Lou, W., Liu, W., Zhang, Y., & Fang, Y. (2009). SPREAD: Improving network security by multipath routing in mobile ad hoc networks. *Wireless Networks, 15*(3), 279–294. doi:10.1007/s11276-007-0039-4.

LTE and the Evolution to 4G Wireless (LTE: 4G). (n.d.). Retrieved April 20, 2013, from http://www.home.agilent.com/upload/cmc_upload/All/Security_in_the_LTE-AE_Network.PDF?&cc=US&lc=eng

LTE Topology Evolving Networks (LTE TEN). (n.d.). Retrieved April 20, 2013, from http://www.rcrwireless.com/mobile-backhaul/lte-topology.html

LTE. (n.d.). *Wikipedia*. Retrieved April 20, 2013, from http://en.wikipedia.org/wiki/LTE_(telecommunication)

LTE: 4gamericas. (n.d.). Retrieved April 20, 2013, from http://www.4gamericas.org/index.cfm?fuseaction=page&sectionid = 249

Lu, R., Lin, X., Zhu, H., Ho, P. H., & Shen, X. (2008). ECPP: Efficient conditional privacy preservation protocol for secure vehicular communications. In *Proceedings of the IEEE Conference on Computer Communications* (pp. 1229-1237). IEEE.

Luo, C. Q. Ji. H., & Li, Y. (2009). Utility-based multi-service bandwidth allocation in the 4G heterogeneous wireless access networks. In *Proceedings of the IEEE Wireless Communications and Networking Conference,* (pp. 1-5). Budapest, Hungary: IEEE.

Luo, H., Zerfos, P., Kong, J., Lu, S., & Zhang, L. (2002). Self-securing ad hoc wireless networks. In *Proceedings of the Seventh IEEE Symposium on Computers and Communications (ISCC'02)* (Vol. 8). IEEE.

Luo, H., Kong, J., Zerfos, P., Lu, S., & Zhang, L. (2004). URSA: Ubiquitous and robust access control for mobile ad hoc networks. *IEEE/ACM Transactions on Networking, 12*(6), 1049–1063. doi:10.1109/TNET.2004.838598.

Luo, X., Dong, M., & Huang, Y. (2006). On distributed fault-tolerant detection in wireless sensor networks. *IEEE Transactions on Computers, 55*, 58–70. doi:10.1109/TC.2006.13.

Ly, H., Liu, T., & Liang, Y. (2010). Multiple-input multiple-output Gaussian broadcast channels with common and confidential messages. *IEEE Transactions on Information Theory, 56*(11), 5477–5487. doi:10.1109/TIT.2010.2069190.

Ma, C. X., & Fang, Z. M. (2009). A novel intrusion detection architecture based on adaptive selection event triggering for mobile ad-hoc networks. In *Proceedings of the Second International Symposium on Intelligent Information Technology and Security Informatics,* (pp. 198-201). IEEE.

Madiseh, M. G., Neville, S. W., & McGuire, M. L. (2012). Applying beamforming to address temporal correlation in wireless channel characterization-based secret key generation. *IEEE Transactions on Information Forensics and Security, 7*(4), 1278–1287. doi:10.1109/TIFS.2012.2195176.

Madlmayr, G., Langer, J., Kantner, C., & Scharinger, J. (2008). NFC devices: Security and privacy. In *Proceedings of the Third International Conference on Availability, Reliability and Security, 2008, (ARES 08)* (pp. 642-647). Barcelona, Spain: ARES.

Makri, E., & Stamatiou, Y. C. (2010). Key management techniques for wireless sensor networks: Practical and theoretical considerations. In A. K. Pathan (Ed.), *Security of self-organizing networks— MANET, WSN, WMN, VANET* (pp. 317–345). Boca Raton, FL: CRC Press. doi:10.1201/EBK1439819197-18.

Malaney, R. A. (2005). *Securing internal wi-fi networks with position verification.* Paper presented at the Global Telecommunications Conference. New York, NY. *NS-2.* (n.d.). Retrieved from http://www.isi.edu/nsnam/ns/

Maltz, D. (1999). *Resource management in multi-hop ad hoc networks.* CMU School of computer Science Technical Report CMU-CS-00-150.

MAN. (2009). *Wikipedia.* Retrieved April 20, 2013, from http://en.wikipedia.org/wiki/Metropolitan_area_network

Manjeshwar, E., & Agrawal, D. P. (2001). TEEN: A routing protocol for enhanced efficiency in wireless sensor networks. In *Proceedings of the 15th International Parallel and Distributed Processing Symposium (IPDPS).* San Francisco, CA. doi:10.1109/IPDPS.2001.925197

Manousakis, K., Sterne, D., Ivanic, N., Lawler, G., & McAuley, A. (2008). A stochastic approximation approach for improving intrusion detection data fusion structures. In *Proceedings of the Military Communications Conference,* (pp. 1-7). IEEE.

Marchi, B., Grilo, A., & Nunes, M. (2007). DTSN— Distributed transport for sensor networks. In *Proceedings of the IEEE Symposium on Computers and Communications.* Aveiro, Portugal. doi:10.1.1.80.4025

Marinelli, E. E. (2009). *Hyrax: Cloud computing on mobile devices using MapReduce.* (Unpublished master thesis). Carnegie Mellon University, Pittsburgh, PA.

Marmol, F. G., & Perez, G. M. (2009). Security threats scenarios in trust and reputation models for distributed systems. *Computers & Security, 28*, 545–556. doi:10.1016/j.cose.2009.05.005.

Marsh, S. (1994). *Formalising trust as a computational concept.* (PhD Thesis). Department of Mathematics and Computer Science, University of Stirling, Stirling, UK.

Martalò, M., Busanelli, S., & Ferrari, G. (2009). Markov chain-based performance analysis of multihop IEEE 802.15.4 wireless networks. *Performance Evaluation, 66*(12), 722–741. doi:10.1016/j.peva.2009.08.011.

Marti, S., Giuli, T. J., Lai, K., & Baker, M. (2000). Mitigating routing misbehavior in mobile ad hoc networks. In *Proceedings of the 6th Annual International Conference on Mobile Computing and Networking (MobiCom'00),* (pp. 255-265). ACM.

Marti, S., Giuli, T. J., Lai, K., & Baker, M. (2000). Mitigating routing misbehavior in mobile ad hoc networks. In *Proceedings of the 6th Annual International Conference on Mobile Computing and Networking* (Vol. 6, pp. 255-265). ACM.

Masdari, M., Jabbehdari, S., Ahmadi, M. R., Hashemi, S. M., Bagherzadeh, J., & Khadem-Zadeh, A. (2011). A survey and taxonomy of distributed certificate authorities in mobile ad hoc networks. *EURASIP Journal on Wireless Communications and Networking, 1,* 1–12.

Massey, J. (1988, May). An introduction to contemporary cryptology. *Proceedings of the IEEE, 76,* 533–549. doi:10.1109/5.4440.

Mathur, S., Trappe, W., Mandayam, N., Ye, C., & Reznik, A. (2008). Radio-telepathy: Extracting a secret key from an unauthenticated wireless channel. In *Proceedings of the 14th ACM Intl. Conf. on Mobile Computing and Networking (MOBICOM '08)* (pp. 128–139). San Francisco, CA: ACM.

Mathur, S., Reznik, A., Ye, C., Mukherjee, R., Rahman, A., Shah, Y., & Mandayam, N. (2010). Exploiting the physical layer for enhanced security[security and privacy in emerging wireless networks]. *IEEE Wireless Communications, 17*(5), 63–70. doi:10.1109/MWC.2010.5601960.

Mathur, S., & Trappe, W. (2011). Bit-traps: Building information-theoretic traffic privacy into packet streams. *IEEE Transactions on Information Forensics and Security, 6*(3), 752–762. doi:10.1109/TIFS.2011.2138696.

Maurer, U. (1993). Secret key agreement by public discussion from common information. *IEEE Transactions on Information Theory, 39,* 733–742. doi:10.1109/18.256484.

Maurer, U., & Wolf, S. (2003a). Secret-key agreement over unauthenticated public channels— Part I: Definitions and a completeness result. *IEEE Transactions on Information Theory, 49*(4), 822–831. doi:10.1109/TIT.2003.809563.

Maurer, U., & Wolf, S. (2003b). Secret-key agreement over unauthenticated public channels—Part III: Privacy amplification. *IEEE Transactions on Information Theory, 49*(4), 839–851. doi:10.1109/TIT.2003.809559.

Maurer, U., & Wolf, S. (2003c). Secret-key agreement over unauthenticated public channels—Part II: The simulatability condition. *IEEE Transactions on Information Theory, 49*(4), 832–838. doi:10.1109/TIT.2003.809560.

Medidi, S. R., Medidi, M., & Gavini, S. (2003). Detecting packet-dropping faults in mobile ad-hoc networks. In *Proceedings of the Conference Record of the Thirty-Seventh Asilomar Conference on Signals, Systems and Computers, 2003* (Vol. 2, pp. 1708-1712). IEEE.

Meghdadi, M., Ozdemir, S., & Guler, I. (2011). A survey of wormhole-based attacks and their countermeasures in wireless sensor networks. *IETE Technical Review, 28*(2), 89–102. doi:10.4103/0256-4602.78089.

Mehmood, R., & Wallace, J. (2011, April). Wireless security enhancement using parasitic reconfigurable aperture antennas. In *Proceedings of the 5th European Conference on Antennas and Propagation (EUCAP)* (pp. 2761-2765). EUCAP.

Mehmood, R., & Wallace, J. (2012). Experimental assessment of secret key generation using parasitic reconfigurable aperture antennas. In *Proceedings of the 2012 6th European Conference on Antennas and Propagation (EUCAP)* (pp. 1151-1155). EUCAP.

Mehranbod, N. (2002). *A probabilistic approach for sensor fault detection and identification.* (Doctoral Thesis). Drexel University, Philadelphia, PA.

Mehuron, W. (1994). *Digital signature standard (DSS).* Washington, DC: NIST.

Mell, P., & Grance, T. (2011). *The NIST definition of cloud computing* (NIST Special Publication 800-145 [Draft]). Retrieved August 10, 2011, from http://csrc.nist.gov/publications/drafts/800-145/Draft-SP-800-145_cloud-definition.pdf

Menezes, A. J. (1993). *Elliptic curve public key cryptosystems.* Boston: Kluwer Academic Publishers. doi:10.1007/978-1-4615-3198-2.

Menezes, A. J., Van Oorschot, P. C., & Vanstone, S. A. (2010). *Handbook of applied cryptography.* Boca Raton, FL: CRC Press.

Menezes, A., Oorschot, P. V., & Vanstone, S. (2001). *Handbook of applied cryptography (discrete mathematics and its applications)* (5th ed.). Boca Raton, FL: CRC Press.

Merwe, J. V. D., Dawoud, D., & McDonald, S. (2007). A survey on peer-to-peer key management for mobile ad hoc networks. *ACM Computing Surveys*, *39*(1), 1. doi:10.1145/1216370.1216371.

Michiardi, P., & Molva, R. (2002). *CORE: A collaborative reputation mechanism to enforce node cooperation in mobile ad-hoc networks*. IFIP-Communication and Multimedia Security Conference. doi:10.1007/978-0-387-35612-9_9.

Min, Z., & Jiliu, Z. (2009). Cooperative black hole attack prevention for mobile ad hoc networks. In *Proceedings of the International Symposium on Information Engineering and Electronic Commerce*, (pp. 26-30). IEEE.

Mingyan, L., Koutsopoulos, I., & Poovendran, R. (2010). Optimal jamming attack strategies and network defense policies in wireless sensor networks. *IEEE Transactions on Mobile Computing*, *9*(8), 1119–1133. doi:10.1109/TMC.2010.75.

Minhas, U., Zhang, J., Tran, T., & Cohen, R. (2010). Towards expanded trust management for agents in vehicular ad hoc networks. *International Journal of Computational Intelligence Theory and Practice*, *5*(1), 3–15.

Mini, R. A. F., Machado, M. V., Loureiro, A. A. F., & Nath, B. (2003). Prediction-based energy map for wireless sensor networks. In *Proceedings of the Simpsio Brasilerio De Redes De Computadores* (pp. 165-169). IEEE.

Mishra, A. (2008). Security And Quality Of Service. In *Ad Hoc Wireless Networks*. New York: Cambridge University Press.

Mishra, A., Nadkarni, K., & Patcha, A. (2004). Intrusion detection in wireless ad hoc networks. *IEEE Wireless Communications*, *11*(1), 48–60. doi:10.1109/MWC.2004.1269717.

Misra, I. S., Dey, S., & Saha, D. (2005). *TLMIPv6: A next generation three layer mobile IPv6 mobility management architecture*. WWC.

Misra, S., & Goswami, S. (2010). Key management in mobile ad hoc networks. In A. K. Pathan (Ed.), *Security of self-organizing networks: MANET, WSN, WMN, VANET*. Boca Raton, FL: CRC Press. doi:10.1201/EBK1439819197-10.

Misztal, B. (1995). *Trust in Modern Societies: The Search for the Bases of Social Order*. Polity press.

Mitra, S. (2008). Dynamic mobility management for next generation all-IP wireless network. In *Proceedings of the International Conference on Communication Systems and Networks* (Vol. 1, pp. 165-170). AsiaCSN.

Mitra, S. (2008). Dynamic resource management in next generation all-IP wireless network.[). IEEE.]. *Proceedings of IEEE INDICON*, *1*, 165–170.

Moeller, S., Sridharan, A., Krishnamachari, B., & Ganawali, O. (2010). {Routing without routes: Backpressure Collection Protocol}.

Mohamad, O., Hassan, R., Patel, A., & Razali, R. (2009). A review of security parameters in mobile ad hoc networks. In *Proceeding of the International Conference on Information and Communications Systems (ICICS2009)* (Vol. 7). ICICS.

Mohapatra, P., & Krishnamurthy, S. (2010). *Ad hoc networks: Technologies and protocols*. New York: Springer Publishing Company, Incorporated.

Mo, J., Tao, M., & Liu, Y. (2012). Relay placement for physical layer security: A secure connection perspective. *IEEE Communications Letters*, *16*(6), 878–881. doi:10.1109/LCOMM.2012.042312.120582.

Molina-Gil, J., Caballero-Gil, P., & Caballero-Gil, C. (2010). Enhancing collaboration in vehicular networks. In *Proceedings of International Conference on Cooperative Design, Visualization, and Engineering* (pp. 77-80). IEEE.

Montavont, N., & Noel, T. (2002). Handover management for mobile nodes in IPv6 network. *IEEE Communications Magazine*, 38–43. doi:10.1109/MCOM.2002.1024413.

Mookiah, P., & Dandekar, K. (2010). Enhancing wireless security through reconfigurable antennas. In *Proceedings of the 2010 IEEE Radio and Wireless Symposium (RWS)* (pp. 593-596). IEEE.

Moore, T., Raya, M., Clulow, J., Papadimitratos, P., Anderson, R., & Hubaux, J. P. (2008). Fast exclusion of errant devices from vehicular networks. In *Proceedings of the IEEE Conference on Sensor, Mesh and Ad Hoc Communications and Networks (SECON)* (pp. 135-143). IEEE.

Moore, D., Shannon, C., Brown, D. J., Voelker, G. M., & Savage, S. (2006). Inferring internet denial-of-service activity. *ACM Transactions on Computer Systems*, *24*(2), 115–139. Retrieved from http://doi.acm.org/10.1145/1132026.1132027 doi:10.1145/1132026.1132027.

Mui, L., Mohtashemi, M., & Halberstadt, A. (2002). A computational model of trust and reputation. In *Proceedings of the 35th Annual Hawaii International Conference on System Sciences (HICSS)*, (pp. 2431-2439). IEEE. Chen, L., Xue, X., & Leneutre, J. (2006). A lightweight mechanism to secure OLSR.[IMECS.]. *Proceedings of IMECS*, *2006*, 887–895.

Murthy, C. S. R., & Manoj, B. S. (2004). *Ad hoc wireless networks: Architectures and protocols*. Upper Saddle River, NJ: Prentice Hall.

Nadkarni, K., & Mishra, A. (2004). A novel intrusion detection approach for wireless ad hoc networks. In *Proceedings of the Wireless Communications and Networking Conference*, (Vol. 2, pp. 831-836). IEEE.

Nagatani, T. (2002). The physics of traffic jams. *Reports on Progress in Physics*, *65*(9), 1331 1386. doi:10.1088/0034-4885/65/9/203.

Nagpal, A., Sanders, L., & Dobsonm, J. (2010). *Liberalising 2G spectrum and GSM refarming*. Analysys Mason Limited.

Nakamoto, S. (2009). *Bitcoin: A peer-to-peer electronic cash system* (Technical Report). Retrieved from http://www.bitcoin.org

Nan, X. H., & Chen, Z. (2006). *Identifier-based private key generating method and device*. WO Patent WO/2006/074,611.

Nasreldin, M., Asian, H., El-Hennawy, M., & El-Hennawy, A. (2008). WiMAX security. In *Proceedings of the Advanced Information Networking and Applications - Workshops, AINAW* (pp. 1335-1340). AINAW.

Negi, R., & Goel, S. (2005). Secret communications using artificial noise. In *Proceedings of IEEE Vehicular Technology Conference* (pp. 1906-1910). Dallas, TX: IEEE.

Newsome, J., Shi, E., Song, D., & Perrig, A. (2004). The Sybil attack in sensor networks: Analysis and defenses. In *Proceedings of the 3rd International Symposium on Information Processing in Sensor Networks*. San Francisco, CA. doi:10.1.1.3.1233

Newsome, J., Shi, E., Song, D., & Perrig, A. (2004). The sybil attack in sensor networks: Analysis defenses. In *Proceedings of the Third International Symposium on Information Processing in Sensor Networks, 2004 (IPSN 2004)* (pp. 259-268). IPSN.

NFC Forum Technical Specifications. (2006). *NFC data exchange format (NDEF)—Technical specification*. Retrieved March 29, 2012, from http://www.nfc-forum.org/specs/spec_list/

Ngadi, M., Khokhar, R. H., & Mandala, S. (2008). A review current routing attacks in mobile ad-hoc networks. *International Journal of Computer Science and Security*, *2*(3), 18–29.

Ngai, E. C., Lyu, M. R., & Chin, R. T. (2004). An authentication service against dishonest users in mobile ad hoc networks. In *Proceedings of the Aerospace Conference*, (Vol. 2, pp. 1275-1285). IEEE.

Ngai, E. C. H., Liu, J., & Lyu, M. R. (2007). An efficient intruder detection algorithm against sinkhole attacks in wireless sensor networks. *Computer Communications*, *30*(11), 2354–2364. doi: doi:10.1016/j.comcom.2007.04.025.

Nguyen, T. (2009, April 20). *A survey of wimax security threats*. Retrieved April 20, 2013, from http://www.cse.wustl.edu/~jain/cse571-09/ftp/wimax2.pdf

Nguyen, H. L., & Nguyen, U. T. (2008). A study of different types of attacks on multicast in mobile ad hoc networks. *Ad Hoc Networks*, *6*(1), 32–46. doi:10.1016/j.adhoc.2006.07.005.

Ni, J., & Chandler, S. A. G. (1994). Connectivity properties of a random radio network. *IEEE Proceedings-Communications*, *141*(14), 289-296.

Ni, X., & Luo, J. (2008). A clustering analysis based trust model in grid environment supporting virtual organizations. In *Proceedings of the 22nd International Conference on Advanced Information Networking and Applications - Workshops (Aina Workshops 2008)* (pp. 100-105). Okinawa, Japan: Aina.

Nichols, R. K., & Lekkas, P. C. (2002). *Wireless security.* New York: McGraw-Hill.

Nokia Siemens Networks. (2008a). *WCDMA frequency refarming: A leap forward towards ubiquitous mobile broadband coverage.* Nokia.

Nokia Siemens Networks. (2008b). *Extending 3G coverage with cost-efficient WCDMA frequency refarming.* Nokia.

Nokia Siemens Networks. (2008c). WCDMA frequency refarming overview. In *Proceedings of the Mobile World Congress.* Nokia.

Noubir, G. (2004). On connectivity in ad hoc network under jamming using directional antennas and mobility. In *Proceedings of the 2nd International Conference on Wired and Wireless Internet Communications* (pp. 54–62). IEEE.

Nowatkowski, M. E. (2010). *Certificate revocation list distribution in vehicular ad hoc networks (Technical report).* Atlanta, GA: Georgia Institute of Technology.

Nuaymi, L. (2007). *WiMAX: Technology for broadband wireless access.* Hoboken, NJ: Wiley. doi:10.1002/9780470319055.

Oggier, F., & Hassibi, B. (2008). The secrecy capacity of the MIMO wiretap channel. In *Proceedings of the IEEE International Symposium on Information Theory,* (pp. 524–528). Toronto, Canada: IEEE.

Olsson, M., Sultana, S., Rommer, S., Frid, L., & Mulligan, C. (2009). *SAE and the evolved packet core driving the mobile broadband revolution.* Elsevier.

Openmobster. (2010). Retrieved August 10, 2011, from http://code.google.com/p/openmobster/

Osipkov, I., Vasserman, E., Hopper, N., & Kim, Y. (2007). Combating double-spending using cooperative P2P systems. In *Proceedings of the 27th International Conference on Distributed Computing Systems, ICDCS'07.* Washington DC: IEEE CS Press.

Ozharar, S., Reilly, D. R., Wang, S. X., Kanter, G. X., & Kumar, P. (2011). Two dimensional optical code-division modulation with quantum-noise aided encryption for applications in key distribution. *Journal of Lightwave Technology, 29*(14), 2081–2088. doi:10.1109/JLT.2011.2156760.

Padmavathi, G., & Shanmugapriya, D. (2009). A survey of attacks, security mechanisms and challenges in wireless sensor networks. *International Journal of Computer Security, 4*(1), 117–125.

Palomar, E., de Fuentes, J. M., Gonzlez-Tablas, A. I., & Al-caide, A. (2012). Hindering false event dissemination in VANETs with proof-of-work mechanisms. *Transportation Research Part C, Emerging Technologies, 23,* 85–97. doi:10.1016/j.trc.2011.08.002.

Panichpapiboon, S., & Atikom, W. P. (2008). Connectivity requirements for self-organizing traffic information systems. *IEEE Transactions on Vehicular Technology, 57*(6), 12–22. doi:10.1109/TVT.2008.929067.

Panichpapiboon, S., & Pattara-Atikom, W. (2008). Connectivity requirements for self-organizing traffic information systems. *IEEE Transactions on Vehicular Technology, 57*(6), 3333–3340. doi:10.1109/TVT.2008.929067.

Papadimitratos, P., & Haas, Z. J. (2002). Secure routing for mobile ad hoc networks. In *Proceedings of the Communication Networks and Distributed Systems Modeleing and Simulation.* CNDS. Ning, P., & Sun, K. (2003). How to misuse AODV: A case study of insider attacks against mobile ad-hoc routing protocols. In *Proceedings of the IEEE Systems, Man and Cybernetics Society, Information Assurance Workshop (IAW'03),* (pp. 60-67). IEEE.

Papadimitratos, P., & Haas, Z. J. (2003a). Secure link state routing for mobile ad hoc networks. In *Proceedings of the 2003 Symposium on Applications and the Internet Workshops, 2003* (pp. 379-383). IEEE.

Papadimitratos, P., & Haas, Z. J. (2003b). Secure data transmission in mobile ad hoc networks. In *Proceedings of the 2nd ACM Workshop on Wireless Security* (pp. 41-50). ACM.

Papadimitratos, P., & Haas, Z. J. (2002). {Secure Routing for Mobile Ad hoc. *Networks.*

Papadimitratos, P., & Haas, Z. J. (2003). Secure link state routing for mobile ad hoc networks. *IEEE Wksp. Security and Assurance in Ad hoc. Networks.*

Papadimitratos, P., & Haas, Z. J. (2006). {Secure Data Communication in Mobile Ad hoc Networks}. *IEEE Journal on Selected Areas in Communications, 24*(2), 343–356. doi:10.1109/JSAC.2005.861392.

Papoulis, A. (1983). *Probability, random variables and stochastic processes* (2nd ed.). New York: McGraw-Hill.

Papoulis, A., & Pillai, S. U. (2002). *Probability, random variables and stochastic processes* (4th ed.). New York: McGraw-Hill.

Pareek, D. (2006). *WiMAX: Taking wireless to the max.* Boca Raton, FL: CRC Press. doi:10.1201/9781420013436.

Parhami, B. (1994). Voting algorithms. *IEEE Transactions on Reliability, 43*(4), 617–629. doi:10.1109/24.370218.

Paris, J.-F. (1986). Voting with witnesses: A consistency scheme for replicated files. In *Proceedings of the 6th International Conference on Distributed Computing Systems* (pp. 606-612). Cambridge, UK: IEEE.

Parkey, T. (2012, November 14). *LTE networks are easy prey for jamming attacks.* Retrieved April 20, 2013, from http://www.fiercebroadbandwireless.com/story/lte-networks-are-easy-prey-jamming-attacks/2012-11-14

Park, M., Gwon, G., Seo, S., & Jeong, H. (2011). RSU-based distributed key management (RDKM) for secure vehicular multicast communications. *IEEE Journal on Selected Areas in Communications, 29*(3), 644–658. doi:10.1109/JSAC.2011.110313.

Partridge, C., Cousins, D., Jackson, A. W., Krishnan, R., Saxena, T., & Strayer, W. T. (2002). Using signal processing to analyze wireless data traffic. In *Proceedings of the 1st ACM Workshop on Wireless Security* (pp. 67-76). ACM.

Patwardhan, A., Joshi, A., Finin, T., & Yesha, Y. (2006). A data intensive reputation management scheme for vehicular ad hoc networks. In *Proceedings of the 3rd Annual International Conference Mobile Ubiquitous System* (pp. 1-8). IEEE.

Patwardhan, A., Perich, F., Joshi, A., Finin, T., & Yesha, Y. (2005). {Active Collaborations for trustworthy data management in ad hoc networks}.

Patwardhan, A., Perich, F., Joshi, A., Finin, T., & Yesha, Y. (2006). {Querying in Packs: Trustworthy data management in ad hoc networks}. *Wireless Information Networks, 13*(4), 263–274. doi:10.1007/s10776-006-0040-3.

Patwari, N., Croft, J., Jana, S., & Kasera, S. K. (2010). High-rate uncorrelated bit extraction for shared secret key generation from channel measurements. *IEEE Transactions on Mobile Computing, 9*(1), 17–30. doi:10.1109/TMC.2009.88.

Pazynyuk, T., Li, J., Oreku, G. S., & Pa, L. (2008). QoS as means of providing WSNs security. In *Proceedings of the Seventh International Conference on Networking.* Cancun, Mexico. doi:10.1109/ICN.2008.22

Pei, X. B., Jiang, T., Qu, D. M., Guangxi, Z., & Jian, L. (2010). Radio resource management and access control mechanism based on a novel economic model in heterogeneous wireless networks. *IEEE Transactions on Vehicular Technology, 59*, 3047–3056. doi:10.1109/TVT.2010.2049039.

Pei, Y., Liang, Y.-C., Teh, K. C., & Li, K. H. (2011). Secure communication in multiantenna cognitive radio networks with imperfect channel state information. *IEEE Transactions on Signal Processing, 59*(4), 1683–1693. doi:10.1109/TSP.2011.2105479.

Pei, Y., Liang, Y.-C., Zhang, L., Teh, K. C., & Li, K. H. (2010). Secure communication over MISO cognitive radio channels. *IEEE Transactions on Wireless Communications, 9*(4), 1494–1502. doi:10.1109/TWC.2010.04.090746.

Penrose, M. D. (1999). On k-connectivity for a geometric random graph. *Random Structures and Algorithms, 15*(2), 145–164. doi:10.1002/(SICI)1098-2418(199909)15:2<145::AID-RSA2>3.0.CO;2-G.

Perkins, C. E., & Royer, E. M. (1999). Ad-hoc on-demand distance vector routing. In *Proceedings of the Second IEEE Workshop on Mobile Computing Systems and Applications,* (pp. 90-100). IEEE.

Perkins, C., Belding-Royer, E., & Das, S. (2003). *Ad hoc on-demand distance vector (AODV) routing.* Retrieved from http://tools.ietf.org/html/rfc3561

Perkins, C. E. (2001). *Ad hoc networking.* Reading, MA: Addison-Wesley.

Perkins, C. E., & Bhagwat, P. (1994). Highly dynamic destination-sequenced distance-vector routing (DSDV) for mobile computers. *Computer Communication Review*, *24*(4), 234–244. doi:10.1145/190809.190336.

Perrig, A., Stankovic, J., & Wagner, D. (2004). Security in wireless sensor networks. *Communications of the ACM*, *47*(6), 53-57. doi:10.1.1.4.9059

Perrig, A., Zewczyk, R., Tygar, J. D., Wen, V., & Culler, D. E. (2002). Spins: Security protocols for sensor networks. *ACM Journal of Wireless Networks*, *8*(5), 521-534. Retrieved from http://link.springer.com/journal/11276

Perrig, A., Canetti, R., Tygar, J. D., & Song, D. (2002). The TESLA broadcast authentication protocol. *RSA CryptoBytes*, *5*(2), 2–13.

Perrig, A., Szewczyk, R., Tygar, J. D., Wen, V., & Culler, D. E. (2002). SPINS: Security protocols for sensor networks. *Wireless Networks*, *8*(5), 521–534. doi:10.1023/A:1016598314198.

Pierrot, A., & Bloch, M. (2011). Strongly secure communications over the two-way wiretap channel. *IEEE Transactions on Information Forensics and Security*, *6*(3), 595–605. doi:10.1109/TIFS.2011.2158422.

Pirzada, A. A., Datta, A., & McDonald, C. (2006). Incorporating trust and reputation in the DSR protocol for dependable routing. *Elsevier Computer Communications*, *29*(15), 2806–2821. doi:10.1016/j.comcom.2005.10.032.

Pirzada, A. A., & McDonald, C. (2006). Trust establishment in pure ad-hoc networks. *Wireless Personal Communications*, *37*, 139–168. doi:10.1007/s11277-006-1574-5.

Pirzada, A. A., McDonald, C., & Datta, A. (2006). {Performance Comparison of Trust-based Reactive Routing Protocols}. *IEEE Transactions on Mobile Computing*, *5*, 695–710. doi:10.1109/TMC.2006.83.

Poortinga, W., & Pidgeon, N. F. (2004). Trust, the asymmetry principle, and the role of prior beliefs. *Risk Analysis*, *24*(6), 1475–1486. doi:10.1111/j.0272-4332.2004.00543.x PMID:15660605.

Prabhu, V. U., & Rodrigues, M. R. D. (2011). On wireless channels with M-antenna eavesdroppers: Characterization of the outage probability and ε-outage secrecy capacity. *IEEE Transactions on Information Forensics and Security*, *6*(3), 853–860. doi:10.1109/TIFS.2011.2159491.

Premnath, S., Jana, S., Croft, J., Lakshmane Gowda, P., Clark, M., Kasera, S., & Krishnamurthy, S. (2012). Secret key extraction from wireless signal strength in real environments. *IEEE Transactions on Mobile Computing*, *12*(5), 917–930. doi:10.1109/TMC.2012.63.

Preuss, P. (2009). *NFC forum: NFC use cases*. Retrieved May 10, 2012, from: http://www.nfc-forum.org/events/oulu_spotlight/Forum_and_Use_Cases.pdf

Prieur, E. (2009, September). Developing a fully inclusive mobile broadband strategy: Bring mobile broadband to remote and rural areas. In Proceedings of Mobile Broadband World. IEEE.

Przydatek, B., Perrig, A., & Song, D. (2003). SIA: Secure information aggregation in sensor networks. *Journal of Computer Security*, *15*(1), 69–102. Retrieved from dl.acm.org/citation.cfm?id=1370616.

Public Key Infrastructure (PKI). (n.d.). *Wikipedia*. Retrieved April 20, 2013, from http://en.wikipedia.org/wiki/Public_key_infrastructure

Public-Key Cryptography Standards (PKCS). (n.d.). Retrieved April 20, 2013, from http://www.rsa.com/rsalabs/node.asp?id=2124

Puterman, M. L. (1994). *Markov decision processes*. New York: Wiley Inter-Science. doi:10.1002/9780470316887.

Qazi, Q., Alshaer, H., & Elmirghani, J. M. H. (2010). Analysis and design of a MAC protocol and vehicular traffic simulator for multimedia communication on motorways. *IEEE Transactions on Vehicular Technology*, *59*(2). doi:10.1109/TVT.2009.2033278.

Qiao, D., Gursoy, M., & Velipasalar, S. (2011). Secure wireless communication and optimal power control under statistical queueing constraints. *IEEE Transactions on Information Forensics and Security*, *6*(3), 628–639. doi:10.1109/TIFS.2011.2155650.

Qin, Z., Jia, Z., & Chen, X. (2008). Fuzzy dynamic programming based trusted routing decision in mobile ad hoc networks. In *Proceedings of the Fifth IEEE International Symposium on Embedded Computing* (pp. 180-185). IEEE.

Quercia, D., Hailes, S., & Capra, L. (2006). B-trust: Bayesian trust framework for pervasive computing. In *Trust Management: Proceedings of the 4th International Conference iTrust,* (LNCS), (pp. 298-312). New York: Springer.

Quist, B. T., & Jensen, M. A. (2012). The impact of multiple antennas in physical layer encryption key establishment. In *Proceedings of the IEEE International Workshop on Antenna Technology (iWAT)* (pp. 24-27). IEEE.

Rachedi, A., & Benslimane, A. (2009). Toward a cross-layer monitoring process for mobile ad hoc networks. *Security and Communication Networks, 2*(4), 351–368. doi:10.1002/sec.72.

Raffo, D., Adjih, C., Clausen, T., & Muhlethaler, P. (2004). An advanced signature system for OLSR. In *Proceedings of the 2nd ACM Workshop on Security of Ad Hoc and Sensor Networks,* (pp. 10-16). New York: ACM.

Raj, P. N., & Swadas, P. B. (2009). Dpraodv: A dyanamic learning system against blackhole attack in aodv based manet. *arXiv preprint arXiv:0909.2371.*

Ramachandran, C., Misra, S., & Obaidat, M. S. (2008). FORK: A novel two-pronged strategy for an agent-based intrusion detection scheme in ad-hoc networks. *Computer Communications, 31*(16), 3855–3869. doi:10.1016/j.comcom.2008.04.012.

Ramanathan, N., Chang, K., Kapur, R., Girod, L., Kohler, E., & Estrin, D. (2005). Sympathy for the sensor network debugger. In *Proceeding of the 3rd ACM Conf. Embedded Networked Sensor Systems* (pp. 255-267). ACM.

Ramanathan, N., Schoellhammer, T., Estrin, D., Hansen, M., Harmon, T., Kohler, E., & Srivastava, M. (2006). *The final frontier: Embedding networked sensors in the soil (CENS Technical Report #68).* Los Angeles, CA: Center for Embedded Networked Sensing, UCLA.

Rangara, R. R., Jaipuria, R. S., Yenugwar, G. N., & Jawandhiya, P. M. (2010). Intelligent secure routing model for MANET. In *Proceedings of the 3rd IEEE International Conference on Computer Science and Information Technology (ICCSIT), 2010* (Vol. 3, pp. 452-456). IEEE.

Rawat, D. B. (April 15, 2013). *Computer and network security: An experimental approach.* CreateSpace Publishing Platform.

Rawat, D. B., Bista, B. B., Yan, G., & Weigle, M. C. (2011). Securing vehicular ad-hoc networks against malicious drivers: A probabilistic approach. In *Proceedings of International Conference on Complex, Intelligent and Software Intensive Systems (CISIS),* (pp. 146-151). CISIS.

Rawat, D. B., Yan, G., Bista, B. B., & Chandra, V. (2013). *Wireless network security: An overview.* Boca Raton, FL: CRC Press.

Raya, M., & Hubaux, J.-P. (2005a). The security of VANETs. In *Proceedings of the 2nd ACM International Workshop on Vehicular Ad Hoc Networks.* Cologne, Germany: ACM.

Raya, M., & Hubaux, J. P. (2007). Securing vehicular ad hoc networks. *Journal of Computer Security, 15*(1), 39–68.

Raya, M., & Hubaux, J. P. (2007). Securing vehicular ad hoc networks. *Journal of Computer Security, 15*(1), 39 68.

Raya, M., Papadimitratos, P., Aad, I., Jungels, D., & Hubaux, J. P. (2007). Eviction of misbehaving and faulty nodes in vehicular networks. *IEEE Journal on Selected Areas in Communications, 25*(8), 1557–1568. doi:10.1109/JSAC.2007.071006.

Raymond, D., & Midkiff, S. (2008). Denial-of-service in wireless sensor networks: Attacks and defenses. *IEEE Pervasive Computing / IEEE Computer Society [and] IEEE Communications Society, 7*(1), 74–81. doi:10.1109/MPRV.2008.6.

Razak, S. A., Furnell, S. M., & Brooke, P. J. (2004). Attacks against mobile ad hoc networks routing protocols. In *Proceedings of the 5th Annual Postgraduate Symposium on the Convergence of Telecommunications, Networking & Broadcasting (PGNET'04).* PGNET.

Razak, S. A., Furnell, S. M., Clarke, N. L., & Brooke, P. J. (2008). Friend-assisted intrusion detection and response mechanisms for mobile ad hoc networks. *Ad Hoc Networks, 6*(7), 1151–1167. doi:10.1016/j.adhoc.2007.11.004.

Razavi, R., Fleury, M., & Monaghan, S. (2007). Multimedia performance for IEEE.802.11 DCF RTS/CTS with varying traffic conditions. In Proceedings of 2007 European Wireless (pp. 1-5). IEEE.

Reindl, P., Nygard, K., & Du, X. (2010). Defending malicious collision attacks in wireless sensor networks. In *Proceedings of the IEEE/IFIP 8th International Conference on Embedded and Ubiquitous Computing*. Hong Kong, China: IEEE Press.

Ren, W., Ren, K., Lou, W., & Zhang, Y. (2008). Efficient user revocation for privacy-aware PKI. In *Proceedings of the 5th International ICST Conference on Heterogeneous Networking for Quality, Reliability, Security and Robustness*. Hong Kong: ICST.

Ren, K., Li, T., Wan, Z., Bao, F., Deng, R., & Kim, K. (2004). Highly reliable trust establishment scheme in ad hoc networks. *Computer Networks, 45*(6), 687–699. doi:10.1016/j.comnet.2004.01.008.

Ren, K., Su, H., & Wang, Q. (2011). Secret key generation exploiting channel characteristics in wireless communications. *IEEE Wireless Communications, 18*(4), 6–12. doi:10.1109/MWC.2011.5999759.

Rivest, R. L., Shamir, A., & Adleman, L. (1978). A method for obtaining digital signatures and public-key cryptosystems. *Communications of the ACM, 21*(2), 126. doi:10.1145/359340.359342.

Rizomiliotis, P. (2010). On the resistance of boolean functions against algebraic attacks using univariate polynomial representation. *IEEE Transactions on Information Theory, 56*(8), 4014–4024. doi:10.1109/TIT.2010.2050801.

Roberti, M. (n.d.). *The history of RFID technology*. Retrieved March 29, 2012, from http://www.rfidjournal.com/article/view/1338/1

Rongxing, L., Xiaodong, L., Haojin, Z., Pin-Han, H., & Xuemin, S. (2008). *ECPP: Efficient conditional privacy preservation protocol for secure vehicular communications*. Paper presented at INFOCOM 2008. New York, NY.

Roshan, P., & Leary, J. (2004). *802. 11 wireless LAN fundamentals*. New York: Cisco Systems.

Roy, S., Addada, V. G., Setia, S., & Jajodia, S. (2005). Securing MAODV: Attacks and countermeasures. In *Proceedings of the IEEE International Conference on Sensing, Communication, and Networking*. IEEE.

Roy, D. B., Chaki, R., & Chaki, N. (2009). A new cluster based wormhole intrusion detection algorithm for MANET. *International Journal of Network Security & Its Applications, 1*(1).

Ruan, G., Jain, S., & Zhu, S. (2009). *SensorEar: A sensor network based eavesdropping system*. Paper presented the 8th IEEE International Symposium on Reliable Distributed System. New York. doi:10.1.1.210.9177

Ruj, S., Cavenaghi, M. A., Huang, Z., Nayak, A., & Stojmenovic, I. (2011). On data-centric misbehavior detection in VANETs. In *Proceedings of the IEEE Vehicular Technology Conference* (pp. 1-5). IEEE.

Saad, W., Han, Z., & Poor, H. (2012). On the physical layer security of backscatter RFID systems. In *Proceedings of the 2012 International Symposium on Wireless Communication Systems (ISWCS)* (pp. 1092-1096). ISWCS.

Saaty, T. L. (2008). Decision making with the analytic hierarchy process. *International Journal of Services Sciences, 1*(1), 83–98. doi:10.1504/IJSSCI.2008.017590.

Sacco, A. (2012, August 14). *NFC not just for mobile payments: Six future uses*. Retrieved January 28, 2013, from http://www.cio.com/article/713618/NFC_Not_Just_for_Mobile_Payments_Six_Future_Uses?page=2&taxonomyId=3045

Sakran, H., Shokair, M., Nasr, O., El-Rabaie, S., & El-Azm, A. A. (2012). Proposed relay selection scheme for physical layer security in cognitive radio networks. *IET Communications, 6*(16), 2676–2687. doi:10.1049/iet-com.2011.0638.

Salimi, S., Salmasizadeh, M., & Aref, M. (2011). Rate regions of secret key sharing in a new source model. *IET Communications, 5*(4), 443–455. doi:10.1049/iet-com.2009.0777.

Salimi, S., Salmasizadeh, M., Aref, M. R., & Golic, J. D. (2011). Key agreement over multiple access channel. *IEEE Transactions on Information Forensics and Security, 6*(3), 775–790. doi:10.1109/TIFS.2011.2158310.

Sami, D., Al-Wakeel, S., & Al-Swailem, A. (2007). PRSA: A path redundancy based security algorithm for wireless sensor networks. In *Proceedings of the Wireless Communication and Networking Conference (WCNC 2007)*. Hong Kong, China: ACM Press.

Santi, P., & Blough, D. (2003). The critical transmitting range for connectivity in sparse in wireless ad hoc networks. *IEEE Transactions on Mobile Computing*, 2(1), 25–39. doi:10.1109/TMC.2003.1195149.

Sanzgiri, K., Dahill, B., Levine, B. N., Shields, C., & Belding-Royer, E. M. (2002). A secure routing protocol for ad hoc networks. In *Proceedings of the 10th IEEE International Conference on Network Protocols (ICNP'02)*, (pp. 78-89). IEEE.

Sayeed, A., & Perrig, A. (2008). Secure wireless communications: Secret keys through multipath. In *Proceedings of the 2008 IEEE International Conference on Acoustics, Speech, and Signal Processing* (pp. 3013-3016). Las Vegas, NV: IEEE.

Scarfone, K., Tibbs, C., & Sexton, M. (n.d.). *Guide to securing WiMAX wireless communications*. Retrieved April 20, 2013, from http://csrc.nist. gov/publications/nistpubs/800-127/sp800-127.pdf

Schmidt, R. K., Leinmueller, T., Schoch, E., Held, A., & Schaefer, G. (2008). Vehicle behavior analysis to enhance security in VANETs. In *Proceedings of the IEEE Vehicle-to Vehicle Communications Workshop*. IEEE.

Scoville, A.W. (1999) Clear signatures, obscure signs. Retrieved from http://www.bc.edu.bcorg/avp/law/st.org/iptf/articles/content/ 1999070101.html

Seeling, P., Reisslein, M., & Kulapala, B. (2004). Network performance evaluation using frame size and quality traces of single layer and two layer video: A tutorial. *IEEE Communications Magazine*, 6(3), 58–78.

Segala, R. (1995). *Modeling and verification of randomized distributed real-time systems*. (Ph.D. thesis). Laboratory for Computer Science, MIT, Cambridge, MA.

Seigneur, J.-M., Abendroth, J., & Jensen, C. D. (2002). Bank accounting and ubiquitous brokering of trustos. In *Proceedings of the 7th Cabernet Radicals Workshop*. Cabernet.

Sen, A., & Huson, M. L. (1996). A new model for scheduling packet radio networks. In *Proceedings of the IEEE Infocom*, (pp. 1116-1124). IEEE.

Sen, J. (2013). Security and privacy issues in wireless mesh networks: A survey. In *Wireless Networks and Security* (pp. 189–272). Berlin, Germany: Springer. doi:10.1007/978-3-642-36169-2_7.

Sen, S., & Clark, J. A. (2011). Evolutionary computation techniques for intrusion detection in mobile ad hoc networks. *Computer Networks*, 55(15), 3441–3457. doi:10.1016/j.comnet.2011.07.001.

Sesia, S., Toufik, I., & Baker, M. (2011). *LTE—The UMTS long term evolution—From theory to practice* (2nd ed.). New York: John Wiley & Sons. doi:10.1002/9780470978504.

Seyfi, M., Muhaidat, S., Jie, L., & Uysal, M. (2011). Relay selection in dual-hop vehicular networks. *IEEE Signal Processing Letters*, 18(2), 134–137. doi:10.1109/LSP.2010.2102017.

Shafiee, S., Liu, N., & Ulukus, S. (2009). Towards the secrecy capacity of the Gaussian MIMO wire-tap channel: The 2-2-1 channel. *IEEE Transactions on Information Theory*, 55(9), 4033–4039. doi:10.1109/TIT.2009.2025549.

Shaikh, R. A., Jameel, H. d'Auriol, B. J., Lee, H., Lee, S., & Song, Y.-J. (2009). Group-based trust management scheme for clustered wireless sensor networks. *IEEE Transactions on Parallel and Distributed Systems*, 20(11), 1698–1712. doi:10.1109/TPDS.2008.258.

Sha, K., Wang, S., & Shi, W. (2009). RD^4: Role-differentiated cooperative deceptive data detection and filtering in VANETs. *IEEE Transactions on Vehicular Technology*, 59(3), 1183–1190.

Shaked, Y., & Wool, A. (2005). Cracking the bluetooth pin. In *Proceedings of the 3rd International Conference on Mobile Systems, Applications, and Services* (pp. 39-50). ACM.

Shamir, A. (1984). Identity-based cryptosystems and signature schemes.[Berlin: Springer Verlag.]. *Proceedings of CRYPTO*, 84, 47–53.

Shannon, C. E. (1949). Communication theory of secrecy systems. *The Bell System Technical Journal*, 28(4), 656–715. doi:10.1002/j.1538-7305.1949.tb00928.x.

Sharif, W., & Leckie, C. (2006). New variants of wormhole attacks for sensor networks. In *Proceedings of the Australian Telecommunication Networks and Applications Conference*. Melbourn, Australia. doi:10.1.1.122.2838

Sharma, R., & Wallace, J. (2010). Bit error rate and efficiency analysis of wireless reciprocal channel key generation. In *Proceedings of the 2010 IEEE International Conference on Wireless Information Technology and Systems (ICWITS)* (pp. 1-4). IEEE.

Sharma, R., & Wallace, J. (2011). Physical layer key generation methods for arbitrary fading channels. In *Proceedings of the 2011 IEEE International Symposium on Antennas and Propagation (APSURSI)* (pp. 1368-1371). IEEE.

Sharma, S., Baek, I., Dodia, Y., & Chiueh, T.-C. (2007). Omnicon: A mobile IP-based vertical handoff system for wireless LAN and GPRS links. *Software, Practice & Experience, 1*(37), 779–798. doi:10.1002/spe.790.

Sharmila, S., & Umamaheswari, G. (2012). Defensive mechanisms of selective forward attack in wireless sensor networks.[**Retreived from** http://research.ijcaonline. org/]. *International Journal of Computers and Applications, 39*(4), 46–52. doi:10.5120/4812-7048.

Shimizu, T., Iwai, H., & Sasaoka, H. (2011). Physical-layer secret key agreement in two-way wireless relaying systems. *IEEE Transactions on Information Forensics and Security, 6*(3), 650–660. doi:10.1109/TIFS.2011.2147314.

Shim, K. (2003). Some attacks on chikazawa-yamagishi id-based key sharing scheme. *IEEE Communications Letters, 7*(3), 145–147. doi:10.1109/LCOMM.2003.809992.

Shin, K., Choi, H., & Jeong, J. (2009). A practical security framework for a VANET-based entertainment service. In *Proceedings of the 4th ACM Workshop on Performance Monitoring and Measurement of Heterogeneous Wireless and Wired Networks (PM2HW2N)* (pp. 175-182). Las Vegas, NV: ACM.

Shin, D., & Ahn, G. J. (2005). Role-based privilege and trust management. *Computer Systems Science and Engineering, 20*(6).

Shiu, Y.-S., Chang, S. Y., Wu, H.-C., Huang, S.-H., & Chen, H.-H. (2011). Physical layer security in wireless networks: A tutorial. *IEEE Wireless Communications, 18*(2), 66–74. doi:10.1109/MWC.2011.5751298.

Shnayder, V., Hempstead, M., Chen, B.-R., & Welsh, M. (2007). *Power TOSSIM: Efficient power simulation for TinyOS applications* (Report No. CS263). Retrieved from http://www.eecs.harvard.edu/~shnayder/ptossim/

Sichitiu, M. L., & Kihl, M. (2008). Inter-vehicle communication systems: A survey. *IEEE Communications Surveys & Tutorials, 10*(2), 88–105. doi:10.1109/COMST.2008.4564481.

Simon, D., Aboba, B., & Hurst, R. (2008). *The EAP-TLS authentication protocol*. Retrieved April 20, 2013, from http://tools.ietf. org/html/rfc5216

Singh, R., Vatsa, M., Noore, A., & Singh, S. K. (2006). Dempster-Shafer theory based classifier fusion for improved fingerprint verification performance. In P. Kalra, & S. Peleg (Eds.), *Computer vision, graphics and image processing* (pp. 941–949). Berlin, Germany: Springer. doi:10.1007/11949619_84.

Singh, V. P., Jain, S., & Singhai, J. (2010). Hello flood attack and its countermeasures in wireless sensor networks. *International Journal of Computer Science, 7*(11), 23–28. Retrieved from www.ijarcs.info/.

Smart Card. (2012). *Wikipedia*. Retrieved May 10, 2012, from http://en.wikipedia.org/wiki/SmartCard

Smart Dust Mote. (n.d.). Retrieved December 2012 from http://robotics.eecs.berkeley.edu/~pister/SmartDust/

Smith, A. (1776). *An inquiry into the nature and causes of the wealth of nations*. London: Strahan and Cadell.

Soliman, H., Castelluccia, C., Malki, K., & Bellier, L. (2001). *Hierarchical MIPv6 mobility management*. IETF, draft-soliman-mobileip-hmipv6-05.txt.

Song, Q., & Jamalipour, A. (2005). Network selection in an integrated wireless LAN and UMTS environment using mathematical modeling and computing techniques. *Journal of IEEE Wireless Communication, 12*(3), 42–48. doi:10.1109/MWC.2005.1452853.

Soosahabi, R., & Naraghi-Pour, M. (2012). Scalable PHY-layer security for distributed detection in wireless sensor networks. *IEEE Transactions on Information Forensics and Security, 7*(4), 1118–1126. doi:10.1109/TIFS.2012.2194704.

Springer Reference. (2013). Retrieved from http://www.springerreference.com/docs/html/chapterdbid/317535.html

Srinivasan, V., Nuggehalli, P., Chiasserini, C. F., & and Rao, R. R. (2003). Co-operation in wireless adhoc networks. *IEEE INFOCOMM*.

Srivastava, V., Neel, J., MacKenzie, A., Menon, R., DaSilva, L., Hicks, J., & Gilles, R. (2005). Using game theory to analyze wireless ad hoc networks. *Communications Surveys and Tutorials, 7*(4), 46–56. doi:10.1109/COMST.2005.1593279.

Stajano, F., & Anderson, R. J. (2000). The resurrecting duckling: Security issues for ad-hoc wireless networks. In *Proceedings of the 7th International Workshop on Security Protocols* (pp. 172-194). Cambridge, UK: IEEE.

Stallings, W. (2005). *Cryptography and network security principles and practices* (4th ed.). Upper Saddle River, NJ: Prentice Hall.

Stallings, W. (2009). *Wireless communications & networks*. Delhi, India: Pearson Education India.

Stamouli, I., Argyroudis, P. G., & Tewari, H. (2005). Real-time intrusion detection for ad hoc networks. In *Proceedings of the Sixth IEEE International Symposium on a World of Wireless Mobile and Multimedia Networks (WoWMoM'05)*, (pp. 374-380). IEEE Computer Society.

Stavrou, E., Pitsillides, A., Hadjichristofi, G., & Hadjicostis, C. (2010). Security in future mobile sensor networks: Issues and challenges. In *Proceedings of the International Conference on Security and Cryptography (SECRYPT)*. Athens, Greece: Springer.

Std, I. E. E. E. 802.11i/D30. (2002). Wireless medium access control (MAC) and physical layer (PHY) specifications: Specification for enhanced security. IEEE.

Stewart, W. J. (1994). *Introduction to the numerical solution of Markov chains*. Princeton, NJ: Princeton University Press.

Studer, A., Shi, E., Bai, F., & Perrig, A. (2009). Tacking together efficient authentication, revocation, and privacy in VANETs. In *Proceedings of the IEEE Communications Society Conference on Sensor, Mesh and Ad Hoc Communications and Networks* (pp. 484-492). IEEE.

Subramanian, A., Thangaraj, A., Bloch, M., & McLaughlin, S. (2011). Strong secrecy on the binary erasure wiretap channel using large-girth LDPC codes. *IEEE Transactions on Information Forensics and Security, 6*(3), 585–594. doi:10.1109/TIFS.2011.2148715.

Subramanyan, R., Wong, E., & Yang, H. I. (Eds.). (2010). *Proceedings of the 34th annual IEEE computer software and applications conference workshops (COMPSACW 2010)* (pp. 393-398). Seoul, South Korea: IEEE Press.

SUMO. (n.d.). Retrieved from http://sumo.sourceforge.net/

Sun, J., Zhang, C., & Fang, Y. (2007). An ID-based framework achieving privacy and non-repudiation in vehicular ad hoc networks. In *Proceedings of the IEEE Military Communications Conference* (pp. 1-7). IEEE.

Sun, X., Wu, X., Zhao, C., Jiang, M., & Xu, W. (2010). Slepian-wolf coding for reconciliation of physical layer secret keys. In *Proceedings of the 2010 IEEE Wireless Communications and Networking Conference (WCNC)* (pp. 1-6). IEEE.

Sun, X., Xu, W., Jiang, M., & Zhao, C. (2011). Improved generation efficiency for key extracting from wireless channels. In *Proceedings of the 2011 IEEE International Conference on Communications (ICC)* (pp. 1-6). IEEE.

Sun, J., & Fang, Y. (2009). Defense against misbehavior in anonymous vehicular ad hoc networks. *Ad Hoc Networks, 7*, 1515–1525. doi:10.1016/j.adhoc.2009.04.013.

Sun, J., Zhang, C., Zhang, Y., & Fang, Y. (2010). An identity-based security system for user privacy in vehicular ad hoc networks. *IEEE Transactions on Parallel and Distributed Systems, 21*(9), 1227–1239. doi:10.1109/TPDS.2010.14.

Sun, Y. L., Han, Z., & Liu, K. J. R. (2008). Defense of trust management vulnerabilities in distributed networks. *IEEE Communications Magazine, 46*(2), 112–119. doi:10.1109/MCOM.2008.4473092.

Sun, Y. L., Yu, W., Han, Z., & Ray Liu, K. J. (2006). Information theoretic framework of trust modeling and evaluation for ad hoc networks. *IEEE Journal on Selected Areas in Communications, 24*(2), 305–317. doi:10.1109/JSAC.2005.861389.

Suryanarayana, G., & Taylo, R. N. (2004). *A survey of trust management and resource discovery technologies in peer-to-peer applications* (Technical Report UCI-ISR-04-6). Los Angeles, CA: University of California.

Svecs, I., Sarkar, T., Basu, S., & Wong, J. S. (2010). XIDR: A dynamic framework utilizing cross-layer intrusion detection for effective response deployment. In *Proceedings of the 34th Annual Computer Software and Applications Conference Workshops (COMPSACW),* (pp. 287-292). IEEE.

Swindlehurst, A. L. (2009). Fixed SINR solutions for the MIMO wiretap channel. In *Proceedings of the IEEE International Conference on Acoustics, Speech, and Signal Processing* (pp. 2437–2440). Taipei, Taiwan: IEEE.

Szewczyk, R., Mainwaring, A., Polastre, J., Anderson, J., & Culler, D. (2004). An analysis of a large scale habitat monitoring application. In *Proceedings of the 2nd International Conference on Embedded Networked Sensor Systems* (pp. 214-226). New York: ACM Press.

Taghavi Zargar, S., & Joshi, J. B. D. (2010). A collaborative approach to facilitate intrusion detection and response against DDoS attacks. In K. Aberer, & J. B. D. Joshi (Eds.), *Proceedings of the 6th International Conference on Collaborative Computing: Networking, Applications and Worksharing (CollaborateCom2010).* Chicago, IL: IEEE Press.

Taghavi Zargar, S., Takabi, H., & Joshi, J. B. D. (2011). DCDIDP: A distributed, collaborative, and data-driven intrusion detection and prevention framework for cloud computing environments. In D. Georgakopoulos & J. B. D. Joshi (Eds.), *Proceedings of the 7th International Conference on Collaborative Computing: Networking, Applications and Worksharing (CollaborateCom2011).* Orlando, FL: IEEE Press.

Taghavi Zargar, S., Joshi, J. B. D., & Tipper, D. (2013). A survey of defense mechanisms against distributed denial of service (DDoS) flooding attacks. *IEEE Communications Surveys and Tutorials,* (99): 1–24. doi:10.1109/SURV.2013.031413.00127.

Takabi, H., & Joshi, J. B. D. (2012b). Toward a semantic based policy management framework for interoperable cloud environments. In *Proceedings of the International IBM Cloud Academy Conference (ICA CON 2012).* IBM.

Takabi, H., Joshi, J. B. D., & Ahn, G. J. (2010a). SecureCloud: Towards a comprehensive security framework for cloud computing environments. In S. I. Ahamed, D. H. Bae, S. Cha, C. K. Chang (Eds.), *Proceedings of the Computer Software and Applications Conference Workshops (COMPSACW),* (pp. 393-398). COMPSACW.

Takabi, H., & Joshi, J. B. D. (2012a). Semantic based policy management for cloud computing environments. *International Journal of Cloud Computing, 1*(2), 2012.

Takabi, H., & Joshi, J. B. D. (2012c). Policy management in cloud computing environment: Challenges and approaches. In D. G. Rosado, D. Mellado, E. Fernandez-Medina, & M. Piattini (Eds.), *Security Engineering for Cloud Computing: Approaches and Tools.* Hershey, PA: IGI Global. doi:10.4018/978-1-4666-2125-1.ch010.

Takabi, H., Joshi, J. B. D., & Ahn, G. J. (2010b). Security and privacy challenges in cloud computing environments. *IEEE Security and Privacy, 8*(6), 24–31. doi:10.1109/MSP.2010.186.

Takabi, H., Joshi, J. B. D., & Ahn, G. J. (2013). Security and privacy in cloud computing: Towards a comprehensive framework. In X. Yang, & L. Liu (Eds.), *Principles, methods and service-oriented approaches for cloud computing.* Hershey, PA: IGI Global. doi:10.4018/978-1-4666-2854-0.ch007.

Tamilselvan, L., & Sankaranarayanan, V. (2007a). Prevention of blackhole attack in MANET. In *Proceedings of the 2nd International Conference on Wireless Broadband and Ultra Wideband Communications,* (pp. 21-21). IEEE.

Tamilselvan, L., & Sankaranarayanan, D. V. (2007b). Prevention of impersonation attack in wireless mobile ad hoc networks. *International Journal of Computer Science and Network Security, 7*(3), 118–123.

Tang, C., & Raghavendra, C. S. (2004). Correlation analysis and applications in wireless micro sensor networks. In *Proceeding of Mobile and Ubiquitous Systems: Networking and Services (MOBIQUITOUS 2004)* (pp. 184-193). MOBIQUITOUS.

Tangpong, A., Kesidis, G., Hsu, H. Y., & Hurson, A. (2009). Robust Sybil detection for MANETs. In *Proceedings of the 18th Internatonal Conference on Computer Communications and Networks,* (pp. 1-6). IEEE.

Tao, L., Huang, D., & Hong, L. (2010). Research of subjective trust comprehensive evaluation model based on multi-element connection number. In *Proceedings of the 2nd International Conference on Information Science and Engineering 2010* (pp. 1433-1437). Hangzhou, China: IEEE.

Taylor, S., Young, A., Kumar, N., & Macaulay, J. (2011). The mobile cloud: When two explosive markets collide. *Cisco IBSG*. Retrieved August 10, 2011, from http://www.cisco.com/web/about/ac79/docs/sp/Mobile-Cloud-Overview-POV.pdf

Telosb Mote. (n.d.). Retrieved December 2012 from http://www.willow.co.uk/telosb_datasheet.pdf

The Apache Hadoop Project. (n.d.). Retrieved August 10, 2011, from http://hadoop.apache.org

Theodorakopoulos, G., & Baras, J. (2006). On trust models and trust evaluation metrics for ad hoc networks. *Journal on Selected Areas in Communications, 24*(2), 318–328. doi:10.1109/JSAC.2005.861390.

Tmote Sky. (n.d.). Retrieved December 2012 from www.snm.ethz.ch/Projects/TmoteSky

Toh, C. K. (2001). *Ad hoc mobile wireless networks: Protocols and systems.* Upper Saddle River, NJ: Prentice Hall.

Tolle, J., Polastre, J., Szewczyk, R., Culler, D., Turner, N., & Tu, K. … Hong, W. (2005). A macro-scope in the redwoods. In *Proceedings of ACM Conference on Embedded Networked Sensor Systems (SenSys'05)* (pp. 51-63). ACM.

Trappe, W., Poor, V., Iwai, H., Yener, A., Prucnal, P., & Barros, J. (2011). Guest editorial special issue on using the physical layer for securing the next generation of communication systems. *IEEE Transactions on Information Forensics and Security, 6*(3), 521–522. doi:10.1109/TIFS.2011.2160572.

Tsang, P., Au, M. H., Kapadia, A., & Smith, S. W. (2007). Blacklistable anonymous credentials: Blocking misbehaving users without TTPs. In *Proceedings of the ACM Conference on Computer and Communications Security* (pp. 72-81). ACM.

Tseng, C. Y., Balasubramanyam, P., Ko, C., Limprasittiporn, R., Rowe, J., & Levitt, K. (2003). A specification-based intrusion detection system for AODV. In *Proceedings of the 1st ACM Workshop on Security of Ad Hoc and Sensor Networks (SASN'03),* (pp. 125-134). ACM. Adjih, C., Clausen, T., Jacquet, P., Laouiti, A., Muhlethaler, P., & Raffo, D. (2003). Securing the OLSR protocol. In *Proceedings of Med-Hoc-Net,* (pp. 25-27). ACM.

Tseng, Y. C., Ni, S. Y., Chen, Y. S., & Sheu, J. P. (2002). The broadcast storm problem in a mobile ad hoc network. *Wireless Networks, 8*(2/3), 153–167 doi:10.1023/A:1013763825347.

Tuan, T. A. (2006). A game-theoretic analysis of trust management in P2P systems. In *Proceedings of the First International Conference on Communications and Electronics* (pp. 130-134). IEEE.

Tun, Z., & Maw, A. H. (2008). Wormhole attack detection in wireless sensor networks. *World Academy of Science. Engineering and Technology, 28*(2), 545–551.

Ukkusuri, S., & Du, L. (2008). Geometric connectivity of vehicular ad hoc networks: Analytical characterization. *Transportation Research Part C, Emerging Technologies, 16*(5), 615–634. doi:10.1016/j.trc.2007.12.002.

ULOOP Consortium. (2013). *EU IST FP7 ULOOP: User-centric wireless local loop.* Retrieved from http://uloop.eu

Uppuluri, P., & Basu, S. (2004). Lase: Layered approach for sensor security and efficiency. In *Proceedings of the IEEE International Conference on Parallel Processing Workshops.* doi:10.1109/ICPPW.2004.1328038

Urpi, A., Bonuccelli, M., & Giordano, S. (2003). Modelling cooperation in mobile ad hoc networks: A formal description of selfishness. In Proceedings of WiOpt'03: Modeling and Optimization in Mobile, Ad Hoc and Wireless Networks. WiOpt.

Vahedi, E., Shah-Mansouri, V., Wong, V. W. S., Blake, I. F., & Ward, R. K. (2011). Probabilistic analysis of blocking attack in RFID systems. *IEEE Transactions on Information Forensics and Security, 6*(3), 803–817. doi:10.1109/TIFS.2011.2132129.

Van Assche, G., Cardinal, J., & Cerf, N. (2004). Reconciliation of a quantum-distributed Gaussian key. *IEEE Transactions on Information Theory, 50*(2), 394–400. doi:10.1109/TIT.2003.822618.

Vanghi, V., Saglam, M., & Jindi, J. (2007). Frequency coordination between UMTS and GSM systems at 900 MHz. In *Proceedings of the IEEE 18th International Symposium*. IEEE.

Vartiainen, E., & Väänänen-Vainio-Mattila, K. (2010). User experience of mobile photo sharing in the cloud. In C. Mascolo & E. O'Neill (Eds.), *Proceedings of the 9th International Conference on Mobile and Ubiquitous Multimedia (MUM '10)* (pp. 1-10). Limassol, Cyprus: ACM Press.

Vazquez-Briseno, M., Hirata, F. I., Sanchez-Lopez, J. d., Jimenez-Garcia, E., Navarro-Cota, C., & Nieto-Hipolito, J. I. (2012). Using RFID/NFC and QR-code in mobile phones to link the physical and the digital world. In I. Deliyannis (Ed.), *Interactive Multimedia*. Janeza Trdine, Croatia: InTech. doi:10.5772/37447.

Velloso, P. B., Laufer, R. P., Cunha, D. d., Duarte, O. C., & Pujolle, G. (2010). Trust Management in Mobile Ad Hoc Networks Using a Scalable Maturity-Based Model. *IEEE TRANSACTIONS ON NETWORK AND SERVICE MANAGEMENT, 7*(3), 172–185. doi:10.1109/TNSM.2010.1009.I9P0339.

Venkataraman, R., Pushpalatha, M., & Rama Rao, T. (2012). Implementation of a Regression-based Trust Model in a Wireless Ad hoc Testbed. *Defence Science Journal, 62*(3), 167–173.

Verma, M., & Huang, D. (2009). SegCom: Secure group communication in VANETs. In *Proceedings of the 6th IEEE Consumer Communications and Networking Conference (CCNC)* (pp. 1-5). Las Vegas, NV: IEEE.

Vieira, R. D., Paiva, R. C. D., Hulkkonen, J., Jarvela, R., Iida, R. F., & Saily, M. … Niemela, K. (2010). GSM evolution importance in refarming 900 MHz band. In *Proceedings of the 2010 IEEE 72nd Vehicular Technology Conference*. IEEE.

Vigna, G., Gwalani, S., Srinivasan, K., Belding-Royer, E. M., & Kemmerer, R. A. (2004). An intrusion detection tool for AODV-based ad hoc wireless networks. In *Proceedings of the 20th Annual Computer Security Applications Conference (ACSAC'04)*, (pp. 16-27). IEEE Computer Society.

Vilela, J., Pinto, P., & Barros, J. (2011). Position-based jamming for enhanced wireless secrecy. *IEEE Transactions on Information Forensics and Security, 6*(3), 616–627. doi:10.1109/TIFS.2011.2142305.

Vulimiri, A., Gupta, A., Roy, P., Muthaiah, S. N., & Kherani, A. A. (2010). Application of secondary information for misbehavior detection in VANETs. In *Proceedings of the IFIP International Conference on Networking* (pp. 385-396). IFIP.

Vural, S., & Ekici, E. (2007). Probability distribution of multihop distance in one-dimensional sensor networks. *Computer Networks: The International Journal of Computer and Telecommunications Networking, 51*(13), 3727–3749.

Vuran, M. C., Akan, O. B., & Akyildiz, I. F. (2004). Spatio-temporal correlation: Theory and applications for wireless sensor networks. *Computer Networks Journal, 45*(1), 245–261. doi:10.1016/j.comnet.2004.03.007.

Wagner, D. (2004). Resilient aggregation in sensor networks. In *Proceedings of the Security of Ad Hoc and Sensor Networks* (pp. 78-87). New York: ACM Press.

Wallace, J. (2009). Secure physical layer key generation schemes: Performance and information theoretic limits. In *Proceedings of the 2009 IEEE International Conference on Communications (ICC)* (pp. 1-5). Dresden, Germany: IEEE.

Wallace, J., Chen, C., & Jensen, M. (2009). Key generation exploiting MIMO channel evolution: Algorithms and theoretical limits. In *Proceedings of the 3rd European Conference on Antennas and Propagation (EUCAP '09)* (pp. 1499-1503). Berlin, Germany: EUCAP.

Wallace, J. W., & Sharma, R. K. (2010). Automatic secret keys from reciprocal MIMO wireless channels: Measurement and analysis. *IEEE Transactions on Information Forensics and Security, 5*(3), 381–392. doi:10.1109/TIFS.2010.2052253.

Walters, J. P., Liang, Z., Shi, W., & Chaudhary, V. (2006). Wireless sensor network security—A survey. In Security in Distributed, Grid, and Pervasive Computing, (pp. 208-222). Boca Raton, FL: Auerbach Publications, CRC Press. doi:10.1.1.77.3003

Wang, H., Lightfoot, L., & Li, T. (2010). On phy-layer security of cognitive radio: Collaborative sensing under malicious attacks. In *Proceedings of the 2010 44th Annual Conference on Information Sciences and Systems (CISS)* (pp. 1-6). CISS.

Wang, H., Zhang, D., & Shin, K. G. (2002). Detecting SYN flooding attacks. In *Proceedings of INFOCOM 2002,* (Vol. 3, pp. 1530-1539). IEEE.

Wang, J., Liu, Y., Liu, X., & Zhang, J. (2009). A trust propagation scheme in VANETs. In *Proceedings of the IEEE Intelligent Vehicles Symposium* (pp. 1067-1071). IEEE.

Wang, T., Song, L., Han, Z., Cheng, X., & Jiao, B. (2012). Power allocation using vickrey auction and sequential first-price auction games for physical layer security in cognitive relay networks. In *Proceedings of the 2012 IEEE International Conference on Communications (ICC)* (pp. 1683-1687). IEEE.

Wang, X., Feng, D., Lai, X., & Yu, H. (2004). *Collisions for hash functions MD4, MD5, HAVAL-128 and RIPEMD.* Cryptology ePrint Archive, Report 2004/199.

Wang, Y., Attebury, G., & Ramamurthy, B. (2006). A survey of security issues in wireless sensor networks. *IEEE Communications Surveys and Tutorials, 8,* 2-23. doi:10.1.1.133.6857

Wang, H.-M., Yin, Q., & Xia, X.-G. (2012). Distributed beamforming for physical-layer security of two-way relay networks. *IEEE Transactions on Signal Processing, 60*(7), 3532–3545. doi:10.1109/TSP.2012.2191543.

Wang, K., & Wu, M. (2010). Cooperative communications based on trust model for mobile ad hoc networks. *IET Information Security, 4*(2), 68–79. doi:10.1049/iet-ifs.2009.0056.

Wang, Q., Xu, K., & Ren, K. (2012). Cooperative secret key generation from phase estimation in narrowband fading channels. *IEEE Journal on Selected Areas in Communications, 30*(9), 1666–1674. doi:10.1109/JSAC.2012.121010.

Wang, X., Tao, M., Mo, J., & Xu, Y. (2011). Power and subcarrier allocation for physical-layer security in ofdma-based broadband wireless networks. *IEEE Transactions on Information Forensics and Security, 6*(3), 693–702. doi:10.1109/TIFS.2011.2159206.

Wang, X., & Yi, P. (2011). Security framework for wireless communications in smart distribution grid. *IEEE Transactions on Smart Grid, 2*(4), 809–818. doi:10.1109/TSG.2011.2167354.

Want, R. (2011). Near field communication. *Pervasive Computing, 10,* 4–7. doi:10.1109/MPRV.2011.55.

Wasef, A., Jiang, Y., & Shen, X. (2008). ECMV: Efficient certificate management scheme for vehicular networks. In *Proceedings of the IEEE Globecom.* New Orleans, LA: IEEE.

Wasef, A., Rongxing, L., Xiaodong, L., & Xuemin, S. (2010). Complementing public key infrastructure to secure vehicular ad hoc networks. *IEEE Wireless Communications, 17*(5), 22–28. doi:10.1109/MWC.2010.5601954.

Watanabe, S., & Oohama, Y. (2011). Secret key agreement from vector Gaussian sources by rate limited public communication. *IEEE Transactions on Information Forensics and Security, 6*(3), 541–550. doi:10.1109/TIFS.2011.2132130.

Wei, K., Chen, Y.-F., Smith, A., & Vo, B. (2005). *WhoPay: A scalable and anonymous payment system for peer-to-peer environments* (Technical Report No. UCB/CSD-5-1386). University of California at Berkeley, Berkeley, CA.

Wei, L., Zhu, H., Cao, Z., & Shen, X. (2011). MobiID: A user-centric and social-aware reputation based incentive scheme for delay/disruption tolerant networks. In *Proceedings of the International Conference on Ad Hoc Networks and Wireless,* (LNCS), (vol. 6811, pp. 177-190). New York: Springer.

Weimerskirch, J. J., Hu, Y.-C., & Laberteaux, K. P. (2009). Data security in vehicular communication networks. In H. Hartenstein, & K. Laberteaux (Eds.), *VANET: Vehicular applications and inter-networking technologies.* New York: John Wiley.

Weiss, M. (2010). *Performing relay attacks on ISO 14443 contactless smart cards using NFC mobile equipment.* Retrieved April 26, 2012, from http://www.sec.in.tum.de/assets/studentwork/finished/Weiss2010.pdf

Wen, Y.-J., Agogino, A., & Goebel, K. (2004). Fuzzy validation and fusion for wireless sensor networks. In *Proceeding of ASME International Mechanical Engineering Congress and RD&D Expo (IMECE2004).* Anaheim, CA: ASME.

White, I. M., Rogge, M. S., Shrikhande, K., & Kazovsky, L. G. (2003). A summary of the HORNET project: A next-generation metropolitan area network. *IEEE Journal on Selected Areas in Communications, 21*(9), 1478–1494. doi:10.1109/JSAC.2003.818838.

Wikipedia. (n.d.). *Advanced encryption standard.* Retrieved April 20, 2013, from http://en.wikipedia.org/wiki/Advanced_Encryption_Standard

Wilson, R., Tse, D., & Scholtz, R. (2007). Channel identification: Secret sharing using reciprocity in ultrawideband channels. *IEEE Transactions on Information Forensics and Security, 2*(3), 364–375. doi:10.1109/TIFS.2007.902666.

WiMAX Forum PRNewswire. (2011). Retrieved April 20, 2013, from http://www.prnewswire.com/news-releases/wimax-forum-celebrates-10-years-of-driving-broadband-innovation-123463264.html

WiMAX Forum. (n.d.). Retrieved April 20, 2013, from http://www.wimaxforum.org/

WiMAX Public Key Infrastructure Users Overview (WiMAX PKI). (n.d.). Retrieved April 20, 2013, from http://www.wimaxforum.org/sites/wimaxforum.org/files/page/2009/12/wimax_pki_users_overview_4_28_10

WiMAX. (2013). *Worldwide interoperability for microwave access.* Retrieved May 5, 2013, from http://www.wimax.com/

WiMAX. (n.d.). *Wikipedia.* Retrieved April 20, 2013, from http://en.wikipedia.org/wiki/WiMAX

Winsborough, W. H., Seamons, K. E., & Jones, V. E. (1999). Automated trust negotiation. In *Proceedings of DARPA Information Survivability Conference and Exposition, DISCEX'00,* (pp. 88-102). DISCEX.

Wisitpongphan, N., Bai, F., Mudalige, P., Sadekar, V., & Tonguz, O. (2007). Routing in sparse vehicular ad hoc wireless networks. *IEEE Journal on Selected Areas in Communications, 25*(8), 1538–1556. doi:10.1109/JSAC.2007.071005.

Wohlmacher, P. (2000). Digital certificates: A survey of revocation methods. In *Proceedings of the 2000 ACM workshops on Multimedia* (pp. 111-114). ACM.

Wong, C. W., Wong, T., & Shea, J. (2011). Secret-sharing LDPC codes for the BPSK-constrained Gaussian wiretap channel. *IEEE Transactions on Information Forensics and Security, 6*(3), 551–564. doi:10.1109/TIFS.2011.2139208.

Wongthavarawat, K. (2005, March 28). *IEEE 802.16 WiMAX securit.* Retrieved April 20, 2013, from http://www.nectec.or.th/nac2005/documents/20050328_SecurityTechnology-05_Presentation.pdf

Woo, A., Tong, T., & Culler, D. (2003). Taming the underlying challenges of reliable multihop routing in sensor networks. In *Proceedings of the 1st International Conference on Embedded Networked Sensor Systems.* New York. doi:10.1.1.1.5480

Wood, A. D., & Stankovic, J. A. (2002). Denial of service in sensor networks. *Computer, 35*(10), 54–62. doi:10.1109/MC.2002.1039518.

Wu, H., Fujimoto, R., & Riley, G. (2011). Analytical models for information propagation in vehicle to vehicle networks. In *Proceedings of IEEE Vehicular Technology Conference* (pp. 26-29). Los Angeles, CA: IEEE.

Wu, X., & Yau, D. K. (2007). Mitigating denial-of-service attacks in MANET by distributed packet filtering: a game-theoretic approach. In *Proceedings of the 2nd ACM Symposium on Information, Computer and Communications Security* (pp. 365-367). ACM.

Wu, B., Chen, J., Wu, J., & Cardei, M. (2007). A survey of attacks and countermeasures in mobile ad hoc networks. In *Wireless Network Security* (pp. 103–135). New York: Springer. doi:10.1007/978-0-387-33112-6_5.

Wu, B., Wu, J., & Dong, Y. (2009). An efficient group key management scheme for mobile ad hoc networks. *International Journal of Security and Networks*, *4*(1), 125–134. doi:10.1504/IJSN.2009.023431.

Wu, B., Wu, J., Fernandez, E. B., Ilyas, M., & Magliveras, S. (2007). Secure and efficient key management in mobile ad hoc networks. *Journal of Network and Computer Applications*, *30*(3), 937–954. doi:10.1016/j.jnca.2005.07.008.

Wu, Y., & Liu, K. J. R. (2011). An information secrecy game in cognitive radio networks. *IEEE Transactions on Information Forensics and Security*, *6*(3), 831–842. doi:10.1109/TIFS.2011.2144585.

Wyner, A. (1975). The wiretap channel. *The Bell System Technical Journal*, *54*, 1355–1387. doi:10.1002/j.1538-7305.1975.tb02040.x.

Wyner, A. D. (1975). The wire-tap channel. *The Bell System Technical Journal*, *54*, 1355–1387. doi:10.1002/j.1538-7305.1975.tb02040.x.

Xenakis, C., & Merakos, L. (2004). Security in third generation mobile networks. *Computer Communications*, *27*(7), 638–650. doi:10.1016/j.comcom.2003.12.004.

Xiaodong, L., Rongxing, L., Chenxi, Z., Haojin, Z., Pin-Han, H., & Xuemin, S. (2008). Security in vehicular ad hoc networks. *IEEE Communications Magazine*, *46*(4), 88–95. doi:10.1109/MCOM.2008.4481346.

Xiao, L., Greenstein, L., Mandayam, N., & Trappe, W. (2009). Channel-based detection of sybil attacks in wireless networks. *IEEE Transactions on Information Forensics and Security*, *4*(3), 492–503. doi:10.1109/TIFS.2009.2026454.

Xiaopeng, G., & Wei, C. (2007). A novel gray hole attack detection scheme for mobile ad-hoc networks. In *Proceedings of the IFIP International Conference on Network and Parallel Computing Workshops,* (pp. 209-214). IEEE.

Xing, K., Srinivasan, S. S. R., Rivera, M. J., Li, J., & Cheng, X. (2010). Attacks and countermeasures in sensor networks: A survey. In S. C.-H. Huang, D. MacCallum, & D.-Z. Du (Eds.), *Network security* (pp. 251–272). New York: Springer. doi:10.1007/978-0-387-73821-5_11.

Xiong, W. A., & Gong, Y. H. (2011). Secure and highly efficient three level key management scheme for MANET. *WSEAS Transactions on Computers*, *10*(1), 6–15.

Xu, Q., Mak, T., Ko, J., & Sengupta, R. (2004). Vehicle-to-vehicle safety messaging in DSRC. In *Proceedings of 1st ACM workshop on Vehicular Ad-hoc Networks* (pp. 19-28). ACM.

Xu, S., Matthews, M., & Huang, T. C. (2006). Security issues in privacy and key management protocols of IEEE 802.16. In *Proceedings of the 44th Annual Southeast Regional Conference* (pp. 113-118). New York: SRC.

Xu, W., Ma, K., Trappe, W., & Zhang, Y. (2006). Jamming sensor networks: Attack and defense strategies. *IEEE Network*, *20*(3), 41–47. doi:10.1109/MNET.2006.1637931.

Xu, W., Trappe, W., & Zhang, Y. (2008). Defending wireless sensor networks from radio interference through channel adaptation. *ACM Transactions on Sensor Networks*, *4*(4), 1–34. doi:10.1145/1387663.1387664.

Yamamoto, T., Fukuta, Y., Mohri, M., Hirotomo, M., & Shiraishi, Y. (2012). A distribution scheme of certificate revocation list by inter-vehicle communication using a random network coding. In *Proceedings of the Information International Symposium on Theory and its Applications (ISITA)*. Honolulu, HI: ISITA.

Yang, B., & Garcia-Molina, H. (2003). PPay: Micropayments for peer-to-peer systems. In *Proceedings of the ACM Conference on Computer and Communications Security (CCS'03)* (pp. 300-310). New York: ACM Press.

Yang, M., Feng, Q., Dai, Y., & Zhang, Z. (2007). A multi-dimensional reputation system combined with trust and incentive mechanisms in P2P file sharing systems. In *Proceedings of the Distributed Computing Systems Workshops*. Washington, DC: IEEE CS Press.

Yan, G., Olariu, S., & Weigle, M. C. (2008). Providing VANET security through active position detection. *Computer Communications*, *31*(12), 2883–2897. doi:10.1016/j.comcom.2008.01.009.

Yang, H., Luo, H., Ye, F., Lu, S., & Zhang, L. (2004). Security in mobile ad hoc networks: Challenges and solutions. *IEEE Wireless Communications*, *11*(1), 38–47. doi:10.1109/MWC.2004.1269716.

Yang, H., Ricciato, F., Lu, S., & Zhang, L. (2006). Securing a wireless world. *Proceedings of the IEEE*, *94*(2), 442–454. doi:10.1109/JPROC.2005.862321.

Yang, H., Shu, J., Meng, X., & Lu, S. (2006). SCAN: Self-organized network-layer security in mobile ad hoc networks. *IEEE Journal on Selected Areas in Communications*, *24*(2), 261–273. doi:10.1109/JSAC.2005.861384.

Yang, J., Chen, Y., Trappe, W., & Cheng, J. (2013). Detection and localization of multiple spoofing attackers in wireless networks. *IEEE Transactions on Parallel and Distributed Systems*, *24*(1), 44–58. doi:10.1109/TPDS.2012.104.

Yang, Y., Wang, W., Zhao, H., & Zhao, L. (2012). Transmitter beamforming and artificial noise with delayed feedback: Secrecy rate and power allocation. *Journal of Communications and Networks*, *14*(4), 374–384.

Ye, C., Reznik, A., & Shah, Y. (2006). Extracting secrecy from jointly Gaussian random variables. In *Proceedings of the 2006 IEEE International Symposium on Information Theory* (pp. 2593-2597). IEEE.

Ye, C., Reznik, A., Sternberg, G., & Shah, Y. (2007). On the secrecy capabilities of ITU channels. In *Proceedings of the 2007 IEEE 66th Vehicular Technology Conference* (pp. 2030-2034). IEEE.

Ye, C., Mathur, S., Reznik, A., Shah, Y., Trappe, W., & Mandayam, N. B. (2010). Information-theoretically secret key generation for fading wireless channels. *IEEE Transactions on Information Forensics and Security*, *5*(2), 240–254. doi:10.1109/TIFS.2010.2043187.

Yi, S., & Kravets, R. (2003). MOCA: Mobile certificate authority for wireless ad hoc networks. In *Proceedings of the 2nd Annual PKI Research Workshop Program (PKI 03)* (pp. 3-8). Gaithersburg, MD: PKI.

Yi, S., & Kravets, R. (2004). Composite key management for ad hoc networks. In *Proceedings of the First Annual International Conference on Mobile and Ubiquitous Systems: Networking and Services* (pp. 52-61). IEEE.

Yi, S., Naldurg, P., & R.Kravets. (2001). {A Security-Aware Routing Protocol for Wireless Ad Hoc Networks}.

Yi, S., Pei, Y., & Kalyanaraman, S. (2003). On the capacity improvement of ad hoc wireless networks using directional antennas. In *Proceedings of the 4th ACM International Symposium on Mobile Ad Hoc Networking & Computing*. New York: ACM Press.

Yi, P., Zhong, Y., Zhang, S., & Dai, Z. (2006). Flooding attack and defence in ad hoc networks. *Journal of Systems Engineering and Electronics*, *17*(2), 410–416. doi:10.1016/S1004-4132(06)60070-4.

Yonggang, Z. (2004). *Measurement and monitoring in wireless sensor networks*. (PhD Thesis). Computer Science Department, University of Southern California, Los Angeles, CA.

Yoo, Y., & Agrawal, D. P. (2006). {Why Does It Pay To Be Selfish In A MANET?}. *IEEE Wireless Communications*, *13*(6), 87–97. doi:10.1109/MWC.2006.275203.

Yu, H., Shen, Z., Miao, C., Leung, C., & Niyato, D. (2010). A survey of trust and reputation management systems in wireless communications. *Proceedings of the IEEE*, 1755-1772.

Yu, F. R., Tang, H., Mason, P. C., & Wang, F. (2010). A hierarchical identity based key management scheme in tactical mobile ad hoc networks. *IEEE Transactions on Network and Service Management*, *7*(4), 258–267. doi:10.1109/TNSM.2010.1012.0362.

Yuksel, M., Liu, X., & Erkip, E. (2011). A secure communication game with a relay helping the eavesdropper. *IEEE Transactions on Information Forensics and Security*, *6*(3), 818–830. doi:10.1109/TIFS.2011.2125956.

Yu, M., Zhou, M., & Su, W. (2009). A secure routing protocol against Byzantine attacks for MANETs in adversarial environments. *IEEE Transactions on Vehicular Technology*, *58*(1), 449. doi:10.1109/TVT.2008.923683.

Yu, P., & Sadler, B. (2011). MIMO authentication via deliberate fingerprinting at the physical layer. *IEEE Transactions on Information Forensics and Security, 6*(3), 606–615. doi:10.1109/TIFS.2011.2134850.

Yu, Z. (2008). A key management scheme using deployment knowledge for wireless sensor networks. *IEEE Transactions on Parallel and Distributed Systems, 19*(10), 1411–1425. doi:10.1109/TPDS.2008.23.

Zafer, M. A., Agrawal, D., & Srivatsa, M. (2009). Bootstrapping coalition manets: Physical-layer security under active adversary. In *Proceedings of the Annual Conference of ITA (ACITA) 2009*. ACITA.

Zapata, M. G., & Asokan, N. (2002). Securing ad hoc routing protocols. In *Proceedings of the 1st ACM Workshop on Wireless Security (WiSE'02)*, (pp. 1-10). ACM.

Zaplata, S., & Lamersdorf, W. (2010). Towards mobile process as a service. In *Proceedings of the ACM Symposium on Applied Computing (SAC '10)*. New York: ACM Press.

Zeng, Q., Li, H., & Peng, D. (2012). Frequency-hopping based communication network with multi-level qoss in smart grid: Code design and performance analysis. *IEEE Transactions on Smart Grid, 3*(4), 1841–1852. doi:10.1109/TSG.2012.2214067.

Zeshan, M., Khan, S. A., Cheema, A. R., & Ahmed, A. (2008). Adding security against packet dropping attack in mobile ad hoc networks. In *Proceedings of the International Seminar on Future Information Technology and Management Engineering*, (pp. 568-572). IEEE.

Zhang, S., Zou, Y., & Wang, B. (2009). A novel grid trust model based on fuzzy theory. In *Proceedings of the Third International Conference on Network and System Security* (pp. 203-207). IEEE.

Zhang, Y., & Lee, W. (2000). Intrusion detection in wireless ad-hoc networks. In *Proceedings of the 6th Annual International Conference on Mobile Computing and Networking* (pp. 275-283). ACM.

Zhang, Y., Liu, W., & Fang, Y. (2005). Secure localization in wireless sensor networks. In *Proceedings of the IEEE Military Communications Conference* (Milcom'05). Atlantic City, NJ: IEEE Press.

Zhang, Z., & Zhang, X. (2009). Realization of open cloud computing federation based on mobile agent. In *Proceedings of the IEEE International Conference on Intelligent Computing and Intelligent Systems (ICIS '09)* (Vol. 3, pp. 642-646). IEEE.

Zhang, L., Wu, Q., & Solanas, A. (2010). A scalable robust authentication protocol for secure vehicular communications. *IEEE Transactions on Vehicular Technology, 59*(4), 1606–1617. doi:10.1109/TVT.2009.2038222.

Zhang, L., Zhang, R., Liang, Y.-C., Xin, Y., & Cui, S. (2010). On the relationship between the multi-antenna secrecy communications and cognitive radio communications. *IEEE Transactions on Communications, 58*(6), 1877–1886. doi:10.1109/TCOMM.2010.06.090063.

Zhang, Y., & Joshi, J. B. D. (2009). Access control and trust management for emerging multidomain environments. In S. Upadhyaya, & R. O. Rao (Eds.), *Annals of Emerging Research in Information Assurance, Security and Privacy Services*. London: Emerald Group Publishing Limited.

Zhang, Y., Lee, W., & Huang, Y. A. (2003). Intrusion detection techniques for mobile wireless networks. *Wireless Networks, 9*(5), 545–556. doi:10.1023/A:1024600519144.

Zhang, Y., Lin, L., & Huai, J. (2007). Balancing trust and incentive in peer-to-peer collaborative system. *Journal of Network Security, 5*, 73–81.

Zhao, Y. (2004). *Measurement and monitoring in wireless sensor networks*. (PhD Thesis). Computer Science Department, University of Southern California, Los Angeles, CA.

Zhao, F., & Guibas, F. (2004). *Wireless sensor networks: An information processing approach*. Burlington, MA: Morgan Kaufmann.

Zheng, G., Arapoglou, P.-D., & Ottersten, B. (2012). Physical layer security in multibeam satellite systems. *IEEE Transactions on Wireless Communications, 11*(2), 852–863. doi:10.1109/TWC.2011.120911.111460.

Zheng, G., Choo, L.-C., & Wong, K.-K. (2011). Optimal cooperative jamming to enhance physical layer security using relays. *IEEE Transactions on Signal Processing, 59*(3), 1317–1322. doi:10.1109/TSP.2010.2092774.

Zhou, H. (2008). Secure prophet address allocation for mobile sd hoc networks. In *Proceedings of the International Conference on Network and Parallel Computing*, (pp. 60-67). IEEE.

Zhou, H., Mutka, M. W., & Ni, L. M. (2005). Multiple-key cryptography-based distributed certificate authority in mobile ad-hoc networks. In *Proceedings of the IEEE Global Telecommunications Conference* (Vol. 5). St Louis, MO: IEEE.

Zhou, J., & Yung, M. (2010). Applied cryptography and network security (LNCS, vol. 6123). Berlin: Springer-Verlag.

Zhou, L., & Haas, Z. J. (1999). {Securing Ad hoc Networks}. *IEEE Network, 13*, 24–30. doi:10.1109/65.806983.

Zhu, C., Lee, M. J., & Saadawi, T. (2003). Rtt-based optimal waiting time for best route selection in ad hoc routing protocols. In *Proceedings of the Military Communications Conference,* (Vol. 2, pp. 1054-1059). IEEE.

Zhu, S., Setia, S., & Jajodia, S. (2003). {LEAP: Efficient security mechanisms for large-scale distributed sensor networks}.

Zhuo, C., Fan, H., & Liang, H. (2005). A new authentication and key exchange protocol in WLAN. In *Proceedings of the International Conference on Information Technology: Coding and Computing, ITCC,* (pp. 552-556). ITCC.

Zugenmaier, A., & Aono, H. (2009). Security technology for SAE/LTE. *NTT DOCOMO Technical Journal, 11*(3), 27–30.

About the Contributors

Danda B. Rawat received the Ph.D. in Electrical and Computer Engineering from Old Dominion University, USA. He is currently with the Department of Electrical Engineering at Georgia Southern University. His research focuses on wireless communication systems and networks. His current research interests include design, analysis, and evaluation of cognitive radio networks, vehicular ad hoc networks, wireless sensor networks, telecommunication networks, network security, and cyber physical systems. He has published over 65 scientific papers on these topics. He has served as a Lead Guest Editor, Guest Editor, Editor, and Editorial Board Member for several international journals in the area of wireless communication systems and networks. He has also served as a workshop chair and session chair for numerous international workshops and conferences, and served as a technical program committee member for several international conferences including IEEE GLOBECOM, GreenCom, WCNC, and VTC conferences. He is the recipient of the Best Paper Award at the International Conference on Broadband and Wireless Computing, Communication & Applications 2010 (BWCCA 2010) among others. He has previously held an academic position at Eastern Kentucky University, Old Dominion University, and Tribhuvan University. He is a Senior Member of IEEE and a member of ACM.

Bhed Bahadur Bista received the B.Eng. degree in Electronics from the University of York, England, and the M.S. and Ph.D. degrees in Information Science from Tohoku University, Japan. After his Ph.D., he worked at the Miyagi University, Japan, for one year as a Research Associate and moved to the Iwate Prefectural University, also in Japan, in 1998 as an Assistant Professor. Currently, he is an Associate Professor with the Department of Software and Information Science at the same university. His research interests include computer networks, vehicular networks, sensor networks, ad hoc and cognitive radio networks. He has organized International Workshops and has actively taken part as an area chair and a program committee member in international conferences.

Gongjun Yan received his Ph.D. in Computer Science from Old Dominion University in 2010. He is currently an Assistant Professor in University of Southern Indiana and has been working on the issues surrounding Vehicular Ad-Hoc Networks, Sensor Networks, and Wireless Communication. His main research areas include intelligent vehicles, security, privacy, routing, and healthcare. Dr. Yan applies mathematical analysis to model behavior of complex systems and integrates existing techniques to provide comprehensive solutions. He has published more than 60 journal papers, book chapters, and conference papers, and has been the best paper award winner in international conferences (BWCCA and SOLI). He has served as grant reviewer, article/paper reviewer, session chair, and keynote speaker in international conferences and editor in journals. He is associate editor of *IEEE Transactions on Intelligent Transportation Systems*.

* * *

Ibrahim Abualhaol received the B.Sc. and M.Sc. degrees in electrical engineering from Jordan University of Science and Technology, Irbid, Jordan, in 2000 and 2004, respectively, and the Ph.D. degree in electrical engineering from the University of Mississippi, Oxford, MS, in August 2008. He worked as Research Assistant with the Center for Wireless Communication at the University of Mississippi, MS, and from Jan 2005 until Aug 2008. From May 2008 to Sep 2009, he worked as Wireless System Engineer with Qualcomm Incorporation and then with Broadcom Corporation in San Diego, CA. He is currently an Assistant Professor at Khalifa University of Science, Technology, and Research at Sharjah, United Arab Emirates. His research interests include OFDM, spaceñtime coding, cooperative networks, and MIMO wireless communications. He is a senior member of IEEE, a member of Phi Kappa Phi, and a member of Sigma Xi.

Alessandro Aldini is Assistant Professor of Computer Science at the University of Urbino, Italy. He received the Laurea degree summa cum laude in Computer Science in 1998 from the University of Bologna at Cesena and the Ph.D. degree in Computer Science in 2003 from the University of Bologna. In 2002, he joined the University of Urbino where he is currently Researcher of the Department of Basic Sciences and Foundations. He is co-chair of the International School on Foundations of Security Analysis and Design (FOSAD) and member of the Scientific Committee of the Workshop on Quantitative Aspects of Programming Languages. In the field of formal methods for the design and verification of complex systems, he has co-authored more than 50 peer-reviewed publications.

Awny Alnusair is an Assistant Professor of Applied Computing at Indiana University, Kokomo. Previously he was a lecturer at Northwestern University and a senior fellow at Robert Morris University. Alnusair received his Ph.D. in Computer Science from the University of Wisconsin-Milwaukee, MS in Computer Science from Illinois Institute of Technology, and BS in Computer Science from Yarmouk University. His research interests include program comprehension, information retrieval, programming languages and security, and the Semantic Web.

Yaqoob Juma Alraisi received his BE, Electrical & Electronics Engineering, and his ME, Telecommunication Engineering in 1991 and 2001, respectively. Both degrees were from Sultan Qaboos University, Oman. He earned PhD in Network Engineering from Loughborough University in 2007. Yaqoob served Sultan Qaboos University Hospital as Director from 2008 until 2011. From October 2001 until present he joined The Research Council of the Sultanate of Oman, as Director of Information Technology. Apart from abovementioned experience, Dr. Alraisi served Sultan Qaboos as Telecom expert and director of administration affairs between 1997 and 2008. His research interests include but are not limited to: (1) network security and performance, (2) information security management, (3) enterprise IT strategy, (4) wireless network, and (4) cloud computing.

Hamada Alshaer (M'04-SM'12) is currently a senior researcher in the Etisalat BT Innovation Center (EBTIC), Khalifa University, Abu Dhabi, UAE. He received a BEng degree in electrical engineering and computer science from Birzeit University, Palestine, in 2001, an MS (DEA) degree in Information Technology and Systems (ITS) from Compiegne University of Technology, France, in 2002, and a PhD degree in computer science and telecommunications from Pierre et Marie Curie University, France, in 2005. He then joined the Electronic and Electrical Engineering Department at Brunel University, in west London, as a postdoctoral research fellow. He later worked as a research scientist at INRIA, France. Between November 2007 and September 2009, he worked as a research fellow in the School of Electronic and Electrical Engineering at the University of Leeds, UK. His research interests include QoS, optical communications and networking, wireless sensor networks, and intelligent transportation. He has served on the technical program committee of various IEEE conferences, including the Intelligent Vehicles Symposium, Vehicular Technology Conference, Globecom, ICC, and WCNC, and chaired some of their sessions. He is the recipient of the 2009 Royal Academy of Engineering travel award, as well as scholarships from UNRWA, the French government, and Pierre et Marie Curie University for academic distinctions.

Alessandro Bogliolo, Associate Professor of Computer Systems, is the Coordinator of the Information Science and Technology division of the Department of Basic Sciences and Foundations of the University of Urbino, Italy. He got a Laurea degree in Electrical Engineering (1992) and a Ph.D. in Electrical Engineering and Computer Science (1998) from the University of Bologna, Italy. In 1995 and 1996, he was with the Computer Systems Laboratory of the Stanford University, Stanford (CA). From 1999 to 2002, he was Assistant Professor with the University of Ferrara, Italy. In 2002, he joined the University of Urbino where he is currently leading a research group focused on Internet models, multimedia, mobile applications, and wireless sensor networks. In these fields, he has co-authored more than 140 peer-reviewed publications. In 2010, he founded NeuNet, a non-profit cultural association aimed at promoting interdisciplinary studies and technology transfer in ICT.

Özge Cepheli has received her Bachelor's degree in electronics engineering in 2009 and her Master's degree in communications engineering in 2011, both from Istanbul Technical University, Turkey. She is currently a Ph.D. candidate in the Department of Electronics and Telecommunications Engineering at ITU and a member of Wireless Communications Research Laboratory (http://www.thal.itu.edu.tr). Her research interests include wireless communication systems, physical layer security, and security issues in cognitive radio networks.

Lei Chen received his B.Eng. degree in Computer Science and Applications from Nanjing University of Technology, China, in 2000, and Ph.D. degree in Computer Science from Auburn University, USA, in August 2007. He has been with Sam Houston State University as an Assistant Professor in Computer Science since 2007. Dr. Chen is expected to become Associate Professor with tenure in August 2013. Dr. Chen's research interests focus on network/information security and digital forensics, mobile, handheld, and wireless security. His extended research reaches the areas of computer networking, multimedia networking, network routing, and artificial intelligence. He was a graduate research assistant for 5 years at Auburn University and worked as Vodafone Research Fellow ($20,000 per year plus tuition waiver) in the last year of his Ph.D. study. Between September 2007 and May 2013, he has authored or co-authored 50 peer-reviewed scholarly works, including 8 journal papers, 12 book chapters, and 30 conference proceeding papers. His edited book *Wireless Network Security: Theories and Practices*, published by Springer (U.S.) and Higher Education Press (HEP), is available in 2013.

Manik Lal Das received his Ph.D. degree from Indian Institute of Technology, Bombay, in 2006. He is an Associate Professor in Dhirubhai Ambani Institute of Information and Communication Technology, Gandhinagar, India. He is a member of IEEE and Cryptology Research Society of India. His research interests include Cryptography and Information Security.

Mehrdad Dianati received the B.Sc. degree in electrical engineering from Sharif University of Technology, Tehran, Iran, in 1992, the M.Sc. degree in electrical engineering from K. N. Toosi University of Technology, Tehran, in 1995, and the Ph.D. degree in electrical and computer engineering from the University of Waterloo, Waterloo, ON, Canada, in 2006. From 1992 to 2002, he was a Hardware/Software Developer and a Technical Manager. He is currently a Senior Lecturer (Assistant Professor) with the Centre for Communication Systems Research, Department of Electronic Engineering, University of Surrey, Surrey, UK.

Kamlesh Dutta is an Associate Professor & Head, Department of Computer Science & Engineering at National Institute of Technology, Hamirpur (India). Her major research interests include Network Security, Software Engineering and Artificial Intelligence. She visited Singapore and Australia regarding Training under UNDP and Cisco. She is the recipient of awards from CISCO and ISTE Conventions for her extraordinary contributions in the technical arena. Dr. Dutta is a lifetime member of ISTE, SIGSEM, and SIGDIAL. She has published more than 80 research papers in national and International Journals and Conferences. Quite a few of her technical papers have been awarded "Best paper award." She worked in a number of IEEE, ACM, and other important International Conferences as a Member in the Working Committees. She reviews manuscripts on behalf of a large number of international journals.

Nazar Elfadil received his BSc (Hon.) degree in Science and Technology in 1993 from Geizra University, Sudan, and his Master and PhD in Computer Science (network security) and Computer engineering from University Technology of Malaysia in 1997 and 2002, respectively. Dr. Nazar served Nottingham University, Malaysia, as an Assistance Professor until 2003. In 2003, he joined department of Electrical and Computer Engineering, Sultan Qaboos University, Oman. He is currently serving Fahad Bin Sultan University as an associate professor since 2008. Since 2010, he is serving Fahad Bin Sultan University as an acting dean for college of computing. His research interests include: (1) network security and performance, (2) machine learning, (3) knowledge engineering, (4) wireless network, and (5) artificial intelligence.

Mohamed Amine Ferrag is a PhD student (3rd year) in Networks and Computer Security at University of Badji Mokhtar, Annaba, Algeria. He received his bachelor in Computer Science in 2008 and his master in Networks and Computer Security in June 2010 at University of Badji Mokhtar. His research publication background is mostly in the areas of security in Ad Hoc Networks. He is the first author of 5+ journal/conference/book chapter/white paper/book publications in the areas of security in Ad Hoc Networks. He currently works in the computer department as a researcher in LRS (Laboratory Network and System) to meet the security concerns of mobile social networks.

M. S. Gaur is presently Professor in Department of Computer Engineering, MNIT, Jaipur (India). He completed his B.E. (Electronics & Communication) from JNVU, Jodhpur (India) in 1988 and M.E. (Computer Science Engineering) from IISc, Bangalore (India) in 1993. He was awarded the PhD degree from University of Southampton (UK) in 2005. His research interests include network security, network on chips, and VLSI design.

Salim Ghanemi is an associate professor at the Computer Science Department of Badji Mokhtar University, Annaba, Algeria. He received his Ph.D. in Computer Science in 1987 at Loughborough Univ., England, following his Master's degree in Computer Science at Aston Univ. in Birmingham, England, in 2005, and bachelor of science degree in Computer Science in 1981 from University of Constantine, Algeria. His research publication background is mostly in the areas of parallel programs, program broadcast, operating systems, and security of systems. He is the first author of 20+journal/conference/white paper/book publications in design and analysis of parallel program. He currently teaches Computer Science and supervises three PhD students in network security.

Ji Guo (S'11-S'12) received the B.S. degree in communication engineering from National University of Defense Technology, China, in 2008, and her Ph.D. degree in electronic and electrical engineering at Queen's University Belfast, UK, in 2013. Her research interests include security in wireless networks, trust model for distributed systems, as well as design of algorithms using Grey theory and Fuzzy mathematics.

Chong Han received the B.Eng. and M.Eng. degrees in electrical engineering from Harbin Institute of Technology, Harbin, China, in 2005 and 2009, respectively. She received her Ph.D. degree in Electronic Engineering from University of Surrey, Surrey, UK, in 2012. She is currently working as a research fellow in the Centre for Communication Systems Research (CCSR) in the Department of Electronic Engineering, at the University of Surrey, UK. Current research interests are in the area of Radio Resource Management, particularly in random access control, including Medium Access Control (MAC) protocol design (multichannel MAC scheme for dense and large-scale vehicular networks), performance analysis for Vehicular Ad Hoc Networks, heterogeneous networks for vehicular environment, simulation platform and application development for Intelligent Transportation System (ITS).

Shefali Jain is currently working with TATA Consultancy Services Limited as an Assistant System Engineer. She has received her MTech degree in ICT with computer networks and security specialization from DA-IICT Gandhinagar in 2012. She has received her Bachelor's of Engineering in Computer Science from Rajiv Gandhi Proudyogiki Vishwavidyalaya, Bhopal (M.P.) in 2010. Her area of interest is VANET and cryptography and network security.

James B. D. Joshi is an associate professor and the director of the Laboratory for Education and Research on Security Assured Information Systems (LERSAIS) in the School of Information Sciences at the University of Pittsburgh. His research interests include role-based access control, trust management, and secure interoperability. Joshi has a PhD in computer engineering from Purdue University. He is a member of IEEE and the ACM.

Sunil Kumar is at present working as Associate Professor & Head, Department of Computer Science & Engineering at HCTM Technical Campus, Kaithal (India). He received his B.Tech Degree in Computer Engineering from the Kurukshetra Univesrsity, Kurukshetra (India) in 2002 and M.Tech. Degree in Computer Science & Engineering from the Guru Jambheshwar University of Science & Technology (India) in 2007. He has been awarded the Gold Medal for standing first in 2005-07 Batch of Master of Technology Computer Science and Engineering, Guru Jambheshwar University of Science & Technology (India). He has published research papers in various International Conferences & Journals. His research interests include Wireless Networks, Information Security, Quality of Service, and Distributed Networks. He is working toward his Ph.D. degree in Computer Science & Engineering at National Institute of Technology, Hamirpur (India).

Güneş Karabulut Kurt received the B.S. degree with HH in electronics and electrical engineering from Bogazici University, Istanbul, Turkey, in 2000. She received her M.Sc. and Ph.D. degrees both in electrical engineering from the University of Ottawa, Ontario, Canada, in 2002 and 2006, respectively. She was with TenXc Wireless between 2005 and 2006, where she worked on location estimation systems. She was with Edgewater Computer Systems Inc. from 2006 to 2008. From 2008 to 2010, she was with Turkcell R&D Applied Research and Technology, Istanbul. Currently, she is working at Istanbul Technical University as an Assistant Professor where she set up Wireless Communications Research Laboratory (http://www.thal.itu.edu.tr) and working on PHY security solutions.

Vijay Laxmi is currently Associate Professor and HOD, Department of Computer Engineering, MNIT, Jaipur (India). She did her B.E. (Electronics & Communication) from JNVU, Jodhpur (India) in 1991 and M.Tech. (Computer Science Engineering) from IIT, Delhi (India) in 1992. She completed her PhD from University of Southampton (UK) in 2003. She has 15 years of teaching experience. Her research interests include security and image processing applications in surveillance.

Qingzhong Liu is currently an assistant professor in the Department of Computer Science at Sam Houston State University. He received his B.E. from Northwestern Polytechnical University in 1993 and M.E. from Sichuan University in 1997, and PhD in Computer Science from New Mexico Institute of Mining and Technology in 2007. His research interests include computational intelligence, data mining, digital forensics, information security, biomedical informatics, multimedia computing and analysis, and computational applications.

Chitra Singh Budhathoki Magar is working as a Section Chief of RF planning and services sales at ZTE India. He is responsible for overall radio network planning and network planning and optimization services sales support of ZTE India market. Chitra has been working in India since 2008 and has an extensive experience of GSM/UMTS design, optimization, and rollouts in India. Prior to working in India, Chitra was working as RF planning expert in Shanghai, China, for ZTE Corporation. His research interests include design, analysis, implementation, and optimization of mobile communication networks, wireless sensor network, and wireless multimedia. Chitra received the MS degree in Signal and Information Processing from the East China University of Science and Technology, Shanghai, China.

Alan Marshall is Professor of telecommunications engineering at the Queen's University of Belfast, where he is Director of the Advanced Networks Group. He is a Senior Member of IEEE, and has spent over 20 years working in the tele-communication and computer communications industry and in academia. Since 1993, he has been a Lecturer, Senior Lecturer, and Professor, respectively. From 1988 to 1990, he was employed by the Admiralty Research Establishment, UK, where he worked on the development of real-time communications networks for surface vessels. Between 1990 and 1993, he was employed as a Senior Systems Engineer with Northern Telecom, UK, where he worked on 2nd generation cellular (GSM), and high-speed transmission (SDH) products. He holds joint patents and applications in the areas of spread spectrum communications, packet scheduling, and wireless network architectures. His research interests include network architectures and protocols, high-speed computer and telecommunications networks, mobile and wireless networks, switching, Quality of Service (QoS) architectures, and network management systems and architectures.

Anish Mathuria has been a faculty member at DA-IICT since 2003, where he is Professor and Dean of Research and Development. His main research interests are in the design and analysis of security protocols. He has a Bachelor's degree in Electronics from University of Bombay, and Master's and PhD degrees in Computer Science from University of Wollongong, Australia. Prior to joining the DA-IICT faculty, he has held visiting positions at IBM Tokyo Research Laboratory and a tenure-track faculty position at University of Massachusetts Dartmouth, USA. Dr. Mathuria is co-author of the book *Protocols for Authentication and Key Establishment*, which was published in 2003. He has served on the technical program committees of conferences in cryptography and security, such as Indocrypt and ICISS. Dr. Mathuria is a member of IEEE and ACM, and a life member of the Cryptology Research Society of India.

Sulata Mitra received B.E. degree from Bengal Engineering College (India) in 1986 and PhD degree in Mobile Computing from Bengal Engineering College (D.U.), Shibpur (India) in 2005. She joined the Indian Institute of Technology, Kharagpur, in 1989 as Senior Research Assistant and moved to the Regional Institute of Technology, Jamshedpur (India), in 1991 as Lecturer. Dr. Mitra has published 50 technical papers in journal and international conference proceedings. Her current research interest is QoS issues in 3G/4G cellular network, VANET, Multihomed mobile network. She is currently with the Computer Science and Technology Department of Bengal Engineering and Science University, Shibpur (India) as Associate Professor.

Maria Moloney is head of Research in Digital Services at Escher Group (IRL) Ltd, located in Dublin, Ireland. Her research interests span various domains such as e-government, informational privacy, design science research, security, and wireless communication. She has over 10 years industry experience in the field of Information Systems and conducted her PhD in Trinity College Dublin, Ireland. The topic of her PhD involved the engineering of informational privacy principles into Information systems. She has published in various academic journals and conferences in the discipline of Management Information Systems. Her latest publications include a paper presented at the International Conference of Information Systems (ICIS) 2012 in Orlando, Florida, and another paper presented at the 46th Hawaii International Conference on System Sciences, in January 2013.

Sami Muhaidat received the Ph.D. degree in Electrical and Computer Engineering from the University of Waterloo, Waterloo, Ontario, in 2006. From 2007 to 2008, he was an NSERC postdoctoral fellow in the Department of Electrical and Computer Engineering, University of Toronto, Canada. From 2008-2012, he was an Assistant Professor in the School of Engineering Science, Simon Fraser University, BC, Canada. He is currently an Assistant Professor at Khalifa University and a Visiting Reader in the Faculty of Engineering, University of Surrey, UK. Sami's research focuses on advanced digital signal processing techniques for communications, cooperative communications, vehicular communications, MIMO, and space-time coding. He has authored more than 75 journal and conference papers on these topics. Sami is an active Senior IEEE member and currently serves as an Editor for *IEEE Communications Letters* and an Associate Editor for *IEEE Transactions on Vehicular Technology*. He was the recipient of several scholarships during his undergraduate and graduate studies. He was also a winner of the 2006 NSERC Postdoctoral Fellowship competition.

Mehdi Nafa is an associate professor at the Computer Science Department of Badji Mokhtar University, Annaba, Algeria. He received his Ph.D. in Computer Science in 2009 at University Evry, France, following his Master's degree in Computer Science at Poitiers, France, in 2005 and Engineer's degree in Computer Science in 2003 from University of Badji Mokhtar. Now his main research and teaching interests are around Networks, Security, and Cloud Computing. He currently teaches Computer Science at University of Badji Mokhtar and is Head of MobiMADD research team laboratory part of Network and Systems Lab (Laboratoire Réseau & Systèmes).

M. Pushpalatha is working as Assistant Professor in the Department of Computer Science and Engineering, SRM University. She is doing her PhD in Computer Science and Engineering in SRM University. Her research interests include wireless networks and distributed computing, file replications, and mobility prediction in ad hoc networks. She was a visiting research faculty at the Electrical Engg dept, Viterbi School of Engineering, University of Southern California for a duration of six months. Her other research interests are wireless ad hoc and distributed network testbed developments.

T. Rama Rao currently workis as Professor & Head, Department of Telecommunication Engineering, Faculty of Engineering & Technology, SRM University, India. He received his PhD degree in "Radio Wave Propagation studies for Fixed and Mobile Communications over Southern India" from Sri Venkateswara University, Tirupati, India, in the year 2000. He worked with Aalborg University, Denmark, as Assistant Research Professor; with Universidad Carlos III de Madrid, Spain, and at the University of Sydney, Australia, as Visiting Professor. He served as a PostDoc Research Fellow at National Chio Tung Univeristy, Hsinchu, Taiwan. He has a long-standing research history on Radiowave Propagation Studies for Wireless Communications. His research interests are, Radio Channel Measurements & Modeling, Broadband Wireless Communications/Networks, and Wireless Information Networks.

Rajesh K. Sharma is a Postdoctoral Researcher in the Cognitive Radio Network Group (CRNG) within the International graduate school on Mobile Communications at Ilmenau University of Technology, Germany. He received the B.Sc. degree (with honors) in electrical engineering from the University of Engineering and Technology (UET), Lahore, Pakistan, in 1998, the M. Eng. degree in telecommunications from the Asian Institute of Technology (AIT), Thailand, in 2002, and doctoral degree in Electrical

Engineering from Jacobs University, Bremen, Germany in 2010. Before joining CRNG in February 2011, he was a postdoctoral researcher at Jacobs University, Bremen, where he worked on physical layer security problem. From 1999 to 2007, he was a full-time faculty in the department of electrical and electronics Engineering, Kathmandu University, Nepal. His current research focus is in cognitive radio, especially on the physical layer issues including sensing and reconnaissance, RF frontend, antennas, over-the-air test in virtual electromagnetic environment, physical layer security, and cognitive radio application scenarios including disaster situations. His other research interests include MIMO communications and wireless channel modeling.

Moein Shayegannia received his B.S.c in Electrical Engineering with Cum Laude from American University of Sharjah, UAE, in 2009. He received his Master of Science studies at Simon Fraser University, Canada, in the area of multimedia communications in 2012. In particular, Moein focused on Wireless Transmission of JPEG2000 images with Unequal power allocation over frequency selective channels. His master thesis contributed several conference papers, a journal paper, and a book chapter to the literature. Since 2012, Moein has been pursuing his PhD studies in the area of Nanofabrication at Simon Fraser University. Currently, his focus is on highly sensitive and highly selective fabrication of Nano sensors for either medical or environmental applications. Moein is a winner of Petrofac Endowment scholarship and several Merit and graduate scholarships. He has been a reviewer for some IEEE conferences, and served as a chairman in ICWMC.

Raed Shubair received his B.Sc. degree (Distinction and class Honors) in Electrical Engineering from Kuwait University in June 1989 and his Ph.D. degree (Distinction) in Electrical Engineering from the University of Waterloo, Canada, in February 1993. He has been with the Electrical and Computer Engineering Department of Khalifa University (formerly Etisalat University College) since August 1993. Dr. Raed Shubair is affiliated with the University of Waterloo as a Visiting Professor at both Centre for Intelligent Antenna and Radio Systems (CIARS) and Centre for Bioengineering and Biotechnology (CBB). His current research interests include wireless sensor networks localization, smart antennas and MIMO systems, implanted antennas for bioengineering applications, guided-wave optoelectronics, computational electromagnetic modeling of RF and microwave circuits. He has published extensively in refereed technical journals and international conferences. Dr. Raed Shubair is a Fellow of MIT Electromagnetics Academy since 2007 and a Senior Member of IEEE since 2001. He is a founding member of the IEEE-UAE Signal Processing and Communications (SP/COM) Joint Societies Chapter and IEEE-UAE Engineering in Medicine and Biology Society (EMBS) Chapter. Dr. Raed Shubair serves currently as Vice-Chair of the IEEE Conference on Communications. He is an Associate Editor for the *Journal of Communications*, Academy Publishers, and *Progress in Electromagnetic Research Journal*, Electromagnetics Academy, MIT.

Rahim Tafazolli received the Ph.D. degree from the University of Surrey, Surrey, UK. He is currently a Professor of Mobile/Personal Communications and the Director of the Centre for Communication Systems Research, Department of Electronic Engineering, University of Surrey. He has been active in research for more than 25 years. He has been an author or a coauthor of more than 500 papers in refereed international journals and conference proceedings. He is a consultant to many telecommunication companies. Dr. Tafazolli is a Fellow of the Wireless World Research Forum. He has lectured, chaired, and served as a keynote speaker to a number of Institution of Engineering and Technology and IEEE workshops and conferences. He is the Chairman of the European Union Expert Group of Networks Technology Platform.

Hassan Takabi is a PhD student in the School of Information Sciences and a member of the Laboratory of Education and Research on Security Assured Information Systems (LERSAIS) at the University of Pittsburgh. His research interests include access control models; trust management; privacy and Web security; usable privacy and security; and security, privacy, and trust issues in cloud computing environments. Takabi has an MS in information technology from Sharif University of Technology. He is student member of IEEE and the ACM.

Meenakshi Tripathi is presently Assistant professor Department of Computer Engineering, MNIT, Jaipur (India). She completed her B.E. (Computer Engineering) from IET, Alwar (India) in 2003 and M.Tech. (Computer Science Engineering) from Banasthali Vidyapith (India) in 2005. She is pursuing her Ph.D. from MNIT, Jaipur (India). Her research interests include Wireless Sensor Network Security and Wireless Network Routing Protocols.

Cihan Varol is an Assistant Professor of Computer Science at Sam Houston State University. He received his Bachelor of Science degree in Computer Science from Firat University, Elazig, Turkey, in 2002, Master of Science degree from Lane Department of Computer Science and Electrical Engineering from West Virginia University, Morgantown, WV, USA, in 2005, and Doctor of Philosophy in Applied Computing from University of Arkansas at Little Rock in 2009. Dr. Varol's research interests are in the general area of information (data) quality, VoIP Forensics, and risk management with specific emphasis on personal identity recognition, record linkage, entity resolution, pattern matching techniques, natural language processing, multi-platform VoIP applications, VoIP artifacts data cleansing, and quality of service in business process automation. These studies have led to more than 20 peer-reviewed journal and conference publications, one book chapter.

Revathi Venkataraman is working as Assistant Professor in the Department of Computer Science and Engineering, SRM University. She completed her PhD in Computer Science and Engineering in SRM University. Her research interests include wireless networks and security, trust computing, and routing in wireless ad hoc networks. She was a visiting research faculty at the Electrical Engg dept, Viterbi School of Engineering, University of Southern California for a duration of six months. Her other research interests are wireless ad hoc and sensor network testbed developments which are ongoing research activities funded by Indian Government.

Saman Taghavi Zargar is a PhD candidate in the Telecommunications and Networking program and a member of the Laboratory of Education and Research on Security Assured Information Systems (LERSAIS) in the School of Information Sciences at the University of Pittsburgh. His research interests include network security; intrusion prevention, detection and response; security, privacy, and trust challenges of Software Defined Networking (SDN); security, privacy, and trust issues in Cloud Computing environments; security, privacy, and trust issues in Dynamic Spectrum Access (DSA); distributed, mobile, and pervasive/ubiquitous computing. Zargar has an MS in computer engineering from Ferdowsi University of Mashhad, Iran. He is also a graduate student member of IEEE and the ACM.

Bing Zhou is an assistant professor in the Department of Computer Science, Sam Houston State University, Huntsville, Texas, USA. Her publications cover various topics on intelligent security data analysis, soft computing, rough set theory, data mining, machine learning, information retrieval, and cognitive informatics. She has served as a program committee member of many international conferences and workshops. She is a reviewer of many international journals and an editorial board member of several books.

Bosheng Zhou (M'03) received his B.S. and M.S. degrees from Nanjing University, China, in 1986 and 1989, respectively, and his Ph.D. degree in electrical engineering from Southeast University, China, in 2003. He has been a Research Fellow at Queen's University of Belfast since 2003. His research interests include wireless networks, sensor networks, mesh networks, and smart networks.

Index

CPSIA information can be obtained at www.ICGtesting.com
Printed in the USA
BVOW05*2353150114

342032BV00009B/100/P